STATISTICS

OF

MINES AND MINING

IN THE

STATES AND TERRITORIES WEST OF THE ROCKY MOUNTAINS;

BEING THE

EIGHTH ANNUAL REPORT

OF

ROSSITER W. RAYMOND,

UNITED STATES COMMISSIONER OF MINING STATISTICS.

WASHINGTON:
GOVERNMENT PRINTING OFFICE.
1877.

LETTER

FROM THE

ACTING SECRETARY OF THE TREASURY,

TRANSMITTING

The report of the Commissioner of Mining Statistics.

APRIL 13, 1876.—Referred to the Committee on Mines and Mining, and ordered to be printed.

TREASURY DEPARTMENT, *April* 13, 1876.

SIR: I have the honor to transmit herewith the report of Rossiter W. Raymond, Commissioner of Mining Statistics.

Very respectfully,

CHAS. F. CONANT,
Acting Secretary of the Treasury.

Hon. M. C. KERR,
Speaker of the House of Representatives.

CONTENTS.

INTRODUCTORY.

WASHINGTON, *April* 11, 1876.

SIR: I have the honor to transmit herewith my report on mines and mining in the States and Territories of California, Nevada, Idaho, Oregon, Montana, Utah, Colorado, Wyoming, New Mexico, and Arizona, for the year ending December 31, 1875. This year was generally a prosperous one for the gold and silver mining industry, although several untoward events diminished the product of bullion in comparison with what might have been expected from a perfectly successful season. Chief among these were the disastrous fire at Virginia City, Nev., in October, which destroyed the machinery of three principal mines on the Comstock lode, and the scarcity of water-supply in California, affecting both the placer and hydraulic mines, and also, to some extent, the quartz-mines of California, many of which are dependent upon stamp-mills run by water-power. The scarcity of water did not however amount to a a drought, but rather to a shortening of the working season, an effect which was aggravated somewhat by the extreme cold of the early part of the year.

From the best attainable authorities, I estimate the product of gold and silver in the United States for the year 1875 to have been as follows, in United States coin value:

California	$17,753,151.
Nevada	40,478,369
Idaho	1,750,000
Oregon and Washington	1,246,978
Montana	3,573,600
Utah	3,137,688
Colorado	5,302,810
New Mexico	325,000
Arizona	750,000
All other sources	500,000
	74,817,596

The authorities upon which this estimate is based are given in the respective chapters of the report, and in the appendix will be found a statement of the product of former years compared with that of 1875.

The most striking new developments of the year were those connected with the great *bonanza* in the California, Virginia Consolidated, and Ophir Mines on the Comstock lode. Besides these, the State of Nevada furnished several other important discoveries, such as the *bonanza* of the

Northern Belle Mine, in Esmeralda County, and the new, large, and rich ore-body found in the Eberhardt and Aurora Mine, in White Pine County, at the greatest depth yet attained in the mines of Treasure Hill. From Inyo County, California, the discovery of rich argentiferous lead-ores is reported in the New Coso district. It is affirmed that one of the mines in this district is the famous "Gun-sight lode," so named because, according to a legend current for many years upon the Pacific Coast, it was first discovered by a party of famishing overland emigrants, who melted silver out of the outcropping ore to make sights for their rifles, but who, being obliged by want of food to leave the place, could never find it afterward. The search for this lost lode has been prosecuted by many a prospector during the last twenty-five years, and it may be confidently predicted that if the mine now declared to be the true "Gunsight" should fail to prove "fabulously rich," its identity will be at once denied, and the zealous pursuit of the genuine, original deposit will begin again; for it is only by its fabulous richness that this vein will ever be recognized.

The San Juan region in Colorado has been steadily growing in importance during the year, and is evidently destined to become the seat of an active and productive silver-mining industry, including smelting as well as amalgamating works. Some of the districts yield gold.

Of improvements in the metallurgy of the West, I would mention particularly, as a considerable advance, the introduction and extended use of water-jackets around the smelting-zone of lead-smelting blast-furnaces. This is specially advantageous in Utah, where fire-proof materials are of indifferent quality and very costly. The jackets are usually of cast-iron, but wrought-iron ones have been introduced at several works. The danger of explosions caused by the formation of steam in the closed jackets first employed has led to the construction of such as are partly open at the top. There is undoubtedly a loss of heat in such appliances; but it cannot possibly be so great, in lead-smelting at least, as to counterbalance the great advantage of preserving the interior lines of the furnace, prolonging the campaign, and decreasing the serious item of cost in repairs. With the view of diminishing the waste of heat, it is customary to run the water through tuyeres and jacket just fast enough to keep it almost boiling. Hence the danger of steam-explosions, which, as I have said, is obviated by using jackets not tightly closed.

This principle of cooling by means of water the surfaces of metallurgical apparatus exposed to the highest temperatures is one of the most important in modern metallurgy. It is destined to complete the revolution in that art which the invention of the Siemens furnace inaugurated. The latter invention made constant high temperatures feasible in metallurgical practice; but, although in the Siemens furnace the heat is concentrated upon its work and measurably directed away from the furnace-walls, yet its intensity is so great as to make repairs of the furnace frequently necessary. The cooling of all these parts and of the hearth-walls of iron blast-furnaces with water is, in my judgment, almost certain to be the practice of the future, and to constitute the solution of what has been called the problem of fire-proof materials. That is to say, we are to meet the high temperatures of modern metallurgy, not by inventing new and even refractory materials, but by effectively cooling and thus preserving the apparatus built of such materials as we have.

An interesting application of this principle has been made by Mr. Steitz at the Saint Louis Smelting and Refining Works, in the cupellation of rich lead upon an iron hearth, kept cool with water, instead of a hearth of bone-ash, according to the immemorial practice. This improvement offers several advantages. Much labor is saved in the preparation of cupels. There is no danger of losing the charge through a defective cupel, or by unskillful handling. There is no difficulty about drawing off the litharge. Above all, there is no chance for a dishonest workman to steal fine silver, for the silver cannot be cupelled on the iron hearth to perfect fineness. That can be done on a bone-ash cupel only, the porous material of which absorbs the last portion of the litharge. Hence the argentiferous lead is cupelled with successive additions of lead on the English plan, until the full charge is on the iron hearth and has reached a certain degree of fineness. This is then removed to a bone-ash cupel, and refined in the ordinary manner, the superintendent or other trusty overseer being present throughout this final operation. When the cupellation is, on the other hand, carried on upon an English bone-ash hearth throughout, it is possible for the workmen at any time, in the absence of the overseer, or by the connivance of a corrupt overseer, to allow the bath to become fine, abstract a portion of silver from it, and then resume the regular addition of lead, leaving no trace of the robbery. The stealing half-refined bullion from the bath on the iron cupel is an operation to which no workman is tempted, since it is nearly impossible to dispose of such material without detection, almost the only buyers of it being parties who would at once be able to trace and willing to report the theft. Mr. Steitz's very useful improvement will doubtless be introduced, sooner or later, in all silver-reduction works, unless its continued use in practice should develop some disadvantage not now foreseen.

The complete and interesting system of metallurgical processes administered at the Boston and Colorado works, in Colorado, is fully described and illustrated in the present report, which contains also practical hints of importance from trustworthy experts concerning methods and apparatus now in successful use in the West. The professional gentlemen to whom I am indebted for these chapters, as well as those who have contributed to the statistical and descriptive account of the mines, are named in connection with their contributions in the body of the report.

In view of the circumstance that this report, like several of its predecessors, contains a number of chapters which have appeared, or will appear, as papers in the Transactions of the American Institute of Mining Engineers, I think it well to repeat the explanation made in a previous volume, that the authors of these papers prepared them at my request and without expense to the Government, on condition that they should be free to lay them before the Institute also, as a special and professional public, while the council of the Institute, in which the copyright of all papers is vested, has pursued the wise and liberal policy of permitting their free publication for the benefit of all persons interested in such subjects.

Since this report is the last which I shall have the honor to submit to the Department, I take this opportunity to renew my thanks to the large number of my professional colleagues and of other citizens to whose cordial assistance the value of this series of publications is chiefly due. The means at the disposal of the Commissioner would have been ludicrously inadequate to his work without such co-operation. Even this hearty and general aid has not fully supplied the lack of a thoroughly organized, paid, and responsible corps of reporters. But I think it may be said that no public documents have ever been prepared at so little expense which contained so much information of practical importance to the Government and the country. I am justified in believing, also, that these reports have been influential in producing and advancing improvements in mining and metallurgical practice by which much money has been saved to those industries.

My sincere acknowledgments are due also to the Treasury Department, and to the Director of the Mint, since my work was placed under his supervision, for the enlightened support extended to me in the execution of such plans as the means at disposal permitted me to form. It is not without regret that I terminate the public labors represented by these eight volumes. I trust that in this form, or a better one, the work may be resumed by other and abler hands; and I shall be well content to have contributed something, however imperfect, to the progress and prosperity of the country in that department to which, by profession, I am attached.

Very respectfully, your obedient servant,

R. W. RAYMOND,

U. S. Commissioner of Mining Statistics.

Hon. CHAS. F. CONANT,

Acting Secretary of the Treasury,

Washington, D. C.

PART I.

CONDITION OF THE MINING INDUSTRY.

CHAPTER I.

CALIFORNIA.

Mr. W. A. Skidmore, of San Francisco, who has been for many successive years my deputy in this State, has manifested this year, as heretofore, great zeal and industry, coupled with skill and tact, in the collection of materials for my report. His efforts have been seconded by the friendly co-operation of many gentlemen, whose names are mentioned with due credit in the following pages. In addition to the statements of this chapter, some industrial and commercial statistics of California will be found in the chapter of miscellaneous statistics at the end of this volume.

The product of bullion, as given by Mr. Valentine, superintendent of Wells, Fargo & Co.'s express, was as follows:

Gold dust and bullion by express	$14,842,010
By other conveyance	1,484,201
Silver bullion by express	387,768
Ores and base bullion by freight	1,039,172
Total, (coin value)	17,753,151

Such details of production as could be obtained by correspondence or personal inquiry will be found under the heads of the respective counties. The water-supply for placer-mining was in general deficient.

Of new metallurgical processes which have attracted attention during the year in California I need say little in this place. The most famous is the Fryer process, which has been passing for many months through experimental stages in works erected for the purpose near Grass Valley. Probably much has been claimed for this method by enthusiastic reporters, which would not be seriously expected of it by its manager and owners. So far as it is not kept secret, it embraces simply roasting and amalgamation, and has been applied chiefly to gold-ores. The roasting is effected in a peculiar water-jacketed furnace or kiln, with a removable bottom; the amalgamation takes place in a cylinder, or set of cylinders, set radial to the axis of revolution, like the spokes of a wheel. It is said also that a heavy die or loose piston slides from end to end of the cylinder as it revolves, thus crushing or grinding, as well as mixing, the pulp. Reports of results from numerous small lots of ore tested in this apparatus have been extremely favorable. That such reports, however, are not trustworthy indications of the working value of a new process has been abundantly shown. In the first place, both parties to such a test are frequently interested in a favorable result: the ore-owner, because it may lend new value to some hitherto refractory and unprofitable material; the process-owner, because it may enlarge the field of his operations. They may be sincere and honest, but they are sure to be sanguine, and to overlook rather than take pleasure in detecting slight indications of trouble or loss. In the second place, the conditions of such a test are usually overfavorable to the process. No account is taken of the wear of machinery. Often surplus labor and fuel are employed, and always greater care is bestowed than would be the case in steady running on a large scale. The results, moreover, are compared with "the ordinary process," a vague term, which usually means the method unsuccessfully tried on similar materials previous to the test. I have frankly expressed, as an individual, in another place my doubts of the advantages claimed for the Fryer process—doubts based upon the apparently ineffective and costly roasting-apparatus and upon the apparently unnecessary devices for securing a "close" amalgamation, such amalgamation having been frequently effected already by simpler arrangements, and having usually cost more than its admitted advantages would counterbalance. The test of experiment is, however, the best; and as Mr. Fryer is continuing to perfect the details and operations of his works, it would be both unnecessary and ungracious to judge him in this report upon *a priori* grounds.

Another process which is said to have attracted much notice in California is the Mindeleff process for treating copper ores. The process proper deals with oxidized ores only; but the inventor purposes to bring out also a special roasting-furnace, by means of which he can suitably prepare sulphides. The reduction is to be effected by light hydrocarbon procured from illuminating-gas, by means of which the copper will be reduced to the metallic state, to be subsequently extracted and refined. The objections to the plan are that a direct smelting of oxidized ores to black copper would be cheaper and simpler; that the reduction by gas would include the oxide of iron as well as of copper, leaving iron-sponge in the ore, which would greatly complicate the subsequent treatment; that if gas-reduction were practicable, carbonic oxide would be much cheaper and probably better than hydrocarbon; and, finally, that the process offers no advantages in treating very poor and sulphurous ores, which is the chief direction in which improvements are needed.

QUICKSILVER.

The annual report for 1875 of Mr. J. B. Randol, superintendent of the New Almaden Quicksilver Company, presents so complete a view, not only of the operations of the company, but also of the conditions of quicksilver-mining in California, the nature and amount of expenses, and the course of the market, that I quote it and the tables which accompany it with slight condensation only.

The net receipts for the period named were:

From sales of * 13,353 flasks of quicksilver	$661,657 77
From advances on quicksilver consigned	57,600 00
From interest and discounts on deposits and purchases	3,394 66
From rents and privileges	20,241 44
From profit on materials sold	1,229 73
From woodlands, profit on wood cut	2,106 71
	746,230 31
From credits to New York office for materials and supplies purchased east	2,846 50
Total net receipts	749,076 81
Balance cash in hands of the manager to the company's credit, December 31, 1874	15,364 99
Total	764,441 80

* Includes 30 flasks lost by fire in Virginia, Nev.

The net expenditures during the year were:

For materials and supplies	$134,699 24
For mine pay-rolls	324,577 21
For hacienda pay-rolls	57,181 23
For improvement pay-rolls	25,051 76
For miscellaneous expenses and taxes	26,539 65
For miscellaneous property	4,700 84
For woodlands	1,569 14
Total expenditures	574,309 07
For remittances to New York office, including premiums on exchange	135,675 00
Total disbursements	709,984 07
Balance cash in hands of manager to the company's credit December 31, 1875	54,457 73
Total	764,441 80

Compared with last year, the net receipts, $749,076 81, exhibit a decrease of $181,966.99; the net expenditures, including remittances to New York, an increase of $7,153.78; and the sales of quicksilver reported were 13,353 flasks, of 76½ pounds each, netting $661,657.77, against $815,320.72 for 9,475 flasks sold in 1874.

The quicksilver on hand December 31, 1875, exhibits a decrease of $63,270, the ore, an increase of $20,098.60; materials and supplies, an increase of $14,374.81; cash, an increase of $39,092.74; a total net increase of assets to the amount of $10,296.15.

The improvements made at the mines and furnaces were on an extensive scale, and of a character to add largely to the productive capacity of the works. A new engine, 16 by 30, was erected at the Randol shaft, the iron-clad furnace mentioned in the last report was completed with condensers, roofs, &c., and started in operation at a total cost of $19,727.39. No. 5 furnace was altered to roast tierras without the expense and delay of making them into adobes, the plans were prepared for a new furnace for the same object, with a daily capacity of 30 tons, and the condensers for the samo were partly built; work was commenced on an iron-clad furnace, the duplicate in every respect of the one now working so successfully, and new condensers were added to the several old furnaces, which were also improved by the prolongation of flues, increasing height of chimney-shaft, &c. A new boarding-house was built at the hacienda, to replace one destroyed by an incendiary fire, and the number of tanks, reservoirs, flumes, hose, and pipes, for protection against fire, were increased and made more efficient. The aggregate of these expenditures for the current year were $52,650.56, showing an increase of $7,331.58 over 1874.

The following is a statement of the amounts expended on the several works:

FOR THE MINES.

Hoisting-engine, pumping-gear, foundations, &c	$10,894 32
Sheds over planillas at Day tunnel and Deep Gulch tunnel and house on hill	1,504 56
Roads	726 79
	13,125 67

FOR THE HACIENDA.

Iron-clad furnace, No. 7	$15,419 65
Iron-clad furnace, No. 9	303 49
Tierras furnace, No. 8	1,902 61
Altering No. 5 to tierras furnace	3,176 77
Wooden condensers, No. 5	1,572 05
Brick condensers, No. 5	1,831 54
Elevating chimney, No. 5	678 07
Brick tower and flume, Nos. 1 and 2	1,850 97
Wooden condensers, No. 1	635 70
Iron condensers, No. 6	1,737 26
Prolongation of flues, Nos. 3, 4, and 6	2,969 87
Adobe store-house	692 70
Coal-sheds	126 31
Roofing, ore, and tierras chutes	357 30
Tanks, flumes, hose, and pipe	2,755 14
Boarding-house	3,515 46
Total	39,524 89

The total earnings and expenses of the mines for 1875 were as follows:

EARNINGS.

From 13,648 flasks of quicksilver, the production of 1875		$680,567 37
Of this quantity—		
11,563 flasks were sold at current market rates, netting		586,937 37
1,884 flasks are consigned to Thomas Bell, esq., upon which Advances have been had	$57,600 00	
And it is estimated that the amount realized over advances will be	26,685 00	
		84,285 00
171 flasks are on hand at the hacienda, estimated value		7,695 00
30 flasks were destroyed by fire at Virginia City, October 26, 1875, and are credited, estimated value		1,650 00
13,648 flasks		680,567 37
Ore-account increased		20,098 60
Rents and privileges		20,241 44
Miscellaneous sources		5,161 96
Total net earnings		726,069 37

EXPENSES.

Hacienda pay-rolls	57,181 23	
Mine pay-rolls	324,577 21	
Miscellaneous expenses, including taxes	26,539 65	
Miscellaneous property	4,700 84	
Materials and supplies consumed for current use of mines and furnaces	92,715 63	
		505,714 56
Leaving net earnings, 1875		220,354 81
Deduct for difference between estimated value of 1,760 flasks on hand December 31, 1874, and amount realized	22,929 60	
For 30 flasks destroyed by fire	1,650 00	
		24,579 60
Balance to credit income account 1875		195,775 21

Compared with 1874, the production of quicksilver exhibits an increase of 50 per cent.; in the quantity sold of this year's product, an increase of 75 per cent., and the amount on hand December 31, 2,055 flasks, an increase of 295 flasks.

The net value of the quicksilver product of 1874, after deducting for overestimated value of quantity in hand at close of that year, averaged $98.80¾ per flask, and deducting from the expenses the increase in ore-account and amounts to credit of rents and miscellaneous sources, its cost was $43.85 per flask. The product of 1875 shows a net value of $49.86½ per flask, with a cost of $33.72 per flask; this exhibits a decline in net value of $48.94¼ per flask, or 50 per cent., accompanied by a decreased cost of $10.13 per flask. The course of prices for quicksilver was rapidly downward for the first quarter of 1875, and low prices were current for the remainder of the year. The appended statement gives the highest and lowest prices per pound in San Francisco, as shown by our sales accounts for the several months of the year, and table No. 1 of this report shows changes of prices in London and New York for the same period.

	Highest.	Lowest.
January	$1 55	$1 55
February	1 40	1 40
March	1 60	0 70
April	0 70	0 65
May	0 65	0 65
June	0 70	0 65
July	0 70	0 70
August	0 70	0 70
September	0 75	0 65
October	0 85	0 70
November	0 70	0 65
December	0 70	0 62½

Opening, \$1.55 per pound, equal to \$118.57½ per flask.
Closing, \$0.62½ per pound, equal to \$47.81 per flask.
Range, \$0.92½ per pound, equal to \$70.76 per flask.

On the company's product for the year, 13,648 flasks, the difference in price is equal to \$965,732.48.

The causes for the great decline in value are to be found in the exceptionally high prices ruling in 1873 and 1874, which stimulated the working, and increased the production of mines at that time in operation, and led to the discovery, opening, and developing of many new mines throughout this State.

The aggregate production of the quicksilver-mines in California for 1875 is estimated at 53,000 flasks, against 34,000 flasks for 1874. The increased number of sellers, and consequent active competition, favored and accelerated the fall in price, which it is to be hoped has now touched the lowest point. Many of the new mines have discontinued operations, finding no profit in prevailing prices, and it is believed that the small producers, taught by the experience of the past year, will be less eager to force the sale of an article that does not deteriorate with age, and for which a demand at paying rates is certain to arise. While prices were falling, it was impossible to make sales, except in small lots; thus our share of sales for the first quarter of the year were only 1,191 flasks, or 569 flasks less than the number carried over from 1874, and therefore the product of 1875 only found a market when prices were low. For the last quarter of the year the company's share of the sales reported was 4,654 flasks, and on the 31st December the total quantity of quicksilver held by Mr. Bell, at home and abroad, for joint account, was 2,907 flasks, against 2,816 flasks at the same time last year. During the past year the exports to China were 18,190 flasks, against 1,200 for 1874, and were $62\frac{48}{100}$ per cent. of the total exports reported by sea. As quicksilver is used by the Chinese almost exclusively for the manufacture of vermilion, of which their make commands the highest price and largest sale throughout the world, on account of its superior quality and rich and durable color, it may be that the selection of an intelligent chemist for a thorough and exhaustive study of their method of manufacturing it would enable the company to establish improved works for the making of vermilion at the hacienda, employing Chinese labor. The duty on quicksilver having been removed, and that of 25 per cent. left on vermilion, the question of thus converting a portion of the quicksilver product is worthy of attention at the present time.

It appears from the official reports of the Idria quicksilver-mine, in Krain, Austria, that for the years 1870, 1871, and 1872 there was an average annual manufacture at that mine of 56 tons of quicksilver, or 1,464 flasks of 76½ pounds each, and $5\frac{1515}{2000}$ tons of sulphur into $56\frac{441}{2000}$ tons of vermilion, which, in comparison with the year 1869, was an average decrease in the annual production of 31 tons of vermilion. The cause for this decreased production is said to lie in the steady rise in the price of quicksilver during the three years named above. As quicksilver has rapidly declined in price during the past year, it is very probable that their production of vermilion will be increased, they evidently finding it more profitable when prices are low to market their quicksilver in the form of vermilion.

The ores produced at the New Almaden mines in 1875 were 116,048 cargas,* equal to $17,407\frac{400}{2000}$ tons of cleaned ore of all qualities.

Of this quantity there were produced:

	Cargas.
Ores from the Old Mine	13,237
Ores from the San Francisco	6,384½
Ores from the Cora Blanca	6,262
Ores from the Enriqueta, &c	534½
Tierras from the mines	67,761
Tierras from the dumps	7,919
Terrero from the dumps	13,950
Total	116,048

The cleaned mine ore and mine tierras are estimated to be about one-fifth of the total quantity of stuff brought to the surface; therefore, the expenses attending their production include the extraction and removal of a much larger quantity of waste vein-matter, which has to be examined and passed over the planillas or cleaning-floors, and the rock

*A carga is a Mexican load of cleaned ore, ready for the furnaces, weighing 300 pounds avoirdupois.

mined in the dead-work of sinking shafts, running drifts, &c., is also all brought to the surface, the ground in all cases, where it is required, being well timbered and carefully looked after.

The following statement gives the expenditures for labor, as shown by mine pay-rolls, for the year 1875:

Miners for ore by the carga	$137, 587 61
Cleaning ore by the carga	13, 811 69
Terrero ore by the carga	18, 335 01
Tierras ore by the carga	11, 284 90
Transportation by wagons by the carga	4, 149 89
Yardage by contract and rock-drills	75, 872 00
Timbermen and miners by the day	15, 736 24
Tramming	27, 322 31
Skilled labor and laborers	16, 125 56
Foremen	4, 352 00
Total	324, 577 21

Compared with the preceding year, these pay-rolls exhibit a decrease of $4,435.26; the amount for yardage, as in previous years, includes powder, fuse, and candles furnished by contractors and paid for as labor. The average cost for mining and cleaning ore was $5.73 per carga, or $1.15 per carga less than in 1874, and the cost of terrero and tierras, as compared with the same year, shows a decrease respectively of 20 cents and 7 cents per carga.

The number of men engaged in the work of the mines during 1875 were equal to an average daily force of 457, and an average of 75 were employed at the Hacienda, making a total of 532 men. Of the number at the mines, 50 were Chinamen, of whom but few were employed at the Hacienda, as white labor could be used to better advantage on furnace-work, &c.

The outside mines, other than the San Francisco and Cora Blanca, gave but little ore, 534½ cargas being their product. Work was discontinued at the Enriqueta mine at the end of March, the price of quicksilver not encouraging further prospecting at a point so remote from our general work.

For the Hacienda (reduction-works) pay-rolls the expenditures were $57,181.23, as follows:

General	$33, 609 33
Adobes	3, 991 21
Furnaces	15, 821 94
Railroad	3, 758 75
Total	57, 181 23

The general expenses named above embrace a large amount of work done for account of the mines, and the railroad charges are for the transportation of ore, tierras, &c., from the mines.

Six furnaces were in operation from January to March, when the continuous furnace was put in use, making seven furnaces running for the remainder of the year, excepting stops for repairs and alterations.

The furnace-returns for 1875 give the following result:

Number of furnaces in operation	7
Number of charges* made	301
Number of tons mine-ore roasted	3, 918 $\frac{400}{2000}$
Number of tons terrero-ore roasted	2, 199 $\frac{1600}{2000}$

*For the purpose of making comparison with furnace-charges of former years, the quantity of ore treated in the continuous furnace is reckoned in this number as equal to 36 average charges of No. 6.

Number of tons tierras-ore roasted	$9,435\frac{200}{2000}$
Number of tons total ore roasted	$15,553\frac{200}{2000}$
Cost of fuel * per ton roasted	$\$1.71\frac{60}{100}$
Cost of labor per ton roasted	$\$1.01\frac{73}{100}$
Cost of labor and fuel per ton roasted	$\$2.73\frac{33}{100}$
Number of flasks of quicksilver produced from mine-ore	9,924
Number of flasks of quicksilver produced from terrero-ore	1,150
Number of flasks of quicksilver produced from tierras-ore	2,467
Number of flasks of quicksilver produced, total	13,541
Average yield of quicksilver per ton of mine-ore—9.688 per cent	$193\frac{76}{100}$ pounds.
Average yield of quicksilver per ton of terrero—2 per cent	40 pounds.
Average yield of quicksilver per ton of tierras—1 per cent	20 pounds.
Average yield of quicksilver per ton of all—3.33 per cent	$66\frac{60}{100}$ pounds.
Average yield of quicksilver per ton for mine-ore and terrero—6.92 per cent	$138\frac{40}{100}$ pounds.

Compared with 1874, the above results show an increase in—

Quantity of mine-ore roasted	$1,012\frac{1100}{2000}$ tons.
Quantity of tierras-ore roasted	$3,355\frac{600}{2000}$ tons.
Total	$4,367\frac{1700}{2000}$ tons.
Less decrease of terrero roasted	$541\frac{1500}{2000}$ tons.
Total increase	$3,826\frac{200}{2000}$ tons.

The furnace percentage for all ores worked, 3.33, was a gain of $\frac{45}{100}$ per cent., and the mine-ore and terrero together exhibit a gain of 2.63 per cent. over 1874. The increase in percentage and amount of ore worked is largely due to the successful operation of the continuous furnace, No. 7,† of which the record, as well as the quantity of ore produced and roasted monthly, with percentages, &c., is shown in tables Nos. 5, 6, and 7 annexed to this report, to which reference is made, as also to tables Nos. 7, 8, and 9, which present the comparative cost per ton, &c., in the old and new furnaces for the year's work. Of the total furnace-product—13,541 flasks—the old furnaces, six in number, gave 5,828 flasks, and the new continuous furnace, No. 7, gave 7,713 flasks, the latter running only ten months. The average cost per flask made in No. 7 was 65 cents, and per ton of ore worked it was $1.69 for furnace labor and fuel. No. 6, the largest and best working furnace of the old style, produced 2,806 flasks, at an average cost for furnace labor and fuel of $2.94 per flask and $2.13 per ton of ores worked, while No. 4, a fair representative of the other five furnaces, produced 618 flasks, at an average cost per flask of $9.18 and $3.44 per ton of ores. This last-named furnace was employed for the first quarter of the year on mine-ore and terrero, with the required quantity of adobes (tierras) to make the necessary flues in the furnace for the free passage of the flame and fumes; the best results obtained were in January, at a cost of $3.10 per ton of material treated. No. 6 furnace was engaged on mine-ore with adobes for flues in January and February, at a cost of $2.05 and $2.04 per ton of stuff worked. The most favorable returns of the operations of the old-style furnace for the year, compared with the average of No. 7, gives an advantage for the latter of $1.41 per ton over No. 4, 36 cents per ton over No. 6, in addition to a better percentage return.

The erection of a second iron-clad furnace of the same class and capacity of No. 7 has been commenced, and it will be completed in March next. With the two continuous furnaces 19 tons of mine-ore can be properly treated per day of 24 hours, and as the cost for labor for the double quantity roasted will be increased only 50 per cent., the average cost per ton worked will then be $1.44, or 25 cents less than the present cost. A trial-furnace for continuous treatment of tierras as they come from the screens, without working into adobes or stamping, has been completed and put in successful operation, roasting 10 tons per day, or 300 tons per month, while not more than 120 tons of adobes could be roasted in the furnace monthly previous to the change made by which No. 5 furnace was altered into the trial-furnace. A large double furnace on the same principle, with a capacity of 30 tons daily, is now under way, and the two will give us a long-desired improvement in the handling and roasting of low-grade ores.

The three new furnaces will enable us to treat twice the quantity of ores roasted in 1875, or 30,000 tons; and as it is estimated that the quantity of tierras in the old workings of the mines and on the dumps is about 150,000 tons, there will be no difficulty in keeping all the furnaces running on full time, for which object it will be necessary to make adobes for the five furnaces of the old style.

* To the actual quantity of wood consumed 15 per cent. is added to cover waste, depreciation, &c., and is included in this cost.

† Built after the plan of a furnace erected at the Royal Imperial Quicksilver Mine of Idria, Austria, in 1871, by Herr Adolf Exeli, principal mining manager, with modifications and improvements suggested by the experiences of New Almaden.

Table No. 10 appended to this report shows the cost of tierras, their transportation, making into adobes, and roasting in the old furnaces, to average $6 per ton, treated. With quicksilver at 60 cents per pound, the profit is equal to the cost. In the new tierras-furnaces it is estimated, based on the working of the trial-furnace, that the cost per ton treated will not exceed $3.42, including cost of tierras, transportation, fuel, labor, &c.

In addition to the quicksilver produced by the furnaces, 13,541 flasks, the sluicings of old mortar, lutings of condenser-doors, dirt, &c., gave 107 flasks, making a total of 13,648 flasks.

For this the costs were as follows:

Hacienda pay-rolls	$57,181 23	
Mine pay-rolls	324,577 21	
		$381,758 44
Materials and supplies		92,715 63
Miscellaneous		31,240 49
		505,714 56
From which is to be deducted:		
Increase in quantity of ores on hand at the furnaces	$20,098 60	
Receipts from rentals and miscellaneous	25,403 40	
		45,502 00
Net cost		460,212 56

or $33.72 per flask, against $43.85 for like items in 1874, a decrease of $10.13 per flask.

The furnace-records show that in the 22$\frac{3}{12}$ years, counting from July 1, 1850, to December 31, 1874, but omitting the period from October 30, 1858, to January 31, 1861, 2$\frac{3}{12}$ years, when the New Almaden mines were closed through litigation, the production of quicksilver from ores mined on the company's property has been a total of 592,805 flasks; adding the product of 1875, 13,648 flasks, the aggregate is 606,453 flasks of 76½ pounds each, or 46,393,652½ pounds of quicksilver. The details of this furnace-work will be found in table No. 11.

At the commencement of 1876, the mine may be said to enter on a new career of prosperity, so far as the prospectus of an increased production of ore and an improved method of treating it in larger quantities at a lessened expense is considered. The question of price is one of demand and supply that time will regulate, undoubtedly to the advantage and profit of the mines that continue in operation, and maintain their connections with consumers at home and abroad.

From the tables appended to Mr. Randol's report, I select the following:

Fluctuations in price of quicksilver during the year 1875.

Months.	In San Francisco.	In New York.	In London.	Months.	In San Francisco.	In New York.	In London.
	Per pound.	*Per pound.*	*Per flask.*		*Per pound.*	*Per pound.*	*Per flask.*
January 1	$1 55		£24 00	July 3		$0 77¼	
January 2		$1 65		July 10	$0 70		
February 1			22 00	August 1			£10 00
February 5		1 55		August 6		75	
February 6	1 40			September 1			11 11
March 1	1 30		21 00	September 3	65	75	
March 5		1 35		September 4	70		
March 13	1 00			September 10	67½		
March 18	90			September 17	68		
March 19			16 00	September 20	75		
March 23	85			October 1			14 10
March 29	70			October 2		85	
April 1			15 00	October 11	80		
April 2		1 05		October 18	85		
April 21	68			October 30	70		
April 30	65			November 1	70		12 00
May 1			14 15	November 5		77½	
May 7		85		November 13	65		
May 14			12 00	December 1	70		13 00
June 5		80		December 2		70	
June 28	70			December 22	65		
July 1			11 00	December 31	62½	75	11 00

Table showing wages per diem to miners, mechanics, laborers, &c., in various parts of Nevada and California, December, 1875.

	No. of hours worked.	Carpenters.	Masons.	Blacksmiths.	Engineers.	Hard-rock miners.	Gravel-miners and pipemen.	Timbermen and pumpmen.	Trammers.	Laborers.	Foremen in mine.
Spring Valley Water Company, San Francisco.	10	$4 00	$5 00	$3 50	$3 50	......	......	......	......	$3 00	......
North Bloomfield Gravel-Mining Company, Nevada County, Cal.	8	......	......	......	......	$3 00	......	......	......	......	......
	10	4 00	......	4 00	......	......	$3 00 to 3 50	......	......	3 00	$5 00
	12	......	......	......	......	......	3 75	......	......	......	......
Idaho Gold-Quartz Mine, Nevada County, Cal.	8	4 00	......	......	......	3 00	......	$3 50	......	......	......
	10	4 00	......	3 50 to 4 50	3 50	......	......	......	$3 00	2 75 to 3 00	......
	12	......	......	......	3 50 to 4 00	......	......	......	......	......	......
Sierra Buttes Gold-Quartz Mine, Sierra County, Cal.	8	......	......	......	......	2 73	......	......	......	......	......
	10	3 42 to 4 92	......	......	4 42	2 35 to 2 73	......	3 12	2 15	1 80 to 1 96	5 42
Eureka Plumas Gold-Quartz Mine, Plumas County, Cal.	8	......	......	......	......	3 00	......	......	......	......	......
	10	3 75 to 5 41	......	......	4 86	2 58 to 3 00	......	3 43	2 36	1 98 to 2 15	5 96
Chollar Potosi Silver-Mine, Virginia, Nev.	8	......	......	......	5 00	4 00	......	......	......	......	6 00
	10	6 00	......	5 00 to 6 00	......	......	......	5 00	4 50	3 50	*9 60
(Other mines at Gold Hill and Virginia City pay the same rates as those given for the Chollar Potosi, and there has been no considerable change made in the rate of wages at above localities during the past two years.)							Machinists.				
Risdon Iron and Locomotive Works, San Francisco, Cal.	10	......	......	3 50 to 4 00	3 33 to 5 00	......	$3 00 to 4 00	......	......	2 00 to 2 50	......
Guadalupe Mine, Santa Clara County, Cal.	10	3 50 to 4 00	3 00 to 6 00	3 50	3 50 to 4 00	3 00	......		2 50	2 00	......
New Almaden Mine, Santa Clara County, Cal.	10	3 00 to 4 00	4 00 to 5 00	3 30 to 4 00	......	......	3 00 to 5 00	3 00 to 3 50	2 50	2 30	......
	12	......	......	......	3 00	......	......	......	......	†2 50	6 00

New Almaden Mine, Santa Clara County, Cal., August, 1874, 267 miners on contract and tribute, average earnings per day of ten hours........ $2 11
New Almaden Mine, Santa Clara County, Cal., December, 1874, 289 miners on contract and tribute, average earnings per day of ten hours........ 2 84
New Almaden Mine, Santa Clara County, Cal., August, 1875, 324 miners on contract and tribute, average earnings per day of ten hours........ 1 95
New Almaden Mine, Santa Clara County, Cal., December, 1875, 333 miners on contract and tribute, average earnings per day of ten hours........ 1 62

* Clerks. † Furnace-hands.

Statement of the progress and expenditures made in the Hacienda tunnel, New Almaden, during the year 1875.

Month.	Paid for—		Total time and materials.	No. of feet driven.	Cost per foot.		Total cost per foot.
	Time.	Materials.			Labor.	Materials.	
January	$1,434 85	$1,038 16	$2,473 01	103	$13 28	$9 61	$22 89
February	1,418 56	1,829 56	3,248 12	124	11 44	14 67	26 11
March	1,404 93	1,444 59	2,849 52	131	10 72	11 03	21 75
April	1,278 24	1,648 70	2,926 94	135½	9 44	12 16	21 60
May	966 35	1,266 12	2,232 47	94	10 28	13 47	23 75
June	1,075 59	1,238 11	2,313 70	85½	12 58	14 48	27 06
July	1,335 00	1,402 35	2,737 35	103	12 96	13 61	26 57
August	1,381 00	1,094 84	2,475 84	121½	11 36	9 01	20 37
September	1,261 37	1,195 75	2,457 12	112½	11 21	10 63	21 84
October	797 50	796 36	1,593 86	65½	12 17	12 16	24 33
Total cost with machine-drills	12,353 39	12,954 54	25,307 93	1,080½	11 43	11 99	23 42
HAND-LABOR.							
October	540 01	126 56	666 57	26	20 77	4 87	25 64
November	1,437 63	188 23	1,625 86	68½	20 98	2 75	23 73
December	1,441 75	411 01	1,852 76	80½	17 91	5 10	23 01
Total cost with hand-labor	3,419 39	725 80	4,145 19	175	19 54	4 14	23 68
Grand total	15,772 78	13,680 34	29,453 12	1,255½	12 56	10 90	23 46

Labor includes two engineers, running compressors, four drillmen, four assistants, four trammers, time of blacksmith, machinist, and carpenters for drills, and twelve miners and two trammers on hand-labor, with time of timbermen and blacksmith.

Materials include fuel, oil, lights, rails, air-pipe, steel, explosives, exploders, timber, &c.

Statement of the number of cargas and tons of ore of all qualities reduced and flasks of quicksilver produced at New Almaden Mine in 1875.

Months.	Ore, cargas.	Terrero, cargas.	Tierras, cargas.	Total, cargas.	Total.		Furnaces, number of flasks.	Sluicings, number of flasks.	Total, flasks.
					Tons.	*Pounds.*			
January	1,770	1,893⅓	4,100	7,763⅓	1,164	1,000	836	14	850
February	1,966⅔	1,486⅔	4,633	8,086⅓	1,212	1,900	795	5	800
March	2,499⅓	1,750	3,846	8,095⅓	1,214	600	1,033	......	1,033
April	1,514⅔	805⅓	6,596	8,916	1,337	800	810	40	850
May	1,984	526⅔	6,627	9,137⅔	1,370	1,300	1,088	7	1,095
June	1,920	1,083⅓	5,447	8,450⅓	1,267	1,100	1,050	......	1,050
July	2,812	1,016⅔	5,580	9,408⅔	1,411	600	1,213	7	1,220
August	2,160	1,250	5,973	9,383	1,407	900	1,100	......	1,100
September	2,040	1,150	5,507	8,697	1,340	1,100	1,192	8	1,200
October	1,984	900	5,297⅔	8,181⅔	1,227	500	1,250	......	1,250
November	2,886⅔	1,250	4,620	8,756⅔	1,313	1,000	1,674	26	1,700
December	2,584	1,553⅓	4,674	8,811⅓	1,321	1,400	1,500	......	1,500
Totals	26,121⅓	14,665⅓	62,900⅔	103,687⅓	15,553	200	13,541	107	13,648

NOTE.—Percentage of all reduced, including sluicings, was 3.35.

The following table, compiled from three given by Mr. Randol, exhibits the comparative efficiency and economy of these furnaces. Of these, No. 6 is provided with Fiedler condensers and a Root blower, as described below, and No. 7 is the new continuous furnace, to which reference is also made below. It should be remembered that No. 7 was running but ten months, having started in March. Its superiority is apparent.

Comparative statement of the class and quantity of ores burned in furnaces Nos. 4, 6, and 7 during the year 1875, with the percentages and number of flasks produced, the cost of labor and fuel, also the cost per flask produced and per ton of ore worked.

Furnaces.	Class and quantity of ore.				Yield of quicksilver.		
	Granza, pounds.	Terrero, pounds.	Tierras, pounds.	Total, in pounds.	Per cent. of all.	Per cent. of granza and terrero.	Number of flasks.
No. 4	38, 000	285, 000	2, 971, 000	3, 294, 000	1. 43	5. 44	618
No. 6	1, 781, 000	2, 229, 000	3, 691, 000	7, 771, 000	2. 76	4. 36	2, 806
No. 7	5, 871, 400	121, 600	....	5, 993, 000	9. 85	9. 85	7, 713

Furnaces.	Cost of labor.	Cost of wood.	Cost of coke and charcoal.	Cost of all fuel.	Total of fuel and labor.	Cost per flask.	Cost per ton of ore.
No. 4	$2, 220 00	$3, 240 00	$216 00	$3, 456 00	$5, 676 00	$9 18	$3 44
No. 6	3, 127 50	4, 744 00	391 50	5, 135 50	8, 263 00	2 94	2 13
No. 7	3, 030 00	1, 365 75	670 55	2, 036 30	5, 066 30	65	1 69

NOTE.—Tierras estimated at 1 per cent.

The following is a statement in detail of the working of the new "iron-clad" furnace, No. 7:

Months.	Pounds of ore roasted.	Flasks produced.			Percentage.	Cords wood burned.	Charcoal and coke burned, pounds.
		Free.	Soot.	Total.			
March	501, 800	449	21	470	7. 17	19⅛	5, 886
April	576, 000	503	23	526	6. 98	20¾	8, 640
May	595, 200	738	29	767	6. 85	22	8, 928
June	576, 000	713	31	744	9. 88	20⅞	8, 640
July	793, 600	810	52	862	8. 31	24¼	11, 904
August	608, 000	658	41	699	8. 78	22½	9, 120
September	576, 000	744	23	767	10. 18	22¼	8, 640
October	595, 200	862	29	891	11. 45	25	8, 928
November	576, 000	1, 066	46	1, 112	14. 76	24½	8, 640

Statement of the cost of tierras, their transportation, making into adobes and roasting, with estimate of profit per ton.

Furnaces.	Number of adobes per charge.	Number of pounds.	Wood—cords per charge.	Wood—cost per charge.	Labor—cost per charge.	Wear and tear, per charge.
Furnace No. 1	5, 500	66, 000	12	$78 00	$40 00	$10 00
Furnace No. 2	9, 250	111, 000	14	91 00	50 00	10 00
Furnace No. 3	5, 700	68, 400	12	78 00	40 00	10 00
Furnace No. 4	5, 500	66, 000	11	71 50	40 00	10 00
Furnace No. 5	5, 000	60, 000	12	78 00	40 00	10 00
Furnace No. 6	13, 500	162, 000	18	117 00	55 00	10 00
Totals	44, 450	533, 400	79	513 50	265 00	60 00

44,450 adobes, 12 pounds each = 533,400 pounds, or 266 $\frac{1400}{2000}$ tons, of tierras.

Tierras, cost at mine	$1. 53⅓	per ton, or	$9. 20	per 1,000 adobes	$408 94
Tierras, transportation	36⅓	per ton, or	2. 18	per 1,000 adobes	96 90
Adobes, making	50	per ton, or	3 00	per 1,000 adobes	133 35
Adobes, handling	45	per ton, or	2 70	per 1,000 adobes	120 01
Wood consumed, cost	1 93	per ton, or	11 55	per 1,000 adobes	513 50
Labor, charging, firing, and discharging	1 00	per ton, or	5 96	per 1,000 adobes	265 00
Furnace, wear and tear	22½	per ton, or	1 35	per 1,000 adobes	60 00
Total cost of 266 $\frac{1400}{2000}$ tons	6 00	per ton, or	35 94	per 1,000 adobes	1,597 70

Calculating the yield of quicksilver at 1 per cent., the product will be 5,334 pounds, at 60 cts.	$3,200 40
Leaving net margin profit for 6 charges	1,602 70
Or for 24 charges, one month's work, 6 furnaces	6,410 80
At ¾ per cent., the profit per month would be	4,808 10
At ½ per cent., the profit per month would be	3,205 40

Value of quicksilver produced, 1 per cent., is $12 per ton of tierras-ore worked.
Cost of quicksilver produced, 1 per cent., is $6 per ton of tierras-ore worked.
Profit of quicksilver, at 60 cents per pound, $6 per ton of tierras-ore worked.

Statement of production of quicksilver at New Almaden, for twenty-three years and three months.

Dates.	Class and quantity of ore.				Flasks from furnaces.	Flasks from sluicings.	Total flasks.	Average amount per month, flasks.	Percentage, including all.	Percentage of tierras.	True percentage of ore, excluding tierras and sluicings.	Number of months.
	Grueso, pounds.	Granza, pounds.	Tierras, pounds.	Total, pounds.								
From July, 1850, to June, 1851	......	......	......	4, 970, 717	23, 875	....	23, 875	1, 989½	36. 74	......	36. 74	12
From July, 1851, to June, 1852	......	......	......	4, 643, 290	19, 921	....	19, 921	1, 660	32. 82	......	32. 82	12
From July, 1852, to June, 1853	......	......	......	4, 839, 520	18, 035	....	18, 035	1, 503	28. 50	......	28. 50	12
From July, 1853, to June, 1854	......	......	......	7, 448, 000	26, 325	....	26, 325	2, 193¾	27. 03	......	27. 03	12
From July, 1854, to June, 1855	......	......	......	9, 109, 300	31, 860	....	31, 860	2, 655	26. 75	......	26. 75	12
From July, 1855, to June, 1856	......	......	......	10, 355, 200	28, 083	....	28, 083	2, 340¼	20. 74	......	20. 74	12
From July, 1856, to June, 1857	......	......	......	10, 299, 900	26, 002	....	26, 002	2, 167	19. 31	......	19. 31	12
From July, 1857, to June, 1858	......	......	......	10, 997, 170	29, 347	....	29, 347	2, 445½	20. 41	......	20. 41	12
From July, 1858, to October, 1858	......	......	......	3, 873, 085	10, 588	....	10, 588	2, 647	20. 91	......	20. 91	4
From November, 1858, to January, 1861*	......	......	......									
From February, 1861, to January, 1862	......	......	......	13, 323, 200	32, 402	2, 363	34, 765	2, 897	19. 96	......	18. 64	12
From February, 1862, to January, 1863	......	......	......	15, 281, 400	39, 262	1, 129	40, 391	3, 366	20. 22	......	19. 65	12
From February, 1863, to August, 1863	......	......	......	7, 172, 660	17, 316	2, 248	19, 564	2, 795	20. 86	......	18. 46	7
From September, 1863, to October, 1863	......	......	......	2, 346, 000	4, 820	700	5, 520	2, 760	18. 00	......	15. 67	2
From November, 1863, to December, 1863	54, 800	1, 586, 500	718, 000	2, 359, 300	4, 040	407	4, 447	2, 223½	18. 65	3	17. 52	2
From January, 1864, to December, 1864	1, 259, 400	18, 730, 300	3, 287, 900	23, 277, 600	42, 176	313	42, 489	3, 540¾	13. 96	3	15. 64	12
From January, 1865, to December, 1865	2, 288, 900	25, 749, 000	3, 910, 500	31, 948, 400	47, 078	116	47, 194	3, 933	11. 30	3	12. 42	12
From January, 1866, to December, 1866	1, 506, 000	19, 939, 100	5, 440, 200	26, 885, 300	34, 726	424	35, 150	2, 929	10. 00	3	11. 62	12
From January, 1867, to December, 1867	731, 500	15, 689, 288	9, 603, 145	26, 023, 933	23, 990	471	24, 461	2, 038⅓	7. 19	3	9. 42	12
From January, 1868, to December, 1868	2, 274, 208	14, 566, 600	12, 564, 722	29, 405, 530	25, 557	51	25, 628	2, 135⅔	6. 66	2	10. 12	12
From January, 1869, to December, 1869	150, 000	11, 942, 175	13, 366, 000	25, 458, 175	16, 898	......	16, 898	1, 408	5. 07	2	8. 48	12
From January, 1870, to December, 1870	30, 000	12, 531, 900	8, 535, 800	21, 097, 700	14, 423	......	14, 423	1, 202	5. 23	2	7. 42	12
From January, 1871, to December, 1871	......	13, 661, 700	8, 373, 000	22, 034, 700	18, 563	5	18, 568	1, 547⅓	6. 44	2	9. 16	12
From January, 1872, to December, 1872	142, 000	12, 777, 000	8, 497, 600	21, 416, 600	18, 391	183	18, 574	1, 548	6. 63	2	9. 57	12
From January, 1873, to December, 1873	......	8, 492, 375	8, 838, 000	17, 330, 375	11, 042	......	11, 042	920	4. 87	2	7. 86	12
From January, 1874, to December, 1874	......	11, 294, 000	12, 160, 000	23, 454, 000	8, 867	217	9, 084	757	2. 96	1. 59	4. 29	12
From January, 1875, to December, 1875	......	12, 236, 000	18, 870, 200	31, 106, 200	13, 541	107	13, 648	1, 137⅓	3. 35	1	6. 92	12
Totals and averages	8, 436, 808	179, 195, 938	114, 165, 067	406, 457, 255	587, 148	8, 734	595, 882	2, 135¾	11. 21	1. 99	14. 58	279
Product of Enriqueta from 1860 to 1863							10, 571					
Total product of the mines on the company's property							606, 453 flasks, of 76½ lbs. each, or 46,393,654½ lbs.					

*Closed by injunction.

During the year 1875 the following principal improvements and alterations were made at the Hacienda:

A new tank, 32 feet long, 10 feet wide, and 9 feet high, was erected 300 feet above the level of the furnace-yard, and connected with a tank of the same dimensions, situated at the same height, built previously for the purpose of supplying with water the compressors of the bottom tunnel, both together containing about 36,000 gallons of water. A 5-inch pipe leads from these tanks toward the furnace-yard, and is connected with branch pipes which supply eight hydrants distributed through the yard, and which promise a complete insurance against any material damage by fire, on the northwest side of the Alamitos Creek.

A round tank 12 feet in diameter was added to the already existing water-works on the northeast side of the creek; 350 feet of carbolized hose is kept in readiness for any emergency, and the many roofs and sheds, all constructed of wood, and scattered over the yard, to which additions are continually being made, are now completely safe compared with former years, as a few small tanks then existing were allowed to decay for want of proper repairs.

The discovery of rich bodies of ore in the "Cora Blanca," which is isolated from the main works and arteries of communication, necessitated the construction of a wagon-road, also the building of a large platform, serving as a discharging-depot, which is situated at a point where the main tramway joins the newly-made road; the ore and tierras are then shoveled into the cars of the main railroad, and distributed in the usual way. A new wagon-road, leading through the farming-lands of the company, was constructed in conjunction with parties living in the mountainous districts of the Uvas and Llagas, who supply this company with redwood timbers, lagging, &c., for the use of the mine. This road shortens the distance between the different points and the Hacienda considerably, and enabled the contractors for timber, lagging, &c., to deliver the same at the usual rate, as the gain in time by the finishing of this road amounts to one trip a week for each team. Without this road all the materials mentioned would have commanded an advanced price, as the sources of supply become more distant and more inaccessible every year.

The destruction by fire of the old adobe-house and outside buildings used as a boarding-house, on the 6th day of August last, made the building of a new boarding-house a great necessity, and as soon as materials could be obtained a new building was begun and opened during November last. Although an additional building, to be used as a dormitory, will have to be erected hereafter, the structure so far finished answers for the immediate wants. A new warehouse for storing adobes was constructed, 120 feet in length and 30 feet wide. The starting of the iron-clad furnace, which nearly absorbs all the mine-ore, left the old-style furnaces for the roasting of adobes and terrero ore. To meet this increased demand a great amount of adobes had to be made during the summer, and the old sheds not proving adequate to store the amount required, this new warehouse was built. The coal-shed, burned partially at the fire of the former hotel, had to be entirely rebuilt.

The flue mentioned as commenced in last year's report, serving as a conductor for the fumes of Nos. 3, 4, and 6 furnaces, and extending 1,000 feet further up the mountain than the original chimneys of these furnaces, was completed early in the year. The expectation of saving thereby all the wood formerly consumed in the draught-fire-chimney has been only partially realized, but the additional time gained for the condensation of the mercurial and other obnoxious vapors, before their exit to the open air, has proved this a wise investment, and encourages the extension of all the other flues leading from the furnaces. The two wooden condensers for No. 5 furnace, mentioned in last year's report as partially finished, were ready for use, as promised, at the end of January, and an additional one of the same dimensions, namely, 12 feet wide, 12 feet long, 20 feet high, with 34 large windows and divided into 4 chambers, was also completed soon thereafter.

Two brick towers, each 7½ feet wide, 12 feet long, and 26 feet high, and two brick condensers, one 27 feet long, 10½ feet wide, and 27 feet high, the other 20 feet long, 20 feet high, and 10 feet wide, were finished for the iron-clad furnace. This furnace, which was started on March 4 last, has proven to fill, not only all the surmises and expectations formed, and which led to its construction, but has surpassed all of these, and stands to-day unrivaled on this continent, and from all accounts has given better results than the original furnace put up at Idria, in Austria. The furnace-reports amply show that this eulogium of its advantages and successes is fully verified.

A large wooden condenser, giving an additional condensing-space of 4,640 cubic feet, was constructed for No. 1 furnace. This condenser is built on the same plan as those erected for No. 5 furnace. They seem to answer fully their purpose, and on account of their cheapness of construction, durability of their material, and great facility of cleaning their walls, and freeing the whole structure from the adhering quicksilver, (so difficult a task in the old brick condensers,) should supersede, wherever convenient or practicable, the brick or iron condensers. The old wooden flues connecting Nos. 1 and 2 furnaces and condensers with the main flue leading up the mountain-side to the chimney, were replaced, on account of debility and rottenness, by new flues, and in order to give additional condensing-space for these furnaces, a large brick tower was erected on the hill-side, into which the new flues land, and the fumes, before passing into the main flue, have to traverse the same. The gain in quicksilver secured by this additional condensing-space has amply paid for the outlay.

In the report for last year mention was made of a wooden tower erected for Nos. 1 and 2 furnaces with upcast and downcast shaft, the latter supplied with a spray of water. This tower, with water-arrangement, was found to operate badly, and was therefore removed. The brick chimney serving as outlet for No. 5 and the iron-clad furnace was raised from its original height of 30 feet to 62 feet, securing thereby a stronger draught for the "Monitor." Two large shoots were built for the iron-clad furnace, and these, as also all the other ore-shoots, were covered with roofs in order to keep the ores dry during the rainy season. Two new iron condensers, after Fiedler's patent, were purchased this year, and connected with a Root blower, which was driven by a small engine. This apparatus was put up at No. 6 furnace condensers, and intended to withdraw from the furnace, after the firing had ceased, and the complete roasting of the ores secured, any mercurial vapors which should remain in the mass of hot ore, and which would be lost when the furnace is discharged. The time between the closing of firing and the opening of the furnace, would not give time enough for these fumes to pass into the condensers, as the draught diminishes rapidly after the firing has ceased. This experiment has been a success, and proven that any outlay for this object for the other furnaces would not only shortly pay for itself, but show a handsome profit at the end of the year. The foundation for a new iron-clad furnace, to be erected this year, was laid at the end of December. Numerous tests, trials, and experiments were made, with the object to discover some method of constructing a continuous furnace for the burning of the tierras and obviating the great expense of making them into adobes, but all of these but one offered too many objections for their acceptance.

There was only one experiment which promised success, and No. 5 furnace was changed so as to allow a test of its merits to be made. This proved successful enough to warrant the enlargement of the furnace for a trial on a larger scale, and on the 28th of December last the furnace was started once more. The time elapsed between that day and the date of this report has been too short to form a conclusive opinion, but enough has been ascertained to believe that no formidable obstacle will interfere with its complete success, and the erection of a furnace on the same principle is fully warranted.

The large amount of tierras on hand, and the assurance that the mine could furnish as many as 60 tons per day, made the construction of a new additional furnace for the burning of the adobes an imperative necessity. Plans of a double continuous furnace for the purpose were made, and condensers for the same, designated as No. 8, were commenced during the year, but a successful experiment with the tierras in their natural state, as above described, forced the abandonment of this plan, and a new tierras-furnace will take its place, and the condensers already commenced will be finished for the same.

Since August, 1874, no general clean-up of condensers has taken place until December, 1875. At the first clean-up mentioned, and more so in all previous undertakings of the same kind, a great quantity of quicksilver was found in the flues leading from the last condenser to the chimneys situated on the mountains surrounding the furnace-yard. The construction of additional condensers wherever it was necessary, during the last two years, has shown at the last general clean-up, at the end of the year, a most satisfactory result, and has proven that the outlay for these structures was a wise and necessary one, as hardly any quicksilver was found in the different flues, and in their whole aggregate length of 1,463 feet (leaving out joint flue of Nos. 5 and 7, which could not be cleaned, as both furnaces were in operation and are continuous in their action) only six flasks of quicksilver were collected as the result of sixteen months' operations.

Statement of the business of the Quicksilver-Mining Company for 1875.

DR.			CR.
To quicksilver and ore on hand per last yearly report, and cost of quicksilver and ore produced and mined in 1875	$753,083 00	By balance to the credit of income-account, January 1, 1875	$1,318,013 44
To materials and supplies used in improvements	27,598 80	By sales of quicksilver	719,257 77
To legal expenses	3,023 77	By rents and privileges	20,241 44
To interest on funded debt	59,500 00	By materials and property sold	1,229 73
To taxes	4,892 81	By interest on call-loans, &c	15,944 36
To exchange	675 00	By premium on gold sold	12,658 12
To general expenses	11,493 35	By ore on hand	179,410 69
To net allowance in value of assets at the mine, per inventory	9,959 79	By quicksilver on hand	34,380 00
To balance to the credit of income-account, January 1, 1876	1,430,909 03		
Total	2,301,135 55	Total	2,301,135 55

Balance-sheet December 31, 1875.

Dr.		Cr.		
Real estate and mining property..	$11, 047, 875 60	Capital stock, preferred	$4, 219, 300	
Convertible-bond stock	71, 000 00	Capital stock, common	5, 708, 700	
Houses and lands	148, 066 12			$10, 000, 000 00
Railroads	75, 603 33	Second-mortgage bonds..........		700, 000 00
Furnaces	128, 858 33	Income-account..........		1, 430, 909 03
Virginia City property..........	1, 500 00			
Furniture, Hacienda, &c..........	4, 000 00			
Machinery and tools..........	55, 546 67			
James B. Randol, manager, cash...	54, 457 73			
David Mahany, treasurer, cash and loans..........	206, 327 39			
Materials and supplies..........	99, 375 68			
Ore-account..........	179, 410 69			
Quicksilver on hand	34, 380 00			
Miscellaneous property	8, 507 49			
Woodlands	16, 000 00			
Total	12, 130, 909 03	Total		12, 130, 909 03

The following summary of the quicksilver industry of California is taken from the Commercial Herald of San Francisco:

The quantity of quicksilver produced on the Pacific coast in the year 1875 amounted to about 54,000 flasks. In this estimate is included an allowance of 500 flasks made to cover various small lots of metal ranging from ten to fifty flasks each, run out by parties owning deposits of limited extent or not yet much opened up, and who have mostly been restricted to the use of retorts alone. This is wholly the fruit of California mines. None of the other Pacific States or Territories have yet made any quicksilver, though cinnabar in small quantities has been found in some of them. The total production of this metal throughout the world now reaches about 100,000 flasks, of which California is at present turning out fully one-half. In a few years more the yield of this State will be likely to greatly exceed that of all the world besides. This commodity has been to us for more than a quarter of a century an element of large wealth, and in the aspect of its indispensable use and late high price, may almost be ranked as a royal metal. Until about ten years ago the New Almaden mine was the principal, as it had before been almost the exclusive source of quicksilver production in California. In 1850 heavy production began here, 20,000 flasks having been run out that and the following year. In 1855 the quantity reached 31,860 flasks, falling to 10,588 four years after. In 1860 and 1861 the mine produced nothing, having been closed by injunction. In 1862, 34,765 flasks were made; in 1863, 40,391, and in 1865, 47,194, after which the yield gradually declined year by year, until it reached its lowest point, 9,084, in 1874. The ore from this mine yielded at the start as high as 36 per cent. of metal, but afterward declined with slight fluctuations until it fell to 4.87 in 1873 and 2.96 in 1874, all the low-grade ores being included. Of the entire world's production, England takes, on an average, about 45,000 flasks annually. The consumption on this coast absorbs about one-third the product, leaving the balance for export. The quantity used here is increasing rapidly every year, promising to keep pace proportionately with increased production, even should prices remain at present figures.

From 1858 to 1870 the prices of quicksilver here ranged from 40 to 55 cents per pound, averaging about 47 cents. For the next three years the average price was 93 cents; in 1874, $1.37½, and last year about 80 cents per pound. For some time to come the price will not be likely to go much above 75 to 80 cents, nor will it probably fall below 55 or 60 cents, as the rapidly-increasing demand for mining-purposes will prevent such accumulation as would tend to force prices downward, while the great abundance of the ore and the widely-distributed proprietorship of the mines will defeat combinations for controlling the market. Owing to the extent and richness of the cinnabar-deposits on this coast, and the facility with which the ores can be utilized, quicksilver can be made here with fair profit when the price does not fall below 60 cents. Heretofore the markets of the world have been affected by certain speculative influences, rather than by the natural agents of demand and supply. Domestic combinations and foreign monopoly have kept them in a state of tension or relaxation, as best suited their purposes. If small lots of quicksilver were thrown upon the London market, the Rothschilds at once depressed prices until they had secured these lots and checked further outside importations, when rates were again advanced to former figures. Under the enormous production hereafter to be made, this style of controlling either the home or foreign market will hardly be practicable. The exports of quicksilver from 1859 to 1874, inclusive, amounted to 365,430 flasks, and, including exports of 1875, give a total of 394,390 flasks, valued at $14,289,591. The exports last year were 28,960 flasks, not including several thousand flasks shipped east by rail. The area of production has recently become so enlarged as to require some detailed notice of the more important cinnabar localities lately discovered.

Beginning at the most northerly point in the State, where extended work is being carried on, we find a number of parties actively engaged opening up the rich deposits that for a long time have been known to exist in Trinity County. During the early days of gold-gathering on the upper waters of the Trinity River, fragments of a crimson-colored rock were found by the miners, intermixed with the gold-dust, its weight being such as to prevent their easy separation. This "red stuff," so called, bothered the honest diggers not a little, interfering with their operations much after the manner of the celebrated "blue stuff"—the rich sulphurets of silver—at a later day vexed and bewildered Comstock and his companions, when working below the great Washoe lode, the tracing up of which led afterward to the discovery of that widely-famed deposit. To this material—the red sulphuret of mercury—little attention was paid for many years, no attempts at utilizing it having been made until 1873, when the high prices of quicksilver induced parties to commence gathering it in the vicinity of the locality now known as Cinnabar, where the surface-soil over a considerable area contained these particles of rich ore, much of which had been carried by the water and lodged along the adjacent ravines. Washing these ravines with rockers afforded the miners good wages for some time, when they finally came upon the veins from which these fragments had escaped, and which were found to be large and well charged with metal. In the early part of 1875 the reported richness of these deposits attracted the notice of certain San Francisco capitalists and miners, and they purchased the largest and most promising claim in the district, and, having organized under the name of the Altoona Quicksilver Company, proceeded to outfit it in first-rate style. This mine is situated about 20 miles from Trinity Centre, and only 18 west from the line of the California and Oregon Railroad. The ore occurs in a regular contact-vein, lying between serpentine and sandstone. It varies from five to twenty feet in width, the matrix being a decomposed sandstone. As the whole of this mass consists of workable ore, carrying from five to twelve per cent. of metal, this may be considered one of the most valuable discoveries of cinnabar yet made in the State. It is a most remarkable fact that the entire mass of material standing between the walls of the lode is here removed and sent to the furnaces, none of it yielding less than four per cent. of metal. The surface of the vein has been uncovered for a distance of 400 feet, showing the ore deposit of uniform dimensions throughout. It has also been opened to a depth of 50 feet by means of tunneling, a second tunnel being now in progress to intersect it at a much greater depth. The drifts and cross-cuttings made show the ore on the lower levels in increased volume and richness, the regularity of the walls and the many stringers coming in pointing to continued fertility and permanence. The ore-body also undergoes a marked expansion with depth attained. In running the lower tunnel several blind lodes have been cut of such power as to raise the question whether the one already opened is the dominating vein of the series, if, indeed, a mineral-belt of extraordinary dimensions does not here cross the face of the mountain, carrying an indefinite number of heavy veins. The ore in these lateral fissures is all of high grade, varying from two to four per cent., some rich streaks going as high as twenty. Coming into possession of this property in July, the owners, running three small retorts, making from three to six flasks per day, have since realized over $32,000 from the product of their quicksilver, the ore for supplying these retorts having been packed a distance of ten miles on mules. Having constructed a wagon-road to the mines, a furnace has since been erected on the ground, which is now operating with a capacity to run out 300 flasks per month. As additional furnaces will probably be built very soon, there being an abundance of ore, there is no calculating what the yield of this mine may be before another year has passed by. The country here is heavily timbered and abounds in fine streams of water, affording every facility for the cheap operating of the mines. Not far from the Altoona are situated the mines of the Boston Company and several other promising claims, some of which are already outfitted with reduction-works, the most of them being yet of limited capacity, running only from ten to forty flasks per week. On the most of these claims systematic work is being done, and there is little doubt but some of them will prove to be valuable properties, the Boston claim being considered of scarcely less prospective value than the Altoona. It is, in fact, evident that a very important quicksilver-field is about to be opened in the far north, and from which a heavy contribution to the yearly out-put of this metal may hereafter be looked for. The entire yield of Trinity County the past year was about 1,500 flasks, which amount, it is believed, will be six-fold greater next year. Coming south from Trinity, the next quicksilver-producing locality met with is in the Coast Range, Colusa County, where, but a little more than a year ago, much activity prevailed in the way of prospecting, locating, and developing the quite numerous but not very heavy deposits of cinnabar there occurring. In consequence of the decline in the price of this metal that took place early last year, this activity soon abated, only two or three claims continuing afterward to be worked. During the year the Abbott Mine, with one small furnace, turned out about 250 flasks, the Buckeye made about 50, and the Sulphur Spring 100 flasks, to which the Elgin and some other small claims added perhaps 25 more, making a total production for the year of 425 flasks on account of the mines in this county.

In Napa, Sonoma, and Lake Counties a great cinnabar-region is being opened up, although the prospects, considered so bright a year ago, have here, too, been somewhat obscured by the declining price of quicksilver. The Redington Mine, the largest producer in that section, makes, as it was expected it would do, a good showing for the past year, having taken out, during ten months' actual running, 8,080 flasks of metal, their furnaces having remained inactive for the first two months' of the year to admit of needed alterations and additions. Toward the close of the year the out-turn was at the rate of over 1,000 flasks per month, an increment due to the more effective style of furnace introduced for treating a class of ores difficult of successful reduction by those formerly in use. Six furnaces, capable of handling 120 tons of ore per day, are now run on this mine, the ore-supply for which is taken wholly from the stopes above the 200-foot level. Exploration is, however, kept well in advance of extraction, the reserves here holding a two years' supply of ore. This company were fortunate in having a contract to supply 400 to 500 flasks per month during 1875, with Flood & O'Brien, at current market-rates of quicksilver. Owing to their prosperous financial condition at the beginning of the year, having large accumulations of cash brought over from the preceding year, this company claim to have been able to disburse dividends during 1875 to the amount of $453,600, besides defraying costs of many important improvements. Next to the Redington on the list of largely-producing mines in this section stands the Sulphur Bank, in Lake County. This company own at that point what promises to be very valuable deposits of cinnabar, the ore being of good grade and easily extracted. The mine has been well opened and outfitted, and will hereafter be able to make a large and profitable production. The metal turned out last year amounted to 5,215 flasks, a quantity that will be materially increased the current year. The yield of the other more actively-producing mines in that section for the past year may be stated as follows: The Great Western, 3,384 flasks; the Manhattan, 437 flasks; the Buckeye, 700 flasks; the Saint John, 2,100 flasks; the Cloverdale, 714 flasks; the Phœnix, 300 flasks; the Great Eastern, 413 flasks; the additional small lots produced in this vicinity having amounted to about 1,000 flasks. The New Almaden Mine made last year 13,648 flasks; the New Idria, 8,800 flasks; the Guadaloupe Mine, with but one small furnace, having turned out 3,415 flasks. The other small lots of metal produced elsewhere in the State will probably be covered by an allowance of 500 flasks. In San Luis Obispo County, another new field which this industry has invaded, a number of cinnabar-deposits are being developed and furnished with reduction-works, the most noteworthy of this group consisting of the Oceanic and the Sunderland, the only ones that have as yet been brought into a condition of considerable production. The Sunderland, with a furnace of 15 tons of daily capacity, ran out 1,500 flasks last year, a yield that will probably be doubled the present year. The Oceanic, with three furnaces, disposes of 75 tons of ore per day, turning out 200 flasks per month. This is a big mine and has sufficient ore developed to run the present furnaces profitably for years. The distinguishing feature of this property consists in the great amount of ore contained between the walls of the lode and the facility with which it can be extracted. About 14 feet of ore is here broken down and passed bodily to the furnaces, being so nearly uniform in quality as to admit of little selection. This is probably the cheapest mine to work in the State, the labor-force numbering scarcely more than half the usual average in mines of equal capacity. The product of this mine amounted last year to about 2,000 flasks, a quantity that might easily be, as it most likely soon will be, largely extended through the erection of additional furnaces and an increase of the working-force. There are two or three other mines in this part of the State making more or less quicksilver, their aggregate product reaching, perhaps, two or three hundred flasks per month, or 2,500 flasks for the past year. In at least a dozen other counties, scattered throughout the length and breadth of the State, cinnabar-deposits have been discovered, some of which show good indications for permanence and wealth. A few of these have been partially opened up and outfitted with retorts, and have produced from 10 to 50 flasks of metal each, an allowance of 500 flasks being enough, no doubt, to cover all the quicksilver made during the year by this class of mines.

From Horatio P. Livermore, treasurer of the Redington Company, we have received in manuscript the following report of that mine. It is as follows:

"The Redington Quicksilver Company during January, February, and a portion of March, 1875, were not producing quicksilver, being engaged in adding to and changing their reduction-works. In March they got their reduction-works well under way again, and their reduction for the current year ending December 31, 1875, (say ten operative months,) has been 8,080 flasks quicksilver. Since September 1 their production has been upward of 1,000 flasks per month, at which figure it closes the year. This increase of product is in a great degree due to the marked success of two new furnaces for the reduction of fine ores or tierras. These furnaces are the invention of the superintendent of the company, Charles E. Livermore, and they may safely be said to introduce a new element into quicksilver-reduction, making it possible to profitably utilize material largely produced by all quicksilver-mines, but heretofore handled always at no profit, and frequently at an absolute loss. The Redington Quicksilver Company have now in active, continuous operation four of the Knox & Osborne patent furnaces, and two of the Livermore patent fine-ore furnaces, their total reducing capacity being upward of 120 tons of ore per day. This large quantity of ore is easily yielded by the upper levels of the mine, none having been drawn from below the 200-foot level. The mine has, however, been opened by shaft to the depth of 400 feet, and constant prospecting-work is maintained in advance, so as to insure a supply of ore for at least two years ahead of requirements. The company employs 300 men in its various departments, and has very extended works, the whole affording a most striking example of what careful management on a strictly business basis may accomplish. Such results have been attainable by reason of the fact that the management of the mine has been carefully attended to by the comparatively few individuals who own it; and the property, though incorporated as a stock company, has never been on the stock-market for sale and speculation, but has always been handled as a legitimate operative business. It has during the past year enjoyed a profitable contract with Flood & O'Brien, to supply them with 500 flasks per month, and this contract is still in force. The capital stock of the company is $1,260,000, in 1,260 shares of $1,000 each, and regular monthly dividends of $30 per share have been paid thereon during 1875, or $37,800 per month, making a total of $453,600 divided profits for 1875. Besides this, at least $125,000 has been invested in new land-purchases, buildings, machinery, new reduction-works, and other appliances, adding largely to the value and future productiveness of the property."

We learn from an official source that the total available cash of the Redington Quicksilver Company during 1875, including a surplus brought forward January 1, amounted to $780,134.28; dividends in 1875, $453,600; leaving balance $326,534.28 for running-expenses. This is certainly a very handsome exhibit for the company, when we recall to mind the fact that in January, 1875, prices ruled as high as $1.50 to $1.55; February, $1.30 to $1.35; March, $1.15 to 75 cents per pound; April, 70 cents to 65 cents; and these were ruling rates during the balance of the year; closing price, 62½ cents. It should be stated, moreover, in justice to the Redington Company's exhibit, that they claim to have had on hand a year ago a large surplus stock of quicksilver, which they sold at $1.50 to $1.30, cleaning all out before the great decline, and leaving them in possession of a monthly contract at a fixed price, and which, we understand, has been extended for another three months with the same parties, contracting with them a year ago; probable price, 70 cents.

The San Francisco Bulletin gives the following as the production:

New Almaden, flasks	13,648	Brought forward	46,642
New Idria, flasks	8,800	Sunderland, flasks	1,500
Redington, flasks	8,080	Cloverdale, flasks	714
Sulphur Bank, flasks	5,215	Buckeye, flasks	700
Guadaloupe, flasks	3,415	Manhattan, flasks	437
Great Western, flasks	3,384	Great Eastern, flasks	413
Saint John, flasks	2,100	Phœnix, flasks	300
Oceanic, flasks	2,000	Various, flasks	3,000
Carried over	46,642	Total	53,706

PETROLEUM.

I am indebted to Mr. Fred. A. Clarke, late of the Geological Survey, for the following notes on this subject:

Some ten years ago petroleum-springs were discovered in California, since which time there have been found divers deposits, but not in quantity or quality sufficient to make the subject worthy of investigation or experiment, save in the coal-oil districts of Sespe and San Fernando.

Here lies a section of some fifty miles square, over the face of which are prominent evidences of the existence of a large petroleum-deposit.

The *San Fernando petroleum district*, lying in the northwest corner of

Los Angeles County, at its farthest point not more than ten miles from the Southern Pacific Railroad, is located on the foot-hills and northeast slope of the San Gabriel Mountains, having the Santa Clara Valley to the north. The main belt of oil-bearing shale is readily traced from 400 feet to 500 feet wide, for some six miles, trending northwest and southeast, and inclosed in wall-rocks of sandstone. The dip of the shale is southwest at an angle of 32°. On the east flank of the shale, in cañons and on spurs, are numerous small oil-springs.

The *San Buenaventura petroleum district* lies to the west of the San Fernando district and is in San Buenaventura County, distant from the Southern Pacific Railroad some thirty miles, forty miles from Los Angeles, and adjacent to tide-water at the port of San Buenaventura. The district is located about Sespe Creek, in San Gabriel Mountains, and is mountainous in its topography. Santa Clara River runs through the locality. There are here large petroleum-springs, the oil from which is carried down to and out upon the ocean for miles.

It is only of late that developments in these districts have been carried to a successful issue. The crude petroleum is found of 40° gravity. In San Buenaventura district there is a small refinery, producing from the crude petroleum of the supply-wells 59 per cent. of illuminating-oil of 130° fire-test, and of water-white and odorless qualities, said to be up to eastern standard. In the San Fernando district there is a flowing well of forty barrels per day, and a refinery producing from this oil 60 per cent. of illuminating-oil of 120° to 130° fire-test, and of high grade; 25 per cent. fine-grained lubricating-oil, 18° gravity. The remainder is fuel. None of these wells carry paraffine. A large refinery is going up at Newhall, on the Southern Pacific Railroad station on Santa Clara River, and a narrow-gauge railroad from Newhall through the oil-section to the Pacific Ocean, some 50 miles, is in contemplation.

Developments carried on with the advantage of the experience of Pennsylvania give good reason to expect here the successful establishment of a commercial industry of especial benefit to the California market, with the additional attraction of an outlet furnished by the islands of the Pacific and Japan, China, and India.

ALPINE COUNTY.

The most important work in the county has again been done by the Exchequer Company, under the management of Mr. Lewis Chalmers. The perseverance of the company has at last been rewarded by the discovery, at the 300-feet level, of a very large body of exceedingly rich silver-ore, and at the end of the year Mr. Chalmers was preparing to start his mill, after first introducing into it furnaces for chloridizing the ore. The following account of the mine, transmitted to me by Mr. Chalmers, contains all of importance in regard to the enterprise.

The development of the mine was commenced by the old-time method of running a tunnel 800 feet long immediately under the croppings of the ledge, at no point cutting the vein at a greater depth than 125 feet below the surface. With the exception of showing the ledge to be regular in its course, from north to south, with a dip of nearly 45° to the south and east, and to contain spots of rich ore, this work was almost entirely thrown away. An incline winze was then started on the ledge at a distance of 120 feet from the mouth of the tunnel. This winze has been sunk a depth of 300 feet, following the inclination of the ledge the entire distance in ore of good milling quality, and which has grown richer as the shaft descends. At the depth of 30 feet below the tunnel-level an ore-stope was opened and a considerable amount of ore extracted. Fifty feet lower down another ore-stope has been started, and at the depth of eighty feet a level was opened for working, and the top of a chimney of rich ore struck.

At a depth of 140 feet this chimney of ore was greatly enlarged, and the vein apparently widening and the ore growing so much better that it was resolved to stop work in the tunnel and incline and erect steam hoisting-works and sink a working-shaft at a point 300 feet lower down the mountain-side. This shaft has been sunk to a depth of 300 feet and over. Stations have been opened and drifts run at the 100, 200, and 300 foot levels of the shaft, which places the lowest point at which the ore-vein has been prospected at a depth of 500 feet below the croppings. The ledge continued to look more favorable and the ore to show greater concentration on the 100-foot level. Ore-stopes have been opened at that point on the ledge which descends with the slope of the mountain, and which have proved to be almost entirely rich milling ore to within 40 feet of the surface. On the 200-foot level a drift 6 by 7 feet in size has been run a distance of 400 feet in the ore-vein without touching either wall, the face in rich ore. The ore on this level is very rich, an average assay made by the assayer of the mine showing $85.11 in gold and $5,710.83 in silver to the ton. On the 300-foot level of the shaft a drift has penetrated the vein 100 feet, showing the ore to be of even a finer quality than it is on the 200-foot level.

The ore contains base metals in quantities sufficient to require roasting before its reduction in the mill. The body is composed of silica mixed with magnesia, iron, antimony, and sulphur. Much of the ore has so strong a resemblance to actinolite, a greenish species of hornblende, that good judges would be puzzled to discern a difference. On the lower levels the ore is interspersed with quantities of beautiful ruby-silver, of the light-red kind, being a combination of silver, arsenic, and sulphur. Average samples, sent to a friend in Gold Hill, were assayed by Mr. Christopher James, the assayer of the Crown Point and Yellow Jacket Mines, one of the most competent assayers on the coast, and gave the following results: That taken from the 140-foot level of the upper works gave $241 per ton, all silver; that of the 100-foot level of the new shaft, $1,019.63, of which $30.13 was gold and the balance silver. The samples from the 200-foot level of the new shaft gave $852.49, of which $20.09 was gold and the remainder silver. The ledge on the lower levels is from 4 to 15 feet in thickness, and is all ore. Both above and below it is separated from the country-rock by heavy clay seams.

The present hoisting-works are entirely too light to prosecute the development of the mine with the required vigor, and the work is confined at present to the sinking of the shaft for opening another level. It is the intention, as soon as spring opens, to commence the erection of new and powerful steam hoisting-works. Three miles from the mine the company have a first-class eight-stamp mill erected. To this are now being added furnaces for roasting the ores and an additional battery of ten stamps, making eighteen in all, which will commence crushing ore from the mine in a very short time. There are now at the mill ready for reduction 700 tons of ore, and, with the present facilities for extracting and the large amount of ore uncovered ready to take out, there will be no trouble whatever in keeping the mill running for at least a year to come.

INYO COUNTY.

Inyo County lies east of the main crest of the Sierra Nevadas, bordering on the State of Nevada. The Inyo Mountains, running north and south, traverse the center of the county. The Panamint, a higher range, lies farther to the east. The country has an area of 4,680 square miles, and contains several mining-districts, the most important being Cerro Gordo, Panamint, Kearsarge, and Darwin. The silver-lead mines of Cerro Gordo produce about $1,000,000 of bullion annually. Panamint and Kearsarge districts contain fissure-veins of silver-bearing ores, and Darwin district (discovered in 1874) large masses of argentiferous galena and carbonates, which have not at this date been sufficiently developed to determine their character. The county contains seven quartz-mills, aggregating one hundred and twenty stamps and ten furnaces. Other furnaces are in process of construction in Darwin district, and a large bullion-production may be anticipated for the year 1876 from the ore-bodies already developed.

This county was visited and described by Mr. C. Luckhardt in 1870, (see Report of 1871, pp. 17–27,) and by Mr. A. Eilers in 1872, (see Report of 1873, pp. 17–21 and 354–357.) Subsequently, in 1874, Mr. C. Stetefeldt visited Panamint and made a report, which will be found in my Report of 1875, p. 33. (See also report of William Crapo, on p. 27 of the same volume.) The developments in Darwin district at that time, although promising, were not sufficiently advanced to render the inspection of a special agent necessary.

I am indebted to Mr. C. Weberling, of the Surprise Valley Mill and Water Company, Panamint district, for the following valuable summary from that locality.

The principal mines worked are the Wyoming and Hemlock, now 450 to 500 feet deep. The ore is taken to the mill by a Hallidie wire tram-way. Average assay-value as delivered to mill, $80 to $100 silver per ton. The mill contains twenty stamps, (900 pounds, drop 9 inches, eighty-five to ninety per minute,) crushing (dry) 22 to 25 tons per twenty-four hours; 100-horse-power engine; ten pans, holding 1 ton each of dry pulp, (revolutions fifty-eight per minute;) a Stetefeldt furnace of the newest construction, (capacity 40 tons per twenty-four hours.) The consumption of wood in the furnace is three to three and one-half cords per twenty-four hours. From 2.7 to 3 per cent. of salt and 2 per cent. of iron pyrites are added to the ore before roasting. The average results of four months' running have been: Chlorination, 93 to 94 per cent.; amalgamation, 91 per cent.; fineness of bullion, .964. The ores being highly cupriferous, these favorable results are mainly attributable to the excellent working of the Stetefeldt furnace. The direct costs for reduction have been from $18 to $20 per ton, wages being $4 to $5.50 per day, and wood $12 per cord.

Mr. J. Neiswander reports concerning the Sunrise and Twilight Mines, owned by the Sunrise Company:

Length of location, 1,500 feet each; course, east and west; country-rock, limestone; vein-matter, quartz; depth of shaft, 50 feet; two levels, total length, 175 feet; twenty miners, at $4 per day; cost of mining, $5 per ton extracted; of milling, $8; average yield, about $80 per ton. The company mill (40-horse steam-power) has five stamps, (900 pounds, eighty-five drops of 8 inches per minute;) three pans, and two concentrators; cost, $35,000; capacity, 10 tons per twenty-four hours.

The latest reports from Panamint district indicate a danger of exhaustion of the ore bodies, though the veins seem to continue in depth. Some miners assert that the argentiferous gray copper ores, which here predominate, are always treacherous in this way. If this be a fact, it is only of local application—say in a certain belt of country; and I cannot see, even in that case, why the blame should be laid on the mineral, rather than on the general formation, which may have resulted in detached bodies rather than continuous seams of ore.

The economy of silver-lead mining in Darwin district will be fully understood upon perusal of the able and comprehensive report of Mr. L. L. Robinson, president of the New Coso Mining Company, dated December 15, 1875, from which I make the following extracts:

Mr. Robinson says: Our deepest working (on Lucky Jim Mine) is 137 feet, on Christmas-Gift Mine, 95 feet. At these depths the two mines show great strength and richness, and at all other openings they also show the same peculiarities, and give every evidence of permanence in depth. At the Christmas-Gift Mine there are five shafts, varying in depth from 35 to 95 feet.

The opening up of such an extent of ground as we have been working on is necessarily slow, and as no reliance could be placed upon any one shaft or opening, there have been five shafts sunk on one mine and four on the other mine, the Lucky Jim. From these shafts drifts have been run on the veins and cross-cuts have been driven to prospect the ground, until we have sunk in all 625 feet of shaft, and run 620 feet of drifts and cross-cuts, besides work on surface in open cuts and tunnels to an extent of 150 feet more in length.

Near the surface the mines turned out considerable heavy lead-ores, which were taken to the furnace and smelted. As the workings attained depth the nature of the ores kept changing, and although they were always rich in silver, yet what are called "dry ores" became predominant, and for a time it looked as if the mines would turn entirely to milling-ores. Deeper workings and more extensive openings have, however, again developed large bodies of heavy ores, and although large amounts of dry ores were also developed, yet these are left standing in the mines for future workings and attention is turned to following the heavy ores which answer for smelting. With our heavy ore we now mix at furnace a percentage of dry ore, and so consume constantly quite an amount of ores of this class.

In a section of country where everything is so expensive, and where it is not advisable to take any risks that can be avoided, and where open surface-excavations are not objectionable, it is good policy to follow the veins, and particularly is this the case where the heavy lead-ores are encountered, as such deposits are generally apt to be eccentric. Finding, as we do, so large an amount of dry ores in our mines at present depth, and not knowing what developments may take place in greater depths, I deemed it my duty to examine the country pretty thoroughly, in order to ascertain where facilities, if any, could be found for a mill-site. The result of these examinations develops excellent locations some three or four miles from the mines, where water can, it is believed, be had in sufficient quantities. The location is easy of access from the mines, and a road with a descending grade the entire distance, some three or four miles long, can be cheaply constructed over hard ground for almost the entire distance.

In the future operations of the company, should it be deemed best to erect a mill, it will also probably be advisable to move our furnaces to the same location. Should such a course hereafter become necessary, our supply of coal and wood can be delivered at such location as cheaply from Owens Lake as it is now delivered at the present furnace from Coso Mountains.

Iron-ores are expensive to procure, and by the time they are delivered at the furnace for use cost us not far from $20 per ton. Our want of iron-ore stimulated prospectors, and during my stay I personally examined two other deposits, one of them on top of Coso Mountain, some fourteen miles from furnace; the other between Darwin and Owens Lake, about eight miles from Darwin, and gave discoverers a contract to take out of each mine and deliver fifty tons of the ore at a point where our teams can reach it. The price agreed to be paid is $5 per ton from one mine and $6 per ton from the of working our furnaces, consequent upon frequent stoppage. These stoppages are caused by changes in our ores and fluxes, which have been constantly varying.

Water can be found in sufficient quantity to supply all the furnaces at Darwin within five or six miles of their location. As the three furnaces will pay, running steadily, at least $40,000 a year for water, they can afford to expend money liberally in cheapening this cost. My belief is that water can be had which shall cost, including large interest on the outlay, less than one-half of this amount yearly.

We canvassed the economy and necessity of erecting a litharge furnace in connection with our present works. With such a furnace we could reduce our bullion in bulk and weight, but increase it largely in value per ton, making it some 200 fine in silver instead of 7 fine as now, and using the litharge in smelting our dry ores as well as flux. To erect such works will cost at least $2,000, or possibly $2,500.

Windlass-men constitute a large portion of "mine-labor account," as it takes four men per day at each windlass, costing $16 per day for hoisting at each shaft. Taking the Main shaft and Yellow shaft at Christmas-Gift Mine, as also the Cactus, or No. 2 shaft, on the same mine, where we are hoisting from drifts, and the New shaft and Footwall shaft at Lucky Jim, requires an expenditure of $80 per day, or nearly $2,500 per month, which is over one-third our labor-account at mines. There is no way to decrease this large expense until we decide upon our main working-shafts and erect horse-whims.

The ore-sorters constitute quite a large force, but they are absolutely necessary, as it is not economy to transport valueless material to furnace, and it is certainly most expensive to put such material in the furnace. To avoid this last danger we keep one ore-assorter at the furnace. I found at times eight or ten men at work sorting ores, costing $32 to $40 per day, or say $1,000 to $1,200 per month.

Our pay-roll at mines varies from $6,000 to $7,000 per month.

At the furnace, the regular force consists of—

1 day-foreman, at $6 per day; 1 night-foreman and chief smelter, $200 per month—per day		$13 00
2 engineers, day and night, $5 and $4.50		9 50
3 smelters, eight-hour shifts, day and night	$5 00	15 00
3 helpers	4 50	13 50
3 chargers	5 00	15 00
2 coal-passers, 12-hour shifts	4 00	8 00
2 slag-men	4 00	8 00
1 ore-assorter, day-man	4 00	4 00
2 rock-men at crusher, day and night	4 00	8 00
1 general workman and blacksmith, day	4 00	4 00
1 brick-maker	4 00	4 00
1 furnace builder and repairer	4 00	4 00
23 in number, costing per day		106 00

The official staff consists of a superintendent, with a salary of $5,000 per year; assayer, at $300 per month, and book-keeper, at $150 per month.

I made an approximate estimate of cost of everything on hand, as also cost of our works to December 1, 1875, with following results:

Mining-timbers, wood and lumber on hand		$3,500
Coal, estimated		19,500
Supplies of various kinds		1,000
Mules, wagons, horses, harness, &c		10,000
Cost of headquarters, offices, assay-office, with cost of lot, $165		1,500
Corral lot, fence, building, &c		1,500
Boarding-house at mine		1,000
Water-tanks, &c		750
Ore-platform, shoots at mines		1,250
Hay, grain, &c		500
Cost of furnaces and appurtenances		45,000
Ores on hand at furnace, cost, say		2,000
Bullion on hand at furnace	350 bars..	
Shipped	650 bars..	
Total bars	1,000, value..	15,000
Cost of everything as above, approximate		102,500
Add cost of 650 feet shafting, $25, estimated		16,250
Add cost of 650 feet drifts, $15, estimated		9,750
Add cost of 150 feet tunnels, $10, estimated		1,500
Add cost of timbers, ladders, &c		2,500

Add cost of wagon-road	$3,000
Add cost of Cuervo spring	1,500
Add cost of interest in Tiger Mine	217
Add cost of interest in iron-mine	600
Add cost of sundry expenses	2,183
Total expenditure	140,000

Not including cost of running furnace and expenses connected with same, nor transportation-account, nor general expenses.

Our expenses at Darwin for November were approximately as follows:

Mine pay-roll	$6,000
Furnace pay-roll	1,800
Iron-mine pay-roll	300
Stables pay-roll	300
Buildings	150
Salaries	850
Mine-supplies	1,000
Furnace, (coal, wood, &c.)	3,000
Iron-mine	300
Stable and team expenses	800
Contingent expenses, estimated	300
Estimated for water, &c	1,200
Total for November	16,000

The assay-book shows from October 15 the assay-value of the ores from all parts of the company's mines at different intervals. Previous to that date a large number of assays were made, but no record was kept of them. Now a complete record is kept, and analyses are being made continually of our ores and fluxes in order to know what fluxes and proportions of ores and fluxes to use in the furnace, but no record is kept of these.

The exhibit certainly shows great richness in our ores, and when it is taken into consideration that we have produced over 6,000 bars of bullion, worth some $100,000, out of our shafts and drifts alone, without stoping, and all this within less than 100 feet from the surface, it certainly speaks well for the richness of our mines. They appear to gain in strength and richness as we get deeper upon them.

The result of the last analyses, made with reference to establishing proportions to use in furnace, gave the following:

FURNACE-CHARGES, DECEMBER 2, 1875.

	Pounds.
7 shovelfuls of ore, average 19 pounds	133
½ shovelful of iron-ore, average 19 pounds	10
Charcoal	35
2 shovelfuls of slag, 15½ pounds	31
1½ shovelfuls of lime, 13 pounds	20
Total weight of charge	229

Of this total weight for charge 194 pounds is ore and fluxes.

Running steadily, about 300 charges per day are required. This would require 20 tons of ore, 1½ tons of iron, 4½ tons of slag, 3 tons of lime, 5¼ tons of coal—giving 34½ tons, gross weight. This should turn out of our ores, if furnace runs without interruption, 150 to 175 bars bullion per day, weighing 12,000 to 14,000 pounds, or six to seven tons, worth nearly $2,000 in silver alone.

The above proportions of course are varying constantly, as is the yield, as our ores vary in richness in silver and lead. The above charges and results are with ores carrying not less than 40 per cent. in lead.

Quite a percentage of our ore is carried into the flues in a mechanical state from the blast. While I was there the flues were cleaned and assays made of the dust, showing in vertical flue $79 per ton in silver, and a large percentage of iron, and in horizontal flue $55 in silver, and but little iron. This material, of which there is quite a large amount now on hand, is steadily increasing; it is all saved, and will, in due time, be put in shape to extract the silver from it, by combining it with lime or by some other process, and passing it again through the furnaces. This material, in connection with a furnace, is like the slum or tailings from a mill, only it is much richer in silver.

Nothing is lost about a well constructed and managed furnace. In time everything is utilized. This dust will require experimental examinations and tests which are in progress.

The matter of cost of charcoal at furnace at $38 per ton, delivered, also of wood at

$11 per cord, attracted my attention, and I investigated it closely, with the following results, which I submit to the board for general information. The following is a memorandum of actual cost:

COST OF TWO PITS OF COAL TURNING OUT 20 TONS, REQUIRING 50 CORDS OF WOOD.

Cutting and gulching 50 cords of wood, at $2.50 per cord	$112 50
Placing wood in pits and covering, 8 days, at $3	24 00
Board, 8 days, at $1.25	10 00
Cutting boughs for covering coal-pits and covering the same with earth, 16 days, at $3 per day	48 00
Board, 16 days	20 00
Cost of pits ready to burn	214 50
Burning two pits takes 20 days' labor, at $3	60 00
Board, 20 days	25 00
Add lost time and delays	10 50
Sacking, 41 sacks per ton, 20 days' labor, at $3	60 00
Board, 20 days	25 00
Wear and tear of sacks, twine, &c	10 00
Actual cash cost at pits, in sacks	405 00
Equal to $20.25 per ton	20 25
To this must be added for contingencies, such as bad burning, lost time, and other matters, say per ton 75 cents	75
Profit of master coal-burner per pit $20, equal per ton to	2 00
Fair cash cost per ton in sacks at pit	23 00
Add for packing to wagon-road, and from thence to furnace 15 miles, per ton	12 00
Cost to contractor, delivered at furnace	35 00
To this add for profit to contractor to pay him for his time, opening roads, &c	3 00
Makes total cost at furnace, present price	38 00

It cannot be done for much less, and if any change takes place it will probably be an increase in price, as the wood nearest to furnace and easiest of access is of course first taken. The foregoing prices are actual cash cost.

Cost of 1 cord of wood at furnace:

Cutting cord of wood	$2 50
Gulching it to wagon-road	1 00
Transportation	7 50
Cost at furnace	11 00

The cord does not contain 128 cubic feet. It is generally short of four feet in length, and I should say the average cord contains 100 to 110 cubic feet only. This cost will not decrease.

I examined the supply of timber on Coso Mountain, where present supply of coal, wood, and timber is drawn from. It may last the drain upon it for two years, not more, with three furnaces running.

The certainty that the supply will be exhausted within a comparatively short time, and with increased cost, consequent upon exhaustion of timber easiest of access, led me to examine other sources of supply. On the eastern side of the Sierra, west of Owens Lake, in the cañons and along spurs of the mountains there are very large quantities of timber. It is, however, far removed and difficult of access. Mr. Stevens, who lives on the eastern side of the lake, owns a large amount of this timber-land and has constructed a flume from it, some fourteen miles long, to the foot of the mountain, within two miles of the lake, and at present floats large quantities of lumber down the flume from his saw-mill.

He will contract to deliver 100,000 bushels of coal, not less, but as much more as we want, on the east shore of the lake, about seventeen miles from furnace, for 25 cents per bushel, in sacks, we to return the sacks. He will erect fixed kilns of brick and furnish kiln-burned coal instead of pit-burned coal.

The present coal weighs about 17 pounds per bushel, and there is quite a loss in fine coal and dirt. Kiln-burned coal would, it is estimated, weigh 20 pounds per bushel, and there would be less loss in dust, as it would be entirely clean.

Taking the cost of this coal in sacks, at the embarcadero on eastern shore of lake, at 25 cents per bushel, it would amount per ton to	$25 00
It would cost us with our own teams, so arranged as to take 10 tons at a load, to transport to furnace, per ton	6 00
Making total cost at furnace	31 00

The transportation might be done for less, but it would be safe to assume it at above rates. This coal would certainly be worth 5 per cent. more, and I think 10 per cent. more, than pit-burned coal, if made from same quality of wood, and it would be safe to assume kiln-coal at $30 per ton, as against present coal at $38 per ton, making a saving to us in coal of at least $1,200 per month in each furnace running steadily. If we hired the hauling it would cost more. There is no danger of a dearth of coal, or wood, or timber for our uses and purposes for many years to come.

The average of twenty-five assays of ore from December 1 to December 15 was $258 per ton; the highest being $1,379, and the lowest $5.65. Bullion-assays were as follows: November 19 to 24, 300 bars No. 1, (24,484 pounds,) $313; in December, 500 bars No. 2, $295.94; in December, 1,000 bars No. 3, $326.81.

In the same district (Darwin) the Coso Consolidated Company have erected furnaces and developed its principal mine, the Bella Union. This mine is reported as yielding ores which assay from $200 to $300 silver per ton.

In the absence of a report from the company's engineer, I have condensed the following description of the Defiance Company's works from the Coso Mining News of December 24, 1875:

The main building is in size 60 by 80, and 27 feet in height from the floor to the comb of roof. The material used in its construction is all lumber excepting the roof, which is covered with heavy sheet-iron. The frame of the building is of solid timbers securely fastened together, and the outside is sheathed with boards set upright. The ore and feeding room is inclosed and separated from the other portions. It occupies nearly one-third of the building, and is conveniently arranged for the reception of the ore and charcoal. On this floor is placed one Wheeler's patent rock-breaker, through which all the hard ore will be passed and reduced to facilitate smelting. It is driven by a belt running over a pulley attached to the main shaft, and can be run or stopped at pleasure. From this floor the ore and coal are fed into the furnace through an opening in the stack 2 by 3 feet in size, and drops a distance of 13 feet to the bottom of the furnace within the fire-chamber. On the lower floor of the building are situated the engine and boiler, the blower and the furnace. The engine is of 30 horse-power, and is supplied with steam from boilers of sufficient capacity to generate all that is required. Its principal use will be to drive one of Baker's (No. 5) patent blowers, which will furnish a blast of thirty-six ounces to the square inch. From this blower a galvanized-iron tube 15 inches in diameter leads to the furnace, conveying the blast to the five tuyéres that lead to the flame.

The furnace is constructed with great care, to insure perfect success in working the Defiance ores. Its foundation is of brick, raised but a few inches above the floor. The lower part of the fire-chamber is of fire-brick, 13 inches in depth, upon which rests the water-jacket, 34 inches in height. It is constructed of the heaviest boiler-iron, is steam-tight, and about 5 inches in thickness. A cold stream of water is forced into this constantly by a force-pump, and as fast as the warm water is displaced it is conveyed by pipes back into the tanks from whence it first came. Any steam that is generated passes through other pipes into a steam-drum situated just above, from which it is conveyed by steam-pipes to the principal boiler. Above the water-jacket is a section of fire-brick, 16 inches in thickness, forming a portion of the main stack, and connecting this portion with the brick chamber above the diaphragm is a tubular casting 3 feet in length, so constructed because at this point the most friction is created when the furnace is charged. Above the diaphragm, which is supported by four cast-iron tubular columns, is a brick chamber 5 feet in height, on top of which rests the down-cast, a large hollow chamber in which the smoke-stack enters and ends near the top in an open hood that catches and precipitates the dust in the chamber, which terminates at the top in a funnel shape, to which the smoke-stack is attached, and continues a distance of 30 feet higher. This makes the entire height of the stack, from foundation to summit, about 53 feet. The down-cast is the peculiar feature of this furnace, for by its use is obviated all necessity for long and expensive flues or fume arresters, in which to catch the finely-pulverized dust which is carried upward by the intense heat and violent draughts. The dust is in this precipitated when it strikes the open hood, and, falling into the chamber, is drawn off through a spout placed at the extreme termination of its inclined base and saved for manipulation. Among the improvements deserving of mention, is an improved truck and slag-pot. The truck is so constructed as to be evenly balanced when carrying the empty slag-pot, and is easily handled by an ordinary workman. The slag-pots are quadrilateral in form and composed of five iron slats kept in place by bolts. If either of these plates are broken, they can be duplicated without the loss of all, and are thereby made a great improvement over the old style, which is conical and cast in one piece.

From assays made recently the galena and carbonate ores mingled showed returns of 55 per cent. lead and $218.70 silver per ton. The galena-ore alone gives 58 per cent. lead and $139.17 silver per ton, while the carbonates yield 7 per cent. lead and $78.50 silver per ton. The raise at the further end of the tunnel is being driven vigorously, and has now reached a point 55 feet above the tunnel. The winze in the south drift is progressing finely in ore of good quality. At a point 55 feet below the drift a level is now being run south, which is now in 15 feet. It is being driven across the ledge diagonally from the hanging wall to strike another winze 100 feet farther south that is to be sunk on the foot-wall at that point. The light carbonate-ore found in this winze assays 40 per cent. lead and $81.68 in silver. The main south drift is still yielding ore of heavy galena mingled with spar. The assays from this part of the mine yield a higher per cent. of lead than any other point, and show as follows: Cube galena, 70 per cent. lead and $89.52 silver per ton; fine galena, 58 per cent. lead and $96.81 silver per ton. The average assay of samples taken from all parts of the mine and pulverized together gave the following result, viz, 60 per cent. lead and $85.84 silver per ton, which is far beyond the average results obtained from mines of this character. A rich body of carbonate-ore has been struck in the drift leading south from the winze, which is now the point of deepest working in this mine. Assays from the ore taken from the face of this drift gave the following result, viz, $1,225.29 in silver, and 56 per cent. lead to the ton, which is the highest yet obtained. Another assay, made from ore apparently containing nothing but iron, which overlies this rich deposit, gave the result of 68 per cent. lead and $196 in silver per ton.

Cerro Gordo district.—I am indebted to Mr. E. F. A. Hehner, of Cerro Gordo, for the following statement and tabular returns of mines in that district. Cerro Gordo is situated on the ridge of the Inyo Mountains, opposite Owens Lake, at an altitude of about 8,000 feet. The district has now been in existence about ten years. Like most camps in this part of the country, it was discovered by Mexicans. They worked the ores in a very primitive manner for some time by *vasos*, until Messrs. Beaudry and Belshaw arrived here, put up smelting-works, and after a great deal of experimenting succeeded in fluxing the ores. Since that time they have been the only company here doing business of any amount, running two furnaces. About four years ago another company, the Owens Lake Silver and Lead Company, was started, and erected smelting-works at the shores of Owens Lake, some 8 miles from Cerro Gordo. Their ores, however, are obtained from Cerro Gordo, from the Santa Maria and San Felipe Mines. Outside of these two companies no smelting-works have been erected, and no mines, except such as they control, have been worked to any extent.

The character of the ore, with the exception of the San Felipe, San Lucas, and San Ignaçio Mines, is argentiferous galena, averaging very high in silver and lead. The Union Mine, the principal one of the district, is valued by the owners at $1,500,000, and has been famous for its large chimneys of lead-ores and the facility for extraction. It has been said that half a dozen men could take out enough ore to keep two furnaces running. The profits of the mine have been very great, and a large amount of bullion has been shipped. For months the average yield of bullion of the two furnaces has been over 500 bars of from 90 to 100 pounds each, every 24 hours, the bar being worth over $100.

For about two years past, however, the camp has been very dull, in consequence of litigation between the San Felipe and Union Mining Companies for the possession of the Union Mine. As a result, the Union Mine has been shut down, and only one furnace is in operation at present. The ores worked now are mostly of very low grade, obtained by the overhauling of old dumps.

Although there are a great number of very promising prospects and claims owned by other persons, the policy pursued by the owners of the two furnaces rendered it impossible for mine-owners to work their claims.

Some 3 miles east of Cerro Gordo are the silver-mines of Belmont. From here Messrs. Beaudry and Belshaw received their supply of silver-ore. The character of the ore there is a high-grade copper-silver-glance, and a very good free-milling ore. The ores will average from $200 to $300 per ton, assay-value; but the veins, though well defined, are small. The principal mines there are the Buena Suerta, Belmont, Wedekind, Nettie, and Gracewood. A large amount of work has been done there, the Belmont, Wedekind, Nettie, and several others, as well as the Buena Suerta, and the Gracewood. There must have been at least from $60,000 to $70,000 worth of labor done there; but, with the exception of the Buena Suerta, which is worked alone by the owner, they are all lying idle, and have been so for years. If the miners want to dispose of their ores, they must do so to Messrs. Beaudry and Belshaw, and they cannot afford to take the ore out at the prices offered to them. The price charged for reduction is (according to Mr. Hehner) $50 per ton.

During the last three or four months quite an excitement has prevailed in the camp in consequence of the finding of very rich specimens of a porous iron-ore coming out of the casing of the Jefferson lead-mine, which is exceedingly rich in free gold. A great number of specimens have been picked up on the old dump of that mine, which were worth from $5 up to $80 and $90 each. Here, also, Mexicans were the discovers, and it is the current opinion of well-informed persons here that from $20,000 to $25,000 of gold must have been taken out. All the ores contain more or less gold, and probably this made the value of Cerro Gordo bullion so high in San Francisco.

There is another difficulty which Cerro Gordo is laboring under, viz, the scarcity of water. Two years ago Mr. Temple, of Los Angeles, and Mr. Craig bought some springs, 7 or 8 miles distant, and brought the water to town, but they were obliged to give up the business this summer on account of the dullness of business and the scarcity of water in their springs. Since then Messrs. Beaudry and Belshaw have laid pipes from another spring some 4 miles distant, and are now also supplying the camp with water, which is sold for 3 cents per gallon.

In the early part of November two or three gold-bearing ledges were located, assaying about $15 to $20 per ton, but as a matter of course they cannot as yet be profitably worked. When the two, or rather three, furnaces were running—the one at Swansea included—and the Union, San Felipe, and Santa Maria Mines were being worked, the place gave employment to from 500 to 600 men—miners, furnace-men, coal-burners, and packers. Now there are not 60 men employed. Charcoal is worth about $35 per ton. The wages of miners and furnace-men are $4 to $5 per day for eight-hour shifts. Mining is, however, mostly done by contract; and good workmen may earn as high as $10, or even $15, per day on contract-work.

Mr. William Crapo, of Cerro Gordo, has furnished me the following statement of the shipments of bullion from that district during the year 1875:

From Belshaw & Judson's furnace 2,937$\frac{218}{2000}$ tons, containing an average of 126 ounces of silver per ton of 2,000 pounds. From Beaudry's furnace 661$\frac{371}{2000}$ tons, containing an average of 147 ounces silver per ton. Total, 3,598$\frac{589}{2000}$ tons.

The lawsuits which have been hindering the bullion-production for several years past having been finally settled by a consolidation of all the interests, there is a probability of a greatly-increased production during the coming year.

Description of leading mines in Cerro Gordo district, Inyo County, California.

(Reported by E. F. A. Hehner.)

Name.	Owners.	Length of location.	Course.	Dip.	Length of pay-zone.	Average width.	Country-rock.
		Feet.			*Feet.*	*Feet.*	
San Felipe	Swansea Silver-Lead Mining Company.	....	N. W. and S. E.	80° S. W.	200	2	Limestone and slate.
Gracewood	Mr. Helmer	1, 500	N. E. and S. W.	70° S. E.	300	2	Syenite.
Union	M. W. Belshaw and V. Beaudry.	1, 800	N. and S.	80° W.	300	10	Limestone.
Buena Vista	H. W. Gould	1, 400	N. W. and S. E.	70° N. E.	150	2	Syenite.

Name.	Owners.	Vein-matter.	Cost of hoisting and pumping machinery.	Greatest depth attained.	Greatest length of horizontal exploration.	Number of levels.	Length of tunnel.	Cost of tunnel.
				Feet.	*Feet.*		*Feet.*	
San Felipe	Swansea Silver-Lead Mining Company.	Argentiferous quartz.	None.	80	200	1	100	$1, 500
Gracewood	Mr. Helmer	Argentiferous gray copper.	None.	150	350	1	650	7, 000
Union	M. W. Belshaw and V. Beaudry.	Argentiferous galena.	$10, 000	700	400	7	300	4, 000
Buena Vista	H. W. Gould	Auriferous and argentiferous quartz.	None.	150	300	6	600	7, 000

The operations of the Union Mine are reported as follows: About fifty miners, at $4 per day; cost of sinking, per foot, about $10; of drifting, about $7.50; of stoping, per ton, about $2.50; of mining, per ton, $5; of smelting, about $15.

The Mineatta Mine is situated in *Lookout district.* Length of location, 1,500 feet; course, N. and S.; dip, 42° W.; average width, 30 feet; length of pay-zone unknown; formation, limestone; vein-matter, silver-bearing quartz; worked by shaft to depth of 100 feet. Mr. James Dolan, the superintendent, says this mine has been opened in three different places, and at each point large chimneys of very high-grade ore have been exposed. It is difficult to estimate the quantity in sight on the surface near these openings, but the closest surveys show not less than 3,000 tons of ore that will yield fully $100 to the ton. Much of it is rich in galena, but the higher grades carry a combination of gray carbonates and chlorides, while the latest developments show extremely rich black sulphurets. The Mineatta shows prominent croppings for a distance of 3,000 feet.

MONO COUNTY.

This county lies on the eastern slope of the Sierra Nevada, bordering on the State of Nevada. It is situated immediately north of Inyo County and east of Tuolumne and Fresno. It lies wholly beyond the main ridge of the Sierra, the crest of that range forming its southwestern border. Its easterly portion is traversed longitudinally by the White, the Inyo, and several other chains of mountains, and its western portion contains several of the highest peaks of the Sierra, some of them having an altitude of 15,000 feet. The mineral resources are extensive and but slightly developed, but are now attracting considerable attention in consequence of the remarkably favorable development of the Indian Queen, the Comanche, or Mack, and other mines in the White Mountain range near Benton. The ores of this county are argentiferous.

Since 1870 there have been erected six mills, aggregating fifty stamps. During the past year about 5,000 tons of ore was crushed. The ores are of high grade and require roasting. One of the most important districts is Oneota, situated in the White Mountains. This is not a recently-discovered mining-district. The mines in this section have been worked more or less for the last twelve years. Yet it is comparatively unknown outside of the county, and it is only within the last eighteen months that any real mining has been done or capital invested in this section. Heretofore the mines have been worked only in a small way and have been entirely self-sustaining. But now, with the aid of steam hoisting-works and better mills, the mines are yielding remarkably well.

The principal mines worked here at present are the Indian Queen, owned by a San Francisco company; the Comanche, owned by Albert Mack, of Benton, Cal., and the Diana, owned by A. W. Williams, of Benton. The Diana runs a five-stamp mill. The Comanche and other mines support a ten-stamp mill. The Indian Queen has at present only a four-stamp mill, but it is the intention of the company to erect next spring much larger works, as the mine can now easily produce twice the amount of ore the present mill can reduce. Yet even with these small and insufficient reduction-works, the Indian Queen is paying dividends of $30,000 per month.

Mr. John Howell, superintendent of the Indian Queen, writes as follows concerning that mine:

The Indian Queen Mine, situate in the White Mountains, about fifteen miles east of Benton, Mono County, California, is a vein of from 2 to 3½ feet in thickness. Course of vein northwest and southeast; dip, 30° east; country-rock, talcose slate. It is a well-defined fissure-vein. The ore is a heavy base sulphuret, of about the following proportions: Lead, 37 per cent.; copper, 7 per cent.; iron, 12 per cent.; zinc, from 8 to 14 per cent.; antimony, 3 to 7 per cent.; sulphur, 8 to 10 per cent.; a little arsenic; no gold, and about $200 per ton in silver, the remainder being clay and quartz. The ore is very rebellious and difficult to work, but when properly treated yields a high percentage of the precious metal. Our average yield of silver is about 90 per cent. We chloridize our ores in a Howell's improved White's furnace, which is also the method of treating ore at Mack's Mill in Benton. Within the last year several mines have been discovered between here and Owens River Valley, on the western slope of the White Mountains, and in the near future this promises to be a rich and extensive mining-section.

The Indian Queen employs 20 miners, at $4 per day; cost of sinking, $6 per foot; drifting, $3.50; stoping, $5.50 per ton; mining, per ton, $8 to $10. The cost of milling, including roasting, is stated to be $32 per ton. The average yield per ton is $180. The present mill has a capacity of 5 tons per day. This company may be relied on for a large bullion-production in 1876, when the new mill will be in operation.

There are several other valuable mines in the county, among others, the Comanche, from which no returns were received. The Dunderberg, a promising property, was described in the report of 1873, page 17. Since that time nothing has been done on this mine in consequence of the failure to obtain profitable results by the common mill-process.

SAN DIEGO COUNTY.

The important gold-producing regions of Southern California are within the limits of San Diego and Kern Counties. San Diego has eight quartz-mills, and during the last two years has crushed about 10,000 tons of quartz per annum. From 1870 to 1873, during the prevalence of a quartz excitement, there were erected in this county ten mills, aggregating 60 stamps, at a total cost of $80,000. Most of these mills are idle, and none of the mining operations have proven permanently profitable. The characteristics of the quartz-mines and the record of the principal ores may be found in the reports of 1871 and 1873. Since that period the gold product has materially fallen off. The principal mine, the Chariot Mill and Mining Company, has since its incorporation levied $48,000 in assessments and disbursed $51,000 in dividends, the last dividend having been declared in 1874. This mine has attained a depth of 300 feet and has a fine 10-stamp mill. Prospecting has been actively resumed during the past year, in some cases with favorable results. The Ready Relief Mine recently crushed 100 tons of ore yielding $30 per ton, and has large reserves in sight. Several other mines have developed extensive reserves of ore which will yield from $20 to $30 per ton.

KERN COUNTY.

Kern County, having an area of 8,000 square miles, comprises within its limits the southern terminus of the great valley of the San Joaquin; it contains valuable gold-mines, both quartz and placer, and large deposits of salt, sulphur, petroleum, and other minerals. The county had in 1875 twelve quartz-mills, which are reported as having crushed 25,000 tons of ores for the fiscal year ending June 30, but as the mill of the Sumner Mine commenced crushing about that time, the product for the year ending December 31 would be largely increased. This mine, one of the most important in the State, by reason of the great width of its vein and the magnitude of its operations, was fully described in the report for 1875.

A correspondent says of this property:

> The Sumner Mining Company is doing a great deal of work. It employs 170 men. The eighty-stamp mill, which is the largest and most complete on the coast, is in constant operation, crushing from 100 to 120 tons per day. The mine is situated about three-fourths of a mile above the mill, and the machinery, including the pump, hoisting-works, &c., is in all respects first class. We entered the first or 80-foot level through a tunnel of about 300 yards in length, through which the ore is taken out, and the mine drained of the water. A great quantity of ore has been taken from this level. From this point we descended 80 feet in the hoisting-works to the 160-foot level. This level has been worked at a distance of 500 feet on the other side, embracing an entire length along the body of the ore of 1,000 feet, and measures wherever cut through from 30 to 40 feet in thickness, although the pay-rock in some places appears to run in strips or veins, and again widens out to the entire thickness. A depth of 200 feet has been reached, and the prospects continue to improve. The east casing of the quartz-vein is clay. At the mouth of the tunnel before spoken of is a large dump, where the car from the mine is unloaded, and a chute from this opens into a car that runs to the mill. The road from the dump to the mill is laid with small iron railing, and the grade is such that the car runs with its own momentum, and is drawn back by horse-power, so that the cost of carrying the rock to the mill does not exceed $5 to the one hundred tons. The rock enters the dump at the mill, where it is deposited above the level of the building, and at an opening at the bottom of the dump the rock is taken out and passes through a rock-breaker and then drops into a car, which passes along the line of eighty stamps, and is deposited into a hopper provided for each five stamps. From here it is thrown into the battery by a self-feeder. The whole works, from the mine until the gold is extracted, are constructed on the most simple and economical plan, The quartz-mill is run by water, which is abundant at all seasons of the year. There is one difficulty attending the work in the mine, and that is the great amount of water.

It requires a pump with an 18-inch pipe, making fifteen strokes per minute, working continuously night and day to keep the water out of the shaft. Several other shafts and tunnels are being run on the same lead, and the erection of other mills and works is contemplated.

The trouble from water, as I learn from the best authority, has seriously hindered the operations of the Sumner Mine. At the end of the year the water was 130 feet below the adit-level. A 16-inch pump, in addition to the 12-inch now running, was to be put in. The new mill was run from June to the end of the year on the very low-grade ore, (partly above and partly below adit-level,) which has yielded not quite $1,000 per day. The bottom of the shaft is in ore of high average, and the water once controlled, large returns are expected.

The Consolidated Bunnell has made arrangements for a ten-stamp mill, which will be in running order by the 1st of February, 1876. The main tunnel was run in 148 feet and tapped the vein. From this point the company turned at right angles, and is running a tunnel along the foot-wall and following a rich vein of ore about two feet wide. They have thus followed the lead about 35 feet and have taken out three hundred tons of rich ore. The vein contains horn and ruby silver. The remainder of the lead is not so rich, but will pay well for working. J. S. Colling, in prospecting the lead, found croppings extending two miles beyond the 12,000-foot location. At one place the croppings were about ten feet wide on the surface, and pieces taken from them assayed $137 to the ton. These croppings run in a straight line, passing directly over the top of the mountain. The other side is covered with the *débris*, and the vein is lost.

Mr. Jacobs, who represents a San Francisco company, has recently visited the Hot Springs Valley and the placer-mines on Kern River below, examining the mines with a view to putting through the McCann ditch, which will be about nine miles long, and will cost about $18,000. It is designed to supply all the placer-mines of that country with water, and will also furnish water in all probability for irrigating purposes in Hot Springs Valley. There are about forty acres on this claim, all rich gravel-diggings. It includes three or four different bars, among which are Oiler Bar and China Bar. The gravel is supposed to be from 5 to 95 feet deep. The bars and small gulches on Kern River in this vicinity are being worked by the Chinese, who are seen everywhere with their rockers and sluice-boxes.

The Saint John Mining Company, at Sageland, expended from $50,000 to $60,000 in putting up hoisting-works, pump, &c. They are now down 720 feet, where the vein is from 4 to 4½ feet wide, and said to be very rich. This is the deepest mine in the county. A twelve-stamp mill with three batteries was reported ready to start up; but at the close of the year I learned that the mine was shut, and that it was somewhat doubtful whether it would ever be opened again. Of the precise nature of the disappointment or difficulty which led to this suspension I am not advised.

The Bright Star Mine, located at Piute, eighteen miles from the Hot Springs, is running fifteen stamps on rich ore. The shaft is down about 350 feet on the vein, which is 8 to 12 feet wide. The company has already realized from this mine from $250,000 to $300,000. A number of other mines are worked in the same neighborhood with arrastras.

San Bernardino attracted some attention last year as a field for quartz-mining operations, and a forty-stamp mill was erected by the Gold Mountain Company, near Bear Valley, at a cost of $100,000, and with a crushing-capacity of 100 tons per day. The enterprise proved a failure, owing to the indiscriminate working of masses of barren quartz. The quartz-zone of this district is of great width, but the system of pay-shoots, if such exists, was not discovered by the managers, or at least was not developed.

San Luis Obispo, a southern-coast county, has lately been the scene of great activity in quicksilver-mining. The principal mine, the Oceanic, was described in our last Report, (for 1875.) The Tribune of December 25 says: The mining-interests of the county are growing brighter with every month's development. There is not a remaining doubt as to the fact of there being one of the richest and most extensive quicksilver-belts running through the entire length of the county that is to be found in any portion of the State. The development of these mines will greatly quicken every other industry in the county. At the present time there are probably 250 men at work in these mines, and the amount of money put in circulation through their earnings is already considerable; but let the number be increased to one or two thousand, as it well might be, then everybody would feel its influence. The Oceanic company for months in succession last summer paid as high as $10,000 a month for wages and material, which gave a great impetus to all classes of business in and about Cambria. The Ocean View Mine has now employed 60 men, and must keep up as large a force until the works are all completed.

MARIPOSA COUNTY.

The following table, compiled from the official returns of county assessors, shows the condition of mining from 1870 to date:

Year	Quartz-mills.	Tons crushed.	Mining-ditches.	Length, in miles.	Miner's inches used per day.
1870	30	35,000	10	66	3,500
1871	34	24,000	10	66	3,500
1872	34	18,000	10	66	3,500
1873*	....	....	....	....	....
1874	23	15,000	7	45	....
1875	20	....	7	45	....

* No returns.

The principal source of gold-production up to the year 1870 was from the Mariposa estate, known as the Frémont grant, and now the property of the Mariposa Land and Mining Company. The leading mines of the company were described in the Reports of 1869 and 1871, and again in tabulated form in the Report of 1874, pages 67, 68. During the past few years the company's energies have been devoted to the running of a long adit from the mound to strike the principal mines at great depth.

As early as 1858 or 1859, the late Dr. Justus Adelberg suggested the advisability of a tunnel from the Merced River, at the Benton Mills, along the line of the vein of quartz which was known to exist from the river to the Pine Tree and Josephine Mines, and from these last continuing southwardly to Mount Ophir, Princeton, Agua Frio, and even to the extreme southerly limits of this estate. The suggestion was not acted on at the time, but some years after was again brought to the notice of the Mariposa Company. A tunnel was commenced and then abandoned, and the enterprise was permitted to rest until June, 1873, when the work was in reality commenced. The tunnel was carried on with occasional interruptions until June, 1874, and then, after a rest of six months, was again resumed. When it had reached a length of 1,000 feet a vein was intersected, supposed to be the continuation of the Pine Tree. The work at the commencement was easy, but as the drift advanced the ground became harder, until, at 440 feet, hard blue slate was encountered, and has since continued. The course of the tunnel being parallel to this stratification, in blasting the powder loses 75 per cent. of its effective force on the "center cuts." The length of the tunnel at the end of the year was reported about 1,300 feet, and the rate of progress as rather less (owing to the extreme hardness of the rock) than the previous average of 90 feet per month. A visitor informs me that the rock in the heading was so hard that a continuous circle of flame issued from the drill-holes till they had attained the depth of five or six inches, although water was poured into them while the drills were in motion. Had it not been for the Burleigh rock-drill the work would have been abandoned long since, as competent miners estimate the cost of running it at $70 per foot. This tunnel once in, the cost of carrying it on will be defrayed out of the vein itself, for, with a down-grade to the mill, and no necessity of handling the ore twice, the quartz can be delivered at the "spaller" for less than $2 per ton, and the cost of milling will not exceed that amount, as the principal item of expense in milling is reduced to a minimum by using the water-power of the Merced. Steps are now being taken to bring in a ditch, which, besides furnishing power to the Benton Mills, will also supply the means of working the placers above the banks of the river, which are now useless for the want of water. The amount of power to be derived from the increased fall will be nearly 3,000 horse-power. It is part of the policy of the company to utilize this power by milling the quartz furnished by the series of veins from the Merced River to Agua Frio, thus avoiding the enormous expense for fuel of about $20,000 yearly for each mill. The canal will have a capacity of 20,000 cubic feet per minute.

During the year just past the company has driven the main drain and working-tunnel above alluded to 750 feet, but the real working-time has been but little over six months, as the old Benton dam had to be rebuilt, thus taking away for a considerable period the power used in compressing air, &c. The Pine Tree fissure was cut and crossed at 1,000 feet. It showed a small vein of about six inches, well defined and carrying sulphurets. Assayers at the New York assay-office pronounced it regular ore and containing $9 per ton in gold. The position of the vein is the same as had been calculated according to the surveys and surface-observations. Now, following on the vein, which widens as it advances, there are still 200 feet to drive before reaching a point under the first outcropping. The drifts will then have "backs" of 500 feet vertical height, with a 3-foot vein on the surface. Parallel to this and 250 feet distant is a 4-foot vein, for which a cross-cut is now running, and toward which it has advanced 126 feet.

From these outcroppings to the old Pine Tree the surface-indications are continuous and well-defined.

Prospecting-drills will be used after January 1, to make a thorough examination of the best-appearing veins on the whole estate. Preparations are making to sink on the well-known Princeton vein to the depth of 1,200 or 1,500 feet. This will allow an undercutting of the old works from 800 to 1,000 feet. At the time this mine was closed, it is said an extensive 4-foot vein of $12 to $15 rock was abandoned. This was six years ago, when the cost of mining was high, but by means of the Burleigh drills and compressed air from the Merced the cost has been greatly reduced.

In the River tunnel, with a heading 8 feet by 12 feet, the lowest offer by hand labor is $70 per running foot, while by machinery the *total* expense is $34.50, as shown during the past six months. This includes everything—rails, ties, car-repairs, some timbering, powder, &c.

The principal mines near Coulterville, in this county, were described in tabulated form in the report of 1875. During the past year but little has been done in this portion of the county. There are many valuable mines in this district lying idle owing to litigation and bad management. The Douglass and the Maxwell Creek Mines will resume operations early in 1876. Their mills are only one mile from town. These mines have a good record. The Hasloe and Bandereta Mines are ten miles from town, and have ten stamps each running. The Martin & Walling Company will resume early in 1876. The Ralston Marble Spring Mine, two miles from Bower Cave, is said to be valuable. The McAlpine, five and a half miles from Bower Cave, has turned out well. Dr. McLean's Mine, near the last, looks well. The Coulterville Mill and Mining Company, ten miles from Bower Cave, is running a ten-stamp mill. The Crown lead is three miles from town. There are some others of less note in this vicinity. Coulterville is a distributing-point for a large region, supplying camps twenty or twenty-five miles around.

The principal mines in the vicinity of Hornitos are the Washington, Hardwick No. 9, the Spring Ledge, Gulch, Silver Lead, the Gaines, Campidonico, Dause, and a few others of less note. The Washington, one and a half miles from town, is a good mine. They are working on the 700-foot level. Their last clean-up (November, 1875) yielded $7,800 from 350 tons of rock. They work 75 men—25 Chinese. Their greatest drawback is fuel. Wood costs $50 per day. Their rock is sulphuret, and they have extensive chlorinating-works. Their engine for pumping is 70 horse-power; for quartz-mill, 70 horse, and for the hoisting-works, 25 horse. The engine for the mill will drive forty stamps; they now run but twenty stamps. The Campidonico runs five stamps; the Hardwick, five stamps, and the Gaines, ten stamps. The Gulch Mine will erect a ten-stamp mill early in 1876.

Through the courtesy of the owners and of Capt. J. H. Riley, of San Francisco, I am enabled to present an abstract of the report of Mr. James D. Hague, M. E., on the Hite's Cove Mine, which was described in the report of 1875, and which may be considered as one of the leading quartz-mines of the State.

The Hite Mine is at Hite's Cove, on the South Merced River, three or four miles above the junction of that branch with the main stream flowing out of the Yosemite Valley. A sharp ridge, 1,500 to 1,700 feet high, here divides the two streams. The vein on which the mine is worked crops out high up on the north side of this ridge, overlooking the South Branch. The outcrop of the vein follows an early east and west line along and dipping (northerly) steeply into the hill. The mine is opened by two tunnels, which enter the hill through country-rock at right angles to the vein. Both tunnels are so situated that they cut the vein near the center of the claim, which is 1,000 feet in length; there are, therefore, about 500 feet of ground on either side of the points in the vein thus intersected. The lower tunnel, through which the mine is now chiefly worked, is about 500 to 550 feet vertically above the bed of the river. The upper tunnel is about 565 feet above the lower, or about 586 feet when measured on the dip of the vein, say 75 degrees. The croppings are from 125 to 200 feet above the upper tunnel.

The upper tunnel is about 300 feet in length. From the point of its intersection with the vein a drift has been driven along the vein east and west over 300 feet in each direction, developing two shoots of ore, one in each end of the mine. These shoots have each been stoped out for a considerable length between the tunnel and the surface. The lower tunnel is about 1,400 feet in length. From its point of intersection with the vein drifts have been run each way nearly, if not quite, to the boundary-lines. The two tunnels (586 feet apart on the dip of vein) are connected by the works in the western half of the claim, where a fine body of ore has been developed and partly worked out. The eastern half of the mine is not so far developed. The lower tunnel shows a strong vein of quartz that assays well, but the ground there between the two tunnels remained almost untouched at the date of the writer's last visit, June, 1875. Below the lower tunnel no work whatever had then been done.

The nature and extent of the development in the mine in June, 1875, may be partly described as follows:

On the level of the lower tunnel, drift west to boundary-line, nearly 500 feet.

On the level of the lower tunnel, drift east about 400 feet.

Above the level of the lower tunnel a series of winzes connect with the upper tunnel, starting from the lower level at a point 150 feet west of the lower tunnel.

On level 84 feet above lower tunnel, drifts east and west from winze, aggregating 184 feet.

On level 190 feet above lower tunnel, drifts east and west from winze, aggregating 430 feet.

On level 265 feet above lower tunnel, drifts east and west from winze, aggregating 100 feet.

On level 343 feet above lower tunnel, drifts east and west from winze, aggregating 335 feet.

On level 432 feet above lower tunnel, drifts east and west from winze, aggregating 208 feet.

On level 496 feet above lower tunnel, drifts east and west from winze, aggregating 256 feet.

On upper tunnel, 586 feet above lower tunnel, drifts east and west from winze, aggregating 700 to 750 feet.

These drifts, with their connected winzes, cross-cuts, and stopes, afford the following observations on the character of the vein. The inclosing country-rock is black slate; general course of vein regular, and nearly east and west; dip to the north 75 degrees from the horizon; width, varying between extremes of a few inches to over 20 feet, averaging where stoped 5 to 6 feet. The quartz occurs in shoots, pinching and widening at greater or less intervals. The main west shoot, which has been thus far the chief source of quartz, has been opened in length from 100 to 250 feet on different levels. On the bottom level this shoot has a continuous length of 250 feet. The quartz also sometimes forms two or more parallel veins or seams, so that within the space included between the main hanging and foot walls of the vein there may be two distinct bodies of quartz separated by a horse of slate. In the upper works there have always been three separate seams recognized, although only two have been much worked. In the bottom level the vein, which is 15 to 20 feet wide where cut by the tunnel, is divided by a large horse in the western portion of the ground. The general character of the quartz throughout the mine is moderately hard, white or bluish-white, sometimes mixed with seams of slate, frequently showing free gold, with some iron sulphurets and a little galena. The quality varies between wide extremes, say from $10 to $100 per ton. The average of several years' operations appears to show a yield of $30 to $40 per ton. At the end of 1874, a careful estimate of the amount of quartz thus far worked showed a product of, say, 30,000 tons, yielding over $1,250,000, or something over $40 per ton. According to the reported operations of this year, (1875,) this yield has been fully sustained. It is specially noteworthy that nearly all the quartz taken from the mine is crushed without any discrimination or assortment. The dumps show very little or no quartz. The yield obtained is the result of milling the whole vein.

The mine has been known and worked since 1862. Its early history is unrecorded, and its production can only be stated in general terms. In later years the bullion-production is given as follows: 1869, $39,171; 1870, $126,902; 1871, $138,567; 1872, $133,782; 1873, $136,125; nine months of 1874, $112,942. The total product from the beginning to the end of 1874 is placed at something over $1,250,000.

The costs of operation are known in detail for only two or three years. Including all expenses for mining and milling, dead-work, permanent improvements, &c., these were reported as follows:

In 1872, $42,792.78, estimated per ton at $17.11.

In 1873, $53,585, estimated per ton at $17.86.

In 1874, (9 months,) $31,063.32, estimated per ton at $10.

The estimated net profits per ton of quartz crushed during the same period were as follows:

In 1872, $36.38; 1873, $27.51; nine months of 1874, $30.33.

The net proffts of the year 1874 are reported at $120,000.

The mine is provided with a mill, which is situated near the river-bank and directly below the tunnel-mouth. The ore is brought out from the mine on a tram-way, and is sent down to mill by an inclined road without change of cars. The mill has twenty stamps; but as all the ore is ground in pans for the purpose of dividing it finely, and of affording abundant opportunity for amalgamation, the duty of the mill is very light, not exceeding (in 1874) 330 tons per month. The cost of milling alone is said to average about $3.75 per ton. The mill is driven by water-power, obtained in abundance, during most of the year, from the South Merced. At the present date (1875) the milling-facilities are being increased by the addition of twenty new stamps. With these in operation it is expected that the monthly production will be from $30,000 to $40,000.

The mine in its present condition is able to furnish a much larger supply of ore than is called for by the present scale of operations. In 1874, when visited by the writer, the total force employed was 34 men, of whom only 10 were miners; the remainder comprising 9 trammers, 6 mill-men, 1 tailings-man, carpenter, smiths, foreman, cooks, and jobbers. Of the mining-force, only 4 were stoping, 5 were breaking quartz in opening ground, and 1 on dead-work. This force, without working nights or Sundays, kept the mill fully supplied.

At that date the developed reserves of quartz standing in the opened ground were estimated at 30,000 to 40,000 tons, and valued at $750,000 to $1,000,000 net.

The promise of the mine for the future, beyond these developed resources, was unusually good.

TUOLUMNE COUNTY.

This county was described at length in my report for 1872, since which time there has been little change in the condition of mining there. There are in the county twenty quartz-mills, most of them working irregularly, and crushing about 15,000 tons per annum. The bullion-yield from this source will be materially increased next year (1876) by the working of the Confidence Mine, which has developed large ore-bodies during the past year. This important mine was fully described in my last year's report by Professor Ashburner. The principal mines are the Confidence, Spring Gulch, Golden Gate, Soulsby, and a group of mines on the Mother lode, which passes through this county, all of which have been described in former reports. Gravel-mining under Table Mountain has been carried on extensively, but no returns can be obtained. The system of working is the same as in 1872.

Mr. H. G. Wetmore, superintendent of the Golden Gate, makes the following report of his mine:

Golden Gate Mine—length of location, 2,600 feet; course, northeast and southwest; dip, west 70 to 80 degrees; length pay-zone, 100 feet; average width, 6 feet as far as explored; are still in pay-ore; country-rock, slate; vein-matter, flinty quartz; no machinery yet erected; greatest depth attained, 210 feet; greatest length horizontal exploration, 285 feet; 2 levels opened by tunnel, 285 feet long; miners' wages, per day, $3; cost sinking, per foot, from $15 to $30; cost drifting, per foot, average, $20; cost stoping, per ton, from $1.50 to $2; cost mining, per ton extracted, $3.20; cost milling, per ton, $1.25 at company's mill; number tons extracted and worked, about 500; average yield, per ton, $14.50; percentage sulphurets, from 1½ to 4 per cent.

Golden Gate Company's mill—water-power, 300 inches, 40-foot fall; 10 stamps, at 720 pounds, dropping 7 inches 83 times per minute; no pans; 5 concentrators; cost of mill, $10,000; capacity, 20 tons per 24 hours; cost treatment, $1.25 per ton; during the past year have only been experimenting; up to date the sulphurets have been sold.

Mr. Jesse Holladay, president of the Confidence Mine, makes the following return, (the bullion-product given below is the total yield since the mine passed into the hands of the present owners, in 1871:)

Confidence Mine—location, 2,500 feet; course, north 25 degrees west, dip 22 degrees east; length pay-zone 246 feet, average width 7 feet; country-rock, granite; vein-matter, quartz and sulphurets; worked by shaft 870 feet deep; 9 levels open; total length drifts, 3,300 feet; cost of hoisting-works, $11,500; 18 miners employed, at $3 per day; cost of sinking, per foot, $10; of drifting, $8; of stoping, per ton, $1.50; of mining, per ton extracted, $3; of milling at company's mill, $2.50; average yield, per ton, $16; total bullion-product, $550,000; kind of power, and amount, steam, 80-horse; number of stamps, 40; weight of stamps, 650 pounds; number of drops per minute, 70; height of drop, 7 inches; cost of mill, $30,000; capacity per twenty-four hours, tons, 50; cost of treatment, per ton, $2.50; tons crushed during the year, uncertain; making developments.

CALAVERAS COUNTY.

The assessment-list of this county shows the following valuation for 1875:

Mining-claims	$118,785
Improvements on same	110,175
Mining-ditches	94,155
Total	323,115

The comparative condition of the mining-interest is shown by the following table, compiled from official statistics:

Year.	Quartz-mills.	Tons crushed.	Mining-ditches.	Length, in miles.	Miners' inches of water used per day.
1870	24	11, 536	22	598	6, 300
1871	28	....	19	515	5, 800
1872	26	37, 105	22	482	3, 050
1873	34	28, 960	22	490	3, 670
1874	40	31, 000	22	490	3, 090
1875	40	30, 500	23	510	3, 160

From the above it appears that there has been but little change in the general condition of mining for the past five years.

In crossing this county from the foot-hills bordering the San Joaquin Valley toward the summit of the Sierras, we find the belt of auriferous metamorphic rocks, which forms the great mining-field of Central California, having a general course of northeast and southwest. The lower portion in the foot-hills is covered only by superficial *debritus*, which seems to be the remnants of broken channels which existed higher up and flowed in a general direction from north to south. In the higher portions of the county, near the junction of the slates and granite, there are isolated patches of these ancient channels covered by basaltic lava, and below these, on the limestone belt, superficial placers, which are still worked during the rainy season.

In the extreme western portion of the slate-belt we find the copper-belt, in which are situated the Union, Keystone, and other mines of note, which have remained closed for several years in consequence of the low price of copper. The ores are yellow sulphurets, known as "bronze-ores," and are inclosed in chloritic slates and serpentine. They are said to have occurred in lenticular masses and to have deteriorated in depth.

The great quartz-vein, or zone of veins, known as the Mother lode, enters this county from Tuolumne and crosses it into Amador. It makes strong croppings at Carson Hill, Albany Hill, Angel's, near San Andreas, and at Lower Rich Gulch, on the Mokelumne River. Carson Hill alone is credited with the production of $4,000,000, but active operations have been suspended for several years, as the free-gold-bearing character of the rock changed in depth and was succeeded by tellurides and arsenical compounds. My report of 1875 contains the results of tests of these refractory ores, but nothing has yet been done toward the permanent development of these claims. At Angel's, arrastras only are running. This place, a few years since, had five quartz-mills, aggregating 60 stamps. The condition of quartz-mining near San Andreas is noticed below in a communication from Mr. J. Rathgeb. This portion of the Mother lode carries low-grade oars near the surface, but its character at lower levels has not yet been demonstrated by deep development. The reason assigned is want of capital.

The most extensive quartz-mining operation of the county at present is the Gwin or Paloma Mine, owned by Messrs. Gwin, Coleman, and others. This is situated at the head of Lower Rich Gulch, a deep ravine debouching on the Mokelumne River. The mine has attained a depth by shaft of 1,100 feet, the lowest level yet opened being at 1,000 feet. The company owns two mills, both run by water-power, and the property is economically managed. It is to be regretted that statistics, such as are cheerfully furnished in the same character of mines on the Mother lode in Amador County, cannot be obtained from this source. They would be valuable as furnishing information on the economy of mining in low-grade ores, for the ores of the Gwin Mine have been of low grade for the most part down to present depths, and yet the business of mining has been successfully prosecuted since the property passed into the hands of the present owners. The vein is well defined and sometimes of great width. On the 800-foot level it attained a with of 18 feet, with high-grade rock. The rich-ore bodies, however, seem to occur in lenticular masses, and alternate levels are sometimes in low-grade ore. The cost of milling and mining probably does not exceed $6 or $7 per ton.

West Point district is situated in the eastern portion of the gold-bearing belt, in a granite formation. As a general rule the veins are narrow, but of high grade, ($30 to $40 per ton,) the walls hard, and the pay-shoots contracted in length. Nearly all these veins paid well until depth was attained, and mining and pumping became expensive. Many are now idle, on which expensive machinery has been erected. This is not owing to the exhaustion of the mines, but to the fact that the pay-shoots are limited in length, and can only be found by continuous sinking of the main shaft.

Several mines noticed in former reports have suspended operations, and others have been resuscitated with favorable results. Among these the Mina Rica and Cheeno are prominent. The principal works of the Mina Rica are situated on an ore-body 232 feet in length, which averages 4 feet wide, and was worked years ago to the depth of 135 feet. The new shaft is 12 feet by 4, in the clear, and is now 175 feet deep. Sinking progresses at the rate of 9 feet per week. The 40 feet of backs attained show a uniform width of 4 feet, containing 18 inches of very high-grade ore. The whole is estimated at $40 per ton. The hoisting-works are driven by a 16-horse-power horizontal engine, consuming three-fourths of a cord of wood in twenty-four hours. Engineers act as "tub-landers." A pump is employed two hours out of twenty-four in emptying a water-tank placed at a depth of 150 feet. The company owns another mine, the Maria, about one mile west of the Mina Rica. A transverse tunnel taps the first vein at a considerable depth, and has been extended on the lode 120 feet. The ore averages 2 feet in width, and is estimated to yield $15 per ton. The main tunnel will be extended shortly to nine other lodes, which crop east of, and parallel with, the vein now being developed. About 400 yards south of the Maria is located the company's 8-stamp mill, driven by a large overshot wheel and free water. A Hepburn settler and two Wheeler pans are employed. This mill has done well for prospecting-purposes, but the extensive and valuable backs of the Mina Rica alone necessitate the erection of a large new mill near the mine.

A group of mines in the slate-formation has been described in former reports. The most prominent is the San Bruno, described in the report of 1875, which has been steadily worked during the present year.

The Calaveras Chronicle, a careful and reliable mining-journal, makes the following statement of the condition of the principal quartz-mines of Sheep Ranch district, near Murphy's:

"Powerful steam hoisting-works have been erected on the well-known Wallace & Ferguson Mine. The engine is 45 horse-power, of sufficient capacity to admit of sinking to any required depth. The ledge—the yield of which has been remarkable from the outset—has been mined to the depth of 125 feet, a distance of 1,400 feet in length, without the aid of machinery. The mine has been very successfully worked for a number of years, and is to-day one of the most valuable mining-properties in the State. When the new hoisting-works are completed, operations will be pushed with greater vigor, and on a more extensive scale than ever.

"Work is going actively forward at the Woods Mine. Sinking has reached a depth of about 200 feet, the quartz having been of a fair quality from the surface down. The scarcity of water during the dry season rendered it impossible to run but a portion of the stamps of the mill connected with the mine, but as that impediment no longer exists, the entire battery will be kept in motion in the future. Splendid ore is being taken from the Calaveras Mine, located near the Woods. A new shaft is being sunk, which has reached a depth of about 175 feet. The old shaft is 400 feet deep. The ledge is a very wide one, all good-milling ore. A fine 20-stamp mill is owned in connection with the mine. Work is being energetically pushed with good results. This company are successfully using the Paul process, described under the heading of Butte County."

To Mr. J. Rathgeb, of San Andreas, I am indebted for the following statement of mining-operations in his vicinity:

"SAN ANDREAS, *October* 20, 1875.

"The owners of the two principal water-ditches supplying water to this vicinity have opened hydraulic claims, and are using nearly all of the water themselves, which fact causes interruption of work of many claims formerly worked, and also this year's exceptional scarcity of water, in a district that has scant facilities and short seasons for water-supply, causes a deficiency of information from mining-enterprises from this vicinity.

"Messrs. Wyllie & Treat have opened their hydraulic-mining claim near Cave City, using the water of the Table Mountain Ditch, which they own, and Terwilliger & Co. are using the water of the San Antonio Ditch on their hydraulic claims on Tunnel Ridge. Drift-mining on hydraulic claims is taking the place of hydraulic washing in many places for those reasons, and large piles of wash-dirt are accumulated to be washed in the winter. Lloyd Brothers, owners of the Garnet claim at San Andreas, have been running a bed-rock tunnel through the rim-rock, and have found the channel with good pay, and are about moving their arrastras for disintegrating gravel-cement to the new location. These arrastras are worked by water-power, and are efficacious for grinding off the cement from the quartz pebbles without crushing them, liberating the gold contained in the cement, consisting of clay, quartz-sand, and oxide of iron. They have given better satisfaction to the owners than their 5-stamp mill, erected to crush the cement. Small-size garnets are found, also pieces of magnesium, in this claim. At Central Hill the drift-mining claims have been steadily worked with varied success. The Machiavelli, Clary, Benson, Cole, Dyas, Harkins, and Shears are locations on the Dead River channel; the pay-streak is drifted out, hoisted by horse-power to the surface, dried, exposed to the influence of the atmosphere, and washed.

"Quartz-mining on the Mother lode, which runs through this district in this county, is limited, from the fact that the capital has not aided it; private labor and the yield of the mines have developed them; its growth and development have been slow, but progressing. The Pioneer Chief, B. K. Thorn, owner, was developed to the depth of 260 feet; the Union Mine was sunk to the depth of 175 feet, with two levels 150 feet in length, and has a 10-stamp quartz-mill. Captain Thorpe's Mine has several shafts with levels, and a 5-stamp quartz-mill. Beckman's, Illish's, and Rathgeb's are worked with good results. Many other locations are lying idle for want of capital."

AMADOR COUNTY.

This county has long ranked as second in the State as a quartz-mining county. It has two systems of ledges traversing it from north to south, one at or near the point of contact of greenstone and slate, known as the Mother lode, the other higher up, in the granite formation. The latter has not been actively worked for several years, and it is doubtful whether upon the whole its mines have proved remunerative. Prior to 1870 there were twelve mills on this belt, aggregating 135 stamps, and twenty-four mills on the Mother lode, aggregating 422 stamps, making a total of thirty-six mills and 547 stamps; but it is not probable that more than two-thirds of these were running at any time. At the present time, according to the returns of the county assessor, there are but seventeen mills in the county, but as many of these are large mills, the number of stamps has not been correspondingly diminished.

The following table, compiled from the official returns of the surveyor-general, will show the relative condition of mining since 1870:

Year.	Quartz-mills.	Tons crushed.	Mining-ditches.	Length in miles.	Miners' inches of water used per day.
1870	29	69, 240	35	427	5, 575
1871	27	70, 360	32	405	5, 450
1872	24	252, 000	....	470	5, 980
1873	15	81, 000	....	....	12, 000
1874	15	83, 450	11	296	15, 830
1875	17	85, 780	11	340	15, 830

The quartz-crushing of 1872, as given above, is either the result of error or of some very wild "guessing." The number of tons crushed was probably between 80,000 and 90,000. The great discrepancies in the returns of mining-ditches is the result of the consolidation of many of the smaller ditches into the Amador Canal, which now controls the principal water-sources of the county, and the abandonment of many surface-placers which were worked up to the year 1870.

West of the Mother lode there occurs a belt of copper-veins, the same as that worked several years since at Copperopolis, in Calaveras County. Only one mine of this class is now worked. This is the Newton Copper Mine, owned by John M. Glidden & Co., of Boston, Mass. The length of location is 1,300 feet; the course north 25 degrees west; dip 68 degrees east; length of pay-zone, 500 feet, with an average width of 2 feet. The vein occurs in metamorphic slate, and the ore is a sulphuret of the class known at Copperopolis as "bronze-ore." Four levels have been opened, and the ground explored to a depth of 400 feet and a horizontal distance on the vein of 588 feet. The mine is provided with powerful hoisting-works, and the ores are treated by the leaching-process. This property has been actively worked for several years, and with presumed profit to the owners; but as they reside in the Eastern States, no details of their operation can be obtained on the ground.

The Amador Canal, which is one of the most extensive water projects in the State, has been described at some length in my reports of 1874 and 1875. This great work was completed in 1875, and is now selling water as power to the quatz-mills on its line. The company already supplies nine mills, having an aggregate of 320 stamps, with a crushing-capacity of about 450 tons per day. Water is sold by the inch, the quantity used depending on the available fall. The Keystone Mill, with a 40-stamp mill, uses 180 inches for milling and hoisting purposes, while the Oneida, with 60 stamps, uses the same quantity. The principal ditch of the Amador Canal Company has a length of forty-five miles, exclusive of the branch ditches. Water is taken from a series of lakes in the high sierra, where it is retained for use in the dry season by the construction of dams. The largest of these lakes has an area of 640 acres, and its capacity has been increased during the past year to an additional depth of twelve feet by the construction of a dam at the outlet. There are two belts of auriferous gravel traversing this county, both of which will be extensively worked during the year 1876. Water is sold at 10 to 12½ cents per inch to hydraulic miners. The quartz-mills, taking small quantities, pay from 20 to 25 cents per inch.

There are about 100,000 linear feet of locations on the Mother lode between the Mokelumne and Cosumnes Rivers, which form the southern and northern boundaries of Amador County. Many of these are parallel locations; one line of locations on the hanging-wall, and another in the slates forming the foot-wall, or west country. In some cases, as at the Keystone, Consolidated Amador, and Oneida, both lines are owned by one company. The vein-system of the Mother lode varies in width, sometimes expanding to half a mile, and again presenting the features of a true fissure. Where these expansions occur the veins are always broken and of low grade.

I append, in the form of a tabulated statement, a review of the condition of quartz-mining on the Mother lode in this county, embracing a linear extent of 94,925 feet of ground. We may safely estimate the total length of locations at 100,000 feet, and of this great extent of ground it will be perceived by reference to the statement that but one-tenth, or about 10,000 feet, is now energetically worked with hoisting-works and mills. About 10,000 feet is worked irregularly, by means of arastras or custom-mills.

The Hardenbergh Mine is located at Middle Bar, on the Mokelumne River, three miles from Jackson. It was opened in 1851 and worked successively by several owners, with reported profit, a large amount of pay-rock being extracted, of the yield of which no record is accessible to me. In 1871 it was closed on account of the financial embarrassment of one of its proprietors. The present shaft (now 506 feet deep) was then under way. In 1875 the mine was re-opened by Mr. J. R. Hardenbergh. The location is 2,400 feet long. The property includes a 20-stamp mill, with rock-breakers, pans, &c., run by water-power. A ditch brings 2,000 miners' inches of water from a point on the Mokelumne three miles above the mill. The fall is 27 feet, and the power is communicated through a turbine. Mine, ditch, and mill-site, with ground for surface-purposes, amounting in all to 31 acres, are covered by a United States patent.

The Kennedy Mine, near Jackson, which was described in detail in the report for 1874, is being prospected on the 800-foot level. The mill has not run during the year, and therefore I have no returns. The large body of ore found in the southern portion of the company's ground, adjoining the Pioneer line, was of such low grade as to prove unprofitable in the company's mill, and prospecting was continued northward in the expectation of developing a chimney of high-grade rock which was worked in the upper levels.

The Consolidated Amador, of Sutter Creek, better known as the Hayward or Eureka Mine, ranked for many years as the leading quartz-mine of the State. During this period, from 1866 to 1872, the mine yielded quartz averaging $20 per ton, and supplied a 40-stamp mill, earning large dividends for the owners. The history of this mine may be traced in the reports of Hon. J. Ross Browne and myself from 1868 to 1875. It appears that with increasing depth there occurred an impoverishment of vein-matter and a horizontal contraction of ore-chimneys. The lowest level opened in the mine was at a depth of 1,665 feet. The company are now sinking their main shaft to a depth of 2,000 feet, when the intervening ground will be exposed from the 2,000-foot level. Meantime the mine has in reserve a large amount of low-grade ore, which can be profitably worked by water-power, whereby the cost of milling is reduced to one dollar per ton.

The Oneida Mine, situated between the Kennedy and Consolidated Amador, two miles north of Jackson, was discovered in 1851, and has been worked since that time with varying results. Within the past two years, however, this property has been placed on a paying basis. The Oneida Company's mill started in March, 1875, on rock from a new level, (the 1,000-foot,) which has been opened through a new three-compartment shaft with a powerful set of hoisting-works erected during the previous fall and winter. The shaft is sunk nearly the entire distance through the country-rock, which relieves it from the pressure so detrimental to shafts sunk in the vein-matter of the Mother lode. The 1,000-foot level is now well open, and sinking of the shaft for another level is under way. (See tabular returns.)

The Lincoln Mine, of Sutter Creek, is owned abroad, and its agents decline to make a statement; but it is known to be in a prosperous condition, and now ranks among the leading producing mines of Amador County. The shaft is down 750 feet, and the mill crushes 80 tons per day.

The original Amador is the oldest quartz-mining location in the county, and one of the earliest in the State. The ledge was discovered at a point where it was denuded by Amador Creek, and its location was the nucleus of a group of mines which for many years yielded large profits to the owners. Those on the south bank of Amador Creek have been consolidated under the name of the Keystone Company. The yield of quartz from the Original Amador was for many years about $10 per ton, but recently a body of high-grade ore has been struck, which promises to be remunerative to the owners. This mine was fully described by Mr. James D. Hague in my report for 1873. Since that time its prospects have materially improved by the discovery of new ore-bodies of high grade. Mr. Hague found the cost of mining (including necessary dead-work in developing new ground) to be $6.13 per ton, and the cost of milling, (steam-power,) $2.25. The recent completion of the Amador Canal, affording the company ample water-power for crushing, has reduced the cost of milling to $1.75 per ton.

The Keystone Mine, of Amador City, has for several years held the position of the leading mine on the Mother-lode belt, by reason of its great production, the magnitude of its operations, and the economy of its management. Since 1870 its production has averaged $1,000 for each working-day. The Keystone is a consolidation of three parallel claims—the original Keystone, the Geneva, and the Spring Hill. The total length of location is 1,800 feet horizontally from north to south, but the company owns 3,100 feet by virtue of the purchase of the parallel ledges. The east country is greenstone, and the west a black, talcose slate. Three veins occur in the company's ground—one on the greenstone hanging-wall, and the other two in the west country-slate, which can scarcely be called a foot-wall, as there seems to be no distinct line of demarkation of the quartz-veins in this direction, they being in fact blended with the talcose slate in a very irregular manner with respect to dip and width, but preserving a uniform course of northwest and southeast. The ore-bodies in the slate, which form the principal source of the company's revenue, are of variable extent, sometimes expanding to a width of twenty feet and again contracting to a mere seam. It has been noticed that the expansion generally occurs when the vein "flattens," and contracts where it approaches a vertical dip. In consequence of this marked peculiarity in the west veins, the ground is prospected by vertical winzes which answer the purpose of horizontal cross-cuts in more regular veins. By this means, the result of long experience and close observation of the peculiarities of the vein-system, the mine always presents large bodies of reserves which would almost invariably have remained undiscovered by the usual system of prospecting by horizontal drifts and cross-cuts. In several instances levels would have passed through nearly barren ground, leaving large ore-bodies between them. The Keystone has been explored to a depth of 750 feet and a length of 900 feet. The longest cross-cut is about 300 feet, cutting the three veins at right angles. On the east is found a well-defined hanging-wall of greenstone, carrying with it a vein of low-grade quartz.

There is properly no foot-wall, but a well-marked line of fracture is found, presenting the peculiar feature known as "slickensides," about 300 feet west of the greenstone. Beyond this exploration has failed to disclose bodies of quartz, although a cross-cut has been run 120 feet beyond the line of fracture. The yield of the quartz in this mine varies from $10 to $20 per ton. The average for the year 1875 was nearly $17, but I learn it run somewhat higher toward the close of the year. There are two working-shafts, and a third is sinking. The hoisting is done by water-power. One hundred and eighty inches of water are used, at an expense of about $40 per day, for both hoisting and crushing. The mine has now in reserves at least one year's supply of ore for its 40-stamp mill. The completion of the Amador Canal insures a constant supply of water for the future as a motive-power. This with the adoption of self-feeders reduces the expenses of treatment of ores to about $1 per ton, and affords a margin of profit on a class of ores hitherto considered as too low in grade for working

Between Amador City and Plymouth we find about 15,000 feet of ground which has been worked only on the surface, the rock being crushed in custom-mills or arastras. The Bunker Hill and the Gover are the only claims working with machinery. Near Drytown two claims, the Gold Mountain and the Belding, are each running a 10-stamp mill. As these claims are not on the line of the Mother lode, they are not mentioned in the tabulated statement.

The Phœnix Mine, of Plymouth, was opened in 1859, and has been continuously worked since that time. There are two working-shafts, 200 feet apart, each having attained a depth of 900 feet. This mine presents a large body of low-grade quartz, which is extracted and milled at an expense of $5.50 per ton. On the 800-foot level the ore-breasts are about 100 feet in width, with but little waste-rock, as the slates carry a large proportion of auriferous sulphurets. The works are run by water from the company's ditch, the power being supplied by a turbine wheel. By means of water-power and automatic feeders the minimum of economy has been reached in this mine, and quartz yielding $10 per ton is worked with large profit to the owners.

Water-power, where there is sufficient fall, is utilized by turbine or "hurdy-gurdy" wheels, the latter class being effective with a small quantity of water where the nature of the ground admits of a fall of about 200 feet. One of these runs the 60-stamp mill of the Oneida Mining Company. It is of cast iron, 8 feet in diameter and 4 inches in width. On the periphery of the wheel are cup-shaped buckets, which receive the water from a three-inch nozzle. Against these buckets one hundred and eighty inches of water, with a fall of 230 feet, is projected by means of the nozzle. The wheel-box occupies a space of 12 feet in height by 4 feet in width.

Automatic ore-feeders are coming into general use, and have an important bearing on the economy of quartz-milling. The favorite one in Amador County is the invention of Mr. James Tulloch. It consists of a hopper mounted on a strong frame-work. Beneath this hopper is the tray which receives the ore from the hopper as fast as may be desired, a suitable regulating-gate being employed. The tray is inclined as much as may be desired, and is suspended by links from the frame, so that it can receive an oscillating motion forward and back. Beneath the tray a rock-shaft crosses the tray transversely, and an arm extends upward and is secured by a pin passing through the lugs in the bottom of the tray and through the slotted upper end of the arm. The end of the shaft has a crank formed upon it, and from this crank the rod connects with one end of a lever-arm. The lever is pivoted near its middle to the frame, and the other end extends to a point near the stamp-stem. An adjustable collar is secured to the stem, and whenever the stamp falls, the collar will strike the end of the lever, and through the connecting-rod the rock-shaft will be operated so as to draw the tray back. When the stamp is again raised, the tray will be allowed to swing forward until the lugs on the bottom of the tray strike a bar or post, which will abruptly stop the tray, and thus tend to loosen and throw forward its contents, this feature being especially valuable when the ore is wet. In practice it is found that the force of gravitation is sufficient to operate these parts, no springs being used; a spring is placed upon the end of the lever which is struck by the collar, so as to relieve the strain and transmit the force gradually. The adjustable bar serves to regulate the movements of the different parts, and the amount of ore beneath the stamps will regulate the amount fed.

Both the quartz and accompanying slates of the Mother lode contain sulphurets. The proportion is from 1 to 2 per cent., and the value when concentrated about $100 per ton. Concentration is effected by means of Hendy's apparatus, supplemented by long lines of sluice-boxes. The concentrated sulphurets are sold to chlorinators.

The condition of quartz-mining in Amador County is exhibited in the following tables, compiled during the month of October, 1875:

Exhibit of the condition of quartz-mining on the Mother lode in Amador County.

Name of mine.	Length of location.	Depth attained.	Position.	Mill.	Remarks.
	Feet.	*Feet.*			
Marlette	800	200	East vein	None	Work discontinued; mill dismantled. Cause, low grade of rock.
Hardenberg	2,400	506	...do	20 stamps	Work resumed in 1875, after four years' stoppage.
Hathaway			...do	None	Not worked during past ten years. No record accessible.
Howard	*5,210		...do	...do	Do.
Moore		250	...do	...do	Do.
Sutter	1,500	100	...do	...do	Do.
Zeile, or Coney	800	600	...do	...do	Work discontinued; mill dismantled. Cause, refractory rock; sulphurets rich.
Blue Jacket	590	150	...do	...do	Work discontinued; mill dismantled. Cause, low grade of rock.
McKinney & Stewart	2,000	150	West vein	Arrastras	Engaged in prospecting, with good results; several shafts.
German Claims	1,000	100	...do	...do	Do.
Spanish Claims	2,000	150	...do	...do	Do.
Sylvester Ground	4,800	100	...do	...do	Do.
Burling	1,500	100	...do	None	Desultory prospecting.
Bacon	1,500	100	East vein	...do	Do.
Good Hope	2,000	100	...do	Custom-mill	Rock crushed at custom-mill.
Trowbridge	1,200	100	West vein	None	Idle; situated in Jackson Basin; vein low grade and broken.
Adams	800	100	...do	...do	Do.
Roberts	2,200	100	East vein	...do	Do.
Pioneer	1,590	150	West vein	...do	On hill-side; abundance low-grade rock; not worked.
Kennedy	2,000	850	...do	20 stamps	Prospecting low levels; no milling this year.
Volunteer	1,080	150	East vein	None	Actively prospecting; vein narrow and rich; rock worked at custom-mill.
Clyde	1,200	100	...do	...do	Desultory prospecting.
Oneida	3,000	1,000	Both veins	60 stamps	Actively and profitably worked. See returns elsewhere.
Tunnel Hill	2,118	100		None	Not worked; no record accessible.
Summit	1,166	500		...do	Works dismantled; no pay-shoot found.
Amador, Consolidated	1,850	2,000	Both veins	40 stamps	Deepest mine in California. Prospecting lower levels. See returns elsewhere.
Maxwell	1,441	150	East vein	None	Work suspended; has yielded good rock.
Railroad	1,697	400	West vein	...do	Parallel to above; has yielded good rock.
Wildman	1,069	500		Custom-mill	Desultory working; past record good.
Mahoney	1,122	600		16 stamps	Do.
Lincoln	1,798	750	Both veins	20 stamps	Actively working, with good prospects. Decline to make returns.
North Lincoln	1,100	100		None	Not worked; no record accessible.
Comet	720	150		...do	Do.
North Star	1,113	100		...do	Do.
Herbertville	1,781	600		...do	One of the earliest locations in the State; not worked for many years.
Median	1,320	300		...do	Not worked for many years; no record accessible.
El Dorado	1,200	300		...do	Do.
Keystone, (including Spring Hill)	3,100	750	Both veins	40 stamps	Three shafts actively and profitably worked. See returns elsewhere.
Eclipse	494	100	West vein	None	Slightly explored; not working.
Golden State	360	100	...do	...do	Do.
Original Amador	1,436	650	East vein	40 stamps	Working actively; condition prosperous. See returns elsewhere.

* Estimated.

Bunker Hill	1,115	450	do	10 stamps	Work resumed this year; quartz low grade, but profitable.
Mayflower No. 1	1,520	100	do	None	Slightly explored; not working.
Last Chance	1,220	200	West vein.	do	Do.
Nevada	1,700	100	do	do	Do.
Hazard	1,328	200	One ledge.	do	Has yielded good milling-rock; not working.
Frémont	1,600	100		do	Prospected at intervals; not working.
Gover	879	700		10 stamps	Work resumed this year; low-grade quartz.
Loyal	1,056	100		20 stamps	Mill idle; rock worked in arrastras from surface-shafts on tribute.
Italian	302	100		None	Desultory surface-workings; paid near surface.
Seaton, or Drytown	1,260	500		do	Ledge wide; low-grade rock. Not worked for ten years. Mill destroyed by fire.
Chili	1,200			do	Prospected on surface; not working.
Mayflower No. 2	1,200			do	Do.
Potosi	840	200		16 stamps	Mill idle; past record of mine good; not working.
Webster, Clay, Dry Creek, and Hercules	Aggregating 4,800	From 100 to 200		None	No active prospecting carried on for several years. Low-grade rock.
Phœnix	1,850	900	West vein.	40 stamps	Great width of vein; quartz low grade, but profitable. See returns elsewhere.
Alpine	800	400	do	10 stamps	Work suspended; results unprofitable; low-grade rock.
Enterprise	1,200	300	do	8 stamps	Do.
Bay State	1,500	100		None	Desultory prospecting at intervals; no record.
Richmond	1,600	200		20 stamps	Work suspended for several years; low-grade rock.
Spanish, or McGettigan	1,200	400		None	Work resumed, with new hoisting-works; prospects good.
Lady Bedford	1,000	200		do	Ledge narrow; rock pays $20 per ton; working.
Total length of claims	94,945				

List of mills in Amador County, California; reported by W. A. Skidmore.

District.	Name of mill.	Owners.	Kind of power and amount.	Number of stamps.	Weight of stamps.	Number of drops per minute.	Height of drop.	Number of pans.	Number of concentrators.	Cost of mill.	Capacity per 24 hours, in tons.	Cost of treatment per ton.	Tons crushed during year.	Method of treating sulphurets.
					Lbs.		*Inches.*							
Sutter Creek	Oneida	Oneida Mining Company.	Steam and water	60	600	80	9	2	2	$60,000	100	$1 25	....	Buddles and concentrators.
Do	Consolidated Amador	Consolidated Amador Mining Company.	... do	40	700	80	9	2	None.	60,000	80	$1 00 to 1 50	....	Chlorination.
Amador	Original Amador	London and California Mining Company.	... do	40	700	80	8 to 10	1	3	55,000	80	1 50 to 1 75	....	Roasting and pans.
Do	Bunker Hill	Bunker Hill Mining Company.	Water, 70 inches, 275 feet fall.	10	750	80	9	12	None.	8,000	16	1 00 to 1 25	....	Pans.
Do	Keystone Consolidated	Keystone Mining Company.	Water, 96 horse-power.	40	750	86	8	......	22	60,000	90	1 21	25,579	Chlorination.
Plymouth	Phœnix Consolidated	Phœnix Gold-Mining Company.	Water, (turbine)	40	600	84	7	None.	None.	35,000	65	1 00	16,000	Do.
Drytown	Gover	Gover Mining and Milling Company.	Water, 100 inches, 84 feet fall.	10	600	80	9	None.	5	7,000	15	1 00 to 1 25	....	Do.

List of mines in Amador County, California; reported by W. A. Skidmore.

District.	Name of mine.	Owners.	Number of miners employed.	Miners' wages, per day.	Cost of sinking, per foot.	Cost of drifting, per foot.	Cost of stoping, per ton.	Cost of mining, per ton extracted.	Cost of milling, per ton.	Company or custom mill.	Number of tons extracted and worked.	Average yield per ton.	Percentage of sulphurets.	Total bullion-product.
Sutter Creek.	Oneida	Oneida Mining Company.	60	$2 50 to $3	Varies largely.	....	......	$6 00	$1 25	Company.	70 per day.	$12 00	......	....
Do	Consolidated Amador.	Consolidated Amador Mining Company.	50	2 50 to 3	$20	$8	$12 00	5 00	$1 00 to 1 50	....do....	....	10 00	¼	....
Amador	Original Amador.	London and California Mining Company.	34	3	35	15	3 00	5 00	1 50 to 1 75	....do....	....	28 00	2	....
Do	Bunker Hill	Bunker Hill Mining and Milling Company.	8	2 50 to 3	15	6	2 00	5 00	1 00 to 1 25	....do....	....	18 00	1½	....
Do	Keystone Consolidated.	Keystone Mining Company.	100	2 50 to 3	$7, $15, 30	$6 to 7	......	4 89	1 21	....do....	25, 579	16 90	2	$432, 637
Plymouth	Phœnix Gold	Phœnix Gold-Mining Company.	90	2 50 to 3	13	9 to 10	1 20	4 50	1 00	....do....	65 per day	6 00	1½	....

List of mines in Amador County, California; reported by W. A. Skidmore.

District.	Name of mine.	Owners.	Length of location.	Course.	Dip.	Length of pay-zone.	Average width.	Country-rock.	Character of vein-matter.	Cost of hoisting and pumping machinery.	Greatest depth attained.	Greatest length of horizontal exploration.	Number of levels opened.
			Feet.			*Feet.*	*Feet.*				*Feet.*	*Feet.*	
Sutter Creek	Oneida	Oneida Mining Company.	3,000	N. & S	65° E.	500	6	Greenstone and slate.	Blackstone and quartz.	$30,000	1,000	700	3
Do	Consolidated Amador	Consolidated Amador Mining Company.	3,291	N.W. & S.E.	70° E.	600	3 to 30	do	Gold-bearing quartz.	50,000	2,000	1,200	10
Amador	Original Amador	London and California Mining Company.	1,350	N.W	N.E	250	8	do	do	12,000	650	1,200	8
Do	Bunker Hill	Bunker Hill Mining Company.	1,400	N.W. & S.E.	65° E.	150	2 to 16	do	do	2,000	450	270	3
Do	Keystone Consolidated	Keystone Mining Company.	1,800	W. & S	45° E.	400		do	Quartz and slate	40,000	740	900	6
Plymouth	Phœnix	Phœnix Gold-Mining Company.	1,900	23° W. of N.	70° E.	W. 250	30	do	Gold-bearing quartz.	15,000	900	400	8
Drytown	Gover	Gover Mining Company.	879	N.W. & S.E.	65° E.			do	do	3,000	700	800	3

EL DORADO COUNTY.

The following table indicates the condition of mining in this county during the past five years:

Year.	Quartz-mills.	Tons crushed.	Mining-ditches.	Length in miles.	Miners' inches of water used per day.
1870	32	3,730	53	853	5,365
1871	44	21,645	58	966	9,450
1872	40	No returns..	54	850	6,720
1873	40	....do	54	850	6,720
1874	30	....do	50	900	....
1875	27	.... do	50	900	7,500

During 1875 but three mills were engaged in crushing, while the assessor's returns showed that there are 27 quartz-mills in the county, equivalent to a total crushing-capacity of 500 tons per day.

Many of the idle mills are among the most expensive erected in the State; three of the number cost from $40,000 to $60,000 each. The aggregate cost of the mills now standing idle is not less than $250,000. The falling off in this branch of mining is attributable to the impoverishment of the quartz in depth. Several of the mines formerly noted for their production of free-gold, such as the Cederberg, have suspended operations, this class of ore running out at a depth of about two hundred and fifty feet, and the quartz below that level being of too low grade for profitable working. The belt of auriferous rocks in this county is nearly thirty miles in width, and contains several systems of quartz-veins, among others the so-called Mother lode, but the formation is much broken and the ore of low grade. The geological features of this county were fully described by Mr. Amos Bowman in my report for 1875. Since that time there has been no important change in the condition of the mining-interest.

An important claim not heretofore noticed is the Dry Gulch or Crawford Gravel claim, situated near Pleasant Valley. It was discovered in the early days by following up the several rich gulches that head from it, and was covered by innumerable square locations of the early miners, which were afterward consolidated under a United States patent. It forms a depression or "sag" in the main ridge between Clear and Sly Park Creeks, and embraces 160 acres of land, of which from 90 to 120 are estimated to be deep, rich gravel-channel. The depth varies from 60 to 260 feet, the average being about 110 feet. It has been prospected by eleven shafts, sunk for drifting purposes. The deepest is 128 feet, and did not reach bed-rock. In the early days it was drifted by several tunnels, the largest being about 700 feet. The character of material in shafts and tunnels is quite uniform. By drifting it yielded over $10 per ordinary car-load, the gold being coarse and selling readily at stores for $18.70 per ounce. It has all the characteristics of an ancient channel, and is plainly traceable, in the form of a letter S, from the southeast to the northwest corner.

It is finely located for extensive hydraulic working, and possesses two unrivaled outlets. The Clear Creek or northwest outlet permits a sluice-line of ¾ mile, of any grade desirable, and an eight-inch sluice-grade would give it a 140 feet drop into Clear Creek, which falls on an average eighteen inches per rod. No bedrock-tunnel is necessary, since the rim-rock is low, so that only a short rockcut is required. As determined by the prospect-shafts, the channel falls toward this end on a steep grade.

The Park Creek or southeast outlet possesses a magnificent fall of over 450 feet. This end has been altogether worked by the hydraulic system, and probably two acres have been washed off. The company is extending and straightening the bed-rock tunnel, so that it will be 5 by 6 feet in the clear and 240 feet in length, and will "bottom" all the land on this end of the claim. It has a grade of 8-inch fall to each 12 feet.

Previous to 1874 a small head of surface-water and a hand-nozzle were employed. By this crude apparatus nearly 10,000 cubic yards of earth were removed in two seasons, and produced $8,770. Last year a new 400-inch (4-inch pressure) ditch was completed, but owing to the scarcity of water, on account of the slight rain and snow-fall, not over 150 inches were available for about four hours of thirty days. During this time 2,005 cubic yards were washed, and yielded $3,140.

This year the claim is being put in good shape for extensive working, which was impossible last year by reason of the season of the year (December) when it was acquired by the present proprietors. A line 500 feet long of 36 by 30 inch sluices is being placed in the tunnel and beyond, when the *débris* is thrown into a rocky ravine and allowed to tumble among the rocks for a distance of 300 feet, when it is again caught up, the bowlders precipitated over a "grizzly" into the cañon below, and the disintegrated gravel permitted to deposit its gold in a 600-foot flume, after which the tailings escape. One more Giant will be added to the two already in use. Next year it is contemplated to work the northwest end. The present face of the gravel on the southeast end is 68 feet in height, and is but a short distance from the southern boundary of the ancient channel. The bed-rock dips rapidly to the north, so that in a distance of 215 feet the depth of gravel is 85 feet. The first or top stratum of gravel (10 to 30 feet) is of a yellow and reddish cast, and seems to be equally rich as the substrata or "blue gravel." Here and there are short, unconnected streaks of a white clay, that yields readily to the pipe. The bowlders, composed of quartz, "nigger heads," and micaceous schists, are not large, but very irregular in form, and show but little wear from attrition. Bank-blasting is practiced. The gravel washes easily, but runs rather sluggishly; hence a heavy grade is necessary. The "backing" of the black sand is thereby also avoided.

On the northwest end about one-half acre was washed away by parties on a lease, but I have been afforded no means of ascertaining its yield. It is regarded as the richest portion of the mine.

The hydrostatic pressure at the southeast works is 176 feet, and on the northwest end 240 feet. A reservoir of a capacity of 600 inches for 10 hours is on the claim. The water is delivered to the machines through a 15-inch pipe and an 11-inch pipe.

Park Creek is capable of supplying 4,000 inches of water for five months of the year, and yields over 1,000 inches for 7 months. The above-mentioned 400-inch ditch has been enlarged this fall to 2,200 inches capacity, at a cost of $13,000. It is 5½ miles in length, and has been cut mostly through blasting-ground.

The Eureka Water Company's ditches and water-rights to the waters of North Fork of the Cosumnes, Steeley's Fork, Van Horn Creek, Baltic

Creek, Camp Creek, Stonebreaker's Creek, and Park Creek have been purchased of D. O. Mills & Co. These ditches aggregate 276 miles of main and distributing lines, and supply all that region between the American River and its North Fork and the Cosumnes, and from the higher foothills to within 15 miles of Sacramento City. They were constructed at an early date, at a cost of $3,400,000, and they are too low for the great amount of deep gravel east and west of Pleasant Valley. These ditches have been consolidated with the Crawford Gravel claim, and work on the new high line has already been commenced. The Park Creek branch will be increased from 2,200 to 4,000 inches capacity, and the Camp Creek line will be completed early in the spring, while the North Fork line will be finished in September, 1876. These will have a capacity of 4,000 inches, and a length of 21 miles. These improvements, together with the contemplated reservoirs, will cost about $160,000.

During the year 1874 cinnabar was discovered in this county in the second range of foot-hills north of the Cosumnes River, and about 800 or 900 feet above sea-level. The vein lies between serpentine on the west, forming the foot-wall, and slate on the east. The vein-matter is composed of sandstone and quartz. The vein or ledge stands nearly vertical, and has been cross-cut 80 feet. The ore is diffused throughout the mass in irregular quantities, some strata being exceedingly rich. At the present point of development, about 80 feet vertical, a high grade of ore has been cross-cut, which occurs in alternate bands of sulphurets of iron and cinnabar-bearing quartz. This ore ranges in grade from 10 per cent. upward. The gangue-matter is, however, principally sandstone. A bench of three retorts was erected in 1875, but the predominance of iron-sulphurets in the ore rendered some other method of treatment advisable, and work was suspended.

Mining-statistics of El Dorado County, California; reported by W. T. Gibbs and William Teague.

DESCRIPTION OF LEADING MINES.

Name.	District.	Owners.	Length of location.	Course.	Dip.
			Feet.		
Woodside	Georgetown	Company	1,500	N. W. & S. E	65° E.
Taylor	....do	....do	3,000	....do	75° E.
Mount Pleasant	Mountain	O. D. Lambard.	5,280	N. 16° E.	80° E.

Name.	Length pay-zone.	Average width.	Country-rock.	Vein-matter.	Cost of hoisting and pumping machinery.	Greatest depth attained.	Greatest length horizontal exploration.	Number of levels opened.
	Feet.	Feet				Feet.	Feet.	
Woodside	100	3	Talcose slate	Aurif. quartz	$10,000	300	150	2
Taylor	250	....	Slate	....do	1,000	400	300	4
Mount Pleasant	200	3	Granite	....do	*Tunnel	300	350	2

* Length, 500 feet; cost, $1,500.

Mining-statistics of El Dorado County, California—Continued.

OPERATIONS OF LEADING MINES.

Name.	Number of miners employed.	Wages, per day.	Cost sinking, per foot.	Cost drifting, per foot.	Cost stoping, per foot.	Cost mining, per ton extracted.	Cost milling, per ton.	Company or custom mill.	Number of tons extracted and worked.	Average yield per ton.	Percentage of sulphurets.	Total bullion-product, 1875.
Woodside	20	$3	$30	$10	$4	$6	$2	Company	1,500	$35	1¼	$35,000
Taylor	25	3	30	12½	2½	5	2	....do	5,000	$7 to 18	1	50,000
Mount Pleasant	8	3	6	4	2	$3 to 5	2¼	....do	700	47	1⅓	31,000

STATEMENT OF QUARTZ-MILLS.

Name.	Kind and amount of power.	Stamps.				Number of pans.	Number of concentrators.	Cost of mill.	Capacity per 24 hours—tons.	Cost of treatment, per ton.	Tons crushed during the year.	Method of treating sulphurets.
		Number.	Weight, lbs.	Drop, inches.	Drops per minute.							
Woodside	Steam, 40 h. p.	5	650	7	84	1	None	$5,000	7	$2 00	1,000	Pan-grinding.
Taylor	Steam, 35 h. p.	10	700	7	80	....	......	20,000	15	2 00	5,000	Do.
Mount Pleasant	Water, 30 miner's inches.	10	750	7	80	....	2	5,000	12	2 50	....	None.

PLACER COUNTY.

Next to Nevada County this is the most important hydraulic-mining county in the State. Its physical characteristics and the nature of its mines, both quartz and gravel, have been amply described in former reports. The principal quartz-mining districts are in the vicinity of Auburn, in the foot-hills bordering on the Sacramento Valley. The formation here is granite and slate. A tabulated description of the developed mines will be found in my Report of 1874, pp. 98, 99. Since that time no new mines of any importance have been discovered, and with one exception, the St. Patrick, but little progress has been made in development. The official returns of the county assessors for the past five years contain so many evident inaccuracies that I have refrained from tabulating them.

The St. Patrick Company, near Ophir, owning four ledges and a 15-stamp mill, has made a remarkable development during the past year in its Crater Mine. Large bodies of ore were discovered between the 200 and 300 foot levels, and the mill is driven to its full capacity on rock yielding an average of $30 per ton, giving a daily gross product of from $900 to $1,000. There are over twelve months' reserves or backs of this class of ore in the mine. The company presents the following statement of operations for the year ending October 30, 1875:

Receipts.

From bullion	$73,951 66
From assessment	19,920 00
From milling-ores, &c	495 00
Balance on hand October 30, 1874	731 41
Total	95,098 07

Expenditures.

Mine and mill labor and supplies at mine	$68,036 03
Mine and mill supplies, San Francisco office	12,262 89
Contingent expenses	2,403 81
Cash in bank	12,395 34
Total	95,098 07

The superintendent says:

The 212-foot level, No. 2 shaft, is in east of shaft 288 feet; ledge in drift, 2 feet wide; on stope, 2 to 2½ feet wide. The rock shows well in sulphurets of a good quality, and has the appearance of good milling-rock. The 312-foot level, No. 1 shaft, is in east of shaft 413 feet; ledge in drift, 2½ feet wide; on stope, 2 to 2½ feet. The rock looks good, both in drift and on stope. The rock in drift I think is the best in the mine. It shows well in sulphurets, and some gold. I think we are coming to a fine body of rock going east. It is the same worked last winter on the 150-foot level, No. 2 shaft. The 440-foot level, No. 1 shaft, is in east of shaft 226 feet; ledge in drift, 20 inches wide; on stope, 20 inches to 2 feet. The rock continues to look good, shows plenty of galena and sulphurets, and some gold.

The $19,920 raised by assessment during the past year was expended in the erection of powerful hoisting-works and in deep explorations of the mine.

The Saint Lawrence Mine is situated in Ophir mining-district, one mile and a half from Newcastle Station, on the Central Pacific Railroad, and comprises 1,000 feet on the Saint Lawrence ledge or lode, 800 feet of the mining-ground known as the Mammoth or Boulder, neither of which are being worked at this date; and 2,500 feet of mining-ground known as the Hathaway-Swift, upon which a shaft has been sunk to the depth of about 150 feet, and two levels run from the outside, intersecting the shaft, each of which is about 400 feet long. Five shoots of pay-ore have been cut in running these levels, each of which is over 75 feet in length on the vein. The ledge has well-defined walls, and the pay-ore in the shoots averages over 2 feet in width. The ores raised assay high in gold-value, but are found rebellious in working by ordinary gold-milling process. This company has a well-built water-mill of 12 stamps, with the necessary appliances, Hendy concentrators, reverberatory-furnace, and grinding-pans, and capable of milling 18 tons of ore per day.

The Julian Mine, near Newcastle, also in the foot-hills, has been in a prosperous condition, but no returns have been received. The rock is of low grade, yielding from $8 to $12 per ton, but the pay is uniform and the ledge of fair width. With the exception of the three claims above mentioned, but little has been done in quartz-mining in the vicinity of Auburn.

The following are the returns furnished by J. H. Neff, superintendent of the Rising Sun Mine, near Colfax, in Illinoistown district, owned by Coleman, Neff & Co.:

Length of claim, 3,000 feet; course, east and west; dip, south; length of pay-zone, 800 feet; average width, 15 inches; country-rock, greenstone; vein-matter, quartz; cost of pumping and hoisting machinery, $4,000; greatest depth attained, 520 feet; greatest horizontal exploration, 1,000 feet; 6 levels opened; 28 miners employed, (1875,) wages, $3; cost of sinking, per foot, $28; of drifting, $12; of mining, per ton, $9; of milling, in company's mill, $3.; number of tons extracted and worked in 1875, 4,880; average yield per ton, $21.50; sulphurets, 5 per cent.; total bullion produced, $104,920; steam-mill, 60 horse-power; 10 stamps of 900 pounds, dropping 14 inches 60 times per minute; 5 pans; cost of mill, $20,000; capacity, 20 tons per 24 hours; tons crushed in 1875, 4,880.

The mining prospects around Gold Run and Dutch Flat were never brighter. The Miners' Ditch Company commenced washing through its new bed-rock tunnel on December 15, and is now running night and day, using 900 inches of water.

The Gold Run Hydraulic Mining Company is about ready to commence washing. The gravel at the shaft is 180 feet deep. The tunnel is 950 feet in length, and has a 5-foot flume, with two under-currents and three 2-foot dumps. The tunnel empties into the Miners' Ditch Company, 700 feet from the main tunnel, and 1,200 feet from its mouth in Cañon Creek. The company will open through an incline, 250 feet through gravel and 80 feet through bed-rock. The dirt on the bed-rock is very rich, having prospected from $5 to $10 to the pan in places.

A description of the ground of the Indiana Hill Cement Mill and Mining Company, near Gold Run, with statistics of the yield of this mine and others of its class, will be found in the report of 1875. The following record of the present year is given by Mr. J. N. Jensen, the secretary of the company:

Work was commenced on November 8, 1874, and the first run of one thousand car-loads was made December 1. The following is the record from that time:

No. of run.	Date.	Quantity.	Value.
1	December 1, 1874	1,000 car-loads	$3,065 72
2	December 27, 1874	1,048 car-loads	3,370 13
3	January 25, 1875	1,000 car-loads	3,622 97
4	February 19, 1875	1,000 car-loads	4,028 28
5	March 15, 1875	1,000 car-loads	5,125 50
6	April 5, 1875	1,000 car-loads	6,134 72
7	April 26, 1875	1,081 car-loads	6,354 67
8	May 22, 1875	1,081 car-loads	8,279 66
9	June 19, 1875	1,440 car-loads	6,184 08
10	July 17, 1875	1,160 car-loads	5,867 60
11	August 21, 1875	1,400 car-loads	4,403 14
		11,210 car-loads.	56,446 47

The gross amount of expenses for extraction and milling, including material of all sorts, such as powder, fuse, candles, timber, coal, &c., was $24,000, or a fraction over $2 per car-load, leaving a profit of $32,446.47. The amount of ground moved has been 201 feet in length, average width 90 feet, and from 7 to 8 feet in height. Our work for the past season has been close to the west rim of the channel, where the bed-rock was found about 15 feet higher than the average level of the bed-rock in the main channel, and running at that height in a long flat bench or bar. It is green slate and very soft, the gravel also becoming somewhat softer than it is nearer the mouth of the channel. Work was stopped on the 11th of August last, for lack of water and for such repair as was necessary. The company commenced crushing again on the 17th of November, 1875.

The car-load above referred to contains about 20 cubic feet. The cement is run through an 8-stamp mill, with a crushing-capacity of about 40 loads per day.

Cañon Creek, which heads about ten miles northeast of Gold Run, flows down a steep cañon just to the east of the Gold Run gravel district, and is the natural outlet for its mines. Col. Jonathan Moody and W. H. Kinder own about two miles each of this cañon. They are both valuable tailing-claims. Colonel Moody has two 8-foot flumes, side by side, 8 feet deep, and three-fourths of a mile long, and four under-currents, from three of which he has taken this season, in three weeks' time, the sum of $1,200. His claim has averaged a yield of $14,000 per year for the last eight years. The Kinder claim is provided with eight under-currents, and does equally well, if not better. The Cañon Creek claim and the system of gold-saving in this class of ground are fully described in my report of 1875.

Attention has recently been attracted to a section of mining-country situated in the southern portion of Placer County, near the line of El Dorado County, lying between the North and South branches of the Middle Fork of the American River, (locally known as *Long Cañon Divide,*) but until the last two years very little work has been done, on account of the absence of mining-ditches. The gravel-deposits of this section are very extensive, commencing at Pennsylvania Point—the lower end of the district—and extending up the ridge a distance of 25 miles At Pennsylvania Point, forming the apex of the ridge, the gravel-deposits are from 20 to 40 feet in depth. Three miles above, at Pennsylvania Flat, the deposits are from 200 to 300 feet in depth. Masses of auriferous-gravel deposit of unknown extent, and belonging to the same channel-system, are exposed at Lynchburgh and Blacksmith Flat. This region has an elevation of from 3,000 to 4,000 feet above sea-level, and the channel here exposed is probably the head of one of the ancient tributaries of the great Pliocene river-system of California. The bed of rock of the higher portion is granite, and of the lower, slates. This auriferous belt is situated higher than the lava-flow.

The country between the Middle and North Forks of the American River contains vast deposits of auriferous gravel of great richness. At Bath during the past season the Paragon Company, using 400 inches of water, took out $30,000 in 30 days. Wheeler & Breeze took out a large amount of gold during the season—their ground having yielded by the hydraulic process at the rate of from $70,000 to $100,000 per acre. The adjoining claim of Rousch & Grinnell is also noted for its large yield. The completion of several ditches on this divide and the consolidation of mining-ground promise a much larger bullion-product for the future.

Dutch Flat and Gold Run districts.—Mr. C. J. Brown, of Dutch Flat, has kindly contributed the following comprehensive review of the condition of gravel and hydraulic mining in these districts.

I will confine myself to a section from Indiana Hill on the south to Thompson's Hill on the north, and its tributary, known as the Dutch Flat Channel, from the latter place eastward one mile, in all, six linear miles of these two channels of ancient rivers long since extinct. Twenty years ago they were filled and overspread with auriferous gravel to the depth of from 350 to 500 feet, upon which grew a forest of gigantic pines.

It will be observed that I locate this section of mining-lands on the divide between the North Fork of the American River and Bear River, in Placer County, and that the Central Pacific Railroad crosses it between Gold Run and Dutch Flat at an altitude of 3,420 feet above the sea.

As the ancient channel ran its waters toward the north, Indiana Hill (which is one mile southeast of Gold Run) is located on the inlet, and Thompson's Hill (one mile west of Dutch Flat) on the outlet of its old channel across the divide. I use the words inlet and outlet, because to the south of Indiana Hill the North Fork of the American River has crossed the ancient channel and cut a cañon to a perpendicular depth of 1,500 feet below the old channel, completely obliterating all evidence of its former existence between the latter place and Iowa Hill, a distance of four or five miles, and to the north of Thompson's Hill Bear River crossed it in like manner, and cut a cañon to a perpendicular depth of 1,000 feet below its channel, destroying about two miles of it. This hill was extensively worked as drift-ground by the Yankee, Potosi, Why Not,

Badger, and Ohio Companies from 1856 to 1863, and proved immensely rich in heavy gold of a very fine quality. This is at the lower or southwest extremity of what is known as the Dutch Flat Mines proper, which extend from thence about one and a fourth miles northeast, to where the old channel has been cut off and destroyed by a tributary of Bear River known as Little Bear River. This Dutch Flat gravel-bed was formerly located and claimed by many different mining companies under different names, and the claims they so located still retain their distinctive appellations, though now owned by but few companies. Except at Thompson's Hill, where the ground was drifted, the former owners and locators have washed by hydraulic process and mined away the top or red gravel, leaving a surface of gravel and *débris* one-fourth of a mile wide, and a depth over the center of the channel of about 200 feet.

Here is located the Yankee claims, the main hydraulic works of the Cedar Creek Gold-Mining and Water Company, (limited,) an English corporation, which purchased from the Dutch Flat Water Company, in the spring of 1872, extensive ditch-property and large tracts of mining-ground. It is now the owner of a compact continuous tract of mining-ground from the outlet at Thompson's Hill up along the Dutch Flat Channel and southward along the channel of the South Blue, aggregating an area of 229 acres, and is about three-fourths of a mile in length, covering the deepest portion of the channel all the way. This company sank a deep shaft at the confluence of these two channels about two years ago, and struck very rich prospects. It commenced a bed-rock tunnel from the cañon of Bear River low enough to tap the whole of this tract of land. This tunnel is 8 by 9 feet in dimensions, and when complete will be 3,000 feet long with a grade of eight inches to twelve feet. About 1,285 feet of it is completed. The work is done with Burleigh drills, driven by air compressed by a hurdy-gurdy water-wheel, and costs on an average $30 per linear foot. After running about 600 feet, a branch 36 feet long was run to the right, on an angle with the main line of about 45°, at the head of which a shaft was sunk 145 feet deep. A fine flume six feet wide was laid in the tunnel, (four feet only of which has as yet been used,) and extended down from its mouth some distance; a side flume was also constructed along the side of the cañon, with under-currents, five in all, and everything arranged in the most complete order to open up the Yankee claim from the bed-rock. Washing was commenced about the 1st of August, 1874, with one Little Giant, carrying 500 inches of water, under a pressure of 500 feet. In February last another Giant was added, and the water-supply increased to 1,250 inches. The work was continued both night and day for one year, at an aggregate expense—including cost of running 1,032 feet of main tunnel and 62 feet of branch tunnel and necessary fluming, erecting derrick, &c.—of $35,000. The company took out in the mean time $55,000 in gold. The use of water averaged not more than twenty days, of twelve hours each, per month, and a space of bed-rock, not over three hundred feet square, was denuded of gravel. The bank will now average about one hundred and thirty feet in height, the lower forty feet of which is the rich blue-gravel stratum, the remainder being barren detritus, the remnant of a land avalanche containing large erratic bowlders. The bed-rock is trap and generally very hard. Two hundred feet of tunnel was run at an expense of from $60 to $100 per foot; but this was exceptionally hard and refractory. Six hundred and thirty-five feet beyond the Yankee shaft is another short branch to the Badger shaft, where another claim will soon be opened. Two Giants will be placed in position and a derrick erected with a mast 100 feet high and boom 85 feet long. A new derrick is also being erected in the Yankee with a 90-foot mast and 80-foot boom. The derricks are all guyed with wire-rope and operated by hurdy-gurdy wheels. It is the intention of the superintendent to wash through each shaft alternately, night and day, which will allow half the time in each claim for blasting and removing the large bowlders. The tunnel can be run ahead at the same time and with greater facility while washing, for the car runs over the flume and the *débris* is dumped into the flume and carried off by the current, instead of being run out of the tunnel on the car.

This company will soon erect a stamp-mill to work the cement-gravel, and will, no doubt, in time, enlarge its water capacity. Its ditches have a present capacity of 6,000, but they will supply this amount to the mines, in average seasons, for from three to four months only each year. Its chief reliance is in the Placer County Canal, which is about fifty miles long, and has a capacity of 2,250 of water, which it will furnish—including the reserve from its reservoirs—for seven months each year. The reservoirs situated along the line of this ditch are three in number, with an aggregate capacity of 50,000 inches, which will supply the ditch a full head for three weeks.

There is no doubt that one of the months from April to December is, on an average, as valuable for hydraulic mining as the three months of January, February, and March. One reason is that the days are much longer. True the work goes on both night and day, still much more and better work can be accomplished in the same number of hours by natural light than by the artificial light used in the mines. But the greatest difference is caused by temperature. It is not only difficult and disagreeable for men to work in a hydraulic claim, especially at night, in weather when it is snowing, blowing, raining, and freezing, but the quicksilver used in the sluices to amalgamate the gold congeals in cold and snowy water, and loses, to a large degree, its amalgamating properties, resulting in the washing away and loss of a much larger per cent. of quicksilver and gold in the winter than in the summer months. Consequently a good supply of water during the summer and autumn is, to every hydraulic mine, a great desideratum.

This company owns also other large and valuable tracts of mining-ground in this section, and is working three or four other claims with full forces. It has a valuable property, but it is as yet undeveloped.

The Polar Star Hydraulic Mining Company is a California corporation, composed of J. S. Colgrove, of this place, Alvinza Hayward and other San Francisco capitalists. It owns the old Buckeye mining-claim and contiguous ground, aggregating fifty acres, lying about one and one-fourth miles above the Yankee shaft, covering the entire Dutch Flat Channel at the inlet thereof. A portion of this claim has been drifted for many years, and has proved very rich. The surface-gravel has also been washed off. Adjoining this claim on the west or down the channel lies the Southern Cross, embracing the old Dutch Flat mining-claim of 40.2 acres, from which the surface has been washed, yielding $155,000, one-fourth of which was paid out for water alone. The bottom has never been drifted. This claim is owned by some of the same parties, including Messrs. Colgrove and Hayward. Both claims cross the channel from river to river, and are second to no mining-ground in this district. Mr. Colgrove, who has been a resident of this place for many years, and is a thorough and practical hydraulic miner, is the general superintendent of both claims. He contracted with the Gold Run Ditch and Mining Company, which owned a Burleigh drilling-machine, to run a tunnel for each claim, including 600 feet for the Polar Star and 1,050 feet for the Southern Cross. The Polar Star tunnel was commenced on the 20th of August, 1875, and is now complete. It is 9 by 9 feet on a grade of 10 miles to 12 feet, and is a splendid piece of work. The head of the tunnel is under the center of the channel, 34 feet below the surface of the rock and 209 feet below the surface of the gravel. Instead of a vertical shaft, an incline is raised through the rock 46 feet and through gravel 250 feet, linear measurement. The flume is 5 feet wide. And it is the intention of Mr. Colgrove to put large-sized railroad-rails lengthwise of the flume on top of the blocking, along the whole length of the tunnel, as a conductor for the large bowlders. This is a novel idea, and I believe will prove an economical and beneficial one, at least till such time as a derrick can be worked.

The hydraulic pipe is made of No. 14 and No. 16 sheet-iron, is 4 feet in diameter at the head, and tapers to 22 inches in 500 feet; thence 2,800 feet to the "twin," from which two 15-inch pipes lead into the diggings. Two thousand inches of water will be delivered from the two Giants under a pressure of 500 feet, with the line of pipe nearly straight from head to tail. The tunnel of the Polar Star opens to the cañon of Bear River, along the steep side of which a system of flumes and under-currents is being built. The work is being pushed with commendable energy, that washing may commence at the earliest possible day.

The Southern Cross tunnel opens to the same cañon, 1,200 feet west of the Polar Star. In size and grade the tunnels are the same. Over 200 feet of the latter is now completed, and the whole will be finished by the 1st of July, 1876. It is estimated that the head of this tunnel will be 40 feet below the surface of the rock and 260 below the surface of the gravel. The appointments for this claim will be the same in every particular as provided for the Polar Star. Water for each is to be furnished by the South Yuba Canal Company, under contract, I believe, and is drawn from one sand-box. All the iron pipe will be painted heavily with red lead, to protect it against corrosion.

The measuring and sand boxes are the most elaborate and the best arranged of any I have ever seen. More than 12,000 feet of lumber was used in their construction. The measuring-box is 18 by 21 feet, and the sand-box is 12 by 24 feet and 9 feet deep, divided into two 12 by 12 feet compartments.

The Franklin Gravel-Mining Company is a corporation, composed of James Teaff, of Dutch Flat; Col. J. D. Fry, L. A. Booth, Joseph Sharon, O. F. Giffin, Robert Graves, and others, of San Francisco. It owns a claim of 28.7 acres, west of and adjoining the Southern Cross, which crosses the channel from rim to rim. The gravel, no portion of which has ever been drifted, is 220 feet at the deepest, and will average about 190 feet. Mr. Teaff, who is an old and experienced miner, and who is now the superintendent of this company, was formerly the owner of this claim. He commenced working the surface as early as 1854, and is estimated to have taken out about $200,000, spent $55,000 in fitting up, and paid $75,000 to $100,000 for water alone. Under the present ownership, 400 feet of new rock-tunnel, 6 by 8 feet, opening to the cañon of Bear River, has been run this year, by hand-drilling, at an expense of about $30 per foot. This tunnel is designed, however, not to tap the bottom of the channel, but to wash a top bench about 150 feet in depth. The flume is 4 feet wide, provided with three under-currents. This claim has a splendid hydraulic rigging, placed thereon in 1871 by the Dutch Flat Blue-Gravel-Mining Company. The pipe is 3,500 feet long, constructed of Nos. 8 and 16 sheet-iron, 5 feet in diameter at the head and 22 inches at the tail, having a fall of about 500 feet. Mr. Teaff proposes to use 1,000 inches of water and commence washing by the 1st of March, 1876.

Indiana Hill Blue-Gravel-Mining Company is an incorporate company, having its principal place of business at the town of Gold Run, and all of the stockholders reside in the district, some of whom labor in the mine, which is located on the American River side of the divide, and embraces the very inlet of the "South Blue Channel." Many years ago the front along the rim was worked by hydraulic process on a small scale. In 1865 A. Mallory and J. Stone commenced a drift-tunnel and erected an 8-stamp mill. In 1869 it fell into the hands of the present management, and since then has produced $150,000 up to December 18, 1875, at an expense of about $65,000. The car contains about twenty cubic feet of earth. In the month of May, 1875, 1,000 loads, which included 150 loads of bowlders, yielded the respectable sum of $8,100. The ground is easily worked, and averages about $3.50 per car-load. The claim is run night and day for nine months each year, with a force of from forty to fifty men, and at the present rate of drifting the ground will last for twenty years to come. The mill is run by a hurdy-gurdy water-wheel, and the company owns nearly all the water it uses.

The Miami claim, adjoining the Indiana Hill claim on the east, comprises sixteen acres. Washing was commenced on the 1st of March, 1875. The mine produced in four months $15,500, and to Joe Mallory about $1,000, caught in his under-current in the cañon below. The claim used 550 inches of water, under a pressure of 250 feet, through 2,500 feet of pipe and a 4½-inch nozzle. The owners, J. and R. Hoskin, netted $3,500, exclusive of $1,700 worth of new pipe and other movable improvements.

The Gold Run Ditch and Mining Company is an incorporation; all or nearly all of the stock is owned by residents of Gold Run and Dutch Flat. James L. Gould, one of the principal owners, has for years been the superintendent and general business manager. The company's mining-lands reach (if we except the Cedar and Sherman ground) from the claim of the Indiana Hill Blue Gravel Company north one and a quarter miles along the channel and across it from rim to rim. Including the Gold Run claim of about 50 acres, owned jointly with the Cedar Creek Gold-Mining and Water Company, (limited,) this company owns at this one place about 350 acres. All of the surface has been washed, and in many places two benches; still the gravel is at the deepest 250 feet. It is much lighter than the Dutch Flat gravel, and easier to wash. North of the railroad the company owns still another large tract of ground, covering the same channel. Some three years ago it commenced a tunnel to tap the bottom of the channel along the whole line of its principal claim. This tunnel opens into Cañon Creek, which, a short distance below, unites with the North Fork of the American River. The main tunnel, 10 by 12 feet, is now advanced 600 feet. A branch from this, 8 by 9 feet, and 1,300 feet long, has been run to open up a portion of the ground known as the Indiana Hill claim, which is now in successful operation. The aggregate cost of the tunnel and branch was about $85,000, including the first cost of Burleigh machines, compressor and engine. This company also owns about 30 miles of ditch, which furnishes 2,200 inches of water for over seven months each year. The head of the branch tunnel for the Indiana Hill claim is 80 feet below the surface of the rock and 250 feet below the surface of the gravel. An incline was raised through the rock 125 feet in length, thence by shaft to the top. Seventy feet below the top of the shaft an incline was run to the surface, through which to wash. The flume is 6 feet wide, on a grade of 7 inches to 12 feet. Washing was commenced on the 14th of December, 1875, with 700 inches of water, under a pressure of 200 feet. From 1,200 to 1,500 inches will eventually be required. The blue bottom stratum is very hard, of course; but the bowlders are small and easily disposed of. Other claims also are worked by this company.

The Gold Run Hydraulic Company (limited) is an English corporation, owning the two claims known as the Cedar and the Sherman, comprising about 65 acres, lying next north of the Indiana Hill claim. It is most advantageously situated, nearly the whole claim lying on the deepest portion of the channel and over the line of connection of the slate and trap; consequently its bed-rock is liable to be uneven, rough, and rich. This company opens through a tunnel run for it by the Gold Run Ditch and Mining Company from the branch tunnel of the latter. It is 8 by 8 feet in size, and 950 feet long, on a grade of 8 inches to 12 feet. It has two falls, 300 feet apart, of 2 feet each, provided with under-currents. The flume is 5 feet wide, and the three tail-boxes are paved with cross-riffles 3 inches wide, faced with inch iron and set 1½ inches apart. The head of the tunnel is 52½ feet below the surface of the rock and 232 feet below the surface of the gravel, which will average in depth about 220 feet. The gravel is washed down through an incline on an angle of 50°. This claim has a superb "rigging"—2,200 feet of iron pipe, all in fine order, the upper half being new pipe, made of No. 16 iron and heavily coated with red lead. It is 4 feet in diameter at the head and tapers to 16 inches 400 feet below. It has a fall of 225 feet, and, under the pressure attainable in the sand-box, is capable of receiving 3,000 inches of water. Heretofore miners have puzzled their brains to devise the best means of keeping out of their pipes the air-bubbles which are forced into the water by the stream falling into the sand-box. They have now concluded that the most natural and efficient remedy is to construct their sand-boxes so large and in such a manner that the bubbles of air will rise to the surface before reaching the pipe. Strange that so simple an idea should be so long developing! The sand-box built for this company is 10 by 12 feet, and 8 feet deep. The water flows into the box at the northeast corner, and strikes against a solid bulk-head about midway of the box. It is thus turned to the west end, passes through a grating, and is received by the pipe at the southwest corner, relieved of all air.

The extinct rivers of the auriferous belt of California.—I am indebted to the same gentleman (Mr. C. J. Brown, of Dutch Flat) for the following interesting discussion of the ancient river-system of this region. Mr. Brown is an active and intelligent investigator in the field, and I consider his views worthy of attention, though they differ in some respects from those of other observers. I do not undertake, from limited personal knowledge, to decide between opposing theories. Mr. Brown holds that the waters which deposited the ancient gravel-beds in Placer County ran northward. His provisional location of the channels may be, he admits, in many points erroneous, but his main proposition he believes he has proved. Other trustworthy students confirm it, particularly with regard to what he calls the "South Blue," which, they say, undoubtedly ran from south to north, and intersected another channel somewhere between Dutch Flat and Nevada City:

The great auriferous belt of California is situate upon the western slope of the Sierra Nevada. The bed-rock of this belt consists principally of trap, serpentine, and talcose slate. Its average width from east to west may be estimated at forty miles, and it extends from Fresno County on the south to the southwest corner of Oregon on the north, a distance of several hundred miles. Narrow at the south, where it dips beneath the alluvial deposit of the San Joaquin Valley, it gradually widens to the northward, till it is lost beneath the waters of the Pacific.

A line drawn through its center would run north-northwest and south-southeast, parallel with the western summit of the Sierra Nevada, forty miles to the westward thereof, at an average altitude of about 3,000 feet above the sea.

Within this belt are three distinct talcose-slate strata—the western or lower, the middle, and the eastern or upper, which are separated by strata of other rock.

The rock separating the lower and middle slate is highly metamorphic, and is not distinct or continuous along the whole line of the auriferous belt, but contains, in places, rich-quartz veins, as at Colfax, Placer County. Upon the lower or western belt of slate are situated many mining-towns of note. It passes under Oroville and dips beneath the valley of the Sacramento, cropping out again in the counties to the north-west. This stratum all along from Amador County on the south to Yuba County on the north is rich in its numerous gold-bearing-quartz ledges and veins. As it was not eroded by the old Pliocene rivers, except where the Big Blue and the San Juan Channels crossed it, it has been extensively worked for its rich, shallow placer and ravine mines. It is highly probable that the deepest auriferous-gravel banks lying along this stratum in Tehama, Shasta, Trinity, and Klamath Counties are, in part at least, sub-marine; but, however this may be, it is foreign to my purpose to discuss at length the character and features of this slate-stratum.

I purpose to speak more particularly of the middle and upper slate-strata, since along these the extinct rivers are most distinctly marked. They are separated by distinct strata of trap and serpentine, the latter skirting the upper slate and the former the middle slate. These different strata run parallel, so to speak, to each other, length-wise of the belt.

It must not be supposed that the different strata of rock can be correctly represented in their exterior individual limits by arbitrary lines; at places they are narrow, and again expand to a greater width.

In Nevada, Sierra, Plumas, and Lassen Counties, the slates are found even to the summit of the mountains, while in Shasta and the eastern portion of Tehama County they are narrowed by the lava-field which caps them.

In the vicinity of Nevada City granite predominates. A little to the southeast, and between Green Horn River and its tributary—Little Green Horn—exists a mountain of syenite. So at other places along the auriferous belt we find other varieties of rock.

The slate-strata are largely composed of talc and are quartz-bearing, containing all the principal gold-bearing-quartz ledges and veins, from which, in part, the gravel and gold filling the old channels came.

Miners, at one time, very generally held the opinion that the old channels were worn in the bed-rock by ocean-currents, and that the deep gravel and *débris* which fill them were the deposits of the sea. They did not comprehend the fact that the quality of gravel they were daily washing away refuted such an hypothesis; nor that their deep beds of pipe-clay, which would preserve in fossil the most delicate fern for an eternity, if undisturbed, were pregnant with fossilized earth but no sea-vegetation, nor any marine remains of any kind. Moreover, in the ancient gravel-deposits there are no lava bowlders or pebbles.

Superficial reasoners who held to the marine theory were occasionally confirmed in their opinions by newspaper articles upon the gravel-deposits of Shasta County or the gold-coast of Klamath and Del Norte, and at once jumped to the erroneous conclusion that the gravel there found was the *product* of the ocean, and as the coast-deposits were in some sense submarine, so too must be the gravel-deposits along the Sierras in Central California.

At the present time, however, it is generally admitted by all who reason upon the subject that these old channels are remnants of ancient and extinct river-systems, of which there are three or four, distinct and separate. I shall write of only one of them, known among the miners as the Big Blue.

The Blue Lead occupies the central portion of the great auriferous belt, from Calaveras County on the south to Plumas County on the north, and drained a country two hundred miles, and possibly more, in length.

Within the last few years a number of writers well known among the literati of California have published essays upon these extinct rivers. They, with but one exception, write of the so-called Big Blue as being at one time a very large river which flowed southward through Sierra, Nevada, and Placer Counties. The one exception says: "I have arrived at the conclusion that the Pliocene rivers have not varied in their general course from that of the present rivers;" meaning, of course, the "present rivers" crossing the auriferous belt.*

The idea that the Big Blue flowed southward is not new. All these writers are compelled to admit that great changes have taken place in the altitude and general topography of this entire region since the now extinct rivers flowed through it, since it would be highly unreasonable to suppose that a stream of any magnitude would flow for miles along the side of a high mountain-chain parallel with the trend of its main summit at an altitude of from three to five thousand feet above the level of the sea. And yet they base their assumption that the so-called "Big Blue" flowed through these counties to the southward upon the single fact that there is at present a down grade toward the south along the line of the deepest gravel-deposits.

The theory which I have entertained for many years may be explained by our present river-system, which, though larger, is copied from the ancient one. We now have the Sacramento from the north, and the San Joaquin from the south; their waters meet and flow into the ocean through the Golden Gate. All their principal tributaries take rise in the mountains to the eastward.

The middle slate-stratum of this auriferous belt was probably no higher above the level of the ocean at the time the cañons of these extinct rivers began actively to fill with gravel, than the valleys of the Sacramento and San Joaquin are at present; Sacramento City being but 65 feet in altitude. These two large valleys were then a part of the ocean, and the Coast Range of mountains cropped out of it a long line of island reefs.

What in Sierra County and the northern portion of Nevada County has been known as the Big Blue, I call the North Blue. *It flowed southward.* What in Placer County and the southern portion of Nevada County has been called the Big Blue, I call the South Blue, because it flowed *northward.* This truth could have been easily ascertained by all of the writers who have preceded me upon this subject had they taken sufficient pains to gather the evidence. The deposit of gravel, sand, and gold, and the position of the bowlders upon and near the bed of the old river at Yankee Jim's, Iowa Hill, Indiana Hill, Dutch Flat, Little York, You Bet, and Red Dog all tell the same tale and point the index-finger northward as unerringly as the needle of the mariner's compass.

The North and South Blue, corresponding to the Sacramento and the San Joaquin Rivers, were the two main branches of the Big Blue, which took their rise, as did also their tributaries, in what was then the rising hilly upland to the eastward. They ran down upon, and for many miles along, the soft rock of the upper slate; thence across the intervening, non-gold-producing strata of serpentine and trap—which latter strata average about seven miles in width—to the middle slate; thence generally along this

* It is a fair presumption that the writer of the sentence above quoted did not mean the "present rivers crossing the auriferous belt," but the present system of drainage, *i. e.*, the Sacramento and San Joaquin, which flow respectively from N. to S. and from S. to N. and nearly at right angles to their tributaries, the Feather, Yuba, American, Stanislaus, &c., the general course of which is from E. to W.—R. W. R.

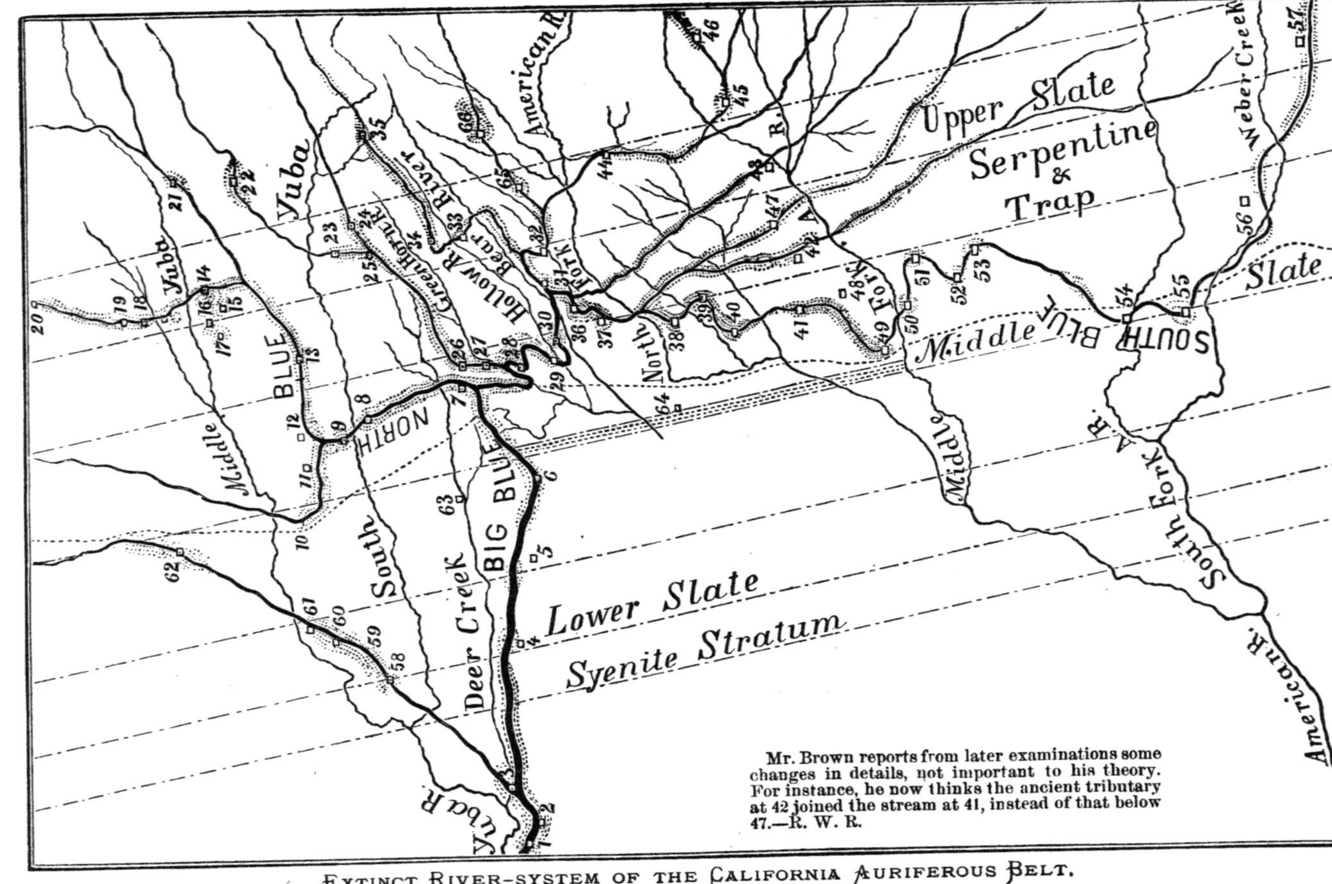

Extinct River-system of the California Auriferous Belt.

stratum to their confluence, a short distance south of Scott's Flat, in Nevada County, forming the Big Blue, which ran thence for eight or nine miles southwesterly to Buena Vista Slide; thence north of Grass Valley to Alta Hill, down north of Rough and Ready to Mooney's Flat, Smartsville, and Timbuctoo, emptying thence into the then ocean not far to the west of the latter place.*

The locality of the confluence of the North and South Blue is now occupied by a high mountain of volcanic origin. The stage-road from You Bet to Nevada City crosses the channel of the Big Blue just to the northwest of Gregory's old saw-mill site. It is a very wide channel, and is deeply covered with lava for seven or eight miles, but as it nears the town of Grass Valley it has become obliterated by erosion.

The accompanying sketch is intended to represent my theory of the extinct river-system which once drained the central portion of the great auriferous belt, with the rivers of the present system crossing the same. It includes a tract of country sixty miles north and south and forty miles east and west. The courses of the present streams, the locality of the towns, and the relative distances are taken from the United States survey. The principal strata of rock are represented by arbitrary lines, merely to convey a general idea of their approximate relative positions, regardless of their irregular widths and sinuous exterior limits as represented by the dotted line which shows more correctly the western boundary of the middle slate-stratum. The dotted streams represent the extinct rivers filled with gravel. It must not be supposed that all or even a major part of the Pliocene streams are traced on the sketch. Many of the smaller and shallower ones are wholly obliterated by erosion, and many are buried under the lava and await discovery by the prospector. At many places along the line of those traced, as at Forest Hill and Deadwood, two, three, and sometimes four channels are known to exist, usually running in the same general direction and within a mile of each other, made, no doubt, by one and the same stream at each locality, but at different periods; the water being forced from its channels successively by the deposition of gravel, and compelled to cut a new channel. The wide dotted space just west of the town of Colfax I pronounce a sea-beach. It is very ancient, having the same trend and strike as the contiguous rock. It is a stratum of sand and bowlders about three-fourths of a mile wide, but in truth is now a stratum of bed-rock, so to speak, for it underlies the deepest of our present streams. I mention it here as a curiosity only, not knowing that any mention of it has heretofore been published. The old village of Illinoistown is located upon it, and it is easily traced by any one curious enough to inspect it.

The towns and important localities are numbered thus:

No. 1. Timbuctoo.
2. Smartsville
3. Mooney's Flat.
4. Rough and Ready.
5. Grass Valley.
6. Buena Vista Slide.
7. Scott's Flat.
8. Blue Tent.
9. Grizzly Hill.
10. Cherokee.
11. North Columbia.
12. Kennebec Hill.
13. North Bloomfield.
14. Snow Point.
15. Orleans Flat.
16. Moore's Flat.
17. Woolsey's Flat.
18. Allegany.
19. Forest City.
20. Downieville.
21. Bunker Hill.
22. Gaston Ridge.
No. 23. Phelps Point.
24. Alpha.
25. Phelps Hill.
26. Quaker Hill.
27. Hunt's Hill.
28. Red Dog.
29. You Bet.
30. Little York.
31. Dutch Flat.
32. Alta.
33. Lowell Hill.
34. Remington Hill.
35. Diamond Creek.
36. Gold Run.
37. Indiana Hill.
38. Iowa Hill.
39. Wisconsin Hill.
40. King's Hill.
41. Yankee Jim's.
42. Forest Hill.
43. Michigan Bluffs.
44. Damascus.
No. 45. Deadwood.
46. Last Chance.
47. Bath.
48. Todd's Valley.
49. Peckham Hill.
50. Gravel Hill.
51. Bald Mountain.
52. Mamaluke Hill.
53. Georgetown.
54. Coloma.
55. Gold Hill.
56. Placerville.
57. Newtown.
58. French Corral.
59. Birchville.
60. Sweetland.
61. North San Juan.
62. Camptonville.
63. Nevada City.
64. Colfax.
65. Blue Bluffs.
66. Lost Camp.

Thus I have set forth what I believe to be the true theory of the formation of the ancient channels which underlie, are filled with, and in many places are deeply buried beneath the auriferous earth and gravel whichconstitute our hydraulic and drift mines.

---

* The present course of the San Joaquin and Sacramento Rivers is apparently the result of the position of the Coast Range, offering only one outlet to the sea at San Francisco. It is difficult to see how a similar course of the Pliocene rivers could have come to pass with the Coast Range out in the ocean.—R. W. R.

These ancient river-channels became filled with auriferous earth, gravel, and *débris* during the slow upheaval of the land. This rise was most rapid to the eastward, along the line of the summit of the Sierra Nevada, and required a great many thousand years for its accomplishment; for if we allow a rise of two and one-half feet every century, (a very high estimate if we allow no interval of repose,) it would require four thousand centuries, or four hundred thousand years, to elevate the land ten thousand feet and place the summit where it stands to-day.

Evidently the land rose more rapidly toward the north than to the south, which action gives a present grade southward of many feet to the mile. It also had the effect, from the first, of lessening the grade of the South Blue. If we allow a slightly more rapid elevation at and near the junction of the North with the South Blue than at other points along the middle slate—and such an assumption may not be unreasonable—the effect would be to lessen the grades of both these large streams, while, as the land arose to the eastward, the currents of all the tributaries to the South and North Blue, and even theirs, from their sources for some miles along their courses, were accelerated from century to century, and the land reaching gradually into the higher, consequently the colder, regions of atmosphere, condensed continually more and more moisture, which fell as snow and rain, thus increasing the volume of water, which alone would increase the rapidity of the currents. Their channels were deeper; the quartz ledges and veins were cut down; slides occurred on all sides; trees slid into the streams, and the entire surface of the land became in time denuded. This mass was deposited in these old streams, washed away, redeposited and rewashed at each succeeding freshet, over and over again and again, till it found its final place in the Big Blue, the North Blue, and the South Blue, whose currents were too sluggish to carry it along to the ocean. It blocked up these streams, (and set back into the mouths of the tributaries,) spreading out to a great width along nearly their entire course, but principally along the middle slate stratum, where it accumulated, at least in Placer and Nevada Counties, to the depth of eight hundred feet, and extended toward the east a level plain for a distance of from three to five miles.

It should be borne in mind that the grades of the main streams along the middle slate-stratum were yearly lessening by the continuous deposition of this great mass of gravel, earth, and *débris*. Judging from the depth of vegetable soil which accumulated upon its surface, this enormous deposit of alluvium must have remained for centuries a verdant field crowned with a luxurious forest. It was subsequently desolated by volcanic overflows.

Great lava-fields extended from Central Oregon to Tejon Pass, from the summit of the Sierra Nevada to the valleys of the Sacramento and the San Joaquin, and eastward throughout the Great Basin. During this long era the lava from hundreds of volcanoes or craters poured over the land, filled the old channels left unfilled by gravel, covered the lateral mountain-ridges to a level, flowed over and covered up the ancient gravel-deposits, of which those now lying along and to the east of the upper slate stratum are mostly still covered by it, in places to the depth of a thousand feet or more.

It is my opinion that during this epoch the ancient rivers were obliterated; and it is possible that the heat was so intense as to vaporize and drive away all moisture, to the extent that no stream of any magnitude existed upon this desert waste.

It is patent to the most superficial observer that our present rivers had their origin upon the surface of the lava, down through which and into the underlying strata of rock they have eroded immense cañons, in some instances to the depth of 3,000 feet below the present surface, and more than 2,000 feet below the bed of the extinct rivers. Along the middle slate-stratum every stream dignified as a *river* crosses it at a depth of from five to fifteen hundred feet below the old river-channels. The effect, after these streams had cut down through the lava and into the deep gravel-deposits, can readily be imagined. The earth and gravel slid into the cañons from beneath the lava, which, left without support, broke down of its own weight, and was, together with nine-tenths of the alluvial deposit along the middle slate-stratum, swept into the valleys to the west, partially by the rivers, but principally, no doubt, by the great ice-drift which, during a long glacial epoch, scoured these mountains from summit to base. Thus we are enabled to comprehend why these old gravel-deposits are free from volcanic lava and detritus, while the lateral mountain ridges or present river-divides terminate to the east of them abruptly, capped with lava three or four hundred feet in depth.

NEVADA COUNTY.

This county, situated in the central portion of the State, has maintained its position as the leading mining-county since the discovery of gold. It derives its importance both from the extent of its deposits of auriferous gravel and the number and richness of its quartz-lodes. The following table, compiled from the official returns to the surveyor-general, will exhibit the condition of mining from 1870 to 1875:

Year.	Quartz-mills.	Tons crushed.	Mining-ditches.	Length, in miles.	Miners' inches of water used per day.
1870	73	125,000	53	875	....
1871	60	190,000	70	946	42,400
1872	46	105,633	74	637	36,225
1873	......	....	76	707	38,000
1874	43	100,000	78	730	40,000
1875	46	80,000	75	625	40,000

The above returns are approximately correct, so far as active mining-operations are concerned. Langley's Directory of the Pacific Coast shows a larger number of mills for corresponding years, but in many instances the mills were idle.

The principal quartz-mining district is Grass Valley. This branch of mining commenced here in 1851 and has been prosecuted with great regularity since that time. In 1867 there were twenty-two quartz-mills in operation, with 280 stamps, and a crushing-capacity of about 400 tons per day. These mills cost, in the aggregate, $140,000. While at the present time there are fewer mills in operation, they are more effective, and the results and general product per year do not vary greatly from that of former years.

Grass Valley is distant from Sacramento sixty-five miles, and twelve miles from the line of the Central Pacific Railroad, with which it is connected by a branch narrow-gauge railroad. The elevation is 2,300 feet above the level of the sea; the climate pleasant and salubrious, and favorable for mining-operations throughout the entire year. Snow rarely falls, and remains on the ground but a few days. Wood is abundant and cheap, and in many instances water-power is available for crushing the ores during more than one-half of the year.

Quartz-mining forms the principal industrial interest, and has been continuously prosecuted with a uniform degree of success nowhere else attained. The aggregate product down to the present time of the quartz-veins of the district, situated within a radius of four miles, may be estimated at thirty millions of dollars. Of this amount nearly one-fourth was produced from the Massachusetts Hill, New York Hill, and Gold Hill veins, which are supposed to be continuous veins of the same system.

The gold-bearing rocks of Grass Valley are mostly metamorphic schists or greenstones, alternating with belts of syenite. The quartz-veins are generally not large. Two feet is probably a full average thickness, while some of the most productive have not averaged over one foot. The metallic contents of the veins of the district vary to an extreme degree, some carrying little or no visible gold, although the mill-workings are satisfactory and the sulphurets are found to be abundant on concentrating the sands resulting from crushing. The gold is easily saved, being clean, angular, and not very small; hence the proportion saved by the mill-process is notably greater than in any other locality in California. The sulphurets occur as a rule in the proportion of 2 per cent. of the gold-bearing rock. These are easily concentrated, and yield by the chlorination process an average of $100 per ton net, the value of the rock ranging from $25 to $50 per ton. The district contains from ten to twelve mines which are continuously productive, more than half of these being worked with great profit to the owners and the balance being self-supporting. There are also a dozen or more mines in various stages of development, and a few on which work has been temporarily suspended.

The cost of mining supplies and labor in Nevada County is as follows:

Wages of first-class miners, $3 per day; shovelers and car-men, $2.50 per day; surface-laborers, $2 to $2.50 per day; Chinese labor, $1.50 per day; cost of lumber, $15 to $16 per 1,000 feet; mining-timber, 5 to 12 cents per running foot; cord-wood, $4 to $5 per cord; common powder, $2.50 per keg of 20 pounds; giant powder, 50 to 75 cents per pound; fuse, $5 per 1,000 feet; quicksilver, 75 cents per pound; candles, $4 per box.

The operations of the principal mines are shown by the accompanying tables and the annual reports of their officers. The principal mines have been described in detail in my former reports. Within the past year the New York Hill Mine, which had been closed for several years, has been re-opened and actively worked, and promises to rank among the leading mines of the district. The following extracts are taken from a report on this mine by W. A. Skidmore:

The New York Hill ledge is situated two miles south of the town of Grass Valley, on New York Hill, which forms a portion of a continuous ridge lying west of Wolf Creek, and having a general north and south trend. The only topographical feature of importance is the occurrence of several ravines running westward from the creek and intersecting the ridge at right angles. The most deeply indented ravine forms the dividing line between Massachusetts Hill and New York Hill, although this ravine does not cut through the ridge, and the surface of the hill is very nearly level for a distance of one mile on the line of the outcrop of the ledge. The elevation of the summit of the ridge is in no place more than 300 feet above the bed of Wolf Creek, which forms the main drainage of the water-shed of the eastern side of the ridge. A belt of greenstone about one-half mile in width runs in a general northwest and southeast direction diagonally across the ridge. On either side of this belt occur zones of syenite, which have exerted an influence on the metamorphism of the greenstone, which was doubtless of sedimentary origin. The New York Hill ledge runs through this greenstone belt in a northwest and southeast course, starting from Wolf Creek and running thence 2,844 feet toward Massachusetts Hill, and having an average dip of 30 degrees north, and a thickness of from ten to thirty inches. The average thickness of the main vein would therefore be from fifteen to eighteen inches, although at times stringers of quartz are found on the hanging-wall side of the vein, varying in thickness from four to six inches; these are not, however, taken into consideration in the estimation of the average width of the vein.

The quartz is white to dark blue in color, vitreous in texture, more or less sprinkled with gold visible to the eye, uniformly sulphureted to the extent of 2 per cent., and very tractable to the ordinary mill-process. The yield has varied from $20 to $60 per ton, exclusive of the rich specimens of free-gold-bearing rock of which this mine has always been remarkably prolific. It would be difficult to state the milling average of all the rock taken from the mine during the past twenty years. The present yield is about $40 per ton of 2,000 pounds, exclusive of the rich specimens which are sold to jewelers to be manufactured into quartz ornaments. This latter class commands from $25 to $30 per ounce of gold contained in the rock, the value of each piece being determined by its specific gravity.

The New York Hill Company ground embraces a consolidation of the Larimer, Sikes, Wilde, Fricot, and Chavanne claims, together with many claims of lesser note, of which no record of working and production can now be obtained. Locations were made here as early as 1851, under the mining-laws then in force, which required that locations should be made in a square form, and limited each claim to 100 square feet in area. This remained in force for nearly two years, during which period the claims which presented an outcrop were worked out from the surface to the limit of the owners' ground. Subsequently the laws were amended and locations were made on the line of the lode with the dips, spurs, and angles, as at the present time provided for by the general mining-law of the United States. Then followed a more vigorous system of mining; shafts were sunk, and levels run, and the quartz crushed at rude custom-mills, yielding, in all cases, with the imperfect process then in use, a fair and sometimes a large profit. As depth was attained water was encountered, necessitating pumping-apparatus, and the character of the rock changed from free-gold-bearing to sulphureted ores. The average yield declined by reason of the inadequacy of the mill-process then in use, and expenses increased. This was in the era of high prices and high freights, and before the introduction of the powerful pumping and hoisting machinery now in general use. Consequently, when the water-level was reached, (about 100 feet in depth on the pitch of the ledge,) mining-operations were suspended. At this period rock could not be worked with profit which did not yield at least $30 per load, equivalent to $20 per ton. At the present time and under the same circumstances, rock of that grade would yield a large profit.

The total amount of bullion taken from the 2,844 linear feet of ground now owned by the New York Hill Company, from the discovery up to the date of the consolidation in 1865, may be safely estimated at $500,000. During the years 1866 and 1867, the mine produced $106,427.66, from 2,189 tons of rock, or at the rate of $48.98 per ton. The mine then remained closed for several years, when it passed into the control of the late Mr. A. Delano, who opened the mine by a tunnel from Wolf Creek, and struck ore on September 8, 1874. From this time till the close of the fiscal year ending June 30, 1875, the mine produced $57,582.24 from 14,000 tons of ore.

From the fiscal year commencing August 1, 1875, to October 30, 1875, a period of three months, the results were as follows:

Month.	Tons.	Average yield per ton.	Product.
August, 1875	540	$49 20	$26,570 85
September, 1875	422	41 66	17,581 18
October, 1875	365	28 27	10,321 36
Totals	1,327	41 05	54,473 39

The returns for October did not include the proceeds from the sulphurets for that month, and therefore afford an unerring standard of the free-gold value of the rock crushed. The October sulphurets, 22 tons, were worked during the first week in November, and yielded $1,753.17, which should be added to the free crushing, making the yield for the month $12,074.53 from 365 tons of rock, or an average of $33.08 per ton. This makes the true average for the first quarter of the fiscal year $42.37 per ton, instead of $41.05, as appears by the above tabular statement.

The main adit has attained a length of 918 feet. It is 6 feet in height by 4 feet in width, and laid with car-track throughout the entire length. The cost was between $10 and $11 per foot, or say $10,000. This tunnel serves for drainage, and will be carried forward as exploration progresses.

The Snyder shaft has attained a depth of 500 feet, on an angle of 33 degrees, and cost $40 per foot, including timber and track. It is 12 feet wide by 6 feet in height, with three compartments, two for hoisting and one for gangway and pump-rod. The shaft is heavily and substantially timbered from top to bottom. Aggregate cost, $20,000. An 8-inch pump has been carried to the bottom, by means of which the water from the lower levels is lifted to the main adit, discharging in Wolf Creek. A 4-inch-plunger pump on the adit-level station forces water through a 2½-inch pipe to tanks on the surface, supplying the boilers.

The upper tunnel starts from a point on the hill-side above Wolf Creek 200 feet north of the Snyder shaft, and 130 feet higher on the hill, (vertical,) and runs 450 feet to its connection with the Wilde shaft, following the course of the vein and passing through chute No. 3 a distance of 270 feet. This tunnel cost about $3,500, and is an invaluable adjunct to the working of the southeastern portion of the company's ground, by reason of its influence on the ventilation of the mine.

The total cost of the shafts and tunnels constituting the working avenues of the mine was $62,500, and the cost of the machinery constituting the "plant" about $30,000 more. The company has leased a 20-stamp mill, with water-privilege accompanying, for $275 per month. Fifteen stamps are run on the company's rock, crushing 30 tons per day, the remaining five stamps being employed on custom-work, for which $4 per ton is charged. The mill is run by water-power during the greater portion of the year. Sulphurets are concentrated by Hendy's apparatus and sluice-boxes, and sold to the chlorinators.

The expense of milling in Grass Valley district is dependent on the motive-power used and the character of the gold saving and concentrating apparatus. The following are estimates of leading mining-engineers of the Pacific coast. According to the report of Mr. J. H. Boalt on the Empire Mine, made in 1870, and quoted in the Report of the United States Commissioner of Mining Statistics for that year, (p. 49,) the cost of crushing rock, concentrating, and working the sulphurets was at the rate of $2.92 per ton of rock—the motive-power being steam. In the Eureka and Idaho Mills, of the same district, the cost has been about $3 per ton for several years with steam-power. Mr. G. T. Deetkin, in an elaborate paper on the California gold process, published in the Report of the Mining Commissioner for 1873, (pp. 300, 331,) estimates the cost of simple crushing by steam at $2.04 per ton, and by water at $1.63 per ton.

The New York Hill Mill is run alternately by water and steam, according to the season of the year, and sometimes by both powers combined. The cost of milling, including concentration, varies from $1.75 to $2.25 per ton, and $2.12½ per ton is a fair average for the entire year. This, added to the contract-price for hauling—37½ cents per ton—would make the cost of handling and treatment of ore $2.50 per ton.

I quote further from Mr. Skidmore's report:

The labor pay-roll of the company varies from month to month, according to the nature of the work and the condition of the mine. The number of employés at mine and mill is from 100 to 150. Of this number one-half are skilled miners, the others laborers, mill-men, mechanics, &c. For the purpose of estimating the cost of mining, hoisting, and pumping, I have taken as a basis 500 tons of rock raised, and the expenses incident thereto as follows:

Five hundred tons ore.

Labor for mining and hoisting	$6,011 75
Wood for fuel	96 00
Candles, powder, fuse, and cartridges	224 85
Timbers for support of ground	98 40
Iron and steel, charcoal, oil, &c	106 20
	6,537 20

Or $13.07 per ton.

During the progress of extracting ore, dead-work is carried on for the purpose of developing reserves. This class of work consists of sinking main shaft, timbering, running levels, raising waste-rock, pumping, &c.

The following statement, compiled from the company's expense-account, will show the cost, per ton of ore produced, of carrying forward the permanent work of the mine:

Record of four months' dead-work.—Cost of developing 5,760 *tons of ore, including pumping.*

Sinking 100 feet shaft, on contract, $30 per foot	$3,000 00
Timbering same, including material	66 73
Driving 800 feet drifts, on contract, $7.50 per foot	6,000 00
Hoisting, pumping, &c., including labor	3,764 00
	12,830 73

Or $2.22 per ton.

We have, then, the following recapitulation of the expenses incident to mining, milling, and dead-work:

	Per ton.
Mining, hoisting, and pumping	$13 07
Dead-work, or developing new ground	2 22
Hauling quartz to mill	37½
Milling and concentrating sulphurets	2 12½
	17 79

Summary.

Cost mining and milling per ton	$15 57
Cost necessary dead-work in advancing development	2 22
	17 79

Yield of the New York Hill Mine, from September 8, 1874, to November 9, 1875.

1875.			
July 29.	Balance from annual statement		$53,551 69
Aug. 16.	5 bars bullion } from 540 tons of rock		24,745 46
Aug. 16.	18¼ tons sulphurets yielding } from 540 tons of rock		1,825 39
Sept. 29.	3 bars bullion } from 422 tons rock	$15,954 38	
Sept. 29.	15½ tons sulphurets } from 422 tons rock	1,626 80	
			17,581 18
Oct. 7.	2 bars bullion, 365 tons rock		10,321 36
	The sulphurets were worked in November.		
Nov. 9.	3 bars bullion	$17,261 93	
Nov. 9.	22 tons sulphurets, yielding	1,753 17	
			19,015 10
	Yield		127,040 18
	Add premium on gold bars and returns from sales of specimens in San Francisco		2,944 82
	Total yield		129,985 00
	Gold taken out from first striking the ledge up to Mr. Delano's death, September 8, 1874		4,030 55
	Total yield since re-opening of mine		134,015 55

The secretary of the Eureka-Gold Mining Company presents the following report for the year ending September 30, 1875:

RECEIPTS.

Book-accounts:		
Balance of cash on hand October 1, 1874	$90,797 96	
In hand of the superintendent	7,342 40	
		$98,140 36
Bullion-account:		
Proceeds from ores worked	97,801 91	
Proceeds from assay-chips	21 72	
Proceeds from sulphurets worked	820 50	
Proceeds from assay-chips	1 73	
Proceeds from sulphurets sold	1,445 50	
		100,091 36
Milling-account:		
Merchandise sold	332 15	
Grinding sand, &c., for McDougal Works	240 00	
Crushing for outside parties	153 00	
		725 15
Mine-account:		
Merchandise sold		21 00
Wood-ranch:		
For wood sold		100 37
Wood-account:		
For 2,868⅝ cords of wood transferred to sundry accounts		12,897 56
Interest-account:		
For interest received on loans		5,700 00

Premium-account:		
For premium on bars sold		$446 55
McDougal Works:		
For returns of gold saved		450 56
		218,572 91

DISBURSEMENTS.

Mining-account:		
Paid for wood	$8,804 81	
Paid for lumber	769 99	
Paid for poles	762 86	
Paid for charcoal	374 00	
Paid for powder and fuse	1,246 61	
Paid for foundery-bills	102 33	
Paid for hardware and steel	1,657 33	
Paid for merchandise	3,121 61	
Paid for freight and hauling	15 75	
Paid for pay-rolls	50,725 00	
Paid for labor by contract	10,908 00	
Paid for salary of superintendent	6,000 00	
Paid for surveying	15 00	
Paid for iron pipe	70 40	
Paid for tribute-men for mining	1,286 75	
Paid for water	50 00	
Paid for fire-insurance	593 75	
	86,504 19	
Deduct amounts for labor and materials transferred to sundry accounts	47,154 93	
		39,349 26
Dead-work		43,667 50
Wood-account:		
Paid for wood		13,083 41
Eureka No. 2 Mine		18,476 54
Eureka No. 3 shaft		2,840 47
Milling-account:		
Paid for wood	$4,092 75	
Paid for foundery-bills	485 12	
Paid for hardware	357 80	
Paid for sluice-blankets	265 50	
Paid for chemicals and merchandise	454 14	
Paid for water-rent	581 25	
Paid for pay-rolls	8,566 00	
Paid for hauling	13 50	
Paid for fire-insurance	397 50	
		15,213 56
Bullion-expenses:		
Paid for assaying bars	128 90	
Paid for freight on same	259 25	
		388 55
Mine-purchase:		
Paid I. T. McDougal for real estate and royalty to use his patent		800 00

McDougal Works:		
Paid for pay-rolls and grinding sand		$240 00
General expenses		6,163 74
Sulphuret-concentration:		
Paid for pay-rolls		1,042 00
Wood ranch:		
Paid for hauling		88 75
Sulphuret-reduction:		
Paid for working sulphurets		243 00
Discount-account:		
For discount allowed on bars sold		1 96
Book-account:		
Balance of cash on hand September 30, 1875	$72,068 97	
In hands of the superintendent	1,571 17	
Due from the estate of A. Delano, Grass Valley	3,334 43	
		76,974 57
		218,572 91

Assets and liabilities.

ASSETS.

Available.—On hand September 30, 1875.

Book accounts	$76,974 57	
4¼ tons of sulphurets, estimated value	200 00	
100 tons of ore broke in mine, cost $9	900 00	
250 tons of ore on surface, cost $10	2,500 00	
179 cords of wood	792 22	
Supplies at mill	1,100 00	
Supplies at mine	900 00	
		83,366 79

Real estate.

Mill, estimated value	$20,000 00	
Mine improvement and buildings, estimated	15,000 00	
McDougal Works	1,000 00	
Wood ranch, 160 acres	950 00	
		36,950 00
		120,316 79

LIABILITIES.

None.

Mine-statement.

October 1, 1874—Ore on surface		325 tons	
Ore hoisted during the year		4,235 tons	
		4,560 tons	
September 30, 1875—Ore on surface		250 tons	
Ore worked at the company's mill during the year			4,310 tons
September 30, 1875—Ore on surface		250 tons	
Ore broke in mine		100 tons	
Ore reduced during the year		4,310 tons	
		4,660 tons	
October 1, 1874—Ore on surface	325 tons		
Ore broke in mine	350 tons		
		675 tons	
Ore mined during the year			3,985 tons

Sulphuret-statement.

October 1, 1874—Number of tons on hand	16½ tons	
Number of tons concentrated during the year	27¼ tons	
	43¾ tons	
September 30, 1875—Number of tons on hand	4¼ tons	
		39½ tons
Number of tons worked during the year	9 tons	
Number of tons sold	30½ tons	
		39½ tons

Ore-statement.

4,310 tons of ore worked by mill-process, yielded		$97,823 63
Also sulphurets as follows:		
9 tons worked by chlorination, yielded	$822 22	
30½ tons sold yielded	1,445 50	
	2,267 73	
Less 16½ tons on hand October 1, 1874—estimated value	700 00	
	1,567 73	
Add 4¼ tons on hand, September 30, 1875—estimated value	200 00	
		1,767 73
Add result of McDougal Works		450 56
		100,041 92

Or an average of $23.21 per ton.
Average yield of sulphurets, $91.36 per ton.
Average yield of sulphurets sold, $47.39 per ton.

Bullion-statement.

As reduced by mill-process:
Average fineness, .844½—equal to $17.45\frac{92}{100}$ per ounce.

As reduced by chlorination-process:
Average fineness, .985½—equal to $20.37\frac{50}{100}$ per ounce.

Returns from McDougal Works:
Average fineness, .795—equal to $16.45\frac{43}{100}$ per ounce.

Return of bullion:		
5,601.73 ounces, at $17.45\frac{92}{100}$	$9,7801 91	
40.27 ounces, at $20.37\frac{50}{100}$	820 50	
27.34 ounces, at $16.45\frac{43}{100}$	450 56	
1.34 ounces assay chips and grains	23 45	
Sulphurets sold	1,445 50	
		$100,541 92

Weight of bullion before assaying:		
Ounces		5,671.32
After assaying:		
Face of bars, ounces	5,669.34	
Assay chips and grains	1.34	
Loss	.64	
		5,671.32

Cost of mining.

Supplies on hand October 1, 1874	$1,200 00	
Paid for supplies and labor during the year	39,349 26	
		40,549 26
Deduct:		
Supplies on hand September 30, 1875	900 00	
Merchandise sold during the year	21 00	
		921 00
Cost of mining 3,985 tons		39,628 26

Or an average of $9.94 per ton.

Cost of milling.

Supplies on hand October 1, 1874	$1,000 00	
Paid for supplies and labor during the year	15,213 56	
		16,213 56
Deduct:		
Supplies on hand September 30, 1875	1,100 00	
For custom-work done and supplies sold	725 15	
		1,825 15
Cost of milling 4,310 tons		14,388 41

Or an average of $3.24 per ton.

Cost of concentrating sulphurets.

Number of tons concentrated during the year		27¼ tons
Cost of concentrating:		
Labor, as per pay-rolls	$1,042 00	

Or an average of $38.34 per ton.

Statement of receipts and disbursements for the year ending September 30, 1875.

RECEIPTS.

From bullion	$100,091 36	
Amount of sulphurets belonging to last year	700 00	
		$99,391 36
From sulphurets on hand		200 00
From other receipts		6,366 77
		105,958 13

DISBURSEMENTS.

Supplies on hand October 1, 1874	$2,806 37	
Paid to I. T. McDougal	800 00	
Paid for supplies and labor during the year, (including $43,667.50 paid for prospecting or dead-work)	120,272 03	
Paid all other expenses	6,551 89	
	130,430 29	
Off for supplies on hand September 30, 1875	2,792 22	
		127,638 07
Amount of disbursements over receipts		21,679 94

STATEMENT OF BALANCE.

On hand October 1, 1874:		
Balance cash	$98,140 36	
Balance of supplies and sulphurets	3,506 37	
		101,646 73
On hand September 30, 1875:		
Balance cash	$76,974 57	
Balance of supplies and sulphurets	2,992 22	
		79,966 79
Amount of former balance of cash, sulphurets and supplies reduced during the year		21,679 94

Statement showing the receipts and disbursements of the company from the date of its going into operation, October 1, 1865, *to date.*

RECEIPTS.

By bullion taken out	$4,373,239 85	
By other receipts	41,757 15	
		$4,414,997 00

DISBURSEMENTS.

To sundry titles; to paid on the purchase of mine; for Whiting ground or square location; purchase of Mobile and Roannaise Mines and perfecting titles.		$302, 706 50	
To construction		158, 383 71	
To dividends		2, 054, 000 00	
To mining, milling, and all other expenses.		1, 819, 940 00	
		4, 335, 030 21	
On hand September 30, 1875:			
Balance of cash	$76, 974 57		
Balance of supplies	2, 992 22		
		79, 966 79	
			$4, 414, 997 00

Statement of profits from October 1, 1865, *to September* 30, 1875.

RECEIPTS.

From bullion	$4, 373, 239 85	
From other receipts	41, 757 15	
		$4, 414, 997 00

COST OF SAME.

Paid for mining, milling, and all other expenses	1, 819, 940 00
Net profits	2, 595, 057 00

DISTRIBUTION OF PROFITS.

Paid for sundry titles		$302, 706 50	
Paid for construction		158, 383 71	
Paid for dividends, $102.70 per share		2, 054, 000 00	
		2, 515, 090 21	
Balance of cash	$76, 974 57		
Balance of supplies	2, 992 22		
		79, 966 79	
			$2, 595, 057 .00

The superintendent, Mr. William Watt, says:

In Eureka Mine proper we have driven 196 feet of drifts, 879 feet of cross-cuts, and sunk 34 feet of winze; have also sunk 71 feet of shaft on the Roannaise, and 22 feet of shaft and driven 611 feet of drifts in Eureka No. 2.

We have hoisted 4,235 tons of quartz, and crushed 4,310 tons in 214 running days, with 10 stamps, averaging a little over 2 tons per day to each stamp.

We have concentrated 27¼ tons of sulphurets and worked 39½ tons, and have now on hand 4½ tons, which I value at $200 net.

There are 250 tons of quartz on the surface and 100 broke in the mine ready for hoisting.

The amount of quartz extracted during the past year from the various levels has been as follows:

	Tons.
From the fourth level	169
From the fifth level	539
From the sixth level	3, 402
From the Eureka No. 2	125
Making a total of	4, 235

There are upward of 900 tons of ore in sight, which will pay a small profit.

I regret not being able to give a more favorable report of our last year's workings, and the immense amount of prospecting that has been done, and the large amount of money expended without making any favorable developments, make me feel solicitous about the future prospects of the company. There are still three places worthy of a further prospect, viz: The twelfth level, the Roannaise from No. 3 shaft, and the Morehouse claim. The mill, hoisting and pumping machinery, although getting old, are in fair working-order.

The Morehouse claim, of which mention has been made by the superintendent, is located south of and cuts the Eureka ledge at right angles, comprises 1,800 feet in length, and is covered by a United States patent, which includes 12 acres of surface-ground. The explorations in the Eureka would seem to indicate a probability of the ledge having turned south across Wolf Creek into the Morehouse ground, instead of continuing west through the Roannaise ground. The trustees of the Eureka have secured the Morehouse claim on the following terms: When the Eureka Company shall have expended $10,000 in prospecting their ledge, the Morehouse Company will deed to the Eureka Company one-half of the claim. It is further agreed that the Eureka Company have the right to stop work at any time they wish to do so, and to remove any machinery they may have on the claim.

Eureka No. 2 is a ledge east and parallel with the original ledge. Shaft No. 3 is on the Roannaise ground, farther to the east than any previous prospectings.

The Idaho Mine of Grass Valley has for several years been considered the leading quartz-mine of the State. This mine is situated one mile east of Grass Valley, in a contact-formation of slate and greenstone. The president and superintendent, Mr. Edward Coleman, in his annual report for the year ending December 20, 1875, says:

During the year just ended but little has occurred worthy of special notice. You will observe that the pumping-machinery is all complete to the 700 level; and as this is the full depth we expect to require the large pumps, we may consider our expenditures in this connection are met, and no further outlay will be required for several years; also, you will notice the main shaft is completed to the 900 level, and no work has been done below that point.

In view of the large amount of lumber in the mill and hoisting buildings, and the close proximity of those buildings to the pumping-machinery, it was deemed advisable to erect a fire-proof building over the pump-shaft and machinery, in order to secure that most important part of the works against fire and add to the safety of the underground workmen. The building is approaching completion, and but little further expenditure will be required to finish it in all its parts.

In regard to the under-ground work, the drifts have been kept well ahead of the stopes, and the mine may be considered in good working order throughout.

The 500 east backs are worked through to the 400 level, a distance of 144 feet from the shaft, and there still remain about 300 feet in the bottom of the 400 level to work out. The 500 east level is in 371 feet from the shaft, and there still remain about 225 feet to go before exhausting the pay-shoot. The 600 east backs are about all worked out, and a few months more, with a small party of men, will entirely exhaust them. The 600 west backs are also entirely exhausted. The 600 east level is in 1,344 feet from the shaft, the last 555 of which have been either through worthless quartz or barren ground. As this drift is in farther from the shaft than any other, and as there is still a distance of 1,257 feet to our eastern boundary, it is thought best to continue this drift on as fast as possible, with the view of prospecting that part of the claim. The 700 west backs are all worked out, with the exception of a small piece next to the western boundary. The 700 east level is in 712 feet from the shaft, and is still in pay rock; and the backs are worked through to the 600 level 375 feet from the shaft, and there are still remaining about 394 feet to work out in the bottom of the 600 before exhausting the pay-shoot. The 800 west level is in 356 feet from the shaft, the last 150 feet of which have been in rather a small ledge and low-grade ore, and the backs are worked through to the 700 level 35 feet from the shaft. The 800 east level is in 388 feet from the shaft. The ledge is quite large the full length, and the backs also are in a good-sized ledge. It is not worked through to the 700 level at any point.

The ledge in the shaft is of good quality and well defined from the 800 down to about 60 feet below that level. The hanging-wall then goes down very flat and the ledge becomes broken up and makes into several stringers. The shaft was continued down on the same angle as before, 51½ degrees, and after sinking 120 feet from the 800 level a cross-cut was run in, and after drifting 59 feet the hanging-wall was struck, but no quartz was discovered. A drift was then run east on one of the stringers. It is now in 137 feet from the shaft, with a good-sized ledge in the last 10 feet; but it is not next to the hanging-wall, and the quartz is of a low grade, although showing some gold, and we have good reason to hope it will improve as it is continued east.

In looking over this statement, it will be observed we have a large amount of quartz in sight, but not broken; and as the 700, 800, and 900 levels are still in pay-rock, it is impossible to give an opinion as to the amount of pay-rock we may expect to take from the mine, but I have no doubt it will last for several years.

It will also be noticed that the yield per ton has not been so large; neither have the dividends amounted to so much as in previous years. As to the future, it is dangerous to express an opinion; still I am in hope we shall divide as much in the coming year as we did in the past, although the present yield gives but little margin, and any further falling off would be a reduction of dividends.

During the year we have crushed 28,103¼ tons of rock, of which 6,828¾ tons came from the 500 level, 2,096 tons from the 600 level, 10,554¾ tons from the 700 level, 8,485½ tons from the 800 level, and 139¼ tons from the shaft and 900 level.

This gives a total yield of—

27,318 $\frac{68}{100}$ ounces bullion	$478,073 35
147 tons sulphurets	8,936 44
Tailings	7,946 89
Specimens	112 50
Old copper plate	600 42
	495,669 30

Yielding $17.63⅜ per ton.

MILL AND MINING.

Surface-labor	$45,345 63
Under-ground labor	144,186 89
Wood and poles	24,829 60
Hardware	4,646 16
Drill-steel	1,787 90
Powder and fuse	6,454 05
Candles and oil	4,503 76
Lumber	2,146 08
Foundery	8,023 89
Coal	1,969 01
Quicksilver	1,932 87
Superintendent's salary	6,000 00
Sundries	3,027 82
	254,853 66

Costing on an average $9.06¾ per ton.

SAVING SULPHURETS.

Labor	$2,781 00
Repairs and sundries	75 00
Paid chlorination-works for reducing 147 tons of sulphurets	3,675 00
	6,531 00

Grinding sand on percentage, wood, and sundries	965 00
Foundery	246 00
	1,211 00

COMPLETING MAIN SHAFT TO 900 LEVEL.

Labor	$7,236 23
Candles and oil	299 37
Powder and fuse	28 75
Hardware	49 00
Lumber	449 72
Wood and sundries	475 00
	8,538 07

Completing pump-machinery	$7,604 94
New brick pump-house	1,995 98
General expenses	19,913 33

RECAPITULATION.

Mill and mining	$254,853 66
Sulphurets-account	6,531 00
Grinding sand	1,211 00
Completing main shaft	8,538 07
Completing pump	7,604 94
New brick pump-house	1,995 98
General expenses	19,913 33
Total expense for year	300,647 98

I make the following extracts from the report of the secretary, Mr. George W. Hill:

At the commencement of the fiscal year now closed, to wit, the 7th day of December, 1874, there was a balance in the treasury amounting to the sum of $16,505.44. The monthly receipts of the company from all sources for the fiscal year ending December 6, 1875, are as follows, to wit:

Receipts from all sources for—	
December, 1874	$39,471 24
January, 1875	45,158 57
February, 1875	45,208 11
March, 1875	40,792 19
April, 1875	37,542 28
May, 1875	44,823 94
June, 1875	33,279 45
July, 1875	34,884 88
August, 1875	45,992 07
September, 1875	40 884 75
October, 1875	36,829 56
November, 1875	48,058 24
Total receipts for the fiscal year ending December 6, 1875	492,925 28
To which add balance on hand December 6, 1874	16,505 44
Total receipts for the year	509,430 72

The monthly expenditures of the company for the period above, for all purposes, amount as follows, to wit:

Expenses for—	
December, 1874, with dividend 66	$50,927 98
January, 1875, with dividend 67	40,051 41
February, 1875, with dividend 68	43,753 12
March, 1875, with dividend 69	39,176 04
April, 1875, with dividend 70	37,832 41
May, 1875, with dividend 71	42,876 87
June, 1875, with dividend 72	39,585 61
July, 1875, with dividend 73	37,799 92
August, 1875, with dividend 74	40,820 38
September, 1875, with dividend 75	42,276 35
October and November, 1875, with dividend 76	90,094 57
Total expenses, including dividends for the year	505,194 66
Assets brought forward	509,430 72
	505,194 66
Balance in treasury, December 6, 1875	4,236 06

In the foregoing monthly expenditures are included eleven dividends, declared by the board of trustees for the year herein stated, and at the times and amounts as follows, to wit:

No.	Dividend declared.	Per cent.	Amount.
66	January 4, 1875	5	$15,500
67	February 1, 1875	5	15,500
68	March 1, 1875	7½	23,250
69	April 5, 1875	5	15,500
70	May 3, 1875	5	15,500
71	June 7, 1875	5	15,500
72	July 5, 1875	5	15,500
73	August 2, 1875	5	15,500
74	September 9, 1875	5	15,500
75	October 4, 1875	5	15,500
	November passed		
76	December 6, 1875	3	9,300
	Being for the year 55½ per cent. on the capital stock, amounting to		172,050

The secretary presents in epitomized form the aggregate receipts and expenditures of the company for the last seven fiscal years, that being the period in which the mine has paid dividends, and before which only prospecting was done.

Receipts from all sources for the fiscal years—

1869	$306,038 75
1870	183,450 23
1871	407,301 16
1872	404,035 52
1873	1,010,612 20
1874	669,023 03
1875	492,919 27
Total receipts for seven years	3,473,380 16

There has been paid out in dividends as follows:

1869, 11 dividends, aggregating 55 per cent	$170,500
1870, 7 dividends, aggregating 12 per cent	37,200
1871, 12 dividends, aggregating 75 per cent	232,500
1872, 11 dividends, aggregating 52½ per cent	162,750
1873, 12 dividends, aggregating 220 per cent	682,000
1874, 12 dividends, aggregating 102½ per cent	317,750
1875, 11 dividends, aggregating 55½ per cent	172,050
Being 76 dividends, aggregating 572½ per cent. on the capital stock, amounts to	1,774,750

Mr. John C. Coleman, the treasurer, presents the following statement for the year ending December 20, 1875:

RECEIPTS.

Cash on hand December 21, 1874	$16,505 45
From 27,318$\frac{68}{100}$ ounces of bullion	478,073 35
From 438$\frac{15}{100}$ ounces of sulphurets	8,936 14
Percentage from tailings	3,725 36
Pan-rent	1,106 00
From old copper plates	600 42
From specimens sold	112 50
From sale of old material	132 50
From water-rent	233 00
Total receipts	509,424 72

DISBURSEMENTS.

Paid superintendent's check	300,647 98
Paid dividends	172,050 00
Total disbursements	472,697 98
Due from Thomas Findley	32,490 68
	505,188 66
Cash on hand	4,236 06

The Empire Mine, located on Ophir Hill, one mile east of Grass Valley, was discovered in 1850, and has been worked from that period to the present time with almost uninterrupted success. It is situated in a greenstone formation; course, north and south; dip, about 30° west. Up to 1865 its product has been estimated at $1,500,000, and the average yield at $30 per ton. From that time to October, 1868, it produced $100,000, the ore running $29 per ton. Cost of mining and milling, $18.25. Since that time the cost of milling and mining has been materially reduced and the production maintained. The records of the mine were destroyed by fire in 1870, and the product of the mine was not reported until 1873, in which year 8,000 tons were crushed, yielding $240,000, or a net profit of about $16 per ton. The ledge is about fifteen inches in width, and has been explored for a distance of 1,800 feet and to the depth of 1,200 feet. The Empire is in all respects a model mine in the economy of its management, and the skill displayed in its underground workings. Returns for the year will be found in the tabulated statements.

The Howard Hill, the Omaha, and the Ford, the latter an extension of the Allison ranch, have been started during the present year, under favorable conditions. The Howard Hill has attained a depth of 400 feet. The third level has been run horizontally about 180 feet, showing at some points a 5-foot ledge. The company's mill, of fifteen stamps, was started in July, 1875, but has since been closed. The Ford or Jennings claim has been tested by several crushings, which yielded about $100 per ton, but it is to be presumed this is higher than the average. The returns from the Omaha will be found in the tabulated statement. Upon the whole the condition of quartz-mining at Grass Valley may be said to be very prosperous.

In the vicinity of Nevada City are found ten or twelve ledges in the granite formation, but, with one or two exceptions, quartz-mining has not been profitably pursued for several years, owing to the refractory nature of the ores in depth. Professor Silliman, in his notes on quartz-mining in Nevada County, (and his remarks are applicable to other portions of the State,) says:

> In quartz-veins containing a considerable amount of sulphurets, it is evident that the outcroppings should offer much better returns to mining-industry than will follow after the line of atmospheric decomposition has been passed, because above this line nature has set free the gold formerly entangled in the sulphurets, leaving it available for the common modes of treatment, with the added advantage oftentimes that the particles of free gold formerly distributed through a considerable section of the vein are found concentrated in a limited amount of ore. It is easy to reach the conclusion in such cases that the tenor of gold in the vein is less in depth, after the real average tenor is reached, while in fact it is neither greater nor less; but the metal is no longer available by common methods of treatment.

This difficulty in the treatment of sulphureted ores has to a great extent paralyzed the quartz-mining industry of Nevada City, but great hopes are entertained of a revival of the long-neglected quartz-mining interest of this vicinity, through an invention or process discovered by Mr. Robert M. Fryer, who has extensive works in operation between

Grass Valley and Nevada City, in which the most refractory ores are claimed to have been successfully and economically treated. I have made some remarks upon this process elsewhere in the present report.

The leading mine of the district is the Providence, situated on Deer Creek, near the point of contact between slate and granite. This mine is now owned by Messrs. Hunter, Walrath, and others. Mr. R. C. Walrath furnishes the following statements. It will be noticed that the bullion-product is not given. It probably exceeded $150,000.

Providence mine, Nevada district: Length of location, 3,100 feet; course, northeast and southwest; dip 45° southeast; country-rock, slate, and granite; vein-matter, quartz carrying free-gold and abundant sulphurets; cost of hoisting and pumping machinery, $30,000; greatest depth attained, 820 feet; greatest length of horizontal exploration, 700 feet; eight levels opened. Mill, water and steam power; 20 stamps, (750 lbs., dropping 11 inches 72 times per minute;) 1 pan; 4 concentrators; 2 buddles; capacity, 40 tons per 24 hours; cost of mill, $20,000; cost of mining and milling, $2.60 per ton. Sulphurets are treated by chlorination. Number of tons crushed during the year, 10,000.

Mr. Shoemaker, of the Grass Valley Union, says of the condition of this mine in October, 1875:

The incline-shaft is down 800 feet. On this level the drift south has been run 70 feet. On the 700-feet level the drift is in 260 feet, and the ledge is 8 feet wide. On the 600-foot level the drift is in 500 feet, and the ledge 4 feet thick. On the 500 and 400 foot levels the drifts are in 245 feet; on the 300 foot 170 feet has been drifted. On the 200-foot level 259 feet, and on the 100-foot 400 feet have been drifted. The winze on the 700-foot level is down 50 feet. The 600 and 700 foot levels are connected by a winze, which is 175 feet south of the incline. The winze on the 500 and 600 foot levels are 345 from the incline. In short, the ledge for a depth of 800 feet on the south side is ready for stoping, and for a distance of 500 feet, the point now reached with the longest drift, the rock is the best ever found in the mine. The ledge averages about 6 feet in thickness, and much of it is composed of fully 90 per cent. base metal. Professor Price, who recently visited the mine, thought, judging by the weight of ordinary rock, that there are about 25,000 tons of rock ready for stoping in sight. Most of the ledge on the south side is so heavily charged with mineral that it is as heavy as lead. It will take at least two years to work out what rock is in sight without any more dead-work. Mr. Fryer has made tests of some of the ore, and obtained at the rate of $339.50 per ton. A quantity was also worked by mill and chlorination process at the mine, and $225 per ton was the result. The dead-work has been going on so as to open up all this body of ore for work by the Fryer process. There has been none of it disturbed except what was necessary to be taken out in running the drifts and winzes. In running the drift on the 600-foot level there were 120 tons taken out in one week by eight men. The foreman thinks one man can take out from three to four tons a day when stoping is commenced.

The rock in the California Mine, on the south side of Deer Creek, in the granite formation, is paying well. That part of the ledge on the north side of the creek known as the Gold tunnel will soon be ready to be worked through the new incline. The shaft will be 600 feet from the present one, which is on the banks of the creek. It is 600 feet deep. The hoisting-works will then be moved there as soon as possible. The mine has been worked at that point before, and rich rock was taken out. It is expected it will continue to afford better rock than has been found south of it. The shaft is a very fine piece of work. The mill will be left where it is now, so as to be run with water until next spring, when it will be removed up to the new shaft and be run with steam.

The Wyoming and Pittsburgh are worked on tribute, and the Murchie is temporarily closed. The Gold Run is prospecting new ground, and several other mines of former note are closed indefinitely and works dismantled.

Among the noted mines of the county, now closed, are the Pittsburgh, Pennsylvania, and Erie, all of which have been described by Mr. James D. Hague, M. E., of San Francisco. His reports on these properties will be found in my report for 1872, pp. 128–301, and report for 1873, pp. 37–40. But little work has been done on these mines since the dates of Mr. Hague's reports, and they remain substantially in the same condition.

Eureka district is situated twenty miles east of Nevada and Grass Valley, at an elevation above sea-level of 4,600 feet. We find here three systems of quartz-veins: one in the granite; another in the slate; and the third at or near the point of contact of these formations. The ledges in slate are of great width, much broken, and of low grade, but it is apparent that many of them can be worked with profit by the use of water-power, of which this district has an ample supply, being situated near the head of supply of the great mining-ditches of the country. The conformation of the country is such as to permit the opening of this class of ledges by tunnels, and the cheap extraction of ore. Where the ledges occur in the granite formation the hardness of the wall-rock has proved an obstacle to successful mining.

The following is a brief statement of the condition of quartz-mining in this district:

Jim Mine. Depth, 200 feet; 5-stamp mill; yielded $14 per ton. Closed for past year.

Golden Age. Depth, 100 feet. Closed for five years.

Commercial. Depth, 100 feet. Mill destroyed by fire. Closed for five years past. Yield was $8 to $10 per ton.

Birchville. Depth, 250 feet; 5-stamp mill. Rock on bottom did not pay. Closed three years.

Iowa. Depth, 200 feet. Poor on bottom. Mill removed. Closed fourteen years.

Sweet's Mine. Depth, 280 feet. Mine had a good record. Quartz yielded $28 per ton for several years. Mill removed and mine closed.

Black & Young Mine. Temporarily closed. Ten-stamp mill. Rock yielded $10 to $15 per ton.

California. Working. See returns elsewhere.

It seems that in most cases there was an impoverishment of rock as depth was attained; and also that the milling-process was not well adapted to saving the gold when the rock was rich. The mass of tailings below the site of Sweet's Mill assays so high as to show great loss in milling; nevertheless, the mill obtained $28 per ton.

Meadow Lake district is situated in the high Sierra, about thirty miles east of Nevada, at an altitude of 9,000 to 10,000 feet above sea-level. In 1865 this district was the scene of a great quartz excitement. Locations to the extent of 65,600 feet were made during the year, and during that and the next year seven quartz-mills were built, aggregating sixty-two stamps. A town of from 400 to 500 houses arose as if by magic, and as quickly disappeared. According to Mr. Skidmore, who was among the earliest in the district, no crushing paid a profit on milling and mining. The reason was not in the absence of the precious metals but in the refractory nature of the rock, the gold being combined with sulphurets to such an extent as to defeat all attempts at amalgamation. In one instance the clean-up of the first run was $4 per ton instead of $40 to $60 as was anticipated from assays. The ores contained iron-pyrites, arsenical pyrites, and galena. The formation is granite. The heavy snows falling during the winter season in this region must greatly restrict mining-operations, even should the long-looked-for process be discovered which will unlock the hidden wealth of Meadow Lake. During the past year the Fryer Works, of Grass Valley, have successfully treated ores from this district, and most of the old claims have been relocated and will be opened in 1876.

Description of leading quartz-mines in Nevada County, California, 1875.

[Reported by W. A. Skidmore, J. L. Holland, J. Berry, and J. F. Beckett.]

Name of mine.	Owners.	District.	Length of location.	Course.	Dip.	Length of pay-zone.	Average width.	Country-rock.	Vein-matter.	Cost of hoisting and pumping machinery.	Greatest depth attained.	Greatest length horizontal exploration.	Number levels opened.	Length of adit.	Cost of adit.
			Feet.			*Feet.*	*Feet*				*Feet.*	*Feet.*		*Feet.*	
Idaho	Company	Grass Valley	1,112	N. W.	70° S. W.	Unknown.	7	Greenstone and slate.	Quartz	$20,000	900	......	8	......	......
New York Hill	do	do	2,900	N. W.	33° N. E.	500	2	Greenstone	do	35,000	*500	1,000	3	918	$10,000
Eureka	do	do	3,664	N. W.	70° S. W.	......	3	Greenstone and slate.	do	20,000	1,200	......	10	......	......
Empire	do	do	2,800	N.	28° W	Variable	1.5	do	do	20,000	1,200	1,800	12	......	......
Pittsburgh	Sandford & McCook Brothers.	do	1,500	N.	74° W	225	0.9	Slate and granite	do	2,000	185	225	3	......	......
Antelope	Egan & Co.	do	1,500	N. E.	40° N. W.	100	0.9	Granite and greenstone.	Quartz and ocher.	200	70	120	1	140	210
California	Company	Nevada	3,000	N.	40° E	400	1	Granite	Clay, slate, &c.	15,000	420	1,150	3	......	......
Gold Tunnel	do	do	3,200	N.	36° E	500	1.2	do	Clay and quartz.	10,000	425	1,300	3	......	......
Nevada	J. S. Van Winkle	do	320	N.	E	......	5	do	Quartz with pyrites and galena.	......	400	2,000	4	1,400	......
California	McDonald & Lattie	Eureka	3,000	N. W.	45° N. E.	200	3	Granite and slate.	Quartz	......	*180	500	4	......	......

* On incline.

NOTE.—Where the word "Company" occurs in the column of owners, the company bears the same name as the mine. Courses are given in one bearing only, thus: "N. W.," for northwest and southeast; and dips are referred to cardinal points only.

Operations of leading mines in Nevada County, California, 1875.

[Reported by W. A. Skidmore, J. F. Beckett, J. L. Holland.]

Name of mine.	District.	Number of miners.	Miners' wages, per day.	Cost of— Sinking, per foot.	Drifting, per foot.	Stoping, per ton.	Mining, per ton.	Milling, per ton.	Company or custom mill.	No. of tons extracted and worked.	Average yield, per ton.	Percentage of sulphurets.	Total bullion-product.
Idaho	Grass Valley	......	$3 00	......	......	......	$9 00	$2 00	Company	28,103	$17 64	2	$495,669
New York Hill	do	60	3 00	$40 00	$9 00	$3 00	12 00	2 25	do	15,000	40 00	5	100,000
Eureka	do	......	3 00	......	......	......	10 00	3 34	do	4,310	23 21	2	100,542
Empire	do	90	$2 50 to 3 00	20 00	7 00	2 50	$8 00 to 9 00	2 00	do	11,000	22 00	2.5	232,000
Pittsburgh	do	8	3 00	10 00	6 00	4 00	......	4 00	Custom	250	65 00	5	20,000
Antelope	do	3	3 00	2 50	1 50	......	5 00	2 50	do	100	50 00	5	5,000
Omaha	do	40	2 50 to 3 00	35 00	10 00	3 50	9 00	4 50	do	600	60 00	2.5	36,000
California	Nevada	20	3 00	15 00	7 00	5 00	......	2 00	Company	3,940	19 00	3	90,000
Gold Tunnel*	do	15	3 00	15 00	7 00	5 00	......	1 75	do	1,000	17 00	2	18,000
Nevada	do	10	3 00	8 00	4 00	1 25	2 50	75	do	......	10 00	3	......
California	Eureka	20	3 00	4 00	3 00	2 00	5 00	2 00	do	2,000	15 00	1	30,000

*The Gold Tunnel Company raised no ore after April, 1875, being occupied in sinking a new shaft and erecting new works.

NOTE.—The column of bullion-product probably includes proceeds of sulphurets not included in the statement of the mill-yield per ton.—R. W. R.

Statement of quartz-mills, Nevada County, California, 1875.

[Reported by W. A. Skidmore, J. L. Holland, and John Berry.]

Name of mill.	Owners.	District.	Power.	Stamps. Number.	Weight, in pounds.	Drop, in inches.	Drops per minute.	Pans.	Concentrators.	Cost of mill.	Capacity for 24 hours, (tons.)	Cost of treatment, per ton.	Tons crushed during year.	Method of treating sulphurets.
Idaho	Company	Grass Valley	Steam	35	850	10	70	1	Buddle.	$40,000	70 to 80	*$2 00	28,103	Chlorination.
New York Hill	do	do	Water and steam	19	900	9	80	8	6	20,000	45	2 25	25,000	Do.
Eureka	do	do	Steam, (60 horse-power)	30	850	10	62	2	Buddles.	40,000	60	3 34	4,310	Do.
Empire	do	do	Steam	20	900	9	73	4	10	30,000	40	2 00	11,000	Chlorination or pans.
California	do	Nevada	do	10	750	8	78	....	....	7,500	18	2 00	3,940	Chlorination.
Gold Tunnel	do	do	Water	10	750	8	80	....	....	8,000	18	1 75	1,000	Do.
Nevada	J. S. Van Winkle	do	do	15	750	9	85	....	6	20,000	30	75	4,000	Do.
California	McDonald & Lattie	Eureka	Steam, (40 horse-power)	10	750	7	78	1	....	12,000	20	2 00	2,000	None.

* About.

The North Bloomfield Company, the works of which are fully described in the report of 1874, pp. 108–114, and in the report for 1875, owns an interest in three distinct corporations.

1st. The Bloomfield property, consisting of the Bloomfield Mine, 1,580 acres, fully equipped and at work, with a tunnel 8,000 feet long, deep enough to bottom all the workable gravel of the claim, and in successful operation; a ditch 41 miles long, with a delivery-capacity of 2,900 inches, and fed in the dry season from storage-reservoirs holding 496 million cubic feet (or 3,710 million gallons) of water. 2d. One-half the property of the Union Gravel-Mining Company. 3d. One-half the property of the Milton Mining and Water Company.

The Manzanita tunnel, of the Milton Company, with accompanying gold-saving apparatus, is in working-order. The French Corral tunnel of this company will probably be completed early in 1876, and the company will then be in the receipt of a large income.

The Milton Company owns five distinct mining-properties, viz: The French Corral Mine, with deep tunnel partly completed; the Kate Hayes and Troy Mine, (½ interest,) with no tunnel; the Bed-Rock Mine, now in operation, with deep tunnel completed; the Manzanita Mine with deep tunnel completed; the Badger Hill Mine, (⅚ interest,) with tunnel yet to be driven to reach the rich gravel.

The Milton Company also owns a main ditch, 60 miles long, from French Corral to the Middle Yuba, which will have a delivery-capacity of 2,500 inches; the Rudyard reservoir to supply this ditch, containing 535 million cubic feet (or 3,980 million gallons) of water; various distributing-ditches aggregating perhaps 18 miles in length; and other water-rights.

The 15-stamp cement-mill on the French Corral claims, owned by the Milton Company, was run in November, 1875, for twenty-two days on cement, and the result of the cleaning up at the end of the run was $4,550, or an average of $200 per day. The expense of getting out and milling the cement was about $50 per day, leaving $150 per day profit. It is for the purpose of tapping this body of ground that the tunnel is being run at French Corral by the Milton Company. When completed it will allow the whole of the pay-channel, cement and all, to be washed through it. The cement is about 75 feet in thickness, but there has never been over 25 feet in depth worked. It is supposed that the bottom will be much richer than the ground at present worked. The expense of the tunnel, which will be very heavy, is expected to be soon recouped when operations commence.

The following is a memorandum of expenditures made by the North Bloomfield Company, from August 1, 1871, to November 30, 1874:

Bloomfield Mine—Tunnel		$499,000	
Improvements, lands, &c		43,000	
			$542,000
Bowman Ditch—Enlargement		12,000	
Bowman Reservoir—Dam washed away	$12,000		
Present dam, (72 feet)	52,000		
Enlargement to 92 feet	7,000		
		71,000	
South Lakes—Dams built and surveys		7,000	
			90,000
Union Company—Assessments and water			50,000
Milton Company—Total cost ditches, &c		$369,000	
Less cost of reservoir		31,000	
			338,000

San Francisco—Office and interest	$134,000
	1,154,000
Cost to August 1, 1871	725,000
Total outlay, November 30, 1874	1,879,000

The following summary shows the financial operations of the company from September 30, 1874, to October 27, 1875, viz:

Receipts.			
Assessments paid by stockholders		$282,310 00	
Profit in mining:			
Bullion-product	$83,078 63		
Cost of water and mining	61,006 18		
		22,072 45	
Sale of water-right and supplies		25,294 45	
			$329,676 90
Disbursements.			
Bloomfield Mine:			
Tunnel, under-currents, title for United States patent, &c	$25,731 99		
Mining-supplies increased	8,062 35		
		33,794 34	
Water properties:			
Enlargement of dam, new ditches, and land for reservoir-sites		29,709 07	
Union Gold Mining Company:			
Assessments and cost of water	$10,288 40		
Milton Mining and Water Company:			
Ditches constructed	39,378 94		
		49,667 34	
Interest, &c.:			
On bonds and floating debt	$79,277 39		
San Francisco office expense, and salaries manager and secretary	4,947 82		
Mining for 1875–'76, &c	1,514 75		
		85,739 96	
Debt:			
Floating debt reduced	115,124 25		
Bills receivable and cash assets increased	15,641 94		
		130,766 19	
			$329,676 90

Mr. Hamilton Smith, the general manager of the company, makes the following report, dated November 1, 1875:

From January, 1875, until October 14, ultimo, washing through the deep tunnel of the Bloomfield Mine was prosecuted with but few delays, when mining was suspended in order to allow the cleaning out of the main Bowman ditch. There was in this claim 386,972 24-hour inches * of water, producing $74,271.77 of bullion, and showing a yield of 19.2 cents per inch. Very much the larger portion of the material washed was white surface-gravel, containing but little gold, and only a comparatively small quantity of the deep blue gravel was mined. The company from 1870 to 1874 used in its old sluices 710,987 24-hour inches of water in washing similar surface-gravel, and the yield per inch was only 13.6 cents; this improvement of the yield for the past season is chiefly due to the increased richness of the lowest gravel thus far worked, and which has largely added to the average of the entire mass of gravel washed. The

* One 24-hour miners' inch is equivalent to 2,230 cubic feet of water.

lowest point yet reached in the claim is still about 40 feet above the bed-rock of the deep channel, and it is in this stratum of 40 feet where the rich pay will be found. The bed-rock will not be reached before next spring, but from that time forward the yield per inch will be greatly increased. At our prospect-shaft No. 1, situate on the same channel, about two-thirds of a mile distance, over 20,000 tons of gravel were drifted, which yielded $1.53 per ton. Should we be fortunate enough to strike gravel of equal richness at shaft 8, which is the tunnel-opening, the results of the next season's workings cannot fail to be most satisfactory.

The claim at the present moment is looking exceedingly well; the top gravel is unusually free from pipe-clay and bowlders, and the deepest blue gravel thus far reached prospects most promisingly.

The operation of opening up a deep-gravel mine is often attended with great risk and large expense, and we can consider ourselves fortunate in this Bloomfield claim to have so nearly opened the mine to bed-rock in a portion of one season and be able to show a profit of over $22,000.

The tunnel and all the hydraulic machinery attached to the claim thoroughly answer the purposes for which they were designed, and the mine is now in first-class working-order. Two under-currents and a tail-sluice have been built at the lower end of the tunnel, and these will be increased next year, so soon as it may be found profitable to do so.

The company's water-supply from September 30, 1874, to October 27, 1875, was 600,600 24-hour inches delivered at Bloomfield, and which is a larger quantity than has ever before been received. The ditch increases in size with use, and it is therefore practicable to run more water through it the older it becomes.

For a supply of water during the dry season we rely almost exclusively upon our storage-reservoirs, and these are now of too small a capacity to fill the main ditch the entire season. In 1873 the board of trustees determined to increase the capacity of the Bowman reservoir, and work on the enlargement of the two Bowman dams has been continuously prosecuted up to date. On July 16, 1875, the board decided that these Bowman dams should be built of stone up to the final height of 95 feet, and at an estimated total cost of $69,000. Up to October 27, 1875, $22,599.57 had been expended upon this enlargement, and from the present satisfactory condition of the work, I now believe that its entire cost will not exceed $60,000, being $9,000 less than the estimate. The work on the dams is being done in a very substantial manner, and it is expected to have them completed to the full height of 95 feet by October, 1876. The reservoir formed by the existing dams, of 72 feet height, holds 453 million cubic feet of water; when completed to 95 feet it will hold 920 million cubic feet, so that this enlargement will double its present storage-capacity. The company will then have a constant supply, averaging about 800,000 24-hour inches of water per annum for its mining-purposes, and which will allow the constant working of its mines through the entire year. The present supply of water averages about 530,000 24-hour inches per annum, and hence the enlargement of the Bowman reservoir will increase our mining-capacity one-half, and add in fully that ratio to the present value of the property. These dams are now the only constructive works of importance which the company has in hand, and when they are completed our construction accounts can be considered as finally closed.

On August 23, 1875, the board of trustees sold to the Nevada Reservoir Ditch Company the second right to our water after it has been used in the Bloomfield and Union Mines, and emptied into the South Yuba River. The consideration of this sale was $20,000, to be paid in four installments, in 1877-'78-'79-'80, and this amount can be considered clear gain, our company having no further use for the water after its discharge into the river.

Washing in opening the Union Gravel-Mining Company's claim was suspended in May, 1875, the results of mining not having been profitable, owing to the large bodies of pipe-clay encountered in the mine. The Union tunnel is now being extended into the claim for the purpose of prospecting the ground, and by the end of the year the present value of the mine will be definitely determined.

The very extensive works of the Milton Mining and Water Company are now approaching completion, and it is confidently expected that the mines of that company will be largely productive during the coming year.* Its Manzanita Mine is now at last well opened, and affords every promise of becoming an excellent mine. The Bed-

* Bullion-yield from Milton Mining and Water Company's mines, from March 18, 1875, to November 1, 1875:

Manzanita	$45,974 40	
Last clean-up, say	22,000 00	
		$67,974 40
French Corral		39,788 91
Bed-Rock		37,331 59
Total for 7½ months		145,094 90

Rock Mine has rich gravel, but is still troubled with surface-bowlders. Two large and powerful derricks have been erected to remove these floating stones, and the next season's work ought to show a handsome profit. The French Corral tunnel will be completed by next summer, when I feel confident the clean-ups from this mine will be very large. Most of the surface-gravel in the claim has been washed away, leaving only the lower 20 to 40 feet of the blue gravel, which is exceedingly rich, some of it having milled as high as $6 per ton. That which is now being crushed at the French Corral mill is yielding $3 per ton.

The burden of the company's assessments for the past year has been a heavy one to carry, but it must be kept in mind that since January, 1875, when washing through the new tunnel was commenced, all these assessments have been applied solely for the cancellation of the company's debt and accrued interest. Since that date the remittances from the superintendent have considerably more than covered all his expenditures, including the considerable outlay for the work on the Bowman dams and the sluice and under-currents.

Balance-sheet of North Bloomfield Gravel-Mining Company, October 27, 1875.

ASSETS.

Realty at North Bloomfield:		
Cost of mining-claims and improvements	$150, 632 60	
Net cost of prospecting-shafts Nos. 1, 2, 3, and 4	31, 606 20	
Cost of Humbug Creek, and improvements	8, 394 02	
Cost of main tunnel	493, 043 77	
Cost of No. 7 cross-cut, (branch of tunnel)	2, 635 27	
		$686, 311 86
Water-properties:		
Ditches—cost of main ditch and distributors, 55 miles	422, 106 32	
Reservoirs	170, 872 68	
		592, 979 00
Milton Mining and Water Company:		
Cost in cash and property of $\frac{6.126\frac{1}{3}}{12.310}$ its properties		464, 907 00
Union Gravel-Mining Company:		
Cost in cash .. } of $\frac{4.050}{8.000}$ its properties	61, 513 13	
Cost in water. }	11, 749 79	
		73, 262 92
Personal property:		
Quicksilver, mining-tools, &c	7, 527 20	
Pipe in diggings, office and engineer's furniture and instruments	20, 002 47	
Live stock and wagons, saw-mill, supplies, &c	5, 334 85	
		32, 864 52
Operating-accounts, (season 1875–'76:)		
Mining-account—expended on account this season's work		2, 150 00
San Francisco expenses, (since organization)		231, 544 70
Bills receivable		20, 200 00
Cash assets		5, 275 58
Total		2, 109, 495 58

LIABILITIES.

Stockholders:			
Amount collected by assessments			$1, 377, 700 00
Profits:			
Profits from sale Rudyard reservoir	$67, 544 10		
Profits from sale water, season 1872–'73	73, 000 00		
Profits from sale water, season 1873–'74	12, 592 43		
Profits from sale water to Nevada Reservoir Company	20, 000 00		
		$173, 136 53	
Less loss on Milton contracts:			
Cost of work done for Milton Company	251, 621 27		
Amount received for this	202, 000 00		
		49, 621 27	
		123, 515 26	
Profit in working Bloomfield mines:			
Yield previous to season 1874–'75	218, 073 42		
Yield in season 1874–'75	83, 078 63		
Total yield	301, 152 05		
Total cost	276, 846 76		
Profit previous to 1874–'75	2, 232 84		
Profit in season 1874–'75	22, 072 45		
		24, 305 29	
			147, 820 55
Floating debt			146, 551 31
Mortgage:			
Proceeds of loan $500,000 currency			437, 423 72
Total			2, 109, 495 58

Mr. H. C. Perkins, the superintendent, renders the following—

Comparative statement of expenses and yield of the No. 8 mine, season of 1874–'75.

Runs.	Water used.	Time occupied.*	Yield per inch.	Gross yield.	Expenses.	Profit.
	Inches.	*Days.*				
First	61, 000	64	$0 14¼	$8, 700 00	$8, 475 00	$225 00
Second	58, 875	46¼	15. 9	9, 360 00	7, 850 00	1, 510 00
Third †	47, 538	29½	21. 7	10, 300 00	6, 150 00	4, 150 00
Fourth	54, 198	26	15½	8, 550 00	5, 600 00	2, 950 00
Fifth ‡	59, 652	61	20. 4	12, 150 00	11, 150 00	1, 000 00
Sixth	52, 134	33	23. 4	12, 200 00	6, 900 00	5, 300 00
Seventh §	53, 575	35	24. 4	13, 011 77	6, 963 83	6, 047 94
Total	‖ 386, 972	¶ 295	** 19. 3	74, 271 77	53, 088 83	21, 182 94

* "Time occupied" includes every day from the time washing commenced until washing commenced on next run.

† This run washing was chiefly up Hilder Ravine, where bank had very little of top or poorest gravel.

‡ During this run the timbers and blocks were washed out of shaft 8, causing a delay of over three weeks and an extra expense of, say, $3,000.

§ The clean-up for this run was $15,038.06; expenses, $6,963.83; showing a profit of $8,074.23. As, however, this clean-up was a final one, all the sluices being cleaned, a portion of it properly belongs to the preceding runs, and has been credited to them in above statement for the purpose of making an exact comparison.

‖ Inches for 24 hours.

¶ From December 21, 1874, to October 11, 1875.

** Average.

Mining and water cost and yield.

	Labor.	Supplies and tools.	General expense.	Total costs, water and mining.	Bullion-products.	Yield per inch of water.	Net profit.
No. 8 Mine	$22, 790 39	$12, 489 09	$3, 328 95	$53, 088 83	$74, 271 77	$0 19. 2	$21, 182 94
Woodward Mine	1, 982 00	625 00	250 00	4, 786 00	6, 011 60	11. 7	1, 225 60
Eisenbeck Mine	1, 459 75	550 00	100 00	3, 086 35	2, 725 06	10. 4	—361 29
Hilder Tunnel				45 00	70 20		25 20
Total	26, 232 14	13, 664 09	3, 678 95	61, 006 18	83, 078 63		22, 072 45

The extensive gravel-mining operations of Nevada County have been fully described in former reports, and I shall therefore review only the operations of the past year.

One of the most costly and extensive systems of mining-ditches is that of the Eureka Lake and Yuba Canal Company. The company owns three hundred miles of ditch, supplying 6,000 inches of water. Their mining-ground and improvements cost $1,500,000. The main canal commences near the summit of the Sierra Nevada Mountains, and follows the ridge to North San Juan, a distance of about sixty-five miles. This ditch receives its water from several reservoirs, the principal ones being Eureka Lake and Lake Faucherie. They will supply about 3,000 inches of water all winter and during five or six months of the dry season. The ditch is about 8 feet wide, and over 3 feet deep. The company also owns the Miners' Ditch, which is about twenty-six miles in length, and will supply over 700 inches of water; the Middle Yuba Canal, which is over forty miles long and has a capacity of 1,500 inches of water; the Poorman's Creek Ditch, which is twenty-two miles long, with a capacity of over 300 inches; the Grizzly ditches, the Spring Creek ditches, and several others. They were built by different companies, but in 1865 were consolidated, and became the property of the present company, which has a perpetual right to all this water, and a section of over two hundred square miles of rich mining-ground to supply. The company has usually sold all its water to mine-owners, but during the past two years rich mining-ground has been secured sufficient to use all the supply afforded. At Relief Hill the company has a large claim, which has been successfully worked for years. At North Bloomfield, adjoining the North Bloomfield Hydraulic Mine, and on the same channel, it owns 700 acres. At Moore's Flat, one of the proprietors, Marks Zellerback, owns some rich and extensive mines, but the most valuable ground owned by the company is at Columbia Hill. The ground is located on the same channel as the North Bloomfield Mine. The ground, from the surface down, pays largely, and there is enough of it to last fifty years. There are in the claim about 1,500 acres. It extends on the line of the channel a distance of two and one-half miles, and is from one-fourth of a mile to a mile in width. The depth to bed-rock averages from 150 to 400 feet, and as far down as it has been washed there is not a particle of pipe-clay or hardly a rock to make it expensive working. On the east end of the claim there has been perhaps a hundred acres of the ground worked to a depth of about 75 feet, when work was suspended for want of fall.

A tunnel has been commenced which will run into the western portion of the mine known as the Central and Western claims, which will allow them to be worked to a depth of 200 feet. It is now completed a distance of 900 feet, and it will have to be run 1,250 feet farther before finished. It is being run at a rate of 125 feet a month; so it will all be completed in ten months. A flume has been constructed from Spring Creek into the eastern portion of the ground, which is 4,600 feet long, 8 feet wide, and about 20 inches high. It will allow the eastern half of the mine to be worked to a depth of 150 feet below the present grade, or when it reaches new ground to a depth of 225 feet. The banks are composed of fine gravel, without any pipe-clay.

The Nevada Transcript gives the following account of two prominent districts:

Moore's Flat, in Eureka Township, is situated on a bench on the side of the hill south of the Yuba River. It is two miles from the old town of Orleans and one mile from Woolsey's. A gravel-channel follows the bend of the hill, and it has been extensively worked since 1851. The mines at Orleans Flat were long since worked out and the town abandoned, only three or four cabins still remaining to mark the site. Large quantities of gold have been taken out at Moore's, and several good mines are still working, but the place is not as prosperous as it once was. The channel is covered in many places with earth (generally cement) to a depth of 250 feet. In order to work to the bottom of the channel, it is necessary to run tunnels from the hill-side into the mines in order to get a grade. In most cases these tunnels have not been low enough to reach the bottom of the channel; hence, after long and expensive work, owners have found that but about half of the pay-gravel could be washed. Latterly those who commenced a tunnel went far enough down the hill to reach a point many feet below the lowest portion of the bed of the channel in their claims. On the north side of the town the Ohio claims are located. Considerable of the ground has been worked to the depth of a hundred feet or more, until there was no grade, since which the claims have been idle. The ground is very rich, and only needs a tunnel 750 feet long to allow of its being worked again.

Adjoining the Ohio are the Chinese claims, owned and worked exclusively by Chinamen. The ground is rich and pays well. They are the only claims near the town which is in grade. Southwest of them is the Illinois Mine. They have been worked for about twenty years, and have always paid, and the ground is still rich and extensive. A tunnel, however, is necessary to get to the bottom of the channel. The Blue Banks Mine is about half a mile south of the Illinois, and is one of the deepest mines on the flat. There is about seventy feet of blue gravel, on top of which is a bank of pipe-clay 150 feet deep. The gravel is very rich, but it is expensive washing it, on account of the clay, which has to be blasted and pounded up so as to allow it to be worked through the flume. The owners of this claim completed a tunnel 1,000 feet in length this season, and have plenty of fall to work all their ground and some of that adjoining if necessary. The channel here is 300 feet wide and about seventy feet deep in the center.

The hydraulic-mining claim known as the American is situated at Manzanita Hill, near North San Juan. The ground is part of a channel extending from French Corral through Birchville, Sweetland, Sebastopol, and North San Juan. Throughout the whole extent, at different points, mining is prosecuted on a scale of great magnitude. The American Mine consists of the ground of what was originally known as the Gold Bluff, the Badger, and the American claims. Work was first commenced on the Gold Bluff about the year 1869. The company drove a tunnel, through which the western portion of the ground is now washed. The gravel was very rich, and paid heavy dividends. Water at that time cost 75 cents an inch. The gravel in the channel was worked out as far as the tunnels would afford fall, but only a part of the ground could be worked through them. Seven years ago a new one was commenced, which will afford an outlet for all the ground owned by the American Company. It will be 4,000 feet long, and will, when it reaches the point where the shaft will be sunk, be 180 feet beneath the bed-rock. Thirty-seven hundred feet of it is now completed, (December, 1875,) leaving only about three hundred feet yet to run. It will cost in the neighborhood of $172,000. It is expected it will be finished and everything ready for washing in 1876. The dirt and gravel on the unworked ground is about 200 feet deep, and pays from the grass-roots to the bottom. There is about sixty feet of blue gravel on the bottom of the channel that is very rich. The company has ground enough to keep it working for ten or fifteen years. It has been estimated that there has been over two and a half millions of dollars already taken out of these claims, and it is thought as much more still remains untouched. The company has this season added a series of under-currents near the point where the washings empty into the river. These, taken in connection with what were before in use, make a most extensive and complete system. There are over forty under-currents now in working-order; some of them are thirty feet wide and forty feet long. The last one pays well. The superintendent says that but a very small portion of the gold is saved in the long flume. The company has expended in the building of under-currents this summer over $7,000, and it is anticipated that this amount will be saved in one run. Operations of late have consisted in washing the rim of the channel or the ground which has been left while working heretofore, and have paid expenses of working and running the new tunnel. The water used is from the Eureka Lake Company's ditch. About 1,400 inches are used daily with three pipes.

YUBA COUNTY.

This county, covering an area of 600 square miles, is situated in the foot-hills east of the Sacramento Valley. The placer-mines of Sucker Flat, Smartsville, and Timbuctoo, among the most productive in the State, were described by Mr. Amos Bowman in the report for 1875.

In respect to quartz-mining, this county has a poor record. From 1860 to 1865, inclusive, seven quartz-mills were erected, with an aggregate of 70 stamps, and at a cost of $200,000.

In 1870 the product in quartz-mining was only $10,680. The principal mines, situated near Brownsville, proved financial failures, and after a short run in 1873 were permanently closed.

One of the most extensive hydraulic-mining enterprises of the State is that of the Excelsior Water Company, of Smartsville, which was organized in the early part of the summer of 1875, with a capital stock of $2,000,000, divided into 20,000 shares of $100 each, for the purpose of consolidating various properties in Yuba County, owned by different corporations, but by essentially the same individuals. Among the properties so absorbed may be mentioned the noted Blue Gravel Mine, whose owners were the first in the State to complete a bed-rock tunnel and tap one of the channels of the so-called ancient river-system of California, and which has been paying largely for many years. Also, the Rose Bar Mine, which promises to rival the first-named; also, the large property and perennial water-supply of the Excelsior Canal Company. This company also controls several other mines of local fame and great value. Since its incorporation it has paid nearly $90,000 in dividends, in addition to spending a large amount in the permanent improvement and extension of its property.

The Smartsville hydraulic mines are worked with energy and profitable results. This deposit of auriferous gravel is about 15,000 feet long and half a mile wide, on the average, while the depth varies from 50 to 350 feet. The bottom of the ancient channel is several hundred feet higher than the channel of the Yuba River, from which it is separated by a rim of bed-rock. This rim is pierced by several tunnels, of an aggregate length of 12,000 to 14,000 feet. These tunnels are from 6 to 8 feet wide and 7 to 9 feet high. The flumes or tail-sluices are about 4 feet wide and 3 feet deep, lined with rock.

Water is supplied by the ditches of the Excelsior Water Company, which also owns or controls the greater portion of the gravel of the district. These ditches aggregate over 110 miles in length, and can deliver during the winter season from 7,000 to 8,000 inches of water. During the summer season the supply falls to 2,500 inches.

Two more tunnels, each about 2,500 feet long, will be required to furnish outlet for the remaining gravel in place. One of these, known as the Deer Creek tunnel, has been run by hand 950 feet. The company has now in operation an Ingersoll drill, by means of which the remaining 1,500 feet will be completed. The rock of this district is exceedingly hard, and the cost of running these tunnels is very high, varying from $40 to $50 per foot, with diamond-drills, and compressed air for motive-power. In one instance which came under Mr. Skidmore's observations it required two days with a diamond drill to put in 18 holes four feet deep. This number of holes constitutes the usual blasting-face, but in some instances as many as 36 holes are required. The consequence is that progress is very slow, even with the improved power-drills.

In order to work the rich bottom strata of the Smartsville Consolidated Company and adjoining ground, another tunnel of 2,400 or 2,600 feet will be required. This company has a piece of ground 1,200 feet in length by 800 feet in width. Work on the new tunnel was commenced in December, 1875.

The celebrated Blue Gravel claim, frequently noticed in these reports, is situated in this district. This claim, for many years the leading hydraulic mine of the State, after having been worked as deep as possible through the upper tunnel, suspended dividends for a time, pending the completion of a lower tunnel, 1,760 feet in length and 65 feet lower than the former, and through which the company is now working. The bottom proved extraordinarily rich, and some of the "clean ups" of the present year have exceeded anything in the previous history of the mine. It has yielded about $2,000,000, a portion of which (bottom gravel only being worked) has been obtained at the rate of $1,750 per day's washing of eleven hours' run, with 1,200 inches of water.

The Rose Bar claim, from which the top dirt has been entirely stripped, yielded $600,000 to $700,000. This claim is about 1,800 feet in length on the channel, and for most of this distance embraces the entire width of the channel. A lower tunnel 1,100 feet in length has recently been completed and washing commenced. The gravel resembles that of the Blue Gravel Company's ground. The ground on the first run yielded $800 to every 1,000 inches water on eleven hours' run. This product will be exceeded in future runs, as the best ground is not yet accessible.

In this district about 30,000,000 cubic yards of auriferous gravel have been removed by the hydraulic process, yielding, as shown by records, $7,000,000, exclusive of $3,000,000 which was taken out in the early days before the era of deep mining. There are by measurement about 100,000,000 yards in place, which, on a basis of 25 cents per cubic yard—the average product of ground already worked—will yield $25,000,000. But assuming this to be an overestimate as to the value per cubic yard, and placing the yield at 15 cents per cubic yard for the entire mass of ground in place, we have $15,000,000 as the probable future product of the district. The average annual product of the district will be about $500,000 per annum for several years, but on the completion of the great tunnels now in progress this yield will be increased. Under ordinary circumstances it will require about twenty-five years to exhaust this great deposit. The proportion of profit will be about 60 or 65 per cent. of the gross receipts.

BUTTE COUNTY.

This county has ten quartz-mills, but only two are running. About 4,000 or 5,000 tons were crushed in 1875. There are 330 miles of mining-ditch, supplying 8,000 inches of water. The principal hydraulic mining and one of the largest enterprises of the kind in the State is that of the Spring Valley Land and Mining Company, located at Cherokee Flat. This company employed 150 laborers and miners, the usual rate of wages being $3 per day. It owns between 250 and 300 acres of mining-ground, averaging 100 feet in depth—enough of good paying ground for fifty years to come at the present rate of working. This extensive mine has three openings. There are three miles of triple line of flume, two of which are six feet in width and the other four. They are constructed so as to shut off the water and clean up any portion of either at any time. There are also in connection with the flume twenty-four under-currents, ranging from six feet in width to thirty. The company has nine hydraulic chiefs or giants, the streams from which are forced out under a pressure of 250 feet of water, and they are constructing a ditch which will give them a pressure of 302 feet. These giants under the former pressure with seven-inch nozzle will throw 1,000 inches of water; six-inch nozzle, 700 inches; five-inch nozzle, 500 inches.

The sources of water-supply for this mine are Butte Creek and the branches of Feather River, as well as the water-shed of Table Mountain. Butte Creek and the west branch of Feather River furnish the entire summer supply. The former is 26 miles in length from the head dam at Butte Creek to the extensive reservoir at Concord Valley; the ditch is 5 feet wide on the bottom by 3 feet deep. The ditch, in its course, crosses two streams or deep cañons, by means of iron pipes 30 inches in diameter. The first is 1,064 feet in length, with a maximum depression of 150 feet. The second, crossing the west branch of Feather River, is 3,555 feet in length; maximum depression, 650 feet. It flows into the large reservoir at Concord Valley, which covers 320 acres of land.

The Dewey Ditch takes its water from the head of the west branch, up in the regions of eternal snows, is 18 miles in length, and serves as feeder for Butte Creek Ditch, into which it empties. From the great Concord reservoir the water is brought 12 miles in a large ditch 6 feet wide on the bottom by 4 feet deep; it again crosses the west branch of Feather River in a pipe of the same diameter as those mentioned—30 inches—but with a maximum depression of 856 feet, which is believed to be the most severe hydraulic strain which engineers have attempted to control in any enterprise of this kind. The pipe is nearly 3 miles in length; the heaviest iron used is three-eighths of a inch. It has a head of 180 feet perpendicular pressure, and its greatest capacity is 2,200 inches by actual measurement, or 37,445,760 gallons every twenty-four hours. This represents the summer supply of the company. In addition to these extensive ditches and reservoirs, they have about 40 miles of ditches ranging from 2 feet wide and 18 inches deep to 10 feet wide and 4 feet deep, which furnish the mines with a vast supply during the winter months, probably increasing the supply to 5,000 inches.

The tailings flowing from the mines have run down the channel of Dry Creek, and during the winter freshets have been washed out over the adjoining lands, and have damaged them to some extent. Hence the company has adopted the policy of purchasing all the ranches through which the creek flows; and it now possesses some 12,000 acres, which have cost $280,000.

In addition to the product of gold, the mines of Cherokee yield diamonds and platinum. About fifty beautiful diamonds have been found, ranging from about one carat to three and a half. Many have been cut and set as gems. The greater part of the stones possessed at Cherokee were found during the earlier days, when primitive modes of mining were in operation. The present system of hydraulic washing, with its immense streams of water and gravel, flowing away so rapidly, renders a search for precious stones impracticable. But in the black sands which gather in the bottom of sluices, tons of which are shoveled out in the process of cleaning up, may be seen, it is said, with an ordinary magnifying glass, great numbers of perfectly formed diamonds, varying from merest mite to almost a pin-head in size. Platinum is found in considerable quantities, but no effort is made to save it; though it does not amalgamate, it affiliates with the gold amalgam, and is brought in that shape. Small lots have been gathered from time to time. The company has a pound or two in the office.

A full description of the extensive works of this company with details of expenditures will be found in my report of 1874, pages 133-136.

The following is extracted from the annual report of the Spring Valley Canal and Mining Company, for the year ending July 15, 1875:

RECEIPTS AND DISBURSEMENTS.

RECEIPTS.

Gold bars	$401,599 91
Water-sales	73 50
Notes given during the year, (see bills payable)	76,714 38
Cash on hand July 15, 1874	2,079 23
	480,467 02

DISBURSEMENTS.

Current expenditures	$152,964 91	
Less amount now due on pay-roll	1,216 08	
		$151,748 83
Dividends during year		85,000 00
Paid notes to amount of		114,056 88
Paid for ranches and on ranch account	$81,010 70	
Less due C. P. R. R. on said purchases	7,130 87	
		73,879 83

Claims purchased during the year	$26,205 00
Permanent expense account	22,566 69
Quicksilver purchased during the year	1,810 20
Paid the amount due on pay-roll July 15, 1874	2,155 26
Cash on hand	259 74
Paid amount due on current book-account July, 1874	997 91
Paid on current book-account additional	1,786 68
	480,467 02

ASSETS AND LIABILITIES.

ASSETS.

Property-account July 15, 1874		$4,344,496 68		
Less—				
Cash on hand July, 1874	$2,079 23			
Ranches on hand July, 1874	247,490 00			
Residue gold account	199,629 23			
		449,198 46		
Balance			$3,895,298 22	
Claims purchased during year			26,205 00	
Permanent improvement:				
Permanent expense-account		$4,105 78		
Iron pipe		13,010 70		
Dewey Ditch improvement		5,450 21		
			22,566 69	
Quicksilver purchased during year			1,810 20	
Total property-account				$3,945,880 11
Ranch-account			307,706 09	
Ranch expense-account during year			14,092 01	
Ranch interest-account			6,702 60	
Total ranch-expenditures to date				328,500 70
Due on current account balance				1,786 68
				4,276,167 49

LIABILITIES.

Capital stock				$4,000,000 00
Gold bars	$401,599 91			
Water-account	73 50			
Total receipts for the year		$401,673 41		
Less current expenses	$22,068 15			
Less current labor	100,338 52			
Less teaming-account	2,628 52			
Less merchandise-account	15,052 29			
Less lumber-account	3,694 44			
Less interest-account	3,638 46			
Less injury-account	326 00			
Less litigant-account	5,218 52			
		152,964 91		
Balance of actual profit for the year			$248,708 50	
Less dividends			85,000 00	
				163,708 50
Actual liabilities:				
Bills payable			81,314 38	
Due C. P. R. R			30,188 27	
Due on pay-roll		$1,216 08		
Less cash on hand		259 74		
			956 34	
Total				112,458 99
				4,276 167 49

The secretary's report contains the following comments upon these statements:

In the preceding statements, under the head of assets and liabilities, the gold yield for the year aggregates the sum of $401,599.91. Of this amount $363.92 was obtained from tailings of the Cherokee Company's flume by a man who worked the ground for one-third the proceeds, and was by him minted through Rideout, Smith & Co., Oroville. The balance came directly from our mine, and was by us refined, run into bars, and shipped to the treasurer, Mr. Judson, San Francisco.

The water sales made during the year have been exclusively for domestic purposes, to parties who have attached to our office pipe.

Our current labor-account for the year has been materially in excess of our last year's report. This is due, in a great measure, to expenditures upon the Eureka and McDonald tunnels, and upon a deep and expensive bed-rock cut excavated last fall to reach the bottom ground on the upper flat. We have also been obliged to make new openings in Saw-mill Ravine, and the work has been through stratas of pipe-clay, which invariably occur upon the rim, incurring an additional expenditure, not only in labor, but also in blasting material, particularly giant powder, as exhibited in the statements. To the latter cause the decreased yield of bullion is also due—the heavy beds of pipe-clay retarding the rapid washing of pay-gravel.

We have purchased during the year about 2,800 pounds of quicksilver, costing, at 64 cents and 65 cents, $1,810.20. This gives us now on hand and in the sluices 15,882 pounds, or nearly 8 tons. This is arrived at by allowing a loss of 12 per cent. per annum, which we ascertained to be the average waste when it was our custom to shut down the works in the spring.

We hold in Cherokee mining-district 1,210 mining-claims, of 100 feet square each. A portion of these have been worked out, and from those lying in the upper flat the surface has been washed away. No surveys have ever been made to ascertain what proportion of our ground is still untouched. We have about 52 miles of ditch, which conveys water to Cherokee, of an average depth of 3½ feet and 5 feet in width, and 3½ miles of iron pipe, 30 inches in diameter, conveying said water across the various rivers which intercept the line of the ditch. In the claims we have nine hydraulic giants, to which the water is conveyed, and leading therefrom a triple line of sluices, 6 feet and 4 feet in width, for nearly 2 miles.

The two quartz-mills in operation near Forbestown are using the Paul process, which was noticed in the report of 1872, (pages 37, 38.) As the process has been changed and improved since its introduction in 1871, and is now in use in several counties in this State, I insert the following statement concerning its details. The results of practice so far do not in my judgment indicate that the advantages claimed for it counterbalance the extra cost and difficulty of a dry treatment. I need hardly add that I do not concur in Mr. Paul's electrical theories. His process might be good in spite of them; but it must be judged chiefly on mechanical and economical grounds.

The ore must be dried to the complete expulsion of all dampness and should be worked as soon as taken from the calcining-kiln or drying-plates, whichever parties prefer using. The calcining-kiln serves two purposes, one of drying, the other of softening the ore, allowing more to be reduced with the same expense. For hard ore, Mr. Paul recommends the kiln; for soft ore, the plates. For the crushing of ore, he uses and prefers the common stamp-battery. Any style of machinery, however, is acceptable which reduces the ore to fineness suitable for the pulverizer, say 20, 30, or 40 mesh wire-cloth.

The operation begins by filling a hopper with ore to be worked. The stamps, when in motion, operate on an automatic feeder, connected with the hopper holding the ore, and the battery is thus fed with more certainty and regularity than by hand. The stamps reduce the ore coarsely, say to the fineness of No. 30 wire-cloth. The battery is thus enabled to do double the work ordinarily performed by dry-crushing batteries. The crushed ore falls upon a conveying-belt and is carried to the hopper of the pulverizing-barrel, where it is at once delivered inside. This barrel is self-feeding and self-discharging, and contains, together with partially-reduced ore coming from the battery, from 200 to 500 pounds (according to the size of the barrel) of hard quartz in pieces of the size of a fist. The larger pieces are used as pulverizing-material, the coarser pulverizing the finer, as well as reducing itself by attrition. The ore from the battery is thus rapidly brought to a powder fine enough to pass through No. 80 or 90 wire-cloth, No. 90 having 8,100 openings to the square inch. The internal arrangement of this barrel is such that the ore passes through a series of sieves, only the first discharging outward and into the hopper below. The remaining material is returned at each revolution into the center of the barrel for further reduction. To prevent dust flying about, the barrel is inclosed in a tight case, the lower portion of which forms a hopper. Into this the pulverized ore falls, and by means of a small valve is delivered at the will of the amalgamator into the amalgamating-barrel, which is directly beneath it. Into this fine, dry, warm ore from 15 to 20 per cent. of mercury is introduced, together with some simple chemicals, provided the character of ore requires them. The ore, it is claimed, is now freed of all gases or rebellious films and is in the most favorable condition for amalgamation. The pure, electrical, and warm condition of the ore enlivens the mercury, and by a slow revolution of the barrel the mercury and ore play together like water, effecting the most complete intermixture. All base substances in the ore are thrown into a different electrical condition to the precious, and cannot be taken up by the mercury, neither do they have any "sickening" effect upon the mercury, no matter what the ore contains. The time given for amalgamating varies from 30 to 60 minutes, according to the ore. It is usually only 30. This time having elapsed, the ore is then conveyed by its own gravity into a main settler of special construction, also patented by Mr. Paul. Water is introduced simply for the purpose of separating the sands and mercury, and soon the mercury begins to gather and move through a simple device, also patented by Mr. Paul as an "amalgam safe." In this safe the precious metals are deposited as amalgam, while the surplus mercury passes on and out, again to be used in recharging the amalgamating barrel. Two and sometimes three of these settlers are used, according to the value of ore, fineness of reduction, and the quantity which can be worked by one set of barrels. Practice has shown that this system can be carried out to any desired extent by duplicating ten-ton mills. Seven patents, all held by Mr. Paul, cover the process and machinery. The percentage of extraction is simply a question of expense and profit. The more labor expended in the reduction of material, the higher the percentage obtained. Mr. Paul considers that on ordinary gold-quartz 85 per cent. is the most profitable percentage to work for.

As a general thing, he claims California ores can be worked up to this percentage by his process at an expense of about $3.50 per ton where steam-power is used, and less if water can be had for power.

Description of leading mines in Butte County, California.

[Reported by H. E. Vail and Charles D. Smyth.]

Name of mine.	Owners.	District.	Length of location.	Course.	Dip.	Length of pay-zone.	Average width.	Country-rock.	Vein-matter.	Cost of hoisting and pumping machinery.	Greatest depth attained.	Greatest length of horizontal exploration.	No. of levels.
			Feet.			*Feet.*	*Feet.*				*Feet.*	*Feet.*	
Forbestown Consolidated	Company	Oro	12,900	S.W. and N.E.	N.W.		6	Slate	Quartz	$2,500	130	3,500	*4
Mammoth	Electric Mining Company	Mountain Spring	2,700	E. and W		2,000	6	Granite	do		300	100	†2

* Opened by tunnel: length, 1,210 feet; cost, $3,600.

† Opened by tunnel: length, 140 feet; cost, $900.

Operations of leading mines.

Name of mine.	No. of miners employed.	Miners' wages per day.	Sinking, per foot.	Drifting, per foot.	Stoping, per ton.	Mining, per ton extracted.	Milling, per ton.	Tons extracted and worked.	Company or custom mill.
Forbestown Consolidated	8	$1 50 to $3 00	$12 00	$3 00	$1 25	$1 50	$2 00		Company.
Mammoth	4	3 00	5 00	2 50	1 00	2 50	1 50	400	Do.

Statement of quartz-mills.

Name of mine.	Owners.	District.	Kind and amount of power.	No. of stamps.	Weight of stamps.	No. of drops per minute.	Height of drop.	No. of pans.	No. of concentrators.	Cost of mill.	Capacity per 24 tons.	Cost of treatment per ton.
					Pounds.		*Inches.*				*Tons.*	
Forbestown Consolidated	Company	Oro	Steam, 50 horse-power	10	750	85	6	Paul process*	2	$16,500	10	$2 50
Electric	do	Mountain Spring	Water, 2,000 inches	5	650	85	7	do	1	15,000	10	1 50

* Dry stamping and dry amalgamation.

SIERRA COUNTY.

This county has been fully described in the Reports of 1873 and 1875, both from a personal visit of Mr. Skidmore in 1874, and in an elaborate paper of Mr. Charles Hendel, which will be found in the Report of 1873, pages 77 to 91. The principal industry is gravel-mining, which is here carried on by means of tunnels or drifts, the greater portion of the county being covered by volcanic matter. In the lower part of the county, however, near Brandy City, there are extensive ranges of auriferous gravel which are worked by the hydraulic process. The county has 23 quartz-mills and 223 miles of mining-ditches. The gravel obtained by drifting is stored in large dumps until the washing season, when it is run through long flumes, under light heads of water. The principal mining-towns are Howland Flat, Gibsonville, Newark, (Whiskey Diggings,) Port Wine, Monte Cristo, Forest City, and Alleghany, all lying on the great "Blue lead" which traverses this portion of the State in a northerly and southerly direction.

The most productive mine in the county is the Bald Mountain, near Forest City, which was fully described in the Report of 1875. This claim was prospected by a shaft 280 feet in depth and a tunnel 2,000 feet in length run to connect with the shaft. These works required nearly two years for their completion, and cost $20,000. The mine has a frontage of 3,600 feet, and a length of 1¾ miles, the channel running nearly on the line of longest course. The improvements at the mines are very complete and extensive. The main tunnel is now about 3,500 feet long. The washing-flume is 1¼ miles long, 17 inches wide, 18 inches deep, grade 6 inches to 12 feet, paved with blocks, and a larger portion laid with iron riffles. At the lower end of the flume are the tailing-claims of the company, which are 8,000 feet in length. There are two large dump-yards, double planked, of a capacity of 30,000 cubic yards, reservoirs, ditches, and flumes, timber-houses, store-room, and shops, &c.

The Bald Mountain Company commenced operation by sinking a shaft, and at a depth of 268 feet found bed-rock and good pay-gravel. This induced the company in the spring of 1870 to start a tunnel for the shaft, and in April, 1872, the shaft was reached, and drifting commenced. From the first washing enough gold was obtained to pay all expenses of opening the mine. Since that time the mine has paid largely. The following is a summary of operations for three years and a half:

Period.		Car-loads of gravel extracted—1 cubic yard each.	Yield per car-load.	Total yield.	Cost per car-load.	Total expense.	Dividends.	Per cent. of dividends to yield.
From—	To—							
April, 1872	July, 1873	50,168	$2 62	$131,781	$1 55	$77,781	$54,000	40.9
July, 1873	July, 1874	65,782	2 98	196,572	1 31	86,572	110,000	55.9
July, 1874	July, 1875	79,590	2 70	215,292	1 19	95,292	120,000	55.8
July, 1875	December, 1875	......	......	53,009	......	22,277	30,721	57.9
Total	......	195,540	......	596,654	......	281,922	314,721	52.7

The product of the last six months was obtained by washing one-half of the dirt on hand. In July, 1875, it was reported that the company had worked 539,354 square feet of the bed-rock of its claim, and had over 6,500,000 square feet remaining, estimated to yield (at the rate of experience to that time) about $1 per foot. The gold is coarse; the largest piece taken out weighed 65 ounces.

I am indebted to Mr. Charles W. Hendel, mining engineer, and United States deputy mineral-surveyor, for interesting information concerning the leading quartz-mines of this county. Besides the often-cited causes of failure in quartz-mining, it is worthy of mention in this instance that those mines which have been worked by associations of private owners, not incorporated, have been less profitable than those worked by companies. This is due to the frequency of disputes concerning the management, leading either to the stoppage of work or to ruinous changes and fluctuations in the administration.

In the southern part of this county, about 10 to 11 miles east of south from Downieville, on Wolf Creek, a tributary of the Middle Fork, we find the Independent and Franco-American quartz-lodes, prominent on account of their large and well-defined croppings. The quartz-rock of the first named, and most developed, was worked by the locators in arrastras as early as 1866. In 1868 they built, at a cost of $6,500, a mill of 12 stamps capacity, containing 2 batteries of 4 stamps each, of 650 pounds weight, having a speed of 70 drops per minute and 8 inches fall. The mill has a crushing capacity of 8 tons in 24 hours; is driven by an overshot water-wheel 20 feet in diameter. The quartz is hoisted in large barrels out of the shaft, and the water is pumped by means of a 6-inch double-acting Hooker pump, all being driven by a 25-foot diameter overshot water-wheel. Pumping and hoisting apparatus cost $2,700. The water to drive both wheels for all kinds of machinery in and around the mine and mill is conducted in a flume 16 inches deep by 18 inches wide, ¼ mile in length, from Wolf Creek, at a cost of $600. The ledge runs S. 16° 30′ east by true meridian. The company owns 1,600 linear feet, for which it has obtained a United States patent. The vein is nearly vertical, dipping about 82° east, and has an average width of 5 to 8 feet. The walls are well defined, the east or hanging wall being dark-blue talcose slate, while the foot or western wall is composed of a dark-colored serpentine rock. The quartz is very hard, white and blue in color, and impregnated with some slate rock, containing abundant free gold, and the slate as well as the quartz contains rich gold-bearing sulphurets and galena. The elevation of this mine is about 3,000 feet above sea-level. The ledge is opened and worked through a shaft sunk on the ledge at the edge of Wolf Creek 5 by 10 feet in size, and is 150 feet deep, with three galleries or levels. The first level or tunnel is 43½ feet below the summit of the ledge at the shaft and 38 feet long; the second level, 55½ feet below the summit and 31 feet long; the third level, 126 feet below the summit and 25 feet long. This shaft and the several tunnels have cost about $10,000 dollars. The quartz in the bottom of this shaft is becoming richer in free gold. Yield heretofore in the mill, $18 to $20 per ton; cost of running, $4 to $5; of milling $1.25 per ton.

The Oro Quartz Company's ledge is situated about 500 feet above Downieville and the North Fork of the Yuba River. It yielded large returns in early days; the vein nearly "perished out" in the second level, and the mine lay dormant for several years. Two years ago some of the old members of the company re-organized it, and have driven a lower adit, in which they have recently found a promising vein about 5 feet, bearing S. 35° E., dipping easterly, but almost vertical, between well-defined walls of talcose slate. The mine now has three levels. The first one, several hundred feet below the summit of the croppings and 170 feet long, has been worked out to the surface. The second level, only 33 feet below the first, is 196 feet long, and between these two the vein has also been worked out in part. The present company has run, 102 feet below the second, the third or lower level, which is now 400 feet long. It is proposed to build a new mill, to be driven by water-power, below the mine on the Yuba River.

The Monte Cristo Company's ledge, formerly the Johnson ledge, which had lain neglected for years, was this year purchased by San Francisco capitalists, who are now driving a lower tunnel 323 feet long to tap the ledge 163 feet below the upper level, which will give them backs or reserves of 175 to 190 feet. Their location is 4,000 feet long, and has an average course of nearly north and south, with a dip of 73° toward the east. This ledge is about 3 miles northwest from Downieville, and is 4,700 feet above sea-level, and about 2,400 feet above the North Yuba River. The former owners drove a cross-adit 100 feet below the highest point of the croppings, and at a distance of 26 feet the vein was cut 6 to 7 feet wide. They then sunk a winze 35 feet deep in the vein, which proved here to be 8 to 9 feet wide. The foot and hanging walls are talcose slate. The quartz in the bottom of the shaft contains much sulphurets and assays from $25 to $30 per ton. It is soft and friable, and hence the cost of the extraction of the ore is expected to be very small after the vein shall have been reached with the lower level. The company purposes then to build a mill, to be driven by water-power, obtained from Goodyear's Creek, a tributary of the North Yuba. The location of this mine, like that of the Oro ledge, is such that the ledges can be tapped by means of lower tunnels at small cost, dispensing with long tram-ways down the hill-side and avoiding the hoisting of the ore in the mine.

The Gold Bluff Mine is 1¼ miles northeast from Downieville, on the west side of the North Fork of the North Yuba River. The location comprises 4,400 feet in length on the vein. This mine was discovered and located in 1854, and received its name on acconnt of the richness of the croppings in free gold. The ore was at that time packed in sacks upon the backs of mules from the summit of the ledge down the steep mountain (which rises at an angle of about 35°) by means of a trail cut around the hill-side; at the mill, 1,000 feet below the croppings, it was worked in a small two-stamp battery, driven by water-power. After having crushed all the ore that could be found near the surface, the owners drove a cross-adit 150 feet below the croppings into the vein, which they found increasing in width. This induced them in 1856 to build a new mill of eight stamps, at a cost of over $20,000. It was provided with old-fashioned square stamps weighing 1,000 pounds. The work is said to have been profitable until 1859, when disagreements among the original owners and the outbreak of the great excitement over the silver-mines of Washoe caused its abandonment. A new company re-opened the mine in 1865, and realized in about two years $35,000, the product of their own labor, from the old works above the tunnel, ground which was supposed to be nearly worked out. In 1864 a new tunnel was run about 600 feet below the old one, on the slope of the mountain, for the purpose of striking the main chimney or pay-shoot at a vertical depth of 300 feet below the old adit-level. The vein was quite narrow when first struck, but soon widened out to from 6 and 8 feet in thickness, standing vertical between its casings and walls of talcose slate. Explorations have exposed a continuous pay-chimney of nearly 600 feet in length. Having satisfied themselves that they had reached an extensive vein of pay-ore, the company built a new mill of 12 stamps of 600 pounds weight, with a crushing-capacity of 16 to 18 tons in 24 hours, driven by water brought ¼ mile in a flume (28 inches by 16 inches, at a grade of ¾ inch in 12 feet) from the Middle Fork of the North Fork of the North Yuba.

After the completion of this mill, the company worked the mine successfully, employing twenty to twenty-five men, until August, 1871, taking out a gross amount of $150,000, besides the tailings, which were worked in two arrastras, immediately below the mill, the owners of the arrastras paying to the company for this privilege a royalty of 25 per cent. of the gross proceeds. The company declared, from January 1, 1870, to July 1, 1871, a dividend of $27,632, besides paying for machinery, driving tunnels, making roads, and outside improvements. The exhaustion in some degree of the stopes above the level, together with quarrels in the company and the want of adequate explorations in depth or otherwise, has caused another suspension of work.

Around the highest and most prominent peak of Sierra County, the Sierra Buttes, (8,800 feet high,) are clustered many quartz-mines, well known for their past and present yield. The leading one of these, and one of the foremost in the State, is the mine of Sierra Buttes Company, which for the fiscal year ending June, 1875, crushed 49,821 tons of ore, yielding $356,420—a little over $7.15 per ton, exclusive of their tailing-assay of $3.76 per ton.

I am indebted to Mr. William L. Oliver, of San Francisco, for the following summary of the operations of the mine and mills of this company for the year ending December 31, 1875. In the Sierra Buttes Mine, 240 men were employed, at $2.50 to $3 per day. The cost of mining per ton extracted was $3.48; number of tons extracted and worked 54,636; average yield about $7; total bullion product $393,089. The three mills of the company are run by water-power, and contain 86 stamps, 3 pans, and 4 concentrators. Weight of stamps, 750 pounds; drop, 8 inches, 80 times per minute; capacity, about 2 tons per stamp per 24 hours; cost of treatment per ton, 77½ cents. The ore contains 0.5 per cent. of sulphurets, which are amalgamated in pans after atmospheric oxidation.

The Independence Mine, belonging to an English company, is on the same lode, and immediately adjoins the three ledges of the Sierra Buttes, which unite near the boundary of these two companies, forming one large vein, 10 to 30 feet in thickness. The company owns 5,000 feet of the vein. It was worked as early as 1851. The first mill erected in 1856 burned down. The second mill was injured twice by avalanches. The third mill, built in 1861, had 24 stamps, and was carried away in March, 1868, by an avalanche, by which several persons were killed. In 1869 the fourth one was built, at a cost of about $25,000, out of reach of snow-slides from the Buttes Mountain, near the entrance of the drainage-adit. The mill contains 24 stamps of 700 pounds weight, and a speed of 70 drops per minute, and 8 inches drop; also 1 Knox pan, and 1 Hendy's concentrator for the purpose of working sulphurets, &c. It has a crushing-capacity of 1,200 tons per month. An additional mill of 20 stamps has lately been erected, which will crush 1,000 tons per month. The Independence vein is worked by a series of levels driven partly alongside and partly in the ledge. Of these there are 5, each one about 100 feet from the next level above. The third level is reached by a cross-adit driven nearly at right angles to the vein from the Independence ravine, a distance of about 600 feet. This is the lowest point of natural drainage which the mine at present possesses, and through this adit all the ore is taken in cars to the mills. The cars are loaded in the levels below the third, and are brought to the hoisting-shaft, where they are hoisted on a cage to the third level, on which the hoisting-works are situated, and are then run through the drainage-adit to the mills, where they are dumped. The batteries are supplied by automatic feeding-apparatus. This mine is kept free from water below the third level by powerful pumps. Adits may be driven from the Yuba, 2,000 feet vertically below the present drainage-level, or over 2,800 feet lower, measured on the dip of the vein, which is over 45° to the north. This mine is situated about 6,000 feet above sea-level. The machinery is driven partly by steam-power, costing $51,000, and partly by water, brought in a large flume seven or eight miles long from several lakes, the capacity of which has been greatly increased by large dams, at a cost of over $25,000. The walls of this mine are well defined. The quartz is very heavily impregnated with rich gold-bearing sulphurets. On account of the great difficulty encountered until recently in clearing the mine from water, the company could crush but little quartz during last year, but is now able to work both mills.

The Keystone Mine is situated about 13 miles easterly from Downieville and about 3 miles southerly from the Independence and Sierra Buttes Mine. It was worked in 1854 by Mexicans with arrastras. In 1860 a quartz-mill with 4 stamps was erected. In 1861 4 more stamps and again in 1866 4 additional stamps were added, making a total of 12 stamps, of about 550 pounds to 600 pounds weight, driven by a 20-horse-power engine. This mill was destroyed in March, 1868, by an avalanche. It was rebuilt the same year in a more sheltered place. In 1871 the company built a new mill below its lowest drain-tunnel, at a cost of $20,000, containing 20 stamps of 600 pounds weight, having a speed of 65 drops per minute and 9 inches fall each, using also 1 Varney pan and settler. This mill has a crushing capacity of about 30 tons in 24 hours, and an average yield of $20 per ton, at a cost of $5 to $8. The machinery is driven by a 50-horse-power steam-engine. The mine is about 6,000 feet above sea-level and 2,000 feet above the Yuba River. The present lower drain-tunnel, began in 1866, was finished in 1870, is about 700 feet below the summit of the croppings and over 1,900 feet long. From this the quartz is transported in cars to the mill, after having been hoisted from the works by a 30-horse-power engine. The location is 3,000 feet in length, with a course of N. 54° 21′ E. true meridian, containing 49.97 acres of land, including the mill-site. It dips about 87° to the south, and consists of 3 pay shoots or chimneys as far as explored, 2½ to 6 feet in width. The first pay shoot is 150 feet, the second 250 feet, and the third 380 feet in length along the vein. The walls are well defined and are a talcose black slate rock. The quartz is a ribbon-rock, and contains rich gold-bearing sulphurets and galena. The gold is fine, free, and evenly distributed through the pay chimneys. This company employs, when the mill is running, about 50 men.

The Phœnix Quartz Mine is situated about 6,000 feet above sea-level, on the eastern slope of the Sierra Buttes Mountain, about one and one-half miles easterly from the Sierra Buttes Mine. The lode courses N. 65° 43′ E., with an average dip of about 78° to the north-northwest. It is incased in well-defined walls of metamorphic slate, with a few inches of gouge between the walls and quartz. The quartz is of white, yellow, and reddish color, containing free gold and rich gold-bearing sulphurets. The company has sunk on the foot-wall a 225-foot double shaft, through which hoisting is done in large buckets by horse-power and a whim. The quartz was in early days conveyed in sacks on mules down the steep hill-side to the company's mill at the river, at a cost of $5 per ton, until the company built a wagon-road three miles long, after which it was hauled to the mill. The company's location on the vein is 1,000 feet long, with an area, including the mill-site, of 19.40 acres. The mill contains four stamps, of 650 pounds weight, having a drop of 8 inches and 65 drops per minute, driven by a 12-foot diameter 3-foot breast overshot water-wheel; the water is brought in a flume 600 feet long, 15 by 13 inches in size, from the South Fork of the South Fork of the North Yuba River, crushing five tons in twenty-four hours, at a cost of $3 per ton for mining and milling and $2.50 for hauling to the mill. There has been about 1,000 tons crushed from this mine, yielding $20,000. This mine is favorably located to drive lower adits, from which the quartz could be cheaply transported in buckets on endless wire ropes or tram-ways, so arranged that the loaded buckets or cars coming down and emptying themselves would return the empty ones.

The Empire Quartz Mine is located on the southwestern slope (near the dividing ridge) of the Yuba and Feather Rivers, on the left bank of the east branch of the North Fork of the North Yuba River, about five miles northwest from the Sierra Buttes Mountain, at and near an elevated mountain-valley, known as Gold Valley. The lowest point, the mill-site, is 5,550 feet above sea-level, while the highest point of the outcrop of the ledge is 6,100 feet in altitude. The average course of the ledge is N. 74° 30′ E., and the length of the claim (as given in the application for patent) is 1,506 linear feet, inclosed in an area (including 5 acres for a mill-site) of 22.25 acres. The dip is from 38° to 55° to the south. The lode is incased in well-defined smooth walls of feldspathic rock on the foot-wall and slate on the hanging-wall. The quartz is mostly of a red and whitish color, and very heavily impregnated with different varieties of refractory sulphurets, predominating in many places over the quartz. This company has expended a great deal of money in extracting ore by sinking winzes and running tunnels following the ledge. The present lower tunnel is 374 feet long, and presents a quartz-vein of 8 to 12 feet in width. The ledge has been worked to a depth of over 200 feet. The mill consists of ten stamps, all machinery driven by an overshot water-wheel. The assorted refractory ore of sulphurets was conveyed to the chlorination-works. This company has made costly experiments in all kinds of gold-saving machinery and apparatus, but have failed to separate the gold from the refractory base metal.

The Four Hills Quartz Mine is located near the head of Little Bear Valley, near the Plumas and Sierra County line, close to the dividing summit of the Yuba and Feather Rivers; it is about midway between the Sierra Buttes and the Plumas Eureka Quartz Mines. The Buttes, Independence, Eureka, and Empire Mines are the most prominent croppings, and are only surpassed by the massive croppings of the Four Hills quartz-ledge. The first three mentioned are owned by English corporations. The Four Hills quartz-ledge is like all the beforementioned ledges, a gold-bearing true fissure-vein. It is well defined, from 5 to 80 feet wide on its croppings, with a dip of 45° to 85° to the southwest.

In close proximity west of this ledge we find a well-defined limestone belt and rich iron veins. This limestone belt apparently runs through California, and along the eastern side of it, within a short distance, runs the above referred to system of quartz-veins, traced by a succession of massive croppings for more than seventy miles, crossing creeks, rivers, and high ridges. About parallel to the limestone belt in this county iron deposits of the best quality occur, bounded on the east by granite and west by slates.

The Four Hills quartz-ledge is incased in well-defined smooth walls of feldspathic granite and sandstone on the foot-wall and metamorphic slate on the hanging-wall. The quartz is of a red and white color, and some a ribbon-rock, heavily impregnated with rich sulphurets and galenas. The red quartz resembles that of the rose ledge of the Sierra Buttes Mine, while the white quartz has the appearance of the Cliff and Ariel ledges of the Buttes Mine. They also appear to be similarly located, the rose-colored rock to the east, the Ariel in the middle, and the Cliff to the west, being here all in one body, while in the buttes they form three distinct different ledges 50 to 100 feet apart and each having well-defined walls. This company has expended a great deal of money in developing their mine, in extracting ore by sinking many wide winzes, opening out the mine from the surface or croppings in a continuous line for about 1,000 feet in length.

They have also run tunnels through hard granite for the purpose of tapping the ledge lower. The lower tunnel started from a small valley on the head of the middle branch of the North Fork of the North Yuba River, and is now 400 feet long, the face being only about 50 feet from the ledge, and will tap the ledge over 200 feet below the croppings. The higher tunnel, near the dividing gap of the middle and east branches of the North Fork of the North Yuba River, is also 400 feet long, and is nearly all run in quartz-rock, on which the company are at present working. The quartz is conveyed on wagons down a steep hill to the mill. The mill contains four stamps, and is driven by a Fredenbass water-wheel under a 225-foot pressure. The first crushing was in 1865. The winters at this mine are quite severe, on account of its great altitude, the highest point of the croppings being 6,870 feet above sea-level. The snow lies often from 10 to 40 feet deep at the company's boarding-house near the mouth of the lower tunnel. This company has 2,615.95 linear feet of the ledge, containing 28.92 acres of area.

PLUMAS COUNTY.

The following account of this county has been contributed by J. A. Edman, of Mumford's Hill. I consider it an extremely valuable discussion, and am very grateful to Mr. Edman for the pains he has taken to add so important a contribution to this report.

From the beginning of the geological survey of California in 1860 to its discontinuance in 1873, though a mass of valuable material was collected in illustration of the geology of the State, but few publications bearing on practical geology and mining have reached the public. The surveys and observations on the ancient auriferous gravel deposits in the central part of the State are still inaccessible to the general reader, and may remain so for some time, until a more far-seeing spirit shall animate our legislators. A comparatively small portion of the gold-mining region of the Sierra Nevada has come within the observations of the members of the geological survey, the field of labor being so immense and the aims of the survey so exhaustive.

Some rapid reconnaissances were made by Professor Whitney and his assistants during the years 1861–'63–'65 of the most prominent points of Plumas County, chiefly on the eastern side of the county, where the important discovery of fossils belonging to the Jurassic period was made, near Taylorsville, all of which is embodied in the few pages devoted to Plumas County found in the first volume of the Geological Survey.

Since that time the extension of the public surveys has done much to increase our knowledge of the topography of the county, and individual explorations and researches, together with the operations of miners, have thrown new light on its geology and mining resources. Although lacking the elaborate accuracy and high authority of the State survey, these may serve a practical purpose in directing attention to a region which offers a rich field alike for the studies of the geologist and for the labors of the miner.

The purpose of this article is to illustrate the geognosy of the south-western portion of Plumas County, from original surveys and explorations made by the writer, and from the most reliable observations obtainable from other sources. An indispensable aid to the comprehension of these will be found in the map designed to accompany this description, to which the reader is referred.

This map has been constructed on the basis of the map made for the county by Arthur W. Keddie, esq., and completed in 1874, a work commendable for its accuracy and finish in all that relates to the general topography of the county. To this gentleman the writer is under obligations for valuable assistance and information. On the geological map herewith given, the underlying rock-formations have been indicated by distinctive markings, and the gravel and volcanic deposits by colors, the same color generally being used for those deposits which appear to belong to a distinctive river-system or to have a common origin.* To avoid needless intricacy, mountain chains and ridges are not indicated, the highest peaks alone being shown.

The region under consideration forms that part of Plumas County embraced between the North Fork of Feather River, with its tributary, the East Branch, on the north and northwest, and the Middle Fork on the south and southeast, extending westerly to the county line and eastward to a point four miles east of Quincy. Within this territory the rock-formations most closely observed by the writter and herein most fully described are situated within and adjoining township 24 north, range 8 east. This township includes within its limits the eastern edge of the great mountain range which here culminates in Spanish Peak, one of the points marking, with Pilot Peak to the southeast and Lassin's Peak to the northwest, the axis of the Sierra Nevada, which after maintaining in the south the character of a high continuous chain here breaks into many irregular ridges, inclosing within their rocky barriers extensive and fertile mountain valleys.

The physical character of the region between the North and Middle Forks of Feather River is that of a broad mountain range rising generally above an altitude of 5,500 feet, its highest point being reached at Spanish Peak, 6,500 feet high. Its general trend is from southwest to northeast; cut by small streams flowing in their lower courses through deep cañons into the North or Middle Fork, respectively, it maintains its character of a continuous range until near the eastern line of township 24 north, range 8 east, where the northern portion, after forming the escarpments of which Spanish Peak is the most easterly, somewhat abruptly sinks into a low ridge separating the East Branch from its main affluent, Spanish Creek, while a southern branch, after suffering a slight depression, continues eastwardly between Spanish Creek and Middle Fork, and rising in Claremont Hill to an elevation nearly equal to Spanish Peak, subsides into lower ridges.

---

*It being impracticable to reproduce these colors in engraving, I must attempt to convey the information (less graphically) by simply saying that on the original map, the spaces numbered 2, 3, 4, 5, 6, 7, 7a, 7b, 8, and 8b are colored alike, and that the same is the case with the spaces *a* and *b*; the spaces 9, 10, and 11; the spaces 12 and 13; the spaces 14, 15, 16, 17, and 18; the spaces 19 and 20; the spaces 23, 24, 25, and 26; and the spaces 27, 28, 29, and 30. Where the spaces are far apart, it is possible that the similarity of coloring may not have been intended as significant.—R. W. R.

The highest points within the region mentioned are generally found to consist of syenite, granite, and syenitic granite, which mostly form broad and rounded ranges with a gentle slope to the south, but presenting abrupt and precipitous slopes to the east and northeast where the slates adjoin them. This condition is caused not only by the upheaval of the granite masses, which appears to have taken place within a comparatively recent period, but also by the wearing away of the softer slates, and not least by glacial action of which indications are found on the eastern and northeastern slopes of Spanish Peak, where large basins now occupied by small lakes are excavated near the junction of the syenite with the slate, and where large fragments of syenite, mostly angular and in unstratified heaps, are found in and near the beds of the streams rising on the flanks of the mountain.

At the foot of Spanish Peak, inclosed by the mountain ranges above described, is a basin of irregularly circular outline and nearly three miles in diameter, forming two valleys, through which flow Spanish Creek and Meadow Valley Creek, and having its present outlet through the gorge cut by Lower Spanish Creek, which, after leaving this basin, pursues a sinuous course of four miles, and then enters the yet larger basin of American Valley, situated at an altitude of 3,400 feet. The Meadow Valley basin will be further described in treating of the geological formations in their order. Further to the west, and near the point where the main range branches off, are found two larger elevated valleys, namely, Buck's and Haskell's Valleys, situated at an altitude of nearly 5,000 feet and parallel in general direction; the former occupying a deep depression in the syenite 5 miles long by from one-half to one mile in width; the latter, situated at the junction of the syenite with the slates, of nearly the same length but somewhat narrower. In both these valleys the bed-rock has but a shallow covering of very recent gravel-beds, and no signs remain of glacial action. It is to be noted that both these valleys open to the south and southwest. Following the main ridge toward the Buckeye house, where the county line crosses it, we find the streams emptying to the North Fork generally flowing with steep descent through narrow and deep gorges, while the tributaries of the Middle Fork, such as the streams of the Gravel Range and Granite Basin, in their upper courses ramify in every direction between low and rounded ridges, and excavate deep cañons first when they approach the gorge of the Middle Fork.

After this general view of the physical geography of this section, we may next consider its geological features, commencing in the review of its rock-formations at the boundary-line between Plumas and Butte Counties and proceeding eastward. As most of the region in question has been little explored and but recently surveyed, the information as to its geology is vague and uncertain, so that but few data can be given as to the position and extent of its formations, and these relate principally to the vicinity of the wagon-road from Buckeye to Quincy, which here follows the summit of the ridge.

The underlying bed-rock near the Buckeye house is a compact granite and syenitic granite, here overlain by a gravel-deposit (No. 1) of limited extent and thickness, consisting mostly of well-worn pebbles of quartz. A sheet of basaltic rock, at this point 30 to 40 feet in thickness, rests on this gravel, forming for more than a mile the flat summit of the ridge, here called Walker's Plain. The basalt is black and compact, exhibiting at some points an irregular columnar structure.

The mass of granite forms the northern point of a great body of the same rock which extends for many miles to the south and southwest into Butte County.

After passing the basalt at Walker's Plain, the ridge is covered by a loose deposit of volcanic material, consisting of the usual tufaceous beds intermixed with blocks of basalt and trachytic rocks, until near Palmetto the bed-rock crops out, here consisting mainly of talcose slates. Continuing in a northeasterly direction, the talcose slates change into a massive talcose rock of fibrous structure, which seems eminently fitted for furnace-linings and fire-proof material, and is used as such to a limited extent. The top of the range, which at a point about four miles east of Palmetto reaches its greatest altitude (5,900 feet) at Frenchman's Hill, is still composed of slates of varying composition, chiefly talcose, until on the slope of Frenchman's Hill toward Little Grizzly Creek true serpentine is observed for some distance. Proceeding southward we find the edge of a body of granite included within Granite Basin, where this rock, generally soft and deeply decomposed, has been formed into broad, low, and rounded ridges, with only occasional outcrops of massive rounded masses. It covers an area of about six square miles, and does not at any point form any high or prominent peak. Gold-bearing quartz-ledges have been found in this formation, among which the Spark's ledge was worked with profit for over two years.

Descending Frenchman's Hill and going eastward we cross Grizzly Creek and enter the western arm of Haskell's Valley, where a branch of Grizzly Creek takes its rise, flowing westward; while in the same valley, separated only by a slight swell of the ground, rises a branch of Buck's Creek, flowing northeasterly. In the extreme western end of the valley, the vast accumulations of loose gravel with angular and slightly worn blocks of a variety of greenstone found *in situ* close by, all of which deposits are devoid of any stratification, seem to indicate the existence of glacial action at a recent period, and before the present gorge of Upper Grizzly Creek was formed. The high and precipitous rock wall bounding the southern side of the valley and consisting of a variety of serpentine, impresses the beholder with a belief in the recent upheaval of the mountain, or a corresponding sinking of this part of the valley. Some isolated patches of basalt, conical in form, are found on the low hills north of the valley.

Following the road on an easterly course we find a magnesian rock, related to serpentine, but possessing a light-gray to reddish-gray color, and of fibrous structure, breaking in large irregular blocks, roughly weathered on the surface, and containing interspersed through its mass many small brownish-black cubical crystals of peroxide of iron.* This rock underlies the greater part of the valley and forms the high ridge on the south, continuing easterly nearly three miles to the head of Willow Creek, where it comes to a point, meeting clay slates on both sides. One mile southeast of Buck's Ranch, and near the gap through which the main stream of Haskell's Valley finds an outlet to Buck's Valley, we reach the southern limit of the great syenitic mass, which extends unbroken northeasterly to Spanish Peak, distant six miles, and to the northwest crosses the North Fork, beyond which it continues for a great distance, forming many of the most prominent mountains near the boundary-line between Butte and Plumas.

Tracing the edge of the syenite from the point above mentioned, its trend is at first nearly easterly through the middle of the eastern arm

---

* Doubtless pseudomorphs after pyrite, and produced by its oxidation.—R. W. R.

of Haskell's Valley; thence it gradually curves to the north, following a northeast course at the divide between Haskell's Valley and the west branches of Bear Creek, sweeping around which it crosses the divide between Bear Creek and upper Big Creek with a northeasterly course, and after entering township 24 north, range 8 east, one mile east of its southwest corner, turns still more, and thence to near Spanish Peak follows a course of north 12° west.

Adjoining the syenite are found near Haskell's Valley quartzites and hard blue clay-slates; at the head of Big Creek a gradual change to hornblende schist, next to mica slate, containing much quartz, which graduates into a hard, nearly black siliceous clay-slate.

Following the edge of the syenite into township 24 north, range 8 east, it is found on the flank of the mountain, which here towers nearly two thousand feet above the Meadow Valley Basin, its upper slope steep and with slightly broken surface, at its foot several lower ridges projecting into the valley. The comb of the mountain, slightly rising, forms Spanish Peak, which seen from any point of the country around it from the southeast to the north-northeast, forms a prominent landmark. A chain of peaks but slightly lower marks the edge of the syenite as it sweeps northwesterly toward the North Fork. The present channel of the East Branch, at Rich Bar, flows nearly four thousand feet below the crest of the mountain at a point between Silver Lake and Mill Creek, which fact would point to the immense denudation effected by that stream (the East Branch) if other causes have not aided to bring about the great difference of level. During late years some great slides from the mountain-side have found their way to the river along the bed of Mill Creek.

Near the head of Eagle Gulch the change from syenite to slates is sudden and without gradation, siliceous clay-slates abutting thereon. The same condition holds good along the eastern flank of the mountain, where slates of the same character adjoin the platonic rocks. The stroke of the slates varies from north 25° west, south 25° east, to north 45° west, south 45° east, of which north 36° west may be taken as the average for the western part of the township. With this stroke they join the syenite at the head of Eagle Gulch, meeting its edge at an angle of 24 degrees, but farther northward they appear deflected to the north and meet the syenite at a less angle, finally becoming parallel near Spanish Peak. The same condition is observable to the south, where the general stroke of the slates is changed near the contact with the syenite.

Near the head of Big Creek the main mass of syenite sends out an arm to the east-southeast, into the Bear Creek Basin. This body, which to a great extent is covered by a volcanic deposit, (No. 10,) appears to be about five miles in length by nearly two miles wide.

The plutonic rocks above mentioned vary considerably in composition and somewhat in structure, being fine-grained syenites chiefly near the eastern edge of the group, occasionally, by an admixture of dark mica, becoming syenitic granites, and toward the western limits showing more fully the composition of granite. Through the parallel arrangements of the hornblende crystals a slight gneissoid structure is often observable. But the most striking feature in the structure of the rocks of this group, particularly in its eastern portion, is their tendency to separate after parallel and nearly vertical planes into large slabs from a few inches to several feet in thickness, which shows in marked manner on the ridges to the north of Buck's Valley, and also on the eastern and northeastern flanks of the Spanish Peak Range. This appearance often causes the syenite to resemble a stratified rock, but we find the planes of separation generally coinciding with the outer edge of the formation and consequently always changing. The planes of separation are rough and uneven, while nearly horizontal joints originate straight and smooth surfaces. At some points, mainly on the northeastern face of Spanish Peak, are found veins and dikes of later plutonic and trappean rocks.

Leaving the syenitic rocks near the head of Eagle Gulch and proceeding northeast, at nearly a right angle to the general trend of the strata, we descend to the basin of Meadow Valley over the upturned edges of formations here free from overlying deposits, and observe now successive belts of auriferous metamorphic rocks, which, in their grand simplicity of position and great extent, well deserve the study of the geologist and the miner.

The first group consists of slates and schists in the following order, (along the line A B C on the map:)

1st. Hard dark-blue clay-slates, alternating with quartzose slates, the former often carrying crystals and impregnations of iron-pyrites; these reach a width of over 3,000 feet.

2d. Green chloritic slates, decomposing into a soft, yellow rock.

3d. Grayish talcose clay-slate, with minute crystals of magnetic iron, and accompanied by a vein of magnetic iron, hematite, and iron-glance, associated with quartz.

4th. Greenish clay-slate. The aggregate width of the last three strata is near 1,000 feet.

Between the last stratum and adjacent talcose slates is found a remarkable ledge, the Diadem, (marked D L on the map,) here 50 feet in average width, noticeable as being in all probability the mother-ledge from which has been derived the principal gold-bearing deposits of the vicinity. The vein-stone of this ledge is magnesian limestone, penetrated by a network of small quartz-veins and filled with lumps of talcose slate rich in crystals of oxide of iron. Through this mass course larger veins of quartz, often swelling to large masses; it is frequently divided by bands or lenticular masses of an altered talcose slate, impregnated by decomposed sulphurets. Near the walls are often found alternating layers of clay and broken quartz and a ferruginous quartz-conglomerate. The magnesian limestone is decomposed to a great depth, forming a soft porous mass of brick-red earth, full of quartz and slate fragments, with rounded bowlders of unaltered vein-stone reposing therein. Massive and crystallized pyrites and the resulting oxides of iron are here abundant. The stroke of the ledge at Mumford's Hill is, with the adjoining slates, north 37° west, and its dip 60° to the northeast.

The explorations on this ledge, mainly at Mumford's Hill, have been carried to a depth of 100 feet, and have demonstrated the presence of fine gold through a large portion of the ledge, with occasional veins of high-grade ore, while the character of the ledge and the frequent occurrence of coarse gold in the gravel deposits situated on and adjoining it seem to point to the existence of rich pockets in the deposit.

The same vein-stone, with similar adjoining formations, can be traced northwesterly for over a mile; then, overland by gravel-beds and slides on the flanks of Spanish Peak, it appears again 4 miles distant, near Burton's Gulch. A ledge of the same character and near the extension of the same stratum occurs also at French Ravine, 1½ miles from Rich Bar, and distant 5 miles from Burton's Gulch.

Apart from the interest which its mineralogical character suggests, it seems strange that this ledge has attracted so little attention and received but few of the benefits which distant and inaccessible regions have derived from capital seeking profitable investment. All the creeks and gulches of both ancient and recent origin, cutting channels through this vein-formation, have been rich in coarse gold at and below the points of intersection; as, for instance, at Mumford's Hill, Eagle Gulch, Lead Point, Deadwood, and Burton's Gulch, as also Rich Bar, through French Ravine, appears to have been fed from the same source. In the palmy days of surface-mining, from the many prosperous camps then existing at those localities, large amounts of gold went out to the channels of commerce, while at this day the mines of this vicinity yield no inconsiderable returns.

Leaving the talcose slates near the Diadem Ledge and continuing our course to the northeast, (along the line A B C on the map,) we pass for 1,000 feet over quartz-schists, alternating with clay-slates, when we find them rather abruptly changing to a rock which may be classed with the greenstones. The slates described may be called the first slate group, have here a general strike of from north 25° to north 40° west, and a dip to the northeast of from 60° to 70°.

Their lateral extent may be estimated at 5,000 feet. In their longitudinal extension they undergo many changes in mineral character, chiefly owing to the intrusion of plutonic rocks. To the south quartzites and siliceous slates represent most of the strata of this group. Quartz-veins are abundant, but with the exception of the Diadem ledge have not been proved gold-bearing. Peroxide of manganese is found in large quantities, and smaller bodies of iron-ores occur in some localities. Native copper, associated with silicate of manganese, occurs near Eagle Gulch. The gold averages 950 thousandths in fineness, at one locality, Taylor's Gulch, reaching .970 fine. At one point only a small body of basalt is found, (near No. 11,) protruding through the edge of the slate, and altering to some extent the contiguous rock. With the exception of the slates nearest to the syenite, the strata of this group are but slightly metamorphosed and seldom bear crystalline structure. Next in the series, and adjoining the slates on the northeast, appears a great belt of homogeneous rock nearly 5,000 feet wide, which may be classed as greenstone or the diabase of some authors. This is light-blue, gray to grayish green, sometimes dark-green rock, hard and tough; generally massive; compact, to faintly crystalline, becoming occasionally porphyritic or amygdaloidal in structure. Although having some characters in common with the volcanic rocks, yet from its position and general appearance this must be classed with the metamorphic strata. By far the larger portion of this greenstone has been decomposed into a yellow or greenish-yellow rock, easily broken with the pick. This change has extended to a great depth, so that it is only in and near the beds of deeply eroded streams that we find the rock jutting out in hard and unaltered masses. The hills composed of this rock consequently are lower, more rounded, and less precipitous than those of the slate formation adjoining, and have a deeper, reddish, often clayey soil. A faint slaty structure is occasionally observable toward the edges of this belt. Quartz-veins found here are generally narrow, short, and irregular, and, with few unimportant exceptions, have not been found gold-bearing. Yet resting on this rock we find many of the richest surface-deposits, as the streams rising in the syenite or in the slates and cutting deep and narrow channels through the latter rocks, here expand into wider beds, forming flats and bars. To the southeast this belt is continuous to the Middle Fork and beyond; also to the northwest, where it, like the strata parallel with it, seems contracted laterally.

The greenstone gradually passing into slate is succeeded by a group of slaty rocks about 2,000 feet in width, consisting, in their order, of soft clay-slates, with chloritic and talcose slates, which finally, taking up quartz, appear as a narrow belt of mica-schist. These imperceptibly change to hornblende-schists, which finally give place to a narrow belt of syenitic gneiss at the junction of this group with the great belt of serpentine. This serpentine belt, underlying the Meadow Valley Basin, forms the largest continuous mass of metamorphic rock in this region, extending its course southeasterly with uncontracted dimensions beyond the Middle Fork, and appearing near the Saw-Pit Flats, not far distant from Pilot Peak, while to the northeast, after crossing the East Branch, it holds its course to the North Fork and beyond without decrease in width.

The last-mentioned group of slates is found at some points to the north, nearly east of Spanish Peak, partly of a crystalline appearance, somewhat resembling protogene granite in structure and composition; but this is only within a limited area.

If we continue on the same course at right angles to the general direction of the strata, we find the serpentine, the edge of which is just met a little to the west of Meadow Valley, overlaid by great volcanic and alluvial deposits, until beyond Spanish Ranch it appears in the foot-hills of that range, where its eastern edge is met, thus showing here a width of three miles. Through its greatest extent within this region it is covered by the older deposits of gravel, and it appears mainly in and near the beds of Spanish Creek, Lower Meadow Valley, and Rock Creek, where it generally forms a massive rock of a dark gray to dirty green color, separating into irregular large blocks, occasionally into flat slabs. When found on the slopes of hills it is often decomposed into a yellowish gray, often very tenacious clay, intermingled with blocks of hard rock, which on the surface are slightly rounded, roughly weathered, and of a yellow to dark-red color. The resulting soil also has a brick-red color.

Few opportunities are presented of observing deep sections through this rock, except as it is cut by the channel of the East Branch, where native copper has occasionally been found in lumps of some size. Chromic iron often occurs in the surface-gravel, as at Green Flat; platinum in small grains occurs sparingly in several localities on Upper Spanish Creek and on Silver Creek.

The eastern edge of the serpentine appears parallel with the western and with the general trend of the strata further west. East of the serpentine, near the eastern line of the township, we again meet a group of slates, mainly thinly laminated clay-slates, occupying a belt nearly 4,000 feet wide. These are again succeeded by a massive rock of the greenstone family, the extent of which is undetermined. This greenstone appears mostly at the bottom and sides of the gorge cut by Spanish Creek, and is scarcely traceable at a higher elevation. Large masses and ledges of limestone occur in the slates.

Next in order we meet talcose clay-slates, which, gradually taking up grains of quartz, change into a metamorphic arenaceous schist, which is found fully developed in the hills southwest of Quincy. This sandstone or quartzite schist appears nearly 1½ miles wide at this point, (on the line A B C,) but to the north and south it narrows gradually by the encroachment of the adjoining slates.

The strata beyond Quincy and underlying American Valley are chiefly clay-slates, often siliceous, for nearly four miles, where a great belt of trap-rock is met with. This region is not within the scope of the present article.

The slate groups east of the serpentine coincide in their strike with the slates on the west thereof; their dip is generally to the northeast at a somewhat greater angle, being found near Quincy at some points almost vertical. Occupying a belt nearly 4 miles wide, they are cut diagonally by the channel of Lower Spanish Creek, and except in its vicinity are in great part covéred by deep gravel-beds, as at Gopher, Badger, and Hungarian Hills, and southerly at Slate Creek and Claremont Hill, localities to be described in the following pages.

After this general review of the rock-formations proper, both igneous and metamorphic, within the region described, the vast gravel-beds and associated volcanic deposits, so frequent within the eastern part of the area comprised between the North and Middle Forks of Feather River, will next claim our attention. A study of these, of the remains of ancient and now obliterated river-channels, and of the evidences of extraordinary volcanic activity, not only furnishes testimony of great geological changes, but is intimately connected with the successful explorations of deep mines and the judicious application of the hydraulic system of mining, now chiefly directed to the deep gravel-beds. The volcanic deposits referred to in the sequel, when not otherwise particularly described, consist of unstratified deposits of volcanic origin, composed chiefly of rough fragments of trap-rocks, mostly trachytes, inclosed in ash-gray volcanic sand or dust, often if not always cemented into a true agglomerate of varying hardness; carrying occasionally a few water-worn rocks, and generally associated with beds of tufa and soft sandstones. They generally form the surface-deposits, filling the upper portions of the ancient river-channels, and even extending over former ridges. Although varying much in color, hardness, and depth, they present a striking similarity of composition, and are found over a vast area in Middle and Northern California. They are frequently but erroneously called "lavas" by the miners.

In examining these deposits we begin at the southwest and proceed eastward, in the manner previously adopted while studying the underlying strata. With the exception of the gravel near Buckeye House, already described, with its basaltic cap-rock, but few and small patches of gravel are found near the summit of the range. Near the heads of Cold Water and Scotchman's Creeks thin beds of gravel occur in many places within the area of Gravel Range indicated on the map. The rocks therein are chiefly composed of rounded quartz-pebbles found in a red sandy soil, containing fine gold through its mass. This gravel seems related to the deposit at Buckeye. To the east of this, on the southern point of the ridge between Willow Creek and Little Bear Creek, at an elevation but little inferior to that of the main divide, we find at Mount Ararat considerable beds both of aqueous and igneous origin, (No. 2.) The lower beds, consisting of ferruginous gravel, often approaching conglomerates in hardness, are covered by clays and tufas, the whole overlain by a sheet of basalt of considerable thickness, extending along the ridge nearly two miles. Considerable prospecting by tunnels has been done in the gravel, but the difficulty of extracting the gold by washing has hitherto prevented work on a more extended scale.

Bear Creek deposit.—It is in approaching the point where the main range divides that we first meet deposits of great depth and extent, of which those situated on the upper branches of Bear Creek (No. 10) cover an area 5 miles long by 2 miles wide. Occupying the top and southern slope of the south branch of the main range, they show but few beds of true river gravel, as the present streams cut but shallow channels through them. The largest masses of free gravel occur in the divide between the middle branches of Bear Creek and Big Creek, (No. 9,) immediately under the steep escarpments of the edge of the syenitic rocks. Here, as everywhere else when found in the same position, they are free from any capping of volcanic material, and consist of gravel-beds, with strata of clay and sandy clay. The creeks and gulches in this vicinity have furnished good placer-diggings. The water-worn rocks found here are of many varieties, chiefly resembling the rocks *in situ* to the south of Middle Fork. With this exception (No. 9) the great Bear Creek deposit consists of volcanic material—tufas and agglomerates—often carrying immense blocks of trachytes on the surface. As but few explorations have been made here, its depth and probable value cannot be determined. At No. 11 an isolated patch is seen, containing some auriferous gravel. Small bodies of basalt rise to the surface at some points.

A small body of gravel, overlaid by volcanic agglomerates, is found on the syenitic ridge between Haskell's and Buck's Valleys, (at No. 3,) and forms apparently the connecting-link between the beds near the Middle Fork (including Mount Ararat) and the great channel of the Spanish Peak Range.

Spanish Peak deposit.—The most elevated of the ancient channels is found in the Spanish Peak deposits, (No. 4,) which mainly consist of alternating beds of gravel and pipe-clay, filling the bottom of a rather narrow channel, and covered by deep beds of volcanic tufas and agglomerates. It forms the eastern comb of the Spanish Peak Range. Its southern portion is on a well-defined channel, and all of it on syenitic bed-rock. Its general direction is from south to north, then deflecting to the northwest; and it covers an area of from 1,000 to 4,000 feet in width, by about four miles in length. That the course of the ancient river was in the above direction is evidenced by the position and lithological character of the gravel-beds.

But few explorations have been made here and these were chiefly confined to the southern end of the deposit, where it attains a depth of 150 feet, the mass of which is volcanic material. Here a distinct channel is found, filled with strata of clay rich in the remains of vegetable life, chiefly the imprints of leaves. The gravel-beds, which are but slightly auriferous, are here 25 feet thick, lie almost horizontal, rest upon the pipe-clay, and are overlain by the tufas and agglomerates. At a point close to Spanish Peak quartz-gravel appears at the surface over a limited area, the rest of the deposit consisting of the volcanic beds. The well-worn rocks in the gravel are of many varieties, partly hard syenites, but chiefly kinds not found in place within the region adjoining, among which hard jaspery rocks and siliceous conglomerates are prominent, thus pointing to a distant, probably southern, origin. A well-defined rim-rock appears on the eastern side of this deposit, descending precipitously toward Gold and Silver Lakes, above which the mountain towers in a precipice 400 feet high. These lakelets are deep, irregular basins, situated mainly on the syenite; their waters have for many years been used for mining purposes, and form now the chief reservoirs of the ditches of the Plumas Mining and Water Company, which convey their waters to an extensive section of gravel-mines, at present chiefly worked at Gopher and Badger Hills, (Nos. 15 and 16.)

To the north, smaller bodies belonging to the same deposit occur at Mountain House (No. 5) and Fale's Hill, (No. 6,) at which points good placer and hydraulic mines have long been worked. The Fale's Hill gravel is free from volcanic capping, has been nearly worked out, and has paid well. Small bodies of black basalt, but a few hundred feet in extent, are encountered at the southern end of deposit No. 4, near the western rim, and at the edge of No. 3. On the face of the precipice, near Gold Lake, several dikes of trap-rock intersect the syenite nearly vertically. Traces of copper-ores and gold-bearing quartz have also been found near this point.

Mumford's Hill and Scad Point.—On the belt of argillaceous and talcose slates adjoining the eastern edge of the syenite, and on the edge of the greenstone belt, occur smaller patches of gravel at Mumford's Hill (No. 8) and Scad Point, (No. 7,) the only remains of deposits made by streams which appear to have flowed from the southeast and to have emptied into the Spanish Peak channel, although now situated nearly 1,000 feet below the latter. The gravel in these is largely composed of greenstone and fragments of slate and quartz; on Scad Point, of rounded bowlders of trachyte also. The Mumford's Hill deposit crosses and reposes for some distance on the great mother ledge of this vicinity, the Diadem ledge, which has been described above (on page 114,) and the coarse gold contained therein has been derived in great part from that ledge. Some of the richest placer-diggings of Plumas County (now nearly exhausted) existed in this immediate vicinity, on Taylor's Gulch, Eagle Gulch, and Deadwood, all of which streams have cut their channels through the gravel-deposits last mentioned and also through the Diadem Ledge. Hydraulic mining is yet carried on at Mumford's Hill and Scad Point on a larger scale than formerly, and with profitable result.

The deposit at No. 8a belongs to the Mumford's Hill channel; those at 7a and 7b to the Scad Point deposit.

Gold Bluff deposits.—The gravel-beds adjoining northward at Gold Bluff (Nos. 27 and 28) and between Clear Creek and Silver Creek, (Nos. 29 and 30,) are of limited extent, but were once continuous, and, from the character of the rocks they carry, may be considered as the continuation of the Gopher Hill deposits. They consist of rather loose and small gravel with well-rounded rocks of quartz, slate, and considerable quartzite or metamorphic sandstone, the rocks being nearly identical with those of the Gopher Hill group, but smaller in size. These beds have been cut through and much broken, and in places covered by vast slides from the edge of the syenite to the west. Glacial action also shows itself in well-defined terminal moraines on Clear Creek, remains of glaciers which at a time not very remote, descended from the mountain towering 2,000 feet above, and reached almost to the level of Meadow Valley.

But little mining has been done in these deposits, the broken nature of the ground being unfavorable for mining on a large scale. Some of the gulches paid well in former days. The only place at present worked with profit is at the edge of No. 30, at the head of Scale's Gulch, where the edge of the great Meadow Valley deposit meets the rim-rock of serpentine. The gold is here found partly on the serpentine bed-rock, partly on the cement or conglomerate resting on the serpentine.

Meadow Valley Basin.—Different in character as well as in extent, and forming the most interesting group of deep deposits, are the gravel, conglomerate, and tufa beds of the Meadow Valley Basin, (No. 12,) so named here from one of the valleys contained therein. These deposits being too complicated and diversified to be described in detail, only their most prominent characteristics can be here stated, as only the general outlines of the group have been shown on the map. Beginning at the southeast corner of township 24 north, range 8 east, these deposits extend northward for over six miles into the next township, with an average breadth of more than two miles, within which area bed-rock is not visible except for some distance on upper Spanish Creek. Resting mainly on the serpentine, they occupy a basin irregular in outline, surrounded by a well-defined rim-rock sloping inward from each side, and probably attain their greatest depth midway between Meadow Valley and Spanish ranch. To the east this rim-rock has been cut to slight depth by Spanish and Meadow Valley Creeks, but the lowest levels attained by these streams do not bring to view more than the upper beds of the central basin. The only sections exposed are therefore found on Upper Spanish Creek, and to the south on the upper course of the tributaries of Meadow Valley Creek.

The formations vary much in character in different portions of the basin. The northern half may be described as composed of deep beds of ferruginous conglomerates of different degrees of hardness, forming the lowest beds, on which rest alternating strata of ferruginous clays and gravels. The conglomerates (agglomerates in part) are largely made up of trap-rocks, trachytes and porphyries predominating, which often are found therein in large blocks, rounded but not very smoothly worn. No stratification is visible in the beds exposed, and but little of the quartz, slate or other materials forming the surface-deposits. The cementing material is chiefly oxide of iron, derived from the decomposition of pyrites, which is found in abundance at some depth; near the serpentine, lime occasionally forms the cementing material. As far as explored, the above conglomerate rests on the bed-rock, and are not auriferous, practically speaking, as no gravel-deposits have been found in or under them. The recent channels of the streams which have eroded these beds are generally gold-bearing, and some have furnished rich diggings, as at Mountain House, Middle Spanish Creek, and Silver Creek, where the gold is found deposited immediately on the conglomerates. Shallow beds of gravel occur at many points on the elevated edges of the basin, seemingly derived from the recent streams emptying into it, and these beds are generally-gold bearing, the surface-gravel proving most productive.

Near the center of the basin, between Spanish and Meadow Valley Creeks, a large area of level ground, called Grub Flats, fully 1,500 acres in extent, contains on its surface shallow gravel-beds seldom exceeding six feet in depth, and all more or less gold-bearing. Want of proper grade to carry off the tailings has alone prevented the extensive working of these deposits, which here rest on the above-mentioned conglomerates, on barren pebbly gravel, or on thin beds of red clay.

On the flats near Meadow Valley the surface-gravel rests on tufa-beds of undoubted volcanic origin, being of an ashy-gray color and containing much pumice. These characteristics generally pertain to the deposits of that part of the basin, south of Meadow Valley Creek, where they are mainly made up of finely-divided material, contrasting greatly, both in color and structure, with the coarse fragments of trap-rocks composing the bulk of the deposits of the northern portion. With the exception of a few points to the south of Meadow Valley, but little mining has been carried on in this part of the basin. The general features of the northern basin distinguish the beds near Mountain House, but in this neighborhood the older cement formation (conglomerates in miner's parlance) is often overlain by more recent gravel-beds, which may be referred to the gravels of the Waponseh group, to be hereafter described. At two points, (*a* and *b*,) at Bear Hill and below Mountain House, occur, about two miles apart, deep beds of sandy gravel composed almost entirely of well-worn pebbles and small rocks of white and grayish-blue quartz, which have been mined with profit. No other beds of similar gravel exist anywhere in this region, the nearest deposits of the same materials being found 20 miles distant, in southeastern Plumas County, near La Porte and Gibsonville.

The extreme northwestern arm of the basin approaches at Mountain House within a few hundred feet of an older deposit of volcanic beds (No. 5) occupying the flat top of the dividing ridge between Spanish Creek and the East Branch, and which, as before mentioned, is to be classed with the Spanish Peak deposits.

The highest gravel-beds of the Meadow Valley Basin occur on its rim at Mountain House, at an altitude of fully 600 feet above the surface of the deposit at its center, where it may be assumed to attain a depth of 150 feet. This fact seems to point out the great erosion which has taken place since the first formation of this deposit. A distinguishing feature of this basin is the presence of fine gold in the surface-gravels, especially in the thinner gravel-beds situated on the interior slopes of its rim-rock. The streams which now course through it have for ages been concentrating and reducing the lighter and less cohesive surface-beds, a fact which is attested by the abundance of heavy magnetic iron-sand and pebbles of iron-stone and other heavy rocks found at the surface.

The evidence of geology and present topography points to the probability that the Meadow Valley Basin contains a lacustrine deposit, principally made by a large stream entering the basin from the northwest, and having its outlet at some point to the southwest, near Upper Rock Creek or Slate Creek.

With the exception of a few shafts sunk near Grub Flat, and said to have reached the bed-rock at a depth of 100 feet, no deep explorations have been made in the center of the basin. Fragments of petrified woods, but as yet no other fossils, have been found.

Excepting the claims of the Golden Enterprise, lately opened near Spanish Ranch, no mining operation of magnitude is at present carried on within all this area. Rich placer-diggings existed for many years on Upper Spanish Creek and its tributaries, particularly between Silver Creek and Mountain House; but these are now almost exhausted. The more accessible flats promise the miner a fair profit, if properly opened and worked with the assistance of moderate capital.

The Slate Creek deposits, (No. 13,) although separated by the channel of Rock Creek from the main body of the Meadow Valley Basin, correspond so closely in structure and mineral characters with the latter that they need not here be separately described.

Gopher Hill group.—Subordinate in magnitude, but at present far surpassing the above-described deposits in economic value, are the adjoining deposits in the east—the Gopher Hill group of gravel-beds, (Nos. 14, 15, 16, 17,) found chiefly on the hills to the north of Spanish Creek, which here enters a deep gorge. The gravel occurs at varying heights above the present stream, being 300 feet above it at the eastern section at Railroad Hill, (No. 17,) and but a few feet above it near the western end at Waponseh Creek.

These beds consist mainly of rather loose gravel, free from any covering of volcanic material, that attain an average depth of 100 feet, and are covered by a stratum of pipe-clay in their higher portions, as at Badger Hill, (No. 16.) The rocks they contain, generally smoothly worn, but not fully rounded, are like the bed-rock immediately underlying, such as slate and greenstone, and that to the eastward, in which fragments of the hard sandstone schist of the Quincy belt are particularly abundant. Well-worn quartz bowlders are also numerous. Fine gold is found throughout the gravel, with coarse gold in the bed-rock. Some platina is obtained with the gold—the most at Railroad Hill.

The external character of this deposit is that of a broad channel averaging near 2,000 feet in width, with a well-defined rim-rock on the northern side, the southern rim being cut off by Spanish Creek. Its general course is from east-southeast to west-northwest, and its situation is extremely favorable for successful working, there being abundant discharge for tailings, and no cemented strata to obstruct the washing down of the gravel-banks. The deposit is cut, by Waponseh Creek and some gulches, nearly at right angles to its direction.

For more than 20 years highly remunerative mining operations have been carried on in deposit, chiefly by the hydraulic system. Of late all the modern appliances have come into use, mainly in the claims of the Plumas Mining and Water Company, operating in Gopher Hill. These mines derive their water-supply by means of a ditch from Upper Spanish Creek, and, as already remarked, from the lakes in the Spanish Peak Range. They have already added much to the gold-production of the country, and bid fair to attain still greater importance in the near future. The whole of this deposit is claimed, and worked at several points.

Opposite the most eastern body of this group, at Hungarian Hill, (No. 18,) on the south side of Spanish Creek, is a deposit generally considered as belonging to the Gopher Hill group, although its general features are somewhat different. Its practical importance has been but little inferior to that of the above gravel-beds. Situated on the southern slope of a ridge parallel with Spanish Creek, and on a broad point of the main ridge, extending southeast to Claremont Hill, its most important beds consist of red clayey loam, with gravel sparsely intermixed, the most gold being found on the bed-rock. Further to the south, the gravel becomes deeper, and approximates more to that of Gopher Hill, attaining here a depth of 150 feet, and in parts overlying the conglomerates of Slate Creek.

The ground hitherto worked in this deposit, which yielded rich returns during the last eight years, was situated on its northern edge near the head of Hungarian Gulch, and disconnected from the main body of deep gravel. The depth of the old workings seldom exceeded 40 feet, and offered every facility for rapid washing. At present, the Hungarian Hill Mining Company, working on an extensive scale, has given most attention to the deep gravel further south, with fair prospects of ultimate success. The supply of water for the higher portion of the gravel-beds is derived from Mill Creek, and, being taken at great altitude, is not permanent.

Waponseh group.—Adjoining the Gopher Hill group on the north, but separated from it by a narrow belt of bed-rock, is another gravel-deposit, cut near its center by Waponseh Creek, a tributary of Spanish Creek, which, eroding it to considerable depth, does not expose the underlying bed-rock in its deepest or central portion. Its general direction is from southeast to northwest, and it reaches its greatest altitude at the extremities, chiefly on the northwest, where it is capped by volcanic beds and extends to the top of the main divide, within two miles of the East Branch. Its upper beds are elevated fully 600 feet above its central portion. The general appearance of the gravel is similar to that of the Gopher Hill group, being red in color, but not so loose and sandy, and showing more trachyte, diorite, and porphyry among its rocks.

These deposits, (Nos. 19 and 20,) which may be designated as the Waponseh group, have been but slightly explored in their southern part. Some profitable workings are found in and near the bed of Waponseh Creek. Further north, where cut by some gulches flowing southward, as at Pine-Leaf Ravine, rich placer-diggings have been worked, and operations, by tunneling in the edge of the main deposit, give promise of fair returns. The main channel of this deposit has not yet been found. The gold is chiefly confined to the gravel nearest to the bed-rock.

To the northeast of this group, two basins among the hills, as Snake Lake and Smith's Lake, show recent alluvial deposits on the site of former lakes, where but small ponds now remain. The level surface of the former, about 200 acres in extent, consists of pure vegetable mold to some depth, resting on sandy clays and beds of loose gravel. This region is underlain by the metamorphic sandstones, and shows many outcroppings of quartz-veins.

Still further to the northeast is Butterfly Valley, beyond which an extensive gravel-deposit, but slightly projected, is encountered. Its mineral characters resemble those of the Waponseh group, but not being familiar to the writer, it is only indicated on the map in its general outline.

Equidistant between this and Quincy, extensive gravel-beds occur at Newtown and Elizabethtown. At the latter place, rich placer-mines formerly existed in many of the gulches, and several tunnel-claims in the gravel-hills gave excellent profits. But little mining is done here at present, chiefly on account of the scarcity of water. A branch of the Plumas water-ditch reaches this region, but its water-supply is now utilized at the mines of the Gopher Hill group. Whenever abundance of cheap water can be had, these mines will undoubtedly yield rich returns.

Alluvium of American Valley.—While noting the older gravel-deposits, it may be instructive to mention an instance of a recent formation, or one which is yet in progress on a large scale, as evidenced by the alluvial deposits in American Valley, an outline of which is given on the map. Nearly two miles west of Quincy, Spanish Creek enters the valley, which is at that point narrow, but gradually expands eastward, its greatest width being nearly a mile and a half. Two arms of the valley follow the lower courses of Mill Creek and Spring Garden Creek. The level lands of the valley comprise fully 4,500 acres, all of which are occupied by recent gravel-beds of slight cohesion, the surface being generally a sandy or gravelly loam. As no explorations by deep shafts have been made, their depth is unknown; but from the general contour of the surrounding hills, it must be fully 100 feet in the central part of the valley. The valley appears to have been formed by the general and gradual subsidence of the contiguous country, and to have been gradually filling with gravel, light sand, and sediments from the large creeks debouching into it, even before the mining-operations on Spanish Creek added vast accumulations of tailings. The flat near Lower Mill Creek contains the heaviest gravel-beds, derived from the *débris* of the Claremont Hill deposits, and needs only to be uplifted and broken to resemble many older gravel-beds. No mining is done in the level lands of the valley, and but little in the hills surrounding it.

Claremont Hill deposit.—Nearly four miles south of Quincy, and towering above the valley fully 2,500 feet, is seen the summit of Claremont Hill, a broad, dome-shaped crest, rising to an elevation nearly equal to that of Spanish Creek, and forming the highest point of the dividing ridge between Middle Fork and the branches of Spanish Creek. A low gap to the west separates it from the Bear Creek deposits, and another still lower forms a depression eastward near Willow Ranch. On the highest part of the mountain, chiefly on its southern and western slope, occurs a vast deposit (No. 23) of volcanic beds overlying gravel, which appears in some places where the rim-rock is broken by slides, as at the head of some of the ravines descending to Middle Fork. The explorations which for a series of years have been made here have not reached the center of the ancient channel, but have demonstrated the presence of gold-bearing gravel on the interior slopes of the southern rim, here overlain by heavy beds of pipe-clay and sandy clay. The gravel is largely composed of quartz-bowlders, and resembles in some degree that found in the adjoining Willow Ranch deposit, which probably at one time was connected with it.

Although the mythical "Blue Lead" is supposed to run through this mountain, and a strong probability exists that this channel forms a continuation of the Washington Hill deposits at Saw-Pit Flats, noted for their richness, yet all the prospecting hitherto done here has been the result of the unaided efforts of a few men without means, who are unequal to the task, while the communities who would reap the most benefits from discoveries made here do not show their faith by works.

As but few surveys have yet been made of the Claremont Hill deposit, it is indicated on the map only in an approximate outline, which is the case, likewise, with the gravel-beds adjoining it on the east.

On the northern side of Claremont Hill, where it slopes abruptly to American Valley, rise the branches of Mill Creek, on which stream placer-diggings have been worked for some years. The branches of Rock Creek, on the western slope, have not been thoroughly explored, but have furnished paying surface-mines at some points. In fact the whole region from Claremont Hill westward to the main branch of Bear Creek, a distance of ten miles, covered in most of its extent with volcanic and gravel beds, remains to this day *terra incognita* to all but the hunter and an occasional prospector.

Willow Creek deposits.—The Willow Creek deposits, next to the eastward, extend from a point on the Middle Fork opposite Nelson Point northwardly for three miles, while a branch reaches still further toward Spring Garden Creek. Willow Creek exposes to view the gravel-beds of the southern portion, which here consist of red and gray firm gravels, chiefly made up of large and small smoothly-worn bowlders of white and bluish-white quartz. The extreme southern point of the deposit has been worked successfully near the river opposite Nelson Point, and also along Willow Creek and its gulches, where good placer-mines yet exist. It is only lately that attention has been turned to the deeper beds, which remain almost unexplored. The northern part of this deposit is formed by deep beds of tufas and conglomerates, as seen along Thompson's Creek, where appears also the heaviest bed of basalt in this region, filling for some distance the bed of the creek and spreading over the adjoining hill-sides. The basalt is nearly black, generally quite hard and compact, of a globular, occasionally of a columnar, structure. Its extent to the northeast is not ascertained. A mining-company is at present sinking a shaft through the basalt, in the hope of finding a gravel-channel beneath.

On the south bank of the Middle Fork and close to the water's edge, a rich gravel-deposit, discovered in 1874, is now worked with excellent results. This, although referred by some to the ancient gravel-beds, is probably of comparatively recent origin, and a former channel of Middle Fork.

Saw-Pit Flat deposit.—It would be beyond the scope of this description to enter into a description of the vast gravel-deposits south of the Middle Fork and to the east and south of Pilot Peak, a region which for years has been famous for its deep gravel-mines, worked both by drifting and by the hydraulic process, and second to none in the State in the amount of gold it has produced. It only remains to notice briefly the gravel-beds of Washington and Richmond Hills, near Saw-Pit Flat, which for years have been the scenes of extensive tunnel-mining.

The Washington Hill deposits occupy the divide between the Middle Fork and Onion Valley Creek, at an elevation of nearly 6,000 feet, and fill an ancient river-channel of varying width, seldom exceeding 500 or 600 feet. In the bottom gravel occur enormous water-worn bowlders of white and bluish-white quartz, the finer sand and gravel between them being chiefly derived from the wearing down of the quartz. This gravel averages but 8 to 10 feet in depth and is generally highly auriferous. Beds of clay and soft sandstones overlie the bottom gravel, with occasional beds of lighter gravel on the rim-rock. Over all this rest heavy beds of tufas and agglomerates filled with fragments of trachyte and basalt, having a depth at the center of the ridge of 300 feet, and a width across the channel of from 2,000 to 3,000 feet.

Isolated knobs and masses of basalt appear along the southern edge of the volcanic beds, and at one point near Burg Creek form lines of regular terraces. Basaltic masses are also seen at many points on the hill-sides south of Onion Creek.

The Washington Hill beds extend eastward to Onion Valley, where traces are found of recent glacial action. Active operations are here in progress to reach the eastern end of the ancient channel. In the central portion, most of the channel has been worked out by drifting, the Monitor claims being the only ones now actively worked on the channel west of its center. A large part yet remains of the western extremity of the deposit, which was formerly worked at a few points.

The eastern edge of the great serpentine beds underlies the western end of this deposit. Hornblende rock, talcose slates, and clay slates are found under the largest portion.

The Richmond Hill deposit, although separated from the above by a narrow belt of high bed-rock and free from the capping of volcanic beds, is identical with it in mineral characters, and was probably formed on a branch of the main stream. It is of limited extent as compared with Washington Hill. During late years hydraulic mining has been carried on in the outer edges of the old drift-diggings, and with profitable results, much gold in extremely fine division being found in the upper beds of light sandy gravel.

It will remain for future extended explorations and surveys to accurately map out and trace the connection between the above-described deposits. The aim of this description is chiefly to present a general view of the vast ancient gravel-beds, yet scarcely touched, in which Plumas County abounds, and to contribute in some degree to the explanation of their probable origin and of the causes which have produced the changes in the rock-strata underlying them.

Without discussing the relative merits of the many theories advocated by different investigators regarding the formation of the ancient gravel-beds, the writer is induced by extended observations in this region during a period of twenty years to express his conviction that all the phenomena of the old gravel-beds may be referred to the erosive power of large and rapid streams, acting in a manner analogous to that now observed on this coast and continent. If sufficient time be given, changes in the climate from a dry to an extremely humid atmosphere, from a high to a low temperature, would create the forces necessary to excavate the old channels and to transport the materials found therein. Under such conditions, nearly all the ancient gravels in the Sierra must be considered as of fluviatile and lacustrine origin. In the region described, no gravel-beds of maritime origin have yet been observed. Glacial action has here played a subordinate part in bringing about the great changes of the surface since the deposition of the older gravel-beds.

It must be admitted that a period of extraordinary volcanic activity must have prevailed within the region of the Sierra Nevada subsequent to the formation of the most ancient gravel-deposits and while some of the later beds were in process of formation. In all probability this period was cotemporaneous with the great changes in relative level wrought in the underlying rock-strata, evidences of which are abundant within the region described, especially in the Spanish Peak Range, where a study of the great syenitic mass will show its upheaval along its eastern edge, the adjoining strata being bent, folded, contorted, altered in mineral characters, and changed in both dip and strike near the line of junction, and often for a distance of two miles from that line. On a closer inspection, other well-marked lines of volcanic activity will probably be found. The mountain-range between American and Indian Valleys, the foot-hills of which rise four miles east of Quincy (near Red Hill) and the general direction of which is parallel with the strata above described, appears to be on the next line of upheaval. This range is composed almost exclusively of trap-rocks, such as diorite, dolerite, and basaltic porphyries. Mount Hough forms one of its culminating points.

A comparatively small portion only of the volcanic fragmentary materials, such as tufas and agglomerates, which cover most of the ancient gravel-beds, has been subjected to the action of running water, and where such action has occurred it has been but in slight degree. Although some of the volcanic beds are mingled with a few water-worn pebbles and rocks, there is generally a total absence of these; and the large masses and smaller fragments of trap-rocks scattered through these beds, with an almost total absence of stratification, are irregular in shape and but seldom water-worn. When they are round, they generally owe this shape to the globular structure of the rock from which they are derived.

Most of the volcanic beds must, therefore, be considered as emanating from the direct action of eruptive forces, being accumulations of ejected matter on the sides and slopes of active craters and in their vicinity. That such forces may act from one center and extend over a large area is evidenced within historical times by eruptions of active volcanoes on this continent, as in Central America; and also in Europe, as particularly shown by the recent eruptions in Iceland, when the lighter volcanic ashes were carried as far southeast as the eastern coast of Sweden, distant over 800 miles.

The nearest center of extensive volcanic activity within Plumas County is found in the region surrounding Lassen's Peak, at a distance of 30 miles north-northeast from Quincy, where many traces of quite recent volcanic action may be observed. From here emanate several distinct flows of basaltic lava. Another extensive range of trap-rock, chiefly trachyte, occurs east of Indian Valley, about 12 miles from

Quincy. From these centers all the material for the volcanic beds within the county may have been derived, without accepting the theory of a continuous sheet of volcanic deposits and lava-beds from the summit of the Sierras to the foot-hills of the Sacramento Valley. In contradiction of the latter theory, actual observation of the volcanic beds in their relation to the basaltic masses occurring at so many points within the region above described, (but few of which are shown on the map,) forces the conviction that independent volcanic action took place at many distinct points distant from the great apparent centers of activity. Most of the smaller bodies of basalt are not parts of a great general outflow of melted matter, but the results of direct eruptions at such points, as is evidenced upon closer examination by the protrusion of the basalt through the underlying bed-rock, which is always greatly altered for some distance around such points. This is notably shown in some of the tunnels at Washington Hill and at other localities within the observation of the writer.

Distinct auriferous zones.—Although gold may be found in nearly every portion of the region reviewed, yet certain zones may be traced as eminently auriferous, while others adjoining them are comparatively barren. Little gold, except what has been derived from the overlying gravel, is found in the beds of the streams coursing through the great syenitic mass of the Spanish Peak Range, and no ledge of gold-bearing quartz has yet been discovered in that mass. The most productive zone is within the group of slates situated between the syenite and the belt of greenstone, particularly in the talcose slates. This condition holds good in the southwest at or near the junction of the slates with syenite, granite, and serpentine.

Gold occurs sparingly in the recent alluvium originating in the greenstone belt, or *in situ* in this rock. The next slate group adjoining the serpentine shows but few original gold-deposits of any kind.

Within the great serpentine belt no gold is known occurring in place, and but little in alluvial beds that cannot be traced to the older gravel-deposits situated upon it. This rock has undoubtedly furnished the platina found in the vicinity. The slate group east of the serpentine appears to be auriferous to some extent, particularly near the edge of the sandstone-schist, which latter gives evidence of having originated many auriferous deposits. This contains a number of gold-bearing veins and ledges lately discovered and promising well for the future, which would entitle this zone to be ranked next in importance to the first-mentioned group of slates.

As yet but few data are known from which to determine the relative age of the deep gravel and volcanic beds. At present the following classification may be attempted, beginning with the oldest deposits: Spanish Peak, Bear Creek, and Claremont Hill groups, Saw-Pit Flat and Willow Creek deposits, lower beds of the Meadow Valley Basin, Waponseh group, Gopher Hill deposits, and the upper beds of Meadow Valley Basin, as most recent.

Some vegetable-fossil remains from the Spanish Peak deposit were submitted for examination to the late geographical survey, but were not reported upon. The forms there found are closely allied, if not identical, with the now existing types of plant-life.

It is to be hoped that a thorough explanation and geological survey of this and adjoining counties may take place within the life-time of the present generation, a work that cannot fail to develop facts of practical value for the miner, open a rich field for the student of geology, and furnish important deductions to the man of science. In the mean time, these contributions are submitted by Mr. Edman, who, slightly altering the poet's sentiments, believes that "they serve best who do not stand and wait."

Quartz-mining.—The following data concerning the Plumas Eureka Mine, in *Jamison district*, are furnished by Mr. W. L. Oliver. Number of miners, 175; wages, $3 per day; cost of mining, $5.35 per ton extracted; of milling, $1.25; number of tons extracted and worked in 1875, 28,777; average yield, $13; total bullion-product, $381,317; percentage of sulphurets, 1.25. The company's steam and water power mill has 40 stamps of 750 pounds, falling 10 inches 80 times per minute; 2 pans, 22 concentrators; capacity, 2.25 tons per stamp per twenty-four hours, (or 1.48 tons per horse-power, guaranteed by the fall of stamps;) tons crushed in 1875, 58,823. The sulphurets are roasted in a Brückner furnace and then amalgamated in pans.

SISKIYOU AND KLAMATH COUNTIES.

The northern mining-counties are Siskiyou, Klamath, Trinity, and Shasta, the two first named bordering on the State of Oregon. Almost the entire area of these counties consists of high mountains, deep ravines, gulches, and cañons. The formation is granite and auriferous slates. The physical characteristics of the principal quartz-mining region are described in the Report of 1873, pp. 100 to 200. The most productive mines are the Black Bear and Klamath, each running a mill of 32 stamps. The country-rock in which these veins are found is talcose slate, through which the quartz is irregularly distributed, sometimes to a width of 100 feet. The yield of the mines varies from $12 to $24 per ton. The quartz bears a strong resemblance to that of the Mother lode in the central counties. Klamath County has five mills, which cost in the aggregate $80,000. The total number of stamps is 80. The annual gold-production of this portion of the State is about $2,000,000.

The following data from this county are furnished by the gentlemen named as superintendents:

Klamath Mine, owned by Klamath Company; John Daggett, superintendent; course, northeast and southwest; dip, 20°; pay-zone, 5 feet wide, 1,000 feet long; vein, quartz; country-rock, black slate; greatest depth of mine, 600 feet; greatest horizontal length, 1,200 feet; two levels opened by tunnels, 600 and 1,200 feet long. Cost of tunnels, $20,000; 25 miners employed for 6 months of 1875 and 13 for the remainder; wages, $60 per month and board; cost of drifting, $6 to $7.50 and $10 per foot; cost of mining, $3.50 per ton of ore extracted; cost of milling, $1.50 per ton; hauling, 25 cents; 5,000 tons extracted and worked in 9 months of 1875; average yield, $10; sulphurets, 2 per cent.; total bullion, $250,000. Company's mill, water and steam power; 32 stamps, 600 pounds, 75 drops of 8 inches per minute; 2 buddles; 1 pan, not used; cost of mill, $40,000; capacity, 50 tons in 24 hours. No sulphuret process at present.

Morning Star Mine, owned by Doran & Co.; Richard Doran, superintendent; location, 2,500 feet; course, east and west; dip, north; pay-zone, 2½ feet wide, 1,000 feet long; vein, talcose, in hornblendic slate; two levels, (tunnels,) 130 and 260 feet deep; length of tunnels, 300 and 500 feet; cost, $8,000; length of horizontal exploration of vein, 300 feet; 30 miners, at $50 to $60 per month; cost of drifting, $5 to $10 per foot; of stoping, $2.50 per ton; of mining, $4.50 per ton delivered at mill; of milling, $2 per ton; 420 tons per month for 3 months extracted and milled, yielding $15 to $18 per ton; a high percentage of sulphurets.

Company's mill; water-power; 16 stamps, 90 drops per minute, (weight and height of drop not given;) 2 pans, in which sulphurets are treated; cost of mill, $20,000; capacity, 30 tons per 24 hours. The cost of treatment is given under this head as $4 per ton, and above as only $2. The larger sum probably includes the treatment of the sulphurets, and the smaller one only the crushing and plate-amalgamation.

Mr. W. L. Oliver, of San Francisco, has furnished the following summary concerning the Black Bear mine and mill, owned by the company of the same name: In 1875 there were employed 140 miners, at $3 per day; cost of mining per ton extracted, $6.15; of milling, $1.23; tons extracted and worked, 15,998; average yield, $15.51; percentage of sulphurets, 1.12; total bullion-product, $242,000. Mill, 32 stamps, (700 pounds, 80 drops of 8 inches per minute;) 1 pan, 2 concentrators; capacity, 1.48 tons per stamp per 24 hours; power, steam and water. Sulphurets are roasted in a reverberatory and then amalgamated in a pan.

TRINITY COUNTY.

This county was described at length in a former report. For later information concerning it I am now indebted to Dr. H. De Groot, of San Francisco.

Although hydraulic washing on anything like an extended scale was introduced into this county within the past two or three years only, it has already become the leading branch of mining there, the material being abundant and the natural facilities very great. A number of schemes directed to bringing in a more plentiful supply of water, and to opening up large gravel-claims, have lately been projected in the county. While a few of these remain still in embryo, others are in progress of execution, some being pushed very actively forward.

On the Loveridge Ditch, projected about three years ago, for taking a large volume of water from Stewart's Fork and carrying it into Weaver Basin and intermediate camps, little work has since been done, and the rich auriferous country to be traversed by it remains unworked for want of water. This, though a formidable enterprise, involving the necessity of depressing the conducting-pipes more than a thousand feet below the ditch-level in order to convey the water across a deep gorge that lies in its course, is still one from which California hydraulic miners need not shrink, and which, in Dr. De Groot's opinion, should readily command all needed capital, as it could hardly fail to prove a good investment.

The canal of the Weaverville Ditch and Mining Company was finished during the year, and water has been brought in considerable quantity upon Oregon Gulch Mountain, where the company owns a large tract of auriferous gravel. This claim having meantime been furnished with first-class hydraulic apparatus, washing was here commenced with the opening of the water-season. No clean-up had yet been made at the time of Dr. De Groot's visit, but large results might reasonably be expected, since the material is reported to prospect throughout at the rate of $2 per cubic yard, and was estimated to have an average depth of 300 feet over an area of several hundred acres. Indeed, a large section of the mountain seems to consist of pay-gravel to the depth of two or three hundred feet.

In the spring of 1874, the Buckeye Water and Hydraulic Mining Company, having secured the water-right of Stewart's Fork and its main southern tributaries, surveyed the route of a ditch for conveying the water upon Buckeye Mountain and other auriferous gravel-banks in the vicinity. Some preliminary labor was done on the ditch in the following summer. Last year work was resumed, and with such energy has it since been prosecuted that a section covering nearly twenty miles has been finished on a scale amply sufficient to carry 2,000 inches of water to its lower terminus at Boalt's Hill. This locality, which is included within the company's extensive possessions, is famed for the great quantities of gold-dust gathered there in days gone by, and it is expected by all old residents that the coming clean-ups of the company will give extraordinary results. Before water was delivered on this claim, it had been furnished with Little Giants, under-currents, and other hydraulic appliances of the most approved models, Captain Atkins, the superintendent of the work, having, perhaps, had as much experience in this department of mining as any other man in the State. Washing has just been commenced here, and the water being run through large-sized nozzles under a pressure of 300 feet, does great execution. During the coming summer this company will extend its ditch about ten miles farther up into the mountains, carrying it to Stewart's Fork, its principal source of future supply. It is now fed mainly by Van Matre Creek, a confluent of that stream. It is intended, also, very soon to enlarge the ditch to the capacity of 8,000 or 10,000 inches, a quantity of water which can be commanded under the several franchises for two-thirds of the year. This water would be drawn from the contributing sources in the proportions following: Stewart's Fork, 5,000 inches; Owen's Creek, 2,000 inches; Van Matre Creek, 1,200 inches, and other smaller streams 300 inches, making a total of 8,500 inches. The whole of this water the company will use in washing its own gravel, which has an average depth of 300 or 400 feet, reaching in some places twice that depth, and generally prospecting well in gold, Boalt's Hill and some other portions of their ground having always ranked among the rich spots of Trinity County. So deep and wide-spread are the banks of pay-gravel in this neighborhood, that this amount of water played steadily upon them will be insufficient to cause their sensible diminution in a decade of years.

During the summer of 1875 the firm of Blythe & Bixby, having secured the right to the waters of Coffee Creek, a large branch of Trinity River, in the northeast part of the county, proceeded to survey the route for a canal designed to carry this water as far as Weaver Basin, supplying Trinity Centre and many other mining localities along its line. Fifteen miles along the line were cleared of brush and some grading was done last year, it being the intention of the projectors to commence the work of excavation as early as practicable in the present season, and thereafter to press it with the utmost expedition. For the first fifteen miles this ditch will have the unusual dimensions of 12 feet on the top and 8 on the bottom, being 6 feet in depth, giving it capacity to carry at the start 20,000 inches of water, which quantity it is expected may be increased to 26,000 inches when the banks have settled and become solid. This section will be built during the coming summer, the ditch being next year extended to Weaver Basin, thirty miles further, to which point it will bring 12,000 inches of water. The grade will be high enough to carry it over all intervening divides, while strong iron pipes will be employed to convey the water across the deeper ravines encountered along its course. When the first ten miles are finished the water from Coffee Creek will be turned into the ditch, leaving dry the bed of that stream, which will then be worked for the gold it contains. If found as rich as expected, this will be first worked out, after which the high-lying bars along its banks will be attacked, these being known to abound in gold. The total cost of this undertaking is estimated at $600,000, two years being required to bring it to full completion.

Among the more noteworthy events transpiring in this county during the year may be enumerated the opening of rich cinnabar deposits discovered some time before. The ore found here is said to be mostly of high grade, and as it appears to occur in compact and regular veins, seems likely to hold well in depth. The claim of the Altoona Company, the most extensively developed, and thus far the most productive and promising in the district, is described on a preceding page in the earlier part of this chapter.

While the hydraulic miners of Trinity suffered in common with those in other parts of the State from the prevailing water-dearth, those engaged in river-bed mining, here largely pursued, experienced a successful season; the causes that worked to the detriment of the former having favored the latter class by producing a low stage of water in the streams where their operations are carried on. As this branch of mining is mostly in the hands of the Chinese, it is impossible to say what their individual earnings or the aggregate production from this source may have been, though no doubt it was much larger than usual. Although auriferous quartz-lodes were known to abound in this county, not much attention was paid to them until 1874. In that year the croppings of some of these lodes situated in the vicinity of the rugged eminence known as Bullychop Mountain, having on more careful examination proved to be pretty well charged with free gold, a good many claims were there taken up. On some of these a considerable amount of work has since been done, and generally with encouraging results. A small quartz-mill has been put up here, which, should it meet with the success anticipated, will probably soon be followed by others, nor would it be cause for surprise should Trinity come in the course of a few years to rank among the active vein-mining counties of California.

CHAPTER II.

NEVADA.

This State, which for several years past has excelled all others in the production of the precious metals, has during the last year recorded an increase over the production of 1874 of more than $5,000,000. This large increase is mainly due to the further development of the enormous ore-body met with in the Comstock lode, and its energetic extraction by the Virginia Consolidated and Ophir Companies; but also in a certain degree to other very favorable discoveries and large shipments of product from several "outside districts." Notable among these are Cornucopia district, in Elko County, various districts in Nye County, and the Northern Belle Mine in Esmeralda County.

At the end of the year the prospects for 1876 were very promising in the majority of the districts. On the Comstock, the Virginia Consolidated and Ophir were in position to extract rich ores more rapidly than ever before; the California, which contains a part of the "Big Bonanza," more valuable, perhaps, than the portion in the Virginia Consolidated, was prepared to begin the extraction of ores at a rate unprecedented heretofore; excellent prospects of ore-bodies had been found in several others of the Comstock claims; a large and very valuable ore-body had been found in the Eberhardt and Aurora ground in White Pine at a depth not before explored; the Tybo, Jefferson, Reese River, and Cornucopia Mines were doing well, and the Northern Belle, in Esmeralda County, had exposed such a large body of ore that it was found necessary to erect a second 20-stamp mill with Stetefeldt furnace attached.

Mr. Valentine, superintendent of Wells, Fargo & Co.'s Express, who certainly enjoys the most ample opportunities for making a correct estimate of the production of Nevada, since almost all the silver and gold bullion passes through the hands of that company, reports the product for 1875 as follows:

Gold dust and bullion, by express	$196, 858
Gold dust and bullion, by other conveyances	19, 685
Silver bullion, by express	35, 283, 193*
Ores and base bullion, by freight	4, 978, 633
Total	40, 478, 369

As nearly as possible, this may be divided as follows:

Product.	Gold.	Silver.
Gold dust and bullion	$216, 543	
Silver bullion, by express		$25, 353, 518
Gold in silver bullion, by express	9, 929, 675	
Gold in ores and base bullion, by freight	2, 000, 000	
Silver in ores and base bullion, by freight		2, 978, 633
	12, 146, 218	28, 332, 151

* This item is not strictly silver bullion, but a large part of it is bullion containing both silver and gold.

The following is the detailed report of the State controller of Nevada. His figures do not agree with those of Mr. Valentine, and cannot be expected to do so, because only mines producing over a certain amount are bound to report their product at the office of the county assessor, for the purposes of taxation, and even these, in many cases, do not report full values. The number of mines in Nevada which do not come under the provisions of the tax-laws is very great.

Statement of the proceeds of the mines of the State of Nevada for the first, second, and third quarters of 1875.

EUREKA COUNTY.

ORES.

Name of mine or owner.	Quantity.		Value.
	Tons.	*Pounds.*	
Atlas	5, 877	....	$269, 891 43
Adams Hill Consolidated Mining Company	170	1, 500	10, 000 64
Allen & Bertrand	14	....	676 84
Alforjas Mine	2	539	216 47
Buchanan & Co	6	845	4, 629 04
Bugout	7	1, 350	318 59
Black Hawk	....	1, 908	76 33
Badger	2	1, 140	450 26
Corless	2	1, 349	195 27
Connelly	39	325	2, 835 86
Coffey	10	....	1, 774 00
Dead Broke	7	450	400 47
Ducommons	1	1, 514	410 75
Diamond	3	1, 533	323 97
Eureka Consolidated	37, 188	....	1, 116, 709 34
Eureka	....	992	69 54
Evening Star	6	272	365 74
Fairview	5	1, 315	376 80
Grasshopper	1	1, 830	140 06
Garrison	358	632	13, 500 49
Grant	5	1, 914	294 71
Hamilton	2	....	285 80
Hall & Campbell	1	522	158 45
Ironsides	....	1, 975	101 74
Industry	20	448	1, 105 89
Kentuck	44	....	2, 812 00
Laughlin	....	1, 738	111 38
Laura Mine	....	746	51 50
Lyons	5	714	268 18
Matamoras	25	310	5, 366 99
Mineral Hill Company's Mines	1, 570	979	40, 048 27
Maria	9	1, 019	796 57
Macon City	3	88	233 74
Morning Star	1	1, 864	216 76
Mahogany	1	132	114 54
None Such	1	650	69 13
Oregonian	2	267	212 57
Page & Corwin	....	546	80 30
Poorman	10	....	526 40
Richmond Mining Company	22, 237	....	1, 103, 536 00
Silver West	17	1, 814	820 68
Smith & Co	26	176	6, 430 08
Shoemaker & Lockhart	2	1, 480	599 99
Stanton	....	1, 408	115 01
Tyndal	4	800	332 91
Williams	8	645	714 19
Total	67, 709	1, 729	2, 588, 675 67

Statement of the proceeds of the mines of the State of Nevada, &c.—Continued.

ESMERALDA COUNTY.

ORES.

Name of mine or owner.	Quantity.		Value.
	Tons.	*Pounds.*	
Brown Hope	430	....	$13, 886 52
Bowers	2	500	162 66
Columbia	4	500	382 35
Death Valley	23	1, 500	2, 176 00
Indian Queen	499	....	79, 984 00
Litzen	1	....	132 51
Lida Valley	4	....	1, 295 96
Montezuma	3	250	372 21
Mount Diablo	162	1, 000	9, 700 48
Midas	60	....	1, 620 00
Mersach	3	1, 000	839 00
Martin	8	1, 000	995 31
Northern Belle	6, 982	1, 088	544, 102 32
Pascal Burges	2	666	495 04
Remas	15	500	2, 691 09
Scott	....	286	63 99
Sotro	2	500	403 14
Simonson	1	1, 500	193 14
Travis	61	1, 000	5, 897 31
Thatcher	1	1, 500	197 90
Whitton	3	1, 500	370 33
Wilson	37	500	1, 806 11
Wheeler Company	1, 037	....	1, 637 22
Welsh & O'Keefe	5	1, 000	930 17
Total	9, 352	1, 790	670, 334 76

TAILINGS.

Name of mine or owner.	Tons.	Pounds.	Value.
Brown Hope	100	....	1, 801 00
Sweet Apple	700	....	3, 600 00
Total	800	....	5, 401 00

BORAX.

Name of mine or owner.	Tons.	Pounds.	Value.
Pacific Company	165	....	16, 500 00
Smith Brothers	830	....	105, 765 00
Total	995	....	122, 265 00

CHURCHILL COUNTY.

BORAX.

Name of mine or owner.	Tons.	Pounds.	Value.
Nevada Soda Company	218	....	3, 270 00
Total	218	....	3, 270 00

ELKO COUNTY.

ORES.

Name of mine or owner.	Tons.	Pounds.	Value.
Leopard Mining Company	1, 496	....	173, 420 75
Mineral Hill Silver-Mining Company	3, 890	979	102, 730 56
Young America	250	....	7, 000 00
Total	5, 636	979	283, 151 31

Statement of the proceeds of the mines of the State of Nevada, &c.—Continued.

HUMBOLDT COUNTY.

ORES.

Name of mine or owner.	Quantity.		Value.
	Tons.	*Pounds.*	
Arizona Silver Mining Company	2, 360	1, 500	$60, 016 00
Badger Mining Company	127	....	1, 270 00
Humboldt Mill and Mining Company	224	....	14, 540 00
Jersey Mining Company	196	....	19, 784 00
Luna	32	1, 720	2, 673 73
O. M. Evans	300	....	12, 090 00
Oakland Gold and Silver Mining Company	300	....	6, 000 00
Rye Patch Mill and Mining Company	855	1, 320	51, 824 00
Total	4, 456	540	168, 107 73

TAILINGS.

Name of mine or owner.	Tons.	Pounds.	Value.
Arizona Gold and Silver Mining Company	1, 460	....	8, 100 00
Humboldt Mill and Mining Company	160	....	640 00
Rye Patch Mill and Mining Company	440	1, 167	5, 340 64
Total	2, 060	1, 167	14, 080 64

SULPHUR.

Name of mine or owner.	Tons.	Pounds.	Value.
Humboldt Sulphur Company	300	....	12, 600 00
Total	300	....	12, 600 00

LYON COUNTY.

ORES.

Name of mine or owner.	Tons.	Pounds.	Value.
Cromer	100	....	800 00
Dayton Gold and Silver Mining Company	1, 200	....	20, 599 83
Santiago	300	....	3, 300 00
Total	1, 600	....	24, 699 83

TAILINGS.

Name of mine or owner.	Tons.	Pounds.	Value.
Dorwin, G. W	198	....	3, 148 00
Excelsior Mill	1, 497	....	8, 498 17
Eureka Mill	2, 500	....	36, 000 00
French & Co	241	....	3, 524 00
Humphreys, D. W	400	....	5, 850 00
Hearne, M. A	123	....	1, 254 00
Hayes, Louis	108	....	580 95
Keystone Mill	400	....	3, 673 61
Kelsey Mill	1, 000	....	4, 000 00
Lyon Mill and Mining Company	37, 017	....	126, 671 97
Woodworth Mill	4, 000	....	40, 000 00
Total	47, 484	....	233, 200 70

Statement of the proceeds of the mines of the State of Nevada, &c.—Continued.

LANDER COUNTY.

ORES.

Name of mine or owner.	Quantity.		Value.
	Tons.	Pounds.	
Arthur	4	1, 950	$620 58
Bliss	6	1, 975	865 21
Beefsteak	2	372	337 57
Bozet	3	440	651 23
Battle Mountain Mining Company	572	171	58, 718 63
Beowawa	4	320	1, 642 30
Bowen & Co	....	1, 070	65 20
Canadian	1	1, 650	229 16
Clifford	....	350	146 29
Cook	2	400	297 71
Cassamayo	2	310	198 22
Cooper	15	1, 616	4, 463 63
Chase	13	1, 940	2, 511 05
Dunn	1	930	109 52
Dougherty	1	830	167 83
Dollarhide	1	1, 890	174 20
Defiance	99	1, 270	25, 793 78
Eagle	55	....	5, 000 00
Eclipse	11	1, 730	3, 527 60
Engstrom	9	1, 829	2, 000 88
Ensign	2	1, 200	107 80
Emery	....	1, 900	85 60
Ford & Co	4	1, 130	412 00
Fannie	1	1, 580	104 51
Finnegan	12	840	2, 979 18
Florida	41	1, 784	5, 499 21
Freehold	24	80	2, 084 19
Grove Tunnel	69	1, 732	22, 511 21
Goss Bros	9	1, 370	1, 534 92
Gates & Co	....	750	90 93
Girard	13	790	6, 363 58
Goodwin	8	1, 010	1, 459 09
Gill	1	1, 190	294 58
Grasshopper	1	350	55 65
Genoa	2	1, 436	866 35
Hill	4	620	520 17
Harris	1	1, 160	113 15
Hayter	5	1, 050	500 00
Homestake	1	300	236 20
Jamison	1	1, 948	205 96
Jackscrew	87	1, 966	24, 085 95
J. A. Blossom	19	1, 000	796 00
Keneally	....	770	128 88
Lynch	....	150	136 21
Lee & Co	15	1, 470	4, 054 82
Lund & Co	3	60	702 77
Lone Star	6	1, 330	1, 295 71
Mohawk	....	1, 720	411 00
Morris & Cable	90	1, 700	21, 958 92
Manhattan Silver Mining Company	3, 674	450	450, 533 84
Moss Bros	30	1, 050	2, 538 13
McAfee	1	1, 540	231 31
Mount Pleasant	....	1, 190	47 84
Magnolia	4	1, 940	841 63
North River	11	182	2, 916 05
Osborn	3	1, 310	406 43
Ockaw	2	1, 470	433 50
Nevada Boy	45	210	7, 493 25
Patriot	26	1, 120	5, 784 81
Pacific Mining Company	13	240	1, 216 37
Razor Blade	....	1, 920	421 90
Reed Tunnel	6	1, 102	2, 368 11
Sinnott	4	540	989 94
Sloan	9	1, 870	1, 287 30
Schoof	3	800	844 30
Southall & Co	12	1, 850	2, 455 50
Semanthe	3	1, 240	788 24
Stranger	34	1, 580	2, 886 29
Sonoma	25	1, 490	3, 030 61
Sundry mines	78	1, 268	16, 728 55
True Blue	4	1, 740	835 44
Warren	5	1, 470	1, 038 60
Whitlach	29	18	5, 603 73
Williamson	2	1, 710	274 30
Yankee Blade	17	1, 150	2, 266 15
Total	5, 301	1, 879	721, 407 25

Statement of the proceeds of the mines of the State of Nevada, &c.—Continued.

LANDER COUNTY—Continued.

TAILINGS.

Name of mine or owner.	Quantity.		Value.
	Tons.	*Pounds.*	
Manhattan Mill	20	....	$274 26
Total	20	....	274 26

LINCOLN COUNTY.

ORES.

Name of mine or owner.	Tons.	Pounds.	Value.
Alps	239	1,741	32,554 98
American Flag	263	270	8,191 83
Chance	3	75	604 00
Chapman	64	1,000	5,470 30
Chief of the Hill	77	1,420	6,445 80
Desdamona	7	111	196 56
George May	23	1,300	1,180 00
Great Eastern	13	500	1,171 28
Havana	7	850	368 65
Hercules	195	....	1,950 00
Huhn & Hunt	133	....	3,108 62
Ivanhoe	22	1,544	1,239 82
Jolly Traveller	16	1,500	316 00
Kentuck	12	600	523 00
Monte del Rey	3	1,017	163 84
Mary Haynes	10	233	431 19
Montgomery	48	1,072	3,293 83
Meadow Valley	825	611	102,735 31
Newark	802	888	21,861 73
National	11	1,500	775 14
Ontario	54	333	3,456 41
Pioche	58	293	6,308 49
Pioche West	39	....	1,280 00
Raymond & Ely	6,817	1,740	334,805 15
Spring Mound	44	....	1,983 00
Sunny South	9	1,081	308 00
Towne & Orr	6	1,200	419 85
Vermillion	18	498	624 00
Washington and Creole	78	395	6,207 91
Total	9,906	1,772	547,974 69

TAILINGS.

Name of mine or owner.	Tons.	Pounds.	Value.
Floral Mill	340	....	1,700 00
Magnet	2,500	....	8,495 00
Newark Manufacturing Company	1,300	....	10,155 58
Raymond & Ely	13,681	....	72,170 17
Total	17,821	....	92,520 75

NYE COUNTY.

ORES.

Name of mine or owner.	Tons.	Pounds.	Value.
Austin	9	280	3,656 80
Belmont Mining Company	947	1,115	64,560 29
Barnes and Clark	5	1,700	1,900 00
Brawen & Co	4	1,357	1,291 20
Barcelona	8	414	2,484 74
Carillo	5	1,378	1,255 56
Croce	....	1,330	196 03
Cook	8	1,450	2,024 65
Cammack	5	1,060	861 70
Cooper	....	1,500	78 50
Downey	9	1,790	965 80
Dean	1	1,030	11 89
Gila Silver Mining Company	897	720	213,797 49
Garvin & Co	....	1,905	126 88

Statement of the proceeds of the mines of the State of Nevada, &c.—Continued.

NYE COUNTY—Continued.

ORES—Continued.

Name of mine or owner.	Quantity.		Value.
	Tons.	*Pounds.*	
Glover & Dean	1	335	$268 46
Hayter, F. M.	23	1, 201	2, 083 58
Hathaway	4	25	890 80
Hall, G. C	1	710	405 26
Helvis	2	1, 303	46 65
Jefferson Mining Company	2, 960	1, 296	124, 089 24
Johnson & Co	21	1, 849	2, 556 40
Lopez	8	269	715 51
Ludwig	....	1, 500	66 20
Munro	1	40	150 35
McPherson	3	1, 470	445 80
Morey Mining Company	108	1, 242	9, 299 95
Monitor	8	1, 387	1, 223 56
McCormack	10	1, 713	2, 667 76
Mitchell	....	938	156 78
Malone & Caruthers	15	1, 951	2, 365 72
Nelson	1	594	53 78
Oder	2	1, 814	668 35
Omond	5	1, 808	905 15
Prussian Gold and Silver Mining Company	3, 833	235	66, 604 77
Phillips	1	1, 050	367 91
Peck, O. O	2	1, 314	391 65
Redman & Hart	1	930	158 22
Stowe	3	990	480 92
Spaulding	....	1, 620	137 00
Tybo Consolidated Mining Company	2, 891	1, 500	97, 744 40
Witham	8	750	1, 262 94
West	....	391	134 14
Webber	3	180	535 00
Welch	2	50	218 23
Total	11, 838	1, 484	610, 306 01

TAILINGS.

Name of mine or owner.	Tons.	Pounds.	Value.
Jefferson Silver Mining Company	2, 454	....	28, 411 54
Total	2, 454	....	28, 411 54

STOREY COUNTY.

ORES.

Name of mine or owner.	Tons.	Pounds.	Value.
Andes	876	....	16, 425 00
Bowers	955	....	10, 950 00
Belcher Mining Company	93, 512	....	2, 384, 111 04
Crown Point	125, 617	1, 110	2, 595, 592 06
Chollar Potosi	12, 100	....	206, 491 68
Consolidated Virginia	142, 272	1, 804	13, 710, 099 43
Empire	8, 530	....	114, 240 00
Hale and Norcross	2, 846	250	47, 168 39
Imperial	400	....	8, 000 00
Ophir	37, 511	1, 500	1, 263, 725 57
Woodville	1, 296	....	16, 200 00
Total	425, 917	664	20, 373, 003 17

TAILINGS.

Name of mine or owner.	Tons.	Pounds.	Value.
Express Mill	2, 600	....	39, 579 00
Railroad Mill	8, 800	....	90, 700 00
Stevenson, C. C	1, 200	....	6, 100 00
Total	12, 600	....	136, 379 00

NOTE.—Mines in Storey County that pay no State tax not reported.

Statement of the proceeds of the mines of the State of Nevada, &c.—Continued.

WHITE PINE COUNTY.

ORES.

Name of mine or owner.	Quantity.		Value.
	Tons.	*Pounds.*	
Aultman	30	....	$1,200 00
Alcyon	2	105	187 29
Battery	80	1,893	9,298 86
Bartlett	4	1,151	642 42
Buckeye State	42	....	3,831 41
Caroline	2	1,760	755 61
California North	18	....	193 50
Dictator	4	....	720 00
Exchequer	43	970	2,408 42
Eberhart and Aurora Company	7,220	1,943	390,236 87
Frederick William the Great	130	....	975 00
Grey Eagle	5	....	510 00
Mazeppa	1	....	168 39
Mountain Queen	5	331	1,600 35
Mariposa	16	1,500	1,675 00
Joker	....	1,676	102 00
Oro	149	....	941 00
Paymaster	142	....	16,010 00
Robert Emmett	24	1,600	297 10
Rescue	154	190	33,354 28
Stafford	10	160	393 37
San José	2,036	....	27,297 53
Star	691	....	64,478 10
South Aurora	5	446	1,391 48
Silver Plate	19	1,300	1,140 02
Trench	4	1,080	1,464 65
Tickup	387	583	37,761 07
Vulcan	5	....	1,102 00
Whippoorwill	10	1,500	376 00
Total	11,247	188	600,511 72

RECAPITULATION.

ORES.

Name of county.	Quantity.		Value.
	Tons.	*Pounds.*	
Eureka	67,709	1,729	$2,588,675 67
Esmeralda	9,352	1,790	670,334 76
Elko	5,636	979	283,151 31
Humboldt	4,456	540	168,107 73
Lyon	1,600	....	24,699 83
Lander	5,301	1,879	721,407 25
Lincoln	9,906	1,772	547,974 69
Nye	11,838	1,484	610,306 01
Storey	425,917	664	20,373,003 17
White Pine	11,247	188	600,511 72
Total	552,967	1,025	26,588,172 14

TAILINGS.

Esmeralda	800	....	5,401 00
Humboldt	2,060	1,167	14,080 64
Lyon	47,484	....	233,200 70
Lander	20	....	274 26
Lincoln	17,821	....	92,520 75
Nye	2,454	....	28,411 54
Storey	12,600	....	136,379 00
Total	83,239	1,167	510,267 89

Statement of the proceeds of the mines of the State of Nevada, &c.—Continued.

RECAPITULATION—Continued.

BORAX.

Name of county.	Quantity.		Value.
	Tons.	*Pounds.*	
Churchill	218	....	$3, 270 00
Esmeralda	995	....	122, 265 00
Total	1, 213	....	125, 535 00

SULPHUR.

Humboldt	300	....	12, 600 00
Total	300	....	12, 600 00

Statement of the proceeds of the mines of the State of Nevada for the fourth quarter of 1875.

EUREKA COUNTY.

ORES.

Name of mine or owner.	Quantity.		Value.
	Tons.	*Pounds.*	
Atlas	784	....	$41, 500 00
Allen	5	....	251 32
Adams' Hill	154	....	9, 032 31
Beebe & Sanchez	5	....	436 40
Boulder	7	....	333 44
Cassidy & Co	11	....	1, 191 50
Erie	2	1, 200	223 68
El Dorado	24	....	3, 352 06
Geddes & Bertrand	450	....	45, 000 00
Garrison	134	....	7, 773 00
Hoosac	2	....	124 07
Jenny Lind	3	1, 600	210 89
K. K. Consolidated	2, 089	1, 000	95, 051 00
Laura	2	961	256 64
Laraway	9	....	881 60
Mountain Boy	21	....	3, 058 54
Morning Glory	55	....	8, 299 91
Macon City	9	1, 200	740 53
Mountain View	11	....	1, 507 25
Otho	6	1, 126	429 76
Richmond Consolidated Mining Company	9, 957	....	340, 371 00
Stella	4	1, 650	332 59
Stramboul	16	....	1, 060 94
Total fourth quarter 1875	13, 764	737	561, 419 43

ESMERALDA COUNTY.

ORES.

Indian Queen	397	1, 000	52, 698 96
Midas	62	1, 000	1, 141 43
Mount Diablo	167	1, 800	9, 731 13
Northern Belle	3, 748	....	296, 848 96
Wm. Brannon	6	400	699 94
Wheeler	312	....	8, 756 45
Willis & Milsap	83	....	497 75
Wilson	110	....	1, 852 00
Total fourth quarter 1875	4, 887	200	373, 226 62

Statement of the proceeds of the mines of the State of Nevada, &c.—Continued.

ESMERALDA COUNTY—Continued.

BORAX.

Name of mine or owner.	Quantity.		Value.
	Tons.	*Pounds.*	
Pacific Borax Company	119	....	$11,900 00
Smith Bros. Borax Works	338	....	33,800 00
Total fourth quarter 1875	457	....	45,700 00

ELKO COUNTY.

ORES.

Name of mine or owner.	Tons.	Pounds.	Value.
Leopard	1,600	....	226,879 00
Mineral Hill Mining Company	480	....	14,283 71
Spencer Mine	8	692	933 00
Austin Mine	17	893	1,356 00
Total fourth quarter 1875	2,105	1,585	243,451 71

HUMBOLDT COUNTY.

ORES.

Name of mine or owner.	Tons.	Pounds.	Value.
Arizona Silver-Mining Company	676	....	18,923 00
Badger Mine	57	1,000	679 00
Humboldt Mill and Mining Company	139	....	5,786 00
Rye Patch Mine	74	648	12,996 95
Total fourth quarter 1875	946	1,648	38,389 95

TAILINGS.

Name of mine or owner.	Tons.	Pounds.	Value.
Arizona Silver-Mining Company	2,850	....	19,950 00
Humboldt Mill and Mining Company	300	....	1,500 00
Rye Patch Mine	700	....	6,328 00
Total fourth quarter 1875	3,850	....	27,778 00

LYON COUNTY.

ORES.

Name of mine or owner.	Tons.	Pounds.	Value.
Silver City Mining Company	46	....	1,426 00
Total fourth quarter 1875	46	....	1,426 00

TAILINGS.

Name of mine or owner.	Tons.	Pounds.	Value.
Dorwin, G. W	170	....	2,550 00
Excelsior Mill	300	....	1,263 00
French Greeley	150	....	1,200 00
Hayes, Lewis	13	....	135 00
Humphries, D. M	50	....	750 00
Lyon Mill and Mining Company	12,491	....	47,245 68
Union Mill and Mining Company	1,500	....	21,215 16
Woodworth Mill	4,000	....	40,000 00
Total fourth quarter 1875	18,674	....	114,358 84

Statement of the proceeds of the mines of the State of Nevada, &c.—Continued.

LINCOLN COUNTY.

ORES.

Name of mine or owner.	Quantity.		Value.
	Tons.	*Pounds.*	
Alps Mining Company	137	25	$10, 448 36
Anna	4	....	250 00
Bay State	22	1, 500	549 75
Great Eastern	14	....	941 21
Lehigh	60	....	6, 014 70
Meadow Valley Mining Company	430	1, 796	43, 230 00
Portland	7	334	221 37
Pioche	16	230	1, 510 87
Newark	12	520	737 57
Pea Vine	5	890	539 08
J. R. James	872	1, 558	18, 450 44
Raymond & Ely Mining Company	5, 611	330	284, 897 06
Total fourth quarter 1875	7, 201	1, 183	367, 790 41

TAILINGS

Name of mine or owner.	Tons.	Pounds.	Value.
J. A. Bidwell	171	....	885 00
A. J. Blair	15	....	340 32
J. P. Kelly	3, 617	....	10, 905 21
Total fourth quarter 1875	3, 803	....	12, 130 53

LANDER COUNTY.

ORES.

Name of mine or owner.	Tons.	Pounds.	Value.
Allen & Co	....	1, 080	154 70
Beowawa	4	820	877 80
Bothin, J. C	....	1, 260	50 66
Bozet, George	1	1, 380	177 96
Battle Mountain Mining Company	98	1, 918	10, 981 99
Bowman Dump	1	230	112 10
Cheek, James	....	1, 430	50 34
Casey & Co	2	1, 570	403 14
Campbell, John	....	710	18 74
Cooper, H. H	1	1, 030	905 67
Collins, John	....	770	611 47
Centennial Mine	3	180	901 05
Defiance	102	530	29, 385 15
Dale	4	390	923 68
Dollarhide	....	1, 974	288 38
Eclipse	7	40	1, 261 92
Esther	2	650	449 90
Freehold	2	100	108 24
Crove Tunnel	29	30	6, 628 60
Goodwin	....	1, 490	94 50
Good Hope	4	1, 980	2, 941 94
Hill & Reed	1	850	406 34
Horton & Sawtelle	....	190	139 74
Jackscrew	3	170	454 90
Last Hope	1	80	125 44
Lone Star	2	1, 940	512 26
Lee & Lund	11	910	2, 060 55
Ludolph & Co	4	1, 966	937 40
Manhattan Dump	22	32	2, 553 38
Morris & Cable	17	750	5, 349 00
Mullen, George	5	70	1, 263 50
Moss Brothers	4	1, 790	621 40
Manhattan Silver-Mining Company	1, 145	1, 750	152, 326 29
Nevada Boy	8	320	1, 410 20
North River	1	240	431 44
Old Well	1	1, 970	143 10
Osborne	1	400	120 64
Occidental	15	1, 650	5, 748 31
O'Kane	2	1, 370	256 40
Patriot	11	1, 040	6, 037 70
Pacific	1	1, 270	232 16
Pierce	....	820	56 15
Rudolf	....	850	104 10

Statement of the proceeds of the mines in the State of Nevada, &c.—Continued.

LANDER COUNTY—Continued.

ORES—Continued.

Name of mine or owner.	Quantity.		Value.
	Tons.	*Pounds.*	
Richardson, J	....	720	$35 20
Sinnot	2	1,740	290 74
Stumon	3	150	460 20
Schoof, Louis	2	1,060	254 40
Southall & Co	5	1,090	795 80
Sidnor	....	1,050	61 22
True Blue	5	130	543 64
Troxel	4	1,500	516 55
Turner Bros	5	896	1,415 10
Warren & Co	13	800	2,925 95
Whitlach	3	1,340	466 65
White & Shiloh	437	576	37,109 12
Other mines	10	730	1,939 31
Total fourth quarter 1875	2,029	1,764	284,542 17

NYE COUNTY.

ORES.

Name of mine or owner.	Tons.	Pounds.	Value.
Altozano	....	360	46 36
Barnes & Clark	2	700	670 44
Blackiston & Richards	1	352	222 55
Belmont Mining Company	8	1,118	2,494 61
Dayton, J. B	900	....	16,517 11
Gillian & Co	3	1,560	660 25
Hutchings & Graves	4	110	673 44
Hanchett, L. J	220	820	14,382 00
Hoel, C	....	1,000	81 04
Love, G. J	1	1,230	288 19
Morton, J. C	1	1,425	273 30
Molliston	6	1,380	671 53
Other mines	27	1,092	3,296 69
Peck & Wood	1	1,327	378 37
Reynolds & Co	2	1,770	566 50
Rhoades, M. G	497	1,719	70,055 10
Savolan	1	1,891	508 03
Tybo Consolidated Mining Company	2,041	....	78,771 53
Vaughn	2	1,980	165 68
Witham	1	1,600	262 36
Total fourth quarter 1875	3,728	1,434	190,985 08

TAILINGS.

Name of mine or owner.	Tons.	Pounds.	Value.
Hanchett, L. J	372	740	5,368 00

STOREY COUNTY.

ORES.

Name of mine or owner.	Tons.	Pounds.	Value.
Belcher Mining Company	30,268	....	999,762 51
Chollar Potosi Mining Company	6,750	....	110,890 64
Crown Point Mining Company	29,742	1,660	506,010 79
Consolidated Virginia Mining Company	26,792	....	3,205,906 92
Empire Mining Company	2,560	....	32,720 00
Hale and Norcross Mining Company	2,950	1,100	51,554 20
Imperial Mining Company	2,727	850	74,005 55
Justice Mining Company	729	500	16,865 78
Ophir Mining Company	9,169	1,500	419,264 98
Vivian Mining Company	1,488	....	23,397 00
Yellow Jacket Mining Company	761	....	12,176 00
Total fourth quarter 1875	113,938	1,610	5,452,554 37

Statement of the proceeds of the mines in the State of Nevada—Continued.

STOREY COUNTY—Continued.

TAILINGS.

Name of mine or owner.	Quantity.		Value.
	Tons.	*Pounds.*	
Express Mill	1, 800	....	$17, 100 00
Railroad Mill	4, 000	....	44, 000 00
Total fourth quarter 1875	5, 800	....	61, 100 00

WHITE PINE COUNTY.

ORES.

Name of mine or owner.	Tons.	Pounds.	Value.
Alcyone	36	1, 124	1, 000 00
Boston	8	1, 124	376 32
Buckeye State	40	....	593 33
Consburg	1	1, 500	82 00
Dewitt	8	661	643 20
Eberhardt and Aurora	3, 895	1, 730	226, 578 51
Elko	33	1, 289	1, 526 69
Fay	72	102	5, 040 74
Kellogg	1	488	272 53
Mahogany	18	1, 881	832 10
Mountain Queen	1	1, 808	429 47
Newark Company	11	62	790 18
Pacific	68	148	4, 586 14
Peterson	1	1, 940	157 03
Paymaster	41	....	9, 734 80
Prince	8	1, 250	810 00
Queen	1	664	204 08
Rescue	29	919	3, 400 36
South Aurora	4	210	602 89
Spaulding	1	1, 050	273 32
Stafford	6	1, 950	709 65
Tickup	251	....	15, 060 00
Total fourth quarter 1875	4, 543	1, 840	273, 703 34

RECAPITULATION.

ORES.

Name of mine or owner.	Tons.	Pounds.	Value.
Eureka	13, 764	737	561, 419 43
Esmeralda	4, 287	200	373, 226 62
Elko	2, 105	1, 585	243, 451 71
Humboldt	946	1, 648	38, 389 95
Lyon	46	....	1, 426 00
Lincoln	7, 201	1, 183	367, 790 41
Lander	2, 029	1, 764	284, 542 17
Nye	3, 728	1, 434	190, 985 08
Storey	113, 938	1, 610	5, 452, 554 37
White Pine	4, 543	1, 840	273, 703 34
Total fourth quarter 1875	153, 193	1	7, 787, 489 08

TAILINGS.

Name of mine or owner.	Tons.	Pounds.	Value.
Humboldt	3, 850	....	27, 778 00
Lyon	18, 674	....	114, 358 84
Lincoln	3, 803	....	12, 130 53
Nye	372	740	5, 368 00
Storey	5, 800	....	61, 100 00
Total fourth quarter 1875	32, 499	740	220, 735 37

BORAX.

Name of mine or owner.	Tons.	Pounds.	Value.
Esmeralda	457	....	45, 700 00
Total fourth quarter 1875	457	....	45, 700 00

Total production of gold and silver for the year 1875.

ORES.

Name of county.	Quantity.		Value.
	Tons.	*Pounds.*	
Eureka	81, 474	466	$3, 150, 095 10
Esmeralda	14, 239	1, 990	1, 043, 561 38
Elko	7, 742	564	526, 603 02
Humboldt	5, 403	188	206, 497 68
Lyon	1, 646	....	26, 125 83
Lander	7, 331	1, 643	1, 005, 949 42
Lincoln	17, 108	955	915, 765 10
Nye	15, 567	918	801, 291 09
Storey	539, 856	274	25, 825, 557 54
White Pine	15, 791	28	874, 215 06
Total	706, 160	1, 026	34, 375, 661 22

TAILINGS.

Name of county.	Tons.	Pounds.	Value.
Esmeralda	800	....	5, 401 00
Humboldt	5, 910	1, 167	41, 858 64
Lyon	66, 158	....	347, 559 54
Lander	20	....	274 26
Lincoln	21, 624	....	104, 651 28
Nye	2, 826	740	33, 779 54
Storey	18, 400	....	197, 479 00
Total	115, 738	1, 907	731, 003 26

SUMMARY.

	Tons.	Pounds.	Value.
Ore	706, 160	1, 026	34, 375, 661 22
Tailings	115, 738	1, 907	731, 000 26
Grand total	821, 899	933	35, 106, 664 48

PRODUCTION OF BORAX.

Churchill County, tons	218	$3, 270
Esmeralda County, tons	1, 452	$167, 965
Total, tons	1, 670	$171, 235

PRODUCTION OF SULPHUR.

Humboldt County, tons	300	$12, 600

THE COMSTOCK MINES.

I am indebted for the details of work done at most of the mines on the Comstock lode during the year to Mr. F. F. Osbiston, superintendent of the Savage Mine, who has been assisted by the courtesy of other superintendents. In this connection, reference should be made to the interesting account of the "Great Bonanza" by Professor Rogers, published in the last report of the Director of the Mint, and accompanied with copies of the surveys of the deepest level upon which operations have been conducted.

The product of the Comstock mines in 1875, as reported to me by the State controller, was as follows:

Number of tons mined	539, 856
Number of tons of tailings worked	18, 400
Total tons	558, 256
Total bullion product, ore	$25, 825, 557 54
Total bullion product, tailings	197, 479 00
	26, 023, 036 54

Of this amount the leading mines have produced as follows:

Consolidated Virginia	$16,957,538 00
Ophir	1,817,187 00
Crown Point	3,124,052 00
Belcher	3,107,993 00
All others	1,016,266 54
	26,023,036 54

The following is a summary of the operations at each mine, taken in the order of position from north to south:

Utah.—The vertical depth of the new shaft is 517 feet; drifts have been run north and south the entire length of the claim, finding the vein perfect and over 100 feet in width, containing low-grade ore, but not of sufficient value to mill. Nothing has been done from the bottom of the shaft owing to the destruction of the works by fire in August last and the consequent filling up of the shaft with water. Since then, new works have been erected at a cost of $100,000; the work of pumping out the water is now being carried on, and in a short time prospecting will be resumed.

The above was furnished by Mr. James S. Fair, the superintendent.

Sierra Nevada.—No ore has been extracted from this mine during the year 1875. Great energy has been exerted to open up the mine at a greater depth. The surface-ore was so favorable and the vein so perfect, that the proprietors are now expending large amounts of money in sinking both new and old shafts and otherwise opening the mine to a much greater depth. During the year the old shaft has been sunk 125 feet, making total depth 895 feet, and the new one has now attained a vertical depth of 1,450 feet. On the 1,000-foot level a west drift has been run 450 feet. On the 1,250-foot level another drift has been run 200 feet west and also one 400 feet north and south of shaft. The cross-cuts on both levels show great improvements in the quality of the quartz. The estimated value of the improvements (machinery, hoisting-works, &c.) is $300,000. Number of feet in claim, 3,600.

For these facts I am indebted to Mr. W. T. Wright, the superintendent.

Union Consolidated.—This mine has no hoisting-works, and is being prospected through the Ophir Company's shaft. A drift has been run north the whole length of the claim on the 1,300-foot level, and necessary cross-cuts made, without developing ore of any particular value. Number of feet in claim is 825. Heavy machinery will be erected this year.

Mexican.—Like the Union Consolidated, this mine has no works, and is prospected through the Ophir shaft. A north drift has been run the length of the claim and cross-cuts made, with the same results as in the preceding mine. Machinery will also be erected on this claim at an early date. Number of feet in claim is 600, being a segregation of the north end of the Ophir Mine.

Mr. Samuel T. Curtis, superintendent of the Union Consolidated and the Mexican, communicated the above facts.

Ophir.—The greatest production of this mine heretofore was during the year 1863, $1,514,222.21, while this year it is $1,817,187.19. But with this encouraging outlook, and in the midst of the company's greatest prosperity, while upon the eve of resuming dividends, the dire disaster of fire overwhelmed it, laying its. valuable and costly works in ruins and stopping all operations for more than a month. Works as fine as had ever been erected on any mine had recently been completed at a cost of over three hundred thousand dollars, and the mine was in fine working condition in all its parts, when the fire of October 26 occurred, sweeping off everything consumable, and irreparably damaging a great portion of the machinery. In just one month's time, however, by extraordinary exertions and superior management, Superintendent Curtis had the buildings and works replaced and again ready for hoisting. But after overcoming these serious difficulties yet another disaster had to be met, viz, the flooding of the mine up to the 1,500-foot station, with more or less slight caves from drift-facings, by which there was, no doubt, lost much good ore by being mixed with worthless *débris*, rendering it unfit for milling.

It is encouraging to notice that during the last five months (as will be seen hereafter) the yield, per ton, of ore has largely increased—from $26.94 to $58.54. It is true the assay-value of the ore increased rapidly at the same time, but not in the same proportion as the yield. This points to more tractable ore than was formerly found in the mine.

Mr. S. T. Curtis, the superintendent of the mine, reports at the end of the fiscal year as follows:

During the fiscal year, up to October 26, the date of destruction of the works, 51,322$\frac{1600}{2000}$ tons of ore have been extracted; which, together with 105$\frac{1340}{2000}$ tons on hand at mills at the commencement of the year, have yielded bullion amounting to $1,817,187.19.

During the year a large amount of prospecting has been done on the different levels, several air channels and winzes constructed, making the mine very cool, and producing beneficial results in the increased facilities afforded the miners to work.

The main vertical shaft has been sunk 125 feet, and the upper 400 feet retimbered, before and after the fire. A large station has been cut out on the 1,600-foot level, preparatory to sinking inclined shaft.

The prospecting on the lowest level (1,700-foot) discloses in the west cross-cuts a great disturbance of the west wall of the lode, and the eastern cross-cuts, as far as they have penetrated, have passed through "horses" or masses of west country-rock and entered more favorable formation with strata of low-grade ore following out east, which evinces a "heave" or pushing of the ore-vein, and gives hopes of discovery of ore-deposits on this level farther east.

The ore-bodies on the 1,300-foot level show strength in raising, and the angle of raise proves that the long abandoned 1,100 and 700 foot stations were not prospected far enough east by from three to five hundred feet, if the ore-bodies discovered on the 1,300-foot level raise that high. Two months ago I started a drift southeast from the 1,100 station to test this theory, the last work done in which showed signs of a favorable formation.

Very large and substantial buildings were erected, and a powerful and first-class pumping engine and gearing, incline engines and gear, and tapered reel; to the shaft of the latter were connected two hydraulic engines, worked by the water of the mine, under a pressure of 400 feet head. These hydraulic engines give an auxiliary power of 268 horse while hoisting, and in lowering form a water-balance counteracting-weight of giraffe and steel cable, and are calculated to save considerable fuel.

A large ore-house was constructed alongside of the railroad, to which the ore is to be raised by a water-elevator, using the same power as the hydraulic engines. This system of elevating the ore 47 feet to the railroad was adopted after careful consideration and perfect surveys for line of switch from railroad, which it was found would cost $45,000 for the only practical route, whereas the hydraulic machinery costs but about $6,000.

Two air-compressors were also put up, and compressed air introduced into the mine, which has proved serviceable and economical, running Burleigh drills, air-fans, and hoisting ore from winzes.

A very perfect system of water-works was in process of construction and partly completed at the time of the fire; a 10-inch lap-welded iron pipe had been laid up the mountain a distance of 2,000 feet, with 400 feet pressure, to a water-tank capable of holding 100,000 gallons of water; six hydrants with 2½-inch hose were laid outside the buildings, and twelve small ones with 1½-inch hose inside buildings at convenient points.

The main pipe to tank, besides being available for fire purposes, also supplies power to the hydraulic counter-balance engines connected with steam incline engines, and also to the water-hoist in the railroad ore-house, the water of the mine being used, except in case of fire, when the water from the water-ditch can be turned into the tank through the connections.

All this powerful machinery and first-class buildings, covering an area of 39,522 square feet, and forming one of the most thorough works on the Comstock, were just completed, and three water-hydrants ready for use, when the terrible fire of the 26th of October laid in ashes nearly the whole city of Virginia in a few hours, and swept the Ophir works down in a flash of fire.

Prior to the fire the water in the ditch was very scarce, and I was unable to get water to fill the tank. Fearful of fire, from the long period of hot weather, I had taken the precaution of having extra watchmen at night. I had also put a 2½-inch pipe through the roof of main building, connecting with hose on the roof, the water being supplied by a steam force-pump. I had also been pumping water up to tank on the mountain for a couple of days and the 10-inch pipe was about half full. This water in the pipe and the hose on the roof supplied by force-pump was all the available water I had to fight fire. I blew up several buildings with giant powder around the works in hopes of saving them, but all efforts were futile. The fire came with lightning rapidity in large sheets, sweeping down the immense buildings as if by magic, and in less than five minutes they were laid on the ground a burning pile, increased by the burning of about one thousand cords of wood and nearly 400,000 feet of mining timbers and lumber. The heat was so intense that railroad car-wheels were melted in the open air alongside of the works; but taking all this into consideration, I believe I could have saved considerable property, had I had a supply of water from the ditch, and the hydrants complete as they are now.

When the fire abated, so as to permit me to get to the shaft, I found that the heavy timbers of the gallows-frame, partially burned, had fallen down the shaft, breaking a portion of the platform that had been put in to protect shaft and mine, and the fire was working its way down the shaft. During the excitement of the day and part of the night fire-engines could not be procured from town, and the fire in the shaft had to be fought with water-buckets passed by lines of men standing in the midst of the burning mass, a furious gale blowing at the time carrying showers of burning coal from our own ruins and the burning town. In the middle of the first night fire-engines were obtained, and for thirty-six hours a continuous stream of water was played down the shaft until the safety of the shaft and mine were assured.

On the day after the fire competent men were dispatched to the lumber-yards of Carson and Dutch Flat, Cal., to procure and ship timbers; machinery was telegraphed for; the new double-reel hoisting-engine and cables just completed for the combination shaft of the Chollar-Potosi, Hale & Norcross, and Savage secured, and, through the heaviest storms Virginia has seen for years, the old engine-foundations were torn out, and new ones to suit the combination engine constructed, work was prosecuted without cessation, supplies hauled a considerable distance on account of destruction of railroad tunnel and bridges, the works rebuilt and work through shaft resumed November 25, being inside of thirty days from time of destruction.

While the reconstruction of works was going on, a donkey-engine, furnished through the kindness of the Phil. Sheridan Mining Company, was put in place, with which we were enabled to retimber shaft where it had been burned to a depth of 400 feet from surface, besides hoisting considerable of the water making on the 700-foot level of the mine.

The buildings rebuilt have been made much larger, and more complete and convenient than formerly.

Most of the machinery which passed through the fire has been made available, especially the new incline and pumping engines, which suffered but little damage. From the two hoisting-engines of the vertical shaft, which received most damage, one good engine has been completed at little cost, and foundations are being laid to put in place for hoisting-power for a new compartment of the shaft, which, when completed, will give three hoisting-compartments and one pumping-compartment, and give hoisting capacity of fully 1,000 tons per day.

During the time occupied in reconstructing machinery, the water in the mine rose to 16 feet above the 1,500-foot station, but now it has been reduced by small pumps driven by compressed air and water-tanks 7 feet, and by the 18th instant the large pumping-engine will be completed and started, which will rapidly clear the mine of water and allow us to resume hoisting ore.

RECEIPTS.

Bucks shaft construction:	
Sale of material	$3,556 18
Ophir Mine:	
Sale of material	2,422 98
Assessment No. 29	201,600 00

Expense assessment No. 29:		
Received for advertising charges		$269 75
Insurance		59,000 00
Bullion account:		
Face of bullion	$1,811,084 33	
Assay grains	6,102 86	
		1,817,187 19
Virginia and Truckee Railroad Company:		
Rebate		6,624 27
Union Consolidated Silver-Mining Company:		
Hoisting 2,400 tons of rock		4,800 00
Bucks shaft building:		
Sale of lumber		354 80
Total receipts		2,095,815 17
Cash on hand December 16, 1874		495 07
Total		2,096,310 24

DISBURSEMENTS.

Ophir Mine:		
Surveying	$1,250 00	
Printing	324 00	
Recording	25 75	
Virginia and Storey County taxes	2,306 14	
Horses and feed	2,897 74	
Ore-tax	9,110 62	
Rubber, clothing, blankets, &c	1,329 00	
Purchase of real estate	7,250 00	
Sundries	822 50	
		$25,315 75
Office expense, San Francisco:		
Rent	1,800 00	
Stationery	270 33	
Stock-boards	625 00	
Newspapers, express charges, &c	261 41	
Salaries	8,125 00	
Lithographing and printing	669 50	
Fuel	46 00	
Carpenter's work	29 00	
Donation to Virginia City sufferers	500 00	
		12,326 24
Expense assessment No. 29:		
Amount paid for advertising		106 50
Insurance:		
Premiums		2,400 00
Bucks shaft building:		
Pay-roll	$21,047 75	
Paint and painting	4,276 14	
Freight and hauling	4,183 17	
Lumber, doors, windows, nails, &c	27,801 30	
Hardware	276 75	
		57,585 11
Discount on bullion		80,200 06
Freight on bullion		1,848 10
Melting bullion		5,165 16
Interest		7,623 04
Milling		773,798 50
Virginia and Gold Hill Water Company:		
Water		5,500 00
General expense at mine:		
Salaries	$8,760 00	
Stationery, telegrams, newspapers, &c	2,900 06	
Discount and exchange	7,774 12	
Fuel	99 00	
Donations	220 00	
Matting	38 25	
Safe	575 00	
		20,356 43

Bucks shaft construction:		
Labor	$329,136 35	
Hardware	42,008 84	
Candles	7,850 90	
Freight	3,854 93	
Wood, lumber, and timbers	104,042 17	
Coal and charcoal	2,728 39	
Supplies, clothing, &c	3,254 50	
Surgery	1,751 50	
Foundery work	4,205 20	
Carbons and drills	6,240 50	
Wire cables	21,916 04	
Expense extinguishing fire	1,250 00	
		$528,239 32
Bucks shaft machinery:		
Labor	54,408 68	
Foundery work	24,588 76	
Hardware	10,686 47	
Oil and tallow	5,386 93	
Hauling and freight	30,729 09	
Horses and feed	154 06	
Grading	2,283 76	
Engines and machinery	177,968 74	
Lime	666 50	
Foundations	37,346 92	
		344,219 91
Assay-office:		
Pay-roll	3,056 00	
Scales	283 81	
Material	628 76	
		3,968 57
Legal expense		5,684 25
Traveling expense		900 00
Sutro Tunnel committee		415 80
Total disbursements		1,875,662 72
Superintendent Samuel T. Curtis:		
Cash with superintendent, on superintendent's account, in excess of last year's balance		9,393 40
Cash account:		
Cash on hand December 15, 1875		211,254 10
Total		2,096,310 24

Ore, shipped and worked, assay-values, and bullion returns.

Months.	Ore shipped to mills.		Ore worked.		Assay-value per ton.	Yield per ton.	Yield per cent. of assay-value.	Assay value of bullion.			Value of samples, &c.	Total yield of ore.
	Tons.	Lbs.	Tons.	Lbs.				Gold.	Silver.	Total.		
1874.												
On hand December 1	105	1,340										
December	6,243	950	4,747		$37 77	$28 27	.74 8-10	$57,412 37	$76,155 89	$133,568 26	$645 51	$134,213 77
1875.												
January	3,233	1,700	4,426	900	38 63	26 34	.68 2-10	49,886 25	66,288 97	116,175 22	410 28	116,585 50
February	3,377	800	3,333		36 17	22 18	.61 3-10	32,016 27	41,665 57	73,681 84	241 13	73,922 97
March	3,827	1,750	3,193		41 70	30 36	.72 8-10	43,702 59	52,956 76	96,659 35	290 65	96,950 00
April	4,064	1,650	2,764		40 20	28 17	.70	33,961 79	43,641 43	77,603 22	258 92	77,862 14
May	3,721	1,700	4,372		41 31	29 05	.70	54,826 07	71,752 99	126,579 06	426 71	127,005 77
June	4,928	300	4,527		40 41	26 94	.66 6-10	51,350 08	70,253 91	121,603 99	364 35	121,968 34
July	5,442	700	5,100		45 84	34 82	.76	81,968 35	95,088 48	177,056 83	543 15	177,599 98
August	3,051	800	4,989	1,000	55 30	43 77	.79	97,375 51	120,244 33	217,619 84	792 82	218,412 66
September	5,904	425	4,806	1,500	66 29	52 72	.79 5-10	112,576 13	140,058 31	252,634 44	783 77	253,418 21
October	7,527	825	7,825	540	56 59	43 52	.76 9-10	159,710 95	179,711 16	339,422 11	1,102 64	340,541 88
November			1,344	1,000	61 58	58 54	.95	36,309 66	42,170 51	78,480 17	242 93	78,723 10
Averages and totals	51,428	940	51,428	940	47 45	35 33	.74 5-10	811,096 02	999,988 31	1,811,084 33	6,102 86	1,817,187 19

California.—Mr. James G. Fair, the superintendent, makes the following report:

During the past year the mine has been prospected as follows:

On the 1,300-foot level a drift has been run from the southern to the northern boundary, west of the ore-vein, connecting with the openings of the Ophir Mine.

Cross-cut No. 1 has been run east 213 feet on the southern boundary to the ore-vein. This drift has been extended north in the ore-vein 100 feet, connecting with the winze sunk in the ore-body to the 1,400-foot level. The ore found thus far on this 1,300-foot level has been of moderate quality, but that found in sinking the winze has been good from level to level.

On the 1,400-foot level a drift has been run west of the ore-vein the whole length of the mine connecting with the Ophir Mine on the north. Cross-cuts Nos. 1, 2, and 3 have also been extended from this drift across the ore-vein.

A lateral drift has also been run north from the southern boundary in the ore-vein 560 feet and will soon be connected with the workings of the Ophir Mine. A large amount of valuable ore is already developed on this level, but it is less regular than on the levels below.

On the 1,500-foot level a drift has been run from the southern to the northern boundary, west of the ore-vein. Cross-cuts have been run from this drift, 100 feet apart, making six in all. The ore thus developed shows a width of from 75 to 208 feet. Cross-cuts Nos. 1 and 2 have crossed the ore-vein. Cross-cuts Nos. 3, 4, 5, and 6 have not yet been extended across the ore-vein, and its width is unknown. A lateral drift has been run in the ore-vein from the southern to the northern boundary, crossing all of these cross-cuts and intercepting the openings of the Ophir Mine. The ore passed through the entire length of this drift, except the northern 70 feet, has been of exceedingly high grade, assaying for weeks during its construction $1,000 per ton. Three double winzes have been raised in the ore-body from this level in cross-cuts Nos. 1, 2, and 3 to the 1,400-foot level, all passing through ore of excellent quality.

Four winzes have also been sunk from the lateral drift in cross-cuts Nos. 1, 2, 3, and 5 to the 1,550-foot level, all of them passing through ore of high grade the whole distance. The developments on this level disclose a very large amount of exceedingly rich ore.

On the 1,550-foot level the main drift has been extended north 400 feet from the southern boundary to cross-cut No. 5, in the ore-body, passing through exceedingly rich ore, and the face of this drift is yet in ore of this quality. This main drift intersects all of the winzes sunk from the 1,500-foot level. In cross-cut No. 1 the ore-body has been developed to a width of 130 feet, and the ore-vein is not yet crossed.

Cross-cut No. 3 has been extended 65 feet, and neither east nor west walls have yet been reached.

Cross-cut No. 5 has been developed 75 feet, and both ends of the drift are in high-grade ore, as neither the east nor west walls have yet been reached.

Between cross-cuts Nos. 2 and 3 a double winze has been sunk to the depth of 128 feet, through ore of excellent quality the entire distance, which terminates in ore of the same richness. Another winze has been sunk 320 feet south of the southern boundary to a depth of 147 feet. No cross-cuts have been run from the bottom of these winzes. The developments made by these winzes prove the continuity at these lower depths, of the same ore-body which exists on the levels above, with an appreciation in the quality of the ore, which must be of great width.

The sinking of these winzes has been temporarily discontinued on account of the increase of water and the limited means of hoisting. This difficulty will soon be obviated by the drift that is being run on the 1,700-foot level of the Consolidated Virginia Mine.

This level is but partially explored. The ore found is of better quality than that on the levels above, and there is little doubt but that the ore-body is of much greater width.

My efforts the past year have been to open the mine as thoroughly as possible on all the levels, and, at the same time, to take out as little ore as possible.

The ore thus removed (5,123¾ tons) has been daily hoisted, weighed, assayed, and passed to our credit by the Consolidated Virginia Mine, we not then having the mills to reduce it.

All of the levels are connected with the Consolidated Virginia Mine on the south, and with the Ophir Mine on the north; also by the various winzes referred to, which thoroughly ventilates the mine and makes it cool and pleasant.

At the C. & C. shaft buildings complete in every respect have been erected, and machinery for pumping and hoisting has been put in place, and is now in full operation. In addition to the main building, there is a blacksmith-shop, a rope-house, two large carpenter-shops, and one machine-shop. The carpenter-shops are supplied each with an engine and machinery—one of these shops being intended for the use of the Consolidated Virginia Mine, and the other for the California mine.

The machine-shop is fitted up with engines, lathes, tools, &c., one side of which is for the use of the Consolidated Virginia Mine and the other side for the California Mine. For security against all fires, the works are surrounded by hydrants, with a good supply of fire-hose; and there is an ample supply of water under a very heavy pressure.

A large area of ground immediately surrounding the site of this shaft has been secured, having been purchased at a heavy outlay.

This shaft is situated 1,040 feet east of the Consolidated Virginia shaft.

It is now sunk with three compartments to the depth of 938 feet. The cost of this joint shaft to January 1, 1876, was $436,183.13.

A drift is now being run east from the 1,500-foot level of the mine, which will connect with the C. & C. shaft.

It will reach that shaft and be in readiness for the transportation of ore as soon as the shaft is sunk to that depth.

Two hundred and eighty-eight feet remain to be sunk to reach this drift.

After this connection is made with the C. & C. shaft, I feel safe in saying that our hoisting capacity will be 2,000 tons per day, and as to the supply of ore we have now in sight in the mine a sufficient quantity to last for a long period.

The secretary of the California reports the following receipts and disbursements during the year:

RECEIPTS.

Amount due from Virginia office, last statement, since paid	$1,113 74
Amount due from Bank of California, last statement, since paid	574 12
Amount received January 18, 1876, from sale of ore	453,060 46
Nevada Bank over-draft	28,247 77
	482,996 09

DISBURSEMENTS.

J. C. Flood, amount due him, since paid	$80,500 00
Freight	220 10
Expense	4,756 42
Advertising	101 25
Books and stationery	1,254 90
Salaries and wages	87,473 50
Supplies	12,745 56
Title	25,000 00
Hoisting	2,681 50
Contribution	500 00
Virginia office expense	210 60
Interest and exchange	37,356 59
Sutro committee	129 00
Survey	600 00
Taxes	277 75
Legal expense	10,950 00
C. & C. shaft	218,091 62
Cash on hand	147 30
	482,996 09

Consolidated Virginia.—This mine has been the most prosperous one on the continent during the past year. A regular monthly dividend has been paid to the stockholders, which during the last ten months has been at the rate of $10 per share. Besides an unparalleled extraction of ore, a vast amount of exploring work has been done.

In October, the disastrous fire which destroyed the greater part of Virginia City, swept away also the extensive hoisting-works and buildings at the mine, together with a vast accumulation of supplies and the splendid 60-stamp Consolidated and California mills, the latter of which was about ready to start. This seriously affected the crushing facilities of the mine, and also compelled the stoppage of ore-extraction and nearly all underground work and bullion shipments until the hoisting-works and necessary buildings could be replaced. But in the face of the most serious difficulties, and at the worst season of the year, this was accomplished by the indomitable energy of the superintendent, Mr. James G. Fair, in the short space of not quite two months, the new machinery and buildings being superior to those destroyed.

Mr. Fair's report on the operations at the mine during the past year is as follows:

VIRGINIA, NEV., *December* 31, 1875.

During the past year 169,307$\frac{462}{2000}$ tons of ore have been abstracted from all the levels of the Consolidated Virginia Mine, and 169,094$\frac{1806}{2000}$ tons have been reduced, which yielded $16,731,653.43 in bullion. There are now in the ore-house and at the mills 2,988$\frac{194}{2000}$ tons, valued by assay at $478,080.

This ore has been taken from the 1,200, 1,300, 1,400, and 1,500 foot levels, including a small quantity which has been gathered in the explorations which have been made on the 1,550-foot level.

On the 1,200 and 1,300 foot levels the ore-bodies have not been developed as far as they extend north. On the 1,400-foot level the ore has been explored south 450 feet from the shaft, and it extends north from the shaft to the northern boundary of the mine. On this (the 1,400-foot) level the exact width of the ore-body is known.

On the 1,500-foot level the ore has been traced south for a distance of 480 feet from the northern line, and has been thoroughly explored by cross-cuts from the east wall to the west wall. On this level all the ore is of a high grade and the width of the body varies from 150 feet to 320 feet. The ground south of this is entirely unexplored.

On the 1,550-foot level a lateral drift extends the whole length of the mine. Starting at the southern boundary it runs northerly on the east side of the ore until it reaches a point 400 feet distant from the northern line, where it cuts through the clay, and thence passes all the way through ore to the northern line. This level is only partially developed. None of the cross-cuts have yet reached the eastern boundary of the ore. The ore on this level is of a better quality than that which has been found on any of the levels above. Its width, I have no doubt, will prove greater.

At a point 320 feet south of the northern line a double winze has been sunk from this (1,550-foot) level to the depth of 147 feet. This winze has passed all the way through ore of a very high grade, and terminates in ore of the same quality. The sinking of this winze has been temporarily discontinued on account of the increase of water and our limited means for hoisting. From this same level, north of the northern line, another double winze has been sunk to the depth of 128 feet, through excellent ore the entire distance, which terminates in rich ore. The developments made by these winzes prove the continuity, at these lower depths, of the same ore-body which exists on the level above, with an appreciation in the quality of the ore.

From this level, (the 1,550-foot,) at the southern boundary, a double winze has also been sunk down to the 1,700-foot level. From the bottom of this winze a drift has been run north 107 feet. This winze and drift are both east of the ore-vein, and consequently no information in regard to the ore in this locality and at this depth has been gained by the work. Work on this drift was discontinued two months ago on account of the water which flowed into it from the Gould & Curry Mine. This obstacle will soon be removed, and work will be resumed.

All the levels of the mine are connected by various winzes, reaching from level to level for ventilation and the passage of men and materials. The 1,200, 1,300, and 1,550 foot levels are connected with the Gould & Curry shaft for ventilation, and the 1,200, 1,300, 1,400, and 1,500 foot levels are connected with the Ophir Mine for the same purpose.

There is a large reserve of ore in all the levels of the mine which have been opened. In extracting the ore, instead of trying to show an extraordinary yield by the working of the higher grade alone, it has been my constant purpose to so unite the higher and lower grades of ore as to make the average yield conform to an average standard value. And this I have done, believing such a course to be for the best interest of the company.

The complete destruction of our hoisting-works and ore-house by the disastrous fire which occurred on the 26th of October last stopped all work in the mine from that day up to the 13th day of December, on which date we again commenced to hoist ore, and since that time more than 600 tons of ore have been raised daily. This quantity of ore exceeds our present milling capacity, but in fifteen days more this milling capacity per day will be increased 260 tons.

The entire hoisting-works, with ore-house, have been rebuilt on an enlarged scale, with many improved conveniences in the various departments. A two-story building, 100 feet by 50 feet, is in the process of erection, to be used for the assay and bullion department, and it is now about one-half completed. When finished there will be room and facilities for melting and assaying $5,000,000 of bullion per month.

A large extent of ground around and in the vicinity of the hoisting-works has been purchased to give ample space for the storage of wood, timber, and mine materials.

By the acquisition of this ground the hoisting-works now stand in a comparatively isolated situation, so that there will be but little danger from any fire except that which might originate on our own premises.

For security against all fires, the works are surrounded by hydrants, with a good supply of fire-hose, and there is an ample supply of water under a heavy pressure. I will also add that the city of Virginia is constructing a perfect system of water-works. These works will surround us and give additional protection against fire.

The Virginia and Truckee Railroad encircles us on three sides, so that our mine-supplies are conveniently landed on the west or upper side, and our ore is expeditiously shipped from the east or lower side of the works.

At the C. & C. shaft buildings complete in every respect have been erected, and machinery for pumping and hoisting has been put in place and is now in full operation. In addition to the main building there is a blacksmith-shop, a rope-house, two large carpenter-shops, and one machine-shop. The carpenter-shops are supplied each with an engine and machinery—one of these shops being intended for the use of the Consolidated Virginia Mine and the other for the California Mine. The machine-shop is fitted up with engines, lathes, tools, &c.—one side of which is for the use of the Consolidated Virginia Mine and the other side for the California Mine.

A large area of ground immediately surrounding the site of this shaft has been secured, having been purchased at a heavy outlay. This shaft is situated 1,040 feet east of the Consolidated Virginia shaft. It is now sunk, with three compartments, to the depth of 940 feet. The cost of this joint shaft to this date has been $436,183.13.

A drift is now being run east from the 1,500-foot level of the Consolidated Virginia Mine, which will connect with the C. & C. shaft. It will reach that shaft and be in readiness for the transportation of ore as soon as the shaft is sunk to that depth. Three hundred and thirty-six feet remain to be sunk to reach this drift.

After this connection with the C. & C. shaft is made, I feel safe in saying that our hoisting capacity will be 2,000 tons per day, and as to the supply of ore, we have now in sight in the mine a sufficient quantity to last for many years.

The secretary of the company reports the following receipts and disbursements:

RECEIPTS.

Bullion		$16,953,771 39
Bullion-samples		3,767 60
Assay		1,544 44
Insurance		14,696 25
Balance-account, including balances due at last annual meeting from superintendent, treasurer, and banks, all since paid:		
Bank of California	$82,450 43	
J. G. Fair, superintendent	4,655 80	
	87,106 23	
Less due J. C. Flood, treasurer	03	
		87,106 20
		17,060,885 88

DISBURSEMENTS.

James G. Fair, superintendent	$142,471 29
Cash	639 95
Nevada Bank	40,462 73
Virginia office expenses	6,888 65
Wood, lumber, and timber	285,437 91
Repairs	974 31
Hauling	2,174 18
Freight	5,550 20
Sutro committee	1,998 00
Survey	1,300 00
Books and stationery	937 85
Legal expense	27,505 00
Advertising	288 50
Water	4,500 00
Real estate	15,995 75
Contribution	750 00
Latrobe tunnel	2,942 00
Hoisting	8,382 50
Construction	96,935 53

Taxes	$152,795 13
Bullion reclamation	4,344 18
Reduction	2,198,236 97
Interest and exchange	1,530 50
Bullion freight	56,383 79
Dividends Nos. 10 to 21 inclusive	12,204,000 00
C. & C. joint shaft	201,981 89
Bullion discount	640,715 48
Back dividends	4 50
Supplies	157,519 76
Salaries and wages	760,698 87
Expense	6,540 46
	17,060,885 88

Best & Belcher.—Mr. Fair, who superintends also this mine and the Gould & Curry, makes the following statements: The Best and Belcher has no works of its own, adjoins the Consolidated Virginia on the south, and has 600 feet of ground. A north drift has been run the whole length of the mine, but no cross-cuts made on account of the great flow of water likely to be encountered, and draining being impossible in the absence of machinery. The outside vein-matter is precisely the same as Consolidated Virginia, and assays from $5 to $20 where found. Heavy machinery will shortly be erected.

Gould & Curry.—During the past year the entire shaft has been retimbered and new and larger pumps put in. A heavy flow of water from the 1,500 and 1,700 foot levels prevented any prospecting during the year.

The following is an abstract of Mr. Fair's annual report to the company for the fiscal year ending November 30, 1875:

The superintendent, in his annual report, says that in the previous annual report he recommended that two additional compartments of the main shaft be sunk from the 1,200-foot to the 1,500-foot level, and that during the year the work was done, doubling the hoisting capacity as well as bettering the ventilation of the mine. Work on the shaft between the 1,500-foot level and the surface had been continuous throughout the twelvemonth. Notwithstanding this work the shaft is now in bad condition and extremely dangerous—the swelling ground crushes in the timbers and is a constant source of delay and expense, and Mr. Fair recommends a stoppage of work for a short time and a substantial retimbering of the four compartments of the shaft, from the 1,500-foot to the fifth levels. This can be done at the same time work in the mine is carried on, but, in the superintendent's opinion, the cost by this method would be doubled, and the work would not be as substantial as it would be were all other work stopped. The year has shown a material increase in the flow of water in the mine, three-quarters of it coming from the east side of the shaft over 1,500-foot level. All of the 8-inch pumps have been removed within the year, and a 12-inch pump substituted, but even with this increased capacity he was unable to keep the mine free from water below the 1,600-foot level. The moving of the timbers in the shaft displaces pumps and pump-rods, causing stoppages constantly and the accumulation of water, which can only be remedied by a thorough retimbering of the shaft. On the 1,700-foot level the main drift has been extended to the northern boundary and connected with the Best & Belcher joint winze sunk from the 1,500-foot level, which secured a good ventilation. The east drift on this level has been run east from the incline 1,033 feet to the east wall of the vein, but as it showed strong indications of water, and as the pumps were already working to their full capacity, it was deemed best not to cut into the vein. No cross-cuts have yet been made on this level, and its value, therefore, has not been ascertained. The formations passed through by lateral drifts look favorable and assay from $5 to $20 per ton, but all the work done so far is outside the ore-vein. The winze sunk 182 feet below the 1,700-foot level, designed to connect with the 2,000-foot level of the Savage, is now filled with water. The 1,500-foot level has been thoroughly developed by cross-cuts in all parts, but no ore of value has been discovered. Much work has been done on the levels above, in prospecting new levels, and repairing and extending old ones, but all have failed to disclose ore of value. It is evident, says the superintendent in concluding his report, that the company must look to the 1,700-foot level and further depths for the production of ores. Buildings, engines, and machinery are in excellent order, and there are good supplies of timber and materials on hand for the winter.

The following is a synopsis of the secretary's report: Receipts during the fiscal year amounted to $339,399, of which $97,648 were from an assessment, $222,749 from the sale of 12,000 shares of stock, and $18,466 from various other sources. Disbursements amounted to $328,377, leaving as cash on hand at the close, $11,022. Of the disbursements $280,348 was for labor, $4,090 for sluice-tunnel, $3,503 for legal expenses, $1,174 for exchange, $22,972 for general expenses, $3,766 for interest, $1,752 for taxes, and $29.84 for minor items.

Savage.—This mine has attained a vertical depth by main incline of 2,300 feet. A winze has been sunk 120 feet below that, making total vertical depth 2,420 feet. No cross-cuts have been made during the year, but drifts north and south on the 2,000 and 2,200-foot levels have been run nearly the entire length of the claim. A heavy body of water was encountered at the bottom of the incline, which arose to the 2,100-foot level and filled all the lower levels. By the middle of January the pumps and tanks had so reduced the water as to allow of work being again prosecuted, when a second body of water broke in the north drift, 2,200-foot level, and flooded the mine up the 1,800-foot level, where it now stands. Heavy pumping-machinery is being constructed; until this is completed, it will be impossible to go on with the work.

I owe these facts to Mr. F. F. Osbiston, the superintendent, to whom I am also indebted for most valuable assistance, and particularly for the collection of reports from other superintendents, and for the compilation of the larger part of the material here submitted concerning the Comstock mines.

Hale & Norcross.—This mine is in the same condition as the Savage, they being connected by drifts on each level. The water affects both mines in the same way, which can only be overcome by the application of heavy machinery. James G. Fair is the superintendent.

Chollar.—This mine continues to extract ore from the old workings, the yield for 1875 being 18,850 tons, which milled $317,382.32, an average of $16.84 per ton. There are 1,400 feet in the claim; the vertical depth of the shaft is 1,350 feet. On the 1,050, 1,150, 1,250, and 1,350 foot levels drifts have been run to the south line and the necessary cross-cuts made without discovering any bodies of ore. The indications, however, are very flattering, and the company is confident of yet finding paying ore-bodies on getting deeper.

Mr. I. L. Requa, the superintendent of this and the succeeding company, has furnished the facts concerning them.

Chollar, Norcross, and Savage Shaft Companies.—The Chollar, Hale & Norcross, and Savage Companies have commenced to sink a combination shaft situated 3,000 feet east of the Chollar shaft. This is to be used by the three companies, each bearing its share of the expense of sinking, as follows: Chollar contributes $\frac{14}{26}$; Hale & Norcross contributes $\frac{4}{26}$; Savage contributes $\frac{8}{26}$. This will be the largest shaft on the Comstock; there will be four compartments, three of which will be for hoisting purposes and one for pumping entirely. The hoisting compartments will be 5 by 6 feet, the pump compartment 6 by 7 feet. The shaft will be most substantially timbered with 14-inch square timbers, framed in sets, 6 feet from centers. The pumping-machinery, now under contract, will consist of two lines of 12-inch inside diameter pumps connected with one 14 by 14 inch pump-rod. The machinery is to be of sufficient power to sink 5,000 feet. The pumps will be worked by a compound cylinder engine—initial cylinder 34-inch and main cylinder 68-inch diameter, vertical and direct acting. The contract-price is $260,000. The hoisting-machinery will be of the most improved pattern; in fact, it is to be *the* hoisting-works of the Comstock.

It is calculated that the shaft will cut the Comstock ledge at about

3,500 feet. The shaft is now being sunk in east country-rock about 4,000 feet east of where the vein shows in the croppings. This shaft will be a great saving to the companies when completed to the vein, as it will do away with the inclines now used, which are both expensive and inconvenient.

Bullion.—Although this mine has never yet produced any paying bodies of ore, Mr. E. A. Schultz, superintendent of the Bullion, Exchequer, and Alpha, writes that he considers the present prospect very flattering. The depth of the shaft is 1,400 feet. Drifting on this level (1,400-foot) a distance of 150 feet south and 275 feet north, and making two cross-cuts, one north and one south, some streaks of ore 2 feet wide were found on the hanging-wall assaying from $10 to $120. Pitch of vein 40° east. A drift from the 1,700-foot of Imperial shaft (equal to 1,830-foot level of the Bullion) has been run through the Alpha and Exchequer Companies' ground, and an upraise commenced to connect with the incline at the 1,400-foot level. No explorations have been made on the 1,830-foot level, owing to the insufficiency of air. A drift has been started from the Imperial shaft at the 2,000-foot level, which is the 2,130-foot of the Bullion, by three companies, the Bullion, Alpha, and Exchequer, to prospect their ground. The drift is in west country-rock, not having reached the vein yet. Number of feet in claim, 943$\frac{7}{10}$.

Exchequer.—This mine has 400 feet in its claim. The company is said to be a very close corporation. The ground is being prospected by the combination drift from the Imperial 2,000-foot level. Prospects favorable. The company has no works of its own.

Alpha.—The same as was said of the Exchequer will apply to this mine. The company claims 300 feet adjoining the Exchequer on the south. No hoisting-works.

Imperial.—This mine, as reported by Mr. C. C. Batterman, the superintendent, has reached a vertical depth of 2,150 feet. No prospecting has been done deeper than the 2,000-foot level. No new bodies of ore have been encountered during the past year. The work of developing the ore already in sight has been vigorously carried on, and some ore extracted and milled which yielded an average of about $30 per ton. The width of the vein on the 2,000-foot level is unknown, as no cross-cuts have cut entirely through it yet. During the year there were 1,448 feet of drifts run and 248 feet winzes sunk.

Gold Hill proper.—Under this head come the small claims situated between the Imperial and the Yellow Jacket, varying in length from 10 to 120 feet, all of which are prospected through the Imperial and Yellow Jacket shafts. The situation of these claims on lowest levels is the same as Imperial and Yellow Jacket. A consolidation of these claims is spoken of, which will probably soon take place, when hoisting-works will be erected.

Yellow Jacket.—This mine has attained a depth of 1,940 feet, 100 feet of incline being sunk last year. No ore was produced in 1875. There have been run on the 1,740, 1,840, and 1,940 foot levels about 4,000 feet of drift. The vein varies from 250 to 320 feet in width and pitches 40° to the east. Some seams of ore have been encountered on every level, but not sufficient quantities to pay for extracting. The assay-value averages about $11 per ton. The ledge continues to hold its strength and regularity and is quite free from water. Value of improvements, $400,000, consisting of hoisting-works and machinery. The entire bullion product of the mine, as reported by Mr. Thomas S. Taylor, the superintendent, to whom I am indebted for the above account, has been $14,500,000, and dividends $2,184,000; assessments, $2,349,000.

Kentuck.—This company has for the last five years done no work from and through its own shaft, which is but 700 feet deep. There are deeper shafts on each side of its ground, which contains but 96 feet, and has been thoroughly prospected from both the Crown Point and Yellow Jacket shafts. The vein is very strong, and carries a very large proportion of quartz, which, however, assays but little. No ore has been extracted for the past five years. Mr. S. L. Jones, the superintendent, has charge of the Crown Point also, and has favored me with the accounts here published of both mines.

Crown Point.—This mine contains 600 feet of the length of the lode, and has attained a vertical depth of 1,700 feet. There have been 8,000 feet of drifts and winzes run during 1875 on the 1,500, 1,600, and 1,700 foot levels. The width of the ledge varies from 75 to 150 feet and pitches very regularly 36° east. On the 1,500-foot level the ore is of low grade, containing about $30 in gold and silver to the ton. On the 1,600-foot the quartz is the same as on the 1,500, but contains less metal until it reaches a point 100 feet north of the Belcher line, where a decided improvement takes place, and the ore-body apparently assumes its former size and value. On the 1,700-foot one drift has been run, which is to the east of the incline, and exposes 140 feet of quartz, assaying from $4 to $10, with a base-metal streak of about 4 feet inside nearly in the center. Owing to the great heat, which is 120° Fahrenheit, this drift has been stopped for the present without having reached to east wall. The total amount extracted in 1875 is 155,180 tons, which yielded $3,124,052. The total amount of bullion produced since 1865 is $28,449,387.68. Dividends paid during the same, $11,898. Assessments for the same period, $662,100. Improvements valued at $400,000.

Belcher.—This mine contains 1,040 feet on the lode; vertical depth, 1,650 feet. The width of the ledge varies from 200 to 300 feet, and pitches 37° east. Number of tons of ore extracted in 1875 was 126,350; value of ore extracted during same time, $3,107,993. Total value of ore extracted since 1865, $31,411,938.31; amount of dividends paid during same time, $15,393,600; amount of assessments, $660,400. The width of ore on the 1,500-foot level is about 60 feet, and will yield about $30 per ton. On account of water and the absence of pumps in this mine, but little has been done below the 1,500-foot level, and nothing is known of the value and extent of the ore-body. New pumping-machinery is now being put in place, at a cost of $400,000; expense to be divided between the Crown Point and Belcher Companies. This will enable them to prospect to a depth of 4,000 feet. The pumps will be placed in the air-shaft, which has been retimbered since the fire, and will now be used for pumping as well as ventilation. Mr. W. H. Smith, the superintendent, furnishes the facts as to this mine, and also the Segregated Belcher.

The following is an abstract of the secretary's report for the fiscal year of the company:

The receipts were: From bullion, $3,383,873.55; cash on hand, January 1, 1875, $242,079.15. The principal items of disbursements were: From dividend No. 34, $312,000; the aggregate expenses were $2,846,717.65; cash on hand, $329,759.45, and a time certificate in the Bank of California of $148,952,61. There were 34,117 tons of ore worked during the year, which yielded at the rate of $28.43 per ton.

To this may be added the following:

The drift running south from the incline, 1,500-foot level, is in a distance of 416 feet. The east drift, same level, on the sill-floor, has attained a length of 92 feet. The northeast drift, on the 1,600-foot level, is in 332 feet. The stopes continue to yield well, especially the 1,500-foot level, the ore from which runs very high in gold.

Segregated Belcher.—This mine has 160 feet of ground, and has been prospected of late years through the Belcher and Overman shafts.

Some streaks of very rich ore found on the 1,300-foot level, which is their lowest working level, but not in paying quantities. Mr. W. H. Smith is the superintendent.

Overman.—This mine contains 1,200 feet of ground. The shaft, which is in east country-rock, has attained a vertical depth of 1,168 feet. The mine has been prospected throughout the north 600 feet, on the 700, 900, and 1,100 foot levels. Four hundred feet north of the shaft there has been sunk a winze, which has followed a very regular wall on the west side from the 700 to the 1,100 foot levels. In this winze, and lying on the foot-wall, some very rich seams of ore, varying from 2 inches to 6 feet, have been discovered, of which about 400 tons have been extracted, the value of which is about $20,000. The ore is remarkably free from all base metals. During the past year very little prospecting has been done on the 1,100-foot level, owing to an immense flow of water at the bottom of the shaft. New and powerful pumps, the largest now in use on the lode, are successfully handling the water, and the sinking of the shaft is being carried on. The pumps, which are 14 inches diameter and 8 feet stroke, run at the rate of 6 strokes a minute. The sinking is necessarily slow, and but 5 feet per week are added to the depth of the shaft. There have been 2,500 feet of drifts run on the various levels, none of which, excepting the north drift on the 900-foot level, have developed any ores of value. Mr. Charles Forman, the superintendent of this mine, has charge of the Caledonia also, and has furnished the accounts of both.

Caledonia.—During the past year a new shaft, 1,040 feet east of the old shaft, has attained a vertical depth of 945 feet. No drifting has been done from this shaft, except to cut the vein at a depth of 1,600 feet. Value of improvements on the mine, $240,000. The old shaft is shut down, owing to the ground through which it passed being clay and very heavy on the timbers, which made it troublesome and expensive to keep in repair. Considerable low-grade ore has been extracted from this mine in former years, but not of sufficient value to pay over expenses.

Justice.—This mine, which has heretofore been considered an outside claim, has the past year developed considerable ore, of which assays as high as $7,000 have been procured. The average value, however, of the ore developed so far, being 120 feet long and 15 feet wide, is about $35 per ton. The rock is of a gypsum character. There have been 1,100 tons extracted during the past year, which milled $26 per ton. The ore is found on the 600-foot level, the course of which is north 22° west. The lowest level is the 860-foot; no prospecting has been done at this point. The future of the mine is very encouraging, there being a large quantity of milling-ore in sight. Cost of improvements, $120,000. During the year 1875, 1,500 feet of drifts were run on various levels. Mr. T. J. McClelland, the superintendent, is authority for these statements.

Silver Hill.—This property is a consolidation of the Echo, Saint Louis, and Lucerne claims, and adjoins Justice on the south. The claim embraces 4,075 feet. Two distinct ledges run through this ground, each cropping out prominently at the surface, and can be traced nearly the entire length of the claim. The mine has yielded over $1,000,000 in bullion, principally gold; but as depth is obtained the silver is increasing and gold decreasing. The vein on the 334-foot level is about 120 feet wide and has well-defined walls on either side; the pitch is 45° east. Thousands of tons of ore have been extracted from the first, second, and third levels. The south portion of the mine has been prospected but little. Vertical depth of shaft is 444 feet. An incline was begun here, and is now down 111 feet. The character of the ore is much the same as that of the Justice. For the above description I have to thank Mr. John Van de Water, the superintendent.

Succor.—This company, which has for several years produced considerable bullion, has for the last two years been engaged in sinking a new shaft some 2,000 feet to the east of the old workings. The shaft is now 630 feet deep, and some fine ore, assaying as high as $275, has been struck in the bottom of the shaft. As this development has been made but a few days, it is impossible to state its value. Mr. John Segur, who furnishes the above description, is the superintendent.

Dayton.—As I learn from Mr. N. C. Hall, the superintendent, this mine, situated on the line of the Comstock, has been a producing one for several years, having yielded $340,000; but the ore of the surface-workings to a depth of 300 feet has almost given out, and the company are now sinking their shaft deeper in hopes of the ore coming in again, as the ledge is remarkably well defined and its walls very regular. Depth of shaft, 650 feet; lowest drift, 500 feet.

Kossuth.—This mine has 2,700 feet of ground, and joins the Dayton on the south. The shaft is 600 feet deep. Pitch of vein, 40° east; width of vein, 80 feet. Assay-value of ore, $12. The mine has produced about $50,000 in bullion. Value of improvements, $150,000. Ledge well defined and holds its strength throughout its entire depth. At a distance of 1,400 feet north and south considerable water coming from the 350 and 500 foot levels. The south end of the mine has of late shown considerable improvement on both the 350 and 500 foot levels, the ore occasionally assaying as high as $170. Mr. P. H. Scott, the superintendent, who furnished the above statement, considers the prospects of this mine very encouraging.

Webber contains 1,500 feet, and joins the Kossuth on the south. This being a new location, little can be said. The shaft is down 125 feet. Kossuth's prospects are encouraging for this mine. Mr. J. P. Hutchinson is the superintendent.

Daney.—This mine is next to the Webber on the south, has erected fine machinery, and is now 500 feet deep. Drifting on 400-foot level has developed a large and well-defined vein, but no ore of value has been extracted. The claim has 2,000 feet of ground. The mine has been shut down for several months, but will resume operations about the 1st of March next. Mr. T. J. McClelland is the superintendent.

Quinn.—This, the next mine of importance south, is considered a very promising one. Considerable money has been expended in developing the ledge already found and known to be of value. The croppings are very prominent, and assays as high as $1,000 are obtained from them. The company has strong hope of discovering a bonanza in the claim, and, as the prospects warrant it, no expense will be spared in its early development. The quartz found is very similar to that in the Belcher and Crown Point, being strong and healthy and very free from base metals. Contains about two-thirds silver to one-third gold, and is the only mine on the Comstock that shows bromide of silver. This mine is unlike other mines in the Spring Valley district, as most of them, commencing at the Dayton, north, show but little silver. Mr. F. F. Osbiston is superintendent.

Knickerbocker.—This mine is situated on the southwest branch of the Comstock lode and adjoins the Caledonia on the south. Prospecting is being carried on to a depth of 700 feet, but Mr. H. V. S. McCullough, the superintendent, reports that no ore of value has been found.

Baltimore.—This mine joins the Knickerbocker on the south, and has 1,050 feet of ground. The shaft has attained a depth of 1,100 feet.

Prospecting from the shaft has been carried on from four levels; some ore assaying very high was found on the 300-foot level, the average value of which was $100 per ton. Seventy-five tons were obtained from this level and are now in the company's dump. The vein is quite narrow, but increases in width with depth and pitches 36° east. I have to thank Mr. E. Strother, the superintendent, for the above description.

Rock Island.—This mine is situated next to the Baltimore on the south, and is in about the same condition. The vein is wider, being 218 feet in the south end of the mine. The shaft is down 869 feet; the last 166 feet of the shaft is in the vein. Average assays of quartz, $18, although very fine bunches of rich ore are occasionally found on the 450-foot level. There is considerable water in the vein. Value of improvements, $75,000, consisting of hoisting-works, machinery, &c. Mr. Charles Forman, the superintendent, furnishes the above account.

Florida.—This is the last mine of note on this branch of the Comstock. The shaft is about 700 feet deep; the vein on the 110-foot level is 185 feet wide, and assays very low. Some fine pieces of ore have been found on the 300-foot level, but as a general thing the ore is very base, as I am informed by Mr. J. E. De Noon, the superintendent.

Julia.—This mine is situated east of the Chollar, and in a cañon which runs parallel with the one in which the Yellow Jacket, Belcher, and Overman are situated, but some hundreds of feet to the east. The mine has attained a vertical depth of 1,680 feet; prospecting has been done on several levels without finding ore of value. Their lowest level is the 1,500-foot. Some fine streaks of ore are met with, and judging from the character of the vein, which is one and the same as that of the Chollar, the prospects for a mine are good.

Europa.—This mine is next south to the Julia, and has 1,000 feet in claim. The depth of the shaft is 450 feet. Have drifted on the 310-foot level 450 feet west. Width of vein 85 feet; pitch, 48° east. Assays of quartz from $4 to $25. Ledge strong and well defined; walls perfect and very regular. Mr. John Lambert, the superintendent who furnishes the above facts, reports the influx of water as about 6,000 gallons per 24 hours.

Sullivan.—This is the next claim upon which work is being done. It is on the same vein as the Julia, Europa, and Woodville. A shaft is being sunk to prospect the ground.

Alta.—This claim joins the Sullivan on the south; the shaft is down 355 feet; no drifting done yet; expect to cut vein at 600 feet. This mine has erected very heavy and expensive pumping-machinery, and has started in good earnest to develop its ground. Mr. C. C. Derby is the superintendent.

Lady Washington.—This joins the Alta on the east. The company is engaged in sinking its shaft, which has attained a depth of 550 feet. Width of ledge over 100 feet; pitches 47° east. Will intersect vein at 650 feet. Vein same as Justice. Very heavy machinery on the claim. Mr. R. P. Keating is the superintendent.

Woodville.—This claim lies where the two cañons intersect, and it is here that the trouble occurs as to the title between the Justice and this company. Some authorities express the opinion that the vein here belongs to the Woodville; but the point is a difficult one. The company has extracted a great deal of ore, but most of it is of low grade. Mr. Baldwin is superintendent.

The Sutro tunnel.—The opinion expressed in former reports concerning the importance of this enterprise to deep mining on the Comstock lode is likely to become universal before long. In spite of the positive predictions of many of the superintendents and mining captains, large amounts of water are continually encountered at considerable depth; and it may almost be said that there is no time when some mine on the vein is not in trouble from this cause. Concerning the merits of the legal controversy between the Sutro Tunnel Company and the managers of the mines, I have no opinion to express, except that it is most unfortunate that a work which should have been completed long ago by the joint efforts of all the companies is hindered, delayed, and rendered extremely expensive by quarrels, intrigues, and law-suits.

The following account of the tunnel and its progress to February, 1876, has been prepared, at my request, by Mr. H. S. Drinker, of Philadelphia. It will be found valuable for reference and comparison:

The Sutro tunnel commences at the town of Sutro, which is located in the Carson Valley, 3½ miles from Dayton and 1½ miles from the Carson River. Its general course is west-northwest, with a rise of 3 inches in 100 feet. It will reach the lode at a distance of 19,899 feet from the mouth and 1,970 feet below the croppings on the Savage claim, (1,922 feet below the shaft-mouth of that mine.) Drifts will be driven along the lode from this point both north and south. The act passed by the Forty-second Congress requires that the main tunnel shall, throughout its entire length, have a cross-sectional area of at least 140 square feet, including timbers and space for drainage, and shall on or before its completion be provided with necessary timber-supports, double railroad-tracks, and working-shafts. Work was commenced on this important enterprise on the 19th of October, 1869, at which time but 15 men were employed, and they only on day-shifts. Operations were conducted on this limited scale up to December 1, 1871, at which date the header, the only point where work was prosecuted, had been driven a distance of 2,601 feet. Under the impetus given by the consummation of successful financial negotiations, the force was increased during the month of December, 1871, to 232 men; four shafts were located nearly equidistant from each other along the line of the tunnel, and hoisting engines and pumps purchased for each.

The pumps used are the double-acting cataract steam-pumps, manufactured by Messrs. Allison & Bannan, of Pottsville, Pa. They have steam-cylinders 20 inches by 72 inches and 10-inch discharge-pipes, weighing 20,000 pounds each, and capable of lifting the water from station to station, 300 feet apart. Steam-pumps of this capacity had not been introduced before on the Pacific coast, though they have been in use quite extensively for some years in the coal-regions of Pennsylvania. They prove greatly preferable to the old style of Cornish pump, now in general use, as to simplicity, cheapness, durability, and diminished liability to get out of order. To illustrate the working of these pumps, the following extracts are taken from the report of the superintendent of machinery for the year 1872:

Shaft No. 1—*April.*—"In this month the water caused considerable trouble here, there being over 3,000,000 gallons pumped from the shaft during the month. Much damage was done to the pump by the sand and gravel cutting out the packing and wearing away the cylinder and glands. The brass lining of the pump-cylinder had to be taken out and a new piston made. During these repairs the pump had to be raised by means of a chain-tackle twice (10 feet each time) in order to keep it out of the water, so that the machinists could continue their work, and in the 24 hours that it took for these repairs the water rose 36 feet in the shaft. At the same time the hoisting-engine was raising water as rapidly as possible, in a tub constructed for that purpose."

Shaft No. 2—*November*.—"The chief work done here during the month was fitting up the two large pumps. One of them is in a station 275 feet and the other 550 feet from the surface. Each of these pumps weighs 10 tons, and the bed-plates they rest on are 30 feet long. The pumps are double-acting, constructed with two plungers and two sets of valves, or, otherwise, two single-acting pumps connected to one steam-piston. The column through which the water from these pumps passes to the top of the shaft is of wrought iron with cast-iron flanges, and is 10 inches in diameter. This column is securely braced and supported by the shaft-timbering. The shafts at all places are 10 feet long in the clear by 5 feet wide, and the timbering is 10 inches by 12 inches, in sets 5 feet apart, supported by corner-posts 10 inches by 10 inches. A girt of 10-inch by 12-inch timber divides the hoisting-shaft from the pump-shaft, making the hoisting-shaft 4 feet 2 inches by 5 feet in the clear, and the pump-shaft 5 feet by 5 feet in the clear; boards are nailed on the girts so as to make each shaft independent, and a ventilator-box is carried up through the roof of the building over the pump-shaft. The water-column from the second pump discharges its water into a tank at the first pump-station; from thence it is pumped by means of the pump at that place and discharged into tanks at the surface. * * * The steam-pipe is of wrought iron, and is 6 inches in diameter down to the first pump, 5 inches in diameter to the second pump, and diminished in size proportionately as more pumps are put in. The steam is conducted along the pump-station from the main pipe to the pump by a 3-inch wrought-iron pipe at each pump. The suction-pipe, from the pump to the tank, is 10 inches in diameter, and is chiefly cast iron. The water is made to pass through a condenser before coming to the pump. This condenser is placed at the back end of the pump-station, and can be used at pleasure by opening a valve, which will turn the exhaust-steam through the condenser instead of conducting it to the exhaust-box. The exhaust-box is of wood, 12 inches by 12 inches internal area, and the exhaust-steam from all the pumps is turned into it, and by it carried to the top of the shaft. The water which may overflow from the pump-stations is also conducted into this box, so as to prevent it splashing in the shaft. All the steam and exhaust pipes are covered with thick cow-hair felt sewn upon canvass and painted; and notwithstanding this precaution the heat in these stations is frequently over 100°.

"The condensers are the ones patented by Henry L. Brevoort, of New York. They are made of cast iron, 3 feet in diameter and 6 feet long. The water is taken in from the side, and passes up to the top through an annular space, thence through an annular adjustable valve, where it is formed into a sheet-jet, through which the exhaust steam is made to pass. The amount of pressure to the jet is regulated by a float, and the water can also be regulated by hand.

"The number of hoists made here this month has been 4,297. The two 48-inch boilers were used, and an average steam-pressure of 60 pounds was maintained. The fuel consumed was 99 cords of Carson pine. The quantity of water pumped from the shaft was 68,900 gallons in 24 hours."

The tunnel has now (1876) passed shafts Nos. 1 and 2, which are used for ventilation. The draught ascends very strongly up shaft No. 2, entering at the mouth of the tunnel. Shafts Nos. 3 and 4, the former after reaching a depth of 456 feet, and the latter after being sunk 674 feet, were abandoned, on account of the immense influx of water, which it was impossible to master.

The header had reached, on the 15th day of February, 1876, a length of 12,259 feet, leaving 7,640 feet to be cut. The tunnel for the last 800 feet has been in mineral, assaying from $2 to $20 per ton. It can only be ascertained by actual experiment whether this country-rock will pay for concentration and reduction; if it does, there is enough material already traversed to last for the next hundred years.

At present, natural ventilation takes place as far as shaft No. 2, beyond which mechanical means are necessary until a connection is established with the mines. Two No. 4 Root blowers are used, with 11-inch galvanized-iron tubing, and the air in the header, 3,300 feet beyond shaft No. 2, is perfectly pure and cool. But besides the air delivered by the blowers, there is the condensed air, which is delivered by the use of six machine-drills in operation in the header. The Burleigh drills in use in the header were at first supplied with air by a compressor located at shaft No. 1, which had been constructed by the Société Cockerill, of Belgium. After shaft No. 2 was passed, the air-compressor at shaft No. 1 was exchanged for a new one started at shaft No. 2, constructed by the Humboldt Company, of Kalk, near Dentz, on the Rhine. Both compressors have given great satisfaction.

In bad ground, or wherever timbering is thought necessary, 12-inch by 14-inch posts, with 14-inch by 16-inch caps, are used, placed 5 feet apart, though in some places they are put close to each other. The timber used is sawed pine; and in bad ground the center-piece of a tree is always selected. Timber costs on an average $30 per thousand, delivered at the mouth of the tunnel. Wood is used for fuel, and costs $6.50 per cord, delivered.

In 1874, when machine-drills were first used at the tunnel, the Burleigh drill was adopted, and has thus far done very satisfactory work. From information received at Mont Cenis, Hoosac, and elsewhere, it was supposed that five drills were needed for every one in operation, but practical experience here has shown that for the six drills in use, four or six at most additional ones would keep the heading going without any interruption—that is, provided there is a machine-shop and competent mechanics are employed to keep the machines in repair. English steel was at first employed, but at present Black Diamond steel, made in Pittsburgh, is in use and is considered fully equal to the English.

The heading which is now being driven, 8 by 10 feet, is blasted out by means of a center-cut and "squaring up." This will ultimately be enlarged to a section of 10 by 12 feet. The cut has a depth of from 7 to 8 feet, and a face of from 4 to 5 feet. From 3 to 8 holes are drilled on each side. This wedge being first blasted out, the sides are then squared up by means of one or two series of 4 or more holes each, according to the hardness of the rock. The average time to take out a cut and square up averages about 12 hours.

Before machine-drilling was introduced, the average progress was not over 100 feet per month, while now it is at least 350 feet for every thirty days. Where timbered, the tunnel as far as completed is 12 by 16 feet outside of the timber, which are 10 by 12 inches, except the inside posts, which are 10 inches square. This is divided into two compartments, each 5½ feet wide at the bottom, 4½ at the top, and 10 feet high, with a passage-way between and a drain underneath. The top and sides are covered with lagging of 2-inch plank. The shafts are timbered with sets of 10 by 12 inch timber, placed 5 feet apart from center to center, with 10 by 10 inch posts.

The following table gives the location and depth of the four principal shafts of the tunnel:

	Distance from mouth of tunnel.	Depth of tunnel-level.
	Feet.	*Feet.*
Shaft No. 1, (finished)	4,915	523
Shaft No. 2, (finished)	9,065	1,041
Shaft No. 3, (abandoned)	13,545	1,361
Shaft No. 4, (abandoned)	17,695	1,485

All work on the tunnel has been done by day-labor, with the exception of some very small contracts in the first stages of the work.

The rates of wages are as follows, (in gold:)

Foremen, per day	$8 00
Shift-bosses, per day	6 00
Drill-men, per day	5 00
Laborers, car-men, and all others employed under ground	4 00

In addition to the above rates the following premium has been offered during the past year: For every foot over 300 per month, and less than 400, $5 per foot; of 400 and less than 500, $10 per foot; anything over 500, $20 per foot. The above to be divided equally among the men employed under ground.

In the heading two men are employed to each machine, one drill-man and one miner assisting, making a total of thirty-six per day. These men do all the work of shoveling and loading in the heading, in addition to the drilling. The average number of men employed by the company during the year 1875 was as follows: 1 general superintendent, 1 accountant and paymaster, 1 chief engineer, 1 assistant engineer, 1 carpenter, 1 foreman of tunnel, 3 shift-bosses, 3 blasters, 18 drill-men, 1 drill-boy, 18 miners, 11 car-men, 1 station-tender, 3 track-layers, 4 timber-men, 10 repair-men, 3 machinists, 1 machinists' helper, 3 engineers, 2 firemen, 2 blacksmiths, 2 blacksmiths' helpers, 1 tinsmith, 3 watchmen, 4 teamsters and assistants, 1 hostler, 7 laborers, 1 ranchman, 1 laborer on improvements, 1 mail-carrier; total, 110.

Work on the tunnel is now (1876) being vigorously pushed, and it is expected that it will be completed about January 1, 1878.

The following tables will show the monthly progress made in driving the heading and in sinking shafts, from the beginning of the work up to March 1, 1876. A set of averages is also appended, showing details of work during the year 1875:

Statement of progress of the Sutro tunnel from October 19, 1869, to March 1, 1876.

Month.	Header.			Character of rock.	Remarks.
	Progress.	Total.	Size.		
1869.	*Feet.*	*Feet.*	*Feet.*		
November	254		14 by 16	Conglomerate bowlders and cement.	From October 19 to December 3, 1869.
December	206		14 by 16	do	From December 3 to December 31, 1869.
Total for 1869.	......	460			
Distance January 1, 1870.	......	460			
1870.					
January	201		14 by 16	Conglomerate	
February	136		14 by 16	do	
March	95		14 by 16	Breccia and tufa	
April	110		14 by 16	do	
May	135		8 by 8	do	
June	157		8 by 8	do	Struck 6 miners' inches of water.
July	116		8 by 8	Red clay	
August	82		8 by 8	Blue clay	Timbering.
September	126		8 by 8	Vein-matter	
October	19		8 by 8	do	
November	48		8 by 8	do	
December	65		8 by 8	do	
Total for 1870	......	1, 290			Monthly average, 1870, 107½ feet.
Distance January 1, 1871.	......	1, 759			
1871.					
January	53		8 by 8	Propylite and vein matter	
February	39		8 by 8	do	
March	53		8 by 8	do	Struck 20 miners' inches of water March 1.
April	35		8 by 8	do	
May	116		8 by 8	do	Timbering.
June	135		8 by 8	do	
July	99		8 by 8	do	
August	98		8 by 8	do	
September	80		8 by 8	do	
October	53		8 by 8	do	
November	61		8 by 8	do	
December	93		8 by 8	do	
Total for 1871	......	915			Monthly average, 76¼ feet.
Distance January 1, 1872.	......	2, 665			
1872.					
January	47		8 by 8	Propylite	
February	72		8 by 8	do	
March	29		8 by 8	do	
April	45		8 by 8	do	
May	45		8 by 8	do	
June	40		8 by 8	do	
July	40		8 by 8	do	
August	117		8 by 8	Trachyte	
September	105		8 by 8	do	
October	91		8 by 8	do	
November	91		8 by 8	do	
December	93		8 by 8	do	
Total for 1872.	......	815			Monthly average, 67.91 feet.
Distance January 1, 1873.	......	3, 480			
1873.					
January	90		8 by 8	do	
February	81		8 by 8	do	
March	121		8 by 8	do	
April	116		8 by 8	do	
May	114		8 by 8	do	
June	85		8 by 8	do	
July	109		8 by 8	do	
August	118		8 by 8	do	Drifts east and west from No. 1 begun August 14.
September	123		8 by 8	do	Header to October 27; connected with No. 1.

Statement of progress of the Sutro tunnel, &c.—Continued.

Month.	Header.			Character of rock.	Remarks.
	Progress.	Total.	Size.		
1873.	*Feet.*	*Feet.*	*Feet.*		
October	105		8 by 8	Trachyte	
November	73		8 by 8	do	
December	129		8 by 8	do	
Total for 1873	......	1,264	....	....	Monthly average, 105.33 feet.
November	......	665	....	....	Drifts from bottom of No. 1.
Distance January 1, 1874.	......	5,399			
1874.					
January	134		8 by 8	do	
February	98		8 by 8	do	
March	99		8 by 8	do	Two machine-drills started.
April	136		8 by 14	do	
May	154		8 by 14	do	East and west drifts from shaft No. 2 begun May 10
June	194		8 by 14	do	Four machine-drills started June 22.
July	208		8 by 14	do	
August	300		8 by 14	do	
September	310		8 by 14	do	
October	360		8 by 14	do	
November	270		8 by 10	do	
December	417		8 by 10	do	
Total for 1874	......	2,680	....	....	Monthly average, 223.33 feet.
Distance January 1, 1875.		8,079			
1875.					
January	350		8 by 10	Conglomerate trachyte	
February	289		8 by 10	Trachyte	
March	314		8 by 10	....	March 24, connected with drifts from shaft No. 2.
April	239		8 by 10	....	Blasting down and leveling from No. 2.
May	209		8 by 10	Conglomerate and greenstone.	
June	358		8 by 10	....	
July	358		8 by 10	Andesite porphyry	Rock contains iron pyrites.
August	370		8 by 10	Clay-quartz porphyry	Cut two quartz ledges, 65 feet and 112 feet wide.
September	326		8 by 10	do	
October	285		8 by 10	Clay-slate porphyry	
November	335		8 by 10	Andesite porphyry	
December	195		8 by 10	Greenstone porphyry	
Total for 1875	......	3,728	....	....	Monthly average, 310.66 feet.
Distance January 1, 1876.	......	11,807			
1876.					
January	300		8 by 10	Andesite greenstone	
February	308		8 by 10	Clay-porphyry	
		608			
Total March 1	......	12,415			

Month.	Shaft feet No. 1.			Shaft feet No. 2.			Shaft No. 3 sunk.	Shaft No. 4 sunk.	Remarks.
	Sunk.	Drift east.	Drift west.	Sunk.	Drift east.	Drift west.			
1872.	*Feet.*	*Feet.*	*Feet.*	*Feet.*	*Feet.*	*Feet.*	*Feet.*	*Feet.*	
January	......	......	......	......	......	......	......	......	Work on shaft begun in January.
February	105	......	......	123	......	......	110	110	
March	27	......	......	62	......	......	46	40	
April	44	......	......	122	......	......	63	65	
May	24	......	......	97	......	......	34	30	Air-shaft also begun May 27.
June	63	......	......	......	......	......	......	......	
July	65	......	......	79	......	......	37	45	Air-shaft completed July 12, 210 feet.
August	32	......	......	55	......	......	47	66	
September	57	......	......	62	......	......	29	33	
October	19	......	......	......	......	......	11	1	
November	......	......	......	......	......	......	......	......	
December	21	......	......	41	......	......	......	46	
Total	457	......	......	641	......	......	377	436	
1873.									
Total January 1	457	......	......	641	......	......	377	436	
January	7	......	......	41	......	......	12	31	
February	40	......	......	36	......	......	16	......	
March	15	......	......	16	......	......	......	17	
April	......	......	......	......	......	......	......	......	
May	......	......	......	......	......	......	......	......	
June	......	......	......	......	......	......	......	......	Shaft No. 1 reached tunnel-level June 5.
July	3	......	......	......	......	......	......	......	
August	......	71	54	......	......	......	......	......	Drifts east and west from No. 1 begun August 14.
September	......	180	163	......	......	......	......	26	
October	......	93	94	22	......	......	14	37	
November	......	......	......	24	......	......	37	47	No. 3 shut down November 4.
December	......	......	......	34	......	......	......	57	
Total	522	344	311	814	......	......	456	651	
1874.									
Total January 1	522	344	311	814	......	......	456	651	
January	......	......	......	32½	......	......	......	23	January 9 passed quartz-ledge in shaft No. 4, 3¼ feet wide. No. 4 shut down January 12.
February	......	......	......	50	......	......	......	......	
March	......	......	......	122	......	......	......	......	
April	......	......	......	41	......	......	......	......	
May	......	......	......	......	82	77	......	......	
June	......	......	......	......	89	93	......	......	
July	......	......	......	......	......	......	......	......	July 1 driven from drifts from No. 2 by influx of water west drift.
August	......	......	......	......	......	......	......	......	
September	......	......	......	......	......	......	......	......	
October	......	......	......	......	......	......	......	......	
November	......	......	......	......	......	......	......	......	
December	......	......	......	......	......	......	......	......	
Grand total	522	344	311	1,059½	171	170	......	674	

Table of averages for 1875.

Progress per week, feet	71.69
Flow of water, miner's inches	51.11
Air temperature at mouth, deg. Fahr	59.9
At shaft No. 1 east, deg. Fahr	74.35
At shaft No. 1 west, deg. Fahr	67.65
At shaft No. 2 east, deg. Fahr	79.17
At shaft No. 2 west, deg. Fahr	80.67
At heading, deg. Fahr	82.58

Water temperature at mouth, deg. Fahr	74.89
At shaft No. 1, deg. Fahr	76.86
At shaft No. 2, deg. Fahr	79.39
At heading, deg. Fahr	81.81
Number of holes drilled	308.81
Number of holes blasted	344.62
Aggregate depth, feet	2,092.21
Average depth, feet	6.77
Powder consumed, pounds	2.62
Number of exploders consumed	351.28
Rock extracted, car-loads	521.81
Number of drills sharpened	448.8
Number of men employed	110

	Feet.
The progress of the tunnel-header (10 feet in width and 8 feet in height) for the year 1875 has been	3,728
Giving an average progress per month of	310.66
An average progress per week of	71.69
An average progress per day of	10.24
And an average progress per shift of eight hours of	3.41

Quantity of water.

The average daily flow of water (in miner's inches, allowing 6 inches pressure above the top of the orifice) has been	51.11

	Gallons.
Which is equal (in standard gallons at 12.2 gallons for each miner's inch per minute) to a flow per minute of	623.54
Per hour	37,412.40
Per day	897,897.60
Per month	26,936,928.00
And for the whole year	323,243,186.00

	Tons.
Calculating the weight of each standard gallon at 8.33 pounds, we get an average flow per minute (in tons of 2,000 pounds) of	2.1194
Per hour	155.1644
Per day	3,739.1456
Per month	112,191.1680
And for the whole year, of	1,346,302.160

Air temperature.

	Deg. Fahr.
During the year the average temperature at the mouth of the tunnel was	61.23
The highest temperature was on July 22	86.00
The lowest on January 22	33.00
At a point immediately east of shaft No. 1 the average temperature was	74.35
The highest, (October 8)	79.00
The lowest, (August 1)	62.00
At a point immediately west of shaft No. 1 (there being a slight air-current down shaft No. 1 and up shaft No. 2) the average temperature was	67.65
The highest, (September 15)	76.00
The lowest, (April 15)	56.00

	Deg. Fahr.
At a point immediately east of shaft No. 2 the average was....	79.17
The highest, (October 15)........................	82.00
The lowest..	78.00
At a point immediately west of shaft No. 2 the average was....	80.67
The highest, (October 15 and December 15)........................	83.00
The lowest..	79.00
At the heading the average temperature for the year was......	82.58
The highest, (December 1)........................	88.00
The lowest..	79.00

It is a curious fact that the temperature in the tunnel, especially near shaft No. 1, is lower in the hottest part of the summer than during the winter months.

Water temperature.

The average temperature of the water flowing from the tunnel was:

	Degrees.
At the mouth..	74.89
At shaft No. 1..	76.86
At shaft No. 2..	79.39
At the heading..	81.81

Holes drilled and blasted.

During the last eight months of the year (no account having been kept before that time) there were drilled, by means of six Burleigh drills, a total of 9,882 holes from 2 to 2½ inches in diameter. In many cases, but more especially in hard rock and when in proximity to timbers, holes had to be blasted twice, swelling the total of holes blasted to 11,029. The aggregate depth of all the holes drilled is equal to 66,951 feet, or a line 12.68 miles in length. The average depth of holes was 6.77.

Powder consumed.

To blast the holes above mentioned 25,945 pounds of Giant and Hercules powder was used, the average for each hole being 2.62 pounds.

Exploders consumed.

A total of 11,241 exploders were set off by friction batteries.

Rock extracted.

The number of car-loads of rock removed during the last eight months was 16,698, which, at an average of two tons each, gives a total of 33,398 tons.

Drills sharpened.

The account of the number of drills sharpened was only kept for a portion of the year; at times as many as 110 drills were required for one round of holes, while at others very few were required.

LANDER COUNTY.

The principal mining operations of this county are in the Reese River district, where the Manhattan Company controls nearly all the producing mines. By a steady policy of acquiring contiguous mining-claims, this company has greatly strengthened its position, and avoided conflicts of title which would have been disastrous to the district. I know of no place in the United States where such conflicts could more easily arise, or would be more difficult to decide, than at Lander Hill. The veins are small, numerous, and full of faults and dislocations. More than once, in the earlier days, a rich vein was suddenly cut off by a cross-fissure, beyond which the continuation could not be found. To trace the movement and rediscover the vein was difficult enough, but to prove its identity and so establish ownership against the claim of some adjoining owner was well-nigh impossible. The natural result was, that the miner who had lost his vein pushed boldly into the country-rock to find it, and "recognized" as the missing property the first vein he found which was rich enough to convince him of its identity. The lapse or purchase of one title after another has now made the Manhattan Company the owner of so much ground, that exploration and extraction can be carried on freely. This is not only a good thing for the company: it is the only condition which permits the exploration of the district. These small and broken, though often rich veins, could not support the expense of separate administrations, in addition to the necessary high cost of mining in such ground and of the reduction of refractory ores in a district scantily supplied with fuel and remote from railway communication. The Manhattan Mill, owning the only Stetefeldt furnace in the region, (the company having purchased the exclusive right,) enjoys a considerable custom business, besides its regular work on the ore of the company's mines. The company reports a product of about $600,000 for the year, but the reported product of the county, most of which came, I presume, from the Manhattan Mill, was over $1,000,000. The Battle Mountain Mining Company, (near Galena,) producing during the year $69,700, was the only other considerable enterprise in progress and yielding returns. For the products of smaller concerns, the assessor's report may be consulted, on a previous page.

I regret that the miscarriage of a paper by Mr. Alexander Trippel prevents me from presenting in this place some further notes of technical interest on the experiments in ore-concentration and in processes of reduction carried on during 1875 in Central Nevada. If these should be in whole or in part recovered before the final pages of this report are printed, they will be given in the Appendix.

NYE COUNTY.

This county, which for a number of years back has been comparatively dormant, has during the last year begun again to furnish considerable amounts of bullion. The principal product of this year, however, did not come from the old districts, most of them having, in spite of considerable developments, remained unprofitable. The Tybo district, though comparatively new, has proved itself on the other hand a very important one.

Philadelphia district.—I am indebted for notes on this district to Mr. W. F. Leon, who has also in former years kindly contributed to my reports.

The mineral deposits of the district occur somewhat irregularly near granite rocks on the west, extending in a northerly and southerly direction, and slate and quartz, &c., on the east. There is one main fissure-lode now known, the Highbridge. The principal mining property on this lode is the El Dorado South, on which, with the exception of about 250 feet at the southern extremity, the vein of quartz is plainly traceable throughout its extent. Varying from a bare trace to bold and magnificent cliffs, rising here and there above the surface, the croppings continue even into contiguous lands. Such outcrops are often unusually massive, and consist of a compact white quartz, richly clouded with dark and antimonial ores of silver. In the solid portions of the lode the silver-ores are scattered throughout the whole mass. Nearly the entire contents of this vein, above water-line, are in a more or less advanced state of oxidation and chlorination.

In the old works the vein varies from 15 to 40 feet in width, but the productive portion of the vein, the pay-stratum, also varies from 9 to 20 feet. The ore is found at times permeating the entire vein, at other times it lies nearest the hanging wall on top of the solid ledge. This property is owned by a company of San Francisco capitalists, and is now fairly under way to receive the fullest development. A vertical shaft (the Leon shaft) near the south end of the claim is being sunk to tap the ore-body known to exist from previous developments in the old incline works, but allowed to remain undisturbed until better facilities than those afforded by an incline could be completed. The company has a 20-stamp quartz-mill, with all the modern improvements, steam hoisting-works, with two powerful engines, a 10-inch Cornish pump, and all the necessary materials and machinery to work the property, which is under the immediate supervision of Mr. W. F. Leon, who is also one of the heaviest owners in the enterprise.

The Belmont Mining Company and its properties are next in importance. The works are situated some three or four hundred yards northerly from the property above mentioned, and on the same vein. This company has a vertical shaft, and is developing its mines in a systematic manner. In the earlier times of the district, the Highbridge and Transylvania, belonging to the company, were widely celebrated. The Old Combination Company's mines, situate north of the last-mentioned property, are lying idle, and have been so almost uninterruptedly since 1868. This property consists of a part of the Highbridge, the Constitution, and other mining locations. With the exception of the Highbridge, this property is wholly undeveloped. In consequence of the stagnation of this enterprise, the interests of Philadelphia mining-district have materially suffered. A 40-stamp mill and hoisting-works are still there, though in a somewhat dilapidated condition.

The El Dorado North, Arizona, Monitor-Belmont, Quintera, and other locations, at one time promising good returns to their owners, are now lying idle, the parties owning them preferring to await the development being made by the El Dorado South and Belmont Companies. There are three mills in the district, two of 20 stamps and one of 40, the two former belonging respectively to the El Dorado South Consolidated Mining Company and the Monitor and Belmont Mill Company, the latter to the Combination Company. To the former two mills Stetefeldt furnaces are attached, having a capacity to roast 20 tons of ore each per day. The combination mill has 10 reverberatory furnaces.

The deep workings now in progress in the El Dorado South and Belmont Mines will, it is hoped, prove the beginning of new prosperity for the district.

The ores of this district are of high grade, assaying often hundreds of dollars per ton. Beautiful crystals occur, rendered more beautiful by fanciful twistings and net-work of native silver. Besides the native silver, chloride of silver, antimonial silver, stromeyerite, sulphurets of silver and iron, stetefeldtite, and carbonate of copper occur. In nearly every instance the best ores are associated with oxides of copper and iron, and in such cases the percentage of silver is always large.

Tybo district.—This district has assumed an importance during the last years which puts it second in rank as a lead-silver district in the State. I am indebted to Messrs. W. A. Skidmore and H. Degroot for the following report on the principal mining property, to which the district owes its reputation :

The property of the Tybo Consolidated Mining Company consists of mines and reduction-works, water-franchises, tram-ways, houses, shops, and various other improvements, the whole located along and adjacent to Precipico Cañon, a broad and deep ravine which at this point cuts the easterly slope of the Hot Creek Mountains at nearly right angles. Bordering this ravine on the south, and rising above it to a height of a thousand feet or more, is the rugged eminence known as Precipico Mountain. Striking diagonally across the cañon in a northwesterly and southeasterly direction, the croppings of a heavy mineral-bearing lode are clearly traceable. On this lode the mining-claims of the company (four in number) are located. The Crosby, the most northerly claim of the group, commencing near the center of the cañon, extends thence south 400 feet. As scarcely any work has been done on this ground, not much can be said about it, its value being derived from its position on an ore-channel of known fertility.

Adjoining the Crosby on the south is the Casket claim, embracing within its limits 666 feet. Two perpendicular shafts—one near either extremity of this ground—have been carried down to a depth of about 70 feet, a drift having been run from the bottom of the more northerly for a distance of 20 feet. In this shaft a streak of good ore from 3 to 3½ feet in thickness was struck, and some ten or twelve tons taken out, and there can be little doubt but further exploration will develop here a large and permanent body of good ore. Both of these shafts are well timbered.

On the Lafayette, a few rods to the west of the Casket claim, a shaft has been sunk to a depth of 60 feet on a line of well-defined croppings trending nearly east and west. From the bottom of this shaft a drift has been carried easterly in the vein-matter 70 feet, disclosing a stratum of medium-grade ore from 6 to 3 feet in thickness. The course of this vein indicates that it will intersect the dominating lode a short distance beyond the south boundary of the Casket ground; and it is reasonable to suppose that a marked enrichment of the main lode will ensue at the point of junction. This outlying ledge has not, however, been sufficiently exploited to determine either its course or dimensions with exactness, though its fertility seems to be pretty well assured. This claim is called the Lafayette, and covers a linear section of 1,200 feet.

The Two G Mine, so named from the initials of Gillett and Gally, its former owners, extends south from the Casket 1,200 feet. This, the only one of the company's claims yet thoroughly developed, has been opened up by means of three tunnels driven in and with the course of the ore-channel. These adits stand vertically the one above the other, having been started in the croppings of the lode which here stretch obliquely along the northerly face of Precipico Mountain, crossing it at an elevation of about 300 feet above the adjacent ravine.

This exposure of the lode has greatly facilitated its exploitation by the means here adopted; this series of tunnels, with their various connection, tending also to promote ventilation and the ready extraction of the ores from the mine. The lowest of these tunnels, designated No. 1, is 530 feet long, while No. 2, the next above, is 500 feet; and the uppermost, No. 3, is 200 feet in length. The latter penetrates the lode at a depth of 113 feet below the highest croppings. Tunnel No. 2 lies 100 feet below No. 3, and tunnel No. 1 38 feet below No. 2, these adits being connected by means of inclined winzes opened at suitable points along them. The material through which they are driven has proved so firm that timbering has been required at only a few spots.

The principal ore-bearing deposits in this mine seem to occur in the form of vertical shoots or chimneys standing between and inclining with the walls of the lode, and pitching toward the southeast. The dimensions of these ore-bodies are variable, ranging from 4 to 10 feet in thickness and from 30 to 60 feet in length. They are usually connected by seams of vein-matter or ore, the wall-rock coming in occasionally and compressing the latter to a very narrow limit, and at a few spots displacing them entirely. In the upper workings these contractions are more noticeable, nearly disappearing in the lower levels of the mine.

In the upper tunnel, No. 3, some good ore was encountered at intervals throughout its entire length. At the entrance of tunnel No. 2 the vein-matter, composed mostly of excellent ore, showed a thickness of about 4 feet. Fifty feet in from the mouth of the tunnel an uprise was made, which finally ran into wall-rock. Ten feet farther on the ore came in again rich and heavy, and so continued for ten or twelve feet, when it suffered another contraction, and for fifty feet on was very irregular, narrowing and expanding sharply from 1 to 6 or 7 feet. After a farther advance of 120 feet the ore spread out to a thickness of 7 feet—all high grade—a short stoping having been carried up here to a height of 20 feet. From this point the ore held on contracting and expanding for a distance of nearly 300 feet, when a still heavier body set in, which was cross-cut for 8 feet without arriving at its western limit. Stoping was carried up in this chimney to a great height without reaching its apex.

After holding its lateral proportions for 25 or 30 feet, this chimney narrowed to 4 feet, and 20 feet farther on was cut off altogether by the invasion of lime-rock from the east. Deflecting the tunnel to the right 20 feet carried it through this obtruding mass and into another chimney of high-grade smelting-ore of unascertained thickness, a drift 8 feet in length having failed to cross-cut it. After penetrating this chimney south for a distance of 10 feet, work was here discontinued, leaving the face of the tunnel in the most promising body of ore yet opened up in the mine. As the irregularities of the ore in the tunnel above corresponded with those encountered here, it is inferred that this chimney will be intersected by the upper tunnel when the latter shall have been advanced another 150 or 160 feet.

The first 60 feet of tunnel No. 1 was run outside of and at a slight angle with the ledge. After running 70 feet the latter was reached and a shaft put down at the point of contact to a depth of 30 feet. In this shaft a sheet of good carbonate ore was exposed varying from 8 to 20 inches in thickness. The tunnel carried this sheet of ore somewhat enlarged in for a farther distance of 60 or 70 feet, where a winze was sunk to the depth of 75 feet. Before reaching this point the ore was stoped out nearly up to the middle tunnel, this stope showing good ore on all sides.

One hundred and seventy-five feet beyond the first a second winze was put down to the same depth as the other, and the two connected at the bottom by a drift. Both of these winzes as well as the connecting-drift are in ore. Afterward tunnel No. 1 was pushed ahead until it had reached an entire length of 350 feet. It carries a stratum of ore ranging from 3 to 8 feet in thickness nearly all the way, and ends in a heavy body of high-grade galena and carbonate ores, being unquestionably the same in which the next tunnel above is terminated.

The drift at the bottom of the two winzes mentioned, and which is denominated the first level, has attained a total length of 365 feet. The belt of ore along this level suffers fewer lateral contractions than anywhere above, these shrinkages here amounting nowhere to an entire interruption of the vein-matter. For three-fourths of its length the ore-stratum maintains on this level an average thickness of about 6 feet, and is uniformly of a good, much of it of a very high, grade. Both extremities of this level are in strong bodies of ore; commencing at the innermost winze, a stoping 20 feet high has been carried south for the distance of nearly 100 feet. The face of this stoping is everywhere in ore.

The second level, like the first, is reached by means of two winzes each 60 feet deep put down at points in close proximity to the bottoms of those above. These two winzes have not as yet been connected below, 53 feet of ledge-matter remaining to be excavated between them. From the most southerly a drift has been run southeast 25 feet, making a total of drifting done on this level of 147 feet, nearly the whole of it being in good ore. The ore-bodies here are, in fact, much more compact, and the walls of the lode more regular than in the upper levels, pointing to a continued improvement in this respect. This, the lowest level in the mine, has a vertical depth of 323 feet beneath the highest point of croppings, being 388 feet measured on the inclination of the lode.

The entire length of the tunnels, drifts, shafts, and winzes, excavated in the "Two G" Mine, amount in the aggregate to nearly 4,000 linear feet, the established reserves holding, in June, 1875, about 55,000 tons of medium or high-grade milling and smelting ores, being enough to keep a 20-stamp mill and two furnaces of moderate capacity employed at least two years. Besides these reserves, there are now about 1,300 tons of ore lying in the main bin and on the several mining-dumps. The whole of this ore, both the extracted and that standing in the mine, ought to return an average net yield of $20 per ton, and may be expected to exceed this, insuring a resultant profit of $1,100,000 at the least.

These ores consist of two classes, the one composed of the carbonates and the sulphuret of lead, and the other of the chloride and sulphurets of silver, the former class requiring reduction by smelting, and the latter by the ordinary mill process. These two classes of ores occur in the mine sometimes at points widely separated, and again side by side; the galena usually lying next the foot, while the milling-ores adhere to the hanging-wall, these positions being occasionally reversed. Neither class of ores is difficult of reduction, each being manageable by the mode of treatment especially adapted to it. Being without means for handling them, the company have removed no more of their milling-ores than was necessary in prosecuting the work of exploration. In stoping and raising, only the smelting-ores have been extracted in quantity.

The strike of the Two G lode, as before stated, is nearly northwest and southeast, or, to be more exact, it bears north 43° west, and inclines toward the east at an angle of 76°. It varies on the surface from 4 to 12 feet in thickness, manifestly gaining strength and symmetry with depth. It is a contact-vein lying between a compact, siliceous limestone on the east and porphyry on the west, the vein-stone being composed chiefly of quartz. The walls are cased with a bluish clay, mixed with talc, and in the lower levels exhibit an evenness and solidity not observable above. The ledge can be traced by the croppings for a mile or more, the latter being everywhere well defined, and in some places very bold.

At a properly-selected point a main working-shaft has been started, having already reached a depth of 132 feet. This shaft contains three compartments, two designed for the hoisting and lowering, and the other for the pumping service. It is substantially timbered, and is outfitted with steam-driven hoisting-gear, cages, and other necessary appendages, and is protected by a suitable building. It will intersect the lode at a depth of nearly 500 feet, and through it the ore from the lower levels of the mine will be brought to the surface. At a depth of 125 feet in this shaft a drift has been commenced, and is being carried toward the vein, which will be cut at the present lowest level, 400 feet below the croppings. As the line of permanent water has not yet been reached, no pumping-apparatus will be required here at present, and probably not for some time to come. At the mouth of the lower tunnel a capacious ore-bin has been built, from which two tram-ways have been laid down, the one three-quarters of a mile in length, leading to the company's mill, and the other one-third of a mile in length, leading to the furnaces. Through the aid of these tram-ways the ores can be delivered at points where wanted at a trifling cost. In addition to these, many other improvements have been introduced and devices availed of for facilitating or cheapening the various processes and handlings to which the ores are further subjected.

At a point a little below, and convenient to their entire group of mines, the company has erected a smelting-furnace capable of running through 25 or 30 tons of ore per day. This is a very complete establishment, being supplemented with calcining, refining, and cupelling works, and all other appliances necessary to further operations and add to its effectiveness. The engine and blower employed here have sufficient power to run the additional furnace which the company design putting up very soon by the side of the present one.

At an eligible point on the opposite side of the cañon, and a little lower down, a 20-stamp mill has been erected. The cost of this structure was $75,000. It is driven by a steam-engine of sixty horse-power, and has a capacity to crush and amalgamate 40 tons of ore every twenty-four hours. This mill has been planned and outfitted with special reference to economizing labor and securing the greatest possible efficiency, so that it is one of the best appointed establishments of the kind in Central Nevada.

From a group of springs situate two and a half miles west of the mines, the company has laid down 4-inch iron pipe, conducting a flow of nearly 3 inches of water to the reduction-works, where as much of it as may be required will be collected in large cisterns and retained for use; a tank, holding 20,000 gallons, having already been constructed on an eminence commanding the company's furnace. In order to concentrate and economize this water at its source, various cuts and tunnels have been excavated for gathering it up and carrying it to one spot, whence it is conducted under ground to its principal point of delivery, the several towns of Upper, Central, and Lower Tybo being supplied along the route. The iron pipe through which it is conveyed has been laid throughout its entire length in trenches cut deep enough, often through the solid rock, to protect it from the effects of frost or other causes of disturbance. Owning these springs, which are never-failing, the company will always enjoy a full and steady supply of water.

In addition to the foregoing, the Tybo Consolidated Mining Company has made many other improvements of a useful kind. Roads have been excavated, connecting the mines with the reduction-works; assay-offices and shops, with buildings for storage and business purposes, have been erected; houses for superintendent, workmen, and other employés have been put up; while all needed supplies of tools, coal, iron, and other material have been provided. The total amount of money expended by the company here in the purchase of mines and other properties, and upon improvements made in connection therewith, amounted to the large sum of $500,000, the whole of which appears to have been laid out in a manner well calculated to insure the thorough development of the property and adding to its prospective value.

From Mr. M. D. Howell, the superintendent of the mine and works, I have, at the end of the year, the information that the developments of the mine from June to the date of writing have all been favorable, all the workings being in ore, of which enough was in sight to run the works during the coming year. The product during 1875 is given in the annexed statement.

Furnace and bullion journal, January 1 to December 31, 1875.

Date.	Tons ore.	Bushels coal.	Number of shipments.	Number of bars in the shipments.	Weight of shipments, pounds.	Assay-value, silver.	Assay-value, gold.	Assay-value, silver and gold.	Assay-value of shipments, gold and silver.	Value of lead.	Total assay-value, gold, silver, and lead.
1875.											
January 14 to 31...	476¼	18, 840	4½	843	85, 247	$1, 676 36	$160 50	$1, 836 86	$15, 755 93	$2, 907 46	$18, 663 39
February 1 to 28...	719	26, 301	6	1, 189	120, 120	2, 078 20	221 73	2, 299 93	23, 022 94	3, 900 00	26, 922 94
March 1 to 20......	469½	22, 594	3½	669	70, 280	1, 292 86	146 00	1, 438 86	12, 506 77	2, 280 75	14, 787 52
August 9 to 31.....	549	23, 860	7½	1, 329	130, 144	2, 114 36	244 33	2, 358 69	21, 671 10	4, 219 25	25, 890 35
September 1 to 30..	678	31, 640	8	1, 627	160, 276	2, 571 28	350 28	2, 921 56	29, 264 95	5, 200 00	34, 464 95
October 1 to 26.....	543	27, 800	6	1, 235	120, 319	1, 815 79	212 23	2, 028 02	20, 334 19	3, 900 00	24, 234 19
November 1 to 30..	946	37, 840	12	2, 471	240, 374	4, 337 00	416 89	4, 753 89	47, 712 80	7, 800 00	55, 512 80
December 15 to 31.	559	21, 560	6	1, 236	120, 226	2, 631 17	251 11	2, 882 28	28, 883 78	3, 900 00	32, 783 78

Reveille district, formerly well known on account of its rich but "pockety" mineral deposits, after having lain idle for several years, has again shown some life, of which the developments in the Gila mine were the main cause. On this mine I have obtained the following full report of Mr. H. Degroot, of San Francisco:

This mine is situate in the Reveille district, Nye County, State of Nevada, in a southerly direction from the town of Eureka. The lode on which the Gila claim is located courses along the easterly slope of the Reveille Mountains in a generally north and south direction. It consists of a well-defined belt of quartzite, much of it nearly pure quartz, being composed of 70 or 80 per cent. of silica and highly crystallized. This quartzite has an average thickness of 150 feet, inclines to the east at an angle of 60°, and is inclosed between porphyry on the east and a sienitic formation and porphyry on the west, the vein-matter of the lode being separated from the country-rock by the usual clay partings. About 500 feet to the west of the lode a lime-rock comes in, and overlying the other formations extends thence to the top of the mountain.

The Gila location embraces 1,200 linear feet, running with the course of the ledge. A deep ravine making down the easterly slope of Reveille Mountain cuts across the claim near its center, while a heavy dike of porphyry, having an easterly and westerly trend, covers up its southerly extremity for a distance of several hundred feet.

The lode can be traced north by an almost continuous line of croppings, in places very bold, for nearly two miles. Concealed for a space of 2,000 feet under this superimposed mass of porphyry the croppings re-appear at its further edge, and bearing thence southeast, can be followed for a long distance in that direction.

Upon this ground, though an early location, but little exploratory work had been done prior to January last. The former owners, having made some slight surface-excavations in the quartzite without obtaining any very encouraging show of ore, ceased operations and the claim was suffered to lie for several years thereafter with only this small amount of prospecting done upon it. Having come into the hands of new owners during the early part of the present year, work was resumed on the southerly side of the ravine mentioned, at a point on the lode where some faint traces of float-mineral indicated the existence of ore beneath. Within a foot of the surface, and covered only by the remains of the disintegrated ore-shoot, intermixed with the *débris* washed in from above, a horizontal layer of the carbonate of lead and chloride of silver was cut into. Starting at this spot a tunnel has been driven south into the vein 80 feet, its inner extremity being about 30 feet below the surface. Though of variable thickness along this tunnel the ore-sheet proved to be continuous, some 80 tons of rich carbonates and chlorides having been extracted therefrom. The flat-lying stratum of ore first struck was followed west 35 feet without compassing its limit in that direction. It varied in thickness from three to five feet and yielded a large amount of superior ore; a portion of which having been reduced by smelting returned over $800 per ton. On the east this stratum commenced to pitch near the line of the tunnel, at which point a winze, designated No. 1, has been put down to a depth of 33 feet. This winze carried ore nearly all the way down, the porphyry coming in and cutting it off almost wholly at the bottom.

Thirty feet further in and 10 feet from the end of the tunnel another winze, No. 2, has been sunk to the same depth as No. 1. This winze is in fine ore throughout, the stratum being from 3 to 5 feet in thickness. A small air-drift connecting these two winzes at the bottom traverses a channel containing streaks and bunches, but not an uninterrupted body of ore. From the bottom of winze No. 2 a drift has been carried forward 40 feet, running all the way through and ending in high-grade ore, this body having an average thickness of about 4 feet. From this drift, termed level No. 1, a stoping has been raised to the tunnel above, all the way in ore. The face of this chimney, opening south, is manifestly shaping for increased strength and fruitfulness in that direction.

From level No. 1, and at a point about 35 feet from its southerly terminus, winze No. 3 has been opened to a depth of 60 feet, connecting with level No. 2 at its bottom. It is all the way in ore, the shoot along it varying from 2 to 3 feet in thickness. Through this winze all the ore above will be sent down to level No. 2, where it will be loaded on cars and passed out through the lower tunnel, now completed and traversed by an iron-railed tram-way.

At a point about 60 feet below level No. 1, and 100 feet below the highest croppings, a tunnel was started against the easterly slope of the hill and driven west at right angles with the course of the lode, which it reached at a distance of 142 feet from its mouth. At the point of intersection a body of superior ore from 3 to 4 feet in thickness was cut into. A drift, level No. 2, runs south from the tunnel, carries this body of ore on 40 feet, where it narrows down to a few inches. After holding this size for 5 or 6 feet, it again expands to a width of 1 foot, all of extremely high grade and tending to widen as the drift is being advanced.

About 15 feet from the southerly end of this drift a winze, No. 4, is being sunk, having reached at this time a depth of 10 or 12 feet. This winze is going down in a four-foot stratum of ore of the best quality yet uncovered. Some of this ore is so highly sulphureted that it will require to be roasted before it can be worked with any considerable degree of closeness. A drift extending north 10 feet from the lower tunnel shows the ore-body cut into by the latter to diminish and mix up with porphyry and barren vein-matter in that direction.

At a point about 175 feet north from the entrance to the lower tunnel the sinking of a main working-shaft has been commenced and will be prosecuted with all practicable expedition. This shaft it is calculated will intersect the ledge at a depth of 286 feet, and very near the center of the claim. When down about 100 feet, where it is expected that a good deal of water will be encountered, steam hoisting and pumping gear will be added. From this shaft, which will be put down to the lode in about sixty days, drifts will be run off at suitable intervals to the lode for the purpose of ascertaining its pitch and the character of the ore-bodies.

The ores extracted from the Gila Mine have been nearly all reduced at the company's 10-stamp mill, a structure well outfitted with amalgamating apparatus and the ordinary equipments necessary in an establishment of this kind. When built, this mill was located on the westerly side of Reveille Mountain, at the only point where, as was then supposed, sufficient water for its use could be obtained. It has capacity ample for the present requirements of the mine, and will probably answer every purpose until such time as more extensive ore developments shall have been made. When a demand for enlarged milling facilities shall arise, the proper point at which to erect the new mill will be a little below the mouth of the working-shaft now being put down, and to which the ore-cars could be run, thereby avoiding rehandling and saving wagon-transportation.

The ores of the Gila Mine have heretofore been decomposed ones, usually chloride of silver and the carbonate of lead, with a small percentage of antimonial and a considerable quantity of sulphureted ores, the latter increasing in the lower workings of the mine at a rate that will necessitate the early erection of a furnace for their chloridization. Mixed with these varieties of ore occurs a trifling amount of iron, copper, and arsenical pyrites, galena, black oxide of manganese, calc-spar, talc, &c. The ores are uniformly of high grade, the quantity reduced under the present administration to June 25, 1875, 610 tons, having yielded at the rate of $246.93 per ton. Some small lots of assorted ore previously worked went much higher, running from $325 to $855 per ton. As the quality of the ores here seems to improve with depth, the future promises a higher working average than has yet been attained. Since adopting dry-crushing, the ore has been milled up to 80 per cent. of the pulp-assay, over $60 of every ton of ore being still left in the tailings, which are, of course, preserved for future treatment. With roasting, from 90 to 94 per cent. of the silver contained in the sulphureted ore could be saved. Nearly everything extracted from this mine is sent to the mill, not more than 4 or 5 per cent. of the whole being rejected. The bullion turned out runs generally from .915 to .955, some of it going as high as .989 in fineness.

Starting up the mill in the latter part of March, a run was made on 48 tons of ore, when it became evident that a change from wet to dry crushing would have to be made. In effecting this change the most of the month of April was consumed, the mill remaining idle meantime. During the month of May the mill ran without interruption, turning out $73,367 in bullion, an amount that will be nearly equaled in June, it being estimated that five days will be lost in this month, caused by stoppages for replacing old with new bearings, cleaning up, &c.

Work is now being steadily and vigorously prosecuted in the stopes raised from levels 1 and 2, as well as at the southerly extremities of both; also in winze No. 4 and upon the main working shaft; the business of exploration being everywhere pushed simultaneously with that of ore-extraction. By the observance of this prudent policy, ample provision will have been made for the pumping and hoisting service by the time it will come into requisition, while fresh reserves will be opened up more rapidly than those already established will be exhausted.

The Gila Mine has now been explored to a vertical depth of 130 feet; the amount of ore developed in the various levels, winzes, cross-cuts, and stopings amounting to 2,600 tons.

The actual cost of extracting, hauling, and milling the ore amounts here to about $19.50 per ton, including dead-work.

At the time of the visit of Mr. Degroot the active history of the Gila dated back only five months. Yet results had been attained which in most other cases would have taken years to bring about.

During the latter part of the year the Gila continued to produce considerable bullion, as may be seen in the report of the State controller, given elsewhere in this volume.

EUREKA COUNTY.

The principal district of this county, that of Eureka, has continued to yield argentiferous-lead ores freely. The Eureka and Palisade Railroad having been finished in the last quarter of the year, the camp is now better situated for transportation than it ever was before, and it is now possible to bring fuel for smelting from a distance cheaper than it can be furnished by the district itself. During the year past, however, very little coke has been used except by the Richmond Company.

In the early part of the year, the Eureka Consolidated Company struck in its seventh and eighth levels a body of high-grade lead-ores, which created at the time considerable excitement in the San Francisco stock-market. A very extensive caving of the soft ore and gangue (brown oxide of iron) soon after destroyed the usefulness of the discovery, since ore and gangue had become so mixed as to lower the grade of the former too much to permit much profit in extracting and treating it. Yet the furnaces of the company were employed actively during the greater part of the year. According to a statement kindly furnished me at the end of the year, the total amount of bullion produced was 11,093,169 pounds, valued at $1,869,392.04. No annual report has been published by the company, and further information than the above has been refused. My deputy, Mr. Eilers, having visited the mine shortly after the occurrence of the above-mentioned cave, when the extent of the so-called "bonanza" could not be estimated, although the exposure of good ore could be viewed at several points, I can only say that the rich ore-body seemed at that time to extend vertically from a point a little below the sixth level to the eighth, while its horizontal extent in the seventh level was not over 80 feet, and in the eighth level only strings of rich ore in the brown iron-ore, from a few inches to several feet wide, had so far been found.

With data in regard to the production of the Richmond Mining Company I have been kindly supplied by Mr. O. H. Hahn, who has for years been one of the most highly valued contributors to my reports. The following table is taken from the records of the smelting-works, except the figures for the last week in December, which are estimated:

Month.	Net tons Richmond ore.	Net tons purchased ore.	Total tons ore.	Tons lead in ore.	Ounces—		Tons lead produced.	Contents.	
					Silver in ore.	Gold in ore.		Silver.	Gold.
								Ounces.	*Ounces.*
January	2, 338. 50	106. 75	2, 445. 25	593. 723	75, 691. 98	2, 699. 34	531. 250	70, 243. 00	2, 036. 41
February	2, 537. 25	69. 50	2, 606. 75	565. 145	64, 945. 44	2, 545. 22	471. 000	61, 993. 02	2, 149. 55
March	2, 098. 13	59. 75	2, 157. 88	498. 783	57, 393. 07	2, 854. 03	481. 071	54, 559. 00	2, 740. 60
April	684. 75	90. 00	774. 75	161. 750	19, 798. 99	745. 38	140. 250	17, 268. 48	698. 31
May	1, 677. 44	129. 87	1, 807. 31	389. 291	55, 045. 15	1, 790. 99	391. 000	49, 283. 02	1, 791. 33
June	2, 662. 19	83. 37	2, 745. 56	566. 666	70, 707. 52	3, 194. 48	650. 772	81, 687. 07	3, 221. 77
July	2, 728. 87	62. 42	2, 791. 29	567. 553	75, 457. 01	2, 993. 89	650. 242	86, 895. 48	2, 803. 64
August	2, 667. 04	86. 37	2, 753. 41	522. 309	70, 877. 17	2, 640. 06	550. 202	75, 051. 34	2, 558. 91
September	2, 617. 54	66. 28	2, 683. 82	455. 162	53, 677. 69	3, 384. 04	507. 688	60, 907. 24	3, 433. 97
October	2, 988. 75	166. 55	3, 155. 30	521. 022	60, 727. 06	4, 037. 53	460. 991	52, 342. 46	2, 568. 44
November	2, 750. 27	179. 90	2, 930. 17	558. 096	74, 010. 50	3, 322. 01	467. 800	59, 973. 09	2, 123. 53
December	3, 207. 88	152. 62	3, 360. 50	638. 495	84, 879. 80	3, 809. 88	557. 737	69, 204. 00	2, 331. 34
Total	28, 958. 61	1, 253. 38	30, 211. 99	6, 037, 995	763, 211. 38	34, 016. 85	5, 860. 003	739, 407. 20	28, 457. 80
Deduct contents of litharges, dross cupel-bottoms, &c., smelted with the ore.							1, 083. 648	38, 721. 02	729. 96
Total							4, 776. 355	700, 686. 18	27, 727. 84

Gross value of lead in ore, at $80 per ton	$483, 039. 60
Gross value of silver in ore	986, 755. 99
Gross value of gold in ore	703, 189. 51
Total value lead, silver, and gold in ore	2, 172, 985. 10
Gross value of lead in bullion	382, 108. 40
Gross value of silver in bullion	905, 917. 16
Gross value of gold in bullion	572, 284. 36
	1, 860, 309. 92

About 84 per cent. of this is net.

Losses, lead, 20.9 per cent.; silver, 8.19 per cent.; gold, 18.48 per cent.

The ore is smelted with an addition of from 7 to 10 per cent. of quartz and 20 to 25 per cent. of slag.

Consumption of fuel, 40 bushels of coal, (without waste,) or its equivalent in value in coke per ton of ore.

Cost of extraction, hauling, and reducing the ore and purchasing of outside ores, $39.

Number of furnaces: 3 of a capacity of 40 tons of ore each, with 9 tuyeres; 1 water-jacket furnace of the Kast pattern, with 6 tuyeres, running through from 12 to 18 tons of ore per 24 hours; and 1 other water-jacket of larger size building.

Auxiliary plant: 1 steam-engine, 22 and 34 inch cylinder, making 42 revolutions per minute; 3 boilers; 1 Knowles steam-pump; 2 Cameron steam-pumps; 3 Sturtevant blowers, No. 8, making 2,000 revolutions per minute; 1 Root blower, No. 6, making 110 revolutions per minute; 1 Blake crusher; 1 Howland grinder, and 1 Wagner grist-mill.

The cause of the above enormous loss of gold has not been ascertained sufficiently; it is supposed to be in consequence of fine particles of metallic gold distributed through the ore escaping out of the furnace-chimneys. The flue-dust is worked over in a very crude manner, by mixing it with 20 per cent. of clay in the form of a thick paste, and then throwing it wet into the furnaces along with the ore. Besides the injurious effect of the clay, this method is objectionable on other grounds.

The use of coke has not proved financially economical. It costs about $60 a ton at the works, which would be equal in cost to 200 bushels of charcoal; the metallurgical effect is not in this proportion. It can be used only in admixture with one-half of charcoal, by weight, as the ore is principally pulverulent and packs so tight that the blast cannot penetrate the coke. The coke is charged from the center forward, but has a bad mechanical effect on the furnace-walls, which have to be repaired every day. The water-jacket furnace, a modification (not improvement) of the excellent Kast furnace, was built with a view to avoid these costly repairs, but has proved an economical failure thus far. Its consumption of fuel is 56 bushels per ton, and the mechanical volatilization or formation of dust seems to surpass that of the furnaces of the old pattern. To judge by the consumption of charcoal alone, the Richmond furnaces seem to be the worst-constructed ones of the district, the K. K. furnaces using 31.4 bushels coal per ton, Eureka 32 bushels, and Atlas 34 bushels.

The refinery plant of the company consists of 1 boiler, 6 sets of crystallizers, (a set comprising 1 melting-pot and 1 crystallizing-pot, and 3 steam-cranes serving this apparatus;) 2 softening-furnaces, holding about 35 tons of bullion each; 5 Welsh cupelling-furnaces; 1 dross and litharge reducing-furnace, and 1 kiln for burning bones. The crystallizers are provided with hoods, leading into condensing chambers, for the saving of oxides.

The process is Lucien Rozan's modification of the Pattinson, described in the *Annales des Mines*, tome iii, livr. 2, de 1873, and requires here 10 operations to obtain rich lead on the one hand and market-lead on the other. The gold disappears from the latter only after the eighth operation. The lead to be treated must be pretty well freed from arsenic, otherwise the crystals run out with the rich lead. It takes 48 hours to soften 35 tons, which yield about 11½ per cent. of dross. The refinery is only running at half capacity, one-half of the calcined bullion being shipped to Omaha. The reported cost of separation is $20.42 per ton of lead.

The Atlas Mining and Smelting Company, formerly the Ruby Consolidated, owns, in addition to the mines named in former reports, the Atlas mine, which is the northerly extension of the Dunderberg. The ores treated by the company during the year came mostly from the northern portion of the Dunderberg, in the 200, 300, and 400 foot levels. A small portion was taken from the Pleiades, the ore being poor and the deposit soon exhausted. The 500-foot level in the Dunderberg is opened, running for 470 feet along a clay wall, but up to the time of Mr. Eilers's visit, in September, no ore had been struck, and the company was then running a drift from the 400-foot level across a stratum of shale, from 200 to 300 feet thick, in an easterly direction, in the hope of finding contact-deposits of ore between the shale and limestone on the farther side of the shale. There is the more ground for this hope, as the limestone croppings above are strongly impregnated with oxide of iron. It is contemplated to sink a vertical shaft in the new Atlas ground, on the north slope of the Dunderberg hill, and to remove the present hoisting-works at the incline to this shaft, from which the whole mine can be worked more economically than at present, because all the ore-bodies seem to lie in this direction. The company has bought all the custom-ores it could get during the year at the following prices:

For ores assaying 50 dollars per ton, 16 per cent. of value.

For ores assaying 60 dollars per ton, 25 per cent. of value.
For ores assaying 70 dollars per ton, 35 per cent. of value.
For ores assaying 80 dollars per ton, 43 per cent. of value.
For ores assaying 90 dollars per ton, 45 per cent. of value.
For ores assaying 100 dollars per ton, 50 per cent. of value.
For ores assaying 150 dollars per ton, 55 per cent. of value.
For ores assaying 200 dollars per ton, 58 per cent. of value.
For ores assaying 225 dollars per ton, 60 per cent. of value.
For ores assaying 250 dollars per ton, 62 per cent. of value.
For ores assaying 300 dollars per ton, 63 per cent. of value.

For higher grade ores, rates were establised by special agreement. Lead, over 20 per cent. was paid for at the rate of 40 cents a unit.

As in former years, Mr. O. H. Hahn has furnished me full data in regard to the company's smelting operations.

Average assays per ton.

Atlas fine ore:		
Silver	17.960 oz. =	$23 22
Gold	1.235 oz. =	25 53
		48 75
Lead, 22.6 per cent.		
Atlas coarse ore:		
Silver	29.650 oz. =	38 33
Gold	1.187 oz. =	24 58
		62 91
Lead, 30.6 per cent.		
Average of Atlas ore:		
Silver	23.400 oz. =	30 25
Gold	1.214 oz. =	25 09
		55 34
Lead, 26.32 per cent.		
Purchased ores:		
Silver	49.780 oz. =	6 436
Gold	1.000 oz. =	2 067
		85.03
Lead, 19.58 per cent.		
Atlas and purchased ores:		
Silver	24.340 oz. =	31 47
Gold	1.206 oz. =	24 93
		56 40
Lead, 26.08 per cent.; moisture, 5.9 per cent.		
Average contents of bullion produced:		
Silver	103.310 oz. =	133 57
Gold	5.499 oz. =	113 67
		247 24

Atlas Mining and Smelting Company's smelter's report for the year 1875.

Date.	Tons of ore smelted per twenty-four hours.								Bushels charcoal per 24 hours.		Number of bars produced.	Weight of bullion.	Number of bars in shipment.	Weight of shipment.	Slag used as flux.	Per cent. of slag used as flux.
	Atlas ore.		Custom-ores.					Total.	Received in bin.	Actually used.						
	Fine.	Coarse.	Newark.	Hamburg.												
												Pounds.		*Pounds.*	*Pounds.* *Tons.*	
April	357. 5	344. 2	......	......		....	....	701. 7	22, 750	21, 368	3, 069	262, 738	3, 048	261, 274	463, 620= 231. 81	33. 0
May	771. 5	566. 4	21. 1	......	Nonsuch, 3. 3	....	....	1, 362. 3	43, 015	42, 309	5, 611	483, 243	5, 597	482, 202	1, 044, 000= 522. 00	38. 3
June	720. 4	557. 3	......	......	....	Wide West, 7. 4	....	1, 285. 1	43, 050	41, 928	4, 857	414, 803	4, 932	421, 313	1, 082, 602= 541. 301	42. 1
July	607. 1	472. 1	......	......	Banner, 10. 5	Star of Eur., 8. 9	....	1, 098. 6	38, 570	36, 454	4, 974	422, 715	4, 956	420, 986	941, 270= 470. 635	42. 8
Aug	609. 2	488. 9	23. 8	......	Lee, 1. 8	Orange, 1. 5	French, 8. 1	1, 133. 3	42, 560	40, 350	5, 082	432, 948	4, 944	421, 336	1, 142, 675= 571. 3375	50. 4
Sept	248. 0	117. 2	7. 9	44. 8	Diamond, 6. 3	....	....	424. 2	15, 963	15, 108	2, 364	201, 428	2, 572	219, 112	407, 200= 203. 6	48. 0
Nov	307. 6	325. 4	......	52. 2	Banner, 12. 1	{Morn'g Glory, 6. 4} {Ruth, 11. 8}	San José, 8. 9	724. 4	26, 950	24, 920	4, 792	393, 902	4, 773	400, 764	593, 800= 296. 9	41. 0
	3, 621. 3	2, 871. 5	52. 8	97. 0	34. 0	36. 0	17. 0	6, 729. 6	232, 858	222, 437	30, 749	2, 611, 777	30, 822	2, 626, 987	5, 675, 167=2, 837. 58	42. 16
	6,492.8 tons Atlas ore.		236.8 tons custom-ore.													
											Bars.	Pounds.				
Purchased from									K. K		59	5, 363				
									Moeller		33	2, 985				
									Richmond		..	8, 498				
													92	16, 846		
													30, 730	2, 610, 141		
On hand January 1, 1876													19	1, 626		
													30, 749	2, 611, 767=1, 305. 8835 tons.		

Charcoal purchased, 244,299 bushels; charcoal consumed, (by tally-boards,) 222,437 bushels. Loss, 21,862 bushels, or 8.94 per cent.

Consumption of charcoal purchased, per ton of ore, 36.3 bushels. 5.15 tons of ore produced one ton of lead. 3.5 per cent. of the ore smelted was purchased ore.

Number of furnaces, 2; only one running at a time. Number of runs made during the year, 3, of respectively 100, 49, and 20 days, according to the quantity of ore and coal at hand.

ATLAS MINING AND SMELTING COMPANY.

Contents of ores smelted during the year 1875, according to the weekly assays.

Description of ore.	Tons of ore, gross.	Tons of ore, net.	Tons of lead in ore.	Ounces of silver in ore.	Ounces of gold in ore.
Atlas fine ore	3, 621. 3	3, 267. 90	738. 612	58, 738. 60	4, 037. 019
Atlas coarse ore	2, 871. 5	2, 839. 51	868. 922	84, 197. 18	3, 377. 640
Custom-ores	236. 8	225. 03	44. 080	11, 203. 87	226. 904
Total	6, 729. 6	6, 332. 44	1, 651. 614	154, 139. 65	7, 641. 563

Contents of bullion produced.

Number of bars made.		Weight of bullion in pounds.	Ounces of silver in bullion.	Ounces of gold in bullion.	Total value of bullion in gold and silver.
	30, 841	2, 628, 613	135, 551. 63	7, 203. 394	$324, 235 80
Less bullion purchased	92	16, 846	641. 68	22. 090	1, 286 40
	30, 749	*2, 611, 767	134, 909. 95	7, 181. 304	322, 949 40

* = 1, 305. 8835 tons.

Relation between contents and production.

	Tons lead.	Ounces silver.	Ounces gold.
Contents of ore	1, 651. 6140	154, 139. 65	7, 641. 563
Produced therefrom	1, 305. 8835	134, 909. 95	7, 181. 304
Loss	345. 7305	19, 229. 70	460. 259
Loss in percentage	20. 93	12. 47	6. 02

The average assay of speiss produced during the year was:

Silver, 15.09 ounces	$19 51
Gold, 0.815 ounces	16 86
	36 37

And of slag:

Silver, 0.5 ounces	$0 66
Gold, trace.	
Lead, 2.38 per cent.	

The K. K. Consolidated Mine has been worked throughout the year, at times with very flattering prospects for the future. The fifth level from the vertical main shaft, on which there are splendid hoisting-works, has reached the main ore-channel of Ruby Hill, and a considerable quantity of good ore has been found, though most of the ore is still of low grade, as heretofore. Mr. W. S. Keys, the superintendent, reports the following yield for the year 1875:

Month.	Ore reduced.	Bullion produced.		Gold and silver.
	Tons.	*Bars.*	*Pounds.*	
January	363	883	80, 921	$14, 800 00
July	1, 438½	2, 726	253, 666	48, 188 50
August	194	467	43, 530	8, 161 90
November	1, 230	3, 104	290, 889	28, 600 00
December	1, 445	6, 240	584, 395	66, 251 00
Total	4, 670½	13, 420	1, 253, 401	166, 001 40

The value of the lead at $80 per ton, $50,120, added to the above, gives the total yield of the mine for 1875 as $216,121.

Of the other mines worked in the district during the year, none have reached results worthy of special mention. Their product is included in the returns of the Richmond and Atlas Smelting Companies, but cannot be separately ascertained. At the end of the year none of the principal mines of the district was in very good condition, though all of them had fair amounts of ore in sight. The prospects for the near future of the Richmond Mine, in particular, were considered less favorable than heretofore.

HUMBOLDT COUNTY.

For data on the mining industry of this county I am, as in former years, indebted to Mr. D. Van Lennep, M. E., now of Winnemucca, Nev.

In taking a retrospective view of the mining interests of Humboldt County, one cannot but feel that the final results of several mining and reducing enterprises, promising well at the beginning of the year, are very discouraging at the close, the stringency in the money-market aggravating the gloomy aspect of affairs.

This year, as heretofore, abandoned mills attest to the folly of hastening to build works for the reduction of ore before a steady and adequate supply has been assured. On the other hand, many enterprises have been hindered or ruined by the attempt to make the mines pay their own way from the beginning, and furnish from their profits the necessary capital for machinery and reduction-works. This may in some cases be done, when custom-mills are at hand and the surface-ores are rich. But many valuable mines are unable to carry the burden of self-development; and many are seriously injured by the robbery of their richer ores and the neglect of substantial timbering and systematic working which too often attend the endeavor. If the misplaced or premature expenditure of capital is a frequent source of failure, the withholding of it is often not less unfortunate, as the present condition of many promising mines in this county testifies.

The high price of labor is a great obstacle to the development of the mines of the county, which carry, on an average, low-grade ores in small ledges. The close vicinity to the Comstock lode seems to be in the way of obtaining a reduction of miners' wages.

During the fall of this year, however, there being no demand for miners, many have gone to work at $3.50. Chinese labor is, for these reasons, coming more in favor every year, especially for such mines and works as would have to be closed if worked by high-priced labor.

In *Buena Vista district*, the Arizona Mine has been worked steadily through the year. The mine has not been paying, and two assessments have been levied of $1 each per share. The number of tons extracted during the twelve months amounts to 3,285. The ore was reduced at the Arizona Mill, at Unionville, and about five tons of higher grade were shipped away for reduction. The force at work in the mine has not been as great as in former years, nor has the mine been worked in depth. The new tunnel begun last year, to connect the works west of the McDougal shaft in a nearly level and straight line to the surface of the hill, was finished this year. The ore extracted has been mostly from this portion of the mine, some having been obtained also from the part known as the Eastern spur, from the Stewart ledge, and from the Manitowoc ledge. Another break in the ledge was encountered in the western portion of the mine, beyond the McDougal shaft. The richness of the ledge has diminished at all the points worked, especially on the western side, going up on the ledge toward the outcrop. At the end of the year the average assay of the pulp at the mill is estimated at $30 per ton.

The Arizona Mill has been kept at work on ore or tailings throughout the year with little interruption, except for repairs. The four Varney pans have been replaced with three Wheeler's. The mill has now 20 stamps and 8 Wheeler pans. The silver or tailings mill has not undergone any change worth noticing. At the end of the summer and during the first part of the fall it had to stop on account of the scarcity of water in the cañon. The castings for these two mills (pan and battery dies and shoes) have been cast by the Mill City foundery.

The Henning Mine fell, by reason of an attachment and judgment in favor of J. C. Fall, out of the hands of the Pioneer & Inskip Mining and Milling Company. Two miners and several Chinamen worked the mine the greater part of the year. The portion of the ledge on the south and near the mouth of the south tunnel was found to be rich, and a considerable amount of ore was taken out. Some was reduced at the Pioneer Mill, in the summer, when the supply of water was sufficient to run. About 40 tons was sent to the Humboldt Reduction Works, in Winnemucca, and the remainder awaits reduction at the Pioneer Mill.

The Pioneer Mill is in the hands of J. C. Fall, for the same reason as that stated above in connection with the Henning Mine. The mill was run during the first part of the year on Henning and Millionaire ore until the water failed. Since this time alterations are being made in the mill. The principal one is the replacement of the small engine by a larger one, powerful enough to run the pans and the battery by steam only when the water fails. The mill was nearly ready to run at the end of the year.

Some prospecting has been carried on in the district during the year, but no permanent bodies of good ore have been discovered.

The antimony-mine has been worked steadily, most of the year by Chinese labor, ten to twelve men having been employed, with a white foreman to direct their work. Several hundred tons of sulphuret of antimony were shipped to the Starr Smelting Works in San Francisco. The exact amount is not known, the owner, O. M. Evans, having died suddenly in the month of August. Two months after this occurrence, the mine was leased to the parties who now ship the ore to San Francisco.

The Millionaire was worked by running an incline on the ledge and following the same dipping into the hill (with more than one break) for 100 feet. The ledge widens in places, but is barren.

The principal stockholder, Mr. Hill Beachy, having died suddenly last summer, the work on the mine was stopped. After a while it was resumed, but only to take out the rich ore, which lies between the outcrop and the first break. The ore taken out has been reduced by the Pioneer Mill, the Humboldt Reduction Works, and a few tons by the Torry Mill, near Oreana.

The shipments of bullion from Unionville in 1875 were:

In silver bars	$140,249 40
In gold bars	8,651 00
Total, (coin-value)	148,900 40

The gold comes from the gulch-washings in Indian district, near the Eagle Mine, and also from gulch-washings on a small scale in Congress

lodes are not able to supply, at least for some time to come, all the ore required, it is clearly the interest and the duty of the owners of outside lodes, which, but for his enterprise, would not be worth anything, to do their best for themselves and him by going to work at once and producing as much ore as possible.

Between Banner and Idaho City, about six miles east of the latter, are the Gambrinus, owned by Mr. Plowman; the Sub-Rosa, owned by Mr. Hooten, and the Keep Cool. Some very fine ore has been obtained, especially from the first two lodes, the ore from the Sub-Rosa ranging in value from $45 to $100 per ton. As to the state of development in this lode, I am not informed. The ore from the three lodes is now worked in a 10-stamp mill owned by Mr. Plowman. It is run by water power, and has been in operation not quite continuously all summer.

Quartzburgh district.—The Gold Hill Company, which has thus far worked its mine only above the water-level, stopped work in mill and mine in July and commenced sinking an incline 150 feet long and gaining 100 feet vertical depth at the southwest side of the creek. The mill in the mean time was thoroughly overhauled and improved, the copper plates were exchanged for silver-plated ones, and the length of the sluice-boxes doubled. The old copper plates yielded $12,000.

In sinking the incline the owners had to contend with a very large amount of water, and it was not finished until the latter part of November. A cross-cut was then started, forming a large curve 30 feet long, this shape being chosen for the purpose of doing away with the necessity of a turn-table. The vein was reached in December, and shows as well in width and quality as in any other part heretofore developed.

Very fine hoisting-works, manufactured by Hawkins & Bartrell, of San Francisco, were erected at the mouth of the incline. The 40-horse-power engine is a portable, double-hoisting one, with link-motion and double reels. It takes up, with hoisting-apparatus, only a space of 14 by 20 feet, and works with great precision. The drums are 32 by 36 inches. A circular saw will be run by the engine for the sawing of timbers and lagging, which will save a large amount of work and money. A plentiful supply of everything needed for the mill and mine during the winter has been laid in, representing a cash-value of at least $25,000.

Nothing has yet been done with the large amount of concentrated tailings on hand, estimated at present at from 5,000 to 6,000 tons. The great trouble experienced in disposing of these tailings is that they are probably not rich enough to stand the expense of roasting, and so far no satisfactory results have, to my knowledge, been obained without it.

The Iowa lode is owned and worked by the Boise Mining Company. In the upper level the ore has been stoped out 150 feet high for a distance of 150 feet north and 100 feet south. In the lower level the vein is considerably broken up, and lies so flat that the ore requires much handling to bring it through the shoots. The ore has yielded heretofore from $5 to $18 per ton, averaging from $6 to $7; the expense of mining and milling amounts to $5 per ton. In the present workings the ore has depreciated in value and the additional amount of labor required in handling takes away all profit. Owing to this fact the owners will quit work in the mine altogether for the present and complete the upper cross-cut tunnel on the Gold Hill extension or Growling Go lode, which also belongs to them. The tunnel will have to be extended 50 feet to strike the lode, and when the levels have been run there will be a body of good ore overhead, 100 feet high, ready for stoping. The tram-way over which the ore from the Iowa is brought to the mill will also be used for the Gold Hill ore. If the ore in the upper part of the Gold Hill extension proves of satisfactory quality, the company will also complete the lowest cross-cut tunnel, which is now in 200 feet, and which, when finished, will bring in 400 feet in depth on the south and 600 feet on the north end of the claim. This tunnel is on a level with the mill, and can be finished at a comparatively small expense, the ground being of a character so favorable that 130 feet has been run in one month. The ground in the Iowa is also very soft, only 200 pounds of powder having been used for blasting in the last seven months.

The mill is small, but substantially built and well arranged. It contains 10 stamps, of 650 pounds each, making 80 drops of 8 inches per minute, and crushing 20 tons per day. The engine has 60 horse-power, but the two tubular boilers have only a capacity of 25. Two copper plates are used in each mortar-box, on which 80 per cent. of all the gold extracted is saved, the remaining 20 per cent. being caught on the copper tables. The bullion from the battery is from 850 to 860 fine, while that from the tables is only 800 fine. Russian screens are used, the discharge being 6 inches above the dies when new.

About a mile above Quartzburgh is the Lawyer lode, now owned by Messrs. Hart, Carroll, Dougherty & Morehead. A cross-cut tunnel 500 feet long taps the lode at a depth of 230 feet from the surface. The crevice is well defined and carries a good body of ore, which mills from $10 to $20 per ton.

In Cañon Creek, 4 miles from Placerville, some new lodes were discovered in July, which, by the extraordinary richness of their surface-ore, created a considerable excitement throughout the Boise Basin. The principal locations are the Chief and Ebenezer and some placer-claims below the former. So far very little progress has been made in the development of the lodes, but next spring will probably witness a great deal of activity. A lot of ore was to be taken over to the Boise Mining Company's mill for crushing, but I have not learned anything about the result. In Summit Flat some work has been done on the Golden Era lode by Freeman, Johnson & Charbonneau, and next season several other mines will probably also be worked again.

The prospects for a prosperous quartz-mining season are generally bright through the whole county. The Gold Hill Company and possibly also the Boise Company will work steadily and turn out a large amount of gold. Banner will come in as a silver-producing camp, and if the Cañon Creek mines are only half as rich as reported, they will make a respectable contribution in the bullion product.

IDAHO COUNTY.

Very little work has been done in this county on quartz-lodes, owing to the difficulties attending mining here. The following circular, issued by citizens of Warren's, the principal mining-camp, gives a complete and, as Mr. Wolters attests, also a truthful and in no way exaggerated account of the condition and resources of that district:

Washington quartz-mining district.—Among the many localities where gold and silver quartz veins have been found west of the Rocky Mountains during the past fifteen years, the Washington district, of North Idaho, has received comparatively little or no attention from capitalists, apparently owing to a combination of causes and influences over which those discovering them and holding them have had no control, and yet the few geologists and mineralogists who have visited this district, examined the veins as partially opened, and tested the ores, have universally pronounced it the best district upon the coast, in view of the number of its veins and the average richness of its ores of gold and silver.

This district is situated in what are called the Salmon River Mountains, about 15 miles south of the main Salmon River and about 10 miles west of the main south fork of said stream, in about latitude 45° 30′′ north and longitude 115° west of Greenwich, in Idaho County, Idaho Territory.

The district embraces a basin in these mountains, with the gradual elevations surrounding, and has an area of about 10 miles square. Its elevation is from 6,500 to 7,500 feet above the level of the sea. The hills and valleys are covered with a growth of black pine timber of dimensions from the size of a fishing-rod up to twelve and fifteen inches in diameter, with here and there in the gulches clusters of spruce and white fir, and on some of the points of the hills red fir trees are found of the dimensions of two and three feet in diameter.

It has one main stream cutting the heart of the basin and passing through a gorge in the mountains and emptying itself into the main Salmon River. Many small tributaries from the ravines and gulches supply this stream, and furnish, at all seasons of the year, an abundant supply of water for quartz-mining purposes with steam-power, while the main stream in many places furnishes ample water-power to propel quartz-mills of small capacity during eight months of the year.

This district is located about one hundred miles distant from the agricultural settlement of Camas Prairie on the northwest, and about one hundred and twenty miles from a similar settlement on the Weiser River on the south side of the main Salmon range of mountains, and there are but very few farms or ranches cultivated within that distance of the district, and these are along the cañons of Salmon River and South Fork of said stream.

The nearest mart of importance where supplies can be obtained for the district is Lewiston, at the head of the present navigation of Snake River, at its junction with the Clearwater, a distance of 160 miles. A smaller town at the foot of the mountain, on Camas Prairie, is 100 miles distant, and at present is only reached for supplies by pack-trains over a good mountain-trail, which has been in constant use since 1862 as a thoroughfare for travel and supplies for the placer-mining camps of Florence, 50 miles distant, and for this camp. The district is about 200 miles a little east of north from Boise City, the capital of Idaho Territory, and for most of this distance travel is performed on the backs of animals over a good mountain-trail.

The district is supplied by two mail-routes, one by way of Lewiston and Florence, and the other by way of the Weiser and Payette Valleys. The former makes weekly trips through the year, and the latter weekly for six months of the year and semi-monthly the other six months.

The snow commences to fall about the first of November, and varies in depth in different winters from three to six and seven feet, and seldom entirely disappears till the month of June. The trails leading into the district are generally blockaded with snow against travel with animals about five or six months each year, but could be kept open if the business of the camp was such as to induce daily travel over them. The routes are generally well sheltered by standing timber, so as to protect them from winds and drifting snows. The winter trail to Lewiston reaches the main Salmon River about 35 miles from the district, and from that point to Lewiston and all the lower country of the Snake and Columbia Rivers the routes are always open for travel with animals. The travel in winter in and about the camp is principally done on Norwegian snow-shoes, except when the business of parties is such as to require the use of animals, and then roads are broken and beaten through the snow for that purpose. The difficulty of maintaining good roads for animals during the winter in any part of the district is no greater than in the States of Vermont, New Hampshire, Maine, and many parts of Massachusetts, and not so great as on the prairies of Illinois and other States where the snows are in drifts.

The mean temperature of the weather during the months of December, January, and February, the coldest months of the year, is from 20° to 25° above zero, and seldom is found to be below zero, and then only for a few days of the season, while it frequently will range for days from 35° to 50° above zero. There were two or three days about the middle of January, 1875, when the mercurial thermometer, at 6 o'clock a. m., indicated 35° below zero, which was the coldest period save one ever known in the district since it has been inhabited by miners.

This district has been worked by placer-miners since 1862, and from it has been taken an amount of gold equal to that of any camp of its size in Idaho Territory. It has always been known as "Warren's Camp." Its placers now are nearly exhausted, except for the Chinese, who will continue to make from $1 to $3 per day per man for some years to come.

Wages of white men in the mines during the past season have been from $4.50 to $5 per day, while Chinese labor has been $2.50 per day.

The placer-gold has been taken from the creek-bottoms, gulches, ravines, and points of hills projecting into the creek-bottoms.

The existence of quartz-ledges bearing gold has been known to some placer-miners from the earliest period of placer-mining in the district, but by men who placed but little value upon quartz in any country. In the fall of 1865 a silver-vein was discovered a few miles from Florence, and its discovery awakened some little attention, which afterward induced some prospecting for quartz in the summer of 1866, and first led to the discovery of the Washington gold and silver vein in this district, and soon afterward the Western and a few other veins. In July of that year the few who had made discoveries and locations in this district convened and established the boundaries of the "Washington gold and silver quartz mining district," and framed their laws relative to the discovery, location, and representation of quartz-claims in the district. This action gave an impetus to quartz-prospecting, and before the first of December of that year upward of one hundred distinct veins had been discovered and partially uncovered, and locations recorded upon them all.

Late in August of that year, Mr. George Hearst, of San Francisco, Cal., in company with one Williamson, paid this camp a visit, having previously followed the noted Robeson into the mountains of the northern part of the Territory, till they became satisfied that he was, and had been, deceiving them about the location of his rich ledges. These men spent some twenty days in examining the ledges then partly uncovered in this camp, and Mr. Hearst caused to be published a letter over his own signature, in which he pronounced the surface-prospects of the ledges of this camp equal, if not superior, to those of any other camp he had ever visited upon this coast, and urged the miners to sink down upon their veins and develop them, and if they proved as good below as upon the surface, they might be assured that capital could readily be had to place them in a working condition and bring reduction-works into the camp. He lamented the absence of good wagon-roads, over which proper reduction-works could readily be transported, and the remoteness of the district from San Francisco, the seat of the quartz-mining capital of this coast, and the length of the winters here.

His opinions, however, as then given, inspired much confidence in some miners who had before become interested in quartz, and they commenced with renewed vigor to sink upon their claims. But by far the great majority of the miners of the district could not be induced to co-operate in the development of the ledges, and traders and supply-men, if at all, gave a very reluctant countenance to any and all quartz-men.

As a result of this disposition on the part of the traders, except in a few isolated instances, prospecting for new ledges, as well as sinking upon those found, for the most part ceased in the fall of 1866, and the great mass of the claims then located, recorded, and represented under the district laws, has been left entirely untouched from that day to the present.

But a few men of more faith and energy than others, without means, save their own labor, have persevered, in defiance of the obstacles which beset them on every hand, and have done something toward the development of a few ledges. Shafts have been sunk on some of them varying in depth from fifty to two hundred and fifty feet, and in no one thus opened has the vein disappeared or lessened in size, but with great uniformity they have gradually increased in size of crevice between walls, and thus demonstrated the fact that they are true fissure-veins, giving prospects of still greater size below.

The ores taken from these shafts have proved as good at the bottom as at the surface, and the average yield per ton of the ores in free gold, by battery-mill process, without any attempt to work them for the silver, has been from $12 to $90. The assays made of the silver-ores taken from these different ledges have been returned from $40 to as high as $12,000 per ton. Assays of large samples of the gold-ores have been returned as high as $10,000 per ton. These highest assays, as might be expected, have been made from selected portions of the veins.

Of the ores which have been milled for free gold by the battery process alone may be mentioned ores from the following veins, to wit:

	Tons.	Average per ton.
The Hic Jacet	90	$43 00
The W. B. Knott	350	29 00
The Keystone	50	65 00
The W. Scott	150	56 00
The Alder	20	17 00
The Rescue	3,500	22 50
The Charity	1,000	15 00
The Samson	300	24 00
The Uncle Sam	10	17 00

Several of these veins have produced assorted ores, in quantities of from seven to twenty tons, which have yielded at the rate of from $50 to $270 per ton. The first ten tons from the W. Scott, assorted and milled, yielded $179 per ton. The first three tons assorted from the Hic Jacet and milled in an arrastra, yielded $270 per ton; and five tons afterward, assorted from twelve tons as it came from the mine, were sold in San Francisco for $155 per ton to European shippers, who paid only 60 per cent. of its value as tested by the pan process. Several small lots from the Keystone were milled in an arrastra, and yielded upward of $90 per ton. One lot of assorted ore from the W.

B. Knott yielded $129 per ton. Several lots from the Rescue, assorted, yielded from $50 to $75 per ton by the battery process alone.

Many gold-bearing veins in camp whose surface-croppings, from assay-tests made, appear richer than any of the above-named, have never been worked, and not a ton of their ores has ever been milled by arrastra, pan, or battery process, and are now lying entirely neglected, and some of them abandoned by their former owners, for want of energy in themselves and capital to open and work them.

One man in the district who has a small arrastra has, during the past two seasons, worked with his own hands and alone in gathering up drift-rock and extracting from mines which he owns, hired the ores packed on mules to his arrastra, in some cases for miles at high freights, milled the ores himself, and made more money than any placer-miner in camp, in the same length of time, and could that man to-day command the requisite means to properly open his ledges, and have proper reduction-works for his ores, he would show to the capitalists of the country a greater profit upon his investment than is shown by thousands who invest their money in merchandise, trading, and stock speculations and land.

Of the silver-ledges which have been tested by first burning the ores when extracted and milling them in an arrastra, may be mentioned the Martinas, Bullion, Black Hawk, and the Knott Treasure. The first yielded in that manner $238 per ton; second, $50; third, $65; fourth, $60. With the imperfect means employed in reduction of these ores, these tests made cannot be regarded as full and fair tests of the value of these ores.

The silver-veins are numerous in this district which prospect better than these. A small stratum of ore found in the Martinas has assayed richer than any other silver-ore ever yet tested in the district. But silver-ledges are almost entirely neglected and are in waiting for capitalists to take hold of them and erect the proper machinery for the reduction of silver-ores.

One serious obstacle to the investment of capital in the quartz of this district has heretofore existed in the territorial and district laws relative to the size of an individual claim and the extent and manner of representation. An individual claim upon a vein was only two hundred feet of the length of the vein with fifty feet on each side, which could be held as *real estate*, under the above laws, by the expenditure of twenty dollars upon the claim at any time within twelve months after date of location, and no annual representation subsequent to said twelve months was required to enable the party locating to hold the claim as his property against all others. Under this provision a large number of claims were located upon the best veins then discovered, and were fully represented by the said amount of expenditure, and have never been touched since the first year. These could not be molested by others without violation of district laws, nor could a sufficient number of feet upon any one vein to form a contiguous claim of the proper extent to induce capital to either purchase or expend money to prospect it be united in interest, owing to separate rights and conflicting opinions of the claimants adjoining.

But the law of Congress of May, 1872, making an annual representation requisite, (notwithstanding the several extensions of time for the first representation under the law,) has caused a forfeiture of the rights of these neglecting parties, and now a large number of valuable claims are open for relocation under the laws of Congress. The district has also made its laws to conform in all of their provisions with the laws of Congress.

Some relocations have been made under the act of 1872 and its amendments. Among these are the Martinas, W. P. Hunt, Samson, Hic Jacet, W. B. Knott, Knott Treasure, Winfield Scott, Black Hawk, Washington, Uncle Sam, (now called "Alhambra,") Rescue Extension, (now called "Right Wing,") J. Greenfield, Jennie Leland, I Excel, (now called "Davey,") George Hearst, Hawk Eye, (now called "Blue Bird,") Andy Johnson, Laurel, Emerald, Copper Lead, (now called "Juniper,") Ramey, (now called "Ruby,") and some others.

Several new veins have been discovered; among them are the Alta and Antler, two large gold-bearing ledges, also the Roebuck. All these relocations and new discoveries are now in the hands of parties who have not the means of properly opening the veins, but they have been located with the view of offering the controlling interest in them to any capitalists who will give guarantee of their being well prospected and operated if found to be as good below as they now prospect upon the surface.

It may here be said that the reduction-works which have as yet been erected in the district have all been of a light and rude character, entirely inadequate to the saving of a large percentage of the valuable metals contained in the ores. Before the proper reduction-works can be transported here a wagon-road must be constructed. To construct such a road over which heavy machinery can be transported will cost an expenditure of from $10,000 to $20,000, according to the different estimates made by road-men who have examined the different routes. But the men of the district are not disposed to construct such a road without some assurance that they can induce capital to take hold and develop these mines and place here the proper reduction-works, which the men of the district are entirely unable to place here, even when a suitable road is constructed.

It may here be further remarked that the veins now known to exist here contain gold or silver, or both, and vary in width from 6 inches to 4½ feet upon the surface, and as developed below the surface they have almost invariably increased in width. The walls are granite. The slate formation crops out as descent is made from the summits of the surrounding mountains to Salmon River and the South Fork of said stream.

From the above facts it may be readily inferred that the real wants of the district, to make it highly prosperous and productive in gold and silver bullion, are: first, a sufficient amount of capital judiciously expended to properly open and develop the quartz-veins of the district; second, a good wagon-road into the district, over which proper reduction-machinery can be transported, and supplies furnished for the miners at moderate prices; third, well-skilled and efficient quartz-miners and mill-men to operate the mines and mills when opened and constructed in the district.

WASHINGTON, IDAHO, *November* 17, 1875.

The undersigned, citizens of the Washington quartz district and of Idaho County, Idaho Territory, hereby certify that each for himself has heard read the foregoing statement of facts pertaining to the situation, condition, and prospects of said district, relative to its mines and the requisites of the district to make it highly productive in gold and silver, and that the facts therein set forth are true and nothing overdrawn.

J. W. POE, *Attorney at Law.*
S. P. C. HOWARD, *Member of Legislature.*
GEO. CHURCH, *Treasurer Idaho County.*
A. H. SANDERSON, *Justice of the Peace of Idaho County.*
A. FRIEDENRICH, *Postmaster at Washington.*
NOAH DAVEY, *Superintendent of Rescue Mining Company.*
SAMUEL LARGE, *Miner, of Washington.*
M. STORMS, *Secretary of Rescue Company.*
CHAS. JOHNSON, *Quartz-Miner.*
G. W. DYER, *Mechanical Engineer.*
A. BEMIS, *Amalgamator.*
B. F. MORRIS, *Auditor and Recorder.*
C. W. CASE, *Sheriff of said County.*
L. P. BROWN, *Member of Legislature.*
J. M. CROOKS, *A Citizen and Old Resident.*
CHAS. BENTZ, *A Citizen and Old Resident.*

TERRITORY OF IDAHO,
County of Nez Perces, ss:

I, Hazen Squier, clerk of the district court of the first judicial district of Idaho Territory, hereby certify that I am personally acquainted with the persons whose names are signed to the foregoing certificate bearing testimony to the situation and character of the placer and quartz mines of the Washington district, Idaho County, Idaho Territory; that I know them to be men of good character and standing in said Idaho County, whose word is entitled to full credit among all men wherever given, and that most of them have long been residents and doing business in said Washington district, and are well informed of the facts to which they have certified.

Given under my hand and the seal of the said district court this 21st day of December, A. D. 1875.

[SEAL.]

H. SQUIER,
Clerk of District Court, First Judicial District, Idaho Territory.

Mr. Wolters adds to this statement that he does not know of any mining-camp where such liberal inducements are offered to capitalists as in Warren's. The miners of this camp form an exception to the general rule. They are not sanguine, though they are perfectly aware of the fact that they have a large number of promising veins; they realize the extent of the difficulties with which they have to contend, and know that a company of moneyed men taking hold of their camp will have to spend a considerable amount of money before they can expect to recoup their investment. Knowing all this, the citizens have the good sense not to expect any capitalist to come and offer them large sums of money for their half-developed lodes. They ask only that some one shall come, erect reduction-works adapted to the treatment of their ores, and help them to construct a good wagon-road into the camp. In consideration of this, they will give him a large interest in their lodes; and from personal conversation with the leading men, Mr. Wolters thinks that any company willing to expend from $100,000 to $125,000 for the above purposes could get one-half interest in nearly every lode in the district.

OWYHEE COUNTY.

The past year has not been a prosperous one for the Owyhee mines. Being almost entirely owned and worked by San Franciscans, the failure of the Bank of California and the embezzlement by an absconding defaulter of large amounts of money belonging to the Mahogany, Poorman, and Silver Cord companies, dealt them a severe blow, from the effects of which they have but partially recovered. It will probably require another season before the former activity and prosperity will be restored.

All efforts by Mr. Wolters to obtain reliable data about the mines of War Eagle Mountain, and especially the amount of ore produced, yield, &c., from superintendents and through influential outsiders, have proved a failure. It seems that the Owyhee companies do not want to have anything known about their property, unless they are able to make a very favorable impression; but the bullion production of the camp, which always becomes public, furnishes a very good criterion by which to judge the condition of their mines. The fact that they are so often closed to the public is taken by many as a sign that the property is either not worked with a view to make it pay, but with a view to force stocks up and down, or that it is not in a fit condition to be shown to the public.

For the information given below about the War Eagle Mountain, I have had mainly to rely on the reports furnished by the Silver City Avalanche, from which extracts have been freely made.

While last year the Golden Chariot was the leading mine of the camp, the old Oro Fino has come this year to the front again, and, to judge from present indications, it will retain the lead for some time. In August new hoisting-machinery of 100 tons daily capacity was erected, which is expected to serve all purposes to a depth of 1,400 feet. The main building, containing the engine, boilers, and hoisting-machinery, is 44 by 86 feet, with an addition of 18 by 86, which serves as a coal-shed and blacksmith and carpenter shop. The engine is 35 horse-power, the cylinder 12 by 24 inches. Three boilers of 42 inches diameter and 14 feet length are there, two of which furnish the steam for the hoisting-engine, while the third works the air-compressors for the Burleigh drill. The hoisting-works have only one reel, but there is room enough for another when necessary. Clutch and brake are operated with hand-wheels and screws, and are with ease controlled by the engineer. An indicator is attached to the reel, to show the exact position of the bucket or cage in the shaft. The exhaust steam is condensed in a tank, and serves to heat the water for the boilers.

When mining was resumed after the completion of the works in August, the shaft was down 327 feet, 200 feet of which were timbered and lined ready for the cage. The width of the lode in this shaft varies from 3 to 10 feet, the ore yielding from $25 to $35 per ton, but later in the season it improved considerably in value. Lately the new superintendent commenced underhand stoping in the first level at a point 300 feet south of the shaft, working 20 feet deep and running 40 feet toward the shaft. Here he struck a deposit of very rich ore, and, after having become satisfied of its large extent, raised a winze from the second level, starting 280 feet south of the shaft. This is now in 15 feet, and shows a strong vein of rich ore, assays of which indicate a value of several hundred dollars per ton. The third level also looks well, and in the stopes now worked here the crevice is from 10 to 12 feet wide, yielding a large amount of average milling ore. The shaft is now sinking farther, and the superintendent intends to start two more levels during the winter. If the newly-discovered body of rich ore extends so far down, the Oro Fino will yield a larger amount of bullion next year than it ever did before.

The Golden Chariot and Minnesota Mines have been consolidated this summer, and now form one claim 760 feet long, with two shafts, 1,050 and 900 feet deep, respectively. In the lower workings the lode is from 2 to 4 feet wide, and in the eighth, ninth, and tenth levels a large body of good ore is exposed, which will be extracted next spring. New hoisting-works have also been erected, which are thus described in the Avalanche of January 1, 1876:

The new works at the Golden Chariot Mine are the most substantial and durable in the Territory. They will be ready for operation early in the new year. Several months' time having been unavoidably taken up in the construction of these works, the operations in the mine have during that time been quite limited, but now that everything is in splendid trim for the resumption of work, we expect to see the Golden Chariot take its place, as of yore, and contribute more largely than ever to the bullion-product of the camp. Having been always recognized as a leading mine, embracing rich and extensive ore-bodies, it is a source of gratification to all interested to find that the enterprising company controlling this mine have not lost faith in its productiveness, and have been ready and willing to demonstrate their belief in the existence of unsurpassed mineral resources in this camp. They have expended the sum of $90,000 in carrying out and completing works which will stand as a monument to their energy and enterprise, and we predict that the time is not far distant which will prove to them the judiciousness of their investment, and leave no room for doubt as to the wisdom of their course in taking steps to develop the mine on a large scale. No expense has been spared to make the works complete in all their details, and to combine all the modern improvements requisite for the expeditious working of the mine and the taking out and shipment of the rich rock that is known to exist in abundance here.

The new shaft-house is 86 feet in length, 50 feet wide, with walls 21 feet high. It has a cupola 16 by 48 feet in size, with walls of 16 feet. The gallows-frame is 40 feet high. All the timbers and materials used are of the best and most durable description, and will bear the test of a most critical inspection. In proximity to the shaft is a large tank with two compartments, one of them being designed as a receptacle for clean water and the other for muddy water. There is also a third tank, erected on the platform, into which the water is pumped for use in the boilers. The sheaves are 8 feet in diameter. On the south side of the shaft-house is a building 70 feet long by 18 feet wide, with 12-foot walls, designed for a carpenter and blacksmith shop and coal and wood house.

The engine, which is 144 horse-power, is of great strength and very compact, the bed in which it is located being blasted from the solid granite and anchored to the same by 14 1½-inch bolts 8 feet long. The cylinder is 22 inches in diameter, with 42-inch stroke. The fly-wheel weighs 8 tons, and is 16 feet in diameter. The crank-shaft is 8 inches in diameter, the reel-shaft 10 inches, and 12 feet long.

The hoisting-gear consists of a double reversible reel 8 feet diameter and 16 inches face. The bed for the reel-gear is blasted from solid granite and anchored by 16 1½-inch bolts 8 feet long. The large spur-wheel is 10 feet in diameter, with a 12-inch face, and weighs 5 tons. It is driven by a heavy pinion of 3 feet diameter and 12 inches face. Most of the heavy machinery was manufactured by Prescott, Scott & Co., in San Francisco, and its solidity and strength are unsurpassed in the works of any mine on the Pacific.

The boiler is set in brick and cut granite. It is 56 inches in diameter and 16 feet long, combining 2 large tubular boilers, each containing 42 4-inch tubes. The height of the stack is 60 feet above the breeching. The pump used to supply the boilers is of the new Wilcox pattern, and is arranged to throw water over the entire building in case of fire, and also to carry water from the lower to the upper tank, where it is heated by the exhaust steam from the hoisting-engine and then forced through a heater into the boilers at a temperature of 160°, thereby effecting a great saving in the use of fuel.

The plan originally designed for throwing the reel-clutches in and out of gear has been altered and greatly improved by compounding the levers in such a way as to enable the engineer to adjust them without leaving the engine. Another great improvement has also been made in connection with the furnaces, which consists in supplying a draught of superheated air through a coil of 4-inch tubing placed in the ash-bed, which receives the cold air through a register into the pipe, and discharges it at a very high temperature at the immediate point of combustion.

Concerning the operations which are about to be commenced in the mine, the indications are favorable for a splendid development. In the second level south, from which 25 tons of ore were extracted recently, which yielded $125 to the ton, there is a large space, which has not yet been explored, and from the working of which the most promising results are anticipated. A drift was run in there several months ago, which disclosed a fine body of ore, but in consequence of the removal of the old works operations in this section of the mine were temporarily abandoned. A winze will be sunk on this ore-body from the Minnesota ground, and the superintendent expresses the belief that from the ore which is in sight not less than $10,000 will be realized per month. The ledge is about 2 feet in width and shows up very favorably in rich rock. All the past developments in the Golden Chariot point to the existence of a much wider ledge in this vicinity, the work of opening which will be prosecuted without delay. In a few weeks work will also be resumed on the fourth level, and at points between the ninth and tenth levels, where profitable operations were carried on while a former superintendent had charge of the mine.

In the preparations which have been made looking to the resumption of new and active operations, a great deal of retimbering had to be done both in the mine and shaft. Many of the old timbers have decayed or are weakened by the pressure of the earth, and have consequently been replaced by new material. New rollers have also been put in throughout the mine, and in every section of it there has been a thorough overhauling of the material, and everything has been put in splendid shape and condition.

Mr. Baldwin, the new superintendent, has worked like a beaver since he assumed the management of the mine a few weeks ago. He found matters in rather a chaotic state on his arrival here, with the machinery scattered along the road between here and Winnemucca, and much time was unavoidably consumed in having it forwarded to the mine.

The South Chariot Mine is at present employing 32 men, and looks better than ever before. Between the sixth and seventh levels stoping is going on at a point 450 feet north of the shaft, where the vein is from 1 to 2½ feet wide, well defined, and producing fine milling-ore, with every indication of continuing just as good to the Minnesota line, which is 150 feet further north. This body of rich ore pitches down through the seventh, eighth, and ninth levels, at an angle which brings it within 115 feet from the shaft on the tenth level, where it was struck by running a cross-cut 24 feet long from a drift which, for some unknown reason, was run by a former superintendent through solid granite, almost parallel to the ledge. In the tenth level the vein is larger and richer than in the levels above, the ore showing considerable native gold and silver. The tenth level south will be run into that of the Mahogany, whereby both mines will secure good ventilation. Drifting has been commenced from the cross cut in the eleventh level, and in the cross-cut now run for the twelfth level the same 2-foot vein as in the tenth is expected to be found. A winze sunk from the ninth to the tenth level in September showed the rich ore all through. It will be seen from the foregoing that north of the shaft in the South Chariot a rich body of ore exists, having the shape of a trapezoid, the upper and lower sides of which are 150 and 535 feet in length on the sixth and tenth levels, respectively. Allowing the vein to average 1 foot in thickness, and reckoning 12 feet of solid quartz to the ton, we find that this body of ore will produce 10,552 tons; and estimating that it will pay $40 a ton, (a low estimate,) we have a yield of $442,080 from ore now in sight.

The Mahogany owns a claim of 900 feet, which is opened by a shaft 1,000 feet deep. Down to the seventh level the ore has been stoped out. The eighth, ninth, and tenth levels have been driven 500 feet from the shaft in good ore, and winzes sunk between the two latter, showing good ore all through and effecting fine ventilation. In the bottom of the shaft the vein is 4 feet wide, and a correspondent of the Mining and Scientific Press estimates the ore in sight at 15,000 tons, averaging from $40 to $70 per ton. Before the financial crisis the Mahogany employed over 100 men. Then the company became heavily involved by the failure of the Bank of California and the disappearance of an agent with about $75,000 of its funds. An assessment was levied; but a portion of the stockholders refused to pay it, and instituted suit against the directors on account of alleged fraudulent transactions in buying, for a large amount of money, an adjoining piece of ground, which is claimed to be almost worthless. When the company owed the hands three months' wages the latter became exasperated, forced the superintendent to shut down, and, for a short time, even forbade the hoisting of water from the mine. Up to the close of the year no settlement had been made.

The Silver Cord employed 30 hands, and had its shaft sunk down to the fourth level. New hoisting-works were to be erected, when the crisis came and stopped all operations, which have not yet been resumed.

The War Eagle worked from 15 to 40 men last summer, but is now shut down.

The Ida Ellmore has likewise not yet resumed work. During the summer it employed 35 men. Winzes have been sunk from the eleventh to the twelfth, and from the latter to the thirteenth level, for ventilation. Drifts were being driven ahead on the twelfth and thirteenth levels, and about 100 feet more will have to be run before the ledge can be touched.

The Poorman had to suspend work a while, but made satisfactory arrangements with their men, and resumed work with a dozen hands. There is a good body of ore in the mine.

In the Pauper a fine body of very rich ore was struck in the third level, which runs 400 feet south and 112 feet north of the shaft. In the fourth level the same body was struck 4 feet wide. Stoping was going on between the second and third levels, the richest ore being sacked for shipment to Winnemucca, the second class being piled up on the dump, when the crisis forced this mine to shut down, in spite of the excellent prospect ahead. Two lots of ore, making together 4 tons, were shipped to Winnemucca. One lot yielded $448.21 in gold and $209.46 in silver, the other $105.48 in gold and $104.61 in silver, per ton. Work has not yet been resumed.

In the Illinois Central the shaft has attained a depth of 445 feet, the ground being opened by four levels. The first level is 145 feet below the surface; the other three are 100 feet each deeper than the preceding one. Most of the ore above the first level was stoped out by Sands & Co. previous to the incorporation of the mine. The second level is in 150 feet north and the same distance south; the third level, 100 feet north and 60 feet south; the fourth level, 30 feet north and 35 feet south from the bottom of the shaft. There are four winzes, viz: one from first to second level, 150 feet south of the shaft, there being yet 23 feet to sink to make connection; one from the second to the third level, 50 feet north of the shaft; another from the second to the third level, 60 feet south of the shaft; and the last from the third to the fourth level, 50 feet north of the shaft, 12 feet remaining to be sunk to complete the connection, which will afford excellent ventilation for the mine. Fifteen men were engaged in underhand stoping from the top of winze No. 3, in the third level, and back stoping had also been commenced at the bottom of winze No. 2, in the same level, in the summer. The rich ore-body extends 150 feet in each direction from the shaft, and it is known to exist to the bottom of the fourth level, a distance of

300 feet. Allowing a cubic foot of quartz to weigh 166 pounds, there are now 11,205 tons of ore in sight, which, it is estimated, will mill at least $75 per ton, or a total of $840,375. How much deeper the ore-body extends is, of course, not yet known; but the fact that the lode has increased in size and richness as depth has been attained, taken in connection with what is already in sight, augurs a bright future for the Illinois Central. The character of the ore appears to change the deeper it is worked. In the fourth level it is dark-colored with copper stains, and very much like the rich ore formerly taken from the Golden Chariot and Ida Ellmore. There is no trouble on account of water, the mine being dry throughout. Even from the bottom of the fourth level it is not necessary to hoist more than two bucketfuls of water a day. A little more water, indeed, would be not unwelcome, since the water for the hoisting-engine has to be brought through a flume 1,600 feet long, from the War Eagle Mine.

In August the erection of new hoisting-works was completed, and in all quarters it was confidently expected that the mine would produce a large amount of bullion, the superintendent claiming to be able to produce 30 tons of ore per day; but the crisis came, and this company also succumbed, and nothing is going on now.

The Belle Peck has been steadily worked with good success, and a body of remarkably rich ore has been struck in the second level, the best of which, showing a large amount of native gold, is estimated as high as $500 per ton. The shaft is down 150 feet, and the second-level drift extends 40 feet north and 35 feet south of the shaft. In both ends the ore is apparently equally rich, though gold predominates more in the north end and silver at the south. So far only a few hands have been kept at work, but the owners will now push developments ahead as fast as possible, and increase their force in proportion.

Several new claims have been worked on a limited scale, among them the Potosi, Lorraine, Glenbrook, Chipmunk, Crown Point, and others.

The bullion-product of the mines for 1875 was about $225,000, against $620,000 for 1874.

South Mountain district. — South Mountain is at present a "dead camp." The financial crisis which so seriously crippled mining operations in Silver City, proved altogether too much for the South Mountain Consolidated Mining and Smelting Company, and with the company the whole camp went down, because its prosperity solely depended upon that enterprise. The causes for such an utter failure are several. From my South Mountain correspondence I condense the following:

The company made large expenditures, probably larger than the exigencies of the times warranted. The mines, though first class, were undeveloped; much dead-work had to be done, and they could not be expected to be at once self-supporting, with such a heavy outlay for necessary improvements. The levying of an assessment (the first one) became necessary, which was a serious disappointment to stockholders, since glowing accounts of the excellent prospects ahead had been sent to them, which made them look rather for dividends than assessments. To make matters worse, the Bank of California failed just before the assessment became delinquent. This produced a panic-like consternation, and lack of confidence in mining circles all over the coast, and made money very tight. The action of the miners on War Eagle Mountain in shutting down the mines, when the companies for several months failed to pay off their hands, was imitated here; but while the miners of South Mountain cherished the hope of forcing the company to fulfill its obligations to them, they only succeeded in scaring the stockholders still more, and demoralizing them in such a manner that they refused to pay the assessment, which made the entire suspension of work unavoidable.

These were undoubtedly some of the main causes of the general collapse, but further on the correspondent exonerates the management from all blame. Other parties, however, have adopted a different conclusion, which is largely shared by the public in San Francisco. Large amounts of money have been made by speculating in this stock, though the stockholders got nothing.

South Mountain was run up as high as $13 in the spring, when no results at all had yet been obtained, only to tumble down to nothing by the time the continuity and richness of the mines had been proved. A management which causes or permits such artificial fluctuations in the figures which are supposed to be the index of success, cannot expect to enjoy much confidence in times of real or reported peril. The operations at the works were curiously ineffective. Most of the ores of South Mountain district are of an exceedingly favorable character for smelting, and besides this, they are usually rich, producing argentiferous lead containing from $400 to $550 per ton in silver and lead, as tested by Mr. Wolters. There is an abundance of the finest hematite for fluxing; the lodes of the company have always furnished a steady supply of ore, which varied very little in its composition, thus offering the great desideratum in smelting operations, namely, uniformly-composed charges; the furnaces in use are substantially built and well adapted to the treatment of the prevailing kind of ore. If, therefore, with all these facilities it proved impossible to keep a furnace running longer than a week, when it ought to make campaigns of at least six or seven months, there must have been something wrong in the management. The permanent excuse, that the water-jackets burst, cannot be accepted, water-jackets correctly constructed and treated having no occasion to burst. Besides, if it was impossible for the men in charge to work them successfully, any ordinary manager ought to have been able to run his furnaces without them.

The reason that the whole camp instantly collapsed when the Consolidated Company stopped operations is found in the fact that the latter possessed the only reduction-works in the place, and owned at the same time a number of very productive lodes, abundantly able to supply their works to the full extent of their capacity. The company cannot now afford to do custom-work or purchase ore; and hence the outside mine-owners, being nearly all men of small means, are prevented from working their mines until they are given a market for the product. It is said, moreover, that capitalists have been deterred from investing in the mines by the belief that the company owns all the good lodes in the camp. The fact is, however, that, although the Consolidated Company owns some of the best lodes of the camp, there are many others at least equally good and able to produce the same quantity and quality of ore as any one mine belonging to the company can furnish.

Of the 800 inhabitants claimed by the camp in the days of its greatest prosperity a mere handful is all that is left, but the present state of affairs cannot possibly last long. The mines of the district possess as much real merit and value as those of any other silver-lead camp on the coast; the greater part of the ores raised fulfills every condition for successful and easy treatment by smelting; they are further unusually rich, averaging probably not less than from $60 to $75 per ton; and all that is needed to make South Mountain prosperous and productive is the establishment of works honestly and skillfully conducted, where the product of all the mines may find a ready sale at any time at fair prices.

The town of South Mountain is located about 26 miles south of Silver City, at the head of South Mountain Creek, and though only a little over one year old at the time of Mr. Wolters's visit, presented a respectable appearance. It is picturesquely situated, but being jammed in between high and steep mountains on three sides in a small valley not exceeding 300 feet in width, can command little room for growth without laying out streets on the side of the rather steep hills. The creek furnishes deliciously clear and cool water, sufficient for household and milling purposes, but not for motive-power. Timber is scarce in the immediate vicinity; but on the other side of the mountain, five to six miles northeast of the town, there is a large amount of fir, which makes tolerably good lumber.

Mr. Con. Shea has erected a saw-mill there. All the charcoal needed for the furnaces has to be packed a distance of ten miles at a cost of ten cents per bushel, from the nearest place, where juniper is found in almost unlimited quantity. The cost of living is not very high considering the recent origin of the camp and the absence of ranches in the vicinity; board is $9 per week; rough lumber $50 and clear lumber $100 per thousand; wages for miners are $4 per day. Large quantities of lumber are hauled from Boise City, a distance of nearly 90 miles, since the only saw-mill near the camp is unable to meet the demand.

The lodes are grouped around the upper end of town. Most of them have been described in a former report by Mr. Eilers, but, for the sake of completeness, I will recapitulate briefly on this occasion.

The Golconda is located on the north side of the town. Twenty-three feet north of the point of intersection of the lode by the cross-cut tunnel a shaft has been sunk to the depth of 125 feet. The lode is here 8 feet wide and carries from 2 to 6 feet of ore, a good deal of which by proper assorting will make tolerably good smelting-ore, while the balance consists mainly of pyrites and zinc-blende. The average ore contains from $30 to $35 silver per ton and 15 to 20 per cent. of lead. This lode when properly opened can furnish a very large amount of ore, but, like that of other lodes close by, it is of inferior quality for smelting.

A short distance above is the Original lode. It is very large, but so far carries ore in small seams only, and of very low grade.

Further up the hill are the Galaxy, Jessie, Mono, and Disappointment, all opened by shafts from 40 to 100 feet deep, and having each from 20 to 100 tons of excellent smelting-ore on the dumps, mostly very rich-looking carbonates.

Below the Golconda is the property of the Hastings Brothers. They have run a cross-cut tunnel 200 feet long, which passes through three lodes. The first one, called the Black Giant, is a very large lode, being 60 feet wide, with streaks of ore distributed through the whole width of the crevice. The lode, where struck, is considerably broken up, the ore resembling that of the Golconda. The other two lodes are 3 feet wide each, but not developed. Another tunnel is now being run which will strike the lodes 50 feet deeper, where they will probably be more solid.

The Crown Point, on the hill opposite the Golconda, carries a good body of ore, similar to that of the latter, but somewhat richer in silver and lead. Very little work has been done on it.

On the mountain southwest of the town are a large number of fine lodes, all occurring in limestone and mica-slate, while the opposite ridge nearly down to the Original is formed of granite.

High up on the first-named ridge is the Independent. It has a shaft 60 feet deep, only the upper 25 feet being on the vein, which here slides to one side, while the shaft continues straight down. There is some very fine gray carbonate of lead, 2 to 3 feet wide, in the lode, and a large amount of ore on the dump. At the time of Mr. Wolters's visit it was intended to recommence work on this vein, but owing to the general crash the plan was not carried out.

Next below comes the Bay State, one of the best lodes of the camp. Like nearly all the others, it runs nearly northeast and southwest and dips 78°. The shaft is 148 feet deep. At a depth of 90 feet a level has been run northeast 30 feet, and from the bottom another level extends 378 feet southwest, the heading being 159 feet below the surface. The company intended to sink another shaft several hundred feet southwest next spring, and to keep the old one for an air-shaft. New hoisting-works, driven by a 12-horse-power engine, were being erected while Mr. Wolters was in the camp.

About 100 feet lower down the cañon, and running parallel to the Bay State, is the Yreka lode, formerly known as the Numkeg. It runs northeast and southwest and dips 46° southeast. A drift has been run in on the lode at the discovery. It was last summer about 250 feet long. A winze was being raised 50 feet from the heading and stoping was done both ways on a body of ore varying from 10 to 30 inches in thickness, the crevice being from 4 to 6 feet wide. The ore is principally galena, but contains also a considerable amount of lead-carbonate and hydrated oxide of iron. From the 90-foot northeast level in the Bay State a cross-cut 83 feet long has been run, tapping the Yreka about 180 feet below the mouth of the upper level, and thence following the vein southwest for a distance of 360 feet. In this level the crevice is 12 to 15 feet wide, with 1½ to 6 feet of ore. The latter is raised from this level through the Bay State shaft. The lode can produce about 30 tons of ore a day, sufficient to keep one of the company's furnaces supplied. There were 30 men employed here before the stoppage.

Further down are the General Grant and Robie lodes, both containing strong bodies of good, and some very rich, ore. Very little work has been done on them. Mr. Don Vincent is running a tunnel, which will be completed during the winter, and will strike the lode 100 feet from the surface.

At the close of the year the only work going on was done on the Hastings property, the Polar Star, and the Robie.

A considerable excitement was created during the spring by the discovery of some very promising mines near Wagontown, about 6 miles south of Silver City. The lodes are generally very strong, averaging from 4 to 7 feet in width, with ore-zones from 1 to 3 feet thick, well-defined walls, and the general appearance of first-class veins. The ore is flinty quartz, with ruby silver and silver-glance and some gold. Silver largely predominates. The richest ore, worth probably several thousand dollars per ton, has been produced by the Henrietta Mine. Several lots of it were shipped to Winnemucca, but I have not learned the result. From the Saint Clair, one of the largest and best-defined veins, several lots of ore were sent to Silver City, yielding from $70 to $80 per ton.

The Maggie has been lately incorporated, and bears as high a reputation as any mine in the district. Next year will certainly witness great activity here, since the "prospects" are extraordinarily good; this fall no lode was explored beyond 100 feet in depth. If Silver City does not do better next year than the past one, and Wagontown should become possessed of good reduction-works, the former may have trouble to maintain its leading position as a bullion-producing camp in this county.

LEMHI COUNTY.

It is reported that some good lodes have been found in this as yet rather inaccessible county, but I have not obtained any reliable data in regard to them.

In conclusion, I wish to acknowledge the valuable assistance rendered to Mr. Wolters by Mr. W. B. Morris, agent of Wells, Fargo & Co., and Mr. R. Heuschkel, of Boise City; Messrs. McNally, Newton, Hopkins, Pfeiffer, Anderson, and others in Rocky Bar; Allgewahr, Lantis, and Tillmar, of Atlanta; Coughanour and Mootry, of Quartzburgh; Leland, of Warren's, and Irwin, Wessels, and Cook, of South Mountain.

CHAPTER IV.

OREGON.

From the western part of the State, I have nothing to report in the way of important developments. The coast-diggings in Northern California and Oregon continue to be the objects of fitful enterprise, but I have heard of no undertakings in that quarter which require further mention than has already been given to the subject.

In Eastern Oregon the winter of 1874–'75 was unusually severe. Only the Indians and the former trappers of the Hudson's Bay Company could recall instances of equally inclement seasons. The mercury stood between zero Fahrenheit and 26° below for a period of two months. Such temperatures are not favorable to heavy snows, or perhaps it would be more rational to say that heavy snows would have moderated the weather. Yet the aggregate supply of water, if I may judge from the general reports from the diggings, does not appear to have been seriously deficient. My valued correspondent, Mr. E. W. Reynolds, of Baker City, informs me that the product of gold-dust came fully up to the yield of 1874, while the Sparta and Gem City diggings, in Union County, tributary to the Eagle Canal Company's ditch, were more productive than in the preceding year.

Powder River Valley.—The gulches along the western slope of this valley have paid about as well as usual. Messrs. Andrew Smith & Co., in Washington Gulch; Daniel Carn, in Ruan Gulch, and McCord & Co., in the same locality; Nelson & Co., on Salmon Creek; Crow & Balger, Dare, Kelly, and others, back of Pocahontas; and Ingraham & Co., farther down the valley and on Wolf Creek, are reported as operating with average good results. In Ruan Gulch, McCord & Co. struck during the summer a small vein of very rich gold-ore, which they propose to develop this year.

Conner Creek.—On this creek, an Oregon tributary of the Snake, is located the old Conner Creek gold-bearing lode, now owned by Messrs. White, Myrick, and others. These parties are employing 15 stamps, 10 being driven by steam and 5 by water. They are reported as "doing well." The extension of the Conner Creek claim, operated by Messrs. Sleeper & Co. with the aid, it is said, of eastern capital, employs, apparently with profit, a 5-stamp water-mill, to which it is intended to add 5 stamps this season.

There are also placer-mines in this neighborhood. Mr. C. Hinckle has two ditches, aggregating 1½ miles in length, which take water from Conner Creek and command the Snake River bars. They carry from 50 to 100 inches the year round. The ground covered by this supply is worked with Chinese and white labor by the proprietor of the ditch, who is able to make advantageous use of all the water, and consequently has none to sell.

In *Fox Creek*, 1 mile above Conner Creek, Messrs. Speake & Packer have a ditch, carrying from 50 to 200 inches of water, all of which is utilized by the proprietors.

At *Soda Creek*, 6 miles below Conner Creek, a ditch 1¼ miles long, carrying from 30 to 100 inches of water, is owned by Messrs. Ross, Pitts

& Co., who own also and work to the extent of the water-supply the ground commanded by the ditch. Across the Snake River there are spots which would pay well for working, if similar water-facilities were provided. The bars are from 3 to 30 feet deep, and run back to the hills.

In *Shirt-Tail Gulch*, on the way from Burnt River to Rye Valley, the Lum Davis lode is said to promise well, "prospecting" from $10 to $40 per ton in gold.

Rye Valley district has been retarded in its development by unfortunate dissensions and litigations, by reason of which the fine mill of Green, McDonald & Co., which was formerly run, it is said, with profit, has been standing idle. It is expected that a settlement of difficulties will be reached and a renewal of industry facilitated during the present season.

Granite Mountain district is making but slow progress, though the prospectors and mine-owners do not abate their high opinion of its numerous gold and silver bearing lodes.

Humboldt Basin, *Clark's Creek*, and the little camps along Burnt River are doing about as they did last year.

Auburn still holds out, with a moderate production. The Marysville Company, a California corporation, owning the Blue Cañon flume, will probably increase, with its ditch now in progress, both the extent and the duration of profitable mining in this well-known camp.

New discoveries of rich gold and silver lodes are reported from Fort Sumter and Granite Creek.

Near Baker City, the Virtue Mine (referred to in former reports) is still the principal enterprise. Mr. Hyde, the efficient superintendent, reports the extraction of 4,500 tons of ore during the year, worth about $108,000, or an average of $24 per ton. This estimate of values is considered too low by some competent outside observers. The ore came from all parts of the mine, which is now 500 feet deep. A new shaft is being sunk with Burleigh drills above the old Ruckle main tunnel. It is intended to carry this shaft to the lowest workings, and hoist all ore through it. It will be done by June, 1876. There are 50 men employed at the mine. Wages, $4 per day. Under Mr. Hide's management, the property is said to be earning profits.

The James Gordon Company, working the mine of that name, 4½ miles east of Baker City, took out last year 71 tons of quartz, which, being treated in a custom-mill, yielded nearly $1,900 after paying expenses. The bullion is very fine, being worth $18.50 per ounce. The company is preparing to work on a larger scale.

The Ironstone Mine has a tunnel 80 feet deep. The deepest point attained is 75 feet below the surface. The vein is gold-bearing; width, 3 feet; country-rock, granite; prospects encouraging.

Baker City has been damaged in business prosperity by the failure of Mr. Virtue, a leading banker. But the town is growing, and will doubtless maintain and increase its importance as the business center of Eastern Oregon.

Shasta mining-district, (El Dorado, Malheur, and Amelia.)—Packwood & Carter have completed about 33 miles of new ditch since May, 1874. Their main ditch is now about 135 miles long, 7 feet wide at top, 5 feet at bottom, and 2 feet deep. The net profits of the season are said to have been over $14,000. From the condition of the ditch at this time, water-sales are expected to reach $50,000 to $60,000 this year, and expenses to be about $10,000. About 200 men, both Chinamen and white men, worked last year under the Packwood & Carter ditch. The water-supply was from 1,000 to 1,500 inches for ten hours, at 20 cents per inch; wages earned by Chinamen, $2 to $2.50 per day; by white labor, $3.50 to $4 per day. The gold-yield was not less than $150,000. The mining-season did not begin till about July, owing to the vast amount of work required to put the ditch in good working order; which had never been done heretofore. The ditch is now an assured success, and promises to be a dividend-paying institution for years to come. It is probably the greatest private enterprise ever begun and carried to a successful termination in Oregon. It has been twelve years in progress. The area of the mining-camps commanded by this ditch is larger in extent of territory than what is called "the Black Hills Country" in Wyoming. It is asserted that not a failure has occurred in placer-mining in the ground supplied with water by this ditch. The price paid for water in hydraulic "heads," namely, 20 cents per inch for 10 hours, measured by a 2-inch opening and 4-inch pressure-board, is certainly profitable enough to the ditch-owners; and the fact that it can be paid speaks much for the productiveness of the placers.

Hog 'em district.—The Summit Gold-Quartz Mine, owned by Packwood & Stewart, remained idle, on account of "hard times," from June to fall. Since that time Morgan Keltner has been running the mine and mill at times. The latter is a 10-stamp steam-mill, and when running at full capacity crushes from 10 to 14 tons every 24 hours. Some 400 tons of quartz crushed during the season yielded about $12 per ton. It is Mr. Packwood's intention to move the mill to Eagle Creek, distant from the mine about 1½ miles, and run it by water-power. The mine is now about 350 feet deep. The vein varies from a few inches to 4 feet in thickness. All the quartz is worked without assorting, and will average from $10 to $12 per ton without saving anything from the iron-pyrites, which is said to be rich. The rock is easily taken out, no powder having been used so far on the lower 150 feet. With water-power at the mill and hoisting-works at the mine, it is believed that $6 rock will pay expenses. The upper stopes have been worked for a length of about 600 feet on the vein, and to a depth of from 50 to 100 feet. In this part of the mine the vein varied very much in size, averaging about 15 inches of decomposed quartz, and yielding as high as $60 per ton. The average of nearly 3,000 tons was between $20 and $25 per ton. The present sinking on the mine has been going on for nearly two years on what appears to be the central shoot or "chimney." From this body, below the upper works, about 1,000 tons have been worked, yielding about $12 per ton, the average size of the vein being between 24 and 30 inches. There is now a large amount of quartz in sight in this body, which, so far as developed, in length seems to extend about 200 to 225 feet along the lode. From this the north shoot seems to be divided by a vertical pinch, in which the walls close together, leaving only a small seam. This north shoot has been opened to a depth of 200 feet. The south shoot and the mine farther south have been prospected and traced for about 1,000 feet in length, but no quartz was obtained which yielded in the mill more than $10 to $12 per ton. At the depth of present workings, this vein carries a black-clay "gouge" on the foot or the hanging wall, sometimes nearly one foot in thickness. Large quantities of bright iron-pyrites are found in this clay. The walls in the lower workings are from 3 to 10 feet apart, and appear smooth and polished where the "gouge" is broken off. Mr. Packwood has been four years developing this mine, and deserves great credit for the energy with which he has persevered both in this enterprise and in the still more important and generally beneficial work of the construction of the El Dorado ditch. He intends to have, as soon as practicable, a 20-stamp mill, with pans for the treatment of the pyrites.

CHAPTER V.

MONTANA.

Mr. William F. Wheeler, of Helena, has collected the materials for this chapter, with the assistance of a number of gentlemen residing in the Territory. From his reports on the several districts, it is evident that quartz-mining is on the increase all over the Territory, while the yield of placer-mines is slowly diminishing each year. More retort gold from arrastras and small stamp-mills has been sold in 1875 than ever before, and less dust from placer-mines.

The number of tons of silver-ore worked and shipped in 1875 is very nearly double the quantity worked and shipped in 1874. By the Missouri River about 2,000 tons were shipped, and by the Union and Central Pacific Railroads about 1,000 tons; the average value was $250 per ton, or total $750,000. Refined silver bars by express, value $88,000.

Of copper-ore, 150 tons were shipped, the average value of which was $150 per ton, or $22,500 in all. The copper interest is growing; and while the shipments in 1875 were experimental, the result has been so far satisfactory that they will be continued; but the ores will be more closely assorted hereafter, and only those of a higher grade will be shipped. The almost uniform experience of working our copper-veins has been to demonstrate that the veins improve in width and richness the deeper the shafts are sunk. At a depth of from 80 to 100 feet, several of them now show ore that will average 50 per cent. copper, though near the surface the same openings yielded ore carrying but 25 to 33 per cent. The lodes of copper are abundant and the veins from 4 to 100 feet in width. Several smelters are in course of construction to reduce these ores to ingots at home.

Two mills for working silver-ores have been constructed at Phillipsburgh, or so improved as to make them new. The mill of the Northwest Company, at Phillipsburgh, running 10 stamps and using Bruckner cylinders for roasting, has uniformly produced from Speckled Trout ores about $9,000 per week. The mill of the Saint Louis Company, working Hope and other ores, running 10 stamps and using reverberatory furnaces, produced from $6,000 to $7,000 per week. These results are very uniform, and are expected to be still greater in the course of the next year, since the numerous leads in the close vicinity of the mills will insure an abundance of good ore.

A small one-stack smelting-works, owned and run by William Nowlan, has been very successful in reducing the galena-ores near Jefferson City, in Jefferson County. It is run by water-power, and is inexpensive in its working and profitable in its results. More smelters close to the mines will be erected during the next year.

Taking the Territory as a whole, more arrastras and small and economical quartz-mills are running than ever before, and with almost uniformly profitable results, while many large and expensive mills, erected in early days, are standing idle for want of sufficient ore in their immediate vicinity to supply them. The miners have learned by said experience to adapt the capacity of their mills and machinery to the known productive capacity of their veins. It may be hoped that few mistakes of excessive mill-building will be made hereafter.

Mr. Wheeler estimates the yield of gold, silver, and copper during the year 1875 as follows:

Gold shipped by Wells, Fargo & Co..........	$2,235,600	
Gold-dust and bullion by other conveyance....	500,000	
Total gold*..		$2,735,600
Refined silver-bars, shipped by Wells, Fargo & Co..	88,000	
Silver-ores shipped, 3,000 tons, at $250	750,000	
Total silver..		838,000
Total gold and silver..............................		3,573,600
Copper-ores, 150 tons shipped, at $150..................		22,500
Total gold, silver, and copper......................		3,596,100

The above Mr. Wheeler gives as the actual amount realized; but at the close of the year there were more tons of silver and copper ores at the mouths of the mines prepared ready for shipment, of equal average value per ton, than were shipped during the year; and 100,000 tons of ores, running from $40 to $150 per ton, that will not bear shipment, are piled by the dumps for future working, or awaiting cheaper transportation.

The shipments of ores in 1876 will be limited by want of transportation. If every wagon that brings freight from the railroads or the Missouri River were to take out an equal tonnage of ores, (say about 8,000 tons,) they could not transport the amounts that could be ready for them. This want of means of shipment, and the other want of mills and smelters to reduce the ores at home, prevent the actual working of all but the best mines, and put a limit to their yield.

The demand for more freighting facilities has considerably raised the cost of exporting ores, and the competition has given the monopoly of export-freights into the hands of those who are able to buy the ores, or to make contracts with freighters for the whole season. This enables capitalists to buy up the richest ores of men who produce but comparatively few tons, by their own labor on their own mines, at a price that gives but little profit to the producer. This is a natural consequence and discourages production.

As evidence of the above statement, Mr. Wheeler mentions two claims owned by wealthy men, whose owners have already contracted for the shipment of 500 tons of ore from each, while poor men, owning just as good claims in the vicinity, are unable, for want of money, to ship their ores at all, and are compelled to sell at the purchaser's own price. A remedy is hoped for in railroads, or the improvement of the navigation of the Missouri and Yellowstone Rivers by help of Congress, for which the legislature has forwarded a memorial.

Placer-mining.—As before remarked, the yield of the placer-mines has

* Mr. Wheeler adds another $500,000 for the amount retained in the hands of miners, an allowance which I have assumed to be counterbalanced by a similar amount mined the year before, but included in the shipments this year.—R. W. R.

slowly and steadily decreased for the past six or eight years. The reasons were given in my report of 1874, page 327. Yet there are causes now at work which will in a short time increase their yield, or at least arrest its decline. These are the consolidations of small claims into one ownership or company. Ability is thus acquired to bring in longer and larger ditches, and more water from the large streams. Capitalists are taking up or buying large tracts of mining-ground which could not be worked heretofore for want of water, and building large, long, and expensive ditches to work them. The days of narrow, rich gulches and bars, and short, inexpensive ditches are past, and with them the chances of the "lone and lucky" miner.

Deer Lodge County, as for some years past, has continued to yield more placer-gold than any other, the amount being about $900,000 for the year. Old Alder and other gulches in Madison give about $450,000. The placer-mines at Bannack and vicinity produce about $300,000; the mines of Cedar Creek and Quartz Creek, in Missoula County, $100,000; those of Confederate Gulch and the numerous gulches and bars in Meagher, about $300,000; those of Gallatin County, $50,000; those of Jefferson, $150,000; and those of Lewis and Clarke, $350,000; or, a total of about $2,400,000. The remainder of the gold-yield is from arrastras and quartz-mills, and amounts, according to Mr. Wheeler's estimate, to about $800,000.

At Helena, Mr. Chessman, the owner of the several ditches, is putting down a bed-rock flume, to run up from Ten-Mile Creek four or five miles, so as to drain the bed-rock of the celebrated Last Chance Gulch, on which Helena is built. Seven or eight millions of gold have been taken out of this gulch, and for a great part of its length bed-rock has never been reached, owing to the depth of the gravel and to the water, which rose so as to prevent sinking to bed-rock. It will probably be completed this coming year. Three or four thousand feet of fluming were put down this year, commencing at Ten-Mile and extending up the gulch. After the water has done its work of washing the dirt for the mines at the upper end of the gulch, it will be used next season in cutting down and carrying away the gravel through the flume, so that it can be extended next fall on the bed-rock up the gulch. Mr. Chessman has bought two farms on Ten-Mile for dumping purposes. It is believed that when the flume is completed along the bed-rock of Last Chance, the former prosperity of the gulch will return, and it will yield millions more of gold. I give this as only one instance of what will be done in the future where capitalists or companies own the ground and the ditches, and as what could never be done by single owners of small claims.

BEAVER HEAD COUNTY.

This county, situated in the extreme southern portion of the Territory, is rich in deposits of the precious and useful metals. Gold, silver, copper, galena, zinc, manganese, and iron have been found in every quarter of the county. Sandstone, limestone, granite, trap, and quartzite crop out on every mountain and hill. Lignite, shale, stone-coal, and fire-clay are in place in various localities. The extensive mountain-ranges, covered with dense pine forests, are varied on each side by rolling foot-hills, and clear mountain-brooks, creeks, and rivers traverse the county from south to north.

Since the first settlement of Bannack, in 1862, not less than three millions of dollars' worth of the precious metals have been taken out, principally from the placer-mines. There have been constructed about

90 miles of water-ditches, at a cost of about $110,000. These ditches convey the water to the placer-mines at Bannack, Horse Prairie, Argenta, Bald Mountain, and Wisdom River, which are still actively worked, yielding handsome returns, especially the Horse Prairie placers, which are now extensively worked by Chinamen, who have paid, and are yet to pay, large sums of money for their mining rights, and can now employ 75 to 100 hands. There are probably about 25 white men who own important claims in that locality and are earning fair profits from them.

The placer-mines at Bannack, Bald Mountain, and Big Hole, or Wisdom River, cover considerable areas, and are likewise reported to be profitable to their owners and operators.

According to the most trustworthy information, the gold yield of the past year is estimated at $200,000, and the value of the silver-ore sold and shipped at the same amount, thus giving the total gold and silver production of this county of $400,000. This is said to be a low estimate.

The prospects of mining in this county appear very favorable when it is considered that the placer-mines will continue to be productive for many years to come, and that the numerous silver, gold, and copper veins are yet undeveloped, to say nothing of the large deposits of iron-ores.

Bannack district.—The first veins of gold-bearing quartz discovered in the Territory were located in this district. Exact statements of the quantities and yield of ore worked in the district during 1875 are not attainable. The following summary of operations, though general in terms, is believed to be trustworthy. Messrs. Philip Shenan and John Carhart were the principal operators in gold-veins last season, running their mills on quartz from the Dakota, Excelsior, and other veins. Mr. Shenan has developed and patented a number of valuable mines, among which are the Excelsior, Waddams, Springfield, and Gold Leaf. In some of these other parties are interested with him. Mr. Shenan is the owner of the somewhat famous Dakota No. 6, which once belonged to New York parties, but proved unprofitable under their management. It now has a shaft 310 feet deep, and yields rock which, at the present time, is worked with satisfactory results. Mr. Shenan took out, with a 5-stamp mill, during the past season, $75,000 in gold, from the quartz of the Dakota and Excelsior lodes, a product which, though it might easily fail to cover all the expenses of an absentee company, leaves a reasonable income for a private proprietor.

Mr. Carhart is the owner of Dakota No. 7, and has run his mill on Dakota ore, doing, besides, a considerable amount of custom-work. No. 7 is yielding a good supply of rich ore, and Mr. Carhart's prospects for the future are flattering.

Messrs. Shenan & Waddams worked ore from the Waddams lode on three arrastras, netting $5,000 for the season. The ore from the Saint Paul also was reduced by the owner in an arrastra.

Mr. Shenan is driving a 300-foot tunnel to tap the Hope lead at the depth of 200 feet, and is reported to be extracting already very rich ore. He is also sinking a shaft on the Poor Prospector's lode, and taking rich oxidized ore, which is said to average $500 per ton. He is also taking out considerable quantities of ore from the Excelsior. The ore has changed from the oxidized condition to sulphuret of iron, carrying gold.

Blue Wing district is situated from one to six miles northeast of Bannack. There are probably over one thousand argentiferous lodes recorded in this district. Most of them are in limestone, but a number occur in granite.*

But few of these lodes have been developed sufficiently to be called permanent mines. Only those which have been worked the past season or have been developed will be noticed here.

The Delmonte is in granite. The main shaft has been sunk to the depth of 230 feet, with levels 80 feet long on each side. The vein is of uniform width in the various shafts and levels, averaging six inches. The surface vein is black, decomposed silver-ore. At the depth of 100 feet the ore changes into ruby silver. Messrs. Peck & Bray mined and shipped 100 tons of this ore the past season, assaying $300 per ton. The lode is well prospected 500 feet along its strike from east to west. The dip of the vein is slightly to the south. A. F. Sears and Clark Smith are the owners.

The Huron silver-lode, situated on a high limestone mountain, half a mile south of the Delmonte, strikes east and west, dips south, fluctuates in width from a foot to six feet. The ore is sulphuret and chloride of silver, and assays from $50 per ton to several thousand. There are a number of shafts and levels on this vein. The deepest shaft is 80 feet. Large quantities of ore have been taken out of this lead and shipped or sold on the dump. The owner is Samuel Batchelder.

These two veins have contributed an important service to the district. When, a few years ago, all the furnaces in the county had failed of success and prospects were gloomy, and the miners themselves were ignorant as to the real value of this as well as the other silver-districts of the county, it was determined to make some conclusive test, and a small quantity of selected ores from these two veins was shipped to Swansea, in Wales. The venture returned a profit after deducting all expenses. This gave a new life to mining, and large quantities of ores were shipped to Germany and San Francisco, the result being largely in favor of the latter place.†

The development of mining and smelting in Utah, consequent upon the introduction of railroads, opened a new market for Montana silver-ores, far more favorable to the miners than Germany, Swansea, or California. The shipment of ores from this county has become an extensive and profitable business. There are now on the dumps in the various districts of the county more ores than can be shipped by wagons for the next year. A railroad into the county would greatly increase the value of the mining property in Blue Wing district; but this constitutes a small proportion only of the deposits awaiting developments in all quarters of the county, many of which appear to be capable of large production.‡

Black Hawk No. 2 is in granite, with smooth walls, now reported to be 7 feet wide; strike, east and west; dip, 85° south. The shaft is 275 feet deep. The ore at the surface is black, (stained with manganese,) but gradually changes into predominating iron-pyrites. The value of the ore is but little known. There are large quantities on the dump of $40 or $50 ore. This lead has been prospected for more than 2,000 feet along the course. J. C. Taylor, the owner, has purchased all the con-

* One of my correspondents calls this rock trap, but the reports of others and the probabilities of the case are against him.—R. W. R.

† See my report of 1874, p. 372.—R. W. R.

‡ But the transportation of ores out of the Territory is, after all, but a temporary and wasteful expedient. Their reduction at home will be the ultimate solution; and, as I have indicated in my report of 1872, the copper-ores of the Territory will probably furnish the most abundantly available material for a rational process.—R. W. R.

flicting interests on each side of his mine, among which are the two lodes—the Nodaway on one side, with a shaft 40 feet deep and well-defined vein of black ore 3½ feet wide, and the Queen of the West on the other, with a shaft 35 feet deep, vein and ore the same. His plat covers, also, several other claims, with shafts from 10 to 30 feet deep, all in granite. Black Hawk No. 2 is probably better developed for permanent working than any other mine in this district. Mr. Taylor is now sinking 250 feet west of the deep shaft, with good prospect, having richer ore. All these veins contain a small percentage of galena and gold.

The Don Juan is owned by Messrs. Mead & Bassett. It has a shaft 65 feet deep, and another shaft, 40 feet deep, on the Luzerne, now supposed to be the same vein. This indicates a north and south vein, 4 feet wide, with a dip of 45° west, located on the line between limestone and granite. Twelve tons of this ore have been shipped, assaying about $250 per ton. There are about 65 tons on the dump, one-fourth of which is shipping-ore. The ore is sulphurets and chlorides, with about 10 per cent. of galena.

The Bonaparte is located about 75 feet south of the Delmonte, on the line between limestone and granite. It strikes east and west, stands almost vertical, and is 3 feet in width; regular, with smooth walls. The ore is black, strongly impregnated with manganese, with a small percentage of silver and galena. The main shaft is 35 feet deep. There are 150 tons on the dump, of an average assay-value of $35 or $40 silver per ton. According to early assays, mentioned in my report of 1873, and apparently made on richer specimens, the ore contains gold also. The mine is to be deepened, developed, and tested next season. It is now owned by J. H. Larwill, William Peck, and E. D. Leavitt.

The Pomeroy lode, owned by A. Bassett, is in limestone. It is from 6 to 8 feet wide, and very prominent, the croppings projecting in some places 8 feet above the surrounding surface. The ore is generally free from base metals, and carries metallic silver. This claim is well prospected for 1,100 feet by ten shafts from 25 to 80 feet deep. About one-fifth of the ore is of high grade. Five tons shipped to Utah sold for $250 per ton. There are not less than 600 tons on the various dumps. The average assay-value is about 30 ounces silver.

The True Fissure, a north and south vein, cutting off the Blue Wing lode on the west, was discovered during the past season by Mr. Wybold. He has sunk a shaft 80 feet deep. The vein is 3 feet wide. The ore is high grade, assaying from 100 to 200 ounces silver, and 25 per cent. lead. Some of this ore has been shipped but is snow-bound, as is also the last shipment made by Messrs. Peck and Steel, and a lot of bullion shipped by Dahler, Armstrong & Co.

The New Departure, owned by G. W. Stapleton, is in limestone on the verge of the granite. A tunnel 150 feet in length has been driven, tapping the vein at the depth of 100 feet. The main shaft is 150 feet deep. The vein is 8 feet wide, filled with clay, talc, and ore. The ore is of high grade, but the supply is irregular. Nine tons were shipped to the Bank of California, netting $200 over expenses of shipping. The hanging-wall is smooth, often polished; the foot-wall is not defined. Further developments are in progress.

The Czar, owned by Clark Smith, has a tunnel running in on the vein 200 feet, the vein cropping in granite, and apparently running direct into a limestone mountain. The ore is black and oxidized and some of it is of high grade. On the surface it resembles the Delmonte ore. Improvements are in progress.

Charles Bowman is sinking on the Bismarck lode. The shaft is 80 feet deep and the vein is reported 3 feet wide, yielding about one-quarter of high-grade ore.

Mr. Batchelder is said to be taking very rich ore from the Great West, a vein in limestone.

Bryant or Trapper district.—This district was first brought to notice in August, 1873. About that time trappers brought to Bannack specimens of quartz, which, being assayed, proved rich in silver. The fact was communicated first to a limited circle, and soon the whole community was excited, and a stampede ensued.

About fifty lodes have been recorded, nearly all of which, so far as they have been developed, promise to produce a considerable proportion of ore rich enough for shipment—a severe test.

Bryant (or Trapper) district is situated due north from Bannack 35 or 40 miles. Between the two are Rattlesnake and Birch Creek districts. The rock in Bryant district is said to be wholly dolomitic limestone, the white mountains of which glisten strikingly in the sun. Some of the lodes are more than 10,000 feet above sea level.

The Trapper lode was finally located on the 10th of August, 1873, by Jerry Grotivant, James A. Bryant, and others, who had gone into that region for the purpose of trapping and for pleasure, and, while hunting for their "cayuses" (Indian ponies) accidentally discovered the outcrop of the vein. The claim has been prospected for its entire length, (15,000.) The strike-vein is north and south; the dip at the surface was almost horizontal, but gradually turned in depth, until it assumed a nearly vertical position. The main shaft is 13 by 13 feet in size and 150 feet deep. The width of the crevice is uniformly 13½ feet. There is one tunnel 6 by 7 feet and 290 feet in length, connected with the bottom of the shaft. An ore-house is built at the mouth of the tunnel 32 feet by 26 feet. The ore is reported to be "rough, tinged with varied colors, and containing silver, copper, lead, zinc, antimony, sulphur, and manganese." In 1873 there was shipped to the Bank of California 10 tons, of which the assay-value returned was 140 ounces of silver per ton. In 1874, 101 tons were shipped to Freiberg, Germany, which assayed there 280 ounces per ton. In 1875, 300 tons were sold on the dump to Dahler & Armstrong, of Glendale, Montana, which assayed from 130 to 300 ounces per ton. Fifty tons of first-class ore remain on the dump and about 3,000 tons of second-class ore, valued at 80 ounces in silver per ton. Thousands of tons are said to be in sight in the mine.

The Dubuque lode, owned by Messrs. Terrel, Wilcox, and others, has one shaft 30 feet deep and one level 30 feet. The vein is 5 feet wide. Seventy-five tons were sold to Dahler & Armstrong on the dump, at an assay-value of 90 ounces per ton.

The Minnie Gaffney, owned by Owen Gaffney, has a shaft 60 feet deep, 6 feet by 7 feet, and a four-foot vein. No sale of ore has been made. There are 75 tons on the dump. An assay of sampled ore gives 40 ounces silver and 60 per cent. lead, and zinc, copper, antimony, and arsenic in various proportions. Mr. Gaffney is working eight hands at present.

The Lady Elgin, owned by Messrs. De Lorimer, Forney, and others, is but little developed. One shaft is 30 feet deep. The ore-vein is 18 inches in width. The assay-value of the ore on the dump is 50 ounces silver per ton.

The Forest Queen is owned by Messrs. Keppler, Graster, and others. The vein of ore is 8 inches wide, and assays 300 ounces silver per ton. There is one shaft 23 feet deep and 5 by 7 feet in size.

The Elm Orlon is owned by Messrs. Driscoll, Lowe, and others. They have sunk one shaft 70 feet deep and 6 by 12 feet in size, and driven one tunnel 6 by 4 feet, and 160 feet long, cutting the lode at the depth of 250 feet from the surface; also two levels, 50 feet each, and *stopes* along the levels 30 feet in height. This is a regular contact-vein, 5 feet in width, between the dolomite and quartzite. The ore is 2 feet wide. There were shipped the past season 200 tons to Utah, valued at about $300 per ton. About 50 tons remain on the dump. The following is an analysis of the ore made at Salt Lake:

Copper	12.12
Lead	39.50
Zinc	39.50
Arsenic	12.80
Antimony	1.01
Sulphur	6.82
Iron	10.06
Silver	2.11
Silica	0.97
Lime, not determined.	8.41
	93.80

The proprietors of this mine, like all the owners in this district, are the original discoverers and locators. They are steadily prosecuting its development.

The Oneida and Niagara lodes, owned by R. P. Hopkins, J. C. Kepler, and W. T. Taylor, are prospected by shafts along the strike of the veins, from 15 to 20 feet deep. The veins vary from 1 foot to 2½ feet in width. Four inches of the ore in the Oneida assays from 40 to 500 ounces in silver per ton.

The Pride of the West is owned by Owen Gaffney. The main shaft, 6 by 7 feet in size, is 50 feet deep. The vein of ore is irregular in width, varying from 6 inches to 3 feet. Thirty tons of ore were shipped last season, at an assay-value or 150 ounces silver. There are 30 tons of ore now in the dump.

The Franklin lode, owned by Frank Gilg, Thomas A. Lowe, and Ed. R. Stevens, has a shaft 6 by 7 feet, 60 feet deep, an incline shaft 50 feet deep, and one level 30 feet long. During the past season there was sold from the dump to Dahler & Co. 107 tons, at an assay-value of 90 ounces silver. The ore-vein is 7 feet wide. There are 25 tons of first-class ore on the dump, and 175 second-class. An analysis of the ore resulted about the same as the Elm Orlon, with 40 per cent. lead.

The True Fissure, owned by Messrs. Mead, Larwill, and others, is one of the most remarkable ore-deposits in this district. It is a contact-vein between dolomite and blue limestone. The ore-vein is regular, 8 feet in width, and yields a large portion of "shipping" or first-class ore. The vein crops 1,200 feet in length north and south, and dips westerly into the mountain at an angle of about 45°. The main shaft is 120 feet deep. Two other shafts are 75 feet each. About 300 tons of ore were sold on the dump and shipped the past season, at an average value of $175 currency per ton. There are now about 50 tons on the dump. The ore is hoisted at the shaft by hand, and then conveyed on a tramway down the mountain 800 feet to the ore-house.

The following is the assay of one of the lots sold to Dahler & Armstrong: Moisture, 4.85 per cent.; 42 per cent. lead, 12 per cent. zinc, and 109.35 ounces silver per ton. This had been rated as second-class ore. The first-class ore was shipped to Utah.

The Cleopatra and Ariadne, belonging to Messrs. Taylor and the True Fissure Company, and located on the same mountain, known as White Lion Mountain, the summit of which is 10,000 feet above sea-level. These claims are on the same lode, and the croppings are visible for the entire length of 300 feet. The supply of ore is abundant; reported width of vein, 8 feet. Two shafts have been sunk on this lode, each 6 by 9 feet, and 75 feet deep. The ore is mainly carbonate of lead, assaying 55 per cent. lead, and 45 ounces silver per ton. There are 300 tons of ore on the dumps. Messrs. Taylor & Pease will prosecute mining operations vigorously next season.

This is likewise the intention of the True Fissure Company, which owns also two other lodes, the Mountain Sheep and the Silver Quartz. The first of these has a shaft 50 feet in depth, and the latter two shafts, each 120 feet deep, the veins varying from 2 feet to 10 feet in width. The assay-value of the ore is about 100 ounces silver per ton, and 40 per cent. lead.

The Mark Antony, belonging to Mr. Pease, is prospected by 2 shafts 22 and 28 feet deep. The vein of ore is pretty uniform, 15 inches in width, assaying 60 ounces silver and 55 per cent. lead. There are 10 tons on the dump.

The Keokuk, belonging to G. W. Stapleton, is developed by shaft to the depth of 40 feet. It has a one-foot vein of good ore.

The Atlantis, owned by N. Armstrong & Co., situated on White Lion Mountain, just below the True Fissure and Cleopatra claims, has undergone very extensive developments during the past season. The owners have employed 18 men in mining and prospecting. The vein of ore is from 2 to 3½ feet in width, and the visible outcrop extends through the entire length of the claim, (1,500 feet.) The yield of ore has been not less than 800 tons, assaying high in lead, and from 80 to 160 ounces silver per ton.

The Hecla lode, owned by the same company, is but little developed. The ore assays high in silver and low in base metals.

The Clive and Avon, owned by the same company, are on one lode. The present developments show this to be a remarkable ore-deposit. The former claim has a shaft sunk to the depth of 185 feet, showing a vein somewhat irregular, varying from 7 feet to 22 feet in width. The silver is in the metallic state, and the ore is comparatively free from base metals, and assays from 35 to 200 ounces silver per ton. The latter claim is but little developed, but appears on the surface exactly like the former. This ore from both is of excellent quality for milling. Just below this lode, at the base of the mountain, Armstrong & Co. have located an admirable mill-site and water-privilege, where they will erect a stamp-mill during the coming season to work this ore.

The Chloride lode, owned by A. M. Morrison, and the Gopher and Crown Point lodes, owned by J. W. Earl and W. Sengler, are promising locations, furnishing rich samples of ore, and awaiting development.

About 8 miles below this camp, where the valley of Trapper Creek opens out a little in width, are located the furnace and sampling-mill of Dahler, Armstrong & Co. These works were commenced in the summer of 1874, and completed in 1875. During the past season, although the works were not finished till late, they sampled and reduced more than 300 tons of ore from the Bryant district. They will commence early in the spring of 1876 for the season's operations, which are expected to be largely profitable to this enterprising firm and at the same time beneficial to the miners of the district. The town of Bryant is located at the mines, and Glendale at the furnace and mill. Roads and bridges are constructing for communicating n all directions.

Vipond district is about 8 miles north from Trapper. This is an old district, but has been almost inaccessible till the past year, being nestled among vast and rugged mountains, remote from the lines of public travel. About a dozen poor men have perseveringly stood by these mines for some eight years, and have finally completed a good road, at a cost in labor of not less than $10,000. It is only 5 miles from the mines to large water-privileges on Wisdom or on Big Hole River. This district is in blue limestone. The ores are black sulphurets of silver, with a small percentage of carbonate of lead and copper-glance. There are about 50 acres of ground covered with large quantities of "float" which has been displaced from the various vein outcrops. Large quantities of ore lie on the dumps, and a still greater amount is in sight in the mines. About 30 lodes have been located, and many of them are well prospected. They are owned in 200-foot claims by different parties and companies; and on these claims many shafts have been sunk, from a few feet to nearly 200 feet in depth. The strike of the veins is generally southeast and northwest, and their width is from 3 feet to 20 feet. The general average of the ore assays from $30 to $75 and upward per ton. There are a few veins, however, that yield first-class ore.

The Mewanahawk,* owned by John Vipond, has been opened by a shaft to the depth of 160 feet. Mr. Vipond sold ore to Armstrong & Co. during the past season, at about $150 per ton. His Gray Jockey lode has a shaft 50 feet deep, showing the vein to be 18 feet wide.

Dewey, Brewbake & Leggett, owning claims on the Argentine, Banner, Wassioga, and North Pacific lodes, have done a large amount of work on their several claims.

The Argentine lode has a vein of massive ore 18 feet in width, and is well developed 1,000 feet along the vein.

The Banner lode is 4 feet wide and yields first-class ore, ten tons of which, being shipped, brought $250 per ton.

A five-stamp mill is nearly completed in this district, and will be ready for work early next season. It is confidently anticipated that the energy and perseverance of the pioneers who have prosecuted under so great difficulties the development of mining in this locality will be soon rewarded with success. To those already mentioned should be added the name of Mr. Knabe, an assayer and mining engineer, who has adhered faithfully to the fortunes of the district, opening with his own hands the promising claims of which he is the owner, and to whom I have been indebted for valuable notes.

Elk Horn district is about 25 miles northwest from Bannack, on Grasshopper or Willard Creek, the stream on which Bannack is situated. This is the latest discovered camp in the county, having been first brought to notice in 1874. Only ten claims have been located, 1,500 feet each in length. The country-rock is gray granite. The strike of the veins is northeast and southwest, running at right angles with the ridges; the dip very slight. The croppings are the largest in the county, some of them 15 feet in height, and traceable for a great distance. The veins average 8 feet in width.

The Elk Horn lode, owned by Messrs. Peck & Steel, was opened during the past season to the depth of 50 feet, by a shaft 5 by 14 feet; and

* This is the name as given by Mr. Wheeler. In my report of 1872, what I suppose to be the same vein is called by Mr. Knabe the "Miwanotack." One is as bad as the other; and it would require a Bannack Indian to decide which is correct.—R. W. R.

15 tons of high-grade ore was shipped, assaying from 500 to 800 ounces silver per ton, and 15 per cent. copper, no other base metals being present. There are 75 tons on the dump, that are expected to average 120 ounces silver per ton.

The Storm, Keystone, and Mohawk belong to Messrs. Steel & Shineberger, and have shafts sunk 10 feet deep and 5 by 10 feet in size. The Storm lode crops out boldly through the entire length of the claim, the vein being from 8 to 10 feet wide. The best ore assays 200 ounces silver; that of the Keystone and Mohawk 100 ounces silver, and from 5 to 15 per cent. copper.

The Comet, (Messrs. Mead & Smith,) Calm, (R. P. Shelton,) Comstock, (John Steiger,) and Liberty (Graeter & Co.) resemble the foregoing veins in character and in extent of development.

West Bald Mountain district.—This is still another new district, brought to notice about the same time as the Elk Horn. But few lodes have been located.

The Emerald is owned by C. Mead and O. D. Farlin, who sank a shaft the past season 50 feet deep. The vein is 4 feet wide. They shipped 12 tons to Utah, assaying 125 ounces silver. There is but little base metal in the ore, and the silver is said to be in a metallic state. About 50 tons of ore are on the dump.

The Caroline is owned by Messrs. Steel and Peck. This is a massive vein of ore, 15 feet in width, cropping out through the whole length of the claim. The ore assays from 100 to 150 ounces in silver.

The Elk Horn district is well located for wood and water. Fine pine-timber covers all the slopes of the mountains, convenient to the mining-ground.

Argenta district.—This district, with its 3,000 located claims, is almost deserted. There has been an immense amount of work done here; but the ore is generally argentiferous galena of low grade.

Birch Creek district is also deserted. It contains extensive deposits of copper and iron ores. Shafts have been sunk on some of the most prominent copper-veins from 60 to 75 and even 135 feet in depth. The Greenwich has a shaft 80 feet deep, and a vein 8 feet wide. Some of the smaller veins yield ore that assays from 50 to 70 per cent. in copper. There are also large deposits of magnetic iron-ore. Wood and water are plenty in the district.

The superior attractions of Trapper and other silver and gold districts in the county are sufficient to occupy the miners for years to come; and these older and poorer districts must await further developments and a greater population.

It cannot well be said that the silver-mining of Beaver Head County is permanently prosperous so long as ores carrying from 30 to 100 ounces silver per ton must be discarded as too poor to pay for shipment. Cheaper transportation and labor, and facilities for the reduction of ore at home, will ere long, I trust, give a really substantial basis to this industry, by permitting the profitable treatment of second and third class ores.

DEER LODGE COUNTY.

Atlantic Cable and Georgetown districts.—In my report of 1872, p. 274, will be found a description of the Atlantic Cable lode and other mines near Cable City and Georgetown. It is unnecessary, therefore, to say anything concerning the working of these mines prior to the year 1872. There is, however, much to be added to the reports of former years. Not only has the Atlantic Cable yielded, since the year mentioned, quartz of surprising richness, but three entirely new silver-districts have been discovered in this region which promise to be as valuable as any in Montana.

The Atlantic Cable lode, which was the main stay of Cable City and Georgetown, has been in litigation for several years, and work has been entirely suspended. The Hanauer and Nowlan Mills have been closed, the former almost wholly and the latter entirely. The effect of this has been most disastrous. The two camps have but few inhabitants; the houses are empty and falling to decay; and the scene presented to the traveler is one of ruin and desolation. The direct cause of this is the fact that no wealthy companies are working any of these mines, and there are but few men employed for wages. Thus the prospector has no chance of earning by day-labor the means to prosecute explorations at intervals. Yet the district is one of the best in Montana. The Atlantic Cable is undoubtedly a rich vein, and the most recent developments tend to enhance its reputation. Work was suspended in the summer of 1873, and in the fall of the same year Mr. S. Cameron, while prospecting, struck a body of ore near the surface, about 100 feet south from "discovery" of this lode. From this pocket Mr. C. took out 100 tons of quartz, which yielded, it is said, in the Hanauer Mill, $20,000. From the same body of ore, about two tons treated by hand (mortar-crushing) yielded $8,000. Besides this, Mr. Cameron has a collection of specimens weighing altogether about 200 pounds, and presenting large masses of gold. One piece, almost solid gold, is worth $375. Another about the size of a small hen's egg has projecting from the quartz a mass of pure gold in the shape of a finger, containing the precious metal to the value of $75. There are in the collection numerous pieces of solid gold weighing as much as an ounce each. It is intended to exhibit the suite at the Centennial Exhibition, in Philadelphia. The Atlantic Cable lode will be made the initial point in describing the position of other ledges in this district. It runs northwest and southeast on Cable Hill, lying 15 miles south of Philipsburgh.

Below the Atlantic Cable are the placer-mines, late Kohrs, Bell & Co's. These are now owned equally in undivided interests by Mr. Conrad Kohrs, of Deer Lodge, and Mr. S. Cameron, of Cable, a half interest having recently been purchased by Mr. Cameron. These are "hillside diggings," containing a large amount of "float" quartz, of the same nature as the Cable rock. Work was commenced in 1871 and suspended in 1874, in order to use the water in working placer-mines in Georgetown. The Georgetown mines having been worked out, work has been resumed this summer by Messrs. Kohrs & Cameron, who have constructed very expensive and extensive hydraulic works. Since the opening of these mines about $80,000 have been taken out. It is estimated that the deposit can be continuously worked for five years more. The work is under the personal superintendence of Mr. S. Cameron, assisted by Mr. E. D. Aiken, a miner of experience, as foreman. The little settlement of the hands employed in these mines presents a marked and pleasing contrast to the ruins of Cable City and Georgetown.

The North Pacific lode was located in 1869, and is supposed to be an extension of the Atlantic Cable. This ledge resembles the Cable in all particulars. There are the same white limestone fragments found in the vein-matter, and the environment of the richest by spar is a feature of both lodes. The North Pacific is owned by William Nowlan, S. Cameron, and others. No considerable quantity of paying rock has yet been taken out. Mr. Cameron's theory is that they are below the rich ore, and that they will have to drift up the hill. The shaft on this lead is 125 feet in depth.

The Pyrenees is a gold-bearing vein in the Georgetown district, and is situated a mile and one-half south of the Atlantic Cable mine. It was discovered in May, 1875, by John Murphy, S. Cameron, and Robert S. Kelly, and is now owned by Messrs. Cameron & Kelly. The ledge runs southeast and northwest, up and down the hill. The owners have drifted on it longitudinally about 100 feet, and are now sinking from the end of the drift. The vein lies between two granite walls, with a 6-inch seam of white clay between the quartz and wall-rock, the latter being perfectly defined, and the vein varying in width from 18 inches to 3½ feet. The rock is a dark-brown quartz, showing particles of free gold. There are between forty and fifty tons on the dump, that will yield from $45 to $50 per ton.

The Whin-Doodle is a gold-bearing vein, discovered in 1872, and owned by Charles Jeffries and J. S. Smith. It runs southeast and northwest and lies one-quarter mile southwest of the Pyrenees. This ledge has a 26-foot shaft, showing a 3-foot crevice, and yields a quartz of the same character as the Pyrenees. There are fifteen tons of ore on the dump, that will mill from $40 to $50 per ton.

The Pittsburgh is a gold-bearing vein, running southeast and northwest, and lying 3,000 feet northeast of the Pyrenees. It was discovered in 1871 and is owned by Lewis Reese & Co., of Pittsburgh, Pa., who hold an undivided half interest, and Messrs. Shively and others, who together hold the other half. This ledge has a 100-foot shaft, showing a 2-foot crevice, and yields quartz of the same character as the Pyrenees. There are six or eight tons on the dump, that will mill from $40 to $50 per ton.

The North Atlantic is a gold-bearing vein, situated one mile northwest from the Atlantic Cable. It was discovered in 1867 by George Cater and John McKay, and is now owned by them. The quartz is similar to that of the Atlantic Cable, and will mill about $20 to the ton. There is a 50-foot incline on the vein.

The Four Johns is a ledge on the same hill as the Pyrenees. It is opened by two shafts, 165 and 180 feet deep, respectively. John Murphy is the owner. There is a large quantity of decomposed quartz on the dump, which Mr. Murphy proposes to run through sluice-boxes next spring.

The Rosa Whitford is a gold-bearing vein lying about two miles south of the Atlantic Cable, and running northerly and southerly. It is from 8 to 9 feet in width, with well-defined wall-rocks. The rock is a dark-brown decomposed quartz carrying fine gold. The owners of the ledge are Dr. Whitford, William Foster, and Thomas Stewart. They have put down an incline, at an angle of 45°, to the length of 65 feet. Messrs. Whitford & Co. are engaged in the erection of a 5-stamp mill to work the ore from this mine. There is about eighty tons of ore on the dump, specimens of which assay variably all the way from $10 to $176 per ton.

There are many other claims, but no trustworthy information can at present be had concerning them.

Mr. Charles Jeffries owns placer-mines at Georgetown that will pay from $6 to $10 per day to the hand. The great trouble with working the Georgetown diggings, which are undoubtedly rich, is the level nature of the ground and the consequent want of dumping-room.

Of the two gold-mills at Cable, the Nowlan mill was recently sold for taxes, and was bought by D. S. Corbin, assignee of William Nowlan. It has been entirely idle for several years.

The Hanauer mill, now owned by L. H. Hershfield & Bros., of Helena, is in good running order, and will soon start, crushing Pyrenees rock, under the direction of Mr. S. Cameron.

Silver Lake district, one of the newly discovered silver districts, is beautifully situated on the well-timbered hills, surrounding a very romantic lake of clear water, about one square mile in extent, and of very great depth. The lake has no visible outlet. The district was located in November, 1874, and is about five miles south of the Atlantic Cable lode. The country rock is white limestone. The veins discovered last fall show very rich chloride and sulphuret ores, assaying as high as $3,000 to $10,000 per ton. The two best veins appear to be the Silver Moss, so named from the appearance of the free silver in the ore, and the Romeo. There are shafts sunk from 40 to 50 feet. A considerable quantity of quartz has been taken out that will assay from $400 to $500 per ton; and a few tons are ready sacked for shipment, that will assay $1,500 per ton.

Silver Hill district was discovered in June, 1875, and is situated from four to five miles west of Silver Lake district, in a heavily timbered and exceedingly rough country. There are several narrow veins containing quartz similar to that of the Silver Lake district.

The *Deer Lodge district* was discovered in June, 1875. It is situated about six miles northeast from the Atlantic Cable lode. The principal veins recorded are the Crystal, F F, Beecher, and Moonbeam. There are numerous prospecting shafts sunk from 5 feet to 35 feet. The specimens taken out by Mr. Cameron, one of the original discoverers, resemble the quartz from Silver Lake district.

The ore from these districts is said to be free-milling ore, but that will probably pay better if treated by the roasting process. In many respects it resembles that found on the Comanche Hill, in the Philipsburgh district.

There is no doubt that this section of country is exceedingly rich in both silver and gold. It is gaining the attention of miners and quartz speculators, and will soon rise to prominence as one of the richest sections in Montana.

All that it is necessary to add here is that this neighborhood has not been even fairly prospected; that the water and timber advantages can hardly be surpassed; that the grazing is excellent, and the facilities of communication with Deer Lodge City are good. Wages for miners at quartz and placer mines are $4 per day. Board costs $8 per week.

Philipsburgh district.—The town or village of Philipsburgh is situated near the mouth of Camp Creek (a tributary on the right bank of Flint Creek), in latitude 46° 21′ north and longitude 113° 16′ west from Greenwich. The district (also called, I believe, Flint Creek district) is traversed by three gulches, running from east to west, nearly parallel, and about three-eighths of a mile apart. Of these Camp Creek is the central one, Frost Creek lying to the south and Comanche Gulch to the north of it. These creeks all head in a spur of the Gold Creek Mountains. The mines are located within an area about two miles in length, easterly and westerly, from the base of the foot-hills up the gulches, and two miles in width northerly and southerly across said gulches. The country-rock is limestone and granite, the dividing-line between the limestone and granite running north and south on the eastern edge of the present mining-camp. Some of the mines on Trout Hill lie on this line, having the north wall of limestone and the south of granite.

Camp Creek appears to be the dividing-line between two distinct kinds of vein-material, nearly all north of this line being free-milling ore, while nearly all south of it is roasting-ore. However, nearly all the ores, both north and south of this line, may be advantageously roasted before amalgamation.

The whole of this district is covered with "croppings" and "float," the claims recorded and represented being almost countless. A large amount of work has been done in prospecting. In this report only the most prominent and promising lodes are mentioned. Of those lying south of Camp Creek, and containing ores that can be worked to advantage by the roasting-process only, may be mentioned the following, running easterly and westerly: The Speckled Trout, Gem, Cliff, Pocahontas, Portland, Kitty Clyde, Navajo, Scratch-awl, Franklin, Burr, Algonquin, Overman, Estell, Little Jenny, Caledonia, and San Francisco. Running northerly and southerly: The Golconda, Cordova, Sharktown, Salmon, and Black Tiger.

The Speckled Trout has been mentioned in my former reports. It has a great reputation for width and richness of vein, but the present management (the Northwest Mining Company, to which the mine and mill were sold a couple of years ago by Mr. Cole Saunders, for the reported sum of $250,000) pursues a policy of strict secrecy, allowing no visitors to examine the works, and furnishing no information to inquirers. Opinions are divided as to the condition of affairs indicated by this policy, the majority inclining, perhaps, to infer that the mine is very much richer than the owners care to permit the public to know. The circumstances will, of course, bear another construction. According to information which I receive from a tolerably trustworthy source, the present length of the incline is 237 feet, at an angle of 45°, and the aggregate length of tunnels and levels is about 500 feet. A vertical shaft is now in progress, to strike the incline 150 feet from the surface. The ore is said to be in a continuous vein of great width and high grade.

The Salmon, owned by Messrs. Estell and Holland, of Philipsburgh, is situated on Trout Hill. This is a contact-vein, 8 feet wide, lying between limestone and granite. The claim, located in 1866, comprises 1,200 feet of patented and 400 feet of unpatented ground. The cost of work done in developing it was $3,000, including two shafts, 46 feet at an angle of 45° and 30 feet vertical, respectively. The gangue is quartz; the ore galena, carbonate of lead, with silver sulphurets, &c. The highest assay made from picked rock ran up to $3,500. The amount of ore taken out of this mine and all now on the dump is 125 tons, of an average value of $125 per ton.

The Franklin, owned by various parties, is situated on Franklin Hill on the south side of Frost Creek. It was located in 1866, 400 feet being claimed. About $3,000 worth of work has been done in developing. The shaft is 40 feet, vertical, with a tunnel 50 feet in length. The country-rock is limestone; the gangue, quartz; the ore contains galena, carbonate of lead, manganese, antimony, and sulphuret of silver. The highest assay ever made from picked rock ran $5,000 per ton. About 60 tons of ore have been taken from this mine, with an average value of $130 per ton. There now remain on the dump 20 tons, that will average $100 per ton.

The Gem, owned by the Irvine family, of Deer Lodge City, is situated on Trout Hill. The claim, located in 1867, is 2,200 feet in length, and has had $1,500 worth of work done on it. The shaft is 100 feet, vertical. The country-rock is limestone; the gangue, quartz; the ore contains galena, carbonate of lead, sulphuret of silver, and magnanese. The highest assay made went $600 per ton. There has been 50 tons of ore taken out, of an average assay-value of $125 per ton, which is now on the dump.

The Cliff, owned by the Hope Mining Company, of Saint Louis, Mo., is situated on Trout Hill. It was located in 1866, with a claim of 1,150 feet. The vein outcrops for nearly 2,000 feet, from 8 inches to 2 feet in thickness, running east and west, with dip about 87° south. Value of work done in developing, $2,500. Length of shaft, 28 feet, with 80 feet of tunnels and levels. The country-rock is white magnesian limestone and quartzites. The gangue is quartz; the ore, zincblende and argentiferous galena. The highest assay of picked rock yielded $259.67 per ton. Average assays of the three grades of ore: First quality, $60; second quality, $25; third quality, $17.50. About 25 tons of rock has been taken out, and is now on the dump, of an average value of $20 per ton.

Among the claims deserving at least brief mention are the following:

The Caledonia, owned by W. Graham, of Philipsburgh; $100 expended in development, and 1½ tons of ore extracted, of the average value of $75 per ton.

The Overman, owned by W. Graham, of Philipsburgh; $200 expended in development, and 1½ tons of ore extracted, of the average value of $40 per ton.

The San Francisco, owned by Estell & Holland, of Philipsburgh. This ledge is in the granite, has a shaft 41 feet deep. Development cost $250, and 50 tons of ore taken out have an average value of $40 per ton.

The Estell, owned by Estell & Holland, of Philipsburgh, is in limestone and granite; shaft, 26 feet; cost of development, $200; and 25 tons of ore, of the average value per ton of $50, taken out.

The Navajo, owned by C. V. Timmons & Co., is situated on Trout Hill, in limestone; has shaft 40 feet deep; $300 expended in development, and 5 tons of ore, averaging $100 per ton, taken out.

The Scratch-awl, owned by Murray, Durfee & Co., of Philipsburgh; is in limestone, with a shaft 60 feet deep, and a cut 12 feet long; $700 expended in development, and 5 tons taken out, that will average $100 per ton.

The Cordova (numerous owners) has a 30-foot shaft, and 120 feet of tunneling; 500 tons of ore have been taken from this mine, that will average $50 per ton; there has been $3,000 expended in development.

Of ledges lying north of Camp Creek, and containing ore capable of being worked by free-milling processes, but that can be yet better worked by the roasting process, may be mentioned the following:

The Comanche, Comanche Extension, Hope, Emma, Dead Thing, U. S., Cordova, Whistle-pecker, Mohawk, Willard, Ophir, Mountain Queen, Acquilla, Dashaway, Apache, and Silver Bend.

The Comanche, owned by the Hope Mining Company, of Saint Louis, Mo., is a 4-foot vein, striking east and west, with quartz gangue, and ore carrying sulphurets of silver and copper. The company claims 550 feet, under a location made July 11, 1866. The development consists entirely of open work, and has cost $6,000. The highest assay made from picked rock yielded $1,560.41 per ton. Three grades of ore will average as follows: First quality, $200; second quality, $60; third quality, $25; with a general average of $50 per ton. The rock inclosing the vein is a dark-blue limestone. The quantity of ore taken out since opening cannot now be estimated. There is now on the dump 16 tons, that will average $200 per ton.

The Comanche claim No. 2, owned by Dr. J. M. Merrell, of Philipsburgh, was located in 1866. It covers 200 feet. The country-rock is limestone. Quartz and spar form the gangue, with ore of sulphurets of silver and copper. The shaft is 115 feet deep, on an angle of 45°; $4,000 has been expended in development. The highest assay from picked rock yielded $4,000 per ton. There has been 400 tons taken out, with an average value of $45 per ton; and the dump now contains 150 tons, with an average value of $37 per ton. The vein runs east and west.

The Comanche Extension is held by numerous owners. The vein is traced 2,200 feet, and was located in 1866. There has been fully $10,000 expended in development, and several shafts have been sunk, varying from 20 to 80 feet in depth. There have also been several levels and tunnels run, aggregating 500 feet. The lode is inclosed in limestone, with quartz and spar for gangue, and ore consisting of carbonate of lead, sulphurets of silver, copper, &c., varying considerably throughout the vein. The highest assay made from specimen rock was $2,000 per ton. The average ore is of low grade. There has been about 1,000 tons of ore taken out, that will average about $25 per ton; this is nearly all now on the dump. The vein strikes east and west.

The Hope, owned by the Hope Mining Company, of Saint Louis, Mo., is a vein of free-milling ore, consisting of sulphurets of silver and copper, with ruby silver; quartz gangue, inclosed in white and blue limestone. The vein has an easterly and westerly direction, and varies in thickness from 1 to 20 feet. The company claims 650 feet. The mine was located July 10, 1867. There has been $40,000 spent in development. There are two shafts, respectively 150 feet and 70 feet in depth; an incline of 115 feet, at an angle of 38°, and 550 feet of tunnels and levels. The highest assay that has been made from picked rock yielded $3,851.25 per ton. The three grades of ore yield by assay the following averages: First quality, $200; second quality, $60; third quality, $25 per ton. The amount of ore taken out will reach 2,500 tons, with an average value of $90 per ton. There is now on the dump 500 tons, with an average value of $97 per ton. The working-results of this ore in the company's mill at Philipsburgh show an average yield of $58.14 per ton, although the richest ore has not yet been worked.

The Emma, owned by Estell & Holland, is situated about 400 feet north of the Comanche, with a claim of 1,500 feet; was located in 1872. The gangue is quartz and spar, and the ore contains sulphurets of silver and copper. The highest assay made from picked rock gave $5,000. There have been 120 tons taken out, of the average value of $90 per ton, 108 tons of which are now on the dump.

Deserving a somewhat shorter notice are the following:

The Dead Thing, owned by W. Graham, has $250 expended in development, and 5 tons, of the average value of $45 per ton, taken out.

The Willard, owned by Estell & Holland, has shaft 20 feet deep; $200 expended in development, and 20 tons, worth $100 per ton, taken out.

The Cordova, owned by various companies, has a 30-foot shaft, and 120 feet of tunneling; $3,000 spent in development, and 500 tons, of an average value of $50, taken out.

The Dashaway, owned by the Hope Company, has had $500 expended in development.

The Apache, owned by Murray & Durfee, has a shaft 190 feet deep, and 250 feet of tunnels and levels; $10,000 expended in development, with but small product of ore, according to report, and that of low grade.

This comprises a list of the most prominent lodes in the district, although it gives no adequate conception of the amount of work that has been done in prospecting. Doubtless many important discoveries will still be made in this locality, and the oldest and most experienced residents are exceedingly sanguine.

Messrs. Murray & Durfee have commenced running a tunnel, called the Sharktown tunnel, through the Trout Hill. It starts from about the center of the north side of Trout Hill and runs south. If carried on, it will cut the Speckled Trout and other mines containing the richest ore yet found in the district. The mouth is 900 feet below the level of the summit, far lower than any of the shafts on the hill have been sunk. The tunnel has advanced 60 feet, and has struck an ore-vein consisting of feldspar, manganese, and quartz of poor quality. The tunnel is 6 feet wide by 6 feet 6 inches in height in the clear. The work is pushed forward rapidly, and it is proposed to proceed right through the hill. What result, further than draining the hill, will be obtained by this labor it is impossible to say. The proprietors are old and energetic miners, who feel very sanguine of striking new veins of ore.

The three largest companies working here are the Northwest Company, the Hope Mining Company, and the Belmont Company. Of the results of working in the Cole Sanders Mill, recently purchased by the Northwest Company, the following is worthy of note: That in a three months' run with a 5-stamp battery, and a drop of 46 inches, at the rate of from 110 to 120 per minute, there was a yield of $45,000 from the ore crushed. This ore came from the Speckled Trout Mine. The chloridizing roasting resulted in 85 per cent. saved. This roasting process was first adopted in working the Speckled Trout ore, by the advice of Prof. Charles Speight, and proved a perfect success. Mr. Speight succeeded in chloridizing up to 96 per cent. on one occasion; and during his superintendence of the mill the average was from 90 to 92 per cent.

The Hope Mining Company has in town a fine stone mill of 10-stamps now under repair. New machinery is on the road for this mill, which will start up again before long.

The Belmont Company, of Saint Louis, Mo., is now at work on the Comanche extension. A mill-site has been surveyed, a millwright engaged, and active preparations are making for the immediate erection of a 10-stamp mill for wet-crushing. The company will probably expend $75,000 in these improvements.

The Northwest Company is adding 5 stamps and otherwise improving and enlarging its mill.

Altogether, the camp promises exceedingly well and bids fair to be the most prosperous in Montana.

Of the country surrounding the district, it may be said that the supply of timber, both for building purposes and for fuel, is very abundant, the water-supply is excellent and of large extent, while the foothills and valley are "a paradise for stock."

Butte district.—Activity in this district, both in building and in mining, has advanced daily since the 1st of September, when the population began notably to increase. Notwithstanding the severity of the weather in November, the work of building dwelling-houses, shaft-houses, and mining operations was prosecuted with much energy. Since the 1st of October forty-eight dwelling-houses and six business-houses have been erected at Butte; the new town Travona, three-fourths of a mile distant, has sprung into existence, with 25 or 30 completed buildings, and, in addition to this, 18 shaft and ore houses have been built at the mines. These are mostly of logs, though many are framed, a few being large and fine enough to befit the most pretentious city in the Territory. Two mills, Farlin's and How's, are fast approaching completion. Work has been retarded by the severe weather in November, and by the impossibility of getting lumber as fast as needed. The mills are designed to be of similar capacity, 10 stamps, though the Farlin mill is much superior in size, being 54 by 108 feet, besides a furnace-building, covering a still larger area. The machinery and equipments are all new and first-class. The How mill was removed from Brown's Gulch, 85 miles distant, and is considered as good as new. The main building, now inclosed, is 38 by 70 feet, with a southern projection 24 by 36 feet.

The latest developments in mining have been made principally on the following-named lodes, each of which have shafts sunk 30 to 60 feet and work progressing, with shaft-houses erected or in course of erection:

Late Acquisition lode; Leffler & Clark; ore, rich silver sulphide.

Mount Moriah lode; W. A. Clark; character of ore not determined.

New Era lode; Irvine & Noyes; lead carbonates and sulphides, assaying high in silver.

Late Acquisition Spur lode; Packer and others; two feet of rich quartz, bearing sulphide of silver; assays \$200 to \$600.

Banker lode; Smith & Coughenour; twenty inches of homogeneous quartz, bearing sulphide of silver, with traces of lead and iron; assays, unassorted, from \$200 to \$300.

La Plata lode; Downs, Leary, Jones, and others; 3½ feet of rich silver and gold bearing ore; silver mostly as sulphide; fine prospect for large quantities of free-milling ore.

Buenos Ayres lode; Farraday & Clark; believed to be the western extension of the La Plata; ore similar.

Josephine lode; Butcher, Archibald & Ramsdell; 2½ feet of galena and lead carbonate, assaying high in silver; fine smelting-ore.

Frank Moulton lode; W. A. Clark; 2 to 3 feet of silver-bearing quartz, with some carbonate of lead.

Wappello lode; W. L. Farlin; character of ore not tested.

Anselmo lode; F. Hirsch and others; 2 feet of fine ore, carrying silver sulphide; assays up to \$400 per ton.

Neptune lode; Prowse, Clark, and others; a strong vein of ore, carrying sulphide of silver; assays \$100 and upward.

Stinson (?) lode; Stinson; 2½ feet of quartz, carrying considerable silver; same character as Neptune, of which it is probably an extension.

Mountain Boy lode; Sherr, Bosman, Jockey, and others; 3 feet of quartz, with seams of very rich chloride of silver; assays \$200 to \$800.

Anglo-Saxon lode; W. L. Farlin; a strong vein bearing silver and gold; contract to sink 50 feet nearly completed.

In copper, the development at present is mainly on the Parrot lode. One claim, owned by Parks & Ramsdell, has a shaft over 100 feet, with levels, from which a rich oxide of copper is taken and shipped east for reduction. Another shaft, owned by Downs & Leary, is now leased to Captain Parkinson, who is taking out fine ore from the 100-foot level.

These lodes are undergoing active development; scores of others have had "representation work" done. The rich veins, Travona and others, owned by W. L. Farlin, though better developed than any other silver-mines in the camp, are not raising ore at present, but will resume when the mill starts up and better facilities for removing the water have been applied.

The present status of the camp is very encouraging. Great expectations are indulged for next season, smelters and reduction-works for copper-ores and base silver-ores will probably be built next summer.

These, with the mills now erecting and others projected, will, it is anticipated, make Butte the leading camp of Montana.

In addition to the copper-mines at Butte, in Deer Lodge County, very rich copper-veins have been discovered by Messrs. Arnold & Door, Mr. Chisholm, and others, at the head of Snow-Shoe Gulch, near Blackfoot City. The ore is a beautiful green carbonate, and that selected and sold for shipping averages 50 per cent. copper.

LEWIS AND CLARKE COUNTY.

The mines in this county have been so fully described heretofore that, with the exception of the *Ten-Mile district*, given below, I have not thought it necessary to treat them over again. Some new discoveries of silver and copper veins have been made since my last report.

The most noted silver-vein is called the Lexington, and is situated about four miles northeast from Helena. The vein is about 4 feet wide, and the ordinary vein-matter will average about $150 per ton in assaying. But lately the owners have struck a zone about 12 inches wide that is marvellous in richness. It appears to be composed of horn-silver and native silver in mossy bunches, and net-works of wires crossing each other as large as straws. The specimens are extremely beautiful, and of course yield by assay very high values, (up to $25,000 per ton.) This valuable claim is owned by Mr. W. C. Child, of Helena, and Mr. Benjamin, of San Francisco. Work is being pushed forward on it now, and the mine will be thoroughly tested during the coming year.

A large number of argentiferous galena-lodes in the vicinity of Helena, and some almost within the town limits, have been discovered and proved to be valuable.

Fine copper-veins have been discovered during the past year across the Prickly Pear Basin, within 15 miles of Helena. Some of the veins are from 7 to 10 feet in width, and the ore runs from 20 to 40 per cent. copper. Generally only enough work has been done on them to comply with the laws of Congress and the Territory to enable the discoverers to hold them.

The gold-veins and the working of the quartz-mills at Unionville and Park City, 4 miles west of Helena, have been fully described in my former reports. No new discoveries of importance were made in these localities during the past year; but the mines have yielded about the usual average, and have given steady employment to several hundred men, with profits believed to be satisfactory to their owners.

Ten-Mile district.—This district comprises a somewhat indefinite range of country on Ten-Mile Creek. The principal mines are about 20 miles in a southwesterly direction from Helena. Red Mountain, situated near the center of the district, rears its crest nearly 11,000 feet above the level of the sea and 2,500 feet above the level of the creek.

The geological formation of the district embraces nearly all of the varieties of granite—syenite, perhaps, predominating—traversed by occasional porphyritic dikes. On the north and east is a limestone formation, and about 10 miles northwesterly from Red Mountain the Carboniferous system makes its appearance, in which a bed of coal has been discovered.*

---

*In the absence of a personal examination or a geological survey of recognized authority, I cannot vouch for the accuracy of the geological descriptions furnished by my correspondents, who frequently adopt, without the opportunity of careful verification, the theories and the nomenclature current among the miners. Red Mountain, for instance, has once been reported to me as sedimentary rock, once as porphyry, and once as an extinct volcano. That the "Carboniferous system" here alluded to is true Carboniferous is not likely, because it contains coal, whereas the Carboniferous strata of the Rocky Mountains are deep-water formations and barren of coal.—R. W. R.

The development of the mineral wealth of the district has been very much retarded by a lack of adequate facilities of transportation, a disadvantage indeed which besets the mining-industry of the whole Territory. No ore of less value than $200 per ton can at present be utilized by the miner; and although considerable quantities have been shipped from the district, much of which has yielded as high as $400 per ton, still it is evident that ore of so high a grade can constitute but a very small proportion of the material mined in any district, for the poorer ore is present in predominating quantity, and much of it must be extracted in order that the richest may be sorted out.

The subject of concentration has of late engaged the serious attention of our miners. There is a great deal of ore in this district which will yield from $20 to $80 per ton in silver, but which is at present valueless unless it can in some comparatively inexpensive way be separated from the accompanying gangue.

Mr. J. W. Gonu has recently made some experiments in this district with a view to utilizing, at small expense, his low-grade ore, and has apparently met with an encouraging degree of success, by means of a somewhat rude process, as follows: The ore as it comes from the mine is first crushed in a Chilian mill and run into a large tank. It is then taken out and washed in a large fluming-trough, 12 feet long by 26 inches wide. The heavy ore remains in the box, while the gangue and the proportion of ore that will necessarily go over is run through common sluice-boxes over riffles and blankets. The blankets are washed every fifteen minutes, and what is thus saved is again washed in the head-box. In this way ten to fifteen tons are concentrated into one, which assays $1,560 per ton.

The following is a synopsis of such lodes only as have been to some extent developed:

Hope Ever, situated in the southern part of the district, on Benner Creek, and one of the first discoveries. Its strike is south, 58° east; dip, south. It is a large vein, carrying some lead, copper, and zinc, and gold and silver in small quantities. On the surface some very fair prospects of gold were obtained, on the strength of which machinery was purchased and a mill erected, which was run but a short time, and has since stood a mute monument to the folly of building mills before developing lodes.

North Pacific, discovered May 10, 1873. Course of vein nearly east and west; dip, about 60° south. The crevice varies in width from 4 to 11 feet. The general character of the ore is sulphureted, galena predominating, accompanied by zinc-blende, copper-pyrites and fahlerz. The blue and green carbonates of copper are met with, however, in the higher portions of the vein. This has been the most extensively-worked claim in the district. Two adits have been driven on the vein, the lower one 290 and the upper one 154 feet. A shaft has also been sunk 110 feet. One hundred and thirty tons of ore, taken mostly from the shaft and upper tunnel, have been shipped from this mine, which yielded about $300 per ton. One thousand tons of ore are now on the dump, which will require to be concentrated before it will be valuable at the present rates of freight.

South Pacific; a continuation of the North Pacific, and a very similar vein, but not sufficiently developed to determine its value.

Silver-Glance. This is a 1,500-foot claim, and is situated on Red Mountain proper, about 400 feet south of the North Pacific. Discovered June 25, 1873. Course of vein, east and west; dip, south. Crevice, 7 feet in width, but ore-streak narrow, varying from 6 to 15 inches. An adit has been driven along the lode 300 feet, and a shaft was sunk at the head of the tunnel to the depth of 45 feet. About 100 tons of ore from this lead were worked by the barrel process, but owing to the base metal in the ore, and perhaps somewhat to the inexperience of the amalgamator, the result was in most respects unsatisfactory. Subsequently the owners shipped 10 tons of ore to Swansea, which sampled nearly $400 per ton. The claim has been surveyed and a patent applied for.

Try Again; discovered July 12, 1873. Strike, north 58° east; dip, south. A shaft has been sunk on this lode to the depth of 103 feet, showing an ore-streak 2½ feet wide, which assays from $90 to $350 per ton. The gangue is quartz, carrying fahlerz and brittle silver. Some galena was taken from the top of the mine and shipped, which averaged a little less than $200 per ton. The owners are now concentrating ore from the lowest workings with a view to shipment.

Little Nellie; discovered October 31, 1873. Situated on the west slope of Red Mountain, about 700 feet west of the Silver-Glance. Strike, east and west; dip, south. Crevice 3 feet wide, and filled with ore, comprising lead and iron as sulphides with copper as carbonate, and fahlerz. The ore is of rather low grade and will need to be concentrated.

Caledonia, situated about 1,000 feet west of the North Pacific claim. Strike, east and west; dip, south. This is a large crevice carrying a large body of talc and quartz, with about 6 inches in width of galena which assays on an average about $100. A tunnel has been run on the vein about 45 feet.

Merritt, situated near Ruby Creek. Strike, east and west; dip, south. A tunnel has been run on the vein 75 feet. Width of crevice, 11 feet; width of ore, 4 feet. Gangue, quartz and hornblende, the hornblende being speckled with fahlerz, which I believe is a very rare occurrence. The ore of this mine will require concentrating.

Mammoth, situated 1,000 miles north of the North Pacific. Discovered May 13, 1873. Shaft sunk 45 feet, showing a 12-foot crevice containing talc, quartz, and galena. Some of the galena shipped to eastern reduction-works sampled $111 per ton.

Carbonate, situated east of the Try Again. Discovered August 29, 1874. This vein is 2 feet wide and contains iron-pyrites, carbonate of lead, and galena, the average assay-value of which is $120 per ton. A shaft has been run on the lead 45 feet.

O. H. Bassett, one of the best-looking claims in the district for the amount of labor done. It has been traced for several hundred feet by a succession of shafts, in all of which is exposed a very handsome and well-defined crevice, from 4 to 5 feet wide, containing 2 feet in width of milling-ore, which assays about $100.

S. P. Bassett, situated 200 feet north of the North Pacific, and a well-defined lode, but contains, so far as yet developed, only a small quantity of ore. A tunnel has been driven about 40 feet.

Daniel Stanton, situated 400 feet south of the Caledonia claim. This mine at one time presented the largest body of galena ore that has been developed in the district. The chimney extends about 100 feet along the lode and is from 3 to 5 feet wide. Its extent in depth is not known. Two tunnels have been run on the vein aggregating 200 feet, and a shaft has been sunk 50 feet. Several hundred tons of galena have been taken out, the assay-value of which was about $150 in silver and 70 per cent. lead. Two shipments of ore have been made to Philadelphia, Pa.

Micawber, two hundred feet south of the Silver-Glance. Strike, east and west; dip, south. One of the largest and strongest veins in the district. A shaft sunk at discovery to the depth of 40 feet, and levels driven from the shaft. A large part of the ore is milling-ore, (quartz carrying gold and silver,) while a considerable portion is galena carrying iron and copper pyrites. About 20 tons of this ore, the assay-value of which was $300 per ton, has been shipped to Philadelphia.

Hamlet lode, situated on the west slope of Red Mountain proper. Course, east and west; dip, south. Width of crevice, 4 feet, carrying galena, zinc-blende, and gray antimony, assaying from $40 to $100 per ton. About $1,000 worth of work has been done on the claim.

McDonald; strike, east and west; dip, south. Width of vein, 5 feet. Gangue, quartz, carrying sulphides of lead, zinc, antimony, and silver, of which latter there is about $40 per ton.

Bunker Hill, situated 200 feet north of the South Pacific. Strike, east and west; dip, south. A large well-defined vein, the gangue of which is quartz, carrying lead, zinc, and antimony in the form of sulphides, and assaying $35 per ton in silver. Some specimens of molybdate of lead have been found in this mine. A tunnel has been run on the lode about 30 feet.

Teal Lake, discovered June, 1873. Course, east and west; dip, south; width of crevice, 4 feet. Gangue, quartz and albite, carrying galena, zinc-blende, and carbonate of copper, and assaying as high as $200 in silver per ton; picked specimens assay as high as $1,000 per ton. There has been about $2,000 worth of work done on the claim.

Green Grove; strike, east and west; dip, south; width of crevice, 6 feet; matrix, quartz and talc, carrying galena and carbonate of copper. Some specimens of brittle silver-ore have been found in this mine. A tunnel has been run on the lode about 30 feet.

Free Speech; strike, east and west; dip, south. Ore, argentiferous galena and copper-pyrites, with a sprinkling of brittle silver. Average assay, $100 per ton.

Home Ticket; strike and dip like the preceding. A large vein of talc, containing galena and zinc-blende, but little developed.

Lee Mountain. This claim is 2,200 feet in length, and is one of the oldest locations in the district, having been discovered in 1865. It is a very large vein, and has been traced several hundred feet on the surface. The gangue is talc, in which are imbedded galena, zinc-blende, copper carbonate, copper-pyrites, and iron-pyrites. There are occasional pockets of galena nearly or quite filling the crevice. The average assay in silver is about $80; picked specimens assaying very high. Situated opposite mouth of Beaver Creek.

Sixty-Ninth, discovered in 1875. Situated on the north side of Beaver Creek. A 2,200-foot claim. Crevice, 10 feet wide. The ore in this vein is 6 feet in thickness, mostly milling-ore, assaying from $25 to $80 per ton. Two shafts have been sunk, one to a depth of 25 feet and the other 15 feet.

Robert Lee, a west extension of the Lee Mountain.

Barnum W. Field, supposed to be an east extension of the Lee Mountain.

Evening Shade, situated on the east side of Beaver Creek. Discovered 15th of July, 1873. Crevice, 4 feet wide, carrying galena, which assays $40 per ton in silver, picked specimens assaying as high as $400 per ton. A cross-adit has been driven 184 feet at right-angles to the lode, which it cuts at the depth of 120 feet. Thence a drift was run on the crevice 40 feet. The ore will require to be concentrated.

The foregoing comprise but a small part of the claims located in this district, but it is believed to embrace all those that have been developed to an extent sufficient to permit intelligent judgment as to their permanency.

JEFFERSON COUNTY.

The very numerous silver-lodes in this county were mostly described by name in my reports for 1873 and 1874.

The groups in the vicinity of Jefferson City and in the Boulder Valley have been extensively worked during the year, partly with a view to their development and partly for profit.

Work on the Legal Tender, near Clancy, has been suspended on account of water. New machinery and larger pumps will have to be procured before work can be resumed.

The mine is claimed to be as rich as ever, and able to yield $100,000 per year, as formerly, when the necessary improvements are made. Its neighbor, the Mammoth, is idle because of the lack of mills to reduce its rich ores, and for the want of freighting facilities, as are many others in the vicinity of Clancy.

Five hundred tons of galena-ore have been taken out of the famous Gregory lode, near Jefferson City, and sacked ready for shipment during the past winter. As much more could very soon be prepared, but will wait, for want of transportation, until another year.

The Argentum lode, near Jefferson City, has not been worked during the year, because the owners prefer to wait for the erection of reduction-works at home. In 1873 over 100 tons from this mine were shipped to Omaha. The gross value after reduction was $237 per ton, yet the shippers only received about $100 per ton on the lot for their share, after paying all expenses of mining, sacking, reduction, commissions, &c.

Boulder district.—The Rumley, Comet, and adjoining claims in the district have been pretty extensively developed the past autumn and winter. The Rumley will ship during the summer of 1876 500 tons, worth on the average $300 per ton. The two mines above named could produce, it is claimed, a hundred tons per day each, if the ores could be worked at home, or sold at what the owners consider a fair profit.*

The owners of the Rumley have, during the past autumn, formed a joint-stock company, including themselves and a number of capitalists in Philadelphia, for the purpose of erecting milling and smelting works at the mine during the next year. This mine alone could, it is claimed, keep a hundred stamps at work, and the Comet, with the dozen extensions east and west upon it, is estimated to have equal capacity.

The Boulder silver-district is certainly one of the most extensive known in Montana. The whole eastern side of the main range of the Rocky Mountains, from Helena southward through Lewis and Clarke and Jefferson Counties, including the Little Prickly Pear and Boulder Valleys and Ten-Mile, abounds in silver-quartz veins on almost every slope.

On the eastern slope of the Prickly Pear Divide, which is a high range separating the Prickly Pear and White Tail Deer Creek from the Missouri River, are many fine gold-veins, as the Blacker and Keating, Lead, the Iron Rod, the great gold vein at Saint Louis, and a hundred others, which have been profitable to their owners. For description of these, the reader is referred to my former reports.

---

* I must say in general, without meaning to apply the remark to this case more than another, that these estimates of the capacity of mines are usually, among our western miners, much exaggerated. Engineers will understand that the production of a mine cannot be doubled at will, except for a short period.—R. W. R.

MEAGHER COUNTY.

Several small gold-quartz mills have worked successfully in this county during the past year—one especially, at Duck Creek; but the principal mineral wealth of this county, so far, appears to be in its placer-mines. The celebrated Confederate Gulch, which yielded its millions in gold-dust when first discovered, is still paying handsome profits to its owners. Thompson's Gulch, Eldorado Bar, Cane, Avalanche, White's, New York, and Spring Gulches, American Bar, and the numerous other bars all along down to the Gate of the Mountain and Old Bear Tooth Mountain are yielding well. All along the Belt Range of mountains, north and east from Helena and across the Missouri River, promising silver, gold, and copper veins have been discovered, but not much developed.

From the Newlan Copper Mine, at Copperopolis, in Meagher County, Benjamin Kingsbury shipped during the season forty tons of ore to Baltimore, which gave 33⅓ per cent. copper, and netted him, after paying all expenses, about $25 per ton. He owns three veins contiguous to each other that are wide and appear to be permanent, and increase in value as they are sunk upon. In December he organized a company at Saint Louis, Mo., which will probably erect works to reduce these ores during 1876.

The gold-yield of Meagher County has not been far from $350,000 for several years past, and the promise is better for the future, as small claim owners are selling out and consolidating with large owners, who are bringing in larger ditches. This is taking place, indeed, all over the Territory, and augurs an increased yield of the placer-mines.

GALLATIN COUNTY.

This has hardly been considered as one of the mining-counties heretofore, but is certainly the foremost agricultural county of Montana. Yet it contains some good mines. The large argentiferous galena mine on Sixteen-Mile Creek, mentioned in my last report, bids fair to fulfill all the promise of its first working, and considerable ore has been prepared for shipment to the East next year, to test its value.

The placer gold-mines at *Emigrant Gulch* and the noted *Clark's Fork* galena-silver mines, described in my last report, although on the Upper Yellowstone or its tributaries, are only accessible from Bozeman, in Gallatin County, and may be considered to belong to it.

The yield of Emigrant Gulch the past season has been about $40,000 of gold-dust. The Clark's Fork mines show on the surface large quantities of galena and silver ore, very rich in galena—60 to 80 per cent.—and in silver bearing from $40 to $600 per ton, according to the tests that have been made. These mines are 10,000 feet above sea-level in the mountains, and 120 miles southeast from Bozeman, and accessible only on horseback. A company has been formed to begin their development. But it will take both time and money to make them profitable. The improvement of navigation on the Yellowstone would bring steamboats within 100 miles of them.

MADISON COUNTY.

During the year 1875 there was shipped by Wells, Fargo & Co.'s Express, from the Virginia City office, gold-dust to the amount of $424,628, as reported by their agent, Mr. H. S. Howell. From the different camps within the county the following brief notes have been gathered:

Alder Gulch.—Last season was a favorable one for placer-mining, and it is estimated that the yield from Alder Gulch was nearly or quite up to the average of the last few years. Some portions of it have been worked out; but the prevalence of lower wages and the consolidation of many small claims under the control of a few large companies maintains the yearly product without material decrease. Several tracts of ground in the lower part of the gulch—considered of little value—have been purchased by Chinamen, and are evidently paying them well. With two or three exceptions, the mine-owners along this creek, a distance of 16 miles, have applied for United States patents.

Barton Gulch.—Barton Creek heads at the foot of Old Baldy Mountain, and just over a low divide from the right fork of Alder Creek. Acting upon the presumption that the source of the gold found in the bed of the latter was at its head, and that some of the precious metal would naturally find its way down the channel of Barton Gulch, considerable prospecting has been done in the latter, but with small returns. In the upper portion there is a scarcity of water, and in the lower part the bed-rock lies very deep; still the men at work in it are confident of ultimate success. On a right fork of this stream, Mr. Robert Williamson has discovered and opened a vein from which a considerable amount of good-looking quartz has been taken. A working test next spring will determine its value as a gold-ore.

Bivens Gulch.—In this gulch placer-mining has been systematically carried on, and large "clean-ups" are the results. The yearly yield is on the increase, and the gold obtained is of a fine quality.

Brown's Gulch.—Near the head of this gulch, Mr. M. D. Platner has been successfully treating the rich silver-ores of this district, in which are situated the Pacific, Black, Gould & Curry, and other lodes. By means of a rude but clever arrangement of quicksilver-tanks, steam is generated and the pulp submitted to its action. This suggests that, with proper facilities, these ores might be easily and profitably worked on a large scale.

The placer-mines in Brown's Gulch are being rapidly opened and pay good wages. Several claims are surveyed and advertised for patents.

California Gulch.—In this gulch the water is used to the best advantage, but the supply is limited, and many good claims are lying idle.

Copper Belt district.—This new district is at the south point of the Ruby Mountain, and takes its name from the first lode discovered, the Copper Belt. Several well-defined veins of low-grade copper-ore have been found A sample forwarded to the Baltimore Copper Works was returned as copper-glance, free from antimony and arsenic, assaying 25.2 per cent. of copper, with no silver.

Harris Gulch.—The placer-ground in this gulch is worked so far as the limited supply of water will permit, and on the average pays very well.

Havana district.—In the Havana or Cherry Creek silver-district, work has been suspended on all but the two principal lodes, the Enselman and the Eberhart, both of which are looking very well. A considerable quantity of rich ore has been taken out, but the lack of capital to develop and erect the necessary works retards progress.

Hot Spring district.—In this district the Red Bluff, Silver Shower, and other lodes have produced largely, and it is expected that the product for the next year will be far in excess of this. The fine Midas mill, at Sterling, stands idle, but the Mallory and Olds mills, and the Red Bluff arrastra below, are constantly and fully occupied.

Idaho Gulch.—Idaho Creek heads at the west face of Old Baldy, and empties into the Stinkingwater River above the lower cañon. Messrs. Barr & Heisrick have run a drain, are putting in a bed-rock flume, and expect to work this gulch during the coming summer.

Iron Rod district.—On the Iron Rod lode a tunnel 900 feet in length has been run for drainage and prospecting purposes, in addition to the usual amount of work. A new and rich discovery has been made in Hell Cañon above, and the camp is in a prosperous condition. Messrs. Dahler, Porter & Co. have a good 12-stamp mill at Iron Rod, and in Hell Cañon there is a 6-stamp mill and an arrastra, all driven by water-power.

Meadow Creek district.—In this district the principal lode is the Madisonian, formerly known as the Mother Hendricks, and now owned by Messrs. Merk & Yandes. On this vein a shaft has been sunk to the depth of 220 feet; levels have been run, and at the present time there are 1,200 tons of $20 gold-ore on the dump. A tunnel has been run and a large steam-pump ordered for the drainage of the mine. These gentlemen have a 10-stamp quartz-mill on Meadow Creek, 2½ miles distant, and a 5-stamp battery, driven by the hoisting-engine, at the shaft.

Mill Creek district.—Messrs. Cisler, Zinn & Co., the owners of the Broad Gauge lode, have erected at Brandon, 2½ miles above Sheridan, a fine 20-stamp mill, built by Fraser, Chambers & Co., of Chicago. This Broad Gauge mine is a gold-bearing deposit deserving more than a passing notice. In the absence of foot and hanging walls, it cannot be properly called a vein. The ore, an ocher-colored earth, is found evenly deposited upon a hill-side, from which it is removed with pick and shovel. The average yield does not exceed $7 per ton, but the ore is so easily worked that the mine pays monthly dividends.

Norwegian Gulch.—The placer-mines on this stream are extensive. During the past season a joint-stock company dug a large ditch 5 miles in length, through which sufficient water for ground-sluicing will be brought.

Potosi silver-district.—This district, a new one, is situated in the range of mountains known as the South Boulder, at the head of Willow Creek, and bids fair to acquire importance. Work has been commenced on several lodes and some rich rock has been taken out; but the mines are difficult of access, and it is probable they will not be developed to any extent until arrangements have been made to treat the ore near the mines.

Rochester district.—This camp about holds its own, and keeps Dr. Gitchell's 10-stamp steam-mill pounding away on quartz from the few lodes worked.

Silver Star district.—Here there are 25 men employed, and the mines are looking better than ever before. There are two quartz-mills here, the Green Campbell and the Tripp & Ainslee, the former having 10 stamps and the latter 6. Mr. Charles Heineman has opened a new vein, called the Aurora, which is considered the best in the district, and has purchased of Tripp & Ainslee their water-mill, in which to crush the ore taken from it. The Green Campbell mill will probably be started on custom-rock from the other lodes.

Summit district.—The principal lodes in this district are the Oro Cache, Keystone, Rosebud, and Kearsarge. The Oro Cache is the only one worked. During the last summer this mine was prospected, and it is now supposed that another chimney of rich ore has been found. The Keystone and Rosebud are down to the water-level, and must be drained before any quantity of rock can be taken out. There are five quartz-mills in the district, all standing idle. The McClure Chilian mill in Spring Gulch has been put in running order and will start in the spring. Application has been made to obtain patents for the Oro Cache lode and the North Oro Cache lode, with the McClure mill-site attached.

Warm Spring district.—The placer-mines of this district are located along Warm Spring Creek, which rises on the south side of Old Baldy and empties into the Stinkingwater River, of which it is the largest tributary, just above the second cañon. The creek derives its name from the many warm springs found upon its banks. During last summer the gulch was located through its entire length, about 7 miles, and three companies commenced operations; but as yet little progress has been made.

Washington Bar is on Meadow Creek, near its source in the South Boulder range, and pays moderately well. Mr. George F. Cope, who has invested money here, employs several men on the bar. A considerable part of the work this summer was done to get the mines in shape for next season.

Wigwam Gulch, on the Madison slope of Old Baldy, has been abandoned, owing to the great number of large bowlders encountered and the scarcity of water. It is possible that with increased mechanical facilities and water-supply this ground might be profitably mined.

Williams Gulch runs nearly parallel with Alder, and contributes a small stream to the Stinkingwater. Very many lodes have been located in this gulch; a few have been represented by labor done during the year, but none are regularly worked. The ore from these lodes is much like that in Brown's Gulch, near by. Placer-claims have been located in the bed of the creek.

Wisconsin Creek.—The lodes in this district are pretty well developed, and encourage the hope of many that this will make one of the best quartz-camps in the county. The Company lode of the Messrs. Noble continues to pay a handsome dividend, and other mines recently opened promises well.

The placer-mines in Wisconsin Gulch are worked to a greater extent and with better results than ever before.

MISSOULA COUNTY.

This County is situated in the northwest portion of Montana Territory. The principal streams are the Missoula and the Bitter Root Rivers, the latter a tributary of the former. The Missoula is a continuation of the Deer Lodge, being the stream formerly known as the Hell-Gate River. It heads in the Big Hole Mountains, and flows into the Pend d'Oreille Lake. The Bitter Root heads in the Bitter Root Mountains. The county is well watered, the mountains being full of small streams and springs. It is the best agricultural county in the Territory. In the Bitter Root Valley, not only large crops of grain, potatoes, cabbages, turnips, onions, and other vegetables grow, but tomatoes, melons, apples, crab-apples, stawberries, raspberries, gooseberries, currants, and other fruits are successfully cultivated. So successful is the agriculturist in this county, that spare labor nearly always seeks employment on the ranches, and mining receives but a small amount of attention. The result of farming is an almost certain success, while that of mining is exceedingly uncertain. There are also other causes that the mines in this county have not received a larger share of attention. Among these are the circumstances that followed the discovery of the Cedar Creek mines, of which I shall say more presently. Another is the hinderance to prospecting found in the heavy timber that covers the mountains and fills the gulches, and the obstacles to gulch-mining presented by the immense volumes of water that fill the channels in the spring, and by the frequent want of good dumping-ground.

The principal mines, those of Cedar Creek, were discovered in November, 1869. Very soon afterward the report that rich placer-diggings had been struck in Missoula caused a great excitement in Helena, and early in 1870 a "stampede" to the new mines was the result. Large numbers of miners arrived at Cedar Creek to find deep snow and very little provision. Of course prospecting was next to impossible. Still they waited patiently, and while they waited every month added to their number. At last the spring opened, and then came the water, roaring down the creek in such quantities as to render work out of the question. Many left the camp never to return, but others persevered. The gulch was exceedingly rich, but also exceedingly expensive to work, and the mining property soon fell into the hands of a few large companies. Miners departed leaving their debts unpaid, and ruined merchants followed their example.

Among the miners who had "stampeded" to Cedar were many of the best prospectors in the Territory; and the fact that these men left the camp disappointed and with empty purses, has doubtless prevented many others from prospecting in Missoula County. At the present time the effect of the Cedar excitement is wearing off, and some successful prospecting has been done during the past year. Yet the mining interests of this county are still unfairly handicapped when compared with those of other counties in Montana.

Cedar Creek.—A very large amount of gold has been taken from the Cedar Creek Gulch and its tributaries. Claims extending from 50 above discovery to 76 above yielded from $18 to $300 to the set of timbers.* The principal companies now working are the No. 67 and the Home-Stake. The former company is at work on claims from 67 to 72 above discovery. The principal work was done in the years 1871, 1872, and 1873, during which period there was taken out about $50,000 each year, at an annual cost of about $30,000.

The Home-Stake Company is at work on Snow-Shoe Gulch, at the head of Cedar. This company is composed of Messrs. Caplice, Smith, Lynch & Kelly, who bought up the whole gulch last fall, (1874,) together with the water-privileges, for $1,000, and have since expended in improvements $1,000. These are "hydraulic" diggings. There is a flume 600 feet long, which will be increased in length 200 feet next year. It is a 16-inch flume with 9-inch grade. There is water for about three months in the year, running from 50 to 300 inches, miners' measurement. During the summer of 1875 these diggings yielded, with nine men at work, in ten weeks the gross sum of $9,200, and netted the owners $4,600. The proprietors claim, moreover, that between $2,000 and $3,000 was lost by robberies of the sluices. The wages paid are $5 per diem, 8-hour shifts, and 7 days in the week. The company boards the men at $9 per week. There is no feed for horses at Cedar Creek, but plenty of wood and water. Water for mining purposes is scarce at the head of the gulch in the autumn.

With the exception of the few claims now being worked, the mines

* This seems to refer to the timbering of drifts, run for purposes of extraction, in the auriferous gravel of the "pay-channel." It is a vague measurement; but, if my conjecture is correct, the "set of timbers" may perhaps be fairly assumed to represent 50 cubic yards of material removed. This would make the yield stated a very handsome but not an unparalleled one.—R. W. R.

are not remunerative on account of the cost of working, the depth of the ground, and the want of drainage.

Nine-Mile Creek is situated 25 miles nearly due west from the town of Missoula, down the Missoula River, on the right bank of which it enters as a tributary. The diggings are about 27 miles from the mouth of the creek. The creek runs first from west to east, then turns and empties into the Missoula, which runs from east to west. The gulch is heavily timbered and has very slight fall; but the diggings are shallow and tolerably easy to drain, prospect, and work. About 2¼ miles of the gulch are covered by patents, Barrett & Co. having a patent for 100 acres, and Dixon, Kime & Co. having a patent for 40 acres. This patented ground, ranging from 8 to 16 rods in width, was taken up in the fall of 1874. The gulch is claimed under locations for 5 miles below the forks of the creek, and each of the two main forks is claimed for 2 to 3 miles. There are also several short side-gulches claimed. All these claims are represented by annual labor. Barrett & Co. are working their ground, and are said to be doing well, probably taking out from $5 to $6 per day to the hand.

Dixon, Kime & Co. have just commenced to open their ground.

The two main forks of Nine-Mile Creek are called, respectively, Saint Louis Gulch and Eustash Gulch.

A Frenchman, who owned No. 19 on Eustash, recently bought out the adjoining claim (No. 20) for $1,000, and now owns 600 feet. The claims are very rich, and have yielded as high as $100 per day to the hand. One day during the week commencing August 16, 1875, 31 ounces of dust was taken out of No. 19. This dust is very fine in quality, selling at from $20.50 to $21.25 currency per ounce. During the same month a nugget weighing 5 ounces was taken from the same claim. In this gulch there are about 50 located claims of 300 feet each.

The First National Bank of Missoula bought from Nine-Mile district during the week commencing August 16, 1875, 80 ounces of gold-dust, paying from $20.50 to $21.25 per ounce.

At the point where Saint Louis Gulch and Eustash Gulch meet and form Nine-Mile Creek is the mining-camp of Montreal, with a population of about forty souls. The town possesses one hotel, four saloons, one store, two butcher-shops, two blacksmith-shops, one bakery, and two Chinese wash-houses. Wages range from $4.50 to $5 per day, and board costs $8 per week. The grass is not good at the upper end of the gulch, but there is an abundance of water for a long mining-season and a plentiful supply of good timber.

Quartz Gulch empties into the Missoula River, on the left bank of that stream, about 52 miles west of the town of Missoula. This is a heavily-timbered gulch, with deep diggings in the channel, having slight fall, and being consequently very difficult to prospect or work. There are two districts in the gulch, called the upper and the lower. In the upper district there are from 50 to 70 located claims. Claims Nos. 15, 16, 17, 18, and 19, above discovery in this district, being "bar-diggings," were worked in 1872 with drifts from 20 to 30 feet in depth, and yield from $10 to $12 per day to the hand. These claims were all worked out in that year, with the exception of the lower portion of claim No. 15, which was worked out in the summer of 1873, paying well. Below No. 15 the ground has not been worked out, on account of the great quantity of water to be removed and the absence of fall for drainage. Messrs. Boyce & Co., McManus, and others are running a drain-ditch in the deep channel, and will probably commence sluicing this fall.

Messrs. McGraw & Co. have been prospecting the deep channel to a considerable extent, but have, I believe, never reached bed-rock in the main gulch. While working on No. 20 above discovery, in the upper district, (difting,) and running across the mouth of a tributary gulch, in the summer of 1875, they struck bed-rock, and, according to general rumor, obtained as much as $225 to the set of timbers. Messrs. William Losa and Joe Farrell, who had been prospecting on the bar for two years, have now drifted on the deep channel, and are said to be doing well. Bartz & Co., on No. 44, in the same (upper) district, are also reported to be prosperous. There are two flume companies in the upper and one in the lower district, but they only clean up twice a year, and nothing trustworthy can be ascertained as to the result of their labors. It is generally supposed, however, that they are successful.

Quartz Gulch was discovered in the fall of 1870. The gold-dust at the mouth is "flaky" and coarse, and very much resembles "Nine-Mile" dust, while at the head of the creek it is "heavy, well-washed, round gold." The richest ground is in spots, and the channel is deep and hard to work. There is plenty of water up to July, and afterward water is collected in reservoirs in sufficient quantities to run in day-time only. The gold assays, according to returns from San Francisco mint, $19.81 in coin per ounce. The diggings in Quartz Gulch probably yield from $20 to $85 to the set of timbers, the lowest figure being the most common. Wages are $5 per diem. The bar-diggings have been thoroughly prospected, but prospecting has only recently been begun in the deep channel.

In 1874, Mr. Richotte, a Frenchman, discovered a quartz-vein showing considerable free gold, but has not yet done much in developing it. The vicinity has not been prospected for quartz, but pieces of quartz containing free gold have been repeatedly taken out of the placer-mines.

Little Bear Creek is about three miles below Quartz Gulch, on the left bank of the Missoula River. It heads on the summit of the ridge between Quartz Gulch and Trout Creek. This gulch has been worked since the spring of 1870. The dust is .956 fine. Messrs. Foote, Holtz, and Quinn are the principal owners. The two former, who recently purchased half the interest of the latter for $550, now claim 650 feet, and are working with results reported to be satisfactory.

Trout Creek is a left-bank tributary of the Missoula River, about 54 miles west of the town of Missoula. The mines were discovered in August, 1873, when about $2,000 were taken out of a piece of ground 30 by 80 feet on the surface, and from 1½ to 3 feet in depth. This was done by Messrs. Fox & Co., who were prospecting on a point where the creek makes a turn, and struck bed-rock on the edge of the gulch. Bed-rock, however, has not yet been struck in the deep channel of the creek. The mines are deep, the fall is slight, and it is very difficult ground to drain. This makes prospecting difficult and expensive; still a large amount of work is in progress. Lewis & Co. are prospecting and running a drain half a mile in length. They have sunk 30 feet, but have not yet struck bed-rock.

In 1873, Cave, Lodus & Co. ran a drain 400 feet long on claims 17 and 18 below discovery, and attempted to raise the water by "China" pumps. After getting down 20 feet they were overcome by the water, and failed to reach bed-rock. In the same year Davis & Co. undertook to run a drain. They struck the rim-rock, and got good prospects, but could not reach bed-rock in the channel.

Mr. David Thompson also undertook to run a drain on claim No. 9 below discovery. He has not reached bed-rock, but is continuing work, though obliged to stop occasionally for want of means, and will go to work again in the fall. The principal tributaries of Trout Creek are Freeze-out, six miles from the head of the gulch, on the left-hand bank; Deep Creek, three miles below Freeze-out, on the same bank; and Windfall, quarter of a mile below Deep Creek, on the right-hand bank. Of these, Windfall is giving the most favorable results to prospecting and mining operations. The two other gulches are worked, and yield small wages.

These comprise the principal mines now known in Missoula County. There are also some Chinamen working on a bar toward the head of Bitter Root River, where they earn small wages (from $4 to $5 per day to the hand) for a very short time in the spring. It is said by many old residents, especially those who accompanied Governor Ashley in his journey through this county, that rich silver-ledges exist in the northwest corner of the county. Certainly some very good specimens are shown as coming from that region.

Mr. Alvin Lent, of Wells, Fargo & Co., gives the following as the shipments of gold-dust by express from the Missoula office during the years 1873, 1874, and 1875:

Months.	1873.	1874.	1875.
January	....	$2, 375	....
February	$5, 000	2, 750	$3, 000
March	7, 550	4, 700	3, 400
April	3, 500	7, 000	....
May	7, 250	14, 000	3, 800
June	8, 800	8, 500	17, 800
July	13, 150	11, 490	14, 000
August	21, 750	26, 700	*7, 600
September	11, 300	5, 000	....
October	7, 500	5, 900	....
November	8, 320	13, 250	....
December	6, 800	10, 600	....
Total	100, 920	112, 265	49, 600

* This is up to August 22.

Mr. Lent estimates that 20 per cent. may be added to these amounts for the "gold-dust" that is taken out of the county by private hands, or forwarded through the mails.

The quality of the dust from different camps in the county, and the price paid in August by the Missoula National Bank, is found in the following list:

Name of camp.	Price paid in August, 1875.	Fineness.
	Per oz., currency.	
Nine-Mile	$21 00	.967
Quartz Gulch	20 75	.956
Bitter Root	19 00	....
Cedar	20 75 to 21 00	.956 to .970
Trout	....	.984
Sunrise	....	.976

There is every reason to believe that Missoula County possesses her share of mineral wealth, but many circumstances have stood in the way of the development of her mines, and the county to-day remains almost unexplored.

CHAPTER VI.

UTAH.

This Territory was visited by my deputy, Mr. A. Eilers, in the summer and fall, and still later by Mr. T. F. Van Wagenen, who has furnished me with the latest accounts up to the end of the year.

The estimate of the bullion-product of the Territory has been arrived at from detailed data as to shipments of the railroads and of Wells, Fargo & Co.'s express, kindly furnished me at the end of the year by Mr. G. Billing, the proprietor of one of the largest smelting-works in the Territory, and from the values of ores and base bullion, ascertained through the principal ore and bullion buyers of Salt Lake City, Messrs. Hanauer and A. von Weise.

The descriptive text as to the condition of the mining-industry in Utah has been furnished by Mr. Theo. F. Van Wagenen, my deputy, Mr. A. Eilers, and several other professional gentlemen residing in Utah.

The product of gold and silver in 1875 was as follows:

	Currency.	Coin. (Gold 116.)
Silver in 284 tons of copper-ore, at 30 ounces per ton, at 30 cents currency..	$2,556 00	$2,159 82
Gold and silver in 16,330 tons argentiferous lead, at $175 currency per ton.....	2,857,750 00	2,414,798 75
Silver bars	*637,763 00	538,909 73
Silver, value in 4,312 tons of lead-ore, 12 ounces per ton, at $12.60 currency....	54,331 20	45,909 69
Silver, value in 1,000 tons of lead-ore, 100 ounces per ton, at $110 currency......	110,000 00	92,950 00
Gold-dust by express....................	†43,686 00	*35,800 00
Gold-dust by other conveyances........	†4,368 00	‡7,160 00
Total gold and silver............	3,710,454 20	3,137,687 99

This amount can be separated into gold and silver, as follows:

Gold in base bullion	$138,805 00	
Gold-dust............	42,960 00	
		$181,765 00
Silver in base bullion..................	2,233,033 75	
Silver from all other sources............	722,889 24	
		2,955,922 99
Total gold and silver		3,137,687 99

To this may be added the values produced in the Territory in lead and copper:

* Amounts obtained from Salt Lake office of Wells, Fargo & Co. by Mr. Billing.

† Amounts published in January, 1876, by Mr. Valentine, superintendent of Wells, Fargo & Co.'s Express. They were given by him as coin.

‡ Estimated.

	Currency.	Coin.
Lead, 16,330 tons, at $75 currency......	$1,224,750 00	$1,034,913 75
Lead, value in 4,312 tons of ore, 55 per cent., at $12.50....................	53,900 00	45,545 50
Total	1,278,650 00	1,080,459 25
Copper, 284 tons copper-ore, 20 per cent., $1.15 per unit, $23 per ton...........	6,532 00	5,519 54
Copper, 349 tons black copper, at $100..	34,900 00	29,490 50
Total	41,432 00	35,010 04

RECAPITULATION.

	Coin.
Gold..	$181,765 00
Silver..	2,955,922 99
Lead..	1,080,459 25
Copper..	35,010 04
Total metals	4,253,157 28

By comparing these figures with those of former years in previous reports, it will be seen that there has been a considerable decrease in 1875.

The cause of this large decrease is found in the depressed condition of the smelting business during the first half of the year. The prices for ore had been carried up in 1874 to a point which almost precluded any profit to home smelters, and as a consequence most of the works had shut down. This practically forbade the working of many of the mines, the ores of which would not bear transportation for long distances, but which, nevertheless, had yielded quite a large proportion of the annual production.

About May, 1875, however, the condition of the ore-market had improved greatly, so that Mr. Billing, of the Germania Works, first ventured to begin smelting. His example was soon followed by the Saturn Works, and at the close of the year eleven furnaces were in operation, and the ore-supply was as good as ever before, if not better. The ruling prices, though pretty well advanced, were not too high to leave a small margin of profit, and the custom-works appeared to be satisfied, on the whole, with the condition of things. A very important advance in the industry during this year was the successful introduction, in the fall, of Utah coke in the furnaces. Heretofore that class of fuel has been the most expensive item in smelting, costing from $30 to $35 per ton delivered, with all the disadvantages of purchasing at a great distance, (in Indiana or Pennsylvania.) In August the first car-load of San Pete coke was delivered to the Germania Works, and, on trial, was found to answer very well, though not as suitable as the Connellsville coke. The manufacturers (the Fairview Coal and Coke Company) found themselves immediately in receipt of many more orders than they could fill, owing to the fact that the coal-beds were 40 miles from the terminus of the Utah Southern Railroad, by a wagon-road not of the best quality. Late in the year the company was selling all it could bring to market at $28 per ton, a figure which insured a handsome profit. It was the intention to construct either a tram-road or a better wagon-road from the railroad terminus early in the spring of 1876, and it was expected that coke could be delivered at Sandy or Salt Lake for not over $20 per ton. The samples first brought up to the city had the appearance of an excellent material, being clean, resonant, and sufficiently firm to bear the burden of a lead-furnace. There seems to be no reason to doubt that the San Pete coal will make a very good coke; and this fact may be expected to stimulate experiments with many of the other coal-deposits of the Territory, some of which produce an equally promising fuel.

Fully 75 per cent. of the product of metals in Utah comes from Parley's Park, Little Cottonwood, Bingham, and Ophir districts. In Camp Floyd, Tintic, Star, Beaver, San Francisco, and the numerous other southern districts a large amount of work has been done, but it has been mostly in the way of prospecting or developing. Great quantities of ore are already in sight in the mines of Southern Utah; but as it is, as a rule, of low grade, no very large production can be expected until railroad transportation is available. "Milling-ore," which can be reduced by amalgamation to nearly pure silver in the neighborhood of the mines, is not abundant in this Territory at present, and the bulkier product obtained by smelting even rich argentiferous lead-ores can scarcely bear the cost of wagon transportation over long distances.

The following reduction-works have been in operation during the whole or part of the year:

Germania Works, 2 furnaces;* Jordan and Galena, 2 furnaces; Flagstaff Works, 2 furnaces; Saturn Works, 2 furnaces; Waterman Works, 2 furnaces; Chicago Works, 3 furnaces; McHenry Mill, Parley's Park; Pioneer and Enterprise Mills, Ophir district; New Jersey Arrastras, Ophir district; Fairview Mill, Ophir district.

Several of the more important smelting-works have been described in former reports. In the present report I give, as a representative case, the account of the Jordan and Galena Works and their operations for the year, for which I am chiefly indebted to Mr. G. P. Lockwood. These works have two reverberatory roasting-furnaces, built on a plan which may be called a cross between the English smelting and the old German roasting furnace. They are considered too short, and too high between arch and bottom, to be perfectly adapted to the work here required of them. There are, in addition, five elliptical shaft-furnaces, 60 by 30 inches in interior dimensions, 10 feet 6 inches from tuyeres to feed-door, 14 inches from tuyeres to slag-tap, and 24 inches from tap to sole. A sixth furnace is octagonal, 42 inches in diameter, 12 feet 6 inches in height, and like the rest in other dimensions. All are run with closed fronts, and have water-jackets, extending 14 inches below and 2 feet 6 inches above the tuyeres. Above the water-jackets the stack rests on pillars, like a Pilz furnace. The jackets are of riveted boiler-plate, giving an inner annular space 8 inches across, which is closed at the top by a plate riveted on. The water is fed into the jackets 1 inch below the top, and the discharge-pipe is in the top and rises 1 inch before turning. This keeps the jacket constantly full and prevents the accumulation of steam. The jackets are separate segments, held in place by a strip of thin band-iron. When the furnace is run down, and has to be cleaned, this band is loosened, and the front jacket is taken out. This arrangement is unsurpassed for convenience.

There are two engines, of 25 and 35 horse-power, respectively, four Mackenzie blowers, a sampling-mill for ores sent for sale, and a water-

* I do not vouch for the correctness of this statement as to the number of furnaces, not knowing by what rule they have been counted. The Jordan and Galena Works, for example, have indeed but two roasting reverberatories, but they have also six shaft-furnaces.—R. W. R.

ditch 9½ miles long, capable when in use of furnishing 250 horse-power, but now out of repair.

All the matter produced is saved and put again through the furnaces until it becomes rich enough in copper to be marketable. The cost of roasting matter and galena is about $2 per ton for labor, and the same amount for fuel. The works were running but seven months during the year, and treated about 7,350 tons of ore, as is shown by the subjoined table.

Ores, &c., consumed at the Jordan and Galena Smelting-Works, Utah, during the year 1875.

Name.	Gross weight.	Name.	Gross weight
	Pounds.		*Pounds.*
Jordan and Galena *	6, 905, 779	Deseret	131, 460
Utah Queen	12, 175	Mack	27, 220
Belle	38, 028	Coleman	12, 361
Emily	10, 687	Winnemuck	505, 730
Cullen	10, 129	Flagstaff	137, 377
Manganese	15, 980	Western Star	102, 980
Grey Rock	13, 500	Occident	6, 390
Agnes	12, 150	South Star and Titus	700, 753
Sierra Madré	1, 895	Thad. Stevens	21, 700
Green Mountain	8, 991	North Star	32, 621
Bruno	14, 690	Revere	78, 000
Highland Chief of Little Cottonwood	157, 875	Spanish	602, 756
Samuel "A"	6, 950	Equitable	8, 190
Samuel "B"	7, 016	Swansea	92, 027
Evarts	1, 507	Teresa	22, 850
Tenderfoot	8, 220	Sailor Jack	29, 279
Blue Rock	9, 090	Wellington of Big Cottonwood	199, 715
"L" Ore	2, 500	Full Moon	54, 172
Tecoma	708, 606	Old Cross	172, 967
I X L	126, 250	Prince of Wales	60, 217
City Rock	55, 168	Nez Perces	91, 115
Yosemite	1, 073, 381	American Flag	53, 610
Walker & Webster	107, 500	Alabama	29, 928
Ashland & Revere	508, 407	Hidden Treasure	10, 920
Toledo	188, 168	Fred	6, 327
Ophir	11, 994	Victor	9, 000
Ira	34, 385	Dinero	18, 580
Jim Fisk	38, 204	Monumental	47, 330
Richmond	200, 238	Kinner	44, 505
Mount Savage	44, 675		
Victoria and Imperial	48, 521	Total	14, 700, 555
Miller, (American Fork)	19, 043		
Reed & Benson	195, 490	Coke, (Connellsville)	1, 791, 672
Brooklyn	6, 619	Charcoal, (bushels)	140, 649
Neptune	6, 440	Limestone	1, 919, 100
Cincinnati	71, 286	Iron-ore †	2, 498, 980
Vallejo	708, 938	Scrap-iron	12, 235

* Average assay of Jordan and Galena ore: Lead, 35 per cent.; iron, 10 per cent.; silica, 33 per cent.; silver, 16 ounces per ton.

† Hematite from Wyoming and Tintic.

The bullion product of the works was as follows:

	Spring campaign, January 1 to March 9.	Fall campaign, September 13 to December 31.	Total for 1875.
Lead .... pounds..	1, 841, 316	1, 213, 771	3, 055, 087
Silver .... ounces..	87, 057. 42	43, 331. 62	130, 389. 04
Gold .... do....	514. 647	264. 602	779. 249
Number of car-loads of bullion	83	58	141

The idleness of the works from March to September was due to the closing up of the business and its reorganization under a new company.

Much less ore is now shipped from Utah than in former years, partly on account of the improvements in home smelting-works, and partly because the business of smelting in Chicago has not been found very profitable. Still a large proportion of the high grades goes eastward. The two sampling-works of Oliver Durant and Scott & Anderson sampled and sold in 1875 nearly 30,000 tons of ore and 7,000 tons of base bullion. Of the first item all but a little over 5,000 tons was sent to smelting-works in Utah, the remainder being shipped east.

In round numbers, I find the production of the Territory to have been derived from the various districts in about the following proportion:

	Currency.
Big and Little Cottonwood and American Fork	$1,140,000
Bingham	800,000
Ophir, (East and Dry Cañons)	812,000
Parley's Park	440,000
Southern Utah	518,454
	3,710,454

This amount has been produced from a total of nearly 150,000 tons of ore, showing the average value of the ore to the smelter and mill-man to have been in the neighborhood of $24.75 per ton. The assay-value was larger by about 25 per cent.

Little Cottonwood district.—A very large number of mines in this cañon have been worked uninterruptedly during the year, and the results have been, as a whole, extremely satisfactory. As shafts and inclines have been sunk deeper on Emma Hill, and connecting-levels driven between the large claims, every development points to the conclusion that there is at least one large ore-bearing zone crossing the hill diagonally. Not improbably, several parallel zones exist. On the large "vein" are the Emma, North Star, Vallejo, South Star, Flagstaff, and probably the Reed and Benson. What are known as the Grizzly Flat mines, of which the Davenport is the most important, belong, doubtless, to another belt, not as yet so fully explored as the first. The hill on the south side of Alta, on which is the Iris tunnel, has been prospected considerably during the year, with good results. Below Alta, for a distance of three miles and on both sides of the cañon, numerous outcrops have been found, but the ores here appear to be more appropriate for milling than smelting, as they do not contain so high a percentage of lead as the ores nearer the head of the cañon. As they are also of rather low grade in silver, there has not been so much encouragement to mining here, since there is no amalgamation-mill in the immediate vicinity.

Alta City is now connected with the valley by railroads. The Wasatch and Jordan Valley Road (steam) extends about six miles up into the cañon. From that point a single-track mule tram-way has been built to the Emma Mine. All but the last four miles have been inclosed in sheds, and during 1876 the rest will be covered. Freights to Sandy are reduced $2.50 per ton, and as the production of the camp is not less than 30,000 tons, this reduction represents a saving to the producers which is itself enough for a reasonable profit on a number of mining enterprises.

It has been noticed by smelters in the valley that the percentage of lead in the ore is not as large as formerly, and that the percentage of iron is slightly greater. It would be hasty to conclude from this (as some have done) that the character of the ore on Emma Hill (from which place most of the product is obtained) is changing as depth is gained, though this is perhaps not unlikely to occur. But the fact probably is that much more low-grade ore was shipped last year than previously, and a good deal of this has been milling-ore.

So far as an intelligent understanding of the geology of Emma Hill is concerned, the developments made in the Bay City tunnel late in the year are the most important of the year's operations. The company running this tunnel had driven it 1,400 feet without encountering any large or promising bodies of ore until late in December, when, according to surveys almost directly underneath the workings of the North Star and of the Emma Mines, a large body of ore is reported to have been struck. It seems quite probable that this is a continuation of the ore-channel above, and the circumstance affords great encouragement to those who had become skeptical of the permanence of the deposits in Little Cottonwood. The head of the tunnel is fully 1,200 feet (measured on the dip of the rock) beneath the surface, and the general character of the country-rock remains substantially the same as it was at and near the surface. It is the intention of this company to prosecute work until the mountain shall have been bored through, and Big Cottonwood Cañon reached. It is believed that other ore-channels exist beyond those of the Emma.

The Emma has remained idle the entire year. There are many among the miners and residents who confidently assert the abundance of ore in the mine, which can be taken out with great profit under good management. The unfortunate troubles into which the mine has fallen do not give promise of any immediate resumption of work. In the winter of 1874–'75 a portion of the ore-house and concentration-works was carried away by a snow-slide, and it will now require a considerable outlay to put the surface plant in working order.

The North Star and Bruno was sold late in the year for $100,000 to a Chicago company. Since that time it has been producing on an average about 10 tons daily of very good ore, and during the coming year it will probably become one of the largest producing mines in the district. The ore is of average grade, and occurs in large bodies.

The Flagstaff at the close of the year had been sunk to a depth of 450 feet below the tunnel. A fine set of hoisting and pumping machinery has been erected, at a cost of about $30,000, which is operated by compressed air. The engines for compressing the air are located at the bottom of the hill, and the power is conveyed to the mine through a 4½-inch conducting-pipe, at a pressure of 90 pounds to the inch. This pipe is 2,000 feet long and leads to a storing tank at the mine 4 by 10 feet in size. The hoisting-engines are double, 10-inch cylinders, 12-inch stroke, with a 6-foot reel, around which is wound the 2½-inch cable. The latter has a tension of 35 tons, and the engines have a capacity of raising 25 tons an hour from present depth. The tanks and pipes are capable of holding 374 cubic feet of air. The exhaust is emptied at the bottom of the mine, thus affording excellent ventilation. As this mine, in common with many others in the vicinity, is involved in litigation, no official statement of its product during the year is available. I believe it has been about $350,000.

The South Star and Titus Mine is one of the most extensively worked claims on the hill. Its underground workings are a labyrinth of tortuous drifts and chambers, slopes, winzes, and shafts, the equal of which can only be found (if at all) in some others on the same hill.

In the Vallejo Mine the incline was 630 feet from the surface at the close of the year. The mine has produced quite steadily, although not largely. A good deal of prospecting has been necessary. The wire tram way has worked admirably, even in the deepest snows. A portion of it, however, was slightly damaged in a slide last winter.

The Reed & Benson has been worked under lease mostly, and has produced a fair quantity of ore.

The Golconda, which was discovered in June, developed from the start a fine body of ore, and paid, from the beginning, every expense connected with mining. It has been opened by about 200 feet of levels, and showed at the close of the year large quantities of reserves.

The group of mines which includes the Prince of Wales, Wellington, and several others, has been consolidated under one company, controlled by the Walker Brothers, of Salt Lake. The deposit seems to be a stratum, is very regular in its dip and width, and carries richer ore than the majority of mines in the cañon. Throughout the year from 70 to 125 men have been steadily employed, and a large amount of ore has been extracted. A fine set of hoisting-machinery has been erected, at a cost of $30,000. Steam-power is used, the necessary water for the boilers being forced up from the gulch, nearly a mile off, through 2-inch iron pipes. An underground tram-way, 1,800 feet in length, has been laid, on which the ore is carried to a point down the slope of the hill and beyond the reach of the heavy snow-slides, that have during former winters so seriously impeded shipments. At the close of the year the mine was shipping about 18 tons daily.

The Davenport, which, so far as reputation is concerned, is the most important mine in the vicinity of Grizzly Flat, has been idle nearly throughout the year. In its vicinity the Dexter, King of the West, Vanderbilt, Darlington, Olive, Regulator, Imperial, Evergreen, and a number of other claims have been worked with encouraging results, and some ore has been shipped. About 1,000 feet of shafting and drifting will represent the amount of work done.

The Emerald Company struck a large body of ore in the Iris tunnel early in the year, and immediately began the erection of a surface tramway from the mouth of the tunnel to the foot of the hill. It is 1,600 feet in length, well laid, and railed with T-iron.

The Equitable tunnel is reported to have encountered good ore during the fall, but, so far as I can ascertain, none has been shipped.

Of the new discoveries the most important are the Swansea, Golconda, North Star, Gladiator, and Kinney.

American Fork district.—But little work was done in this cañon during the year. The Miller smelter, upon which the miners depended largely for the reduction of their ore, has been idle through the entire year, and though several times there were reports that it was to be re-opened, that much-looked-for event has not yet occurred. Nevertheless, a fair amount of ore has been shipped to Sandy and elsewhere. The mines producing most have been the Wild Dutchman and Sunday. Occasional lots of ore have been shipped from the Miller and others, but it has been the work of prospectors or transient leasers.

The condition of the mines at the close of the year was, therefore, not very different from their condition in December, 1874. The following data represent the state in which they were found by Mr. Van Wagenen: The Miller Mine is opened by about 2,500 feet of tunnel-work, cutting the deposit at six different points on the hill. The underground workings are a complicated combination of shafts, inclines, levels, and stopes, which cannot be clearly described in words. A considerable quantity of ore is exposed, worth, perhaps, $30 to $50 per ton.

The Pittsburgh Mine has been developed by about 2,000 feet of shafts and levels, and an immense body of low-grade ore has been exposed.

Although capable of yielding from 50 to 100 tons per day, it is unworked, probably on account of the low grade of its ores, which cannot be profitably shipped out of the district.

The Wild Dutchman is now reached through a tunnel 320 feet in length. It is developed pretty thoroughly by several thousand feet of workings, and has produced steadily throughout the year.

The Sunday Mine is a vein in quartzite, carrying ore rich in gold. The mine was worked for some time before the true value of the ore was discovered. This did not occur till late in the year, and subsequently a small lot of about 15 tons was shipped to Sandy, which yielded over $500 per ton. From reports received subsequent to Mr. Van Wagenen's visit, I judge that the lot referred to must have been rather an accidental bonanza in the vein, for the second shipment was as great a surprise to the owners as the first, but, unfortunately, in the opposite sense.

Among the other numerous mines of this cañon which are in a promising condition, mention may be made of the Live Yankee, Roessler, Bredemeyer No. 2, Silver Dipper, Wyoming, Caribou, Southern Spy, Comet, and Bullion.

Parley's Park district.—The Ontario is the only mine of note on which work has been prosecuted during the year. There have been numerous prospects in the vicinity, but none, as yet, have attained great prominence. Among them may be mentioned the California Central, Bullion, Flagstaff, Walker & Webster, Pioneer, McHenry, Switzerland, Iron-Horse, General Washington, Hawkeye, Daniel O'Connell, Mountain Top, Great American, Piñon, and Pirate. From most of these ore has been taken and shipped during the year, and some have produced considerably. Their production has, however, been intermittent.

The shaft on the Ontario Mine has been sunk to 400 feet, and the ground explored on either side for a distance of 300 and 500 feet. The vein is a contact one, having quartzite for the foot-wall and porphyry for the hanging. It has an average width of 2 feet, with an ore-seam that has so far shown great regularity. It carries little or no galena, and is a true milling-ore. The mineral is treated in the McHenry Mill by amalgamation. The mill went into operation in June, and has been producing steadily since, having a capacity of 20 tons per day.

The extensive developments on the mine have shown it to be a vein of great promise. The explorations of the year have gone far in advance of the production, while the latter has been much greater than are the company's milling facilities. As a consequence, it is estimated that from $500,000 to $1,000,000 of reserves are in sight, and the owners of the mine are expecting to lease and put in operation the Marsac Mill, which will exactly double the reducing capacity. As the valuable character of this vein has been shown, there has of course been much search after its extensions, and it is thought that these have been found in the Hawkeye and Irish-American.

Although the McHenry Mine has never yet been profitably productive, the company owning it proposes to explore it still farther, and are sanguine of ultimate success. Not less than $300,000 has been expended on the mine and mill. The latter is employed in treating Ontario ore.

The Hawkeye has been developed to a depth of 65 feet, and opened by a 140-foot tunnel.

The Switzerland has a shaft 130 feet deep, with good ore at the bottom. This vein is also cut by a tunnel 175 feet long.

The General Washington shows a good vein of ore of fair grade. A tunnel is being run than will cut the vein 350 feet below the surface.

The Great American has reached a depth of 60 feet, and is quite promising.

The Walker & Webster has produced steadily during the year, shipping its ore, which is suitable for smelting, to the Utah Sampling Works.

Two tunnels, the Washington and the Minnesota, are cutting under the mountains of this district. The former, which is situated a mile west of the Ontario, cut a very promising vein during December, on which work will be immediately commenced. The latter, which is something over 500 feet long, has, after passing across three veins of minor importance and size, intersected a crevice about 10 feet in width, which carries a good body of ore. This property is owned by Dr. Reed, of Wyoming, and promises better results than most enterprises of a similar nature.

This district is under much disadvantage in having no smelting-works. There is apparently an abundance of galena-ores, carrying from 15 to 50 ounces in silver per ton, in the claims of the southern and southwestern part of the camp, which will not now pay for treatment if the ore must be transported to Salt Lake, but which can be made quite profitable if treated in the vicinity. Several parties are considering the erection of works here in the spring.

Bingham, or West Mountain district.—The mines of Bingham Cañon produced last year a total of about 30,000 tons of ore, carrying silver-lead and a small quantity (merely nominal) of gold. The assay-percentage of lead in such ores of this district as come into market is usually estimated at 45. During 1875 so large an amount of milling-ore was produced, and so many new discoveries had been made of this desirable class of mineral, that at the close of the year arrangements had been concluded to erect amalgamation-works at the mouth of the cañon or at Sandy, the main inducement for their erection being the large and steady supply of ore attainable from the Mayflower Mine, which is now shipping all the way to Reno, Nev.. Bingham Cañon annually produces a little gulch-gold. The first discoverers of the gulch extracted a large amount of dust from the creek, but the bars were not deep enough to last long, and are now but little worked. The amount extracted in 1875 did not exceed $30,000. Several companies have been at work in Bear Creek, and some Chinamen have been busy in the main gulch.

The ores of the cañon are treated mostly at Sandy and at the Germania Works. At Bingham Junction the Sheridan Hill Works were running during part of the year.

Early in the year the Winnamuck Company shut down its smelter, and since then it has been shipping ore. The production of the year has been small, and the work has been mainly prospecting. In following the vein into the hill much barren ground has been encountered. Explorations have been continued in that direction perseveringly and are still going on; but more encouraging results have been obtained in sinking below the huge ore-body which was the source of the large former production of this mine. It is now pretty well decided that the outcrop on the other side of the gulch and some little distance up the creek, known as the Dixon, is the same vein as the Winnamuck. The ledge has suffered an unusual amount of distortion, and is probably much faulted in the gulch. The company determined, toward the end of the year, to sink a shaft at the bottom of the hill, and, when this had reached sufficient depth, to drift both ways on the ledge and thereby test whether the Dixon is really an extension, or whether the lode is lost in the gulch. This work is now in progress, and suitable hoisting and pumping machinery is to be built over the shaft. In other parts of the mine about 20 men have been at work.

The Dixon (supposed to be an extension of the Winnamuck) has been opened by a shaft now between 150 and 200 feet deep. In December a large body of rich ore was reported to have been struck. This mine is worked by the Winnamuck Company. An extension still farther north on the same vein has been located, and is said to promise well.

The Spanish Mine has been worked steadily throughout the year, and has maintained a fair production. For many months past more attention has been paid to placing the property in better shape by replacing the old timbers with new square sets than to taking out ore. This has been rendered necessary by the dangerous condition in which the mine was found by its present superintendent, Mr. W. W. Gallagher. In retimbering bad ground and clearing away dangerous *débris*, much valuable ore has been found that had escaped previous notice. There is no lack of good mineral in sight at present. Any attempt to designate the position of the exposed bodies of ore would be unintelligible to the reader, and can only be understood by surveys, as the mine belongs to that class of subterranean quarries consisting mainly of galleries running in all directions, in which the most expert mining-engineer will be lost without his compass. This method of extraction finds, however, in the nature of the ore deposit and the economical conditions of the locality a plausible, perhaps a wholly valid, excuse. The expense of timbering is its great drawback. This is now executed in an extremely creditable manner.

The production of the Neptune and Kempton property has been about 4,000 tons during the year. Ten times that quantity could have been extracted without opening any new ground. The main work of the year has been the driving of the deep tunnel, which is to cut the lode 700 feet below its outcrop. To meet this a shaft has been sunk on the vein and on the line of the tunnel. At the close of the year the tunnel was thought to be in close proximity to the vein, but had not yet reached it. In many parts of the mine the reserves of ore at hand are very great. In that portion around the Galena chamber the body of mineral is apparently 20 feet in width and of excellent quality. Not far off considerable excitement was caused by the discovery of a body of black oxide of copper, which at one place was 14 feet in width. In October the lessees of the mine leased the Sheridan Hill smelter at Bingham Junction, and smelted their own ore during the remainder of the year.

The Jordan Mine has been worked intermittently during the year. When working with full force its production has ranged from 30 to 40 tons a day. The mine shows plenty of ore in sight, and is capable of maintaining the above production at least.

The Utah has been idle during the entire year, excepting that a few parties have been gleaning what little mineral was left in sight.

The Mayflower has reached a depth of 500 feet, and as depth has been gained there appears to be no diminution in the abundance of ore. Expensive hoisting-works have been erected during the year, and the mine throughout is in excellent condition. During the fall a sample lot of the ore, which is milling-ore, comparatively free from lead, was shipped to Fairfield for trial in the mill at that place. The trial having proved a success, the mill is to be removed to Sandy, and the ore treated there instead of being shipped to Reno, as has heretofore been the case. The ore from this mine is worth from $50 to $70 per ton. The production during the year has amounted, as nearly as I can learn, to 3,500 tons.

The Yosemite has developed during the year an extraordinary display of ore. The body of mineral which appeared on the surface has held out almost without interruption to the bottom of the shaft, which is a little over 400 feet deep. In November a body of ore was struck which has proved of great lateral extent, and is from 15 to 25 feet in width. It is of rather low grade, but, owing to the quantity in sight, can be mined at a good profit. The yield of the mine has averaged 15 tons per day, the ore being worth in the neighborhood of $25 per ton.

The Last Chance has been producing regularly. At the end of the year the tunnel had reached a length of nearly 1,000 feet, and was expected shortly to cut the vein.

The Nez Perces Chief has not been doing much during the year, but is expected to re-open early in the spring.

The Aladdin has shipped during the year about 1,000 tons of very good ore.

Among the new discoveries of the year the Albino, Live Yankee, Winnebago, and Tiewaukie are most prominent. A large number of the older mines have been worked with satisfactory results, among which may be mentioned the Revere, Ashland, Bully Boy, Live Pine, Sacramento, Williams, Montreal, Hamlin, and Owyhee. The cheap freights that result from the successful operation of the Bingham Cañon Railroad (narrow gauge) permit the profitable mining of ore of very low grade, and several mines have thus been continued in operation which otherwise would have been forced to shut down.

Ophir district.—This district, including Dry and East Cañons, is undoubtedly one of the best in Utah. Dry Cañon has produced very heavily during the year, and the mines now working are in promising condition. In East Cañon the work has been rather in the nature of prospecting. The rich but precarious deposits of Lion Hill and Chloride Flat have attracted numerous sanguine explorers, but have generally failed to pay for development. Yet the product of much desultory extraction has been the shipment of a considerable quantity of ore, some of which has been of very high grade.

In the Chicago and the Waterman Works, at Rush Lake, almost all the ore of these camps has been treated. The former has been supplied mainly by the Queen of the Hills and the Chicago Mine, but has bought all custom-ore offered. The works were running during the greater part of the year. The Waterman Works were running steadily during the last half of the year almost entirely on Hidden Treasure ore. The Walker Mill at Ophir made a short run during the summer, and turned out about $20,000. The amount of ore treated was 1,600 tons. The Enterprise Mill and Mr. Mayer's arrastras also did a few months' work on ores from East Cañon.

The East Cañon mines produced in 1875, as nearly as can be ascertained, not less than 7,500 tons of ore. Of this amount the Ophir Company (Miner's Delight Mine) produced 3,000 tons, and the remainder came mainly from Lion Hill.

The Ophir Company's operations were not satisfactory. A very large amount of development was done, but the ore found was of so low grade as to be unprofitable. The explorations have been pushed extensively in every direction upon the claim, but with only a moderate degree of success. During the year considerable ore has been extracted and sold. Toward the end of the season it was thought that the incline was approaching a better class of material, and later advices show that the belief was partially realized. The ore taken from the Miner's Delight during the season has averaged about 20 ounces silver and 10 per cent. of lead. The first-class ore, of which but a small quantity was shipped, did not return more than 35 ounces silver and 25 per cent. lead. Over 400 square sets of timber were put up in the mine during the year.

On both slopes of the cañon, from base to crown, the mountain-side is dotted with prospects and mines. Hardly 10 per cent. of the claims located are worked to a depth of 50 feet, and even a much smaller proportion than that would include all operating on any well-defined vein.

On the top of Mountain Lion Hill is a group of mines that have been worked during the year with tolerable persistency. The country-rock is a limestone, between the strata, and in the seams of which occur argentiferous galena, and often horn-silver. Some extraordinarily rich, but small, deposits of the latter mineral have been found. The veins, or lines of deposit, cross each other at every conceivable angle, and, as a consequence, the tenure of mining-property is not well defined. The most prominent of these are the Tiger, Monarch, Zella, Mountain Lion, Silver Chief, Chloride Point, and Sunnyside. The ores average from 2 to 10 per cent. of lead, and are said to carry, besides the chloride, some bromide and iodide of silver.

On the northern slope of the cañon the mines appear in a more regular formation, often occurring as defined zones, and carrying large veins of ore. Of this class the San Joaquin and Little Peru are the most prominent examples. The Jim Fisk, Bonanza, California Boy, and Grey Rock are others of minor note. The ore from these claims carries often considerable arsenical pyrites and manganese.

The two great mines of Dry Cañon—the Hidden Treasure and the Flavilla—have well sustained the reputation of the district. Both mines have been worked uninterruptedly during the year, and, so far as a display of ore in reserves is concerned, are in magnificent condition.

The Hidden Treasure is now developed to a depth of 1,100 feet below its outcrop. A tunnel has been run into the hill which cuts the vein 900 feet in depth, and through which, before long, the entire extraction will be carried on. The vein appears to be a contact layer. It is not very regular, but has usually an upper wall of slate and a lower one of limestone, between which the ore lies, varying in width from 6 inches to 15 feet. The production has been from 30 to 40 tons daily throughout the year, a figure which could now easily be trebled, as the reserves in sight are enormous. The mine is opened very extensively, though rather irregularly. In November a chamber was being cut on the tunnel-level at the head of the main shaft, in which large hoisting-engines were to be erected. Other improvements were being made in order to put the mine in better form than it has shown for several years past. Toward the close of the year the shipments had increased to 50 and 60 tons daily.

The Queen of the Hills and Flavilla, which are now the property of the Chicago Company, are in a very flattering condition. The vein (a layer) dips into the hill at a very slight inclination, and has been followed downward on this incline for 600 feet. From this central work three inclined levels branch off to the east and two to the west, the five having a combined length of 2,600 feet. Between these a vast amount of stoping has been done, especially in the upper "backs" near the surface. The ore ranges in width from 3 to 12 feet, and yields at the mill from 40 to 50 ounces in silver and 30 per cent. of lead. The shipments have averaged about 30 tons daily throughout the year. The surface works of the mine are situated about 300 feet above the "grade," or stage-road, which connects Dry Cañon with the valley. A surface tram-way has been laid on the slope of the hill from the mouth of the mine to the road, and ore is carried down in cars and loaded directly into the wagons.

In driving the upper levels east in this mine, a complete break in the vein was found at a distance of about 800 feet from the shaft. The entire formation appeared to be completely cut off by a cross-course or a fault in the country-rock. After the breast of the level had been driven ahead several feet in the barren rock without finding anything, it was determined to sink a shaft on the edge of the slip. This was done, and at a depth of 20 feet the vein was found again as perfect as ever. On being followed another break was found, and again the same expedient was adopted with a similar result. At the time of Mr. Van Wagenen's visit the level had been driven on for some distance beyond the last fault, and the vein still continued regular. From other explorations above and below, it is likely that this fault crosses the entire mountain and breaks the vein in its path, giving it a displacement of about 22 feet.

The Chicago, which has reached a depth of over 1,200 feet, has been worked continuously throughout the year, but not extensively. It has produced a fair quantity of ore.

The Mono, once a famous mine of Dry Cañon, and supposed to be as good now as ever, has been idle during the entire year, excepting that several parties of lessees have been exploring the abandoned upper workings in search of what ore was left. The vein is reported to be lost, and it is likely that a break or fault has been met with similar to that found in the Queen of the Hills, and perhaps not more formidable.

Of the other mines in the cañon, the Sacramento, Poor-man, Rattler, Dexter, Mayflower, Fourth of July, Emporia, and Eureka have been worked to a considerable extent, and given promising exposures of ore, with some actual production. Beside these a large number of claims have been worked which on account of the insignificance of their development, cannot receive special mention this year.

Dry Cañon will next year be better provided with smelting facilities than it has been heretofore. A movement is on foot to open the old Jacob Smelter at Stockton for custom-work. Mr. John Longmaid, of Ophir City, has charge of the business, and in order to secure to his company a steady supply of ores, has leased a couple of mines in East Cañon that are showing good bodies of galena-ores.

SOUTHERN UTAH.

Under this head are embraced the districts lying on the lower extremity of the Oquirrh range, and between it and the Arizona line. The valleys of Utah have a general north and south trend, and are approximately parallel with each other. Following them toward the south, they lead gradually and imperceptibly into the mesa and cañon lands bordering on the Colorado River. To this boundary-line the prospector has pursued his work, and numerous mineral-districts have been discovered, some presenting an abundance of lead-ores and others a preponderance of copper. All are more or less argentiferous. The most important are Camp Floyd, East and West Tintic, Tom Paine, Star, San Francisco, Granite, and Bonanza City districts.

The distance of these localities from railroads and the average low grade of their ores have retarded their development. Quite a number of mills and smelting-furnaces exist in them, hardly a camp being without a reduction process of some kind; but none have made steady runs, and it is necessary to transport the ores to Sandy or Rush Lake at considerable expense.

Camp Floyd district has produced but little during the year. Its ores, mostly of low grade, (from 15 to 30 ounce,) must be reduced by milling in the vicinity of the mines. The character of the silver-ore deposits also forbids profitable mining except on a large scale and with the aid of capital, there being no distinct veins, but rather an impregnated stratum of quartzite of great width, in the cavities and seams of which chlorides, bromides, and other argentiferous minerals occur. Quite a number of minor claims have been working during the year, among which may be mentioned the Queen of the West, Sparrow Hawk, and Jenny Lind. In the latter cinnabar has been found.

Tintic district, located about 70 miles south of Salt Lake, has improved but slightly during the year. The Utah Southern Railroad is now within 18 miles of East Tintic, while the Utah Western has been surveyed directly through West Tintic, and in a couple of years will doubtless be extended at least so far on its road to Pioche. At present the terminus of the latter road is some 60 miles away, and the former offers the cheapest route for transporting ores to market.

Eureka Hill, on account of the richness of its ores, has attracted more prospecting and development than any other section of Tintic district, and here most of the work of the year was done. The principal mines are, however, still in litigation and idle, (that is, the company is doing no systematic work,) but various lessees have been taking out ore from some of the old works, and some adventurers have been pursuing their vocation on abandoned properties, so that there has been at all times during the year a small but steady production from the camp. The facilities for reducing ores in the camp are represented by four mills and three smelters, all of which have been in operation for a short time during the year. But they have been run with such irregularity and under so many managements that it is impossible to learn anything definite of their operations. The largest part of the production of the mines has been shipped away as ore; but, besides this, there have been shipments of silver bullion, lead bars, and copper-matte.

The Crismon and Mammoth Copperopolis mines have not been worked to any extent during the year, and are practically in the same condition as at the close of 1874.

Among the promising *working* properties of the district are the Bullion, Sunbeam, Brooklyn, Bowers, Morning Glory, Shower, and Gold Hill mines. These have yielded considerably more than one-half of the ore produced, the remainder having come from the work of lessees or poachers, operating intermittently and on a small scale.

Tom Paine district is one of the new discoveries of the year, having been located in the fall. It is 180 miles south of Salt Lake and 108 miles from the terminus of the Utah Southern Railroad. The locations of promise are the Silver Dipper, Blue Jean, Munroe, Hidden Treasure, Mono, Bully Boy, Ingersoll, and Liberal. The ores are galenas and carbonates of lead, carrying from 15 to 40 ounces in silver. Some rich chlorides have also been found.

Star district is slowly developing a regular production. The Sherman smelter, which has been in frequent operation during the year, has treated a portion of the ore produced, but much more has gone to Sandy. The two great mines of the district, the Rebel and the Big Bonanza, have together produced during the year, as nearly as I can ascertain, about 3,200 tons of galena and carbonates. In the workings of the former, which are quite extensive, an immense body of mineral is exposed, and the property is universally held to be of great value. Of the other mines of the camp, the Rainbow and the Minnesota are the most noteworthy.

In *Granite district* about half a dozen mines have been under work during the year, with moderate success, and of *San Francisco district* the same may be said. What has been done in both has been done in the way of development, and with little or no outside aid.

Bonanza City district.—This district, of which Bonanza City is the center, is in Washington County, about 20 miles south of the southern rim of the Salt Lake Basin. Prominence was first given to the district by the discovery of petrified wood, in the seams of which silver chloride and native silver occurred. Further explorations demonstrated that the formations around the city were highly metalliferous, and the camp is now, considering its remote location, one of the most promising in the Territory. The formation is said to be mainly sandstone, but it is probable that quartzite is the predominating rock. There are numerons veins of considerable regularity, and also localities where the formation is impregnated and without system. The ores are, so far, chlorides and bromides, more or less mixed with lead, arsenic, iron, and copper, the latter being the most abundant of the baser metals. Some of the ore is extremely rich, milling from $300 to $1,200 per ton, according to the care with which it is selected or dressed. As yet there are no reducing-works on the spot, but it is expected that in 1876 several mills will be built. The existence of rich mines was not known till the fall of 1875, and consequently the amount of development has been small, though the value of such ores as were shipped amounted in total to between $10,000 and $15,000. The most noted claims are the Pride of the West, Susan, Tecumseh, and Buckeye.

The Grand Gulch Copper Company, having a mine across the border, in Arizona, has erected a furnace near Saint George, in Utah, and will attempt in the coming year to smelt the abundant and rich copper mineral from that claim. The lode has not been developed additionally during the past year, but is reported capable of a large production from the surface.

CHAPTER VII.

COLORADO.

The reports which have been furnished to me in regard to the production of Colorado Territory during 1875 vary somewhat, but not sufficiently, so far as totals are concerned, to render them untrustworthy.

As the values in all business transactions in Colorado are expressed in currency, the statisticians of the Territory have followed the general custom; and I have therefore had to reduce the important amounts to a gold basis, taking gold at the average of $1.16 for the year, in order to bring them into harmony with my previous estimates.

Mr. T. F. Van Wagenen furnished me at the close of the year with a report on the condition of the mining-industry at that time. This report, the notes of my deputy, Mr. A. Eilers, who visited the Territory twice in the summer, and various information kindly furnished to me by different professional gentlemen during the year, constitute the material upon which the present report is based.

Mr. Van Wagenen includes in his report the following exhibit of production, which I adopt as probably nearest to the truth, giving the gold values of my informant's currency figures:

	Currency.	Coin.
Gold-dust and retorts	$1, 641, 109	$1, 414, 636
Gold and silver bars	2, 868, 842	2, 472, 941
Ore shipped from Territory	1, 416, 000	1, 220, 592
Gold consumed at home	150, 000	129, 300
Total gold and silver	6, 075, 951	5, 237, 470
Copper	75, 000	64, 650
Lead	800	689
Total metals	6, 151, 751	5, 302, 810

Arranged according to counties, this yield appears as follows:

	Currency.	Coin.
Clear Creek County	$2, 110, 902	$1, 819, 598
Gilpin County	1, 763, 985	1, 520, 555
Park County	758, 000	653, 396
Boulder County	558, 000	480, 996
Fremont County	234, 200	201, 880
San Juan and southern mines	400, 664	345, 372
Summit County	76, 000	65, 512
Lake County	100, 000	86, 200
Other sources	150, 000	129, 300
Total	6, 151, 751	5, 302, 810

The gold and silver production, $5,237,469.76, shows a decrease of over $120,000 as compared with the previous year, the reason for which may be readily found in the unfortunate litigations at Georgetown, which stopped several mines effectually.

The coal-production during the year is calculated by Capt. E. L. Berthoud at about 75,000 tons, worth at the pit's mouth $225,000.

Dividing the above yield of $5,237,470 into gold and silver, as well as the insufficient data furnished me will permit, we have the following:

Gold	$2,224,568
Silver	3,012,902
Total	5,237,470

Mr. F. Fosset, of the Central City Register, who, to judge from various articles written by him on the subject both in the Central City Register and in the Engineering and Mining Journal, appears to have paid much attention to the yield of last year, gives in one of his latest articles the production in currency as follows:

	Currency.
Clear Creek County	$2,064,863
Gilpin County	1,763,986
Park County	835,800
Boulder County	767,000
Fremont County	342,000
Summit County	142,000
Lake County	120,940
San Juan and elsewhere	263,228
	6,299,817

In this are included, besides gold and silver, the items of copper and lead produced during 1875. Mr. Van Wagenen's currency-estimate for the same items being $6,151,751, it is seen that the discrepancy in the totals is only $148,066, a small sum, when the difficulty of collecting this kind of information from private concerns in the absence of compulsory laws enforcing truthful statements is borne in mind. In the subdivision by counties there are in several cases such large differences in the estimates that it seems difficult to account for them, and I can imagine no other cause than inaccurate reports as to the source of shipments from the railroads.

The receipts of the Denver branch mint during the year were as follows:

First quarter, January to April	$133,446 66
Second quarter, April to July	162,566 72
Third quarter, July to October	243,069 01
Fourth quarter, October to January	218,098 50
	757,180 89

The achievements of the year 1875 in Colorado mining include, aside from a large amount of work performed on the old and well-proven mines, the inauguration of a great number of enterprises, and the opening of several entirely new and apparently important districts, which may be now recorded as among the standard ones of the Territory. At the close of 1874, eight smelting and amalgamating works were in operation, and five parties were shiping ore out of the Territory.

The total metal-yield for that year amounted to $5,362,383. At the present time eleven beneficiating works are in active operation, and eight ore-buyers are shipping the high grades east. There were no concentrating establishments in successful operation during 1874, except the one at Idaho, which ran only for a few weeks. At the close of this year three large works, with a combined capacity of over a hundred tons daily, have been built at Georgetown, and will undoubtedly affect very largely the production of metals during 1876. The Collom Company has been energetically at work during the year on a comprehensive plan, and is just completing its central works at Golden City. This company already has separating and concentrating establishments at Idaho and Black Hawk, and contemplates erecting others at Georgetown and Boulder. The smelting-works at Golden will receive the products from the branch works, and either smelt them into lead rich in gold and silver, or separate the bullion, as may be found most advisable and economical.

The Golden Smelting Company, under Mr. West, the Rosita Reduction-Works, the Mount Lincoln Smelting-Works, and Green & Co.'s Works in Baker's Park have been the year's additions to the smelting-capacity of the Territory. Two new amalgamating-works have been built.

Mr. Stewart, at Georgetown, has supplemented his establishment with the Hunt & Douglas process, and is now treating gold and copper, as well as silver ores. Several attempts have been made at chlorination in Boulder and Park Counties, with no definite success as yet. Several new stamp-mills have been built, and most of the old ones have been working steadily throughout the year. Several entirely new mining-districts have been discovered during the year, viz: The Rabbit-Ear, in Grand County, containing mines of argentiferous galena; the Magnolia, in Boulder County, with ores of gold and silver combined with tellurium; and the Uncompahgre, Gunnison, and Lake districts, in the south-western part of the Territory, where the ores are mostly those of silver; and the districts back of Fort Collins, in which has been found good nickel-bearing pyrites, besides the ordinary galena and pyritous ores, carrying gold and silver.

Four of the older districts, discovered years ago, and the history of which has been one of alternate growth and retrogression, are now showing signs of renewed vigor, and will probably maintain a steady growth hereafter. These are Empire, (gold,) Gold Hill, (gold,) Jim Creek, (gold and tellurium,) and Daily, (silver.)

Six of the districts discovered during 1873 and 1874 have passed safely through the vicissitudes of early age, and are already producing in considerable amounts and with regularity. The Summit and Eureka, (San Juan,) Rosita, (Fremont County,) Sunshine, (Boulder County,) Geneva, (Clear Creek County,) and Hans Peak, (Grand County.)

The proportion of silver to gold produced shows a regular and rapid increase, which fact may be considered as an advantage to the general condition of the industry, inasmuch as silver-mining presents fewer risks and more favorable chances than gold-mining. About three-fifths of the precious-metal production of the mines is now silver, whereas in 1866 that metal bore the proportion of about one-fifth.

In Georgetown and Central, the oldest two camps in the Territory, the fierce litigations that have for many years retarded the development of the mines, and caused so much distrust to investors, show signs of dying out. Though several of the largest and most valuable mines are still hampered by expensive lawsuits, it is not likely that many new ones of great magnitude will arise, as pre-emptors are generally exercising more care in regard to their titles, and are compromising with contestants whenever possible. The demand for patents was never so great as at present, evidencing that owners have confidence in the value of their property, and are willing to expend money in what may be considered a species of dead-work.

The placer interests have enlarged greatly during the year, the amount of ground now under improvement being fully one third more than during 1874. The gain has been in the South Park, Bear Valley, South Clear Creek, Arkansas Valley, and at the base of Hans Peak, where gold has been found to exist over much larger areas than had before been supposed. The successful introduction of the most approved California machinery, and the extension of the "booming" system, (described in a former report,) have made available large districts of comparatively good ground, which may now be washed with profit. While the placer-mining interests of Colorado can never be expected to assume the enormous dimensions of those of the Pacific coast, (because the formations are more local,) they are yet good for many millions of gold, and offer inducements for the investment of capital. Observation during the last twelve years has shown that both the rain-fall and snow-fall have increased, and with each year of ordinary weather a larger quantity of water may be expected. It is true that, at the same time, owing to the removal of large bodies of timber from the mountains, the winters' snows disappear more rapidly, and with a greater tendency to freshets; but this difficulty will be obviated gradually by the construction of reservoirs, and the growth of new forests, already springing up around the older settlements, which were deprived of their trees in the early days of mining in the country.

The production of pig-lead for the year has been small. The Lincoln City Works have been idle for the entire year and the Golden Works did not open till September. Quite a large amount of this metal has been turned out from the new works in Baker Park, and if the run had been one of a year, instead of a few months, the total would have been a large addition to the product of the Territory.

The copper out-put remains substantially as it was last year. The only works saving this metal are at Black Hawk and Golden, and as the source of supply is mainly from the pyritous gold-ores of Gilpin, Boulder, and Park Counties, the production will advance very slowly. Of the copper-bearing veins there are plenty in Colorado, and so advantageously located as to offer unusual inducements for the erection of works to smelt the ores, if the mines were opened sufficiently to supply them. Till this is done, and the necessary works are built, however, the Territory cannot be expected to become a great producer of copper.

Of the rarer metals, tellurium, bismuth, and nickel may be mentioned. The belt of mines carrying tellurides of gold and silver, which last year was supposed to be confined to the veins on Gold Hill, has been traced north and south for a total distance of nearly twenty miles, and as rich ore found as was ever taken from the Red Cloud or Cold Spring. Bismuth has been found to a high percentage in the argentiferous galena of the Geneva and Snake River mines, and nickel, besides, occurring, as was known last year, in Gilpin County and in the Home-Stake lode, has lately been found in veins carrying true copper-nickel in the northern part of the Territory.

One of the most important enterprises of the year connected with the mining-industry was the formation, on June 1, of the Colorado Mining and Exchange Board. At first this institution had to contend with great difficulties, and received but little encouragement; but at the close of the year it had become pretty firmly established. The board now numbers 35 members, and has a list of good mines on which stock-transactions to the amount of nearly $100,000 had taken place between June 1 and the end of the year. The board has a fine room in Denver, meets daily at 11.45 a. m., and attracts always a large crowd of visitors. It is thought that during 1876 its business will have so augmented that it will affect very considerably the introduction of capital and hasten the development of a great number of the mines.

CONDITION OF THE SMELTING BUSINESS.

For the past five years Colorado has been a battle-ground for smelting companies. Its mining-district, situated on both sides of the great continental divide, which at no point sinks to an altitude less than 10,000 feet above the sea, are not easily accessible from any one central point, nor are they conveniently located with respect to each other. But one mining-town in the State is reached by rail, all the others being from 18 to 300 miles away from steam-communication. Several have between them and the rest of the world the barrier of the Great Divide, a wall which in most places is completely impassable for five months in the year. As a result, the utmost latitude has been allowed for competitors in the ore-market. Invoices of ore, like extra-good commercial paper, have been eagerly sought, and buyers, in their anxiety to get hold of them, have decreased the rate of discount on their value until the margins have been swept away, and the once-eager purchasers have found themselves holders of property costing more than it contained. In other words, so ardently have purchasers from Chicago, Saint Louis, Wyandotte, Pittsburgh, Newark, and Omaha sought for Colorado ores, that the price has been run up to figures which preclude any profit to buyers, and which also prevent any healthy competion at home.

This state of the market affects directly only that part of the production which is included within the limits of high-grade silver-ores, the mineral being worth $250 and upward per ton in precious metal. But, as in Colorado, about $1,350,000 of this material is produced annually. It constitutes a considerable item in the total yield of the mines, and the business of handling it indirectly affects all ores of lower grade that are not treated at or close by the mine. In this way the entire system of ore-brokerage—in which a capital of not less than $700,000 is employed—is sadly demoralized, and has in turn demoralized the whole business of smelting. Reducers cannot now buy directly of the miner, but must deal through middlemen, who are constantly quarreling among themselves on the subjects of rates, weights, and freights.

A glance at the map of Colorado will show how much the question of geography enters into the business of mining. For instance, the mines on the Middle Boulder and Left Hand Creeks have a most natural and convenient outlet for their produce by way of the cañons of these streams. But when the plains are reached, the greater part of the ore is brought around to the mouth of the next cañon, (Clear Creek,) and is transported 25 miles up into the mountains again before reduction. Clear Creek County ores have from 15 to 30 miles between them and the nearest smelting-works. Park County mineral is smelted to matte, and then shipped 1[illegible] miles before it is reduced to bullion. Rosita has 190 miles between it and reduction, while San Juan ores have to cross two snowy ranges, and spend ten days at least on the road before the furnaces are reached.

Nevertheless, in the face of these numerous natural disadvantages, ore still keeps going out of Colorado, and the struggle for the possession of it is as brisk as ever. Saint Louis and Pittsburgh at least do not seem to have been injured by the competition, if one may judge by the fact of their continued purchases, even at the highest rates.

The main advantage possessed by eastern buyers has been their command of a cheap fuel—coke. It is possible that when the Denver and Rio Grande Railroad reaches Trinidad, which will be early in the summer, Colorado smelting-works can, by the use of domestic coke, successfully compete with those in the East. Eastern coke now costs from $25 to $30 per ton at the foot of the mountains, while the Trinidad coke, which is believed to be quite as good for the purposes of the smelter as that of Pennsylvania or Indiana, can be laid down in Denver for $10 to $12 per ton.

In the smelting business some important changes have occurred. The persistent effort at Golden City to smelt for lead has not proved successful, and the management, finding that the supply of galena was inadequate, has altered the works accordingly, and is now smelting for copper-matte. This establishment has only been in operation during the last three months of the year, but its campaign was so much of a success that operations will now in all probability be continuous, with none of the discouraging stoppages that have formerly done so much toward discrediting the establishment in the eyes of the miner. The following statement, taken from the books of the company, shows the business of the three months ending December 29, 1875:

Total number of tons of ore bought	660
Total number of ounces of silver	34, 613
Total number of ounces of gold	474
Outlay:	
Cash paid for stock	$34, 801 05
Labor, fuel, flux, &c	16, 241 76
	51, 042 81
Income:	
Receipts from bullion-sales	$37, 464 36
Metal on hand, (lead, gold, and silver)*	20, 322 17
Metallic lead and copper	1, 832 00
	59, 618 53

The amount of lead-ore received was very small, averaging about 7 per cent., or 46½ tons, of which about 25 per cent. was saved.

I may mention here an improvement in the utilization of the lignites of the country lately introduced by Mr. West, the superintendent, which is an important advance in local metallurgy. I refer to his apparatus for using powdered lignite in reverberatory furnaces. Mr. West has

*This item includes an estimate, based on former runs of the same works, of the material in the furnace-hearths.

been experimenting on this subject for a long time, and has his machinery now in operation, having attained, so far as can be judged by outsiders, a perfect success.

The coal is ground to a powder and stowed in a box, in the bottom of which are two outlets. Through these the coal is forced by a right-and-left screw into two upright pipes, through which it falls into the horizontal draught or blast pipes. Here the falling coal is caught by the blast and carried into the furnace, where it ignites immediately on reaching the bridge. When the furnace is first fired up, it is of course necessary to start a fire in the fire-box, but no additional wood is needed afterward, except when, after drawing both slag and matte and recharging, the furnace cools off more than usual.

This device has now been in operation for several weeks without interruption. Although the coal used contains from 20 to 27 per cent. of moisture, and is from one of the second-rate lignite-mines of the Territory, the combustion is far more perfect than can be brought about with lump-coal, and the heat is intense and very even. More striking, however, is the financial success of the machine. It is now running steadily on a 7-ton matte-furnace and saving $30 per day on previous cost. The idea of burning coal, and especially soft coal, in the shape of a fine powder, is of course not new, nor do I think that Mr. West makes this claim. Messrs. Whelpley & Storer have, in fact, for years had a patent on a very perfect device for this purpose, which has been extensively used throughout the country. It consists of a ventilator, the arms of which, at the same time that they furnish the necessary blast for perfect combustion, crush the coal to an impalpable powder, which is continually fed out into the combustion-chamber by the wind.

I cannot close these observations without pointing out the fact that, although a very perfect combustion is accomplished in this way, the employment of the method for the purpose of matte-smelting, with lignites as a fuel, is objectionable on the ground that the very siliceous ashes are carried into the smelting-chamber, thereby increasing the percentage of silica already in the (mostly very siliceous) ore, and thus either occasioning an augmented addition of flux or a direct loss of heat by the higher temperature necessary to liguify a more siliceous slag, to say nothing of a probably greater loss of the precious metals, both through the stiffer slag and mechanically by the draught.

A more proper way of using the lignites for smelting ores of the precious metals in reverberatories is, no doubt, the employment of gas-generators or devices half-way between the common grate and gas-generators, such as have been employed for some time by Mr. Pearce, of the Boston and Colorado Works, and by various works in Utah, in the latter Territory mainly in roasting-furnaces used for slagging. In this method there is not only a perfect combustion reached, but the ashes are also kept separate from the charge and the temperature can be regulated at wi l by a simple damper.

The Boyd Works, at Boulder, have produced about $6,000 during the year. The proprietor has not yet perfected his system, and, moreover, has never succeeded in getting a good supply of galena-ores. He is, however, working a galena-vein in James Creek, and expects to be better supplied next year.

The Denver Works have been idle during the entire year, but are to be opened in the early spring.

The following table gives a list of works in operation during 1875, with their capacity, location, system of reduction, and plant. I include all works that have run at any time during the year, excepting stamp-mills.

Name.	Location.	System employed.	Plant.	Capacity, tons per day.
Batesville Mill	Boulder, (North)	Roasting and amalgamation.	....	15
Boston and Colorado Smelting-Works.	Black Hawk	Matte-roasting	2 calcining-furnaces; 4 matte-furnaces, and complete separation-works.	50
Boston and Colorado Smelting-Works (Alma).	Alma	....do	1 calcining-furnace; 1 matte-furnace.	20
Boyd's Smelting-Works	Boulder	Lead-smelting	1 patent roaster and 1 stack-furnace	12
Golden Smelting-Works	Golden	....do	1 calcining-furnace; 1 slag-furnace, and 2 stack-furnaces.	15
Judd & Crosby Works	Georgetown	Roasting and amalgamation.	20 stamps; 1 triple Stewart furnace	15
Mount Lincoln Smelting-Works.	Dudley	Matte-smelting	1 calcining and 1 matte-furnace	15
Nederland Mill	Nederland	Roasting and amalgamation.	20 stamps; 4 Brückner cylinders, and pans.	20
Pelican Silver-Mining Company.	Georgetown	....do	15 stamps; 5 cylinders, and 8 barrels.	15
Rosita Reduction-Works	Rosita	....do	Ball pulverizer; 1 roasting-furnace and pans.	10
Stewart Silver-Reducing Company.	Georgetown	....do	20 stamps; 2 furnaces and pans	20
Greene & Co	Silverton	Lead-smelting	Roasting and blast furnace	10

GILPIN COUNTY.

The production of the Gilpin County mines during the year has been as follows:

	Currency.
Stamp-mill, gold	$1,240,109 00
Boston and Colorado Smelting-Works	502,000 00
Ore shipped and jewelers' gold	21,876 00
	1,763,985 00
Or, in gold-value	1,520,555 07

The following is the currency and gold value of mill-gold by months:

Months.	Currency.	Coin.		
January	$99,993 33	Gold	$84,901 17	
		Silver	1,201 75	
				$86,102 92
February	72,803 30	Gold	61,908 71	
		Silver	942 93	
				62,851 64
March	87,610 05	Gold	74,431 42	
		Silver	1,132 45	
				75,563 87
April	90,734 97	Gold	77,086 28	
		Silver	1,172 85	
				78,259 13
May	85,097 51	Gold	72,625 83	
		Silver	1,101 47	
				73,727 30
June	110,667 78	Gold	94,022 24	
		Silver	1,428 96	
				95,451 20
July	107,036 60	Gold	99,935 77	
		Silver	1,383 55	
				101,319 32
August	119,034 23	Gold	101,128 83	
		Silver	1,538 51	
				102,667 34

Months.	Currency.	Coin.		
September	$112,775 35	Gold...	$95,794 28	
		Silver..	1,457 47	
				$97,251 75
October	109,563 00	Gold...	101,594 91	
		Silver..	1,545 72	
				103,140 63
November	112,308 90	Gold...	95,594 99	
		Silver..	1,453 21	
				97,048 20
December	132,499 46	Gold...	112,568 40	
		Silver..	1,712 70	
				114,281 10
Total	1,240,109 08			1,087,664 40

Thirty stamp-mills have been in operation during the year, carrying a total of 56 heads of stamps, all that was available without the introduction of new steam-power. Among the mills that have been running are Potter's, Clayton's, Waterman's, Whitcomb's, Buell's, Briggs's Smith & Parmelee's, Black-Hawk, Empire, Wheeler, and Sullivan.

Among the many mines in active operation during the year the following are the principal ones:

Mammoth.—From 1,000 to 1,500 feet of this vein have been worked during the year, mainly by lessees. It has paid well, and has yielded a steady production of 10 to 15 tons daily, worth $10 per ton. Toward the close of the year the production increased, and is now nearly double the above figure. Almost all the ore coming out is from levels and stopes within 200 feet of the surface.

Bates & Hunter.—The amount of work done on this property during the year has been small, and consisted mainly in clearing it of water and placing it in shape for further developments. Its western extension, the German, has received more attention. The latter is proving itself to be one of the best mines on Mammoth Hill. It was opened during the summer, and has been worked continuously since then with good results.

The Mountain City has been successfully worked during the entire year by a small force of men. It has yielded ore worth from $12 to $15 per ton.

The Tiernay lode has produced a fair quantity of $8 to $10 ore.

Work was commenced on the O. K. in July. A new shaft-house has been built, and the shaft sunk to the depth of 165 feet. The ore has averaged, in the mills, about $10 per ton.

The Winnebago mine was worked a little during last year. The shaft was drained and a small amount of ore taken out. From the cañon of Chase Gulch, on the northern slope of Carlo Hill, is running the Belden Tunnel, which, at the close of the year, had attained a length of 100 feet. It is being pushed ahead rapidly, and will intersect the Winnebago about 600 feet below its outcrop.

The Gunnell ranks among the very best mines of the county. Eight hundred feet have been under lease during the year to Kimber & Fullerton, and several other parties have been working on other parts of the vein. The main shaft had reached at the close of the year a depth of 700 feet, and the production amounted to between 25 and 35 tons daily. The Gunnell ore is of rather low grade. That which is milled averages $16 per ton, while the smelting ore brings from $50 to $75 at the Boston and Colorado Smelting-Works. The mine has been much troubled during the year with water, but has, nevertheless, been worked with profit.

The Prize and the Sensenderffer, which are probably southwestern extensions of the Gunnell, have been idle during the entire year. Beyond the latter, however, and still on the same vein, is the Hubert, which has been worked during a portion of the year, and with very satisfactory results. Some of the ore extracted has been of very high grade.

The Fiske is one of the old standard mines, and is still under lease to Mr. George W. Matee. It has produced quite steadily during the year about $5,000 monthly. It is now worked entirely from the surface, instead of from the Bobtail tunnel, as formerly.

The Pleasant View was incorporated in January, 1876, under a stock organization, and the stock was put on the Denver board. It is undoubtedly an extension of the Gunnell, and is a mine of great promise. At the close of the year the shaft was 150 feet deep, and two sets of levels had been started. A good body of ore was exposed along the entire depth of the shaft. No ore, however, has been milled as yet. This mine is one of the old locations of the county; but, though well worth developing, it has lain idle for a number of years.

The Saint Louis lies close to the Pleasant View, and is, probably, on the same vein, or a branch of it. It was re-opened during the summer, after several years of inactivity, and has been sunk upon for over 100 feet. The vein shows good "pay" in considerable quantity. It is taken out as development proceeds, and accumulated on the dump. About 50 tons is the amount thus far extracted. The mine is owned by Wisconsin parties, who are opening it extensively before crushing any ore.

The Leavitt was worked steadily up to the month of June, and produced in that time $55,000. During the remainder of the year the main portion of the mine was idle, but at the close of the year the entire property was leased to the Briggs Brothers, who are preparing now to work the mine on a more extended scale than ever before. As this mine is one of the most largely developed in Gilpin County, it merits a special description. The vein, which has been traced clearly from Clear Creek to Quartz Hill, a distance of about 3 miles, is opened by mine shafts, the deepest of which is now a little over 500 feet down. For 200 feet on either side of this shaft the vein has been worked very extensively, and has produced nearly $500,000 in gold. The entire vein is estimated to have yielded since its opening about $1,000,000, which, considering the desultory manner in which all but that portion around the deep shaft has been worked, and the low grade of the ore, ($7 to $11 per ton,) is an unusually large amount.

The total length of the shafts aggregates 2,210 feet, and of levels far more. The amount of ground broken is enormous.

Six hundred and eighty feet west of the main Leavitt shaft the lode is crossed diagonally by the Kip vein, which is included in the Leavitt property, and which has been opened to a depth of 270 feet. The ore in this vein is similar to that of the main fissure, and is found in bodies of large size. The main feature of interest in this property is the arrangement by which the 60-stamp mill and the boilers of the hoisting-engine are supplied with water. Gregory Gulch does not furnish enough water, even in the Spring, to supply so large an establishment, and, moreover, the stream is so charged with the *débris* of mills farther up the gulch as to be totally unfit for use. It was determined after long consideration, by Mr. Buell, the proprietor, to erect a series of settling-tanks, and use the water from the mine over and over again in the mill until enough was gained for all purposes. The demand for the mill and boilers was from 100,000 to 150,000 gallons each in 24 hours, while the mine furnishes from 25,000 to 50,000 gallons in the same time. The arrangements, now in most successful operation, are as follows:

Tank No. 1, into which the water flows from the pumps, is 25 feet square and 4 feet deep, and is divided into compartments 15 feet long by 3 feet wide.* The water flows from one compartment to another, and in the transit leaves behind the heavier particles of ore and rock brought up from the shaft. From No. 1 the water is carried through a race-way into tank No. 2, which has a capacity of 80,000 gallons. This tank is divided into two compartments, through which the water passes; and out of them by a second race-way into tank No. 3, the capacity of which is 100,000 gallons. From this it passes through a flume 50 feet long into a well underneath the floor of the mill. Here it is quite clear and ready for use in the batteries. Small pumps elevate the desired quantity into circular tanks in front of the stamps, from which it is led to the mortars, to be subsequently returned to the tanks.

The whole distance traveled by the water from the stamps to its return to them again is 400 feet. The tanks are sluiced out frequently, and easily kept clear from waste. In addition to the three tanks above mentioned is a fourth, having a capacity of 250,000 gallons, making the total storage capacity of the system 500,000 gallons. Its advantages are not alone that a small amount of water is made to supply a large demand by using it several times over, but it has been found that even in the coldest days in winter a temperature of 60° to 70° is maintained in the tanks, and thus a comparatively warm water is supplied to the stamps without the use of steam-heating apparatus.

Almost all the work done on the Bobtail Mine during 1875 was below the tunnel-level. The deepest workings are now 700 feet below the surface, or 135 feet below the tunnel. At the depth of 90 feet below the tunnel a continuous level has been driven for more than 1,000 feet, exploring the entire ground owned by the company. About 70 men have been steadily employed during the year, and the production has averaged over 2,000 tons per month. The mill-ore is gradually improving in value, and, owing to the extended developments, many thousand tons are constantly exposed in advance of extraction. At the point where the tunnel cuts the vein, the company is sinking its main shaft, through which hereafter the entire traffic of the mine is to be carried on. A large underground chamber is being excavated, in which heavy hoisting and pumping machinery will be erected. The company has also determined to use machine-drills in the mine, and, after a long examination, has decided upon the Wood drill, and a full set, with a compressor, has been ordered. The Bobtail vein maintains a good width in its lowest workings, at places expanding 15 or 20 feet. The ore as it goes to the mill averages $9 to $11 per ton, and is worked at a considerable profit. The smelting-ore does not assay as richly as last year.

The Gregory lode is at present one of the largest producing veins in Colorado. During 1875 operations have been carried on upon five claims, representing a total length of 2,000 feet. These were the New York and Colorado Company, (500 feet,) the Briggs, (200 feet,) the Black-Hawk, (300 feet,) the Consolidated Gregory, (500 feet,) and the Narragansett, (500 feet.) The product of ore has amounted to 19,000 tons of

*I give these figures as reported to me. The impracticability of making exactly such a division is obvious; but the inconsistency in the account is not important.—R. W. R.

mill-rock, of an average value of $10 per ton, and 485 tons of smelting-ore, which sold for $41,000, making the total yield of the vein for the year $231,000.

The three inside claims—the Briggs, Black-Hawk, and Consolidated Gregory—are now consolidated under one management, that of the Briggs Brothers, who have contracted for a three years' lease on the last named. The combined property has, since the consolidation, been producing 1,800 tons a month, worth about $20,000 to the producer. It will be seen, therefore, that this property alone will, if its present rate of production is continued, yield during 1876 more than the entire vein did during the last year.

The deepest workings on the vein are in the Briggs claim, whose shaft is at present 700 feet deep below the bottom of the gulch. The mouth of this shaft is located at the lowest point of the outcrop of the vein. Its bottom is considerably over 1,200 feet below the outcrop of the Narragansett.

The Narragansett has been worked but slightly during 1875. The main shaft, which was 440 feet in depth at the beginning of the year, is now a little over 500 feet. At the depth of 470 feet a level 115 feet long has been driven west, and one 55 feet east. A stope has been broken above the former, from which a little more than half the production of the mine has come; the remainder has been taken from old stopes nearer the surface.

During the year the main shaft of the New York and Colorado Company has been extended in depth 50 feet. On the large vein 500 feet of levels have been driven and two 60-foot winzes sunk. On the small vein the 350-foot shaft has been straightened and retimbered and 350 feet of levels driven. A large amount of stoping has been done, and the production has more than covered all current expenses, though never pushed beyond legitimate working. The standing of the mine at the opening of the year is such that stockholders may feel that the property is now saved from the wrecked condition in which it was three years ago.

The Quartz Hill mines have furnished during the year about one-third of the stamp-gold product of the county. The Burroughs, Kansas, Gardner, Alps, Illinois, and Kent County have been the prominent producers. A number of minor properties have given a considerable aggregate product. At the base of the hill the Quartz Hill Tunnel Company is still at work, and advancing slowly.

Twenty-nine hundred feet on the Kansas and Burroughs lodes has been operated under one management during the year. To the westward, where the two veins join, nothing has been done, but next year the same company will probably work there. The main shaft, which is on the Ophir claim, is sunk to a depth of 915 feet, and is producing excellent ore in good quantity. This shaft is sinking to gain a depth of 1,000 feet, when an extensive system of drifts will be begun and the property opened through its entire length. This is undoubtedly one of the finest mines in the Territory. It is generally believed that the two veins will not only unite laterally to the westward, but will also join in depth. The latter point of juncture will not probably be reached in the Ophir shaft for several hundred feet.

The Monmouth claim, on the Kansas, which during the year was bought by New Jersey parties for a price not far from $35,000, has been yielding uninterruptedly ever since, and has paid, according to statements furnished me by trustworthy parties, a profit at times as high as 12 per cent. a month on the investment.

The English-Kansas has been allowed to remain idle during the entire year. Almost all the remainder of this great vein is in successful operation under American supervision.

The Illinois, though not wholly neglected, has not been worked very extensively during the year. The mill-ore produced has been of high grade, averaging $20 per ton, and the operations of the year have been financially successful on a small scale. Preparations are making to work the vein more thoroughly during the coming season. It is one of the best lodes on the hill, a continuation of the Mammoth, and possessing all the valuable qualities of that ledge.

The Kent County has yielded steadily throughout the year. At one time the vein showed a width of 3 feet of very rich ore.

On the Gardner operations have not been very extensive. The Clark claim has been worked most, and has repaid the lessees moderately.

Of the other mines on this famous hill but little detailed information can be given. The Louis, Register, Roderick Dhu, Boston, Alps, Wood, and Harsh have been worked intermittently by owners or lessees. That they have not yet proved largely productive is said to be due to the lack of sufficient capital to work them on an extensive scale. The mines of Gilpin County cannot be relied upon to yield much more than $10 a ton, and in order to make this grade of ore profitable, a large amount must be produced, and there must also be cheap means of transportation from the mine to the mill. Lastly, there is a great need of an abundance of water-power, which as yet the county does not possess.

The total production of the Boston and Colorado Smelting Company's works during the year was $1,947,000 currency, of which amount $70,000 was in copper, $527,000 gold, and the remainder, $1,350,000, silver. The ores furnishing this product were derived from the surrounding districts, in the following proportion:

Gilpin County:		
Gold	$357,000	
Silver	94,000	
Copper	51,000	
		$502,000
Clear Creek County:		
Gold	4,000	
Silver	438,000	
		442,000
Park County:		
Gold	41,000	
Silver	618,000	
Copper	19,000	
		678,000
Boulder County:		
Gold	113,000	
Silver	74,000	
		187,000
Fremont County:		
Silver		126,000
San Juan		12,000
Total		1,947,000

The capital of this company was, late in the year, increased to $1,000,000. One 15-ton furnace has been added, and at the close of the season the works had a capacity of 50 tons per day. For some time past Mr. Richard Pearce, who is in charge of the works, has been experimenting to find a process by which the gold left in the matte after the silver is extracted may be economically separated from the copper bottoms, which have heretofore been shipped to Boston. It is now claimed that success has been achieved. The process is reported to be an entirely new one, and is kept rigidly secret. Nothing is now shipped from this establishment but fine bullion. Even the cement-copper which is precipitated in the Ziervogel process is to be melted into ingots hereafter before shipment.

The arrangements and appointments of this establishment are in the highest degree creditable to the management. Receiving as it does ores from all parts of the Territory in very large quantity, it requires extensive sampling-floors. The quantity of telluric ores alone treated last year amounted in value to considerably over $100,000, while about $130,000 worth of silver-ores from the southern part of Colorado were sent here for treatment. The company has been able to build up a large area of ground along the narrow gulch by a proper disposition of its slags, and has utilized to great advantage the space thus gained. At the close of the year several important changes were in progress, which will be carried out before spring, and which will increase facilities and cheapen the cost of handling the ore. A full description of the works will be found in the metallurgical part of this report.

CLEAR CREEK COUNTY.

The production of the mines of this county for the year has been as follows:

	Currency.
Silver bullion from the Stewart Reduction Works, Judd & Crosby Works, and Pelican Mill	$617, 200
Ore shipped to Boston and Colorado Smelting-Works	442, 000
Ore shipped to Golden City Smelting-Works	29, 958
Ore shipped out of the Territory	941, 744
Gold produced from South Clear Creek hydraulic mines and from Empire veins	80, 000
Total	2, 110, 902
Coin value	1, 819, 598

Nearly 12,000 tons of ore was produced and sold, making the average grade of Clear Creek mineral about $175 per ton. Comparing this with results of the previous year, it will be seen that much more ore has been broken, but the increase has been mainly of the lower grades, such as have heretofore been unavailable. This, coupled with the fact that two large concentration-works are now in operation at Georgetown, may be considered as a most favorable indication of the healthy growth of the mining industry.

It may not be amiss in this connection to discuss the peculiar condition of the ore market in Georgetown, which, as much as any one other circumstance, has given unusual prominence to the district, and forced the miners into what now may be considered an unhealthy condition. In addition to the two milling establishments that have sought for all the ore they could get, there have been no less than five parties seeking ore for export, either to works out of the Territory or to works in other districts. The competition consequently has been exceedingly lively, and, as outside purchasers have had the advantages of much larger capital, the result has been that the home reduction-works have made little if any profit, and, moreover, have been driven in great measure to content themselves with the low grades, that would not bear the cost of transportation. Indeed, it is doubtful if outside purchasers have made any appreciable profit, and the only parties who have cause to congratulate themselves are the miners and middle-men. It may be urged that if these have not suffered, the industry is uninjured; but such an assumption is certainly a mistake. Any business, to be in a healthy and prosperous condition, should yield satisfactory returns to both producer and consumer. If the conditions are otherwise, there will come a time when the latter (or most of them) will decline to conduct business without reasonable profits, and the market will fall into the hands of one or two parties whose capital has allowed them to outlast the rest, and who, when their turn arrives, will put down prices to a figure that will not only permit a present profit, but will rapidly make up for all previous losses.

This condition of affairs is, perhaps, not far distant in Georgetown. For some time past Mr. Stewart has seen the impossibility of an amalgamation-works competing for ore in a base-metal district where as high as $1 for each per cent. of lead over 15 has been offered by outside buyers; and he has, therefore, endeavored to protect himself by remodeling his system of reduction so that it would include the separation of copper and a more perfect extraction of the silver. Unfortunately, his works were destroyed by fire on December 19, and all endeavors in that line must, for some time at least, be delayed.

The mines around Georgetown have now been opened to such an extent that the average quality of their production may fairly be gauged. It is evident that not over ten tons daily of ore really suitable for roasting and amalgamation can be produced without having recourse to dump-rock, which had better go for concentration-works. Even this supply, if it be of good grade, (150 to 250 ounces,) will be sought by exporters. Our amalgamation-works is, in fact, all that the present business of the camp can supply, and more will only serve to increase the complications already existing.

The market has further suffered from the wide-spread opinion that a large proportion of the ores were suitable for lead-smelting. While it is true that on an average about 10 per cent. of that metal can be obtained, and from many of the mines even a higher percentage, it must not be overlooked that with the galena occurs so large a quantity of zinc-blende that its value as a smelting-ore, unless separated, is greatly impaired. In spite, however, of this fact, which has been amply demonstrated, there is still a vigorous demand from Pittsburgh, Wyandotte, Chicago, Saint Louis, and Newark for Georgetown ores. This demand, caused at first by a desire to get galena, is now continued from a wish to secure high-grade silver-ore, (which undoubtedly the mines can yield,) and Georgetown, being the only camp of any size on the eastern slope of the range producing such ore, has been the theater of the most active competition. Buyers have been willing to pay nearly the full value of the silver and lead, in order to obtain the ore for mixing purposes.

Mr. Van Wagenen considers this an unfortunate condition of affairs, because it discourages home smelting-works; because it creates fictitious values for the product of the mines, which cannot be expected to last; and because, as soon as any other locality is opened, where true lead-smelting ores can be produced, buyers will have no more need of those from Georgetown and the market will be left in the hands of a few, who can make their own prices.

I am not sure, however, that the demand for the Georgetown ores "for mixed purposes" is unhealthy, or would cease upon the discovery of other districts supplying purer galena.

The following is a list of the important mines that have been worked during the year:

Stevens, Baker, East Roe, Brown, Glascow, East Terrible, Parr, Silver Plume, Queen of the West, New Boston, Comet, Colorado Central, Ocean Wave, St. Joe, Hercules and Seven-Thirty, Coldspring, Dives, Pelican, Payrock, Dunkirk, Fred Rogers, Polar Star, Silver Cloud, Magnet, East Griffeth, Equator, Star, Pulaski, Victor, President, Silver Ore.

In addition to these, a very large number of claims have been more or less under development. The system of leasing is much in favor, and fully one-third of the production is from mines worked in that manner. At the same time, the larger mines are, as a rule, operated on a more comprehensive and better system than heretofore, and as a result their condition has improved. The old tunnel excitement (in regard to which I have expressed my opinion in former reports) has been succeeded by a fashion of deep mining, which has already proved itself a step in the right direction.

The new discoveries of the year have been mainly on Democrat Mountain, where a belt of very strong lodes, carrying rich surface-ores, has been found. The Polar Star and Fred Rogers, which are older locations on this mountain, have been developed considerably, and have yielded good results from both their surface and their deep workings. The newly-discovered mines are apparently of the same class.

The Empire mines, though not producing largely, have not been left idle. Mr. Stewart has been most active in encouraging their development; and had it not been for the destruction of his mill, a large amount of mineral would have been taken out during 1876. As it is, there is little or no market for the ores, which are mainly iron-pyrites, and not very rich in gold. A Bolthoff mill was erected there during the summer.

The production of gulch-gold on and below Spanish Bar has amounted, as nearly as can be ascertained, to $80,000, showing an increase of over $30,000 as compared with last year. Ten claims have been worked intermittently during the season, two of which have done remarkably well.

At and near Idaho the Hukill, Victor, Veto, Queen, Seaton, and a number of other mines have been more or less worked. The yield of the mines of this section of the county has amounted to about $90,000, most of which has been produced at the Boston and Colorado Smelting-Works, which bought the ores.

Mines.—The legal horizon has undergone a little clearing this year, though none of the heavy suits have been definitely settled. The Dives and Pelican fight grew in bitterness and vigor from January, culminating in May in the assassination of one of the principal owners of the latter claim, since which time both parties to the litigation have been earnestly looking for a settlement. The year closed without this most desirable event, but it seems likely that an understanding will be reached within another twelve months. Since the examination of the property by Mr. Clarence King, the attention of San Francisco capitalists has been drawn to it, and at one time the vein was nearly disposed of to a company formed in that city. Of the other large suits none have yet come to a definite conclusion, though all are tending in that direction.

In *West Argentine district* the Stevens and Brooklyn have been continuously worked, with results that have been considered fairly satis, factory, considering the altitude and location of the veins. The Stevens having been purchased by a wealthy company, will doubtless be developed in time to a very valuable property. A tunnel is being driven from the base of the mountain to strike the vein about 350 feet below the outcrop, and at a distance from the tunnel-mouth (so steep is the precipice of the mountain) of not over 400 feet. It will hardly be completed till late in the summer. The main working shaft is being sunk to connect with it, so that in future all operations may be carried on from the base of the mountain. This will lessen the cost of production by fully one-third. The ore produced during the year has yielded in the mill about 120 ounces in silver per ton and 70 per cent. in lead. The vein has proved to be remarkably even and regular in nearly all parts opened, and should the tunnel cut as good a lode below as is opened above, the production can be greatly increased.

The Brooklyn has been worked under lease during a large part of the year, but has not produced any considerable amount of ore. What has come out, however, has been of unusually high grade.

In *Brown Gulch* more development has been effected during the past year than during any previous season. The properties worked have been old discoveries.

Early in the year the east level from the Silver-Ore lode broke into the fourth level of the Terrible mine. Immediately an injunction was issued against the latter, which, after a little preliminary fighting, resulted in the closing of the Terrible mine and an order from the court prohibiting either party from extracting ore from the ground in dispute below the tunnel-level. For several months parties of tributers were at work in the upper and partially-exhausted levels of this famous lode, and the concentration-works were kept running. At the close of the year, however, the entire property was idle, and seems likely to remain so until a compromise can be effected between the English company and Mr. Hammill, of the Silver Ore.

As this property has proved to be one of great value, and has been developed more extensively and in a better manner than any other in the district, its stoppage affected the general business of the town considerably, and has been in every way a misfortune. The great ore-body which gave the mine its reputation was, at the time of stoppage, as finely developed in the seventh (lowest) level as above, and bid fair to extend for a long distance farther. The dip of the chimney was, however, to the west, and for the last 100 feet no ore of any account had been found in the shaft. This circumstance showed that ultimately the body would pass into the Silver-Ore claim, which, during the last months of this year, proved to be the case; and as the eastern part of the mine has so far yielded but little, it is evident that much expensive development must be done before the English Terrible alone can gain the position it held before its stoppage. It has been hoped that this consideration would have had some weight in inducing the English stockholders to buy out the Silver Ore claim.

The Clark Terrible has been worked with considerable steadiness during the year, (mostly by lessees,) and has maintained a moderate production.

The Mammoth and Glasgow have been in the hands of lessees all the year. Meanwhile an Erie (Pa.) company has been running a tunnel to cut these veins, which has already attained a length of about 300 feet.

When finished it will strike the Mammoth at the depth of about 200 feet.

The Atlantic has yielded a small quantity of very rich ore. It has been worked steadily, and is deemed likely to develop into a valuable mine.

The Hercules Company leased its mine for the most of the year, and the production has been small, though not because of any exhaustion of the vein. The Seven-Thirty, which is on the same lode, has been in a similar condition. In the fall, however, the Earl Roe vein, which by some is consdered a continuation of the Seven-Thirty and by others a mere spur from the Hercules, was made the basis of a stock company, which was floated on the Denver exchange. Subsequently the three properties were consolidated, and at the same time passed into the hands of new owners. With the opening of the year it is hoped that operations will be resumed on a large scale, and, judging by the past yield of the claims, a considerable production may be anticipated. For this year the three have not produced over $30,000.

The Bismarck, President, Brown, Coin, Old Missouri, and a few others have been worked mainly under lease and on a small scale, yet their aggregate product forms a considerable item in the total for the district.

Passing eastward from Brown Gulch, a number of claims are encountered, including the Cashier, Cascade, Bush, Mendota, Virgin, Silver Spring, Captain Wells, and Anglo-Norman, each of which has produced a small amount of silver under intermittent working.

The dispute over the Phœnix and Coldstream mines has this year been confined to the courts, and still remains unsettled. Developments on the former have consisted mainly in sinking and drifting from the discovery-shaft and in driving eastward to connect with corresponding workings on the Coldstream. A few bunches of good ore have been found, but most of the vein-matter was of low grade and unprofitable, carrying much iron-pyrites. The main shaft on the Coldstream has been sunk about 100 feet farther, and, besides opening the mine very thoroughly westward, so as to show its course, drifts have been run eastward under Cherokee Flat for nearly 300 feet. There the vein was found strong and fairly good, in places very rich. The production has not, however, been large, since the main object of the owner has been such a development as would give hope of settling the litigation which has been pending so long.

The Pelican and Dives mines are perhaps the most important in the county. It has been impossible to arrive at their exact production, but the amount cannot have been less than half a million dollars, and was probably nearer $700,000. During a large part of the year the richest parts of the mines have been enjoined from both claimants, and this is the present condition of the property. The lawsuit which has been pending for three years concerning this magnificent vein is not yet ended, though both parties seem quite ready to agree to a compromise. Meanwhile the development of the vein has not been neglected. In the Pelican explorations have been pushed westward beyond the No. 2½ tunnel, and into a part of the mine hitherto comparatively barren. In the fall a new chimney of ore was met with, which is now being followed both up and down, with very gratifying results. Up to the close of the year much work had been done in this part of the mine, and the ore-body discovered promises to be fully as large as, if not larger than, any yet opened. Contrary to the general pitch of the chimneys in the Pelican-Dives vein, this one inclines to the west. It has been explored horizontally along the lode for about 75 feet, which is probably nearly its limit, and on the dip of the fissure for about a hundred. The ore is the same as that usually found in this mine, carrying perhaps a trifle more zincblende, and averaging about $110 to the ton, as nearly as I can ascertain. In places it is 6 to 8 feet in width, nearly solid, and averages fully 18 inches for nearly the whole length as so far exposed.

More work has been done on the Dives property than on the Pelican, mainly because the mine has been in leasers' hands. The deepest workings are now about 500 feet below the outcroppings. Ore has been found in abundance, some of it of excellent quality. The immense galena-chimney has been followed downward about 100 feet farther than at the date of my last report, and the pay-seam has been found to maintain its strength with remarkable evenness. So far, this large body of mineral has not been made available, as it carries not more than 40 ounces of silver to the ton, but it is expected that it will be possible to mine this ore with profit as soon as the Silver Plume Concentration Works go into operation. The ore taken out from the several workings on the Dives this year has averaged about the same as that from the Pelican, 110 ounces. During the year a tunnel has been driven from a point on the hill-side about 500 feet down the mountain, which cuts the vein about 250 feet below the surface, and through which all operations are now carried on. The mine is now fitted out with two good hoisting engines and pumps, and operations are carried on consequently at a greatly reduced cost.

Every additional year of development on this lode strengthens the opinion that it is one of unusual value. In time it is to be hoped that the questions of spurs, side-veins, cross-veins, and horses, which are now of the first importance in deciding points of ownership, will be sunk and forgotten in a united development of its lower portions.

Since the above was written, on the basis of Mr. Van Wagenen's report, I have received (October, 1876) from Messrs. Charles A. Martine and Benjamin F. Napheys, of Georgetown, the following letter, which gives the latest description in my possession of this extremely valuable property:

We have jointly examined the lower workings of the Pelican and Dives mines, our purpose being to arrive at a conclusion concerning the supply of ore from both in the immediate future. Our examination of the Pelican Mine was confined to the ground lying below what has been termed the "court level," said level being 90 feet above the main or No. 2½ level, which is connected with the No. 2½ tunnel, and through which the mine is now entirely worked. We also examined the main shaft now being sunk from this No. 2½ level, and the several winzes to the west from said main shaft.

Concerning the several blocks of ground opened up by the court level, and the winzes sunk through to the No. 2½ level, 90 feet below, extending over a length of about 575 feet, we would state that about one-third of it has been worked out. An exceedingly fine body of ore, attaining locally a width of upward of two feet, is now being stoped out to the westward of the "little shaft," (125 feet west of the old whim shaft.) The quality of this ore is fully equal to any heretofore extracted from the mine; 20 tons of the first class, sold last week, averaging above 400 ounces per ton, while the second class (being the ore treated at the Pelican Mill, in Georgetown) contains from 100 to 130 ounces per ton. There is every indication that this body of ore will continue to the west, and that its grade will remain the same.

The ground below the No. 2½ level has been explored by the "main shaft," sunk to a depth of 160 feet below said No. 2½ level, and two winzes, 150 and 450 feet, respectively, west of the main shaft. The main shaft and the two winzes are now being connected by levels. Large amounts of ore are in sight in all the openings, but our attention was specially attracted by a body of unusual width in the drift connecting the main shaft with No. 1 winze, at a depth of 60 feet below the No. 2½ level. Galena predominated largely in this pocket, and a test-run made upon about three tons showed it to contain 51 ounces of silver and 41 per cent. of lead per ton. It is but fair to suppose that large quantities of similar ore will be furnished by this particular portion of the mine.

The sinking of the main shaft has been temporarily suspended, but is soon to be resumed on the approach of colder weather. Besides, it is to be expected that the farther extension of the Diamond tunnel, now being actively driven, will, at an early day, remove all further difficulties in the way of drainage.

From the above brief statements, it will be seen that those portions of the Pelican Mine which are now being worked are all in a promising condition, and that a steady supply of ore is insured for the future beyond all doubt, while the quality of the same remains about the same as heretofore.

The Dives Mine is now being explored by means of two shafts, the mouths of which are reached through a tunnel, opening in what is called the "engine level," which is about forty feet below the court level in the Pelican Mine. These two shafts are called the Purdue shaft, being near the point of intersection of the tunnel and engine level, and the East Dives shaft, about 95 feet to the eastward of the former. Depths of respectively 375 feet and 265 feet have been reached by them, and both have been sunk upon what is called the intermediate ore-vein.

The hoisting through both shafts is done by engines, steam being supplied to both by one boiler. Both shafts may be considered as good specimens of mining work.

A fine streak of ore, varying in thickness from 15 to 18 inches, was observed on the north vein, immediately west of the Purdue Shaft, which appears to be of good quality, the streak extending over a distance of about 60 feet, and reaching up to the court level.

We descended through the Purdue Shaft to the 270-foot level, about three-fourths of the ground being worked out. A cross-cut, 39 feet in length. run to cut the north vein, and connected with a drift 80 feet in length, showed all along a seam of ore 6 to 12 inches wide.

The 340-foot level was next visited, the ground between this and the level next above being almost intact. The same is true of a streak of ore shown up by a cross-cut run north, and a level connected therewith, the ore-vein being from 4 to 6 inches wide.

An exceedingly fine pocket of ore is in sight in the 400-foot level. This bench was fully 15 inches in width, and extended 165 feet east of the Dives shaft. A test-run made upon 10 tons of this ore showed it to contain upward of 200 ounces per ton. The presence of this bunch of ore at so great a depth—almost the greatest so far reached in this mine—is an extremely encouraging sign for the future prosperity of the mines in question. The ore plainly shows the peculiar fahlore, the presence of which, in greater or smaller quantities, determines the richness of the ores in this district, the pure galena or zinc-blende being comparatively barren.

Our examination of both mines was necessarily a hurried and superficial one, but it is quite safe to assert that there is as much and as good ore in sight at present as during any past period of its history, leaving out of consideration the finding of a few large and rich pockets. The further development of the mine could doubtless be carried on in a more expeditious and economical manner if both properties were to come under one management.

Judging from the general appearance of the lower workings in both mines, we could not help coming to the conclusion that its future, as regards economical results, was thoroughly secured.

The Diamond tunnel is an enterprise begun about three years ago for the purpose of prospecting the mountain a little to the east of the line of Cherokee Gulch. The work has been pushed steadily and rapidly, and at present the face of the tunnel is, according to calculations, not over 200 feet from the Dives-Pelican vein. It is expected that the lode will be cut during the coming summer, and as this will take place at a depth of 600 feet, or 100 feet below the deepest present workings, it will open a new era of mining on this part of Republican Mountain. The Diamond Tunnel Company is a Baltimore organization, entirely distinct from either the Pelican or the Dives Company; yet as the company is said to own no property on the line of its tunnel, its only object can be that of draining the developed mines on that line and of offering a thoroughfare for ores. I am told that arrangements to this effect have been concluded with the Baltimore Company by the several parties interested in the Pelican and Dives, and that as soon as the connection is made the upper surface works will be abandoned and all operations will be carried on from below.

The Hermann Silver-Mining Company is one of the new organizations of the year. It was formed on the Dunkirk property, which by many is thought to be the eastern extension of the Dives. This point will, doubtless, be settled before long, as the company is rapidly driving its levels west, and if a connection is made it will probably be done early in 1876.

The Silver Plume, a mine owned by an English company, which has experienced all the vicissitudes that generally fall to the lot of those properties, was idle for the first six months of the year. During the last six months, however, it has been worked by lessees, and has yielded about $25,000. The legal difficulties which have for a long time blocked extensive operations are now somewhat removed, and it is likely that the mine will be worked in the future with more vigor and regularity. The vein belongs to the cross-lodes of Republican Mountain, and has seldom failed to be profitable.

The Payrock, Hopewell, Snowdrift, Tropic, Fingal, Morse, Baxter, and Denver are the other prominent properties of this locality. They have been worked mainly under lease, and with such results as might be expected from a system which throws the mines into the hands of poor men, who are forced to work them for a small but immediate production.

Still farther eastward on the same mountain is the group of veins lying across the line of the Lebanon tunnel. Among these are the South American, Hise, Alhambra, Caledonian, and others. On almost all a little work has been done, but the results have hardly paid the total expense. The Lebanon tunnel has not been driven any farther than as stated in my last report.

Passing around the point on this mountain, and across the ravine separating it from Democrat Mountain, the Beecher and Boston groups of mines are encountered. None of these has been worked during the year, except the Boston. This mine was sold in the spring to a New York company, which immediately began the erection of a concentration-mill at the foot of the mountain. A surface tram-way was built from the mine to the mill, and a number of men were set at work in the mine. The Boston is a very large vein, carrying a low-grade galena, only susceptible of being worked profitably by concentration. The mill was not ready to start until November, and then failed to work satisfactorily. In December a re-organization of the company was effected, and the entire work is now in the hands of Mr. W. W. Rose, who expects to remodel the mill completely.

The *Democrat Mountain* (west side) belt of veins has attracted this year more attention than almost any other in the district. Early in the year the Polar Star was sold, and re-opened under good auspices. The Rogers and Queen of the West experienced the same quickening process, and, to the credit of the mines be it said, the buyers were thoroughly satisfied with their bargains. The production from the camp has been very good, probably amounting to $200,000 during the year, which, considering the nature of the operations carried on, is a fair result. Next year it is hoped that this figure will be doubled. Numerous other lodes of promise have been found, among which may be mentioned the Silver Cloud and Silver Wing. The Fletcher, Hesperus, and Junction have all been worked at intervals. A good road has been built down the western slope, connecting with the county road across the Empire Pass.

On *Griffith Mountain* work has been confined to the Anglo-Saxon, Court, Magnet, Griffith Extension, Homestead, and a few other minor veins. The ore produced has been very small in amount.

On *Leavenworth Mountain* none of the numerous and rich veins have been worked systematically, with the exception of the Colorado Central.

Yet the production has been very good. The Saco, Equator, Gates, O. K., Compass and Square, Alabama, Ni-wot, Welsh, Phalen, Sweepstakes, Argentine, Simpson, and Ocean Wave, have yielded each a moderate quantity of good ore, but operations have been carried on so irregularly that no detailed report of individual progress and production is possible. Each year of work on this mountain adds hundreds of feet to the levels and drifts with which it is honeycombed, but, unfortunately, only a small portion of this labor is expended in deep development. Most of it is consumed in open cuts and surface excavations, so that today but little more is known of the vein-formations than ten years ago.

The Marshall tunnel made no advance in its main line during the year. The following sketch of the property owned by the Marshall Silver-Mining Company was furnished me by General Marshall, the indefatigable proprietor and manager: The majority of the stockholders are citizens of Colorado, residing in the vicinity. The tunnel has reached a length of 1,300 feet, and has crossed ten veins, of which those not already located have been designated by numbers and regularly located. The aggregate length of the lode-claims patented or surveyed and approved for patent to this company is about 11,000 feet. The underground workings comprise, beside the main tunnel, drifts or side-tunnels and shafts on the lodes, intersected as follows: Marshall tunnel, 1,300; No. 2 tunnel, 350; No. 3 tunnel, 200; No. 4 tunnel, 400; McCoy shaft and tunnel, 550; Tobin shaft, 80; shafts, levels, &c., on Compass and Square and Reynolds lodes, 900; Robinson tunnel-level on No. 5 vein, 500; other levels on the same vein, 660; shafts, levels, and cross-cuts on O. K. lode, 250; shafts, levels, and cross-cuts at other places not included in the foregoing, 1,500; total length of underground workings, 6,690 feet. The cost of the dead-work to about the middle of 1876 is given by General Marshall at $165,000; cost of mining ore from the different veins, $65,000; cash yield of the mines to the same date, $155,000. The company intends to drive the tunnel through the whole of Leavenworth Mountain, a total distance of 2,600 feet, and it is expected that on the southeast slope a network of rich veins, carrying silver in combination with gold, will be encountered. It is reported that a Colorado company has obtained a lease from the Marshall company, on one of the veins cut by the tunnel, and purposes to sink to 1,000 feet below the tunnel-level, or 1,400 below the surface at that point. The royalty is to be 25 per cent. of the gross proceeds of the ore mined.

The Ocean Wave tunnel has advanced sluggishly, finding but little mineral in its course, though it runs directly on a vein.

The Simpson Company has done some good work in developing its mine, though as yet it has been unproductive.

The Colorado Central has not been developed much, if any, deeper than at the close of 1874. Connection has been made with the tunnel, and explorations have been carried east and west for some distance on the 200-foot level. No new pocket like the Bonanza, struck directly on the surface, has been found, though ore of good grade and in fair quantity has not been lacking. Mr. Van Wagenen was unable to ascertain the production of the mine from any authority, but estimates that it could not have been over $100,000, a figure which is ridiculously small, compared with what it would be if the vein were developed on an adequate scale.

The project of sinking a 500-foot shaft from the tunnel (Marshall) level was broached this year during the general "deep-mining excitement" consequent on the Comstock discoveries in Nevada. A stock company was formed, composed mainly of Georgetown men, and enough cash has been raised by assessments to begin work. A large chamber has been cut on one side of the tunnel, in which the engine is to be put, and sinking has already begun. The vein in the tunnel is over 25 feet wide and quite soft. This is probably the enterprise alluded to above, under the head of the Marshall tunnel.

BOULDER COUNTY.

The product of the mines of this county, which includes Grand Island, Gold Hill, Sunshine, Magnolia, and Ward districts, has been as follows:

Product of Canton Mine	$210,000
Shipments to Black Hawk	187,000
Shipments to Golden City	5,000
Shipments out of the Territory	100,000
Bullion and silver in lead from Batesville and Boyd's Mills	16,000
Placer-gold	40,000
Total	558,000
Coin value	480,996

These figures show a gain over last year which is perhaps not quite normal, inasmuch as about one-quarter of the product has been from extraordinarily rich surface-pockets, discovered on the "tellurium belt." When my report for 1874 was in course of preparation, Sunshine district was just coming into prominence. The American Mine in that camp had just been sold and placed in charge of Mr. J. Alden Smith. Several other sales had been made, some sacks full of extraordinarily rich ore produced, and a great deal of enthusiasm aroused over new and wonderful discoveries. There appeared, however, such a disproportion between the assays and the mill-returns of these tellurides that many persons doubted the extended distribution and persistency of the ores.

The developments of the year on this class of veins have, however, been surprisingly favorable. The actual amount of telluride ore produced has, as nearly as I can find out, been worth not les than $220,000, while the work done in sinking, drifting, and opening has been immense. Early in the year prospectors set out in every direction from the central camp, (Sunshine,) and since then there has been a steady succession of important new discoveries. At first these were in the vicinity of Four-Mile Creek, at Salina, Camp Tellurium, and along Gold Run. Then came reports from a new camp on the South Boulder Creek, now called *Magnolia district*, after which the Slide lode, on Gold Hill, was found. Lastly the prospectors found ores of the same character in the valley of Jim Creek, a tributary of Left Hand. It now appears, therefore, that this belt of veins extends north and south for nearly 20 miles, being represented at about every mile of its course by discoveries already made. The belt is about 4 miles in width, runs parallel, or nearly so, with the line of the foot-hills, and maintains a distance of from 6 to 10 miles from the plains. Its southern termination, so far as now known, is in Magnolia and its northern in Providence. It therefore crosses the cañons of the South and Middle Boulder and of Left Hand. Within these limits, since the discovery of the Red Cloud in May, 1873, more than 500 locations have been made of veins carrying telluride ores of gold and silver. Of course most of these are as yet mere prospect-holes, and can boast of but little rich ore; yet in all the characteristic tellurium minerals have been found, either in pockets or disseminated through the vein-material, and, unless my informants are greatly in error, the majority promise to become, with development, valuable and productive. These mines are in granite and gneiss, presenting all the features supposed to indicate fissure-veins, and in all respects (excepting the nature of their contents) are like other Colorado veins. They are not, as has been often stated, "knife-blade lodes," but range from 4 to 40 feet width, with well-defined walls, and often extensive slickensides. The ore is generally scattered through the entire width of the fissure in quartz or altered granite, and, being of a grayish color and finely disseminated, is easily overlooked. Occasionally it is found concentrated in seams, streaks, or bunches, and in that case almost invariably yields extraordinary mill returns, causing much excitement among the miners. The most exaggerated case of this kind that has taken place during the year was in the Melvina, where a lot of 1,500 pounds, sold at Black Hawk, brought the enormous sum of $8,300.

Generally, however, the ore is of low grade—from 20 to 50 ounces—and it is this that makes the tellurium district at once so attractive and so disappointing. The miners, who have no possible means of handling their low-grade material, work constantly in the hope of discovering one of these miniature bonanzas. A great number of these have been found and are constantly being uncovered, so that there is always a sufficiency of fuel to feed the flame of excitement in the breast of the sanguine miner.

The amount of low-grade ore that has been taken out is enormous. It constitutes the dump-piles which are rapidly accumulating, and will, in time, produce more metal than the mines have ever turned out. When it is stated that but little rock worth less than $100 per ton can be handled to any profit, it is evident how vast an amount of material is annually thrown to waste. Owing to the wide dissemination of the telluride minerals in these veins, the crevice material will mill from $15 to $30 per ton from wall to wall, and as they are of good width, they are capable of producing immense quantities. There is here a splendid chance for the right kind of concentration-works or for a cheap humid process.

The prominent mines of the telluride belt are the Coldspring, Red-Cloud, Stirling, Osceola, Grand View, John J., Ellen, American, Keystone, Magnolia, Slide, Melvina, Cash, Phil Sheridan, and Victoria. Of the innumerable other discoveries on the belt, the following are worthy of mention as promising, with development, to become properties of value: In Sunshine district, the Charcoal, Surprise, Silver Dale, and Sunshine; in Magnolia, the Little Dorrit, Mountain Lion, Congress, Raven, and American Eagle; in Spring Dale, the J. A. Smith, Gladiator, Providence, and Van Dam; and in Salina, the Loveland, Great Eastern, Phœnix, First National, Henderson, Ringgold, and Bessie Turner. On these mines are shafts ranging from 15 to 100 feet deep. From nearly every one small lots of ore have been taken, that have milled from $500 to $5,000 per ton; the veins are strong, well-defined, and, in many cases, of great width, and while they can hardly be denominated mines, yet they are most excellent prospects, and offer good security for the investment of reasonable sums, so soon as there is provided a means of handling the low grades now thrown on the dumps.

Not one of the older discoveries on Gold Hill is now worked. The Horsfall, which is said to be one of the finest lodes ever found in Colorado, is still idle, though frequent reports are heard of the intention of its owners to reopen it. The Alamakee, Hoosier, Jefferson, Pride of the West, Great Cross, and Forest are in the same condition; and, in fact, so eager has been the search for the new ore that older claims of known worth seem to have been forgotten.

In *Ward district* three mines are now worked, the Ni-wot, Columbia, and Stoughton. A few other claims of minor importance are under development. Some interesting experiments were made late in the year on Stoughton ore with the new Pomeroy percussion-tables, (a description of which will be found further on,) and it seems likely that during 1876 considerable ore will be treated in this apparatus. Farther back on Gold Hill, in what is known as Williamsburgh, the Washington Avenue Mine, one of the oldest discoveries in the county, has been worked during the year with satisfactory results. A description of its condition will be found elsewhere.

At Sunnyside the Milwaukee, a lode of good reputation, has been idle during the year, but is to be re-opened early in 1876.

The Caribou silver belt has been the scene of a great deal of work during the year. The gross production of the mines has amounted to about $450,000, being an increase of more than $100,000 on the figures of 1874. While but a few new veins have been discovered, most of the old locations have been worked with satisfactory results, several sales made by which new capital has been brought in, and those of the mines now sunk to a depth of 200 feet and over have indicated that the veins are to be depended upon, and will return a large profit on judicious working.

The Caribou has labored during the year under the disadvantages of dissensions in a dissatisfied body of stockholders. A struggle has been waged, apparently to determine whether the Dutch or the American party shall rule. So far the former has held the reins. The other side made at the close of the year a vigorous move for the command, but did not achieve success. It is understood in mining circles in Colorado that a strong pool has been formed upon the basis of the stock held by Americans, and that every effort will be made to displace the Dutch management. The mine is undoubtedly one of the best in the Territory, and carries the enormous weight of its $3,000,000 capital better than was anticipated. It has not, however, yielded any dividends.

The following are detailed descriptions of the condition of some of the mines and mills of the county at the close of the year:

Grand Island District.—No mention was made of the Fourth of July lode in my last report, because, though it had been discovered for some time, no development had been made, and no excitement had arisen in consequence. During this year, however, a number of parties have been at work in various places along its outcrop, and have demonstrated that it is a lode of unusual magnitude and value.

The vein lies about two miles west of the town of Caribou, and cuts directly through the main range of the Rocky Mountains, running down on their western slope into Grand County. Its outcroppings have been traced for nearly six miles without being lost, and the vein, by measurement, is from 300 to 500 feet in width. The crevice material is the same as that found elsewhere, carrying, irregularly scattered across its width, numerous seams of ore, varying in width from an inch to a foot, and of all grades. In many places the ore crops out directly on the surface, showing all the minerals peculiar to the Caribou belt, including argentiferous galena, native silver, pyrites, native copper, sulphurets of silver, ruby silver, gray copper, and others.

The vein is divided into a number of claims, eight of which, representing 12,000 feet, have consolidated under one ownership, and will probably during next year be developed to an extent worthy of the magnitude of the property. A lode with such an enormous outcrop, and showing so well in ore directly on the surface, will most certainly develop greater bodies of mineral when depth is gained. It is proposed by the owners of this 12,000 feet to form a company for the purpose of sinking a vertical shaft to the depth of 1,000 feet directly in the lode. The width of the vein will necessitate exploring cross-cuts at regular distances, and probably before the first 500 feet are passed enough ore will have been found (if one may judge by surface indications) to demonstrate that the Fourth of July is one of the most valuable mines on the continent.

Considerable work has been done on other parts of this vein during the past year, but as the workers have been poor miners, and no united attempt has been made in any one part, the results have been simply a half-dozen shallow shafts, where the expenses of hoisting and draining have been so great as to preclude any possibility of profit, though the ore taken out has averaged well.

At the close of the year the shaft of the Caribou Mine was a little over 500 feet deep. The appearance of the mine was as good as ever before, there being plenty of ore in sight of good grade, ($30 to $60,) but the quarrels between the American and Dutch stockholders have prevented harmonious working, and the future of the property is gloomy in the extreme. The production of the year amounted to $204,000.

On the Sherman and No Name Mines work has been carried on throughout the year, but the production has been comparatively small. The mines, although under separate management, are owned by the same men. The workings in each have reached a depth of over 250 feet, and show good veins of ore. The product is now shipped partly to Black Hawk and partly to Batesville, at which place the new mill of the company is located. This mill has been remodeled several times during the year, and is not yet satisfactorily at work, though several shipments of bullion have been made. The process used is roasting and amalgamation, to which is added occasionaley a trial of leaching. Inasmuch as the works can not yet be said to be complete, any detailed description of the machinery used is at present uncalled-for. The shipments of ore from the district outside of the Caribou Mine have been very small. Besides the Sherman and No Name, the Poorman, Grand View, Native Silver, (an extension of the Caribou,) Seven-Thirty, Idaho, Potosi, Sovereign People, and a few others of minor note, have been worked. About three miles east of the town of Caribou, in the valley of the North Boulder, is the Blue Bird, now called the Santa La Saria, a property of which high expectations have been entertained. It has been worked intermittently during the year in the way of development. Some ore has been shipped that milled over $200 per ton. The company owning it has much faith in the property, and proposes to build a mill as soon as enough ore is in sight to warrant the venture.

Prospectors have been exploring the country around the head of the Middle Boulder this year, and a number of good mines carrying gold are claimed to have been found.

Work has been prosecuted in Grand Island district during the year on four tunnels, the Idaho, Two-Seventeen, Red Cross, and Summit. The latter, which is running from the valley of the Middle Boulder for Caribou Hill, is between 400 and 500 feet in length.

The principal mill of the county is the Nederland Mill, belonging to the Caribou Company. The subjoined report has been furnished to me by the courtesy of Mr. N. H. Cone, superintendent of the mill:

JANUARY 1, 1876.

H. J. DE BRUYN PRINCE,

Chief Agent Mining Company Nederland:

DEAR SIR: I herewith transmit to you my yearly report of the operations of the Nederland Mill, embracing the production, loss, and expenses; with a general review of the different departments of the mill, and the changes circumstances have permitted me to make.

In preparing this, I have adopted the same methods of tabulation as in my monthly report. The average assays for the months of January and April were estimated in the same manner as were the months of February and March, copies of which were handed in on the 1st of May. In some of my former reports I have mentioned the inaccuracies that were liable to occur in taking dry weights at the batteries, and, in looking over the figures of those months in which custom-ore and dump-ore were run besides the regular Caribou ore, it appears that dump was credited as Caribou ore, causing a large percentage of moisture for the former and a very small percentage for the latter, when exactly the reverse should be the case, as the dump at no time exceeded 3 per cent. of water.

PRODUCTION AND YIELD.

Number of tons treated	3,819,328
Bullion, (ounces)	169,978
Average assay per ton, (ounces)	46.3
Average fineness	827.3

Making a saving of 82 per cent., or an average loss of 8.4 ounces per ton of ore.

EXPENSES.

In making this part of my report, I have inserted, in place of "apparent loss of quicksilver," the amount of mercury purchased at the average price per pound, and estimated loss a follows:

Quicksilver on hand January 1, 1875, (pounds)	2,287
Quicksilver purchased during 1875, (pounds)	1,989
Total, pounds	4,276
On hand January 1, 1876, (pounds)	2,012
Actual loss, (pounds)	2,264

Corresponding to a loss per ton of 0.59 pounds.

COST OF TREATMENT PER TON.

Pay-roll, salt, wood, oil, candles, &c	$46,201 56
Loss of quicksilver, 2,264 pounds, at $1.19	2,698 88
Castings purchased	3,230 41
Five per cent. on value of mill, $60,000	3,000 00
Total cost	$55,130 65

Corresponding to a cost per ton of $14.43.

I have now ascertained, with as careful and conscientious computation as possible, the two most important results of the year's work, and have mentioned these estimates where inaccuracies are liable to occur.

To me, as superintendent of the mill, the knowledge of these results is of great interest and value, for my predecessor left no faithful record that I have been able to find, and what facts were obtained were too general to be of any material assistance. In milling, as in everything else, perfection is only gained by practice and experience. I desire, therefore, to examine into the items of loss, and suggest what changes are necessary to prevent them in the future.

1st. *Loss occurs in the batteries in the fine dust blown away.*—As yet, I know of no practical means of positively preventing this. Suction-fans have been tried in other mills, but with no flattering results.

2d. *Loss occurs in the smoke-stack.*—It has been claimed that the silver passes off with the volatile gases; but I do not think that can be the case, as we have too large an extent of dust-chambers, but that it is a mechanical loss, as there is a very strong draught, and I think a marked improvement would be seen if the stack were cut down ten feet.

3d. *Loss occurs in the breakage of thebattery-screens*—allowing coarse particles of the ore to pass to the cylinder-hoppers.

4th. *Loss occurs through sintering of the ore in roasting.*

5th. *Loss occurs through grease getting into the amalgamating-pans*—through flouring of the quicksilver, and through insufficient roasting.

The changes I would suggest to prevent these are: 1st, pipes and suction-fans for the batteries; 2d, screening of the roasted ore; 3d, the substitution of barrels for pans in amalgamation. Expenses can further be reduced by drying and pulverizing the salt, and thereby shortening the time of roasting and the consumption of wood.

A conveyor should be built to carry the ore from the cylinders to screens, in order to separate the sintered lumps from the well-roasted fine ore. This does away with three men, and will not cost over $2,000.

RECAPITULATION.

Wet Caribou ore, (tons)		3,769.240
Dry Caribou ore, (tons)		3,171.199
Dry Caribou dump, (tons)		366.155
Total Caribou ore, (tons)		7,306.594
Assay per ton, (ore)	47 ounces.	
Assay per ton, (dump)	28 ounces.	
Wet custom-ore, (tons)		317.893
Dry custom-ore, (tons)		282.040
Total ore treated, (tons)		7,906.527
Average moisture	7.2 per cent.	
Average assay per ton of custom-ore	62.6 ounces.	
Average assay of chlorinations	89.5 per cent.	
Average time of roasting	10 hours.	
Average assay of tailings	5.3 ounces.	
6,680 pans produced of amalgam, (pounds)		27,040
936 pans scraped, of amalgam, (pounds)		30,263
Put in retort, (pounds)		57,303
Weight of crude bullion from retort, (pounds)		12,150
Weight of 112 bricks, (ounces)		169,978
Average fineness		.827.3

EXPENSES.

Pay-roll	$23,600 74
Quicksilver	2,371 32
Salt	7,999 82
Wood	13,111 00
Oil, candles, &c	1,490 00
	48,572 88

CASTINGS PURCHASED IN 1875.

Blake Crusher:		
28 chills	7,391 pounds	$545 46
16 side plates	447 pounds	31 29
Steel lever, toggles, connection and joint	1,866 pounds	182 29
Freight from Black Hawk	3,898 pounds	58 47
Freight from Chicago and Cincinnati	5,806 pounds	130 63
Total	9,704 pounds	948 13
Old iron sold at Black Hawk	6,458 pounds	226 45
Actual cash cost		722 68
Battery:		
47 shoes	5,358 pounds	330 01
30 dies	2,259 pounds	137 54
400 feet wire-cloth, 40x40		368 52
10 cams	1,800 pounds	156 00
2 cam-shaft boxes		26 00
3 cam-shafts		109 75
Freight		216 46
Total		1,344 28
Old iron sold		58 85
Actual cash cost		1,285 43

Cylinders:

Pinion diaphragms	6,539 pounds	537 52
Re-lining fire-boxes		75 00
Re-lining cylinders		100 00
Total		712 52

Pans:

Millers, shoes, shieves, dies, shields, &c	509 78

SUMMARY.

Crusher	722 68
Battery	1,285 43
Pans	509 78
Cylinders	912 52
Total	3,230 41

Ward district is still alive, though not more active than during last year. The Stoughton, Columbia, and Ni-Wot have been worked, the first two with no remarkable results, but the last with more success.

The cessation of continuous work on the Ni-wot several years ago was caused by the disappearance of all ore in the lower workings, the vein having "pinched." The yield of the mine had previously been magnificent, and probably there is no finer hoisting-machinery and no more complete mill in the Territory than this company erected while in bonanza. After a long period of unremunerative work, during which the main shaft was deepened at a cost of from $30 to $60 per foot, the discouraged stockholders discontinued further extensive operation, and for some time the mine has been in the hands of Mr. Tobie, the old superintendent, who has always had unlimited faith in the lode, and who has been exploring the mine little by little in the hope of striking a new body of ore. In August his unremitting labors were rewarded with success. What is supposed to be the continuation of the old ore-body was found some distance east of the main shaft, and has since been opened to a large body of fine "peacock" ore, varying from 2 to 6 feet in width. Besides this rich zone, there is also from 2 to 7 feet of good mill-ore exposed.

A company has just been formed on the Columbia lode, with a capital of $1,000,000.

Some interesting experiments have been made on Stoughton ore in the way of concentration with a new style of machine, known as Pomeroy's percussion-table. On the small scale on which they were made I can report no results of value, but the model-machines worked well and will be replaced by larger ones. A company has been formed on the patent, and large works are to be built at Boulder City, to put the invention in operation. The tables are set on a slight incline, about 2° from a level, and have a horizontal, back, and forward motion. The ore, crushed to a great fineness, is fed in with water at the head, and the motion of the table gives the effect of a wave motion to the water. I need hardly say that the principle is an old and well-known one. Judging from the above description, which is all that my correspondent has furnished me, this apparatus presents features which have been superseded in the best modern percussion-tables. Whether it has any new and counterbalancing advantages I cannot say. Of course, like any other single machine, it will be inadequate for the systematic dressing of ores. The objection, which from the start attaches to its universal use for dressing, is the fine pulverization required for the ore, when no doubt the bulk of the mineral might be saved by jigging coarser stuff, and thereby avoiding the serious losses always connected with fine pulverization.

The Telluride mines.—There are now five districts in the "Tellurium belt," viz: Magnolia, Gold Hill, Sunshine, Springdale, and Providence. Taking them in regular order, as named, the following data will show the condition of the most prominent mines at the close of the year.

Magnolia district.—The Keystone shaft has reached a depth of 75 feet, and levels have been run 35 feet from the surface 50 feet each way. Since its discovery, in August, the mine has produced over $20,000, and has opened a body of very fine-looking tellurides of gold and silver, equal to any yet found in the county. Ore was found without a break from the surface to the bottom of the shaft, where there was a vein of mineral ranging from 2 to 7 inches in width, that would mill as high as $600 per ton. The average value of the ore so far shipped has been about $700.

The Mountain Lion is a northerly extension of the Keystone. Thirty-five feet from the surface pay-ore was found, and has held out well to the present bottom of the shaft, which is 50 feet deep. It has more than paid its own expenses, without any stoping.

The Little Dorrit was discovered in July, and has shipped since then about $4,000, the ore averaging about $300 per ton.

The Dunraven has been opened to a depth of 50 feet, and has turned out some very fine ore. Several shipments have been made, worth from $200 to $300 per ton. The pay-streak is narrow.

The Adabazar is opened by two shafts, each 20 feet deep, and has shown small seams of the usual telluride ore, very rich, but very precarious. The vein is one of six lodes belonging to a company, which also own a site for a tunnel which is to cut them all.

Gold Hill district.—The Melvina, discovered in June, is one of the most remarkable discoveries of the year. It is located on the ridge between the Four-Mile Creek and Gold Run. The first lot of ore shipped weighed 1,500 pounds, and brought $8,360 at the smelting-works. While sinking the shaft the first 25 feet nearly $20,000 was taken out, and from the time of discovery up to the close of the year over $37,000 was produced from developing work only, without stoping. Of course this was the result of sinking directly on the top of a very rich pocket. The mine continues to ship ore with regularity that mills on an average over $600 per ton. The shaft at the close of the year was something more than 100 feet deep.

The Slide is the name given to a new discovery made in July on the northern slope of the hill, and just above the Corning tunnel. Its first ore yielded "in the thousands," being a combination of tellurides and native gold. The vein was developed at first by an open cut. Since then a shaft has been sunk to a depth of 60 feet, and the ore has been found to hold out well. Subsequently the mine was sold for $40,000, and is now being developed by an adit-level, which will intersect the shaft some 10 feet below its present depth.

The Cash, on the north slope of the hill, is an old discovery. Last summer it was "capitalized" and thrown on the Denver Stock Exchange. The transformation has not apparently been a fortunate one, for, although the mine has been considerably developed and has reached a depth of 150 feet, the stock has gone down very much. The average of ore does not carry much of the tellurium minerals, and has yielded in mill about $20 per ton, mostly gold. The vein is one of the strongest on the hill.

The Sterling, probably an extension of the Cash, is at present producing some remarkably rich tellurides, thus leading to the conclusion that the workings of the Cash Mine are on a poorer part of the vein.

The Red Cloud has been idle during the entire year, excepting that in October an effort was made by driving on some of the upper levels to find a continuation of the rich ore-body that had made the mine famous. The effort was, however, unsuccessful. There is no lack of ore in nearly all parts of the mine, but it is of too low a grade to be shipped, and there are no means near by, either to concentrate or to amalgamate. The shaft was at the time work was stopped about 420 feet deep.

The Coldspring continues shipping ore regularly, as it has done for two years past. The actual production of 1875 was small compared with that of previous years, but the grade of the ore remains as high as ever. The main shaft is 300 feet deep, and about 1,200 feet of levels and winzes have been run. Nearly a year ago a cross-cut was driven west from the main shaft, and cut at 20 feet a new vein of tellurium-ores, upon which a new shaft has been sunk to the depth of 230 feet. This cross-cut has been driven 30 feet from the east wall of the vein, (which is porphyry,) but no indications of the foot-wall have been found. The new vein is, therefore, probably but a seam of the main fissure. It is somewhat pockety in nature, like the old one upon which the main shaft was sunk; but the ore is continuous, seldom, if ever, disappearing entirely, and often expanding to a width of several feet. In driving this cross-cut several minor streaks of mineral were intersected, and it appears quite certain that the entire width of the fissure is crossed irregularly by such seams. The experience of the Coldspring Mine has greatly encouraged deep explorations in other telluride veins of the county, for there is at least the proof in this property that the mineral is not found near the surface only.

The Victoria lies about 2,000 feet below the Cash. It was, in common with the Cash, capitalized in the fall and placed on the Denver exchange. It has been shipping ore regularly since then, and is considered one of the best mines on the hill. The workings have been extended to a depth of over 200 feet, and suitable surface improvements, such as hoisting and pumping machinery, have been erected over the shaft.

The Horsfall and Alamakee are still idle, though presenting good inducements to development. West of the town of Gold Hill is the Washington Avenue Mine, a property which many years ago attracted much attention. It was re-opened during the summer, and now is in a condition to ship large quantities of ore regularly. The ore is galena, with pyrites of copper and iron and some zinc-blende. Gold Run is dotted with miners' cabins from source to mouth, and numerous mines of minor note, but of great promise, have been opened during the year. In this gulch are the camps known as Salina and Camp Tellurium. The mines are located on both sides of the gulch, crossing it in every direction and offering excellent opportunities of advantageous development. At the mouth of the gulch, in Four-Mile, are several tunnels, projected to penetrate underneath Gold Hill or Sunshine.

The Corning tunnel, which enters the northern face of the hill from the cañon of Left Hand, has been driven 800 feet, and is steadily advancing. Its objective point is undoubtedly the porphyry dike, on the north side of which is the Cold Spring, and on the south the Red Cloud. Several good veins have been crossed by it already, on one of which work is now prosecuted.

Sunshine district.—The American sustains its reputation more thoroughly than any mine yet opened in the tellurium belt. Under the management of Mr. J. Alden Smith it has been developed systematically and economically; and though the workings cannot yet be considered very extensive, they show the vein-fissure to be well charged with ore and quite regular in its formation. The shaft has been sunk to a depth of 100 feet, and 500 feet of levels have been driven. Good hoisting and pumping works are erected over the shaft, and there are convenient arrangements for sorting the ore, which is an item of great importance in this class of mines.

The shipments of ore have averaged about twenty-seven tons per month, netting about $10,000, the year's production being, as nearly as I can learn, about $125,000. This is certainly, if correctly reported, a remarkable yield for a mine opened to so small an extent. The ore furnished by the American contains all the various tellurium minerals so far found in the county, besides considerable free gold in small grains or scales and filiform segregations.

Of the other mines in Sunshine but little can be said that is new. The Grand View, Osceola, Phil. Sheridan, Consolidated, Glendale, Shoo-Fly, Warsaw, Charcoal, Young America, Little Giant, Augusta, Yosemite, and others are working, and nearly all are doing well.

Springdale and Providence districts.—Springdale is located in a gulch running southward into Left Hand. The number of prospects is legion, but the only mine that has been worked to any great extent is the Ellen. From this a considerable quantity of tellurides of the richest kind has been taken.

Providence is located in Jim Creek, and its mines are the John J. and the Last Chance. Being as yet slightly opened, (neither is deeper than 30 feet,) it can only be said that they have produced some exceedingly rich ore of the usual tellurides. In this camp also the prospector has been busy on every side, and the number of claims staked is beyond the power of an ordinary mortal to enumerate.

LAKE COUNTY.

The valley of the Upper Arkansas is the only mineral district in this large county yet opened by the miner, if I except the workings on the headwaters of the Gunnison and Uncompahgre, which are included in the present report under the head of the San Juan region.

The industry is mainly placer-mining, though a few quartz-ledges are operated. Mr. Van Wagenen gives the product of the county as follows:

	Currency.
Quartz-gold from Printer Boy	$30,000
Quartz-gold from other mines	3,000
Gulch-gold	42,000
Silver-ore	25,000
	100,000
Or, in coin	86,200

Mr. Maurice Hayes, the territorial assayer, at Oro City, gives the production of the county as follows:

	Currency.
Gold from the gulch-mines and Printer Boy Mine	$95,940
Silver, copper, and lead from the lodes	25,000
	120,940

But I suspect that the last item includes ores which, also raised from the mines, have not been beneficiated, but lie probably at the works of the Cincinnati company, (under the management of Mr. Loescher,) which have not been in operation. It is, therefore, to be expected that this item will appear again in next year's estimate.

There is still no market for silver-ores in this county, and this circumstance hinders all mining enterprises in that direction. Several attempts are making to correct this disadvantage, and it is probable that in another year the Arkansas Valley will be supplied with one or more works. In California Gulch Captain Breece is building chlorination-works, under the superintendence of Mr. R. Keck, and expects them to be in operation by February. At the mouth of the gulch another company has put up smelting-works, which have, however, not been in operation, and in Chalk Creek Messrs. Chapman and Riggins are building works of ten tons' capacity to treat ores from their own mines. The plant of this establishment comprises two roasting-furnaces and one blast-furnace. It is not expected to be in operation before the summer of 1876.

In the mines there is but little new. Those which were worked last year are, with a very few exceptions, still in operation, and attaining just the degree of success which encourages a continuation of labor. The experience of years in the gulches emptying into this valley shows that the ores are, as a rule, very low in grade, and require more capital than the prospector and the miner generally possess to develop them to a point where they can steadily pay.

The Printer Boy was worked steadily during the latter part of the year. Developments have not been pushed much below the depth at which work was last stopped, but the mine has been explored laterally with fair results. The yield of the mine was about $30,000. A full account of the workings is given below.

The Berry tunnel, which runs upon a lode of the same name, is one of the important enterprises of the county. The lode has a width of 8 to 12 feet, and carries copper and iron pyrites, partly rich in gold and silver. As far as opened the vein shows plenty of ore, but of low grade. The chlorination-works spoken of above are being built for the special purpose of treating the material from this mine, though if they prove successful they will be enlarged for custom-work.

Excepting a little "gouging" done by lessees, the Home Stake, which at one time was considered one of the finest mines of Colorado—the best certainly on the Arkansas—has been idle during the year. Differences among the owners and disappointment in deep developments have been the cause. The property has now, however, fallen into the hands of one of the former owners, Capt. James Archer, and it has been the expectation to reopen it during the winter. It was currently reported some time ago that the mine was exhausted, but this is not the case. At present there is but little ore exposed in the workings, (which have been quite extensive,) but this is the result of poor management in handling the mine. It will be remembered by readers of former reports that it was from the ore of this mine, treated at the Golden City works, that so much nickel was taken.

The Chalk Creek mines are mainly on galena-veins. A number have been worked during the year by the company which is putting up the smelting-works on the creek, and it is expected that they will in time furnish a large amount of ore, carrying as high as 35 per cent. lead and 40 to 70 ounces silver. At the close of the year several hundred tons were on the dumps and several of the mines were to be worked throughout the winter. Those which the company own, wholly or in part, are the Riggins, Naomi, Tecumseh, Black Hawk, Anna, Mary Murphy, and Mount Yale.

Of the other mines in the Arkansas Valley that have been worked more or less, may be mentioned the Pilot, Yankee Blade, Five-Twenty, American Flag, Mike, Gray Bird, Hidden Treasure, and Mary Francis.

The placer-mines of the Arkansas Valley have produced about $42,000, considerably less than last year. California and Cash Creeks have been the most actively worked; but even in these localities operations have been languid and intermittent, little more being done than was required to procure gold for the immediate personal necessities of claim-owners.

In regard to California Gulch, which is by far the most important mining-camp of Lake County, I have received later notes, which I owe to the courtesy of Mr. Rudolph Keck, M. E., formerly territorial assayer at Fair Play, and now engineer of the beneficiating works connected with the Berry tunnel enterprise.

Near Upper Oro City California Gulch runs east and west. On the mountain-side south of it several parallel lodes running north and south have been discovered in porphyry, the most noted being the Printer Boy, which has produced at least $600,000 during the few years since its location. The vein, like the parallel lodes on both sides, is filled with porphyry, which is, however, softer than the country-rock, and of a different color. It contains, in very irregular distribution, nests of carbonate of lead with native gold, the latter occurring in particles far smaller than those found in the placer-mines of the gulch. In the lowest workings of the mine the same gangue material has lately been reached as was found some time ago on the north side of California Gulch, in the Berry tunnel, namely, a talcose mass of auriferous iron and copper pyrites with a little galena and tennantite. According to a certificate of the territorial assayer of the county, a selected specimen of this ore contained 122 ounces of gold per ton. Several assays by Dr. Loescher, of the Malta Smelting-Works, showed from 3 to 4 ounces of gold per ton.

The vein is opened by means of three shafts and several levels, and that is split in two places for distances varying from 200 to 400 feet.

Most of the mining work has been done between the main and the line or middle shaft in the split highest on the hill and in the eastern branch of the vein. It was here that rich nests of carbonate of lead, filled with leaf-gold, were repeatedly found. The thickness of the vein proper and its branches varies between 1 inch and 4 feet, but may be called on an average 7 inches, the eastern branch averaging 6 and the western 8 inches. Besides the two splits referred to, the vein shows the peculiarity that it is, from the surface down to a depth varying between 100 and 200 feet, filled with cross-seams in the porphyry mass, which are from 2 to 3 feet thick and cut off abruptly by the steep eastern wall, while on the western wall they often continue for a short distance outside of the vein. They are filled with the same auriferous ore as occurs in the vein itself, only of different color and hardness. In addition to this the gangue mass, as far as its contents of gold and the differing hardness are concerned, shows a diverging vein-system within the fissure from the surface toward depth, something like the spread fingers of a hand held downward. Whenever such soft veins are joined by cross-seams the richness of the ore is said to be greatest. The inconsiderable difference of outer appearance between the porphyry of the walls and that of the vein-matter, which can be distinguished with still less certainty in the comparatively dark workings, renders it often very difficult to follow the real ore-deposit.

The line or middle shaft has been sunk on the line between two claims, the upper one of which belongs to the Philadelphia and Boston Gold-Mining Company, and the lower or northerly one to a few inhabitants of the vicinity. The latter is, however, leased to the company just mentioned, and it is here that the rich pyrites spoken of above has lately been found. It is to be regretted that for the present at least it cannot be extracted, because without powerful pumps the water struck at the same time cannot be overcome. The material is much desired and needed by the Malta Works as a flux.

The ore in the western branches of the two splits is decidedly softer than that in the eastern ones, but so far it has not shown any such rich pockets as the eastern upper branch between the line and the main shaft. The eastern lower branch between the line and the lower shaft has so far not been developed. At the lowest depth, just before the rich pyrites was struck, the contents of the ore in gold were very small. At the same time it must be remarked that the vein above this point is by no means exhausted, and, considering the former carelessness of management, this field is very promising. A little over 100 feet deep in the main shaft a mass of bowlders, with a little iron-pyrites and fine gold, was found, which Mr. Keck thinks may either be taken for the bed of a former stream or for the remaining moraine of a former glacier. I do not find it necessary to adopt either hypothesis. The presence of rounded bowlders, unless they are clearly of a material different from the country-rock, may be the result of attrition and water between the vein-walls. This phenomenon is expressly considered by Von Weissenbach, in the classification of "veins of attrition," contained in his Theory of Veins, as published in Von Cotta's *Gangstudien*.

At the depth of 200 feet in the line-shaft, and of 100 in the main shaft, the cross-seams mentioned above were no longer met with, and south of the latter the vein is not split at all. At this point, however, so little systematic work has been done that no conclusions as to increase or decrease of richness can be drawn from the altered geological conditions. Indeed little systematic work has been done on any part of the whole vein. Former operations were principally confined to robbing the rich pockets, while good milling-ore was left standing.

The gold contained in the pyrites just discovered, although it can be partly washed out, cannot be directly amalgamated, behaving in this respect like that in the ores of the Berry tunnel.

Among the veins running parallel with the Printer Boy, the Five-Twenty is at present the most promising. The ore from this mine yielded in the battery alone 8 ounces gold per cord, or about 1 ounce per ton. The mill-gold of these veins is usually worth $15, coin, per ounce, while the wash-gold of the gulch is worth from $17.75 to $19.

Of the production of Lake County during 1875, now estimated at over $120,000, currency, three-quarters are said to come from California Gulch.

The placer-mining of the gulch, an industry which has now been in existence for sixteen years, is really a still worse robbery of the gold-deposits than that carried on so long in the veins. The gold occurs in these placers, notably in the upper part of the gulch, in two different layers. The upper one consists of gravel and conglomerate, and is the deposit which alone has been washed; the lower one consists of so-called cement, a hydrated oxide of iron combined with a feldspathic mass to a very hard layer, which contains not only fine, and very fine, gold-dust, but also coarse gold. As the hardness of this material precludes washing without a preliminary crushing, this layer is to-day virtually virgin ground, a fact which is the more remarkable since assays of average samples have never yielded less than an ounce of gold per ton.

At the Berry tunnel Mr. Keck has completed his beneficiating-works as far as was intended for the present. While up to the end of the year only the common ores of the Berry tunnel (talcose gangue with iron and a little copper-pyrites) were subjected to the process* employed, the mine has been better developed, and now there is a considerable quantity of more solid and richer ore ready for extraction, similar to the pyrites described above in connection with the Printer Boy. This ore is now assorted by hand, dried, in order to stamp it without water, and subjected to the rest of the beneficiating process. It is to be regretted that for the amalgamation of the residues arrastras only are at Mr. Keck's disposal, since the gold is in this way not extracted as perfectly as could be done in pans.

The Malta Smelting-Works are built on the slope of a hill, and intended for lead-smelting. Besides the necessary buildings and apparatus for crushing, sampling, storage of wood, &c., they contain a long reverberatory furnace for roasting, (without a hearth for slagging purposes,) a shaft-furnace of the Kast pattern, of a capacity of at least 15 tons per day, and an English cupelling-furnace. The blast is furnished by a Sturtevant blower, No. 4. The establishment impresses the visitor favorably, and it is only to be hoped that in the coming summer the argentiferous-lead mines of the vicinity (so far containing principally cerussite) may be more energetically attacked than has been the case heretofore, in order that the metallurgical enterprise may not be crippled (as so many in Colorado have been) by the lack of material suitable to the processes employed.

SUMMIT COUNTY.

The metallic product of this county is placed at $76,000, being wholly gold-dust from placers. There has been also a yield of probably $10,000 from the Snake River mines which would belong to Summit, but which is included in the statements of Clear Creek, nearly all of it being sold there. The properties worked during the year are the same as those of last season, with a few additions. The Summit County placers being located at so high an altitude, can be worked successfully in good seasons only. The last season was but a tolerable one, and expectations were, as a rule, not realized. Fully as much ground as usual was opened, but the water-supply gave out nearly a month earlier than usual, and all ground worked by booming had to be abandoned. This system of washing is doing good work in the Blue Valley, and though it may be considered, in comparison with the more extensive and complicated systems of California, as rather primitive, it has peculiar merits of its own not to be despised. It has been described in former reports.

In French Gulch and its tributaries, Dry Mayo, Humboldt, and Nigger Gulches, Calvin Clark, I. H. Fuller, J. J. Cobb, and the Badger Company have been at work as usual. The production of the gulch (which is by far the best at present in the Blue Valley) has amounted to about $40,000. Georgia Gulch and Gold Run have together yielded about $13,000; about $4,000 have come from other minor localities, such as Galena, Iowa, and Lomax Gulches, and Stilson, Buffalo, and Dela-

* The process followed consists in stamping, dressing on fine-grain jigs, roasting with salt, lixiviation, precipitation of copper and silver, and amalgamation of the auriferous residues.—R. W. R.

ware Flats; and $15,000 may be credited to claims located directly in the main valley.

Of the new projects which have developed during the year into a condition of productiveness, the Izzard diggings are the most notable. Concerning them a correspondent of the Alma News reports the following:

Izzard's diggings are located about three miles south of Ten-Mile, on the west side of Blue River, and between 7 and 8 miles north of Breckinridge.

Four years ago if anybody had predicted that valuable and extensive placer-mines would be discovered between Gold Hill and the confluence of Ten-Mile and Blue Rivers and costly improvements added, he would have been considered an idle talker. So little faith had the "prospector" in that particular area that it always received the go-by. It was not until the spring of 1873 that any prospectors ventured a location. A party of two men made a pre-emption in one of the series of gulches, taking up 400 feet in length, with suitable width and 200 feet front, and doing a little work. Mr. J. E. Izzard, a Philadelphian, and a gentleman commanding considerable capital, had been testing lode-property about a mile and a half southwest of Gold Hill. Not meeting with anything encouraging, he abandoned it. His attention was next attracted to the locality now familiarly known by the name which heads this article. After prospecting awhile, he made up his mind that a large area of gulch and hill placer, having gold in paying quantities, existed in that vicinity. His next endeavor would naturally be to pre-empt all the territory that was likely to have pay, and secure the water flowing through that region which could possibly be brought upon the premises. The extent of ground to which he has secured possessory right is about 500 acres, having a front on Blue River of over 5,280 feet, and running west up a number of gulches and over gravel ridges and hills, in many instances as much as 13,200 feet, taking up and securing the water of 20,000 acres, affording during the flush a quantity as much as 4,000 inches, miners' gauge. The principal stream, and that which furnishes his largest supply of water, is called Miners' Stream. Barton, Izzard, and a number of other gulches unnamed, the springs and marshes with which this region is so bountifully supplied, constitute his water-privileges.

Miners' Stream runs north and empties into Ten-Mile. On this stream Mr. I. has put in a dam, conducting the water thence through large and well-constructed ditches, distributing it by a net-work of branch ditches to all his mines, which lie off east, changing the natural water-courses lying north and south, making those of the former flow south and east and the latter north and east. In the spring of 1873 he commenced the preliminary operations of surveying and digging ditches, sinking shafts, delivering lumber, and erecting cabins. At the close of the season he and his family visited their old home. Returning next season, a force of thirty-five men was set at work enlarging and extending ditches, building boom-flumes and reservoirs. The season closed without finding bed-rock. Leaving two men to finish uncompleted work, he and family left for Denver for the winter. This summer he employed from three to eight men, and late in the fall a depth was reached where increased pay came in, but no bed-rock, and in twelve days sufficient gold was taken out to pay the season's expenses, leaving him the net sum of $400. The gold assays 843 fine, and is worth $17.42 per ounce. Since the close of the mining season, a shaft has been sunk reaching bed-rock at 40 feet from the surface, prospecting from 8 to 36 colors heavy gold to the pan all the way down.

Poverty Flat.—In the districts bordering on North Park, in the gulches flowing from Hann's Peak, some very promising placers are being opened. Gold was first discovered in this camp by Sam Conger, of Caribou fame, in the summer of 1869, and, without causing much of an excitement, the district last year developed into what will without doubt prove next year a very valuable addition to our mineral lands. Two large companies, the Hann's Peak and the Purdy, have absorbed, by location and purchase, tho best parts of the district, owning between them about 1,250 acres, located on Poverty Flat and Way's Gulch. Their combined capital is $6,000,000, and the total amount of improvements up to date have cost in the neighborhood of $100,000. Twenty miles of ditches have been dug, and it is proposed this year to build several new ones of a total length of 12 miles, which will bring 5,000 inches of water additional into Way's Gulch.

Poverty Flat is on Beaver Creek, one of the tributaries of the Elk River. The elevation of the Hann's Peak Company's claim, which is on this flat, is about 8,000 feet. The ground is from 10 to 60 feet deep, of gravel, free from large bowlders, and pays well through its entire depth. Last year but one run of 25 days with one hydraulic was made, which washed out $3,500 in gold. The company is now arranging to work 12 hydraulics, and has a constant water-supply equal to about 2,000 inches. Five reservoirs have been built, by which means the supply can be maintained quite late in the year.

The Purdy Company, located in Way's Gulch, will put in this year a bed-rock flume, and probably will not take out much gold till 1877. The ground is as good as that of the Hann's Peak Company, but not so well located as to water. Hence the necessity of the 12-mile ditch from the Elk.

Several very promising gold-bearing lodes have been discovered at Hann's and Way's Peak, upon which work will be done this year. It is expected that the year's work will develop a splendid gold-district in Grand County, which will have the effect not only to draw an agricultural population to the valleys of the Bear and Grand, but to incite further explorations in the numerous mountain-chains around the North and Middle Parks, which are as likely to be rich in minerals as any in the Territory.

The Rabbit-Ear mines.—In the range of mountains dividing Middle from North Park are the Rabbit-Ear mines, about which but little can be said, except that the prospects are fair. The mines are numerous, large, and easily worked. They carry mainly silver-ore, and some of them show good veins of argentiferous galena. But little development has been made, no workings having been extended deeper than 50 feet, and the majority of the claims being only sunk 10 feet. Numerous companies have been organized and several tunnel schemes proposed, and next season will demonstrate whether the discoveries are of any value. The camp is 60 miles from the nearest reducing-works. It is proposed to put up a mill in the district next year, should the supply of ore warrant it.

The Lincoln City Lead-Works have been idle during the year, having fallen into legal troubles.

Snake River district has been steadily but slowly improving, and of *Peru district* the same may be said. The Champion, Tiger, Printer's Pool, Peruvian, Blanche, Orphan Boy, Silver Wing, Potosi, Cony, Sukey, and the Comstock tunnel mines have been worked with considerable regularity during the year, and all but the last have shipped ore.

The Sukey Mill made a short run in the summer, but was unsuccessful. The Saint Lawrence Mill has been transported to Georgetown and sold to the Pelican Company.

The operations of the Boston Silver Company, at Saint John's, have been steadily prosecuted during the season. The company continued to drive its long tunnel into Glacier Mountain until, on the 20th of November, it had reached a length of 1,075 feet. It is well constructed throughout, being 7 feet wide by 9 feet high, and in all places, where the rock is not sufficiently hard, timbered in the most substantial manner. Eight veins have been crossed so far, Nos. 1, 2, 3, 4, and 6 showing at the points of intersection quartzose gangue and iron-pyrites; Nos. 5 and 8, a similar gangue, with zinc-blende and galena; and No. 7, heavy spar, galena, and blende, with little iron-pyrites. All the veins, with the exception of No. 8, are very large, some of them extraordinarily so, as, for instance, No. 5, which at the point of intersection is about 20 feet; and No. 2, which is 83 feet thick. The latter carries such soft vein-material (broken quartz with iron-pyrites) and delivered when opened such volumes of water, that it was found necessary to timber closely the whole 83 feet, sides, top, and bottom, with 12-inch timbers, (sets of 10-inch timbers 3 feet apart, which had first been inserted, having been broken like reeds by the enormous pressure.) Just before the driving of the tunnel was temporarily stopped, a ninth vein had been struck and entered into for 3 feet, which carried quartz and iron-pyrites. The opposite wall not having been reached, the value of the vein is unknown.

At the time above named positive orders from the directors of the company in Boston forbade the continuance of the tunnel for the present, and ordered the development of Nos. 5 and 7 by drifts and rises. This work has since been going on uninterruptedly, 30 miners having been employed on an average, and with most unexpected results. The north drift on No. 5 was 200 feet long at the end of the year, the vein-material having been soft throughout that distance. When the drift had progressed so far, a very serious cave occurred about 170 feet from the entrance of the drift, which delayed further driving for a month, and required timbers 2 feet in diameter for a distance of 50 feet to overcome it. A rise was started at the end of the year a little south of the cave. While at the intersection of the tunnel with No. 5, only galena, blende, and a little iron-pyrites were found, containing, when solid, 60 to 70 ounces of silver per ton; the vein carried beyond a point 75 feet from the entrance northward, besides the minerals named, rich silver-ores, such as ruby silver, stephanite, polybasite and tetrahedrite in considerable quantity, so that the average value of the ores was more than doubled. The south drift on No. 5 was in about 50 feet at the end of the year, and has since been driven to the intersection with No. 7, 140 feet from the tunnel. In this drift only one pocket of ruby silver, stephanite and fahlore was found. The drift on No. 7 north of the tunnel was at the end of the year about 60 feet long, and is throughout in very soft and dangerous ground, carrying no ore. The south drift was in about 200 feet, and showed ore (zinc-blende and galena in heavy spar) for almost the whole distance, the vein being on an average 4 to 5 feet wide, and the ore-streak varying from 1 to 3 feet. At a distance of about 180 feet from the entrance, the drift encountered a horizontal fault of 8 feet, (the vein being thrown to the east,) and 12 feet farther a second fault of 6 feet in the same direction. Between the two the vein carried very good galena. About 6 feet beyond the second fault the galena became very solid and contained much native silver, which continued for a distance of 30 feet. The ore in No. 7, at the intersection with the tunnel, contained in solid galena from 48 to 50 ounces of silver; at the further end of the drift, where native silver was visible, it contained from 100 to 500 ounces, and in ordinary galena from 70 to 80 ounces.

Since the end of the year, two rises have been started on No. 5, 170 feet apart, the northern one being at the time of this writing 80 feet and the southern 114 feet high. In the latter, north and south drifts 100 feet above drift No. 1 are being started. Besides this, stoping ground for 10 men is opened, and extraordinarily rich silver-ores, carrying, however, little galena, are now being extracted.

On No. 7 one rise, now 120 feet high, has been made, and drifts will be started north and south in a few days. There are three stopes opened on No. 7, two of which produce ore.

Little work has been done during the year in the upper mine on the Comstock lode (probably No. 7 of the tunnel) beyond the extraction of about 60 tons of solid galena. The stopes there opened will probably be worked during this year, but no extensive work is intended there, until the connection has been made from the tunnel below.

At the end of the year the company had about 800 tons of ore on hand, about three-fourths of which is dressing-ore, to be concentrated in its very systematic establishment and to be smelted into pig-lead.

A dozen or more veins have been worked in Snake River district by other parties at intervals during the year, and some of the veins have produced rich lead-ores in small quantities. No large developments have, however, been made. The ores mined have mostly been bought by the Boston Silver Company.

PARK COUNTY.

I have nothing to add to what has been said in former reports as to the placers of this county, though I am informed in a general way that they are making satisfactory returns, particularly under a consolidation of ownerships and a more effective use of water. A few words may be said of the quartz-mines. On Mounts Lincoln and Bross the Moose, Dolly Varden, Hiawatha, Lincoln, Russia, Ford, Danville, and Security have been working steadily during the year. It is wholly impossible to give any intelligible statement concerning the developments on any. The entire story will be told by saying that in each case the ore-bodies have been diligently followed wherever they led, and if they suddenly pinched up to nothing, explorations have been turned in other directions. On none of these claims has there been found any regularity in the deposits. The entire stratum of blue limestone seems to be saturated with mineral, segregated in places to bodies of considerable magnitude. So far the Moose has seemingly had the monopoly of the big deposits, but the Ford and Russia promise to equal it shortly in quantity of mineral. The Moose has maintained throughout the year a steady production of about six tons daily, averaging in value about $150 per ton. The Dolly Varden has done well also, and has yielded some exceedingly rich material. The Hiawatha has been under lease, and is consequently not in as good a condition as it might be. The Security has kept up a fair production, and is regarded as one of the coming mines of the district.

In Buckskin and Mosquito Gulches a large amount of prospecting and development has been done, and a number of very good veins have been opened; also plenty of poor ones. At the head of Buckskin is the London lode, a vein which is attracting a great amount of attention, and which undoubtedly is a rich and valuable property. The Phillips has not revived yet, though about five hundred tons of ore have been taken out during the year for fluxing purposes. In Mosquito, the Orphan Boy has been temporarily opened, and a tunnel has been started to cut it some 250 feet deep.

In Sacramento and Horseshoe Gulches a small amount of ore has been produced, mainly galena. The latter has been most productive, if either can be said to have yielded. The amount of prospecting done has also been large, and it is known that the deposits in that part of the limestone belt are large and worthy of better attention. Still, though not lacking in mineral wealth, Park County improves but slowly. This fact may be attributed to the poor ore-market which exists, and to the comparative inaccessibility of the district. The latter drawback to its growth will only be removed when the South Park Railroad, now connecting Denver with Morrison in the foot-hills, is pushed up the Platte Cañon to the Park. The former may be expected to cure itself.

FREMONT COUNTY.

Rosita.—Few mining-camps in the West can show so rapid and so healthy a growth as Rosita. In the summer of 1873 the first discovery of note (the Senator) was made. A little later the Pocahontas vein was found, which, with its extensions, is now one of the most important lodes in the Territory. The Greenhorn range, in which the camp is located, is crossed from the northwest to the southeast by an eruptive mass or huge dike of porphyry,* trachyte, and andesite, which culminates at the south in the Greenhorn Peak, and disappears at the north in Wet Mountain Valley. Within this mass, which is from 3 to 5 miles in width, are located all the mines of importance hitherto found in this neighborhood. Outside of the porphyry, in the granite, veins have been found, but they do not exhibit any permanence of character or any valuable features. Veins are also found on the edge of the eruptive rock, between it and the granite; but these also promise less than others wholly within porphyry.

The Pocahontas vein, which has been called the "mother lode" of the district, has a course approximately the same as that of the "dike," northwest and southeast. There are several fissures having a parallel course with that of the Pocahontas, and presenting many similar features, leading to the belief that this is the line of main fracture and also of first fracture. The latter opinion is confirmed by the examination of several places where these northwest and southeast veins are crossed by others. In every case noticed the latter break through the former with a clean fracture, and generally cause faults of several feet in the older veins.

These secondary veins do not appear to have any marked parallelism of direction, but are claimed by some, who have examined the whole district thoroughly, to bear toward the prominent peaks within the range of eruption; or, in other words, to radiate from these peaks as spokes from the center of a wheel. The only illustration reported to me in support of this theory is the west slope of the peak, on which occur the Invincible, Matchless, Chieftain, and other veins. This is hardly conclusive.

The Pocahontas vein has been traced and claimed for a distance of several miles. Commencing at the southern end, so far as at present known, the first mine is the South African, followed by the South Humboldt, the Humboldt, the Pocahontas, the Leviathan, and the reduction-works Leviathan. In the latter the vein appears to be split, one fork being known as the Leavenworth, the other as the Stevens. The last claims have not been developed sufficiently to show whether this is a real forking of the vein or a division of the ore into two or more seams. The latter is probably the case. The production of the camp in 1875 was as follows:

	Currency.
Pocahotas Mine	$165,000 00
Humboldt and South Humboldt	62,000 00
Other mines	7,200 00
Total	234,200 00
Coin value	201,880 40

* I claim no personal knowledge of this locality, having seen the range at some distance only. But I hesitate to admit without further evidence the eruptive character of the country-rock containing the veins. Nevertheless, I leave the statement in the text as it was furnished to me.—R. W. R.

About 8,000 linear feet of mining-work, including shafts, levels, and tunnels, has been done since the opening of the camp. The production last year was 1,300 tons, showing an average grade of $180 per ton. As the reduction-works were running but a very short time during the year, nothing but high-grade material has been marketed. There are now from 500 to 800 tons of ore, worth from $30 to $60 per ton, lying on the dumps, awaiting the opening of the home-reduction works. The ore is mainly composed of gray copper and copper-pyrites, carried in a gangue of heavy spar. Galena, iron-pyrites, oxide of copper, ruby and native silver, and native copper also occur. The percentage of copper is pretty high, and renders the ore unfit for amalgamation without previous leaching. No veins have yet been found on any part of the Greenhorn range carrying a heavy percentage of lead. There is likely to be some difficulty, therefore, in treating these ores alone by smelting.

Numerous promising discoveries have been made on the western slope of the Greenhorn range, in what seems to be a continuation of the same belt of porphyry. On the eastern slope of the Sangre de Christo range, which lies just across from the Greenhorn, (Wet Mountain Valley being between,) some discoveries of rich argentiferous galena have been made, and early in 1876 a new camp will be started in their neighborhood. On Grape Creek, which flows from Wet Mountain Valley into the Arkansas, there has been a copper excitement, and some outlay has been made for development. The results, however, have not been very satisfactory, and at the close of the year Copper Gulch was almost deserted.

The following is a statement of the condition of the Rosita mines at the latest date, (March, 1876,) received since this report was sent to Congress:

Pocahontas.—This mine is opened by about 1,500 feet of shafts and levels, nearly all of which has been driven since March, 1875, at which time it fell into the hands of its present owners. The mine is now worked through a tunnel 250 feet long. The vein of ore is from 2 to 5 inches in width, very regular and continuous, and mills between $170 and $200 per ton. The ore is a gray copper and copper-pyrites, in a gangue of heavy spar, in which is found, as occasional minerals, oxide of copper, (black,) ruby and native silver, a trace of gold, and often iron-pyrites and galena. Production from March, 1875, to January, 1876, 706 tons, worth $123,408.31. From the latter date to March 1 of this year, 195 tons have been produced, worth about $36,270, making the total yield for the year ending March 1, 1876, nearly $160,000.

Humboldt and South Humboldt.—This property occupies 1,900 feet on the mother lode of the district south of the Pocahontas. It is opened by six shafts, of a total depth of 675 feet, and has 800 feet of levels. Shaft No. 1, which is the main working shaft, is at present 175 feet deep, and is being sunk steadily. The shaft is 30 feet in length, and is divided into a compartment for hoisting and one for ventilation. The ore-vein is steady and continuous in almost every part of the mine, and it is of the same character as that in the Pocahontas. The production of the mine during 1875 was $62,000.

West Virginia.—Shaft 86 feet deep, northwest drift 90 feet long. The parties who have leased the mine are putting up a whim and preparing for extensive work.

Leviathan.—The shaft on this claim is now 65 feet deep and is under contract to 100 feet. A drift 50 feet in length has been driven south on the vein, exposing a good seam of rich ore, which shows extremely well. This mine promises to become one of the most valuable in the camp.

Invincible.—The shaft has been sunk to a depth of 142 feet, and a 60-foot level run 100 feet below the surface. There is a good quantity of ore in sight, but it is of low grade. Better material is expected as greater depth is gained.

Polonia.—The Polonia shaft is 95 feet deep and is to be sunk to a depth of 125 feet before new levels are driven. Seventy-five feet from the surface drifts have just been started, with a good showing of ore.

SAN JUAN COUNTRY.

To the courtesy of Mr. N. A. Foss, superintendent of the San Juan Smelting and Refining Company, and late superintendent of Green & Co.'s works at Silverton, I am indebted for a very interesting report on San Juan, in substance as follows:

The San Juan mining country is situated in the southwestern corner of Colorado, bounded on the west by Utah, on the south by New Mexico, on the east by the one hundred and seventh meridian of west longitude, on the north by a line 20 miles north of the fortieth parallel. This vast region of over 30,000 square miles has never been prospected or explored to any extent outside of the 5,600 square miles relinquished by the Ute Indians in their treaty of September, 1873, and now comprising La Plata, San Juan, and Hinsdale Counties. The country is divided into six mining-districts, all of which, except Lake and Adams districts, are in San Juan County.

The Animas district includes all locations made on the Animas River and its tributaries to a point 2 miles above Howardsville.

The Eureka district joins the Animas at this point and extends to the divide between the waters of the Animas and those of the Gunnison and Uncompahgre.

The Uncompahgre district includes all lands drained by the Uncompahgre and its tributaries as far north as the Ute reservation.

Mount Sneffels district includes the sections drained by the Rio San Miguel.

Lake district includes all the locations made in Hinsdale County, except the mines situated in Burris Park, at the extreme head of the Lake Fork of the Gunnison, which constitute what is known as Adams or Park district.

Much has been accomplished during the last two years, notwithstanding the great distance from railroad communications, the inaccessibility of the country, and the want of capital for the development of a new mining-camp. More than five thousand locations have been recorded; two good wagon-roads have been built into the country, one via Del Norte up the Rio Grande, the other up the Gunnison via Saguache. Several flourishing towns have grown up, of which Silverton, the county seat of San Juan, and Lake City, the county-seat of Hinsdale County, are the principal ones, each having a population of some five hundred. The only mines that have been worked to considerable extent in the country are the Hotchkiss, in Lake district; the Silver wing, in Eureka district, and the Highland Mary, Aspen, Prospector, and Little Giant, in the Animas district.

The Hotchkiss, located by Hotchkiss Finley, is the best developed mine in the San Juan country. The strike of the vein is northeast and southwest; the vein-matter is 60 feet thick, and it was only in the latter part of February that what is considered the true ore-zone was found. There are two tunnels, 50 and 80 feet long, respectively, which give access to the vein. The ore consists of tellurides, containing in value about equal proportions of gold and silver. Specimen assays range from $17,000 to $20,000 per ton; 18 tons of ore shipped averaged $1,318.61; 75 tons remain on the dump, valued at $150 per ton.

The Silver Wing Mine consists of a group of ten lodes, situated on Jones Mountain, one mile above the town of Eureka. It is developed by one tunnel, 100 feet long; a second tunnel is under contract for 1,000 feet. This tunnel cuts all the veins from 300 to 1,000 feet below the outcrop. Assays range from $130 to $2,800; the ore contains iron, lead, and a large percentage of copper.

The Highland Mary, Rob Bruce, and Powderhouse claims are all located on one vein, all situated at the head of Cunningham Gulch, three miles above Howardsville. The workings consist of four tunnels, running in and along the vein, 300 feet apart, one above the other. The crevice is 15 feet wide, with an ore-streak from 9 to 30 inches wide. The ore is argentiferous galena. Sample-assays from first-class ore gave $2,100; second-class, $760; third-class, $170.

The Prospector lode has probably furnished more ore than any other in the San Juan country. The mine is located on Hazelton Mountain, two miles above Silverton. The developments consist of two shafts, 100 and 130 feet deep, with a level 100 feet long connecting the two, 100 feet from the surface.

The Little Giant, located in Arrastra Gulch, was the first location made in the San Juan country. The mine has a pay-streak of 8 inches of gold-bearing quartz. Twenty-seven tons, worked by the arrastra, produced $150 per ton. In 1872 a company was organized in Chicago, known as the Little Giant Company, which erected upon this property amalgamation-works, containing a 12-horse-power engine, Dodge crusher and ball-pulverizer. The works were built 1,000 feet below the mine, with a wire tram-way to bring the ore to the mill. About 100 tons of ore were milled, producing $14,500, or about 65 per cent. of the assay-value. The property has been involved in litigation since the spring of 1874.

List of producing mines in the San Juan country for 1875.

District and name of lode.	Crevice, in feet.	Pay-streak, in inches.	Character of ore.	Percentage of lead.	No. of ounces of silver per ton.	Coin-value per ton of 2,000 pounds.	Improvements.
Animas district:							
Silver Cord	1½	3	Galena	40	85	$109 90	....
Prospector, first class	4	7 to 10	...do	60	375	484 84	....
Prospector, second class	......	....		...	169	218 50	....
Aspine, first class	4½	10 to 15	Galena	60	255	329 69	175 S.*
Aspine, second class	......	....		...	175	226 26	....
Philadelphia, first class	4	10 to 24	Galena	45	501	647 71	70 T.*
Philadelphia, second class	......	....		...	224	289 61	....
Susquehanna, second class	3	3 to 7	Galena	60	147	190 07	90 S.
Little Giant, *a**	......	8	Gold	...	......	225 00	....
Eureka district:							
Lookout, *a*	6	24	Galena	50	225	290 90	....
Mountain Queen, *a*	5	36	...do	75	32	41 36	....
Crispin, *a*	4	20	Gray copper	...	131	169 37	....
Hartman, *a*	6	20	...do	...	69	91 01	....
Uncompahgre district:							
Saxon, first class	15	22	...do	...	1,383	1,788 09	....
Saxon, second class	......	....		...	600	775 75	....
Poughkeepsie, *a*	25	60	Gray copper	...	223	288 31	....
Alaska, *a*	2	3 to 7	...do	...	612	791 25	....
Tribune, *a*	20	24	...do	...	117	151 27	....
Lake district:							
Hotchkiss, first class	60	....	Telluric	...	......	7,155 50	....
Hotchkiss, second class	......	....		...	......	1,100 00	....
Belle of the East, *a*	6	24	Gray copper	...	178	230 13	100 S.
Little Chief, *a*	5	18	...do	...	769	994 24	....
John J. Crooks, *a*	......	....	...do	...	381	492 59	....

* *a* signifies average; S, shaft; and T, tunnel.

Total amount of ore smelted in San Juan for 1875, $172\frac{1051}{2000}$ tons; average value per ton, $216.59; total coin-value.	$37,361 82
Total amount shipped for treatment elsewhere, $48\frac{1153}{2000}$ tons; average value per ton, $805.65; total coin-value.	39,135 06
Total amount of ore extracted, $221\frac{204}{2000}$ tons; coin-value..	76,496 88
Average coin-value per ton of all ore extracted and treated or shipped	345 98
Total amount of bullion produced from the $172\frac{1153}{2000}$ tons was $60\frac{500}{2000}$ tons, assaying $540.35 per ton; coin value..	32,556 10
1,559 ounces silver refined in the country; coin-value....	2,015 63
Total	34,571 73

Loss in extracting, $2,790.05, equal to $7\frac{2}{10}$ per cent. of the ore-value.

The coming season will witness considerable activity in both mining and smelting throughout the San Juan country. Seventeen mines are being worked during the present winter, which will produce by June 1 500 tons in the Animas district and 300 tons in the Lake district.

The next year's product of bullion, it is estimated, will be about as follows: Green & Co., Silverton, 1,000 tons ore, producing 400 tons bullion; value, $550 per ton. San Juan Smelting Coompany, Forks of Animas, 600 tons ore, producing 240 tons bullion; value, $400 per ton. There will be no refining done in the country next season, since the bullion can be shipped out, the lead paying the cost of transportation. Besides the two above works, which will be in operation by the 1st of July, the Rough and Ready Works, at Silverton, which have been lying idle for the want of capital, may be put in operation.

RIO GRANDE COUNTY.

Summit district.—This district is usually classed as part of the San Juan country. For the following very interesting account of it I am indebted to Mr. C. E. Robins, treasurer of the Little Annie Mining Company, at Summit. As will be seen from several dates given below, the account was received after this report was transmitted to Congress. I have felt justified in introducing it because of its value as a careful and, in some particulars, detailed exhibit of the actual condition of mining in that region.

Summit district, which is the leading gold-district of the San Juan country, is situated about 27 miles southwest of Del Norte, and lies just within the southern boundary of Rio Grande County. Its approximate latitude is 37° 30′; approximate longitude, 106° 30′ west from Greenwich, with a mean elevation of about 12,000 feet above the sea. The surface below timber-line is for the most part heavily wooded with spruce and balsam, and covered during the three summer months, both above and below the upper line of the forests, with a carpeting of nutritious grasses, colored by masses of low-growing plants, representing a very large range of the Alpine flora of Colorado. The outlook from Summit Peak, 12,673 feet high, taking in the vast sweep of the Sierra Madre, Saguache, and Sangre de Christo ranges, a hundred miles in every direction, is one of the finest in Southwestern Colorado.

South Mountain, in which the mineral value of the district, so far as known, exclusively lies, is composed mainly of porphyry, quartzite, and feldspar. The quartz is in immense, but as yet undefined, masses, apparently the result of overthrow in later Tertiary time. Whether or not it exists in depth in definte veins, is as yet an undetermined question, and for the present to the owners of rich locations a matter of remote inserest, as there is enough in sight worth $75 per ton in the mills to insure a large profit for a long time to come. The country-rock appears to be all Azoic; no fossils yet found.

Concerning the climate, data covering long periods do not exist. The winter of 1875–'76 was the first during which the summit was occupied by men, so far as known, and it is presumed that it shared in the general mildness of the season throughout the Western Hemisphere. The lowest range of the thermometer was only 9° F., and the mercury passed below the Fahrenheit zero but three times. In February, snow was 12 feet deep on the level, and in drifts 60 to 70 feet deep. On the 1st day of May it was about 7 feet deep on the level, but disappeared rapidly after that time. Snow lies in the upper mountain ravines at all seasons, and there are large fields of it in such locations which have probably preserved their general summer outline during historic time. The ground beneath the surface is all at seasons frozen to an unknown depth, no excavations in mines or foundations having yet passed below the line of perpetual congelation. Winter usually sets in about the 1st of October, and may be said to melt into summer, without the intervention of spring, about the 1st of June. The rainy season lasts about two months, July and August. The winds (westerly) are constant and severe during the winter season, but in summer rarely rise to the height of gales below timber-line. On the mountain summits they blow strongly at all times. In July, 1876, the treasurer of the Little Annie Mining Company obtained from the War Department the location of a recording station of the signal service at the summit, and regular observations have been taken during the month of August. The meteorology of the district, about one thousand observations being taken monthly, will be well defined if continued for a year. Lunar halos are frequent, and one very fine lunar rainbow, with secondary, was exhibited on the evening (9 o'clock) of 4th August. Electrical displays are frequent and strong. On the 11th of August the sun, moon, and several stars were visible together a short time before noon. Average thermometer for August, 1876, was 49.2°+; highest reach of the month, 60°+. Prevailing clouds: lower, cumulus and nimbus; upper, cirrus. Winds, mostly WSW.; force average, 1 mile an hour. Total rain-fall, 3.24 inches. Altitude of observations, 11,089 feet.

The first discovery of gold in the summit district was made in Wightman's Gulch about the last of June, 1870, by a party consisting of James L. Wightman, E. Baker, J. Cary French, Sylvester Reese, and William Boran, Wightman getting the first "prospect." All of the party, with the exception of Wightman and Reese, left by the middle of September, the latter remaining, engaged at sluicing, until the 9th November, when they left, heavily packed, and made their way out through snow waist-deep, reaching the Rio Grande in three days.

In the spring of 1871 a large number of people flocked into the summit, hundreds arriving while the snow was yet very deep and work impracticable. A general disgust soon took possession of the prospectors, and by the last of August there were but three men in the district, J. L. Wightman, P. J. Peterson, and J. P. Johnson. These then remained until about the 20th of October, Wightman and Peterson being the last to leave. They took the gold realized by sluicing to Denver, and had it refined at the mint, dividing $170 between the three after paying all expenses of the season's operations; not a very encouraging yield for a hard summer's work. Several lodes had in the mean time been found, or at least load-locations made. The specimens found in the gulch indicated to the miners that they had not washed far, and they believed that parent ledges in place were close by.

In 1872 a few locations were made, and 1873 witnessed a new emigration into the district, and in that year the richest mines in the summit were located. The Esmond and Summit lodes were staked during the summer, and on September 13 F. H. Brandt and P. J. Peterson located the Little Annie, Del Norte, and Margaretta Mines, the former being named after a daughter of Mr. Peterson, the latter after a sister-in-law of Mr. Brandt.

During 1874 a vast number of new locations were made, and the attention of the owners was turned to the matter of getting in machinery. Dr. Richard F. Adams, after locating the Summit Mine, shipped a small amount of the ore to be tested, and, having become satisfied that the enterprise would pay, located a mill-site and ordered a mill, which was brought in and commenced to run the following spring.

During the winter of 1874-'75 negotiations were opened by the mine-owners with capitalists for the purpose of getting in mills. The owners of the Little Annie, Del Norte, and Margaretta, of the Golden Queen, and of the Golden Star, entered into contracts by which the parties putting in the mills were to have an interest in the mines.

The spring of 1875 marked the opening of permanent mining-operations at the Summit. Dr. Adams's 5-stamp mill began work as early as the advance of the season permitted. In the latter part of May the machinery for the Little Annie and Golden Queen mills reached Del Norte from Chicago, and was drawn by mule-teams on a road cut for the purpose over Del Norte Mountain, 13,000 feet high, and costing over $4,000. The machinery for the two mills weighed more than 50 tons, but was successfully transported above the lower cloud-belt, and placed in position before the close of September. Such other historical matters as properly belong to this sketch will be found under notices of mining companies, mills, or mines.

The chief gold-producing property of Summit district, and of the territory known as the San Juan mining-region, is owned by the Little Annie Mining Company, and comprises the Little Annie, Del Norte, and Margaretta Gold-Mines, and two placer-claims of 20 acres each, situated in the gulch below them, with a 10-stamp mill, business and assay office, store, bunk-house, mess-house, retort-house, charcoal-house, blacksmith-shop, tram-way, substantial mine and mill dumps, dam, flumes, sluices, &c., including all the items to be found in the plant of a first-class gold-mining company.

The ores of the Del Norte and Margaretta Mines have not yet been tested in the mill. Average assay-value of former, $43.37; of latter, $24.20. The Del Norte has yielded exceedingly rich pan-prospects, and on the 26th of August, 1876, a very rich deposit of flour-gold was found on the Margaretta, the extent of which has not been determined.

The chief interest of the district centers in the Little Annie Mine. This lies on the northern slope of South Mountain, the location, for which a United States patent is now sought, being an irregular parallelogram 50 feet wide in its narrowest part, and 1,500 feet long, with a general course north 15° 15″ east and south 15° 15″ west. About 600 feet of its superficial length is below and 900 feet above timber-line. The present opening is 500 feet from its lower end, and 11,920 feet above the sea. The Little Annie has had more development than any mine in the district, some 1,200 tons of ore having been taken out, but it is yet only an open quarry. The rock is a light quartz, with more or less red-

South Mountain and Little Annie Mining Camp, Summit District, Colorado.

dish and purplish stain, derived chiefly from iron, non-pyritous, weighing about 60 pounds per cubic foot, or 33⅓ cubic feet to the ton. Specimens have assayed all the way from $70 to $160,000 per ton at the Denver mint and elsewhere. Two to ten men have been employed in getting out ore during the present season, at an average of 4 tons per day of ten hours to a man; average cost, $1 per ton. Black powder only is used in blasting; cost, $4.50 per keg of 25 pounds. The present cut on the mine is about 75 feet in length, open, and 35 deep from highest point of surface. Average breadth of cut, 30 feet. It is 887 feet in vertical height above the battery-floor of the mill. Hand-drilling used exclusively. The rock is eminently a free-milling ore, no sulphides or other minerals in combination having yet appeared. Wages in mine, $2 to $3 per day and board. No water obstructs working. The average value of the ore is best shown by the result of last autumn's mill-work, in which 306 tons taken from the face of the mine, without any sorting, yielded $31,444 = $102.68 per ton, (currency.) The gold is chiefly in the form of "flour," and for the most part invisible, although fine specimens are occasionally taken, some being of very large size. The fineness of the retorts has been about 980, as shown by certificates from the mint at Denver, and from the United States assay-office at New York.

The ore is delivered from the mine to the mill by a tram-way 2,125 feet long, running down the mountain-side and connecting the two. It was built in the spring of 1876, while there was 6 feet of snow on the ground, and is working constantly and satisfactorily, with a capacity of delivery of 80 tons per day of ten hours. Its operation is automatic, the loaded car pulling up the empty one, controlled by a break at the mouth of the mine. It is furnished with a ⅞-inch steel cable, manufactured by J. A. Roebling's Sons, which passes along the track over wooden rollers. The cars have a capacity of 72⅔ cubic feet, or 4,580 pounds. Before the construction of the tram-way the rock was hauled (last fall) from the mine to the mill by teams, and last spring was brought down over the snow in sleds and raw-hides, the former mode costing $3 and the latter $5 per ton. Two hundred and sixteen tons and four hundred and twenty-eight pounds were brought down in the manner last named, a stout man bringing down a ton to a ton and a half per day. The cost of delivery by tram-way is about 25 cents per ton, the difference being an important offset against its cost, which was about $6,000.

The Little Annie Mill is a 10-stamp outfit, with Blake Crusher; capacity of latter, 30 tons per day of 10 hours. The mill has two batteries of five stamps each, four dolly-tubs, or pans, and one agitator. Amalgamation in batteries, on table-plates, in pans, and on a second set of table-plates on a floor below, over which the slimes pass before going into the discharge-sluice. Fall of stamps, 11 inches. Drop rate, 60. Weight, 530 pounds. Cams, two-armed. Shoes and dies of white iron—weight of former 112 pounds, of latter 84 pounds. Length of cams from point to point, 29 inches. Battery-issue, 10 inches deep. Screens, No. 1 fine, slot. Pan-revolution, 65 per minute; settler, 28 per minute. Engine, 25 horse-power, burning 16 cubic feet of wood per hour. Blankets washed every fifteen minutes. Wood delivered, cut and piled, at $3 per cord; 1,000 cords now under contract, and more than half furnished, at that price. Steam-pressure in boiler, 50 to 55 pounds. Main mill building 32 feet by 42 feet; ell 28 feet by 24 feet; substantially built of frame, the main building two stories, with sharp pitched roof and deep loft; siding, a double thickness of boards with tarred paper between; roof sheathed, then a layer of tarred paper, and then shingles. Large water-tank in loft. Power steam, and fuel wood exclusively; water furnished by Wightman's Fork of the Alamosa, on the south bank of which the structure stands. Frame of mill raised 10th August, 1875. Commenced to run 28th September following, and has been in continuous operation since, except from 8th December, 1875, to 20th May, 1876, during which time there was no ore on hand. Capacity per day of 24 hours, 5.58 tons of ore, or 1,100 pounds per stamp. Running time in 1876, from 20th May to 1st September, (the date of this report,) gross, 103 days; stoppages of all kinds, 470 hours 17½ minutes; net running time, 2,001 hours 42½ minutes = 83 days 9 hours 42½ minutes, during which time the mill has produced 1,710$\frac{125}{1000}$ ounces of gold, worth, in coin, $34,202.50.

The property is favorably situated in regard to fuel. The four square miles immediately surrounding the Annie camp contain over 1,000 acres of heavy, close-standing timber, which will cut 60 to 80 cords per acre. The operations of the mill are constantly checked by assays, the apparatus for which is ample and of the best class, costing about $900. The average of blanket-tailings to date has been $87.61; of sluice, $32.28. Arrangements are now in progress to save a portion of the waste represented by the latter figure. Wear of shoes and dies per month is $133.33. The following are the elements of mill-work for 24 hours:

Wages of amalgamator	$3 33
Wages of two engineers	4 50
Wages of one man at crusher	1 33
Wages of two battery-feeders	4 00
Wages of two blanket-washers	4 00
Wages of one wood-passer	1 33
Board of above at $1	9 00
Total mill-wages	27 49
Fuel, 3 cords, at $3	9 00
Mercury	50
Oils and tallow	50
Cyanide of potassium	25
Lights	35
Incidentals	50
Cost of running mill 24 hours	38 59
Cost of mining ore, with six men employed at mine, at, say, $2.75 each	16 50
Board of same	6 00
Powder, tools, and repair of same	2 50
Average cost of mining	25 00

(This is, of course, only during the season of active operations at the mine, say five months in the year, at present.)

Other expenses:	
Wear and tear of tram-way	$1 50
Wear and tear and replacement of mill and machinery	6 00
Wear and tear, depreciation, repairs and betterments of buildings of company other than mill and tram-way, dam, sluices, &c	2 50
Salaries	11 28
Office-expenses	20
General expenses	50
Blacksmith, charcoal, &c	2 00
	23 98
To this may be added interest at 10 per cent. on cost of the company's permanent improvement, say	15 00

RECAPITULATION.

Mining	$25 00
Milling	38 59
All other out-go	23 98
Total outlay in 24 hours during the season of out-door work, (say five months,) excluding interest on permanent improvements	87 57

Adding to this cost of preparing meals, and all other miscellaneous outlays not heretofore itemized, the cost of running the company for one day, from 1st May to 1st October, may be set down at $95. During the balance of the year, while the production is the same, the expenses are on a greatly-reduced scale.

The cost of board for the hands is 94 cents 6 mills per day, or 31½ cents per meal.

The Little Annie Mill has at present but 10 stamps, but there are 64 stamps working under contract on Annie ore at a cost to the company of $10 per ton. This reduces very largely on the balance-sheet the ratio of cost to yield. With 10 stamps, it costs the Little Annie Mill $12.30 to reduce a ton of ore; with 30 stamps, it is profitably done for $7. The needed increase of mill-capacity will soon be made. Under the above showing, the Little Annie Company's expenses on *its own* work and plant are $34,675 per annum, charging the maximum outlay (that during the summer months) to every day in the year. The product in its own mill (at the average so far made of $3,000 per week) is $156,000 per annum, or a *net* earning of 10 per cent. on $1,213,250. Three-sixteenths of the Little Annie, Del Norte, and Margaretta Mines and the two placers were sold in 1875, before the mill began to run, for $78,000.

The placers have been worked only at intervals, without system and without machinery. In this mode they have yielded some very fine nuggets, and have about returned the expense put on them. Copper is found widely diffused in Wightman's Gulch, also platinum in small acicular bodies.

The Little Annie Company is an unorganized association, the members of which are F. H. Brandt, Johnston Livingston, P. J. Peterson, John J. Crooke, Lucius A. Winchester, Le Grande Dodge, Henry S. Hoyt, jr., Lewis Crooke, Eliza S. Winchester, and Frank W. Winchester.

Its managers are Pear J. Peterson, superintendent, and Charles E. Robins, treasurer. The office of the company is at the mine, Summit, Rio Grande County, Colorado.

The following is its balance-sheet for September 1, 1876:

Debit accounts.

Little Annie Mill	$34,557 42
Machinery-road	2,095 13
Cash on hand in office	12 00
Gold on hand, 105.25 ounces	2,105 00
Cash in bank of San Juan, Del Norte	13,429 35
Gold in transitu, 252 ounces	5,040 00
Notes receivable	953 87
Debts receivable	2,662 37
Merchandise	3,357 73
Miscellaneous property, tools, &c	2,556 96
Office and store building	971 99
Furniture in same	292 66
Patent-expenses	1,317 25
Legal expenses	359 69
Office-expenses	46 76
General expenses	2,825 17
Mill-expenses	904 30
Mill-wages	1,026 90
Mine-wages	873 13
Other wages	2,964 41
Salaries	2,395 22
Assay-outfit	740 09
Tunnel-site	69 25
Placers	123 35

Surveys	1,084 07
Charcoal-house	46 00
Outbuildings	153 10
Retort-house	40 43
Cook-house	71 49
Bunk-house	228 00
Golden Queen Mining Company	878 88
San Juan Consolidated Mining Company	1,000 00
Ore, 1875	1,890 00
Rawhide ore, 1876	1,143 15
Wood, 1875	2,418 13
Wood, 1876	611 45
Charcoal on hand	389 20
Lumber on hand	1,184 26
Tram-way, payments on account	2,787 44
Tram-way expenses	15 00
Dividend No. 1	3,480 02
	99,100 62

Credit accounts.

Loss and gain	$34,374 17
Bills payable	37 00
Assessments	1,485 00
Tram-way earnings	33 00
Retorts, (gold taken from mill,) 3,113.87 ounces	62,277 34
Exchange	894 11
	99,100 62

The Golden Queen Mine was located in the latter part of September, 1873, by Josiah Mann, O. P. Posey, John Grant, and others. It has been extensively worked, and a stamp-mill has been erected 88 feet east of the Little Annie Mill, which is a duplicate of the latter, except that the engine is 20 horse-power instead of 25. Assays of ore in mine have not hitherto run high, and definite information as to mill-results is not at present accessible. The owners are Johnston Livingston, John J. Crooke, Adams & Posey, Arthur Burton, Peter Beeker, Joseph S. Reef, John A. McDonald, Lucius A. Winchester, J. S. Partridge, Lewis Crooke, William Beck, James L. Hill, Henry B. Clark, F. C. Day, L. C. Smith, R. C. Sheppard, and L. C. Baker. Office, Summit, Rio Grande County, Colorado.

The Summit Mine was located in 1873, by Dr. Richard F. Adams, and his 5-stamp mill, erected in the autumn of 1874, was the pioneer of all the machinery now in the district. The mine lies high up on the northeastern face of South Mountain, and a considerable of surface-ore has been taken from it. Various assays have ranged from $10 to $200. Yield in mill not ascertained. Fifteen more stamps designed for the latter are at Del Norte. The power is water, supplemented by a steam-engine. The owners are R. F. Adams, Lewis Crooke, and Le Grande Dodge.

The Golden Star Gold and Silver Mining Company owns three mines, all located by Isaac Garnett; the Golden Star No. 2, staked 19th June, 1874; Eighth Wonder, staked 22d June, 1874; and the Keystone, staked 3d July, 1874. Assays have been had from the former of $20. A superior mill has been erected by the company on Wightman's Fork, with ten 650-pound stamps, and provision for ten more. The building is 32 by 48 feet, with addition for boiler of 15 by 30 feet, substantially constructed with double-board siding inclosing a layer of tarred paper; felt roof. Large Blake crusher; engine, double cylinder and 40 horse-power; single-armed cams. Large grinding-pan, with capacity of eight tons of tailings daily. Drop rate, 90; high mortars; single discharge, (as are all the mills in this district;) width of issue, 12 inches; amalgamation in battery and on table-plates; no blankets. Bumping-table on Rittinger plan for concentration; one Wheeler & Randall pan for working concentrates, with raised patent washers; screens, No. 1 fine, slot. Machinery by Morey & Sperry, of New York. Capital stock, $1,000,000. Principal office, Chicago, Ill.; branch office, New York. Daniel Barnum, president; C. R. Brooke, secretary; J. A. Sperry, builder and agent. Majority of stock held in New York. The mill has just commenced to run; results of work not ascertained.

The San Juan Consolidated Mining Company is a combination owning over 15,000 linear feet on South Mountain, comprising a large number of locations, of which the Ida, staked out by Colonel Gillette, in July, 1874, is at present regarded as the best. A 30-stamp mill has just been erected, and has commenced running. Weight of stamps, 500 pounds; fall, 12 inches; rate, 37 per minute. Double-armed cams; issue, 13 inches wide. Engine, 45 horse-power; steam-pressure, 50 pounds. Amalgamation in battery and on table-plates. Blankets washed every 15 minutes. Four Bartola pans, rate of revolution 35 per minute; one settler, rate 35; screens, No. 1 fine, slot; Dodge crusher, large size. Mill-building, 50 feet square. Capital stock, $3,000,000. Charles W. Tankersley, president; Thomas M. Bowen, secretary. Office of the company, Del Norte, Rio Grande County, Colorado.

Cropsey's Mill was erected by Col. A. J. Cropsey during the present season, to commence operations in the early part of July, 1877. The structure is 32 by 60 feet, substantially built of logs. It has four batteries, of six stamps each. Weight of stamps, 500 pounds; fall, 15 inches; drop-rate, 30 per minute; capacity, twenty tons daily. Water supplied to batteries and pans by a large-sized Knowles steam-pump. Engine, 25 horse-power. The four silvered table-plates have an aggregate surface of 160 square feet. Blanket-tailings run through Bartolo pans. The mill was built for custom-work, and has up to this time been engaged in sampling the ores of various mines.

The foregoing comprises the main points of the developments in the district. Other mines of more or less prominence are the Chicago, located in 1874; present owners, John B. Hoffy, W. W. Park, and J. W. Harris; the Dexter, located October, 1873, by Josiah Mann, Arthur Burton, and John A. McDonald; the Golden Eagle, located May, 1875, by Jos. S. Reef, Josiah Mann, and Peter Beeker; the Highland Mary, located July, 1875, by Josiah Mann, P. Beeker, J. S. Reef, and A. J. Sparks; the Missionary, located by Benjamin Burroughs, June 18, 1874; the Yellow Jacket, Rising Sun, Caribou, Little Jessie, Little Nellie, Goldie May, Mountain Queen, Wisconsin, Poorman, Des Moines, Esmond, Ellen, Odin, Centennial, Princess, Aurora, Narrow Gauge, Grey Eagle, Moltke, Tender Foot, Queen Esther, David Fulton, John J. Crooke, Captain Charley, Golden Star No. 1, Annie E. Benson, McCormick, Independence, Saint Louis, Amazon, St. Mary's, Washington, Columbia, and Major, from the last of which have been taken the finest specimens of free gold yet yielded by Summit district.

The population of the district is about two hundred. Del Norte, 27 miles distant, to which access is had by a wagon-road built this year, and by a trail down Pinos Creek, is its supply-point. Besides the mills and their out-buildings, there are about fifty cabins in the settlement, built of logs and covered with dirt. Freight to Del Norte varies from 1½ to 10 cents a pound. Wood is the only fuel. Cost of lumber, $30 per M; potatoes, 1 to 8 cents per pound; flour, $8.75 per hundred; tea, $1.25 to $1.50 per pound; beef, 7½ cents per pound; bacon, 22½ cents per pound; sugar, 18 to 20 cents per pound; onions, 12½ cents per pound; dried apples, dried peaches, and dried currants, 20 cents per pound; rice, 20 cents per pound; crackers, 20 cents per pound; cheese, 30 cents per pound; kerosene, $1 per gallon. All supplies must be laid in before winter opens. No raising of vegetables has yet been attempted in the district, though it is possible that a very few of the hardier kinds might succeed. There have been so far only two deaths, one from a blast and one from debility—an invalid. Water boils at 182°.

The two accompanying sketches show, one the mountain and camp as seen from the northwest, the other the net-work of locations covering a portion of the northern and eastern face of South Mountain. Although twenty-three hundred claims have been recorded within its limits, the district so far has been orderly and peaceable. The sketch of the mountain and camp is by Henry Learned, associate of the Chicago Academy of Design, and the mine-map by J. F. Sanders, United States deputy mineral surveyor. There are at present 89 stamps in the Summit and one arrastra. Two more mills are under contract. With the reduction appliances now on the spot or coming, the rank of the district as a gold-producing territory will soon be definitely established.

CHAPTER VIII.

WYOMING AND DAKOTA.

From the Territory of Wyoming I have little to report. The Sweetwater region seems to be nearly idle, and discoveries reported in other parts of the Territory have not yet attained the rank of regularly-productive districts, though I hear vaguely of some mines not far from Laramie which are expected to prove extremely profitable. Doubtless before this report appears in print full information will have been furnished by the press as to rumors which I have, at the moment of writing these lines, no opportunity to investigate.

The production of iron ore for shipment to Utah, which is used as a flux in the lead-smelting furnaces, is still continued; but, although I have not obtained the precise figures, I feel sure that this business is declining or about to decline. The transportation for so many hundred miles of a superb, pure red hematite, only to throw away in mattes, slags, and salamanders the iron it contains, is a lamentable waste; and if the discovery and use by the Utah metallurgists of ferruginous fluxes nearer home should result in stopping the shipments of the Rawlings ore, and in leading its owners or others to utilize it in the manufacture of iron and steel, both the country and the individual would be gainers by the exchange. The ore in question could, I think, without doubt, be used in the open-hearth steel-manufacture by the pig-and-ore modification of the Martin process. The only difficulty in the way of utilizing it in the blast-furnace for the manufacture of pig-iron is that of obtaining a suitable fuel. For the present, the coke of Southern Colorado, or charcoal from the Rocky Mountains, seem to be the only available fuel for this purpose. But reverberatories, Chenot or Blair retorts, &c., can be run with Wyoming coal, using the Siemens producer and regenerators if necessary; and hence there will be a chance, whenever the price of iron advances, to start some form of "direct manufacture," or of the fabrication of steel.

The coal-mining industry of the year is shown in the following figures, for which I am indebted to Mr. I. W. Sannett, auditor of the Union Pacific Railroad Company, at Omaha.

Product of the mines of the Union Pacific Railroad Company.	Tons.
Carbon	61,751
Rock Springs	104,667
Almy, near Evanston	42,156
Product of other mines, shipped by railroad.	
Excelsior Company, Rock Springs	6,366
Rocky Mountain Company, Almy	83,917
Coalville mines, near Echo	28,197
Total product	327,054

I believe these are tons of 2,000 pounds.

THE BLACK HILLS.

Mr. Walter P. Jenney, under the direction of the Commissioner of Indian Affairs, has made, during 1875, a careful exploration of the Black Hills of Dakota, and his forthcoming report will doubtless contain a clear and discriminating account of their mineral resources, so far as these can be determined by a general reconnaissance. In the present instance I expect that Mr. Jenney's report will approximately fix the extent and nature of the gold-bearing drift, upon which the placer and hydraulic industry will depend. Of course he could not explore the quartz-veins, nor prophesy whether or not rich mines of that character would be opened there. It is evident that a considerable immigration will pour into that region as soon as the Indian title, or the Indian opposition, is extinguished. Not improbably there will be some excitement; certainly there will be sanguine reports from miners and speculators. But I hazard little in expressing the opinion that the placer and gravel deposits, though they may suffice to open the country to other industries, will not sustain for any considerable period a large and profitable production of gold. A few localities of limited extent will perhaps prove rich, but there is apparently no chance of finding such wide and deep auriferous drift as the western flank of the Sierra Nevada presents.

CHAPTER IX.

NEW MEXICO.

For notes of the mining-industry in this Territory I am chiefly indebted this year to Mr. Theodore F. Van Wagenen, of Colorado, who, as my agent, collected such data as were available with the means at command. According to his reports and estimates, the coin-value of the bullion-product of New Mexico in 1875 was as follows:

Silver bullion	$225,000
Gold-dust	95,000
Gold and silver in ores shipped out of the Territory for reduction	5,000
Total precious metals	325,000
Estimated value of copper in copper-ores and of a small quantity of pig-lead	74,915
Total metallic products	399,915

The small progress of mining in this Territory is due to its remote position and imperfect communication; the indolence or indifference of the Mexicans and half-breeds, constituting the larger part of its population; the great scarcity of water, which, in many localities, forbids placer-mining, and in others enhances the cost of milling quartz; and, finally, the failure to obtain, in many of the mountainous districts, adequate supplies of ore suitable for the simple processes of reduction upon which reliance must be placed in the early stages of development. There is a large area of auriferous alluvium in the Territory; its resources in copper are remarkably extensive; large veins of galena characterize several of the mining-districts; and the supply of coal is both abundant and excellent. As yet, however, no quartz-mines, whether of gold or silver, have been successfully worked for long periods since the days when Maxwell's ranch and the Ortiz Mine grant were under active development. The recently-developed silver-districts contain many deposits of the character of pockets or chambers and much base metal, and the lack of water in most of them increased the cost of operations. Yet it would be unjust to deduce from these results of experience thus far a general conclusion unfavorable to the resources of the Territory. The very predominance of base metals, for instance, which now constitutes a hinderance to rapid development, will become in time an element of prosperity; while, on the other hand, the small amount of successful quartz-mining is to be considered in connection with the small amount of energetic prospecting and of invested capital. These views are illustrated by the details given below.

GRANT COUNTY.

The mines of this county yielded last year about $225,000 in silver and $25,000 in gold. Mining is now carried on in five districts in the county, viz, Pinos Altos, Georgetown, Lone Mountain, Silver Flat, and Chloride Flat.

Pinos Altos district produces gold exclusively. The country-rock is syenite and gneiss, and the deposits have generally the character of gash-veins; but a few are apparently true fissures. The principal veins are the Pacific, Pacific No. 2, Arizona Central, and Atlantic. None of the mines are deeper than 150 feet. The surface-ores assay from $8 to $25 per ton, and consist of a honey-combed quartz in which the gold is comparatively free. Beneath the zone of decomposition the veins carry pyrites worth about $10 per ton in gold and silver. As yet this class of mineral has not been successfully worked, and hence only surface-ores have been extracted. In the gulch are two steam-arrastra mills, one having eight machines and the other four. The district contains about a dozen other arrastras, driven by horse-power. They save from 60 to 70 per cent. of the assay-value of the quartz. During last season a number of Mexicans extracted from the gulch-diggings a small amount of gold.

Georgetown district is at present by far the most promising in Grant County. The country-rock is limestone, and the mines, excepting the Pi-Ute and Naiad Queen, are contact-deposits occurring between limestone and slate. The Pi-Ute and Naiad Queen are on the same lode, which appears to be a contact-vein, having granite for its hanging-wall. The ores of the district have a siliceous limestone gangue, and consist of carbonates of lead, galena, antimonial silver, silver chloride, and native silver. The miners separate their ores into two grades, milling and smelting ore. The separation is effected mainly by washing, by which the finer and poorer material is washed away from the larger and heavier. The former constitutes the milling-ore, and averages about $125 per ton. The latter is smelted into "lead bullion," and averages, as delivered to the furnaces, from $500 to $1,500 per ton. The camp contains two Mexican furnaces, each capable of treating one ton in 24 hours. A stamp-mill is being erected to crush and concentrate.

The two principal mines, aside from the Pi-Ute and Naiad Queen, are the Commercial and McGregor, each of which is between 30 and 40 feet deep. About a dozen more complete the list. Work has been quite continuous in this district during the year.

Lone Mountain district has not prospered greatly during the year. The veins are narrow and poor, and fill the limestone rock like a net-work. A large amount of work, therefore, produces only a small amount of ore. When the district was first opened several rich pockets were found, which caused considerable excitement, but in 1875 the developments were meager. The silver-ore is a mixture of chlorides and sulphides, carries very little lead and not much gold. The principal mines worked during the year were the Durango, Emma, Copper Point, Home Ticket, and Red Lode. They have attained a depth of 30 to 50 feet, and have been producing with more or less regularity during the year. The reducing facilities of the camp consist of two steam-mills of 30 tons capacity each. The system employed is the Washoe raw amalgamation.

Silver Flat and *Chloride Flat* are in the immediate vicinity of Silver City. In the former most of the mines are idle, the ore being of so low grade as to offer no inducements for working at present.

The New Issue and the Legal Tender are the best mines of the district. Chloride Flat has produced a considerable amount of ore during 1875. The deposits are in limestone, and occur with some regularity, though presenting no proofs of permanence. Most of them lie horizontal, expanding at times into large bodies or chambers, and again narrowing to seams quite difficult to trace. The ores are similar to those of Georgetown, containing sometimes, however, a little copper. The gangue is calc-spar.

The Providence, which in 1873 was one of the best mines of the district, has been idle for two years. It is 75 feet deep.

The Two Ikes is worked only by Mexicans. It has produced a small quantity of ore during the year. This was formerly a productive and profitable mine.

The Texas, which has the reputation of being the best mine in New Mexico at present, was worked steadily during most of the year; and the Seventy-Six, on the same vein, has also been tolerably productive.

The Seneca has been idle for four years. The Dexter has yielded nothing for the last six months, but is still prospected.

There are three mills at Silver City—the Tennessee, Bennett's, and the Wisconsin. Their combined capacity is about 15 tons in twenty-four hours, and they have been running with considerable regularity during the year. The Wisconsin amalgamates raw, the other two roast. The Tennessee Mill is supplied with ten stamps, two Brückner cylinders, and six pans. The Bennett Mill carries ten stamps, six triple-hearth reverberatory roasting-furnaces, four 4-foot Varney pans, two 6-foot Wheeler pans, and five 3-ton tanks for leaching. The Wisconsin Mill uses a Bolthoff pulverizer.

What are known as smelting-ores in this district are the richer grades. carrying usually 300 ounces of silver and upwards per ton. They generally contain a little lead, and there is just enough galena in the district to permit (with careful repeated use of the litharge from cupellation) a limited amount of lead-smelting in a blast-furnace. The furnaces used are built of adobe, and are 8 feet high from the bottom of the crucible. They will stand about four days' heat, after which they must be relined. Sometimes a species of refractory sandstone is used instead, of the adobe, which will last for nearly two weeks. One tuyere is used, and the blast is supplied by a common bellows, worked by hand. The fuel is oak or pine charcoal, the former being preferred. The Mexicans make their charge about as follows: one-third ore, one-third old slag, and one-third litharge. This is thoroughly mixed, and fed in by the bucketful alternately with the coal. The cupels are made of adobe lined with loam and ashes.

Santa Rita district.—The Santa Rita Copper-Mine has not done remarkably well during the year. Considerable capital has been expended in building furnaces that have not been run, and in exploring parts of the mine that did not pay. A new surface-body of ore was found during the year, from which most of the ore shipped was taken.

The Chino Mine, in the vicinity, has been worked steadily and with favorable results. It produces mainly the carbonates of copper. The mine has two shafts 150 feet apart, 65 feet deep, and connected by two levels, which show throughout, as is reported, a vein from 2 to 7 feet wide of green carbonate, black oxide, and red oxide of copper. The country is decomposed granite, and requires timbering in drifts and shafts. According to a recent account, Mr. Magruder, the owner, is now sinking in the main shaft, on a vein of 10 to 12 inches, native copper and red oxide, containing 80 to 90 per cent. of copper. This vein is in water, which is raised with a whim. South of the southern or main shaft a drift shows 3 feet, of 30 per cent. carbonate. North of the north shaft a drift, now 75 feet long, shows for part of the distance 7 feet, and for the larger part 3 feet, of black oxide and carbonate.

The San José has been idle for two years. Plenty of ore is in sight, but it is mostly copper sulphide, and too refractory to be treated with the rude appliances used for the oxidized ores.

The Yosemite is one of the promising new copper-mines of the district. It lies about 600 yards south of the Chino, and belongs to the same person. The two shafts have reached 48 and 95 feet, respectively. From the latter a drift 120 feet long, and still vigorously driven, shows a reported average of 3 feet red oxide; from the former a drift northward is said to have an average vein of 2 feet excellent ore.

The Burro Mountains, about 12 miles from Silver City, have been prospected somewhat during the year. A number of the gulches are rich in gold, but there is no water to wash with. Numerous silver-bearing veins have been found, but they are as a rule of low grade. Some very promising deposits of copper discovered in these mountains are not being worked.

Ralston district, 60 miles west of Silver City, has been the scene of some excitement during the year. The veins here are in granite, are large and strong, and carry silver, gold, and copper. They are, however, quite low in grade, not averaging over 25 ounces of silver per ton. There is no supply of wood within 10 miles, and no water (except from wells) within 50 miles.

Socorra district.—The Socorra mines show but little progress during the year. The district is mainly noted at present for its deposits of fire-clay, though there are a number of large galena-veins, carrying from 10 to 15 ounces of silver, some copper-deposits, and some lodes rich in gold-ore.

In *Ute Creek* and *Moreno* the mines have been worked during the year with some diligence. At one time in the summer the production of dust was averaging $10,000 per week; but this yield was not maintained for any great lengh of time. The total product of the district, Mr. Van Wagenen estimates to have been between $50,000 and $60,000. There is a good water-supply and no lack of rich soil. Some new capital has lately come into the district, and it is quite likely that next year will witness a great advance in the industry. Grouse, Michigan, and Humbug Gulches and the Moreno were the localities worked most extensively during 1875.

NORTHERN AND MIDDLE NEW MEXICO.

There is nothing to report from this part of the Territory. The Maxwell, Old Placer, New Placer, Cerrillos, and other grants containing mineral deposits of value have been little worked by their owners, and the scattered results of Mexican labor in the gulches are not ascertainable, and not important. Perhaps some gold from these sources, finding its way to the more active business centers of San Juan, is included in the reports elsewhere given concerning the product of that part of Colorado.

CHAPTER X.

ARIZONA.

For the preparation of this chapter I am chiefly indebted to Hon R. C. McCormick, than whom no better authority can be named. Mr. McCormick desires to acknowledge receipt of information from Governor Safford, John Wasson, esq., of the Arizona Citizen, T. J. Butler, esq., of the Arizona Miner, and W. J. Berry, esq., of the Arizona Sentinel.

After many years of tedious and costly conflict, the Apaches and other hostile Indians occupying this Territory have been forced upon reservations, and so long as Congress furnishes the money for supplying them with food, they will not interfere with mining operations, which heretofore they have at many points impeded and at others absolutely prohibited.

Mine-owners are naturally elated and hopeful under this new and long-wished-for condition of affairs, and prospectors are daily making fresh discoveries of gold, silver, and copper lodes, many of them of exceeding promise.

But the peaceful condition of the country, with all its attendant advantages, and the value of many of the mines, (which is no longer a question of doubt,) are not sufficient to overcome the need of cheap and quick transportation, which, next to the Indian troubles, has ever been the serious drawback to the rapid settlement and profitable development of this remote Territory.

The past year has witnessed an increased attention to mining and the investment of some new capital, but the distances, both from the Pacific and the Atlantic States, are such, and many of the roads to the mineral districts are so heavy or rough, that no expeditious and economical movement of ores, machinery, or miners, no working or shipment of low-grade ores, and no influx of capital (even from California) can be looked for, and consequently no extensive or very important operations can be carried on until at least a trunk railroad crosses the Territory.

At present only such gold and silver lodes as would elsewhere be considered surprisingly rich can be worked to advantage, and scores of lodes that would pay handsomely in California or Colorado are utterly neglected, while the great copper interests of the Territory (for copper is nowhere more abundant or of greater purity) are for all practical purposes without value.

Fortunately, if Congress refuses to aid in the construction of a railroad by the thirty-second or thirty-fifth parallel, or by both, private enterprise will soon supply the great desideratum.

The announcement is made that the Southern Pacific Railroad of California, now extending to Dos Palmas, on the desert, between San Bernardino and the great Colorado River, will be completed to Yuma, on that river, early in the year 1877.

This done, as it doubtless will be, it cannot be long before, with or without a subsidy, the same company or the Texas Pacific Company will connect with the Texas railroads, thus affording Arizona an outlet to East and West, and a trunk-line to which narrow-gauge roads from Prescott and from all the important mining-districts, north and south, will soon become tributary, and thus the solid and lasting prosperity of the Territory will be assured.

The mining-districts in Arizona are now so many in number, that it has been thought best to make reference only to the counties in which the lodes referred to are located, and it must not be understood that all, or nearly all even, of the prominent lodes are herein named. The aim of the writer has been to refer to several representative mines in each county, and particularly to those not mentioned in previous reports; but for this purpose so few owners have furnished material, (in response to urgent appeals through the press and by private communication,) that he cannot claim to have more than partially covered the field.

For some reason or other the miners of Arizona have always been slow to avail themselves of opportunities to make their discoveries and developments known through Government reports, and to this day it is about as difficult to estimate the annual yield of gold and silver in the Territory as it was when the first mining operations were begun, there being as yet no official record kept of the shipments of dust, ore, or bullion either to California or to the East.

PIMA COUNTY.

This was the first settled, and to overland travelers is the best-known part of Arizona, as the route of the Butterfield stage-line (from Saint Louis to San Francisco) was through it, and it was the national highway to the Pacific prior to the civil war. Tucson, the county-seat, and the capital of the Territory since 1867, is the chief town in Southern Arizona, and the largest in the Territory. It was a military post under Mexican rule, and it is supposed to have been founded more than one hundred years since. It is well built, of adobe, and pleasantly situated in the valley of the Santa Cruz. The mines of Pima County were the first open in Arizona, and are yet considered among the best. They are of quartz, but placers have been worked at several points, and recently those at the Santa Rita Mountains have given good returns to quite a large number of prospectors.

The Arizona Citizen of July 3, 1875, has this reference to these new and apparently extensive placers:

Wednesday of this week this town was again surprised at the products of placer-gold in Smith district. David Burroughs brought in from there 9½ ounces of nice placer-gold, the product of three days' work of himself alone, and he carried the dirt three-fourths of a mile in a sack on his back to water, where he washed it under unfavorable circumstances. The gold averages coarse. One piece is worth about $50, another near $35, and others from $1 to $5. His claim is in a gulch making into the main placer-ravine from the Santa Rita Mountain side.

We learn that Horace Arden has regularly made an ounce a day in the Smith district, and that he is not noted for working imprudently hard, but goes along cleverly, making his $16 to $20 per day; the gold being worth these figures per ounce.

Since the above was written, Jack Ralston came in from Smith district with $150 more placer-gold—nuggets we should say. The largest piece is worth just $90.50, and the balance in bits from $1 to $10. This gold was washed, and by packing the dirt a long distance to water. The hills and gulches all about have gold in them, and, with plenty of water, millions could soon be taken out. The gold coming from there brings vividly to mind that seen in every store in the mountains of California from 1849 to 1854. There is no doubt of an immense gold-quartz lead in Smith district, for this placer-gold is evidently not far from its original resting-place.

Southwest of Tucson, in what is known as the Papago country, there are extensive "dry washings," and the Papago Indians have for years brought more or less of gold-dust to the Tucson merchants. In one month of the present year one firm purchased over $3,000 worth from them.

Of the quartz-lodes, the Cerro Colorado and the Patagonia are the best known in Pima County. Work upon them was begun before the organization of the Territory, but for years they were virtually abandoned to the Indians. Now, under new owners and better auspices, they promise good returns. Their characteristics having been fully described in previous reports, it is not necessary to repeat them in this connection.

The Old Mine, supposed to be the old Tumacacori, has recently been re-opened and its shafts and tunnels cleaned out. This is one of the numerous mines worked by the Mexicans many years since.

Already, in cleaning out the mine, Mr. Darrah has found two sacks of silver-ore worth at the rate of $7,000 per ton. He finds the old drill-holes to be 4 inches square, proving that the work was done very many years ago. He also found skeletons in the old works, leading to the belief that the workmen staid by the mine until they were murdered by Indians, and this theory is strengthened by the very rich ore found on the dump, which, in case of abandonment, would very likely have been taken along. The Old Mine is in the Ostrich Mountain range, and is about 75 miles southward from Tucson. Wagons can easily be taken within 2 or 3 miles of the mine. Wood and water are plentiful, and near the works. The natural surroundings are favorable to successful mining, and the owners are confident they have a very valuable property.

The Nequilla Mine is situated 12 miles west of Tucson, in the Amola Mountains. It was discovered in 1865, and has a shaft 120 feet deep, with two short tunnels. On top the vein was 15 inches thick; in the bottom of the shaft it shows 4 feet solid metal with a clean wall, and dips about 45°; mostly amalgamating-ore, which has been worked by the old Mexican process on the patio, and paid over $60 per ton. The general course of the vein is northeast and southwest. This was the first mine patented in the Territory, (1872.)

A 10-stamp mill has been placed upon the Ostrich Mine, located about 80 miles southwest of Tucson, and the mine will be regularly and systematically worked. Developments on the vein consist of one shaft 60 feet in depth, and a drift or level of 40 feet; another shaft 50 feet deep and drift of 60 feet, and another shaft of 35 feet in depth. In all the workings the vein shows permanent walls, and it is beyond doubt a true fissure-vein. The ore paid a handsome profit by the arrastra process. The company have built a fine road from the adjacent valley to the mine. Water for the use of the mine is obtained about a mile from the mine from a spring, which will furnish more water than will ever be needed at the mine.

A shaft to the depth of 60 feet has been sunk upon the Yellow Jacket lode, and at that depth the vein is well defined and increasing in width and richness.

D. C. Thompson writes that from 5,900 pounds of ore taken out of the Arizona Cloud Mine, and worked in the Ostrich Mill, he obtained a result of $579; nearly $200 per ton.

The San Xavier Mine, 18 miles from Tucson, has recently been developed to a considerable extent. The ore is of argentiferous galena and chloride, and a quantity smelted in a Mexican furnace gave fifty per cent. of silver and forty-five of copper.

The Trench Mine, in the Patagonia Mountains, is another of the mines worked by the Mexicans in years past, and (as it is believed) by the Jesuits in the last century.

At the highest point on the vein a shaft is sunk 110 feet. The metal, a rich carbonate of lead, width from 1 to 7 feet, in smooth clay walls. Three hundred feet west, and about 60 feet lower, another shaft is sunk 30 feet; the vein, 3 feet wide, of bright galena. The vein between these shafts has been uncovered, and shows from 3 to 4 feet wide, 150 feet. Farther west, and 60 feet lower, a tunnel is run in along the vein for 40 feet, showing a vein 30 inches wide, mostly a rich carbonate of lead. Ore from this tunnel has assayed $378 per ton. Two hundred feet to the west of this tunnel, and 100 feet lower, another tunnel is run in along the vein 75 feet. The vein here is from 12 to 30 inches wide, bright galena, and increases in width regularly as greater depth is attained. Country-rock, granite and porphyry.

In 1874 two furnaces were erected, and about 100 tons of ore reduced in the Mexican way, and produced 87 ounces of silver per ton.

One mile from the mine is a living stream of water sufficient for all purposes in running large works where steam is used for motive power; timber for coal is practically inexhaustible, and the whole country is covered with nutritious grasses.

About twenty men are now at work upon the mine, and building furnaces, burning coal, &c., preparatory to reducing from ten to twenty tons per day.

The Rusk, France, Florencia, Lost, Salero, Serena, Enterprise, San José, and Santa Maria lodes have been worked to some extent and are well spoken of, and some promising silver-lodes have lately been taken up in the Arabaipa Cañon and some near the Sonora line.

Through Pima County there are signs of unusual activity in prospecting and developing lodes, as far as the limited capital of the people will warrant. The country is so level, and the roads are generally so good, that ores and machinery can be moved with less expense than in many parts of the northern counties, but as yet there is but little machinery in use.

The Arizona Citizen (Tucson) thus refers to the situation:

> Thus far our miners have worked with little means and without machinery or furnaces, and yet we do not know of a single man who is not pleased with his prospects. It is only a little more than one year since the promised peace with the Indians has been believed permanent, and in that short time enterprises have been undertaken and carried to a point where success is now regarded as certain. Shafts have been sunk, cuts made, and tunnels driven into the mountains revealing bodies of ore that bear a world of riches. And this good work goes bravely on. Nearly every range of mountains is filled with hardy prospectors, turning over the treasure-bearing rocks, bringing to light new veins, and preparing for the day when extensive reduction-works will enable them to receive a good return for their present labors.
>
> Had Congress granted us a railroad, our situation would have been second to none of the mining empires growing up on the Pacific coast. As it is, we must still work on hopefully, sowing that we may reap, knowing that we have in abundance the elements of a golden future, and that the better day so long hoped for is not so far away as many would have us believe.

PINAL COUNTY.

This is a new county created by legislative act, approved February 1, 1875, and constituted of parts of Pima, Maricopa, and Yavapai Counties. The county-seat is located at the town of Florence, upon the south bank of the Gila River, about 90 miles north of Tucson and 200 miles south of Prescott by the stage-road.

The first county officers were elected on the first Monday in March following, and at about the same time the denizens of the new county were thrown into a state of great excitement by the discovery of what is now known as the Silver King, a huge vein of silver-ore. The story of its discovery, location, and value is thus told:

Four farmers lived near Florence—Regan, Copeland, Mason, and Long—to relieve the monotony of agricultural labors on the Gila, made occasional prospecting visits in the adjoining Pinal Mountains, and had discovered a copper-vein about 40 miles back in the mountains called the Globe Mine. When Tully, Ochoa & Co. started their copper-furnace in Tucson, Regan and his partners concluded they would have their Globe Mine tested, and fitted out at Florence to go after some ore.

A discharged soldier, who happened to be in Florence enjoying the festivities of the election-day aforesaid, came to the Regan party and "held them with his glistening eye." "I have a tale to tell," said he; and then he told them a dead comrade's story. "When you go up the Stoneman grade," said he, "you will pass the tanks; you will pass old Camp Pickett; then, some five miles on, you will come into a mountainous country; you will see a little valley like, hemmed in with mountains; near the head of the valley you will see some immense bowlders on the side of the road; off just a little bit you will see a little brown hill rising up all by itself, and in that hill, if what my old comrade said is true, you will find the richest mine in the world."

The Regan party heard the stranger's story, but were not much affected by his recital. They went on with their preparations for the copper expedition, passed up the grade, recognized the valley, saw the bowlders and the little brown hill beyond, and laughingly said, "There's our big mine, boys." But not one of the party stopped or appeared anxious to verify the stanger's tale. They had started for copper, and with the dogged persistence and easy incredulity of the old pioneer stock, were not to be turned aside by any tale, no matter how eloquently it might be told. They toiled along up and down the rugged side of the Pinal Mountains until they got to their Globe Copper Mine, dug out what they wanted, loaded their pack animals and returned, and then again they met the little brown hill which the story said contained endless wealth for the fortunate possessor of its contents. Regan, who was the leader of the party, looked at the little brown hill and meditated. It might be as well to look into the matter a little. Having more confidence in Copeland's judgment of mines than his own, he turned to him and said, "Copeland, let's look at this thing; give me the lead-mule, and the rest of us will go on to camp, five miles below, and you go over and see what you think of it." Copeland went over and found croppings immediately. The next day they all went to Florence. Copeland took his rock to a blacksmith's forge and melted out a fine bar of pure silver.

The party had been in great haste to get some copper out from the Globe to test their mine, but it was concluded now that the copper could wait. They procured a wagon, a few mining-tools, and returned next day to the little brown hill, broke off 1,500 pounds of rock from the surface, and took it to Tucson with their copper. The Tucson people admired the ore; so much so, that one of them offered $800 for the 1,500 pounds, which offer was immediatly accepted.

Regan and his party named their discovery the Silver King, and began sinking on it about the 15th of April. There is now a lively little camp near the mine, with a four-horse stage making regular trips to and from Florence, which is 35 miles away.

The Silver King shaft is now down 42 feet, with a drift from the bottom 12 feet. The shaft is 6 by 9 feet, and the drift is 5 feet wide by 6½ feet high. The shaft started on mineral, and as it goes down cuts numerous small seams of rich ore, all pitching toward the main mountain at an angle of about 55°. These seams vary in width from 3 inches to 18 inches. The hill is in a formation of brownish stone, which the miners think is a kind of granite. The vein-matter is quartz. The mineral consists chiefly of chlorides and black sulphurets. Great quantities of nearly-pure silver is found in little black nuggets in the quartz; these nuggets are soft, have coherence like bar-lead, and can be chewed between the teeth without feeling any grit; they assay about $20,000 to the ton. The first lot of ore worked was about 500 pounds, taken from the first 14 feet of the shaft. It was worked in a little furnace built at Florence by Messrs. Airy & Hughes to work ores from this district. This lot of ore yielded over $5 a pound, and 100 pounds yielded over $8 a pound. To work this, they bought in Tucson pig-lead produced from the Patagonia Mine, which is about 80 miles south of Tucson. It is estimated that the ore taken out of the shaft of 42 feet depth,

6 by 9 in size, will, taken as a whole, yield about $50,000; or, in other words, that the original prospecting shaft on the mine has in the first 42 feet given a yield of over $1,000 a foot.

The mine produces mainly a milling-ore, but the richest portions may be best reduced by smelting. Many silver nuggets have been found, which only require the application of heat to reduce them to merchantable silver.

The Silver King has been examined by experts from San Francisco, and it is said that a company will soon be formed in that city (where the ore has attracted much attention) to work it upon a scale commensurate with its size and richness. The ore in sight warrants the immediate erection of extensive works.

Numerous extensions have been taken up, and other lodes have been found in the vicinity. Of these, the Josephine, Iron Horse, Democrat, Fernandez, Hub, and Pike are reported to give rich indications.

The Surprise lode is of the same character as the Silver King. Mr. George Richmond writes that in one day 60 pounds of silver nuggets were taken from it.

The Athens lode, discovered by Mr. Dorsey, is well defined and traceable a long distance, running in a northeasterly and southwesterly direction south of the Silver King.

Mr. C. O. Brown, now one of the owners, recently brought to Tucson 80 pounds of silver nuggets which he picked up from the surface of this ledge. The largest piece weighs 34 pounds, and is believed to be worth $12 per pound, or, in other words, to be nearly pure silver. It has been sent to San Francisco for exhibition.

Northeast of the Silver King about 40 miles, in the *Globe district*, the principal lodes are the Globe, Rescue, Rambo, Alice, Pinal, Champion, and R. C. McCormick. A number of tons of silver-ore, estimated to be worth $1,000 to $1,500 per ton, have been sent to San Francisco from the Rescue.

"The lodes," says Governor Safford, "are regular and give promise of permanency."

South of the Gila River about 30 miles, in the *Quacharty district*, the Quacharty and Sacaton silver-lodes have been opened. Shafts have been sunk and large veins of good ore found, incased in regular walls. The ore yields from $50 to $200 per ton in silver, and is mixed with lead and copper. Many locations have been made in this district.

MARICOPA COUNTY.

This county, which lies between Pinal and Yavapai Counties, and of which the town of Phœnix is the county-seat, is one of the best agricultural districts in Arizona. The fertile valleys of the Gila and Salt Rivers, which form a junction near to Phœnix, are very extensive, and the abundance of water in said streams at all seasons admits of cheap and ample irrigation.

The northeastern part of the Globe mining-district (referred to under the head of Pinal County) is in this county, and its mountains all give evidence of more or less of mineral wealth.

YAVAPAI COUNTY.

This county includes an important part of central and all of northeastern Arizona. Prescott, the county-seat, and for some years the capital of the Territory, is picturesquely located in the mountains, at an elevation 6,000 feet above the level of the sea. It is one of the best built and most attractive mining-towns upon the Pacific slope, and with its fine brick and frame houses and stores it resembles a thrifty New England village much more than the average frontier settlement. The climate, which is never oppressive, and the abundant supply of timber and water, combine to make this part of Arizona especially enticing to miners, and the population is almost entirely American.

The best placers were found in this county in 1863. For several years large quantities of gold were taken from Lynx Creek, the Big Bug, the Hassayampa, and other streams; and now, at certain seasons, the washings are found very profitable.

The county is prolific in quartz-lodes, both of gold and silver, but, unfortunately, the mills first brought in some ten years since, at great expense and great risk, owing to the active hostility of the Indians, were, most of them, put upon veins, the ores of which had been tested only by assay, and naturally many mistakes were made and much time, labor, and money were thrown away upon non-paying lodes, of which even the richest mining-districts of the Pacific coast have a large proportion.

Since there has been less haste there has been less waste, and most of the mills now running are located upon good mines, and pay as well as can be expected at the present cost of working ores.

The Peck Mine, located near the Tiger belt, and about 30 miles east of south of Prescott, is the latest sensation in this county.

C. C. Bean, esq., of Prescott, thus describes the discovery of this mine and its character in a letter dated July 8, 1875:

On the evening of the 16th of June, Mr. E. G. Peck discovered, on War Eagle Creek, in the foot-hills, at the base of the Bradshaw Mountains, three large ledges or lodes of quartzite, which carried mineral, and which had probably, been passed over by a thousand prospectors before him, who regarded them as of no account, except so far as iron was concerned. In one of these ledges he found a crevice of 2 feet in width, which disclosed gray sulphide of silver and other mineral beneath the cropping, and some of the ore being brought to Prescott, it has been pronounced by assayers and competent judges to be of the very highest grade of silver-ore, as good as that taken out of the Eberhardt, at White Pine.

The mineral on these ledges has been traced for nearly 4,000 feet, and the indications are that these ledges form one large and valuable mine—at least, on the discovery and first extension claims. I have been on the ground and assisted in clearing the location for the dump and for sinking the shaft, and between two and three tons of ore was obtained in this little work, and that of the highest grade.

I lifted out myself chunks of pure gray sulphide of silver that would weigh from four to ten pounds, and that would yield at least 84 per cent. of silver.

Col. A. V. Kautz, commanding the military department of Arizona, adds this testimony, in a letter dated at Prescott, July 14, 1875:

The lode is on the summit of a spur of the Bradshaw Mountains, running north of east. There are three massive ledges of purplish quartz, parallel, and projecting above the surface, often 20 feet high. The distance between these ledges is about 50 or 60 feet. On the south side of the south ledge, on the hanging-wall, is the point of discovery, where the discoverers are now working and taking out the wonderfully rich ore from a pay-streak about 2 feet wide. We found several tons of this ore already on the dump-pile, and no signs of running out. Of course it is impossible without work for any one to tell how long it will pay, or how much of this very rich ore exists. The parties at work were apprehensive of its being too rich to last. They stated, however, that the same character of ore had been traced at opposite sides of the mountain on the same side of the ledge. While the very rich ore may be limited, I have every evidence that this discovery will lead to the development of extensive and valuable silver-lodes. In all my experience I have never been in a region where the ledges are so well defined and so extensive. From the point where we struck it to the Peck lode, the trail from Black Cañon passes over one ledge after another, the course and width of which can be traced from one mountain to another as far as the eye can reach. These ledges start within 15° of a vertical position, and dip to the north.

We examined another discovery of the parties interested in the Peck lode, called the William Wallace, and found it to be about 100 feet wide, for which it is claimed that it pays not less than $40 to the ton wherever it has been tested. The appearance of the lode is on the surface that of iron, and there are veins of native silver found in it. These discoveries are difficult of access, and it will be necessary to pack out the ore on mules until roads are made, which will be expensive. There is not much wood or water in the neighborhood, although there is a fine supply for the use of animals and workmen at the Peck Mine.

Col. H. A. Bigelow, of Prescott, a noted pioneer in Arizona, who lately visited the mine, writes of it as follows:

The shaft on the Peck Mine has developed magnificently. Those who have seen the mine will understand its situation when I say that the shaft was started on the east side of the mine, in the open cut on top of the hill, where the ore sent to Prescott has been taken out. It was sunk at the back end of the cut, which was about 20 feet deep, and is now down 32 feet, and the bottom has reached a fine body of ore 2 feet thick, and they have been taking out rich rock all the week. It is the largest and best deposit of ore yet found on this wonderful mine, and Mr. Hogle says (and his varied experience gives weight to his opinion) that it is the richest average ore he ever saw taken out of the ground. The tunnel is to cut the veins at right angles; is in some 25 feet, and in very hard, blue slate. Another tunnel on the north side of the hill, being run in on the Peck vein, is in 70 feet.

Ten tons of ore selected from the first taken from this mine were sold in Prescott for $13,000, which the owners considered much below its real value.

The Silver Prince is but half a mile southeast from the Peck, and in the same belt. Several tons of ore that assays up among the thousands have been taken out and shipped; and at seven different openings on the surface, 1,200 feet apart, there is a show of uniformly rich ore. The Silver Prince (singular number) really consists of two parallel veins 120 feet apart, both of which show rich ore where opened.

Colonel Bigelow, before referred to, says of this mine:

At the Silver Prince the principal work going on is the sinking of a shaft, which is now about 50 feet deep. It is on what they call the little ledge, and follows the vein down, taking out all between the walls, which are from 4 to 5½ feet apart, and as smooth as a bar of soap. At the top of the shaft very rich chloride was found, but as they went down the pay-streaks widened from a few inches to more than a foot, the ore changing to fine milling-ore, good enough, but not sufficiently rich to bear transportation at present rates.

* * * The present cost of getting ore to San Francisco is a great drawback, and even the expense of packing it to Prescott—$50 per ton—is such that it is impossible to do anything with any but first-class ore, say that which will assay from $750 per ton and upward; the rest must be worked nearer the mines or lie on the dumps until a day of cheaper transportation arrives.

The Wallace and the Sulphide, on the same belt, 10 miles east of the Peck, are two mammoth lodes running parallel with each other, and about 400 feet apart. The croppings stand up like immense towers, and are visible for miles.

The Antelope lode is in the same vicinity, and about 4 miles from Big Bug Creek. About 2 miles of this ledge has been located.

The Occident, Black Warrior, Oriental, Old Dominion, Evening Star, Del Pasco, Antelope, and Wild Pigeon are all promising lodes located not far from the Peck and Silver Prince.

The War Eagle lode has been worked for more than a year, and has paid handsomely by the arrastra process. The ore yields on an average $70 to the ton, and there is much free gold.

The Senator Mine is situated in the *Hassayampa district*, about one mile from the creek of that name, and distant some 12 miles from Prescott. The lead runs along with the hill on the backbone of the mountain, and is traceable for about two miles. It is gold-bearing, well defined, and has every appearance of a true fissure-vein. The deepest shaft is 106 feet, and there is an eastward drift 80 feet, and at the end of that lead a body of ore 7 feet wide, and about the same distance west another body 5 feet wide. The late workings of the ore average about $30 per ton, being about 50 per cent. of the contents of the rock. At a depth of 25 feet sulphurets were struck, but are worked by the free-gold process.

The Senator 10-stamp mill is situated on the Hassayampa Creek, and is run by steam, the ore from the mine being hauled by teams over a good road built by private enterprise.

Already about 3,000 tons have been worked at the mill. About one-half of the ore going through the mill is saved by means of riffle-sluices, with a view of reworking it at some future time.

The ores of the General Crook and the Empire Gold-Mines are worked by a 5-stamp mill, and yield a good return.

The Accidental Mine, upon Lynx Creek, from which very rich and beautiful specimens of gold quartz have been taken for years past, is now steadily worked. The vein has an average width of 2 feet, and is extensively tunneled and shafted. Over a thousand tons of ore have been crushed by arrastras run by steam, giving a yield of $25 to $75 per ton.

Of late discoveries in the *Big Bug district*, C. E. Hitchcock, esq., (long identified with the district,) wrote at length in a letter in October, 1875, from which the following is an extract:

The first recent silver discovery was made only a few months since in Big Bug mining-district, about 15 miles southeast of Prescott, where rich silver-ores had been previously known to exist. This first discovery was, singularly enough, named The Silver Belt.

Subsequent discoveries have proved this mine to be on a silver belt 2 miles wide and about 20 miles long, this mine being on the northeastern end of a belt which commences at the Agua Fria Valley, running southwest through the mountains on the head-waters of the Big Bug, Lynx, Turkey, and Hassayampa Creeks to Walnut Grove, a distance of about 25 miles.

The Silver Belt Mine is located about half-way between Agua Fria Valley and the Big Bug Mill, 15 miles southeast of Prescott. On it a shaft has been sunk to the depth of 85 feet, showing a continuous vein with well-defined wall-rock, and, what is considered evidence of true fissure-veins, a continuous gouge of talc. About 10 tons of first-class ore, assaying $600 per ton, has been shipped to San Francisco, and there is now on the dump from 40 to 50 tons of ore that assays from $150 to $300 per ton.

Several extensions have been located on the vein, and parallel with it are several veins located which show ores that assay from $150 to $600 per ton.

The Gopher Mine, situated about 2 miles southwest of the Silver Belt, was discovered the latter part of May. A shaft 60 feet deep shows a continuous vein of ore that assays from $50 to $450 per ton.

Several other veins have been discovered at various points from 3 to 10 miles southwest that show on the surface ores that assay from $30 to $400 per ton. Among these recent discoveries are several galena-veins from 1 to 2 feet wide, the ores from which give assays from $25 to $50 per ton. One of these veins, situated about 4 miles southeast of the Big Bug Mill, crops out about a foot high for a distance of several hundred feet, the vein of solid galena actually forming a dam to the water in a ravine which it crosses. A blind prospector would have tumbled over such a vein.

Of the Silver Belt, T. J. Butler, esq., editor of the Arizona Miner, (Prescott,) writes:

The quality of the ore is no longer a question, and we trust further development may prove the quantity to be equally satisfactory. They have out about 50 tons of ore, procured in sinking a shaft 70 feet on the ledge. This ore varies more in richness than in the character of the metal it carries, and Mr. George Hogle, a practical assayer and mineralogist, who has charge of the work, as well as Mr. Brown, an old silver-smelter, confidently believe that there is nothing in its chemical combination to prevent its being smelted without difficulty. The ores, so far as can be judged without analysis, are sulphurets of silver in combination with galena and a trace of antimony. Yet there are seams all through the rock, and little pockets filled with what appears to be chloride of lead, but upon collecting and washing it is found to contain considerable quantities of metallic silver. A small furnace with a fan-blower, to be run by horse-power, is erected and lined with a fire-clay found in the mine and mixed with quartz-tailings.

Of the Isabella, in the same district, he says:

This is not a large lode, nor extraordinarily rich, but is admirably situated for being worked cheaply, and is well opened on the surface for nearly a hundred feet in all, besides having a shaft down 25 feet in one place, at the bottom of which the vein is about 3 feet wide. A ditch has been brought into the lode and several tons of pay-ore ground, sluiced out, and piled up ready to be sent down on a tram-way to the creek, where the battery from the Big Bug Mill will be set up, and run by water from the ditch to crush it. Mr. Hitchcock informed us that in sluicing out the ore now on hand they saved from $12 to $18 per day, in free gold, to the hand, which is sufficient evidence of the value of the vein-matter, aside from what may be in the rock itself. The Isabella runs parallel with the Eugenia, and dips into the mountain toward the other; is of the same character of ore; and, as the Eugenia is a perpendicular ledge, it is believed that at a depth of several hundred feet they come together and form one ledge; or, in other words, that the Eugenia is the ledge and the Isabella a spur. They have crushed some seven or eight thousand tons from the Eugenia, with good results, but it is quite inaccessible on account of its great elevation, and if it can be reached through the Isabella, it would greatly facilitate its working and render it much more profitable.

The Sexton Mine, in the *Weaver district*, south of Prescott about 50 miles, is in the famous Antelope Hill, from the top of which the largest gold nuggets yet found in the Territory were taken in 1863 and 1864.

The vein runs northeast and southwest. It has been prospected by six or eight shafts, running down small distances, and by a tunnel driven into the hill 100 feet from the surface. The first vein cut by tunnel is 10 feet 9 inches in width. The companion vein has not been cut by tunnel, but appears much larger on the surface. The vein increases in size as it penetrates the ground. Both veins, on the surface, have an apparent width of 30 feet. This is owing to the disintegration of the quartz and the confusion with which it is piled up on the surface. The veins are true fissure-veins, cutting the strata at right angles, and situated at the junction of the primitive and secondary formation, in metamorphosed azoic rocks, on the foot-hills of a large granite mountain on the north and talcose clay-slates south and east. The walls are talcose slate, the same as in the Vulture Mine. The ore, from its disintegrated character, is easily crushed, and 10 stamps would reduce 15 tons in one day of 24 hours. The gold is free, and without the presence of any minerals that would prevent amalgamation. Much "specimen" rock has been found. The surface of the mine is covered with immense croppings, the result of the disintegration of centuries, and plainly distinguishable at a long distance.

Fifty tons of ore taken from croppings indiscriminately, and broken in the Vulture Mill, (at Wickenburgh,) gave a return of $15 per ton. Ore since crushed in arrastras has yielded $37 per ton. Three tons of ore from one of the spurs produced $573 in gold.

Mr. Stanton, one of the owners, writes:

The ore in the tunnel gets better in depth, and, in my opinion, as soon as we get below where the immense body of spurs, which shoot out in all directions, connect with the main vein, it will get much richer. There are over two hundred of these spurs, running out in all conceivable directions from the mother vein, all of which are rich in gold, and vary from 3 to 18 inches in thickness. Some of them run a distance of one mile from the mother vein, others 400 yards, and some not over 250 feet. Generally they give out at a distance of 12 to 25 feet, but some go down to a depth of 70 feet. The Marcus main shaft is down to a depth of 90 feet, and is twice richer than on the surface. The sulphurets yielded $800 per ton. These are all spurs of the Great Sexton. They have no walls, and run straight down without any pitch. The Marcus spur can be plainly traced to where it intersects the Sexton at the tunnel. All these spurs impoverish the main lode on the surface.

The great body of ore in this mine, (even should it not average over $20 to $30 per ton,) and its location upon the highway from Wickenburgh to Prescott, make it a very desirable property, and a movement is on foot to organize a company in New York for its development upon an extensive scale. It promises to be a worthy rival of the great Vulture Mine, from which it is not over 40 miles distant, and which it closely resembles in many particulars.

During the year quite rich placers have been discovered in the *Santa Maria district*, about 80 miles southwest of Prescott. The gold is coarse, but of good quality, and a considerable quantity has been taken out. The lack of water is a drawback, and Americans are not usually expert in the Mexican process of "dry washing." The largest nugget yet found in these placers is valued at between $50 and $60.

The Arizona Miner has the following concerning a discovery of cinnabar:

Everybody about town will recollect that three or four weeks ago there was a little stir on account of some cinnabar-ore that was brought in by some prospectors. Numerous tests were made and quicksilver found in all the rock. John Malcomb and Joe Stone arrived in town Tuesday, having been out to make locations. They brought in about 20 pounds of ore. The lode is situated on the Verde River, which crosses it several miles below Squaw Peak, and shows for a long distance on both sides of the stream. Malcomb and Stone report that there are large holes along the vein, excavated evidently by Indians, who used the ore for paint. The ore is identical in appearance with the pieces which have been found in the old Indian camps for years past in Yavapai County.

MOHAVE COUNTY.

This county embraces the northwestern part of the Territory. Many mineral-bearing lodes have been found within its boundaries, and some near to the Colorado River have been favorably known for a number of years past. The principal mineral belt developed to this time extends from the southern line of the county north about 100 miles, and runs parallel with the Colorado River, and about 30 miles east of the same.

McCrackin district.—Perhaps the most noted lode in the county is the McCrackin, named after the discoverer, a pioneer in Arizona. It was found in August, 1874, and has been quite extensively developed. The lode is well incased in walls, and is from 15 to 39 feet in thickness, and has every appearance of a true fissure-vein. The larger part of the ore taken out is base, containing lead and copper, but yielding an average of about $75 per ton in silver. A San Francisco company is negotiating for the purchase of this valuable property.

One who visited the mine in June last writes:

At present the McCrackin Mine is working some thirty or forty men, which number will be increased as soon as tools and other facilities which are requisite arrive. I was at the mine a few days ago, and was just in time to see a new strike of some of the richest ore ever taken out of the mine. This large body of rich ore was struck on the claim known as the Senator, and was the richest I ever saw. It was about five feet wide and looked more like a mass of chloride of silver than common ore.

The McCrackin bed of mineral has been traced for several miles, and many locations have been made upon it which seem to be nearly as rich as the discovery claim.

The Greenwood Mine is one of the largest gold-mines in Mohave County. There are 1,000 tons of fine milling-ore out on the different dumps at this mine, and many thousand more in sight. The owners of this valuable property intend adding several more stamps to their mill, and are thinking of purchasing another mill of twenty stamps.

Twenty miles north of the McCrackin district is the *Cedar district*, in which the Hope and Hibernia lodes assay from $100 to $1,000 per ton.

In the Wallapai Mountains, 30 miles north of the Cedar district, a shaft has been sunk to the depth of 100 feet upon the Dean lode. It shows a vein about 8 feet wide, with regular walls, and containing silver-ore of a high grade.

The Cupel and Tiger Mine is considered one of the most promising mines in *Wallapai district.*

The Oro Plata Mine is looking remarkably well. There are already 50 tons of ore on the dumps, that will work from $100 to $300 per ton, principally gold. This mine has been extensively worked, and there are now many tons of ore in sight, which the owners expect to have worked in the new mill at Mineral Park.

Mr. Thomas Christie has shipped nine tons of ore from his mine, the Metallic Accident, near Mineral Park, and he confidently expects to get from $1,200 to $1,500 per ton for it in San Francisco.

Cerbat range.—North of the Wallapai Mountains, in the Cerbat range, hundreds of locations have been made, nearly all of which show rich silver-ores. Some promising gold-lodes have also been found. A considable amount of ore has been shipped to San Francisco, and profitably sold.

The mining-towns of Cerbat and Mineral Park are located in these mountains; the former is the county-seat. Several mills and furnaces have lately been erected, but the writer has not been able to secure any report of the amount of ore reduced.

The most important lodes in this district are the Keystone, Lone Star, Shoulder, Empire, Little Grant, and Sixty-three. A fine body of ore is exposed to view in all the drifts and shafts upon the last-named lode. One of the shafts is down to a depth of more than 200 feet, the vein widening and improving.

The Mocking Bird Mine is situated about two miles east of Cerbat. At the bottom of the shaft, now over 100 feet deep, there is a fine body of ore. Two tunnels are connected with the shaft at a depth of 50 feet. From one of these a quantity of rich ore has been taken out.

Peacock range.—Twenty-five miles east of Mineral Park is the Peacock range of mountains, and at the north end of the range is located the Hackberry Mine. The mine is situated on the northeast slope of the mountain, about 1,400 feet above the valley. The rich vein of silver ore is from 10 to 18 inches thick, and will average one foot in thickness, The ore-vein lies upon its parent ledge and cleaves off free from it, so much so that it seems almost independent of the 6 to 8 feet of brown quartz that forms its foot-wall. The hanging-wall is a soft porphyry, with a thick stratum of white clay separating it from the vein. The vein has been opened by six shafts within a distance of 700 feet. The deepest shaft, at about 50 feet, (water-level,) developed a baser ore, and at 62 feet the vein is solid and 14 inches thick, and the ore averages $340 per ton. From 50 feet down the ore will have to be roasted; above that it is free, and will work up to 80 per cent. with the ordinary treatment of salt and sulphate of copper.

Hon. A. E. Davis and W. B. Ridenour, esq., the discoverers, have put a 5-stamp mill on the Hackberry Mine, and have every reason to believe that it will pay well.

The facilities for mining are as good in this district as anywhere in Arizona. Water is abundant, and wood can be furnished at low cost, as there is much of it close at hand.

East of the Peacock range exploration has been extended into a lately unknown region, and a finely-timbered and well-watered country has been found, abounding in game and bearing a rich profusion of grasses.

YUMA COUNTY.

The principal mines in Yuma County, which comprises the southwestern part of the Territory, are those of the *Castle Dome district*, upon the Colorado River. They have so often been referred to in these reports that it will now suffice to say that recent work upon them has abundantly confirmed their permanency and value. Much ore has been shipped to San Francisco, where it has an established reputation, and finds a ready market.

W. J. Berry, esq., the editor of the Arizona Sentinel, published at Yuma, the county-town, recently said of these mines, with which he is personally familiar:

> The whole district is almost one solid mass of metal. Thousands of tons of argentiferous galena have been shipped to San Francisco for reduction, and, after paying all expenses, have yielded a handsome return to the miner. Mr. Miller's furnace is in operation, and has turned out a vast amount of rich bullion, but it will require a hundred furnaces to smelt the ore that can readily be taken from these mines, and that for an indefinite time. And then this district has facilities unsurpassed for the mining and reduction of ores. Wood, water, and grass are abundant, and of the best. Lime and iron and fire-clay are also here in abundance, and a large navigable river runs almost at the base of the mines.

Captain Nagle, an owner in the Castle Dome mines, has lately erected at Yuma works for the reduction of argentiferous galena and all smelting-ores, which are likely to greatly facilitate mining operations in Yuma County.

He considers the location a fortunate one, because it is at a junction where the ores from Castle Dome, in which galena largely predominates, can meet those from Southwestern Arizona near the Sonora line, which are rich in silver, without carrying enough galena to form a flux, and that by combining the two the advantageous reduction of both can be made.

Placers.—New placers have been discovered near Ehrenberg, in this county. Rich gold-dust is found throughout an area about 40 miles in length and 15 in width. Nuggets worth from $2 to $10 have been taken out. There is little if any water, and the dry-washing process is used.

Mexicans continue to bring in gold from the vicinity of Gila City, 20 miles from Yuma, where placers have been worked for many years.

THE BULLION PRODUCT.

Mr. Valentine, the efficient superintendent of Wells, Fargo & Co.'s express business, published December 30, 1875, his annual statement of the product of precious metals on the Pacific coast, including British Columbia and the west coast of Mexico, but excluding New Mexico. In his accompanying remarks he said:

> Prof. R. W. Raymond credits New Mexico (omitted in our statement) and Arizona combined with $987,000, which is a liberal allowance. We have been unable to obtain any data that justify a showing so favorable.

This criticism requires me to state that my figures, referred to by Mr. Valentine, were given for New Mexico and Arizona separately, and not "combined;" that they were for 1874, not 1875; that the $500,000 credited for 1874 to New Mexico was complained of by the citizens generally as too low an estimate; that the $487,000 credited in the same year to Arizona was based largely on detailed reports, which are printed in my volume; that at the time Mr. Valentine compared my returns with his own, I had published no returns for the period he was considering; and that the governor of Arizona reported the product of that Territory for the fiscal year, in an official communication to the Director of the Mint, as $1,000,000.

Mr. Valentine's estimate of the product of Arizona for 1875 is as follows:

Gold dust and bullion by express	$23,500
Ores and base bullion by freight	85,593
	109,093

That this is ridiculously low, no one who knows how many men are mining in Arizona can for a moment doubt.

John Wasson, esq., surveyor-general of Arizona, and editor of the Arizona Citizen, having been requested to furnish an estimate of the gold and silver product of the Territory for 1875, made the following response:

1. There are no express-offices in Arizona through which gold and silver are shipped, and hence no means of procuring reliable figures as to the amount.

2. Nearly every outgoing mail carries gold-bullion by the pound. The letter-postage per pound is only 96 cents, and the mail is regarded cheaper, and by many safer, than any other available way of shipment.

3. Individuals are constantly carrying out bags of gold and gold bricks and some silver bricks, all taking the utmost care, for prudential reasons, to conceal from the public both the fact and amount thereof.

4. Every steamer from Yuma to San Francisco carries considerable silver contained in shipments of ore.

5. The general belief is that the product of gold and silver in Arizona for 1875 was fully $1,500,000; and this has been so often asserted by those most capable of knowing that any other statement would be regarded as not nearly so accurate.

Taking into consideration the natural tendency of resident observers to overestimate the aggregates of an industry which they know only in detail, and also the fact that bullion carried in private hands may subsequently be consigned to some public conveyance and be credited to another source than that of its origin, I think it advisable to set down the product of Arizona at $750,000 for the year 1875; an estimate in which I regret that I must differ widely with Mr. Valentine's usually judicious figures.

METALLURGICAL.

PART II.

CHAPTER XI.

A CENTURY OF MINING AND METALLURGY IN THE UNITED STATES.

BY HON. ABRAM S. HEWITT.*

Mining enterprises were among the motive powers to the exploration, conquest, and colonization of the New World. The desire to find a shorter route to the profitable trade of India, and the desire to conquer new territory, wherever it might be found, in the name of some Catholic or Protestant sovereign of Europe, were accompanied, both in North and South America, by eager hopes of the discovery of gold and silver.

The history of the plunder of the metallic wealth and the development of the mineral resources of Mexico and South America does not lie within my present purpose. The early enterprises of this kind in the northern part of the continent were less successful, though the progress of two hundred years has made them more beneficial, to national prosperity, for reasons which I shall, perhaps, be able to indicate.

Gold was found in moderate quantities in use among the Indian tribes of the present Southern States. The Spaniards under De Soto, following this clew, and led on by stories, exaggerated or misunderstood, of their Indian guides, made a wide superficial exploration in search of the origin of this treasure. They are supposed to have excavated many of the diggings in North and South Carolina and Georgia which are now overgrown with forests; but no rich deposits appear to have been discovered and no permanent operations undertaken.

In the great charter of King James, by which, in 1606, the right to explore and settle the North American continent from the thirty-fourth to the forty-fifth parallel, was granted to the London and Plymouth Companies, it was provided that one-fifth of the gold and silver and one-fifteenth of the copper which might be discovered should belong to the Crown. One of the earliest expeditions of Capt. John Smith, in Virginia, was the exploration of the Chickahominy River, in the hope that it might constitute a water-way to the Pacific Ocean; and one of the next events in the history of the same colony was a mining excitement, such as would be called in our California tongue a "stampede," caused by the supposed discovery of gold; in which, fortunately, John Smith did not avail himself of his official position to take "stock." It is a curious circumstance that gold really occurs in that region, though

* The present chapter was prepared as an address before the American Institute of Mining Engineers, of which body Mr. Hewitt is the president for 1876. In consideration of services which I was able to render in the compilation of materials, and particularly in the tabulation of statistics, it was arranged that the address should also be furnished to me as a contribution to the present report, which, if it had been printed immediately after its transmission to Congress, would have appeared at about the time of the delivery of the address. In consequence of the delay in publishing these pages, Mr. Hewitt's address is already widely known through other mediums; but I do not feel called upon, on that account, to omit it here, since it contains matter of permanent and general interest.—R. W. R.

the glittering dust, of which a ship-load was sent by the deluded colonists to the jewelers of London, proved to be but mica or iron-pyrites; and it seems probable (albeit this suggestion is not based upon any explicit record known to me) that the presence of gold among the Indians, and the discovery of specimens of the quartz or slates of Virginia containing visible particles of it, gave rise to the general excitment, under the influence of which, without further tests of value, a large amount of worthless material was collected, to the neglect of necessary and profitable industry. From this point of view the Jamestown mining fever was the prototype of many that have since occurred—all of which may be summed up in the general expression, that the mine "did not pan out according to the samples."

A more promising industry was inaugurated at the same time by the sending of a quantity of iron-ore from Jamestown to England in 1608. This ore, smelted in England, yielded seventeen tons of metal, probably the first pig-iron ever made from North American ore. In 1620, a hundred and fifty skilled workmen were sent to the colony to erect iron-works; and it is said that a fund, subscribed for the education of the colonists and Indians, was invested in this enterprise, as a safe and sure means of increase. But, in 1622, an Indian massacre broke up the enterprise; and both the manufacture of iron and the education of citizens and Indians have been obliged, ever since, to rely upon other sources of support.

For an interesting collection of facts relative to the beginnings of the iron industry of the American colonies, I refer you to the forthcoming work on that subject, by our fellow-member, Mr. John B. Pearse, to whose courtesy I am indebted for the opportunity to consult the advance-sheets of a portion of the book.

According to the statement of Colonel Spotswood, quoted by Mr. Pearse, it appears that, previous to 1724, neither New England, Pennsylvania, nor Virginia possessed blast-furnaces. Their product of iron was from bloomeries only. According to Professor Hodge, quoted by Professor Whitney, however, a furnace was built at Pembroke, Mass., in 1702; and another authority states that, in 1721, New England possessed six furnaces and nineteen forges. In 1719 was passed the famous resolution of the British House of Commons, "that the erection of manufactories in the colonies tended to lessen their dependency on Great Britain." Only the earnest protest of the colonial agents prevented the prohibition at that time of the American iron manufacture. The next thirty years witnessed two instructive contests. The first was that of the colonial with the domestic pig-iron manufacture—a competion in which America was favored by the abundance of her vegetable fuel (the employment of mineral coal in iron-making not having yet found introduction) in comparison with the rapidly-waning forests of Great Britan. The British manufacture being protected by heavy duties on colonial pig-iron, the latter began to be more and more worked up into bar iron, nails, steel, &c., at home; and this brought on a new competition with the British manufacturers of these articles. In 1750, a further legislative attempt to regulate this trade was made by Parliament, which decreed the admission of colonial pig-iron duty free, but prohibited the erection in America of slitting, rolling, or plating mills, or steel furnaces, ordering that all new ones thereafter built should be suppressed as "nuisances."

It will be recollected that arbitrary acts of this kind, for the destruction of our infant manufactures, were among the grievances cited in the Declaration of Independence. The extent of the American iron manufacture, during the ante-revolutionary period, can be inferred only from scanty records of exports. These, beginning in 1717 with three tons, had increased in 1750 to about 3,000 tons; in 1765, the total is reported at 4,342 tons; and in 1771 at 7,525 tons, the maximum annual export. The outbreak of the war of course put an end to exportation and caused a great demand for war material, which occupied and rapidly extended the means of manufacture possessed by the country. The expanded iron industry suffered a severe collapse when, at the close of the war, not only this demand ceased, but the re-opened ports admitted large quantities of foreign iron—the successful employment of mineral coal, the steam-engine, and puddling having by that time laid the foundation of English supremacy in the iron manufacture.

The earliest copper-mining company of which we find any record—according to Professor Whitney, in his excellent work on the metallic wealth of the United States, the earliest incorporated mining company of any kind—was chartered in 1709, to work the Sinsbury mines, at Granby, Conn. These mines were abandoned in the middle of the eighteenth century, afterward bought by the State of Connecticut, and used as a prison for sixty years. Mining was resumed in them about 1830, and after a few years they were again abandoned. The ores were mostly shipped to England, and seem to have been lean.. The deposit belongs to the class of irregular bunches, nodules, seams, or limited beds, in the New Red Sandstone, near its junction with trap. This formation was the scene in New Jersey, also, of early mining activity. The Schuyler mine, near Belleville, on the Passaic, was discovered about 1719, and proved more profitable to its owners before the Revolution than it ever has been since that time to any of the series of individuals and companies that have expended large sums in its development. In fact, the chief blessing conferred upon mankind by the Schuyler mine arises from the circumstance that the first steam-engine ever built wholly in America was constructed in 1793–'94 at the small machine-shop attached to the smelting-works at Belleville, my father being the pattern-maker in the party of mechanics sent out by Boulton & Watt for the purpose of erecting an engine for the Philadelphia water-works in Center Square. In 1751 a copper-mine was opened near New Brunswick; and the Bridgewater mine, near Somerville, was operated previous to the Revolution, though even then, it is said, with much loss of capital. New Jersey's record in copper-mining is not a cheerful one; but her unsurpassed ranges of iron-ores may well console her. Betrayed by the treachery of Triassic and trap, she can flee to the shelter of the crystalline schists. Pennsylvania was not without her copper-mining in the colonial period, the Gap Mine, in Lancaster County, having been opened in 1732.

Already during the colonial period the first red gleams of the future glory of the Lake Superior mines had appeared. The intrepid Jesuit fathers, Marquette and others, who penetrated the wilderness from Acadia to the Gulf, to carry both the Cross of their religion and the Lilies of their sovereign, had made extensive explorations on the Upper Peninsula, and published glowing accounts of the abundance of copper, to which later travelers added legends of gold and precious stones. Before them, the Indian tribes, whose stone tools now furnish subjects of inquiry to the archæologist, had wrought rudely upon the deposits which nature had left in a condition so exceptionally pure as not to need, for the production of limited amounts of metal, the intervention of metallurgical processes. The first recorded mining operations on the part of white men were those of Alexander Henry, near the Forks of the Ontonagon, in 1771. As is well known, however, the active development of this region dates from the publication of Houghton's Geological Report, in

1841, and the extinguishment of the Chippewa title by the treaty of 1843.

Lead-mining in this country may also claim an ancient origin—as we reckon antiquity. As early as 1651, Governor John Winthrop received his famous license to work any mines of "lead, copper, or tin, or any minerals, as antimony, vitriol, black lead, alum, salt, salt-springs, or any other the like," and "to enjoy forever said mines, with the lands, woods, timber, and water within two or three miles of said mines." As he received also a special grant of mines and minerals in the neighborhood of Middletown, Conn., it is not unlikely that the old Middletown silver-lead mine, the date of the discovery of which is not precisely known, was opened by him or his successors. The nickel and cobalt mines near Chester, in Connecticut, once held to be very promising deposits, are also believed to have been originally worked by Governor Winthrop; but nickel was not valuable in those days; and the lead and copper in these ores do not seem to have been abundant. Unfortunately, now that nickel and cobalt are so valuable as to repay amply the cost of extracting them when they are present in a small percentage only, these Connecticut ores no longer correspond (if indeed they ever did) to the analysis and accounts formerly given as to their nickeliferous character.

The old Southampton silver-lead mine in Massachusetts, well known to mineralogists, was commenced in 1765 by Connecticut adventurers; but its operations were suspended by the revolutionary war. Lead mines in Columbia and Dutchess Counties, New York, were also worked at an early period; and, no doubt, all over the country occupied or controlled during the war by the American forces, there were small and desultory surface operations, furnishing lead for the use of the Army.

The Indians inhabiting the Mississippi Valley before the advent of the whites probably did not understand the metallurgy of lead. Galena has been found in the western mounds, but, it is said, no lead. In 1700 and 1701 Père Le Sueur made his famous voyage up the Mississippi, discovering, as he claimed, many lead mines. Lead mining was begun in Missouri in 1720, while that country belonged to France, and under the patent granted to Law's famous Mississippi Company. Mine la Motte, named after a mineralogist who came over with Renault, the superintendent, was one of the first discoveries. It has been in operation at intervals ever since, and is now successfully managed by Mr. Cogswell, a member of our institute, who may, I think, truthfully claim that he has charge of the oldest mining enterprise still active in the United States. The ores yield a small percentage of nickel and cobalt, as well as lead.

It was in 1788 that Dubuque obtained from the Indians the grant under which he mined, until the year of his death, where the city now stands which bears his name. The land was subsequently ceded to the United States by the Indians, and the representatives of Dubuque were forcibly ejected.

Such, then, was the condition of our mining industry at the commencement of our national existence. We occupied but a strip of territory on the Atlantic; and even in that limited area we had scarcely learned the nature and extent of the mineral resources to be utilized. Anthracite and petroleum, quicksilver and zinc, were unknown as treasures within our reach. The rapid extension of possession, government, population, and industry over plains and mountains to the Pacific, which has been effected in a hundred years, is but the type of a conquest and progress which has advanced with equal rapidity in every department of human labor, and nowhere more notably than in the departments of mining and metallurgy. The tables which Dr. Raymond has prepared, and which will be printed to accompany these remarks, show that this country has produced during the century ending with 1875, of gold, about 66,680,000 troy ounces, worth about $1,332,700,000; of silver, about 201,300,000 troy ounces, worth about $261,450,000; of quicksilver, 840,000 flasks, or 64,206,000 pounds avoirdupois; of copper, 200,000 tons; of lead, 855,000 tons; of pig-iron 40,000,000 tons; of anthracite coal, 351,521,423 tons, (the ton in all these cases being 2,240 pounds avoirdupois;) and of petroleum, 76,594,600 barrels. The product of these leading industries for the year 1875 were: gold, $33,400,000; silver, $41,400,000; quicksilver, 53,706 flasks; copper, 15,625 tons; lead, 53,000 tons; pig-iron, 2,108,554 tons; zinc, about 15,000 tons; anthracite, 20,643,509 tons; bituminous coal, about 26,000,000 tons; petroleum, 8,787,506 barrels.

In order that a clear idea may be formed as to the relative position now held by the United States in the world of mining and metallurgy, I have selected the production of coal, which is the main reliance for power of all organized industry, and of iron, which is the chief agent of civilization, as the basis of comparison with other nations, using, so far as coal is concerned, the figures given in the Forty-second Annual Report of the Philadelphia Board of Trade, for the year 1873.*

	Tons.	Per cent.
Great Britain	127,016,747	46.4
United States	50,512,000	18.4
Germany	45,335,741	16.5
France	17,400,000	6.4
Belgium	17,000,000	6.2
Austria and Hungary	11,000,000	4.0
Russia	1,200,000	0.5
Spain	570,000	0.2
Portugal	18,000	—
Nova Scotia	1,051,567	0.4
Australia	1,000,000	0.4
India	500,000	0.2
Other countries	1,000,000	0.4
Total	273,704,055	100.0

The following estimate, in round numbers, of the world's present production of iron is taken from various sources, and may be considered approximately correct. The figures for Great Britain and France are those of 1874, and the product of the United States for the same year has been taken. For other countries the estimates are principally for 1871 or 1872, except Austria and Hungary, for which the official returns for 1873 have been taken.

The quantities are given in tons of 2,240 pounds.

	Tons.	Per cent.
Great Britain	5,991,000	45.2
United States	2,401,000	18.1
Germany	1,600,000	12.1
France	1,360,000	10.3
Belgium	570,000	4.3
Austria and Hungary	365,000	2.7
Russia	360,000	2.7
Sweden and Norway	306,000	2.3
Italy	73,000	0.5
Spain	73,000	0.5
Switzerland	7,000	—
Canada	20,000	0.2
South America	50,000	0.4

* I wish to acknowledge, for these and other figures relating to coal, my obligations to Mr. R. P. Rothwell, who has freely placed at my disposal the very extensive and elaborate compilations of statistics which are to form the basis of an exhaustive paper by his experienced hand on that subject.

	Tons.	Per cent.
Japan	9,000	0.1
Asia	40,000	0.3
Africa	25,000	0.2
Australia	10,000	0.1
Total	13,260,000	100.0

An examination of these tables will serve to show that in the products which measure the manufacturing industry of nations, Great Britain stands first and the United States second on the roll, and that there is a clear and almost identical relation between the product of coal and the product of iron. The United States now produces as much coal and iron as Great Britain yielded in 1850. We are thus gaining steadily and surely upon our great progenitor, and in the nature of things, as the population of this country grows, must, before another century rolls around, pass far beyond her possible limits of production, and become the first on the international list, because we have the greatest geographical extent, and our natural resources are upon so vast a scale that all the coal area of all the rest of the world would only occupy one-fourth of the space in which, within our borders, are stored up the reserves of future power.

In a hundred years we have thus reached a point at which for coal, iron, gold, silver, copper, lead, and zinc, we are independent of the world, with abundant capacity to supply as well our growing wants, as to export these blessings of civilization to other and less favored lands, as soon as our labor and our legislation are adjusted to the conditions which will enable us to compete in foreign markets. One hundred years ago we proclaimed our political independence, and we maintained it by force of arms; we are now in a position to proclaim our industrial and commercial independence, and maintain it by the force of peaceful agencies against friendly competition.

A striking view of this prosperous development is presented by the magnificent mineral collection under the charge of Professor Blake, in the Government building at the neighboring Exposition—a collection which constitutes the first worthy National Museum of Mining and Metallurgy.

Never was a century of free government celebrated under such favorable conditions; never was free government so justified by the material results it has produced. But let us not conceal from ourselves the fact that mere growth in wealth, mere development in industry, mere increase in population are not the best evidences of national greatness; and unless our progress in art, learning, morals, and religion keeps pace with our material growth, we have cause rather for humiliation than for glorification.

"Whatsoever things are true, whatsoever things are honest, whatsoever things are just, whatsoever things are pure, whatsoever things are lovely, whatsoever things are of good report" constitute the real glory of a nation, without which the magnificent material structure which in a century we have reared will disappear "like the baseless fabric of a vision."

In a hundred years, as I have said, we have reached a point at which for every one of the minerals and metals named, we are independent of the world, having the capacity to supply our own growing domestic demand, and also to export to foreign lands.

It is not my purpose to trace in detail the steps by which this degree of progress has been achieved. The narration of successive events alone, without any discussion of underlying causes and accompanying effects, would consume far more time than I could command. So far as the leading epochs of the history are concerned, I think they may be fairly summed up in the following mere catalogue:

1. First of all, must be named the erection in Philadelphia, in 1794, of the first steam-engine in America. We celebrate this year the centennial anniversary of a greater power than the United States of America—a wider revolution than our War of Independence. It was in 1776 that James Watt presented to the world the perfected steam-engine, all the improvements of which since his day are not to be compared with those which he devised upon the rude machines of his predecessors. In one hundred years, the steam-engine has transformed the face of the world and affected to its remotest corners the condition of the human race. Few changes have been so profound; not one in history has been so rapid and amazing. With reference to the special subject now under consideration, if I were asked what elements had most to do with the swift progress of our country, I should answer, freedom and the steam-engine. But deeper even than any organized declarations or outward forms of freedom lies the influence of the steam-engine, which has been from the day of its birth, in spite of laws and dynasties, and all accidents of history, the great emancipator of man.

2. *Gold mining in the South.*—Already Jefferson, in his "Notes on Virginia," mentioned the finding of a lump of gold, weighing seventeen pennyweights, near the Rappahannock; and, about the beginning of this century, the famous Cabarrus nugget, weighing twenty-eight pounds, was discovered at the Reed Mine, in North Carolina. But the great gold excitement in the South followed the discoveries in Georgia from 1828 to 1830. The maximum of production (probably never more than $600,000 in any one year) was from 1828 to 1845, since which time it has declined to insignificance, though a few enterprises, both in hydraulic and quartz mining, are now actively prosecuted.

3. *The opening of the anthracite-coal fields and the use of anthracite in the blast-furnace.*—The first of these events practically dates from the year 1820, although some anthracite found its way to market much earlier, and the second from the year 1839. The latter was followed by the development of the vast anthracite-iron industry, which has contributed so much to the prosperity of Pennsylvania. The connection between anthracite and civilization was long ago pointed out by Sir Charles Lyell, in connection with his visit to this country, when he observed in this State, and in this very city where we now stand, the strange phenomenon of a vast manufacturing population dwelling in neat houses and able to keep themselves and their houses clean. This smokeless fuel is a great moral and æsthetic benefactor. It has also proved specially useful in metallurgy—one process at least, the American zinc-oxide manufacture, being impracticable without it; and in war no one will deny its superiority who remembers how our cruisers, burning anthracite, and hence not traceable at sea by their smoke, were able to spy and pursue the blockade-runners, whose thick clouds of escaping bituminous smoke betrayed them. A table of the production of anthracite is given herewith, and some further observations concerning its control and management will be appropriate under another head of my remarks.

4. *The use of raw bituminous coal in the blast-furnace.*—This was introduced in 1845.

5. *The development of the copper-mines of Lake Superior*, beginning in 1845 and increasing slowly but steadily to 1862, when about 8,000 tons of ingot-copper were produced; then declining for some years, to recover in 1868 and 1869 its lost ground, and since the latter year, by reason of the great production of the Calumet and Hecla Mines, to attain an unprecedented yield. The tables of copper production for

the United States, herewith given, show that our present product is not far from 16,000 tons, of which three-fourths must be credited to the Lake Superior mines.

6. *The discovery of gold in California*, in 1848, or rather its rediscovery, since it had previously been known to both the natives and the Jesuit missionaries, and also to hunters and trappers. The wonderful direct and indirect results of this event have been too often the theme of orators, historians, and political economists to need a further description from me. Its direct result in the way of mining was the rapid exploration of the western Territories by eager prospectors, and the successive development of placer-mines in nearly all of them. It is difficult to fix the dates of these beginnings; but we may assume with sufficient accuracy that gold-mining practically began in Oregon in 1852, in Arizona in 1858, in Colorado in 1859, in Idaho and Montana in 1860. With the completer exploration of the country, and the decline of the placer-mines, stampedes have grown less frequent and extensive than in the earlier days. There is scarcely any corner of the country left, except the Black Hills of Dakota, which has not been ransacked sufficiently to show whether it contains extensive and valuable placer deposits; and those districts which present accumulations of gold in such a way as to offer returns immediately to labor without capital have been already overrun. The principal reliance of our gold-mining industry for the future must be quartz and hydraulic or deep gravel mines. These may be expected to maintain for years to come their present rate of production, if not to increase it. In the table of gold production, herewith given, there is, it is true, a falling off of late years, but this is to be attributed to the placer-mines.

7. *The commencement, about* 1851, *of regular mining operations at the New Almaden quicksilver-mine, in California.*—The production of this metal in the United States has been thus far confined to the State of California, and it will be seen from the table of the production of the New Almaden mine that it has always furnished a large, though of late a waning, proportion of the grand total for the country.

8. The middle of the nineteenth century was crowded with important events in metallurgy and mining. It was in 1856 that Mr. Bessemer read his paper at the Cheltenham meeting of the British Association for the Advancement of Science, which inaugurated for both continents the age of steel. Within sixty days after that event an experimental Bessemer converter was in readiness at the furnaces of Cooper & Hewitt, at Phillipsburgh, N. J. But the experiment was not carried far enough to demonstrate the value of the newly-proposed process, and it was left to the late John A. Griswold and his associates to introduce and perfect this wonderful method in the United States. I speak more briefly on this point than its far-reaching importance deserves; but in the presence of one whose acquaintance with it is so profound, and whose services in relation to it have been so brilliant as those of our honored president, Mr. Holley, and of so many gentlemen as I see before me who are worthily associated with him in its glorious history, I could afford to be silent altogether.

9. *The commencement of the hydraulic-mining industry.*—The position of the auriferous slates and quartz-veins on the west flank of the Sierra, with the precipitous mountains behind them and the broad plain before, has favored exceptionally the formation of deep auriferous gravels in which California far exceeds any other known region. And the same topographical features furnish the two other prime requisites of hydraulic mining, namely, an abundant supply of water and a sufficient

grade of descent to permit the use of flumes and the escape of tailings. These advantages the keen-witted miners of the Pacific coast were quick to make available; and I think we may set down the invention of hydraulic mining which occurred, I believe, about 1853, as an epoch in the progress of American mining. It has given us an entirely new and original branch of the art, involving many ingenious hydrodynamic and hydrostatic contrivances; and it has certainly made possible the exploitation of thousands upon thousands of acres of auriferous gravel which could not have been profitably handled in any other way. The mountain torrents of the Sierra, caught on their way to the Pacific, have been forced to pause and do the work of man. The same agencies that buried the gold among the clay and pebbles of the river-beds are now made to strip the covering from it and lay it bare again. The hydraulic mines produce at present not less than $10,000,000 or $12,000,000 annually; and many enterprises of this kind which have been prosecuted through years of expensive preparation and are now just beginning to touch their harvests of profit, will add henceforward to the product. I may mention as an illustration the extensive operations of the North Bloomfield and its two allied companies in California, which have expended in works $3,500,000, and will have six deep tunnels, aggregating over 20,000 feet, and canals supplying 100,000,000 gallons of water daily.

10. We must turn for a moment to the East again, to note the commencement of iron-mining at Lake Superior, about the year 1856. The extraordinarily pure and rich ores of the upper peninsula of Michigan now find their way, to the extent of a million of tons per annum, in fleets of vessels across the lakes to Cleveland, and are thence distributed to the furnaces of Ohio and Pennsylvania. The similarly pure Missouri ores have built up in like manner their own market. The growth of the Lake Superior iron business is shown in the accompanying table.

11. The next great event in the history of American mining was the discovery, in 1859, that the Comstock lode was rich in silver. This opened an era of activity and speculation which has scarcely ceased since that time. Single districts have been subjected to fluctuating experiences, passing from the first enthusiasm through all the stages of hope to reaction and despair; but though the fortunes of each have risen and fallen like the changing tide, it has nearly always been high water somewhere. Thus we have had a succession of favorites in the way of silver-mining districts, each one crowding its predecessor out of the public notice. Of these the following list includes the most permanently productive: In Nevada, the Unionville, Reese River, Belmont, White Pine, Eureka, Esmeralda, and Pioche districts; in California, the argentiferous district of Inyo County; in Idaho, the Owyhee district; in Utah, the Cottonwood and Bingham districts; in Colorado, the silver districts of Clear Creek, Boulder, and Summit Counties, to which the latest favorite, the San Juan region, may be added. I have named those localities in which mining industry is still active and flourishing. There is a longer and a sadder list, the funereal effect of which I will not intrude upon this festive occasion. But it ought to be remarked that the apparent failure and abandonment of many districts heretofore does not argue their lack of prospective value. It is, on the contrary, amazing that under the adverse conditions surrounding the industry of mining in regions "remote, unfriended, solitary"—though not "slow"—so many communities should have succeeded in taking permanent root. Too much is expected of this industry when it is required to supply the lack of labor, food, transportation, government, and the organized support

which in settled societies all the trades and occupations give to each other. Pioneer work is full of peril and of waste; and in view of the wonderful results achieved by our pioneers in mining, it ill becomes us to sneer at the losses and failures which constitute the inevitable cost of such conquests. When the battle has been gloriously won, and the spoils of victory are ours, we do not greatly mourn over the number of bullets that may have been fired in vain.

But through all the vicissitudes of silver mining in other districts, the Comstock mines have maintained their place, an instance of rapid exploitation, and of aggregated wealth of production unexampled in history. Here, too, there have been intervals of failing hope; but a new *bonanza* has always made its appearance before the resources at hand were entirely exhausted; and we have seen extracted from the ores of this one vein, during the past fifteen years, the round sum of $200,000,000 in gold and silver. Dr. Raymond, in the table herewith given, assumes the product of gold to have been (on the authority of Mr. Hague) about 40 per cent. of the entire value. We have, therefore, from the Comstock mines during the period named, $80,000,000 gold, and $120,000,000 silver.

The swift development of these mines, and the active commencement about the same time, of deep quartz mining operations in California, led to a remarkable progress in mining machinery, and to the perfection of two distinctively American processes. I refer to the California stamp-mill and amalgamation process for gold, and the Washoe pan-process for silver. Neither of these is so novel in principle as the hydraulic-process of gold mining already mentioned; but both of them have received the peculiar impress of an ingenuity and mechanical skill, partly innate in our national character, and partly the product of the stern pressure of economic necessities. Into the fruitful field of further metallurgical improvements born of our Western mining industry—or adopted by it—such as the Blake rock-breaker, the Stetefeldt roasting-furnace, the Brückner cylinder, the Plattner chlorination, and many others less widely known, I cannot enter here. Our people have advanced in this line with headlong energy, and accomplished great results—at great expense. Much, undoubtedly, remains to be done, and it may be hoped that future progress will be equally rapid, but less costly. The introduction three or four years ago of the smelting processes of Europe for the treatment of the silver ores of the West is a striking and encouraging instance of the quickness of our mining communities to seize upon the advantages of experience elsewhere as soon as they are brought to notice. The ignorance which has led to many disasters in such enterprises was not voluntary or obstinate. Give our people light, and they do not keep their eyes shut. I am assured that already the smelting works in the West present many features of interest and suggestiveness even to the study of our skillful colleagues from abroad.

12. I may be permitted, in closing this imperfect review, to refer to the great improvements in mining machinery, in rock-drilling, in explosives, in the use of gaseous fuel, in the construction and management of blast-furnaces, puddling-furnaces, rolling-mills, and other branches of the iron manufacture, which have crowded upon us during the last ten years. It is impossible here to give even an enumeration of them which shall do them justice. They have been worthily commemorated in many papers before the Institute. With regard to one of them, the Martin process for the manufacture of open-hearth steel, I may speak with some personal satisfaction, since I had the privilege of introducing it into this country, after studying its merits in 1867 abroad. I am con-

vinced that it has a great future, as the ally, if not the rival, of the Bessemer process.

Returning now to the contemplation of the general field over which we have passed, we may inquire what the Government of the United States has done with regard to the mining industry. Other nations have elaborate mining codes and bureaus of administration. In comparison with these the meagerness of our governmental supervision of mining is remarkable; yet, in view of the progress I have sketched, may it not be possible that our system has been on the whole the best for us? Certainly a complicated mining code like that of Spain and Mexico, whatever it may have brought to the coffers of the State, seems to have conferred, in centuries of operation, little benefit upon the people.

The common law of England is the foundation of our jurisprudence in this, as in so many other respects. According to that law, as laid down in a noted case in the reign of Elizabeth, all gold or silver ores belonged to the crown, whether in private or public lands; but any ores containing neither gold nor silver belonged to the proprietor of the soil. Apart from the claims of the crown, the property in minerals is, according to the common law, *prima facie* in the owner of the fee of the land, but the property in minerals, or the right to search for them, may be vested in other persons by alienation, prescription, or custom. Since the two latter rights require an origin beyond the time of legal memory, they are practically out of the question in this country. The crown right to the precious metals, as declared in the case referred to, was a survival or remainder of the royalty claimed in ancient times by the sovereign over all minerals. This sweeping claim, born of the despotisms of the Orient and made the subject of much conflict among emperors, feudal lords, and municipal authorities during the middle ages, dwindled at last till it covered only gold and silver. But it disappeared entirely from English America, for the simple reason that there was no private land ownership in this country, and the sovereign of England claimed, by right of discovery, soil and metals alike, barring only the Indian title, which it was his exclusive privilege (or that of his authorized representatives or grantees) to extinguish. After the Revolution, the United States succeeded to the rights of the British crown, and by the treaty of peace and the subsequent cessions by the different States of their colonial claims upon the public lands, the Federal Government became possessed of a vast domain over which, after extinguishing the Indian title, it had complete control. In the territories subsequently acquired from France and Spain, the United States assumed the rights and obligations of those sovereigns; and this circumstance, particularly in the adjustment of Spanish mineral and agricultural grants, has caused some apparent variations from the general policy. But it is sufficiently accurate to say that at the present time, throughout the country, the owner of the fee, or the party who has obtained from him by lease or purchase the mineral right, has supreme control. The mining legislation of the United States, therefore, is simply a part of the administration of the public lands; and for this reason it is executed by the Commissioner of the General Land-Office.

In 1807 an act was passed, relating primarily to the lead-bearing lands of Illinois. They were ordered to be reserved from sale, and leased to miners by the War Department. The leases covered tracts at first three miles square, (afterward reduced to one mile,) and bound the lessee to work the mines with due diligence and return to the United States 6 per cent. of all the ores raised. "No leases were issued under this law," says Professor Whitney, "until 1822, and but a small quantity of lead was raised previous to 1826, from which time the production began to increase rapidly. For a few years the rents were paid with tolerable regularity; but, after 1834, in consequence of the immense number of illegal entries of mineral land at the Wisconsin land-office, the smelters and miners refused to make any further payments, and the Government was entirely unable to collect them. After much trouble and expense, it was, in 1847, finally concluded that the only way was to sell the mineral land, and do away with all reserves of lead or any other metal, since they had only been a source of embarrassment to the department."

Meanwhile, by a forced construction (afterward declared invalid) of the same act, hundreds of leases were granted to speculators in the Lake Superior copper region, which was, from 1843 to 1846, the scene of wild and baseless excitement. The bubble burst during the latter year; the issue of permits and leases was suspended as illegal, and the act of 1847, authorizing the sale of the mineral lands, and a geological survey of the district, laid the foundation of a more substantial prosperity.

This policy of selling the mineral lands has been that of the Government ever since. But it has necessarily been modified in the West by the peculiar circumstances under which that region has been settled. Before lands can be sold they must be surveyed; and before they can be sold as mineral lands, their mineral-bearing character must be ascertained. Our miners and explorers overran and occupied the Pacific slope in advance of the public surveys. They built cities that were not shown on any map; they cut timber, turned water-courses, dug canals, tunneled mountains, bought and sold their rights to these improvements under laws established by themselves, and enforced by public sentiment only. For nearly twenty years the Government looked on, without asserting its dominant ownership of the public lands; and when by the acts of 1866, 1870, and 1872, and other minor enactments, a general system was created, it was necessary to recognize as far as possible the rights which had grown up by general consent, and to seek only to give to them certainty, practical uniformity, and reasonable limitations. It is not my purpose to discuss in detail the mining laws of the United States, or to trace the curiously complicated origins of the local customs on which they are largely based. Suffice it to say that the system recognizes the English common-law principle, that the mineral right passes with the fee to the lands; so that, in the words of the Commissioner, (July 10, 1873,) "all mineral deposits discovered upon land, after United States patent therefor has issued to a party claiming under the laws regulating the disposal of agricultural lands, pass with the patent, and the Land-Office has no further jurisdiction in the premises."

But the principle is also recognized that the mineral right may be separated from the fee by the owner, whether he be an individual or the United States; and this principle is curiously applied in the form of patents for mining claims upon lodes, which, following the form of the possessory title, grant to the patentee the right to follow all veins, the top or apex of which lies within the exterior boundaries of his claim, downward to any depth, though they pass under the surface of the land adjoining.

As the size and the price per acre of the tracts sold under the agricultural laws are different from those to which the mining laws apply, and as, under the homestead law, a certain amount of agricultural land may be obtained without any payment, it is evident that no known mineral deposits can be acquired under the agricultural laws; and this reservation is enforced both in the preliminary proceedings andi n the patents finally issued under those laws.

With regard to the mineral lands, however, it is certain that the patent for a claim carries with it both the fee of the land and also a mineral right, though not the same mineral right as is contemplated by the common law, since it is enlarged on the one hand by the permission to follow mineral deposits beneath the surface of adjoining land, and limited on the other hand by the operation of the same permission in favor of the adjoining owner. The latter limitation is incorporated in agricultural patents also, and may become operative whenever they adjoin mining patents.

Previous to the application for a patent, the law permits free exploration and mining upon the public lands to all citizens and those who have declared their intention to become such. The rights of this class of miners under what is known as the possessory title, are regulated by local laws and customs, subject only to a few simple conditions which the United States enforces upon all, and which chiefly concern the maximum size of individual claims, the definite character of their boundaries and landmarks, and a certain quantity of labor which must be bestowed upon them annually in order to maintain possession. I will not pause to state the different features which these conditions present for lode and placer claims. It is sufficient to say that the miner conforming to them, and thus maintaining his possessory title, may, after a certain expenditure, and upon due application, survey, and advertisement, in the absence of any valid opposing claim, perfect his purchase from the Government, receive his patent, and be thereafter free from the necessity of performing any given annual amount of labor to hold his claim. There are features in the present law concerning the rights of prospecting tunnels which seem both obscure and unwise; and some serious questions remain to be settled as to the precise meaning of the law in these and other respects; but these we must pass by.

Looking at the legislation on this subject as a whole, we see that it is confined to one department—that of title. The whole system is devised to facilitate the purchase of mines by citizens. They are freely permitted to work them experimentally, but it is made their interest to buy them. No inspection, no police regulation, no technical control, is exercised by the Government.

Turning to the State and territorial legislatures, we find that they have, in some cases, provided for inspecting mines in the interest of the safety of workmen. Perhaps the best law of this kind is that of Pennsylvania, in which State the peculiar perils of coal-mining have forced the legislature to take measures of protection. But we find nowhere such a technical control of mining as is exhibited in many European states, where the government requires of the miner that he shall not waste wantonly or ignorantly the resources which, once exhausted, will never grow again. Our people waste as much as they like and no one interferes. Admitting that this is an evil, it still remains a matter of doubt how far, under the circumstances of our particular case, the supervision of authority could remedy it. For my own part, though inclined to restrict as far as possible the functions of government, I am not disposed to say that for so great an end as the conservation of the mineral wealth of the country, it may not properly enforce some measures of economy with as good right as it may forbid the reckless waste of timber or the slaughter of game out of season. But in our nation, at least, governmental interference is the last resort, and a poor substitute for other causes which, in the atmosphere of freedom and intelligence, ought to be effective. We are, perhaps, in our material career as a nation, like the young man who has "sown his wild oats," and now, by mature reflection and the lessons of experience, is likely to be better restrained than by the hand of parental authority.

Permit me, in drawing my remarks to a close, to suggest two agencies which seem to me to be co-operating already, and to open still wider future prospect for the steady social and economical improvement of our mining and metallurgical industry.

The first of these is the spread of knowledge on these subjects throughout the country. Under this head we must recognize the great importance of that series of explorations of our great western domain, which was recommended by Mr. Lincoln, with sublime faith in the salvation of his country, in the midst of the civil war, and which has been, by the liberality of the Government, prosecuted under various departments ever since. I need hardly make special mention, in addition, of the reports of the Commissioner of Mining Statistics, which have appeared annually since 1866, and have reflected upon our own community the light of the gathered technical knowledge of the world, while they have in turn exhibited to the world the resources and the progress of America. Such works as these, together with the technical periodicals and the occasional volumes, translated or original, which have come from the American press, have contributed already a great deal to the education of our mining communities. The Government has not done too much in this direction; but it seems to me that it should continue this most necessary and proper work in a more systematic and uniform way. There ought to be no conflict of authorities, no duplication of work, no unnecessary expenditure of labor and money in the face of a task so great.

Next in order, I may rank the influence of the technical schools. The number of these has rapidly increased during the past ten years; and I venture to say that many of them compare favorably, in theoretical instruction at least, and several of them in the apparatus of instruction, with the famous schools of the Old World. The Massachusetts Institute of Technology, at Boston; the School of Mines of Columbia College, at New York; the Sheffield Scientific School of Yale College, at New Haven; the Stevens Institute of Technology, at Hoboken; the Pardee Scientific Department of Lafayette College, at Easton; the excellent school at Rutgers College, under the direction of Professor Cook; the new Scientific Department of the College of New Jersey; the School of Mining and Metallurgy of Lehigh University, at Bethlehem; the School of Mining and Practical Geology of Harvard University, at Cambridge; the Scientific Department of the University of Pennsylvania, in this city; the School of Mines of Michigan University, at Ann Arbor; the Missouri School of Mines and Metallurgy, at Rolla; the Polytechnic Department of Washington University, at Saint Louis; and the similar department of the University of California, at Oakland; and perhaps some others which I have omitted to name—this is a list of schools for instruction in the sciences involved in mining and metallurgical practice, of which we need not be ashamed. What our schools undoubtedly need is a more intimate relation with practice. But this theme I need not touch. It has been ably and amply discussed at the joint meeting last night of the two bodies most fully aware of all its bearings.

One more agency of the spread of technical knowledge deserves special mention. I refer to the influence of societies like the Institute of Mining Engineers. The five years' activity of this institute has impressed upon the professions which it represents a spirit of union, an enthusiasm of progress, a mutual recognition of the claims of theory and practice, which cannot be too highly estimated. Perfect our schools as much as we may, the association of the young engineer with experienced engineers, the contact of his mind with mature minds, their recognition of his merit, their correction of his errors, constitute the necessary supplement to the school-training. The average man, at least, should not be left to wrestle with his professional career alone. He will make better progress and take more pleasure in it if he calls to his aid the element of social sympathy, and the intellectual re-enforcement expressed in the proverb, " Many heads are better than one."

One further consideration, and I have done. The effect of growing intelligence and knowledge in improving our methods of industry would come short of some great ends if it operated only through the self-interest of the individual. Many reforms are beyond the power of the individual; some are not even to his interest. Thus the miner, under a possessory titlo en a gold-bearing quartz-vein in Colorado, may know that with a greater investment of capital he could manage to reduce his losses of gold in extraction; but the capital may be wanting; or he may know that by robbing the mine of its richest ores only, and allowing it to cave, he is probably destroying more valuable resources than he utilizes; but the mine is only temporarily his, and he prefers quick gains to permanent ones. So long as the anthracite lands of Pennsylvania were leased to countless small operators, who paid royalty only on the coal which they sent to market, it was useless to explain to them that they wasted a third of the coal in the ground, and another third in the breaker, or that they ruined thousands of acres of coal-beds, overlying those which they recklessly worked. If there were no natural remedy for this wicked waste of the reserved force upon which the future prosperity and comfort of mankind depend, it would be the highest duty of Government promptly to take into its own hands the direction and management of the mines of coal which society holds in trust for the future; but already it is easy to detect the operation of a new social law developed within the memory of man, yet the fruit of the preparation of the ages during which society has been slowly built up, and matured into its present form and conditions.

To the philosophic observer, the controlling law which runs through the whole history of man, down to the present century, is the law of dispersion, diffusion, distribution, the centrifugal social force, so to speak, which by its irresistible power has tended not merely to scatter mankind over the face of the habitable globe, but through what are termed civilizing and christianizing agencies to place communities and individuals upon the common plane of equal rights in the domain of nature and before the law.

From the time of the confusion of tongues at the tower of Babel, through the long history of the early oriental empires, which reduced society to the rule of order and then broke up into fragmentary political organizations, retaining, nevertheless, the principles of cohesion acquired by bitter experience; through the Greek and Roman imperial political structures upon which were ingrafted the civilization and the religion which their downfall made the common heritage of the northern barbarians who came for destruction, but were themselves transformed into the apostles of a more liberal and enlightened social organization, this law of dispersion has never ceased to exercise its power and its supremacy. The very inventions of man are only so many proofs of the unceasing operation of this law. In warfare, gunpowder and firearms merely enlarged the area over which it was possible to carry on military operations; the magnetic compass only widened the field of commerce; the printing-press and the telegraph are merely agencies for the diffusion of thought; the steam-engine is but a means whereby it becomes possible to establish local industries in every part of the habitable globe; and the canal and the railway are essentially distributors of the products and the wealth of the human race.

Although there is an impression abroad that this age is one of growing concentration of property, no man can study the history and the facts of the development of society without coming to the conclusion that at no period has there been so general and equal a distribution of rights and property as in the present age. The destruction of the feudal system was, in reality, the establishment of a new and better theory, in regard to the ownership of land, which has borne its legitimate fruits in the subdivision of estates in France, through the convulsions of a revolution; in the more general distribution of landed property in Germany, and in that steady, remarkable, and successful agitation in England, which is now showing its results in the limitation of entail, the simplification of transfer, the enlargement of the suffrage, and the acquisition of small freeholds, whereby political power is being slowly but surely transferred from the great landholders to the middle classes of the most powerful and compact political organization which the world has ever seen.

While, then, there is thus an unmistakable progress in the world towards a juster and more general distribution of the control of the resources of nature and of the fruits of human industry, the present century has, undoubtedly, developed a new and remarkable centralizing tendency, which might be denominated the centripetal industrial force. I speak of the application of the corporate principle to the management of industrial enterprises, producing a concentration of property and management through the diffusion of ownership. Under the corporate system, the number of owners may be unlimited, but the management is necessarily confined to a few hands. It is the political idea of representation applied to industrial enterprises; it is the common wealth in its industrial, and not in its political sense, which is concentrated for the material wants and progress of the human race. Now, this law of universal ownership, under limited management, heretofore applied with marked success during the latter half of the present century to great manufacturing establishments in this country, and of late in Europe, and of necessity to railroads everywhere, has at length, by slow but irresistible steps, taken possession of the great mining enterprises of the United States, and to-day has its strongest and most interesting development in the anthracite coal region, which may be said to be monopolized by six great corporations, administered by a very small number of able officers representing a vast body of owners who rely upon steady but not excessive dividends for their support. It is the fashion to denounce these corporations as monopolizers, but it is only the thoughtless who do not investigate below the surface, who take this view of what is really the most interesting and suggestive application in our day of a powerful and irresistible force originating in the very heart of the social fabric. The monopoly is not the monopoly of ownership, for everybody is free to buy and sell, and there is no day when a man with money may not, at its value, procure a share in these enterprises. And no one familiar with business will pretend that the profits have been out of proportion to the cost and the risk of the undertakings, and no more conclusive answer to any complaint on the score of monopoly can be made, than that to-day the shares in these corporations, in many cases, are selling below the original money cost. These corporations are, in fact, not the creators, but the outgrowth of a new and beneficent principle, which has begun to assert itself in society, and will continue to grow in power until the end of time. This principle is the practical association of diffused capital, through the agency of corporate organization, with labor, for the promotion of economy, for the improvement of processes, and for the general welfare of mankind.

The capital is derived from innumerable sources, just as the little rills, finally, through streams and rivers, constitute the great ocean. The laborer himself may thus be the capitalist, and the capitalist may thus be the laborer, each taking his share of that portion of the fund which is appropriated to labor and to capital, and often in a double capacity taking a share from both.

In its perfect and ultimate development it embodies the Christian idea of "having all things in common," yet "rendering unto Cæsar the things that are Cæsar's."

The rate of profit which may be derived from these great enterprises, subject as they are to the scrutiny, criticism, and judgment of the public, in an age when nothing escapes notice, and all rights and property are virtually subordinated to the popular will, can never be excessive, for two reasons: on the one side the public will inevitably demand lower prices for an article of primary consequence in every household, and these corporations, creatures of the public will as they are, could not successfully resist such a demand, based upon excessive or unreasonable profits. On the other hand, whenever the dividends rise above a reasonable rate of compensation, the laborers engaged in the production of coal, from whom these profits cannot be concealed, will justly claim, and rightfully secure, a larger share of the fruits of their labor. The checks upon any unreasonable exercise of the power conferred by the ownership under limited management of the anthracite coal-fields, are in reality so powerful that the public have nothing to fear from this cause, but the corporations have rather reason to dread that they may not have justice at the hands of the public and the working classes. This justice they can only hope to secure by the wisest, best, and most economical management and administration of the property they control, and whatever profits they may hereafter derive and be allowed to divide among the owners will be rather due to the economies which they may be able to introduce, whereby the article is furnished at the lowest possible rate, than to any fancied monopoly which they may have in the coal itself, or in its transportation to market.

Already, by the application of adequate capital, guided by the largest experience and the highest technical skill, the anthracite coal-mines, from being worked in a wasteful and extravagant manner, are being rapidly put in the best possible shape for the economical delivery of coal at the surface, and for the preservation of every portion of the store upon which the future value of the property must depend. But besides economy in mining and care in preserving, there must be regularity and stability in the operations of the mine. There can be no real profit where these operations are subject to constant interruption, caused by strikes or other artificial impediments. The loss of interest on the plant at the mines and in the lines of transportation, caused by any serious stoppage to the works, would, of itself, be sufficient to render investments of this kind unprofitable. Hence the out-put must be regulated and proportioned to the wants of the market. But this regulation must be continuous and not spasmodic. To enable this to be done, large stocks of coal must necessarily be kept on hand, in order that any sudden demand may be properly met without any serious increase in price; and in dull times the accumulation and restoration of the stock will give steady employment to the miners, to whose families any cessation of work is a calamity of the most serious character, and to society an unmitigated evil. To insure continuous operations, the best relations must exist between the corporate owners and the laborers in their employ. It is notorious that throughout the coal regions these relations have been of the most unsatisfactory character, resulting, at often-recurring intervals, in strikes and lock-outs, which have no redeeming feature, but, on the contrary, have raised the price of coal to the consumer, have impaired the dividends of the owners, and have reduced the workingmen and their families to a condition of suffering and demoralization appalling to every well-wisher of his race. It is fortunate, therefore, that the interests of all classes concur in the prevention of these destructive and demoralizing collisions, and that the owners of the property, for their own self-protection, will be driven to remove the causes which have produced them. It is idle for them to expend their capital for the best machinery, for the highest skill, for the most economical transportation, unless they can, at the same time, insure a continuous production from a contented laboring population.

This they have it in their power to do. If the same spirit of sacrifice which has sent out our missionaries into every heathen land, had been shown in the coal regions, and the same efforts had been made to establish and maintain the school-house, the church, and above all the Sunday-school, which have borne such fruits elesewhere in this broad land; if the hospital for the sick, and the comfortable refuge for the unfortunate had been carefully provided; if reading-rooms and night-schools, and rational places of amusement had from the outset been maintained for a growing and restless population, the coal regions to-day might have been a paradise upon earth instead of a disgrace to civilization. And here it is that this new power of concentrated management can exert itself with sure and absolute success. The appropriation of a few cents per ton on the coal mined to the work of improving the moral and intellectual conditions of the miners and their families will, in a time incredibly short, change the whole face of society in the coal regions.

To be effective, however, this concentration of a fixed amount on each ton of coal sent to market must be as absolute and final as that portion of the proceeds which is devoted to pumping the mines, or driving the gangways. It must not come from grace, but from a sense of duty involved in the ownership of property, and dictated by a wise regard for its preservation and permanent value. Even if this percentage were added to the price of the coal the addition would not be grudged by the public; but in fact no such addition could possibly occur, as there is no surer way of promoting economy in the cost of production than by improving the social condition, the self-respect, and the intelligence of those who are engaged in the work of production, which thus becomes continuous and systematic. Until the great companies thus recognize the duties, the responsibilities, and the opportunities for good, which are offered by the new social development which has rendered their existence a necessity as well as a possibility, they must not complain that they are regarded with distrust, and as enemies, both by the public which consumes their products, and by the working classes who see in them only grasping employers without a conscience. What individual owners could not do, it is easy for these great companies to put in practice; but the effort must be as earnest and serious as is the business of producing the coal and getting it to market. The very best talent must be secured for the organization and management of the various agencies necessary for the moral, intellectual, and social improvement of the working classes, who must be themselves associated in the administration of the fund created and expended for their benefit. Five cents per ton would produce an annual revenue of over $1,000,000 applicable to this necessary and noble use, and five years of its intelligent and conscientious administration would convert what in some regions has been aptly termed a "hell upon earth" into a terrestrial paradise which would be the pride and the glory of the new world.

What more fitting celebration of the centennial year of American Independence could be possibly suggested or devised, or how could the advent of the incoming century be better signalized, than by the foundation on the part of the great anthracite-coal companies of a new department in their administration for the moral, mental, social, and physical improvement of the workingmen and their families, and by the appropriation of a fixed charge on coal for this purpose? Let each of them select a well-paid and competent agent to devote himself to this work; let the various agencies be wisely organized and surely perfected, and there will be realized one of the greatest triumphs of that gospel which proclaimed "peace on earth and good-will toward men." The example thus set will soon extend itself to other industries, and to every branch of business which can adapt the corporate principle of the concentration of management through diffusion of ownership, the result of which will be that the strange phenomenon, now felt throughout the civilized world, of a general glut of products in the face of general want of them, will never again be witnessed; because, when the working classes, through the diviner agencies of Christian effort, shall have constant employment and adequate compensation, the sure results of general enlightenment and a cultivated conscience in the use of property, the power of consumption, now so far in arrear, will surely overtake the power of production, and re-establish the equation which nature intended to subsist between them. Thus may be realized that Christian commonwealth, which has been the dream of the patriot, the philanthropist, and the statesman in all ages, in which every man who is willing to work shall find employment, and in which the products of industry will be so distributed that every man shall feel that he has received his fair share of them; in which there will be neither abject and hopeless poverty on the one hand, nor superfluous riches on the other, because the problem of how to distribute capital through the concentration of management will have been fully solved and be thoroughly comprehended by all classes in the community; in which the quaint questions put by Sir Thomas More, three hundred and sixty years ago, will at length have been answered, and his suggestive commentary thereon have lost its significance:

"Is not that government both unjust and ungrateful, that is so prodigal of its favors to those that are called gentlemen or goldsmiths, or such others who are idle, or live either by flattery, or by contriving the arts of vain pleasure; and on the other hand takes no care of those of a meaner sort, such as plowmen, colliers, and smiths, without whom it could not subsist?

"But after the public has reaped all the advantages of their service, and they come to be oppressed with age, sickness, and want, all their labors, and the good they have done is forgotten, and all the recompense given them is, that they are left to die in great misery. The richer sort are often endeavoring to bring the hire of laborers lower, not only by their fraudulent practices, but by the laws which they procure to be made to this effect, so that though it is a thing most unjust in itself to give such small rewards to those who deserve so well of the public, yet they have given those hardships the name and color of justice, by procuring laws to be made for regulating them."

Although I quote from the Utopia, let it not be supposed that there is anything Utopian or impracticable in the proposition which I have advanced. It seems to me to be the next great step to be taken for the amelioration of the condition of mankind. The law of diffusion which thus far has governed the progress of the human race toward a higher and better plane of civilization, has at length made an effective lodgment in the domain of capital, whereby it is rendered capable of infinite division without impairing, but in effect improving the economy and force of its administration. The reproach that "corporations have no souls," must, and will, next be removed, so soon as the beneficent possibilities inherent in these agencies shall be generally recognized, and those who are called to the management shall see that because capital is aggregated, the primary law on which all property rests, that it is a trust to be administered for the public good, loses none of its force, but can, in reality, only assert itself in all its vigor when concentrated management is brought to bear upon great aggregations of capital. Man did not become a "living soul" until God breathed into him the breath of life. So corporations are mere machines until they are inspired by the associated conscience of society, to which they can give ready and effective expression, and I look for this expression first from the great coal companies, because their property and their peculiar organizations make it easy as well as profitable for them to put in practice the fundamental idea, that a fixed portion of the proceeds of industry should be invariably devoted to the social improvement of those who labor directly for its development.

If the seed here dropped should take root, as I pray and believe it will, then indeed will the country and the world have reason to rejoice at the industrial development of the last hundred years, and the celebration of this Centennial be the dawn of a better day for the patient sons of toil, who, let it be confessed, with all frankness and humility, have not yet been endowed with their fair share of the good things of this goodly earth.

Population of the United States.

[From the United States Census Returns.]

Year	Population	Year	Population
1790	3,929,214	1840	17,069,453
1800	5,308,483	1850	23,191,876
1810	7,239,881	1860	31,443,321
1820	9,633,822	1870	38,558,371
1830	12,866,020		

Table of production of leading metals and minerals in the United States during the first century of National Independence.

[Prepared by R. W. RAYMOND.]

	Anthracite, in tons of 2,240 pounds avoirdupois.	Pig-iron, in tons of 2,240 pounds avoirdupois.	Lead, in tons of 2,240 pounds avoirdupois.	Copper, in tons of 2,240 pounds avoirdupois.	Quicksilver, in flasks of 76½ pounds avoirdupois.	Gold, in dollars, United States coin.	Silver, in dollars, United States coin.	Petroleum, in barrels of 42 gallons.
1819....	18, 000*	....	....	....	....	....	....	....
1820....	1, 965	....	....	....	....	....	....	....
1821....	3, 273	....	....	....	....	....	....	....
1822....	4, 940	....	....	....	....	....	....	....
1823....	9, 023	....	....	....	....	....	....	....
1824....	13, 641	....	4, 432*	....	....	....	....	....
1825....	38, 499	....	1, 281	....	....	....	....	....
1826....	54, 815	....	1, 771	....	....	....	....	....
1827....	71, 167	2, 178, 239*	3, 927	....	....	....	....	....
1828....	91, 914	130, 000	7, 815	....	....	....	....	....
1829....	133, 203	142, 000	7, 824	....	....	....	....	....
1830....	209, 634	165, 000	7, 163	....	....	....	....	....
1831....	230, 320	191, 000	6, 646	....	....	....	....	....
1832....	448, 171	200, 000	8, 888	....	....	....	....	....
1833....	592, 210	218, 000	9, 767	....	....	....	....	....
1834....	456, 859	236, 000	10, 552	....	....	....	....	....
1835....	678, 517	254, 000	11, 696	....	....	....	....	....
1836....	825, 729	272, 000	14, 216	....	....	....	....	....
1837....	1, 039, 241	290, 000	11, 994	....	....	....	....	....
1838....	873, 013	308, 000	13, 512	....	....	....	....	....
1839....	957, 436	326, 000	15, 539	....	....	....	....	....
1840....	1, 008, 220	347, 000	15, 000	....	....	....	....	....
1841....	1, 115, 045	290, 000	18, 171	....	....	....	....	....
1842....	1, 286, 618	230, 000	21, 586	....	....	....	....	....
1843....	1, 478, 926	312, 000	21, 000	....	....	....	....	....
1844....	1, 899, 805	394, 000	22, 000	2, 680*	....	....	....	....
1845....	2, 352, 984	486, 000	26, 500	100	....	....	....	....
1846....	2, 707, 321	765, 000	25, 000	150	....	....	....	....
1847....	3, 327, 155	800, 000	25, 000	300	....	20, 000, 000*	....	....
1848....	3, 572, 695	800, 000	22, 500	500	....	10, 000, 000	....	....
1849....	3, 724, 806	650, 000	21, 000	700	....	40, 000, 000	....	....
1850....	3, 863, 365	563, 755	19, 500	600	25, 424*	50, 000, 000	....	....
1851....	5, 190, 690	413, 000	16, 500	800	24, 000	55, 000, 000	....	....
1852....	5, 725, 148	540, 755	14, 000	1, 000	20, 000	60, 000, 000	....	....
1853....	5, 940, 905	723, 214	15, 000	1, 850	19, 000	65, 000, 000	....	....
1854....	6, 846, 556	662, 216	14, 000	2, 250	27, 000	60, 000, 000	....	....
1855....	7, 684, 542	700, 159	14, 000	3, 000	33, 000	55, 000, 000	....	....
1856....	7, 999, 767	788, 515	14, 000	4, 000	30, 000	55, 000, 000	....	....
1857....	7, 694, 842	712, 640	14, 000	4, 800	28, 000	55, 000, 000	....	....
1858....	7, 864, 230	629, 552	14, 000	5, 500	31, 000	50, 000, 000	1, 000, 000*	....
1859....	9, 010, 726	750, 560	14, 000	6, 300	12, 000	50, 000, 000	100, 000	3, 200
1860....	9, 807, 118	821, 223	14, 000	7, 200	10, 000	46, 000, 000	150, 000	650, 000
1861....	9, 147, 461	653, 164	14, 000	7, 500	35, 000	43, 000, 000	2, 000, 000	2, 113, 600
1862....	9, 026, 211	702, 912	14, 000	9, 000	42, 000	39, 200, 000	4, 500, 000	3, 056, 606
1863....	10, 953, 077	846, 075	14, 000	6, 474	40, 531	40, 000, 000	8, 500, 000	2, 611, 359
1864....	11, 631, 400	1, 013, 837	14, 000	6, 518	47, 489	46, 100, 000	11, 000, 000	2, 116, 182
1865....	10, 783, 032	831, 768	13, 165	6, 811	53, 000	53, 200, 000	11, 250, 000	3, 497, 712
1866....	14, 233, 919	1, 200, 199	14, 342	6, 978	46, 550	53, 500, 000	10, 000, 000	3, 597, 527
1867....	14, 345, 644	1, 305, 015	13, 662	7, 774	37, 000	51, 700, 000	13, 550, 000	3, 347, 306
1868....	15, 810, 466	1, 431, 250	14, 636	9, 407	37, 000	48, 000, 000	12, 000, 000	3, 715, 741
1869....	16, 375, 678	1, 711, 276	15, 653	11, 858	33, 713	49, 500, 000	13, 000, 000	4, 215, 000
1870....	17, 819, 700	1, 696, 429	15, 922	12, 650	29, 546	50, 000, 000	16, 000, 000	5, 659, 000
1871....	17, 370, 463	1, 707, 685	17, 854	12, 546	31, 881	43, 500, 000	22, 000, 000	5, 795, 000
1872....	22, 032, 265	2, 539, 783	23, 106	11, 948	30, 306	36, 000, 000	25, 750, 000	6, 539, 103
1873....	22, 828, 178	2, 560, 962	46, 661	15, 573	28, 600	35, 000, 000	36, 500, 000	9, 879, 455
1874....	21, 667, 386	2, 401, 261	53, 219	17, 548	34, 254	39, 600, 000	32, 800, 000	10, 910, 303
1875....	20, 643, 509	2, 108, 554	53, 000	15, 625	53, 706	33, 400, 000	41, 400, 000	8, 787, 506
Total.	341, 521, 423	40, 000, 000	855, 000	200, 000	840, 000	1, 332, 700, 000	261, 450, 000	76, 594, 600

* Including the whole previous period from 1776.

Production of Comstock lode.

1860	$1,000,000	1869	$7,528,607
1861	2,275,256	1870	8,319,698
1862	6,247,047	1871	11,053,328
1863	12,486,238	1872	13,569,724
1864	15,795,585	1873	21,534.727
1865	15,184,877	1874	22,400,783
1866	14,167,071	1875	26,023,036
1867	13,738,618		
1868	8,499,769		199,824,364

Or, in round numbers, $200,000,000, of which about $80,000,000 has been gold and $120,000,000 silver, according to Mr. J. D. Hague.

CHAPTER XII.

THE BOSTON AND COLORADO SMELTING WORKS.

By T. Egleston, Ph. D.*

Columbia School of Mines, New York City.

The Boston and Colorado Smelting Works are situated in the town of Black Hawk, Gilpin County, Colorado, on the Clear Creek Narrow Gauge Railway, 55 miles from Denver, in the Rocky Mountains, at an altitude of 7,800 feet. It was one of the first works erected for the metallurgical treatment of gold ores, and the only one established in Colorado on a large scale which has been uniformly successful. Both gold and silver ores are treated, and gold, silver, and copper produced. The lead is not separated from the ores nor paid for, if it exists, and is entirely lost in the residues. The works were planned and built by Professor Hill, formerly professor of chemistry in Brown University, Providence, R. I., and is still managed by him, assisted by Mr. Richard Pearce, formerly professor in the School of Mines at Truro, England. They are very advantageously situated with regard to the ore-producing regions, having Boulder County on the north, which produces, besides ordinary gold ores, a series of tellurium minerals, such as altaite, sylvanite, and hessite, which are very rich in gold and silver. They are associated with copper and iron pyrites, blende, galena, and the carbonate and oxides of iron. Gilpin County itself produces for the most part the pyrites of iron and copper, rich in gold, with a small quantity of galena and blende, which is rich in silver. In some mines native gold is found. Clear Creek County to the south furnishes mostly galena and blende, very rich in silver. The works also receive mattes rich in gold and silver made at Alma, in Park County, and tellurium ores, rich in gold, from the southern part of the Territory.

The works are thus located in the very center of the gold and silver producing regions of Colorado, and are also most favorably situated with regard to transportation. They treated in 1874 30 tons of ore and tailings in 24 hours, and produced 700,000 ounces of silver, 12,000 ounces to 15,000 ounces of gold, and 225 tons of copper. With matte from Alma, their production in 1875 will be 110,000 ounces of silver, 25,000 ounces of gold, and 250 tons of copper.

Gold ores.—The gold ores are divided into three classes. The first class consists of auriferous copper pyrites containing from 2 to 10 per cent. of copper, 2 ounces to 10 ounces of gold, and 2 ounces to 10 ounces of silver. These ores average 4 per cent. of copper, 3½ ounces of gold, and 6 ounces of silver. The second class are tailings from the gold

* This chapter was prepared by Professor Egleston as a paper for the American Institute of Mining Engineers, and a duplicate copy was furnished to me for this report, it being anticipated that the report would be printed before the Transactions of the Institute.—R. W. R.

mills, consisting of pyrites with about 1½ per cent. of copper, 1¼ ounces of gold, and 4 ounces of silver. The third class consists of tellurium ores, which have a very siliceous gangue, and contain 100 ounces to 200 ounces of gold, and 6 ounces to 10 ounces of silver. These ores come mostly from Boulder County, and are often worth $10,000 to $15,000 to the ton.

Silver ores.—The silver ores of the first class consist of surface-ores, mostly free from sulphur, containing 70 per cent. of silica. They contain 100 ounces of silver and 5 to 6 per cent. of lead, and no gold. Those of the second class are sulphurets, rich in blende and poor in galena and pyrites; they contain 150 ounces of silver, 15 per cent. of zinc and lead, and no gold.

The cost of material at the works is:

Wood, per cord	$5 00
Fire-brick, per thousand	90 00
Common brick, per thousand	14 00
Iron castings, per pound	08
Wrought iron, per pound	08

The cost of delivering the silver in New York is 1¼ per cent. of its assay value, taken at the valuation of the works. The rate for gold is six-tenths per cent.

The general plan of these works is given in Fig. 1, Plate I. The diagram, Fig. 1*, indicates the various processes, showing what becomes of each of the products in the different stages. The treatment consists of eight distinct operations, most of which are more or less subdivided. These operations are:

1. Sampling the ore.
2. Roasting the ore.
   - A. Large ore roasted in heaps.
   - B. Small ore roasted in a reverberatory furnace.
3. Fusion for matte.
4. Ziervogel's process.
   - A. Crushing and roasting the matte for sulphate of silver.
   - B. Leaching the roasted matte and precipitation of the silver.
   - C. Washing and fusing the cement silver.
   - D. Precipitating the copper.
   - E. Refining cement copper.
5. Treatment of the Ziervogel tub residues.
   - A. Fusion for white metal.
   - B. Roasting the white metal.
   - C. Treatment of the pimple metal.
6. Treatment of the residues of the Ziervogel process by the Augustine process.
7. Treatment of the bottoms.
8. Treatment of the oxidized copper alloy.

I.—SAMPLING THE ORE.

The ore is purchased in large and small sample lots varying from 50 pounds to 6 tons or 7 tons. It is sampled by first taking one-tenth of the lot and putting it through a crusher* and a pair of Cornish rolls, and then sampling as usual. When the ores are sent by the owner for treatment the charge formerly was:

For ores containing		$50,	$35
"	"	60,	36
"	"	70,	37
"	"	80,	38
"	"	100,	40
"	"	200,	50
"	"	300,	60

and so on.

* Dodge's crusher is used in these works, and to some extent in Colorado, though Blake's crusher is preferred where there is a large and constant amount of work to do.

The arrangement of July, 1874, was that the company should pay for gold-ores at the rate of 85 per cent. of the total value of the gold and silver contained (premium added) after deducting $35 per ton currency for treatment. The gold is estimated at $20 gold per ounce, and the silver at $1.25 gold per ounce, with the premium added, 3 per cent. below New York quotations.

The arrangement for silver at the same time is given in the table below. The prices are based on the premium on gold in New York, ranging between $1.10 and $1.15.

For ores containing	40 oz.	per ton,	34 cents	per oz.	in currency.
"	50	"	44	"	"
"	60	"	52	"	"
"	70	"	60	"	"
"	80	"	66	"	"
"	90	"	70	"	"
"	100	"	74	"	"
"	125	"	82	"	"
"	150	"	89	"	"
"	175	"	93	"	"
"	200	"	97	"	"
"	250	"	99	"	"
"	300	"	101	"	"
"	350	"	103	"	"
"	400	"	105	"	"
"	450	"	106	"	"
"	500	"	107	"	"
"	600	"	108	"	"
"	700	"	109	"	"
"	800	"	110	"	"
"	900	"	111	"	"
"	1,000	"	112	"	"
"	2,000	"	116	"	"

The copper is paid for at $1.50 currency for each unit by the dry Cornish assay. The prices given in Georgetown differ slightly from this. Below are given the prices of two different works as they were advertised in July, 1874.

Prices given for silver by W. Bement, Georgetown.

Ounces of silver per ton.	Price per ounce of silver for ores containing from 5 to 10 per cent. of zinc.	Price per ounce of silver for ores free from zinc, or containing less than 5 per cent.
	Cents.	*Cents.*
75 to 100	48	50
100 to 125	55	60
125 to 150	65	70
150 to 175	75	80
175 to 200	82	84
200 to 250	85	88
250 to 300	90	92
300 to 350	93	94
350 to 400	96	98
400 to 450	99	100
450 to 500	102	103
500 to 550	104	105
550 to 600	106	107
600 to 700	107	108
700 to 900	....	109
1,000 and upward	....	110

At Stewart's Mill, Georgetown, the following prices were paid:

	Ounces.		Cents.			
Ore containing	299 silver or less,		105 for each oz.; over	35 oz. no deduction.		
"	300	"	94	"	"	"
"	325	"	95	"	"	"
"	350	"	96	"	"	"
"	375	"	97	"	"	"
"	400	"	98	"	"	"
"	450	"	99	"	"	"
"	500	"	100	"	"	"
"	550	"	101	"	"	"
"	600	"	102	"	"	"
"	650	"	103	"	"	"
"	700	"	104	"	"	"
"	750	"	105	"	"	"
"	800	"	106	"	"	"
"	850	"	107	"	"	"
"	900	"	108	"	"	"
"	1,000	"	110	"	"	"
"	2,000	"	112	"	"	"

The precious metals in the ores were formerly never paid for above a certain minimum, which for silver was 40 ounces, and for gold 1½ ounces. All above this minimum was paid for in currency at the rate of 85 per cent. of its bullion value. For all copper above 2 per cent., $1.50 currency was given for each unit.

All the ores received are piled separately on the sampling-ground. All the large pieces of gold ore are roasted in heaps, and are then passed through a crusher and rolls, and afterward through a screen with four to the inch mesh. The tellurium-ores are only crushed and passed through a ten to the inch mesh screen, and are then ready for smelting. The surface silver-ores are crushed and passed through a four to the inch mesh screen, and then go to the furnace. The ores rich in sulphur are called heavy ores, and are crushed and roasted in a large reverberatory furnace.

II.—ROASTING THE ORES.

A. *Roasting ores in heaps.*—The auriferous pyrites is broken to 2 inches square in a crusher and roasted in heaps of about 50 tons each. The piles are made in the usual way, with a wooden chimney about 7 feet high in the center. Wood is used as fuel. The amount consumed is two cords for 50 tons. The wood is burned out in about twelve hours, at which time the sulphur commences to burn. The pile is lighted at night, because the moisture in the fuel makes sulphureted hydrogen, which would annoy the men in the day-time. The fire, except in case of accident, burns until the roasting is complete. The sampler takes charge of the piles. He has little to do except to throw fine ore on the cover when he sees that there is too much flame. He has two or three assistants, and with them he does all the weighing and sampling, and takes care of the piles. When the pile is finished the outside crust of unburned pyrites is taken off and put onto the next pile. The roasted ore is crushed and goes through a sieve with a four to the inch mesh, and is then ready for the smelter. One man does the whole crushing. The roasting is finished in about six weeks from the time the fire is lit. The amount of sulphur remaining in the ore is 4 per cent. As the ores contain considerable arsenic the pile is frequently covered on the outside with crystals of arsenious acid, which are often white, but generally colored with a slight trace of sulphur. They are generally found when there has been a hole in the cover of the pile, and their usual form is that of an octahedron with hollow faces.

B. *Roasting the ore in a reverberatory furnace.*—The ore submitted to this process is said to be calcined.* The tailings and finely-divided copper-ores are roasted in a reverberatory furnace, called a calciner, till they contain not more than one-half to 4 per cent. of sulphur. There are six of these calciners in the works. They are marked K on the ground-plan, and are shown in detail at Figs. 2, 3, and 4, Plate I. Only three of them are in use at a time; two of these work into the same flue. The total length of the furnace is 40 feet on the outside, including the fire-place. Each furnace has three step-hearths, 10 feet long; they are 11 feet wide, and have six working doors, two doors to each hearth. The hearths are 4½ inches, the one above the other, and are equally divided in the length of the furnace. Each one is rectangular, with the usual waste space at the doors filled up. The two at the end have their corners rounded.

On comparing the relative dimensions of these furnaces, it will be seen that the surface of the hearth is 304 square feet. The surface of the grate is 16 square feet. If the fire-place is taken as unity, the relation between the surfaces will be as 1 to 19.

The fire-place is arranged for long sticks of wood, and has a door at the side. It is 5 feet long and 2 feet 8 inches wide. The bridge has an air-hole in it which is 4½ inches square, and communicates with the interior of the hearth by four openings. The width of the bridge is 28 inches, the height of the roof above the hearth is 28 inches, and at the flue-end it is 18 inches.

The furnace is built of red brick, fire-brick being used only in the fire-place and on the first hearth. A charge of one ton is introduced on the hearth nearest the flue, so that there are three tons in the furnace at a time. The charge of ore on each hearth, spread out after being first put in, is 3 inches deep, but it swells, so as to be 4 inches to 5 inches in depth on the hearth nearest the fire-place; this is particularly true of the tailings. As the charge is drawn once in eight hours, it takes twenty-four hours to complete the roasting of one ton of ore. One man to a shift, who brings his own wood, is all the labor that is required, so that two men work three tons in twenty-four hours. The ore is brought to the furnace-men, who then make the charge. One man brings all the ore for three furnaces. The men from the calciners always assist in charging the calcined ores into the matte-furnaces. The furnace burns 1½ cords in twenty-four hours. One day in a year only is required for necessary repairs.

III.—FUSION FOR MATTE.

The roasted ore is fused in a reverberatory furnace for matte. There are three of these furnaces, which are marked D in the ground-plan, Fig. 1, and are given in detail in Figs. 5, 6, 7, and 8, Plate I. Only two of them are in use at a time. They are constructed to use wood, so that the fire-place, which is 5 feet at the top of the bridge, is only 2 feet 6 inches at the grate; it is 5 feet long, and 4 feet 6 inches deep from the grate to the roof. The opening in the fire-place for charging fuel is at the end of the furnace, and not at the side, as is usual. The fire-place door is of cast-iron; it slides in a groove, and is counterpoised with a

*The word "calcining," as used in these works, means treating the ores or mattes in a fine state in an oxidizing atmosphere. The term "roasting" means the treatment of metal ingots or mattes in large pieces in an oxidizing atmosphere. As these words are not used properly in a metallurgical sense, we shall speak of both as roasting.

weight. The bridge is 2 feet 6 inches wide, the fire-place side is 2 feet 3 inches, and the laboratory side 1 foot 10 inches from the roof. Just above the bridge there are a series of openings in the roof, 3 inches by 1 inch, for the admission of air, which follow on the roof the contour of the laboratory in two rows, the outside having eight and the interior eleven holes each. The laboratory is 15 feet 7½ inches long by 9 feet 9 inches wide. The working door is at the end; the two openings at the side are closed for this operation.

In comparing the relative dimensions of the furnace, we find that the surface of the fire-place at the height of the bridge is 25 square feet, that at the grate is 12½ square feet. The laboratory has 143.18 square feet, so that the fire-place being taken as one, the relation is as 1 to 5.7.*

Each one of these furnaces has its own chimney, which is 50 feet high. The arrangement of the holes in the roof is a very ingenious one, for as the fire-place is very deep, and is constantly filled with long sticks of wood to a depth of over 3 feet, the wood distils and forms gas, which is burned by the air entering through these holes, so that the fire-place is really a generator for burning wood. Before this method was introduced by Professor Pearce there was not sufficient air to produce a perfect combustion. Formerly the flue connected with the chimney was constantly burning out, and needed frequent repairs. The immediate effect of the introduction of these holes in the roof was the saving of fuel and more equal distribution of heat. An opening has recently been made in the foot of the chimney for the introduction of cold air, and both because the combustion is better regulated and because the cold air is mixed with the products of combustion on leaving the furnace, the repairs to the furnace are very much diminished.

The hearth of the furnace is slightly inclined toward the working door and also to one side. It is made of two layers of brick, upon which fine quartz-sand is placed, which is mixed with a small quantity of wood-ashes and then agglomerated. When the hearth is made the temperature is lowered, and the charge is introduced. The charge is made up of—

	Pounds.
Heap-roasted gold-ores	2,000
Roasted tailings	2,000
Oxidized silver-ores	1,500
Roasted silver-ores	1,500
Raw pyrites	800
Fluorspar	250
Rich scorias	500

After the charge is drawn, the furnace is repaired, if necessary, with clay, which is beaten in with a ladle-shaped instrument attached to a long handle. Such repairs are usually not made oftener than twice a week. The charge is introduced with a shovel by a side door. The ore is introduced first and then the rich slags. The charge is so arranged that ten tons of mixed ores will produce one ton of matte. It will not do to make the matte richer, as there are always grains of it in the slag, and the loss would be greater. The slag is carefully calculated, so that it shall not be too basic, or otherwise it would cut the fire-brick to get silica. The charge is evenly distributed over the surface of the hearth, which is almost at a cherry-red heat. It takes six men, working in groups of three at a time, nearly a quarter of an hour to make the charge. As soon as it is made, the charging door is built up and luted or closed

* In all these fire-places with inclined sides, the surface taken as unity is the section at the bridge. As the grate-surface is smaller, the relation between the grate and fire-place surfaces should also be given.

with sand. The fire-place is then charged, and the furnace is left with the full power of the draft for five or six hours. During this time the workmen clean up the slag-bed and tend to the fire, which requires looking after every twenty minutes. At the end of this time they stir the furnace carefully five or six minutes to bring up everything from the bottom, which should be perfectly smooth to the tool passing over it. This produces the reactions. The furnace is now left in repose for twenty minutes to effect the separation of the scoria and the matte. If lumps are found the stirring is done again, and kept up during the firing, or for about an hour. The slag is now drawn with a rabble into molds prepared for it. The operation of skimming the slag takes about twenty minutes. When the door is opened to skim the slag it is quite hot and fluid, and there is a constant but quiet ebullition of sulphurous and sulphuric acid, the bubbles being about 1 inch in diameter and quite uniformly distributed. Professor Pearce asserts that the larger part of the gas is sulphuric acid. At the close of the skimming, as the slag becomes cooler, the bubbles become larger and less uniform. Just before the skimming, pieces of sheet-iron, 3 feet by 2 feet, are placed in front of the slag-bed and to one side of it, to protect the workmen from the heat. The casting-bed is made 10 inches deep in front of the furnace to receive the plate-slag, which ordinarily contains all the grains of matte. This casting-bed has fourteen divisions, which are connected one with the other. When the slag, which covers the matte to the depth of about 3 inches, is being skimmed, it is very easy to distinguish the matte below, which shows of a dark color and a more or less brilliant surface. As the rabble goes backward and forward, the slag does not close at once over it, and the surface is exposed for a very short time. When all the slag is drawn off, a new charge of ore is introduced. Four charges are made in twenty-four hours. During each one of the operations the stirring and rabbling are conducted in exactly the same way. While the slag is tapped the matte is left to accumulate, and is tapped only once in twenty-four hours. When the matte is to be tapped, all the doors of the furnace are to be opened so as to chill the last part of the slag a little, so that it will not flow out from the tap-hole. It is then tapped and made into plates 3 feet long, 14 inches wide, and 4 inches thick in the middle, the bottom being rounded. No slag flows out with it, because it is too much chilled. When all the matte has been tapped, the tap-hole is closed with damp sand. The charge makes about 14 plates. The operation of tapping the matte and stirring takes half an hour. Three men per shift of 12 hours are required to work two furnaces. Eight cords of wood are consumed in 24 hours. The plate-slag contains on an average 5 per cent. of copper, but is often poor enough to be thrown away with the other slags. It is generally a silicate of protoxide of iron, but is sometimes more basic. The poor slag contains about 7 ounces of silver and a trace of gold. It is too poor to treat, and is thrown away. All the slag richer than this is put back into the furnace. The matte contains from 25 to 30 per cent. of copper, 20 ounces to 30 ounces of gold, 600 ounces to 1,000 ounces of silver, and some iron, lead, zinc, and antimony. When the hearth-bottom of the matte-furnace becomes loose and rises, as it sometimes does, the whole hearth material is taken out, crushed, and treated as ore. The flues of the furnace have to be repaired every two or three months. The roof is made over once a year. The outside walls last a number of years before it is necessary to rebuild the furnace. There are produced from this fusion the copper matte, which passes to the next operation, the plate-slag, which is immediately put back into the furnace, and the poor slag, which is thrown away.

IV.—ZIERVOGEL'S PROCESS.

A. *Crushing and roasting matte for sulphate of silver.*—The matte produced from the previous operation must be roasted, and for this purpose it must be crushed fine. It is first broken up with sledges and then crushed in a Dodge crusher, with which one man can crush about 10 tons in a day. After crushing it is put through a twelve to the inch screen, and is then wheeled in a wooden barrow to the calciners, marked K on the general plan, where it is roasted for twenty-four hours, a charge being drawn every eight hours. The charge is 1 ton on each hearth, so that there are 3 tons in the furnace at a time. One furnace working constantly does the whole work of the establishment; 90 per cent. of the sulphur is removed in this operation. The roasted matte contains about 5 per cent. sulphur, partly as sulphides and partly as sulphates. Where the matte is charged on the hearth the furnace is dark. This is necessary to prevent fusion, as there must be rapid oxidation at the lowest possible temperature. When the workman is not attending to the fire he is always rabbling the charge. When the charge on one hearth is finished it is moved to the next one by a spaddelle. On the middle hearth the heat is very dull, and from this temperature it is gradually raised until it is withdrawn from the furnace; on the last hearth the temperature is a bright cherry-red heat. The charge is drawn with a rabble into a "cub" beside the furnace. As there is but a small amount of sulphurous acid given off, the roasted matte remains here until it is cool enough to be wheeled in wooden barrows, when it is taken to the ball pulverizer. One and a half cords of wood in twenty-four hours is all the fuel used in this operation.

The ball pulverizer consists of a stationary horizontal sheet-iron cylinder 4 feet in length and 2 feet 8 inches in diameter, inside of which another cylinder of less diameter revolves. This inside cylinder is made with a cast-iron head-piece, into which cast-iron bars are fitted so as to leave a space $\frac{1}{64}$th of an inch between them. These bars are kept in position by a flange and wedges, and the heads are then securely bolted together. The material to be ground is introduced into the revolving cylinder through a trough in its axis. This cylinder or grinder contains one-half ton of iron balls, which when new are 3 inches in diameter.

The cold calcined ore from the cubs is thrown on to the crusher-floor, and shoveled into bins, from which it is carried by an endless chain to a hopper which communicates with the charging-trough. The charge and balls revolve together at the rate of 37 revolutions per minute. The ore which is ground sufficiently fine, passes through the spaces between the bars and falls into the stationary cylinder, which is hopper-shaped at the bottom, and communicates with a trough, through which an endless chain passes and carries the ore to a 60-mesh screen; what remains on this screen is carried back again to the grinder. The crusher works between 3 tons and 4 tons in twenty-four hours, and has besides plenty of time for the necessary stoppages for repairs. Six tons might easily be put through in ten hours, but from 3 tons to 4 tons is all that is required, so that a single crusher is more than sufficient. Very few repairs are done to the machinery. The bars wear, and when the openings become too wide new bars are put in. Not more than 500 pounds of balls are worn out in the course of a year. The men who do this work are obliged to wear wet sponges over their mouths in order to protect themselves from the dust. One man, who also carries the wood to the calciners, brings the ore, and one man who shovels the ore and tends the grinder, are all that are required for the work.

Roasting for sulphate of silver.—From the ball-grinder screens the ground matte is deposited in a bin ready to be roasted for sulphate of silver. The furnace in which this operation is conducted is called the fine calciner. There are two of them, marked B B in the general plan, Fig. 1, Plate I, and Fig. 12, Plate II. The furnaces are shown in detail in Figs. 9, 10, and 11, Plate II. They connect with four small dust-chambers, which are common to both furnaces and connect with the same chimney. They are constantly in use except when silver is being melted, when only one of them is run. They have but one hearth, which is 11 feet 6 inches long, 3 feet 6 inches deep, and 10 feet 6 inches wide. This hearth is flat. The fire-place is 4 feet 6 inches long, 2 feet 6 inches wide at the bridge. The grate is only 1 foot wide. There are 11.25 square feet surface in the fire-place, and 100 square feet in the laboratory, making the relation as 1:9. The top of the bridge is 8 inches from the roof. The bridge is 2 feet wide, but 14 inches of this width is a curtain arch, the bottom of which is 16 inches above the hearth. Just beyond the curtain in the roof of the furnace there are a series of holes for the admission of air, of the same size as in the matte-furnace. The first line goes straight across the roof, and is composed of five holes. The second follows the contour of the furnace and is composed of nine holes. The hearth of this furnace is made of a bed of old slag or stone covered with sand. On these, bricks placed on end and laid in cement are placed, which form the hearth proper.

The charge is 1,600 pounds of roasted crushed matte, which is thrown in with a shovel and made into a pile on the center of the hearth. Just before it is introduced all the dampers are closed. The hearth of the furnace at this time is dark. The fire-place is, however, glowing, but contains only embers, just sufficient to keep it hot. As soon as the charge is introduced it is leveled with the rabble and spread out over the hearth. When spread out it is about 3 inches thick. It takes about 20 minutes to do this work, during which time the dampers remain closed and no fuel is put into the fire-place. As soon as the charge is completed the damper is slightly raised, but no fuel is charged. In about an hour the charge has a dull, blackish glow. The surface looks black, but it is red when stirred. The fire-place in now charged with a small amount of fuel, and the temperature gradually raised so as to keep it at about a dull-red heat, but raising it slightly. The fire-place door is closed. The supply of air comes from the bridge holes, the working door, and the grate. The work at this stage consists of forming a maximum amount of sulphate of iron and some sulphate of copper, but the silver remains unchanged. The fumes of sulphuric acid commence to be given off from the decomposition of the persulphate of iron, and the charge increases in volume, becoming spongy. As the furnace-door is open the workman is exposed to the acid fumes, and is, therefore, obliged to wear a respirator. The stirring is kept up and the heat gradually increased. From the second hour the grate is kept full until the end of the operation, the temperature being kept as uniform as possible. The ash-pit door is closed after the first hour, the air entering only through the working door and the holes in the bridge. The flame over the curtain arch is curly, blackish, and reducing, but as there is more than 14 inches between it and the charge below, and the working door is constantly opened, it is so fully mixed with air, that in contact with the charge it is oxidizing. At the end of this time the heat is at its maximum, and the charge becomes dry, no longer sticking to the rabble. At this point, which is at the end of three hours, the sulphate of silver is formed. The sulphate of iron is decomposed at the end of two hours. The sulphate of copper, at the time all the iron is decomposed, is at its maximum, which is at the end of the third hour. When the silver is "out" a bar 2 inches square and 14 feet long is used to break up any lumps. The charge is collected with it into the middle hearth. The pile is then, by a sliding motion of the bar on its side, cut down, bruised, stamped, and broken up, and in this way turned over twice from one side of the furnace to the other. In order to facilitate this work, the front of the working door is provided with a roller, on which the bar rests. The whole charge by this means is ground fine and all the lumps broken up, and a perfect oxidation secured. It is essential to have as little sulphate of copper as possible, but about 1½ per cent. is left so as to be sure that no sulphate of silver is decomposed. This operation with the bar lasts one hour, so that at the end of four hours the charge is ready to be withdrawn. At the end of the third hour assays commence to be made, and samples are constantly taken until the end of the operation. The first assay generally shows that the sulphate of silver is free, but it is reduced almost instantly to a metallic state by the suboxide of copper present, and spangles are formed which scintillate and sparkle, forming a most beautiful reaction. To make the assay, a sample of the hot charge is simply thrown into cold water in a small dish. The heat of the ore is so great that the temperature of the water is raised to boiling. Whatever silver is in the state of sulphate is dissolved by the boiling water. If there is any suboxide of copper present, the spangle reaction takes place. At the end of the fourth hour the exposure of the surfaces to oxidation from the action of the bar has converted all the copper from suboxide into protoxide, and no spangles are seen in the assay. The sulphate of silver consequently remains permanent. If any sulphide of silver was present in the charge, it is attacked by the sulphuric acid given off by the decomposing sulphates and converted into sulphate. An average of from 90 to 95 per cent. of silver is thus rendered soluble, the rest being in a condition of arsenides, antimonides, or as fine particles within the sulphate of lead, and is not decomposed. The charges are constantly assayed, and the workmen, as they are skilled men, feel it for their interest to conduct the operation properly. It would not be safe to decompose the whole of the sulphate of copper, since there would be danger that some of the sulphate of silver would be decomposed and pass into the residues. The copper gives a blue color to the solution, so that when the spangles are no longer produced, and the liquor is a very pale blue color, the charge is drawn. None of this work is done at night, as the operation is an exceedingly delicate one and requires to be constantly watched. As soon as the charge is withdrawn, the furnace is cooled by opening the doors and dampers to get ready for another charge. Only two charges a day are made. It takes about ten minutes to discharge the furnace. The charge is drawn with a rabble into an iron barrow, and is wheeled to the brick cooling-floor shown at B′ in the general plan, Figs. 1 and 12. Each furnace is tended by one man only. The two furnaces burn together 1¼ cords of wood in twelve hours; they require only one day's repair in a year.

B. *Leaching the sulphate of silver.*—The charge from the sulphate of silver furnace is allowed to remain for twelve hours on the cooling-floor and is then leached in tubs. These tubs are 3 feet high, 3 feet in diameter at the top, and 2 feet 6 inches at the bottom (see *m*, in the general plan, Figs. 1 and 12, and Figs. 13, 14, and 15, Plate II). They are provided with a double-bottom, pierced with holes, which is covered with a cloth filter. They are charged with 1,500 pounds of the matte which has been roasted for sulphate of silver. The leaching is done by a current of boiling water kept hot by steam. The tubs are kept constantly full and discharged into a series of tanks below. It takes eight or nine hours to leach the charge; at first it is light, but in about an hour it shrinks and the water passes less freely through it.

The residues in the tubs contain all the gold and some silver which has not been separated. They are taken out and put on one side to be treated by the Augustine process to separate the silver, and the residues are afterward treated for gold. All the sulphate of copper is dissolved out in the first stages of the work. In about seven or eight hours, assays of the liquid are made and the hot water stopped, when salt added to it shows no trace of silver. The time required varies according to the richness of the matte. Between 600 pounds and 700 pounds are leached in eight hours; generally about an hour is required for every hundred ounces of silver contained in the matte.

Precipitating the silver.—The hot water charged with the sulphates of silver and copper from the solution-tubs is run into a series of vats, *Sg*, shown in Fig. 12, and Figs. 13, 14, and 15, Plate II, and on the general plan, Fig. 1 at S. These vats are 12 feet long, 4 feet wide, and 2 feet 3 inches deep. Two sets of these vats, one in front of the other, are placed before each series of tubs. Each of them is divided into ten compartments, which are 24 inches by 20 inches and 27 inches deep. The liquid is discharged from the tubs into number one and communicates with number two at the bottom. The partition between two and three is low at the top, so that the liquid overflows into three, which communicates with four at the bottom, and so on. At ten the overflow passes into the tank below and follows the same circuitous course. Each compartment in the tanks is filled, as shown in Fig. 15, with plates of copper ¼ inch thick and 14 inches by 12 inches in size. Twenty of these plates, each having a precipitating surface of nearly 400 square inches, are placed in each compartment. In the bottom of the tank the plates are placed upright and are slightly inclined, being separated from each other by small strips of wood at the top. Over these the plates are laid horizontally, with strips of wood between each to prevent actual contact. This arrangement gives about 100,000 square inches of precipitating surface to each system. Both series of tanks are filled with copper in the same way. The tanks are kept perfectly covered with wooden covers. At the end of a week they are removed, and the copper plates shaken and washed in the liquid, to remove the silver sponge, which falls to the bottom and is taken out. This sponge is very light, and adheres very slightly to the copper. After the copper plates are taken out the liquid is allowed to settle.

The copper solution is drawn into the tanks *nn*, and the silver carried to the tubs *b*, to be washed to remove any traces of copper. It takes about two hours to get the tanks ready for another charge. More than half of the silver is deposited in the first four compartments. Here the copper-plates last about four months. In the other compartments they last twelve months. The amount of copper dissolved is equivalent to the quantity of sulphuric acid set free from its combination with the silver.

C. *Washing and fusing the cement silver.*—The cement silver is washed in a washer invented by Professor Pearce, and patented in England about eight years ago. It is a tub about 4 feet high and 4 feet in diameter at the top, and 2 feet at the bottom. It is, however, sometimes made a little smaller, being 42 inches high, 40 inches in diameter at the top, and 23 inches at the bottom. This tub, with its injector, is shown on the general plans, Figs. 1 and 12, at *b*, in Figs. 13, 14, and 15, and in detail at Figs. 16 and 17, Plate II. Two of these washers are placed on a raised platform having a spout connecting with the sulphate of copper tanks. About 3,000 ounces of silver are placed on the false bottom of the tub. A mixture of one part of sulphuric acid to 100 parts of water is then poured in, in sufficient quantity to cover all the silver. Steam at a pressure of 50 pounds is then turned on through the injector, and the arm *a* moved so as to open the air-holes. The steam and air pass down through the false bottom and up through the silver and sulphuric acid. A very violent ebullition is caused in the liquid by this passage of the air and steam.

The silver is thus kept in constant agitation, and fresh surfaces are continually exposed to the action of the acid. Beside this mechanical effect the current of air oxidizes the metallic copper and transforms it, together with the suboxide, into sulphate.* The cement silver from the tanks still contains some traces of copper, as sulphate, and some metallic copper detached from the plates. At the end of two or three hours the liquid is run off through the spout into the tanks. The silver is washed for half an hour with clean water and steam, and then removed in buckets to be dried on top of the drying furnace, Figs. 18 and 19, Plate II. It requires from three to three and a half hours to completely purify the 3,000 ounces of cement silver. After drying, the silver is melted in graphite crucibles in the furnace, Figs. 20, 21, and 22, Plate III. It is cast into bars in the iron ingot mould, Fig 23, and is found to be 999 to 999.5 fine.

D. *Precipitation of the copper.*—The copper solution from the tanks *gS* runs into the tanks *n*, Fig. 12, which are divided into compartments like the tanks *gS*, and are also covered. These compartments are filled with scrap-iron, which is simply thrown in without any special care in piling. The spent liquor, which is sulphate of iron, when sulphureted hydrogen or a polished-steel plate shows no trace of copper, is discharged into the stream; the velocity of the discharge being regulated according as the action is quick or slow. The copper precipitates on the iron, and is left to accumulate. The compartments are cleaned out about once a month. The copper is removed from the iron by simply moving it backward and forward in the liquid. The iron so cleaned is at once placed in an empty tank to be used on a fresh charge. All the iron used is old scrap-iron, and is therefore not weighed. About 5,000 pounds to 6,000 pounds is used in each tank. The cement copper is allowed to drain and dry, and is then taken to the smelting furnace. It contains about 90 per cent. of metallic copper when it is fresh. The small amount of impurity is owing to the fact that the tanks are closed, thus preventing the precipitation of insoluble compounds of iron. The cement copper oxidizes very rapidly in contact with the air, so that when ready for the furnace it does not contain more than 80 per cent. of copper in the metallic state.

E. *Refining the cement copper.*—The furnace in which the cement copper is refined is shown at A in the ground-plan, Fig. 1, and in detail by Figs. 24 to 29, Plate III. The fire-place is 5 feet long and 28 inches wide at the top of grate. The grate has the same length, but is only 17 inches wide. The bridge is 2 feet wide. The laboratory is 6 feet 4 inches long and 4 feet 4 inches wide, and has two doors, one at the end, which is the charging door, and one at the side, which is the working door. Just over the bridge in the roof there are two rows of six openings each for the introduction of air; these are covered with a hood to prevent the

* This injector is also used in parting the rich auriferous copper alloy, for the separation of gold, and manufacture of sulphate of copper.

introduction of foreign substances. The furnace connects with the chimney by a flue, which is 2 feet square.

The fire-place has 11.65 square feet and the laboratory 21.79 square feet, so that the relation between them is nearly 1 : 2.

This furnace runs once a month for eighteen or nineteen hours. A charge of 2,500 pounds of copper mixed with 50 pounds of refuse charcoal is put in at 6 p. m. The fireman keeps up the fire during the night, and the refiner takes it at 7 a. m., and then skims off the slag and exposes the surface of the bath. Considerable sulphurous acid is given off, probably from the reduction of the sulphate of iron in the cement copper. The charge is worked for a "set," which takes three to four hours. This is done by striking the surface with the rabble and making waves. This is called beating the copper. The copper produced contains from 2 to 3 per cent. of oxide of copper dissolved in it, but it is not necessary to refine it completely, as it is used at once in the tanks G. The copper is taken from the furnace with a ladle, and is poured into a cast-iron mold made of a frame in two parts, held together by clamps, and is slightly tapering, being larger at the bottom than the top. This frame is placed on a cast-iron plate 3 inches in thickness. The ladleful of copper poured in is allowed to set, that is, a film of suboxide of copper is allowed to form, another ladle is poured on, and so on until the mold is full. The cast-iron frame is then removed, and the plates fall out separately, as the oxide prevents anything more than contact. Twenty-five plates are made in this way at a time.

V.—TREATMENT OF THE ZIERVOGEL TUB RESIDUES.

A. *Fusion for white metal.*—The residues from the tubs consist of oxides of copper and iron with 20 or 30 ounces of gold and 40 ounces of silver to the ton. They amount to about 22 tons a week. They are melted in the matte-furnace, Figs. 5 to 8, Plate VII, with rich gold-ores of the first class, containing iron with copper pyrites, and variable quantities of gangue, and highly siliceous tellurium ores. All the siliceous pyritiferous ores are selected for this purpose. The ores are all crushed and put through a four to the inch mesh sieve. The charge is brought to the furnace in alternate barrows of residues and ore, but it is not mixed before charging, as it becomes mixed after it is thrown into the furnace. The charge consists of—

	Pounds.
Tub residues	4,000
Raw gold-ores of the first class	2,500
Gold-ores of the third class	900
Total	7,400

When there are no tellurium-ores the charge of gold-ores of the first class is made to amount to 3,400 pounds. The treatment is exactly the same as before. A poor slag containing only two ounces of silver and a trace of gold is produced; it is very much poorer than those of the previous fusion. It has otherwise very nearly the same composition as the others, but there is no zinc, either as blende or oxide, in it. The matte contains:

Copper	60 per cent.
Gold	55 ounces.
Silver	130 ounces.
Sulphur	30 per cent.

It is called white metal. If the matte was made richer in copper the slag would also be richer, and there would be more loss. The tapping is made twice in twenty-four hours. In other respects the labor, fuel, &c., are the same as in the matte-fusion No. 3. This fusion for the treatment of tub-residues takes place once a month and lasts a week. All the plate-slag produced during this operation is put directly back into the furnace.

B. *Roasting the white metal.*—At the end of a week all the mattes produced are recharged in large lumps, the charge being about 4 tons. It is roasted at a dull-red heat for about ten hours with admission of air. The reaction which takes place between the sulphide and oxide makes a peculiar noise, which can be heard at some distance from the furnace. The operation is termed "roasting" for black copper, but it is stopped half-way. As the sulphur is driven off some metallic copper is liberated.

The slag is very thick, and not more than 200 pounds to 300 pounds are produced. It contains from 8 to 10 per cent. of copper, and is highly basic, often containing crystals of magnetite. At the end of the ninth hour the doors are closed and the fire-place charged. The whole furnace is brought to a white heat, so that the whole charge is in intimate fusion. Just before tapping it is rabbled for five minutes, and then tapped into sand-molds. The tapping is done as before, but molds are made to receive the matte, as the charge is greater. In the first three or four pigs there will be found plates or bottoms of metallic copper containing arsenic, antimony, and lead. These bottoms contain nearly the whole of the gold, with a small quantity of silver, from 3 to 5 per cent. of sulphur, and 80 per cent. of copper. The matte is pimple metal, and contains about

Copper	75 per cent.
Gold	2 ounces.
Silver	140 ounces.

From every charge about 600 pounds of bottoms and 3 tons of matte are produced. This bottom fusion takes three days, making ten days for this treatment of the residues. The labor is the same as in the matte-fusion, but more wood is used, four cords being burned in twenty-four hours. Only two operations are made in twenty-four hours.

C. *Treatment of the pimple metal.*—The pimple metal is roasted again in the same way, treating it nearly five hours, and making four charges in twenty-four hours. Other bottoms are produced poorer in gold, but containing

Gold	60 to 100 ounces.
Silver	200 ounces.
Copper	75 per cent.
Sulphur	25 per cent.

The pimple metal from this fusion contains

Gold	¼ ounce.
Silver	120 ounces.
Copper	80 per cent.
Sulphur	20 per cent.

the iron being entirely removed. This operation takes one and a half days. The bottoms are treated with the other bottoms. The pimple metal goes to the Ziervogel process B, but is kept entirely separate, because it contains no gold as does that of the process A.

VI.—TREATMENT OF THE RESIDUES OF THE ZIERVOGEL PROCESS B BY THE AUGUSTINE PROCESS.

The residues from the Ziervogel process B, which contain 25 ounces of silver per ton, are roasted with salt in one of the furnaces, B, Fig. 12, for roasting for sulphate of silver in the Ziervogel process. The residues are charged moist, a charge being one ton. It is heated for two hours, until it is hot. Twenty pounds of salt are then added, and well rubbed into the charge for fifteen minutes. The charge is then drawn, to prevent the loss of copper, as well as chloride of copper. Three charges are made in twelve hours. This requires one man, and three-fourths of a cord of wood.

Solution.—This material is treated with a hot saturated solution of brine, a tank holding 1,000 gallons of the brine solution being always kept in reserve; 1,600 pounds of the chloridized residues are placed in a vat, and the solution allowed to constantly flow through it by an inch pipe for four hours.

The liquid which runs out of the solution-tubs runs into tanks, Figs. 30, 31, and 32, Plate III, where the silver is precipitated with copper in the tanks *i*, and the copper with iron in the tanks *k*, as in the Ziervogel process. The salt solution containing chloride of iron, is collected in the tank *o*, and is pumped back into the tanks and is used again. Chloride of iron by constant boiling becomes perchloride, and finally sesquioxide is precipitated. The salt solution lasts (with occasional renewals of water) indefinitely. The loss of salt, per ton of residue treated, is about 10 pounds. The residues from this treatment are either reduced and made into ingots, or sold as they are, as residues. The precipitation is the same as in the Ziervogel process, except that chlorides are formed. The material is always kept separate.

VII.—TREATMENT OF THE BOTTOMS.

Four tons of white metal, from the Ziervogel treatment, give 600 pounds of bottoms. These are left to accumulate until they amount to 3,500 pounds, enough for a charge in the small reverberatory furnace. The furnace in which this operation is effected is shown in the general plan, Figs. 1 and 12, at C, and in detail in Figs. 33 to 38, Plate III. The fire-place is 6 feet long, 4 feet deep, 42 inches wide at the bridge, and 20 inches at the grate. The bridge is 2 feet wide. The laboratory is 9 feet long, 6 feet 9 inches wide, and connects with the chimney, 2 feet 6 inches square, by a flue. The surface of the fire-place is 21 square feet, that of the laboratory 46.27 square; the relation, therefore, is 1 : 4. The furnace has a working door at the side and a charging door at the end. On the side opposite the working door there is a spout which ends in a wooden tank sunk in the ground, which is 4 feet 5 inches in diameter and 3 feet deep.

The object of the process is to oxidize the lead and other impurities, and to prepare the metal for treatment for gold. The charge is made at 7 a. m. It is first sweated at a low temperature for two or three hours, during which time some of the lead liquates and runs out of the furnace. It is then left to oxidize for three or four hours. In about seven hours the charge is well melted. The slag, which is skimmed at this time, is composed mostly of oxides of lead and copper, containing from 10 to 15 per cent. of copper, and is sent to operation No. 3. After the slag is withdrawn the bath is beaten with a rabble for about two hours, all the doors being opened to admit an excess of air. It is again skimmed and tapped into water. The "pitch," that is the condition of the copper, must be such that the whole of the sulphur is eliminated before the oxygen is absorbed. If the pitch is right the globules will all be round and hollow. This point must be seized with the greatest nicety, for if the charge remains too long in the furnace the globules will cast solid, and the charge must then be put back and worked with sulphur. The temperature of the water governs the size of the globules. They are small when it is cold and large when it is hot, but it does not otherwise affect it. It takes about ten minutes to do this casting. The copper flowing from the spout falls on to a pole of green wood held underneath it, so as to scatter the copper. Care must be taken that the slag does not flow with the copper. To prevent it, the doors are opened, so that the slag is cooled until it is pasty. One charge is made at a time, and only one or two per month. The globules contain 1,000 ounces of gold, 600 ounces of silver, and a trace of lead. Twenty tons of white metal give one ton of refined auriferous copper. Three cords of wood are used, one man tends the furnace, one man does the firing.

VIII.—TREATMENT OF THE OXIDIZED COPPER ALLOY.

The copper globules are oxidized in one of the fine calciners, in which sulphate of silver is treated. One and a half tons are charged at a time. The oxidation takes thirty-six hours. The globules are put into the furnace in a heap and spread out over the hearth. The charge will be 3 inches deep. The fire-place is charged at once, and the temperature is made as hot as the red bricks will bear, and as oxidizing as possible. It is constantly rabbled. At the end of thirty-six hours a portion is taken out and tested, to see that it will pulverize completely. If it does, the operation is finished; if it does not, the oxidation is continued. The whole of the copper has been transformed by the operation into suboxide, and the charge is increased in weight about 500 pounds by the operation. The grains are black on the outside, but if broken or rubbed the streak is red. The charge is drawn out into an iron barrow and carried to the store-room. It is placed in bags, packed in petroleum-casks, and shipped to Boston. One cask holds 650 pounds. Three cords of wood are used for the process, and two men do the work, one man to each twelve hours' shift. The men are required to bring their own wood.

Solution of the oxidized-copper alloy.—The oxidized product is treated with dilute sulphuric acid. This is done in a conical tub lined with lead, having a false bottom. The bottom is hollowed so as to leave as little space as possible. A charge is 1,500 pounds. Over this, sulphuric acid at 20° Baumé is poured. Steam and air are turned on and the boiling continued for four hours. The whole is not dissolved, but 90 per cent. of the copper will be in solution. It is allowed to settle for an hour, and is siphoned off and a fresh charge put in. Two charges are made in a day. This is repeated until all the oxidized products have been treated. This work is not done at night. The residues are boiled two or three times in the same way to get out all the copper possible. The tub is then cleaned up and what remains is melted in plumbago crucibles. The bullion is from 600 to 800 fine of mixed metals. It contains from 40 to 50 per cent. gold and 20 to 30 per cent. of silver. This is sent to the mint.

The sulphate of copper is crystallized and sold. The mother liquid is used to dilute the acid used for the solution of the oxides.

The working of these alloys of gold, silver, and copper was first tried in the works, and was given up on account of the high price of sulphuric acid. It was carried on for more than a year in Boston, but has quite recently been abandoned, and the separation of gold and silver is now to be done at the works by a process invented by Professor Pearce.

In conclusion, I beg to present my warmest thanks to Professor Hill, who afforded me every facility for making the plans of the works and for taking the drawings of all the furnaces, and to Professor Pearce, who gave all the information which was required, both at the works and after my return to New York, concerning the various processes carried out there.

CHAPTER XIII.

THE HUNT AND DOUGLAS COPPER PROCESS.

For the following account of this process, I am indebted to Prof. T. Sterry Hunt and Mr. James Douglas, jr., the patentees.

This is what is technically called a wet method, because the copper is removed from its ores in a dissolved state, the solvent employed in the present process being a watery solution of neutral protochloride of iron and common salt. Most oxidized compounds of copper—whether obtained artificially by roasting sulphureted ores, or found in nature in the forms of carbonates and oxides—when digested with such a solution are converted into a mixture of protochloride and dichloride of copper, which are dissolved, while the iron of the solvent separates in the form of insoluble hydrous peroxide of iron. When the solution of the chlorides of copper thus obtained is brought in contact with metallic iron, the copper is separated in a metallic crystalline state, while the iron passes into solution, reproducing the protochloride of iron, thus restoring its solvent powers to the liquid which we shall call "the bath," and fitting it for the treatment of a fresh portion of copper-ore. This process of solution and precipitation can, under proper conditions, be repeated indefinitely with the same bath, the only reagent consumed being the metallic iron.

The chief advantage which wet processes possess over smelting lies in the economy of fuel. To extract copper from a low-grade ore by smelting, five or six furnace-operations are necessary, and about one ton of coal is consumed for each ton of ore treated; while for the various wet processes a single calcination, in which not more than three hundred-weight of coa lis consumed for each ton of ore, is the only furnace-operation required to obtain the metallic copper in a precipitated form known as *cement copper*. An important item of cost in wet processes is the metallic iron employed to separate the metallic copper from its solutions. The same amount of iron is required to precipitate a ton of copper whether extracted from a poor or a rich ore, but as for the smelting of the latter much less fuel is required, it follows that rich ores are generally treated by smelting rather than in the wet way, any saving of fuel in the latter being more than compensated for by the cost of iron. No general rule, however, can be laid down to determine what grade of ore can be more profitably treated by one method or the other, inasmuch as circumstances of locality, affecting the cost of fuel and the price of iron, must in each case be taken into account.

The various other wet methods of copper-extraction may be divided into two classes: those in which the previously oxidized ore is treated with hydrocholoric or sulphuric acid to dissolve the oxide of copper, and those in which sulphureted ore, generally after a preliminary roasting, is calcined with an admixture of sea-salt or of sulphate of soda, by which the copper is converted into chloride or into sulphate. All of these methods, when properly applied, effect a pretty thorough extraction of the copper, but the cost of the reagents which have to be added to every charge of ore, preclude altogether the use of some of these methods, except in certain favored localities, and render them in almost all cases, it is believed, less economical than the present one with the Hunt and Douglas bath, for which the following advantages are claimed:

I. It is a general method adapted to all compounds of copper, while that by calcination with salt is only applicable to sulphureted ores.

II. It does not require the addition of reagents, such as acids, salt, or sulphate of soda, to each charge of ore, since in the regular course of the operation the solvent required for the treatment of the ore is constantly reproduced.

III. The bath employed being neutral, certain impurities of the ore, such as arsenic, which pass into solution and contaminate the product in the wet processes, remain undissolved, so that a purer copper is obtained.

IV. As the solution obtained is neutral and free from persalts of iron, there is no unnecessary waste or consumption of metallic iron in the process of precipitation. Moreover, as the result of the action of the protochloride of iron of the bath on protoxide of copper, one-third of the copper is obtained as protochloride, and two-thirds as dichloride. Now since the latter requires for each one hundred parts of copper precipitated only forty-five parts of iron, it is found in practice that not more than three-quarters of a ton of iron are consumed to precipitate one ton of metallic copper, while in the other methods, in which the copper is obtained as protochloride, the consumption of iron amounts to a ton, and in many cases greatly exceeds it.

WORKING DIRECTIONS.

Grinding the ore.—The degree of fineness to which the ore must be ground will depend entirely upon the character of the gangue. If the metal be scattered in fine particles through an impermeable rock, it will be necessary to grind it to the size of sand, so that the copper, if a sulphuret, may be exposed to the oxidizing action of the air during calcination, and to the solvent action of the protochloride of iron bath during lixiviation. If, on the contrary, the copper sulphuret be mixed, as is often the case, with iron pyrites, which by calcination becomes porous, the ore need not be ground so fine. Experiment in each case must determine the point, and upon the decision must depend the machinery which should be chosen to effect the grinding; Cornish rolls being preferable for coarse crushing and stamps for finer work. Two pairs of rolls—one pair of 24 or 30 inches diameter, and one pair of 12 or 15 inches, with a screen between them to sift out what is not broken sufficiently fine by the upper pair, will crush about twenty tons of stuff in twenty-four hours so that it will pass through a sieve of fifteen holes to the linear inch, a degree of fineness sufficient for most ores. A rock-breaker with jaws set close may be substituted for the upper pair of rolls.

Calcining the ore.—It is not necessary to calcine carbonates or protoxides, but mixtures in which there is a large proportion of red or dinoxide need a slight roasting to convert at least a part of this into protoxide; while all sulphureted ores require much more calcination. The mode of effecting this will vary with the character of the ore. When it contains 20 per cent. or upward of sulphur, it may be broken into lumps of an inch or more in diameter, and exposed to a preliminary roasting in heaps or kilns, whereby, without the aid of fuel, the greater part of the sulphur will be driven off, and the metallic ingredients more or less completely oxidized. The lumps thus partially roasted should then be crushed and calcined in a muffle or reverberatory furnace. The calcination of all ores in an earthy gangue must be effected wholly in such furnaces.

The first rule in roasting is to expose the ore at the beginning to a low heat, which is to be gradually increased as the sulphur is driven off. If the temperature be too high at the commencement of the operation, the ore, if highly sulphureted, may become softened and agglutinated or fritted, after which it is impossible to effect a proper roast. But even if this should not happen, too high a heat at first, or indeed at any stage of the process, brings the copper into a condition in which it is difficultly soluble in the bath. A long furnace is more easily managed than a short one, since in the former the fire can always be kept strong and the ore moved forward from a cooler to a hotter portion, while in a short furnace the gradation of heat can only be attained by close attention to the firing.

A long muffle furnace always gives a good roast, as the tile floor protects the ore from excessive heat, and there is sure to be an oxidizing atmosphere in the furnace, which is not always the case in a reverberatory, where the flame comes in contact with the ore. But the construction of the muffle furnace is expensive, and a cheap and efficient furnace is a three-hearth reverberatory. When a number of such furnaces are needed, they may be built side by side, in a row, the rabbling-doors opening before and behind, and the arches of the whole row being supported by a stone buttress at each end—the only binding necessary. The fire-boxes of adjacent furnaces are placed side by side. The dimensions which have been found advantageous for these furnaces are as follows: Lower hearth 10 feet wide by 16 feet long; upper hearths 12 feet wide by 15 feet long. The lower hearth is contracted in width by the fire-place, and the upper hearths in length by the flues which lead from hearth to hearth.

The advantages of such a form of furnace are cheapness of construction and economy of heat, on account of the exposure of a less amount of cooling-surface than in the long reverberatory with rabbling-doors on the side. On the other hand the upper hearths are not very accessible to the rabblers. If such a furnace be used, the heat should only be sufficient to thoroughly dry and warm the ore on the uppermost hearth. Oxidation should take place, with the elimination of the greater part of the sulphur, on the second hearth, so that when the ore is exposed to the higher temperature of the lower hearth there may be no danger of fritting. The quantity of ore which may be roasted in such a furnace will depend on the character of the ore and the proportion of sulphate of copper which it may be desirable to obtain. If the ore is highly sulphureted and has not received a preliminary roast before grinding, only two or three tons can be calcined in twenty-four hours, whereas double that quantity may be treated if the ore be poor in sulphur. An ore with from 15 per cent. to 20 per cent. of sulphur may be added in charges of 2,500 pounds, and shifted from hearth to hearth every eight hours, while one containing from 5 per cent. to 7 per cent. of sulphur may be shifted every five hours.

If the ore contains no carbonate of lime or magnesia, (which will deprive the bath of the chloride of iron in the subsequent operation of solution,) the roast need not contain over one-fourth of its copper in the state of sulphate. This will be more than sufficient to repair unavoidable losses in the iron-chloride of the bath. The presence of portions of these obnoxious elements may, however, make it desirable to obtain in the roast a larger proportion of sulphate of copper, (which is soluble in water and by its precipitation by metallic iron yields an iron-salt.) To obtain this the ore should be roasted more slowly and in larger charges, say of 5,000 pounds each, in which case the yield of ore from the furnace will be somewhat diminished.

The quantity of fuel consumed will vary with the different ores, but as a rule one cord of wood will suffice for three tons, and one ton of coal for eight tons of ore.

When a sulphureted ore has been properly roasted it loses, when being rabbled, that apparent fluidity which ore still giving off sulphurous acid exhibits, and when withdrawn and cooled should have a bright-red color. If the heat has been too great, the color of the cooled ore will vary through dull-red to black. There is more danger of having too much than too little heat in the furnace. The ore on the upper hearth should never be in a glow, and that on the lower hearth should never attain a higher heat than dull redness. Besides regulating the heat, it is important to attend to the admission of air. As the roasting of the ore is an oxidizing process an abundance of air is essential to the operation, and that this may be supplied, the furnace must possess a good draught and be provided with openings sufficiently large and numerous. If the furnace be defective in these points the ore will be scorched and its copper rendered insoluble by a reducing action on the lower hearth, while the upper hearth will be liable, at the same time, to become too hot.

The more completely the sulphuret of copper is oxidized in the roasting, the more thorough will be the subsequent extraction of the copper, but to oxidize the last traces of sulphuret requires a disproportionate expenditure of time, labor, and fuel. Upon the relative value of the raw ore, and of labor and fuel, will therefore depend the degree of thoroughness to which it may be profitable to carry the extraction of the copper at any given reduction-works. While it is desirable to oxidize as completely as consistent with economy the sulphurets of the ore, it should be borne in mind that a *dead roast*, as it is called, or the elimination of that portion of sulphur which, after oxidation, remains combined as sulphate of copper, is to be avoided, since, as already pointed out, to provide for unavoidable loss of chloride of iron, it is desirable to leave a portion of sulphate of copper in the roasted ore. The composition of the roast may be seen from the following examples:

At the Ore Knob Mine in North Carolina, the average of the ore roasted by this process was, according to Mr. Olcott, (Trans. Amer. Inst. Min. Engineers, vol. iii, p. 395:)

Copper as sulphate	3.76
Copper as oxide	7.75
Copper as sulphide	.39
	11.90

At Phœnixville, Pa., where the ore contains a considerable quantity of carbonate of magnesia, the effect of which has to be neutralized by a large proportion of sulphate of copper, and where charges of 5,000 pounds of ore are calcined for twenty-four hours on each hearth of the dimensions above given, the roasted ore has the following average composition:

Copper as sulphate	1.25
Copper as oxide	1.10
Copper as sulphide	.40
	2.75

Dissolving the copper.—The solvent or bath employed for the extraction of the copper is, as has been stated, a neutral solution of protochloride of iron with common salt. This protochloride may be obtained in various ways. In localities where acids are cheap it is easily made by dissolving scrap-iron in diluted muriatic or sulphuric acid; the first yields directly protochloride, the second protosulphate of iron, which when mixed with a solution of salt gives rise to the protochloride, together with a portion of sulphate of soda. In places where acids are not so easily had, the commercial protosulphate of iron (green copperas) is the most convenient source of the protochloride, as explained in the specification. One hundred pounds of the commercial acid and 56 pounds of scrap-iron will make 280 pounds of copperas. Knowing the relative cost of these substances at any locality, it will be easy to calculate whether it is cheaper to make the copperas or to purchase it. Where highly sulphureted copper-ores or copper-pyrites are to be had, these, by calcining at a low red heat, (as already stated,) yield large proportions of sulphate of copper and sulphate of iron, both of which are soluble. By leaching these roasted ores with water, and digesting the solution thus obtained with scrap-iron, the dissolved copper is thrown down as metal, and a solution of protosulphate of iron obtained, which may be mixed with salt to form the bath.

In the original specification of the process it was directed in making the bath by the use of protosulphate of iron to take 280 pounds of this (equal to 56 pounds of metallic iron) and 120 pounds of salt, sufficient to convert it into protochloride. These dissolved in 1,000 pounds of water (100 imperial gallons) with a further addition of 200 pounds of salt made the strongest bath, but a weaker one was also recommended in which these same ingredients were to be dissolved in 2,000 pounds of water. Experience has shown that the latter is strong enough for the treatment of all ordinary ores.

The bath may be brought in contact with the ore either by percolation in leaching-tanks, or by agitation in vats arranged with stirrers. If the ore be finely ground and slimy, the latter must be used; but if it is coarse, and contains nothing which when wetted will form mud, it is best treated by leaching. When agitation is required the tank should be round, 10 or 12 feet in diameter, and 5 or 6 feet high, and made of 3-inch staves. A convenient stirring-apparatus consists of two oblique blades fixed to the base of a vertical shaft, which rests on the vertex of a conical bottom. The tips of the blades should reach to within an inch of the sides of the tank, and be raised about 15 inches above the level of the bottom of the tank at the periphery. The object of thus elevating the stirrer on a cone above the bottom is to permit the ore to settle below the blades, so that the stirrer, after having been stopped, can be started at will; whereas, were the bottom flat and the distance between it and the blades the same at all points, the ore would accumulate around the shaft and thus escape agitation. The stirrer should make about twenty revolutions a minute. A vat of the above dimensions, having a capacity of about 3,000 gallons, and two-thirds filled with bath, will serve to agitate and dissolve the copper from 3,000 pounds of roasted ore, containing five or six per cent. of copper oxide, in six to eight hours, the temperature being from 120° to 150° F. The stirrers are then stopped, the whole allowed to settle, the clear liquor drawn off into the precipitating-tanks, and the muddy portions into settling-tanks, after which the residue may be washed, first with bath, and then with water, to remove the adherent copper solution.

When percolation can be adopted it is preferable to stirring, since, though the operation is slower, we are enabled to dispense with the settling-tanks, which the latter plan requires, and the handling of the slimes which accumulate in these. Moreover, as the solution of the copper takes place in the mass of ore out of contact of air, a larger proportion of dichloride of copper is found and less iron is lost by oxdation than when the solution holding the dissolved iron and copper salts is exposed to the air by constant agitation.

The vats for filtration are made of wood or of brick. For the latter the bricks are laid in Roman cement and coated within by a layer of the same cement mixed with silicate of soda. This, when afterward washed with a solution of chloride of calcium, forms a coating which resists the action of the metallic salts of the bath. If wood be used the vats may either be square or round, but in any case they should be somewhat wider at the top than at the bottom, otherwise the settling and contraction of the moistened ore will leave a space along the walls through which the bath may descend without percolating the mass. Filtering-vats need not be more than three feet high. The filter may be made by laying on the bottom of the vat three inches of small stones, broken cinder or coke, and covering this by a layer of coarse sand, upon which the ore may be laid to the depth of one or two feet according to its coarseness or fineness. Instead of this arrangement a false bottom, consisting of perforated planks or of narrow boards loosely laid together, may be covered over with coarse sacking, upon which the ore is spread. A hole in the side near the bottom of the tank, into which is fitted an india-rubber tube provided with a squeezer or pinch-cock, gives vent to the liquor after its passage through the ore. The vats should be fitted with close covers so as to exclude the air and retain the heat; these are provided with a small hole through which enters a tube to supply the bath. It is well to spread the ore in the vats already partially filled with heated bath, as when thus wet down it will not cake, but will permit the bath to percolate uniformly through it. When the desired quantity of ore has been added a wooden float should be secured beneath the opening in the cover so that the bath, as it flows in, may fall thereon, otherwise it would make a depression in the mass and thus the percolation would be unequal. About two or three inches of bath should be kept on the top of the ore, and it should be supplied as rapidly as it escapes from the tube below. When the outflowing liquid is found, by testing with a bit of iron wire, to contain no more copper than the liquid entering above, we know that the soluble copper has been removed and it only remains to stop the supply of bath, allow the layer above to filter through, and then displace that which remains in the pores of the exhausted mass by the addition of a little water. The extraction of the copper by filtration may not be completed in less than three or four days, the time of course depending on the richness of the ore and the strength and the temperature of the bath.

The solution of the copper is much accelerated by heating the bath, which may be done by the injection of steam. If the liquid be heated to from 120° to 180° F. it will flow through the ore in the leaching-tanks with a very little reduction of temperature, and the heat generated in the process of precipitation will, if the tanks for this operation are well covered, maintain the bath in these at a sufficient temperature to insure a quick separation of the copper, so that it is only the liquid in the store-tanks that will require heating by steam.

The bath after it is withdrawn from the precipitating-tanks generally contains a little copper. If, however, care be taken to leave it there till the whole of the copper is separated, the liquid will then be without action on metallic iron, and steam coils may be used to heat it in the store-tank, or in passing from this to the leach-vats it may be made to pass through a coil of iron pipe heated by a stove.

Where kilns are used for roasting, the heating of the liquors, as well as the evaporation of the excess of liquid derived from the wash-waters, may be effected in Gay-Lussac towers, which are small brick or stone chambers, tall and narrow, filled with fragments of coke or broken bricks, in which an ascending current of the hot air and sulphurous vapors meets a descending current of the liquid. The hot gases from the kiln or from a muffle may also be utilized by drawing them through a pipe from 4 to 6 inches in diameter by means of a small steam-jet introduced at the bend in an injection-pipe, which at that point should be contracted to 2 inches, and may dip 2 feet or more into the liquid in the store-tank. Such an arrangement saves steam and serves to impregnate the bath with sulphurous acid, which in its passage through the ore in the filtering-vats serves to attack the separated peroxide of iron, converting it into soluble protosalt.

The use of the sulphurous acid fumes, which thus serve to supply the losses of protochloride of iron, need not be resorted to except in treating native carbonates or oxides of copper, or such ores as contain carbonates of lime or magnesia or oxide of lead or of zinc, all of which cause a loss of the protochloride of iron. In such cases the best mode of applying the sulphurous acid is by using stirring-tanks and passing the gas over the surface of the liquid, which is agitated during the solution of the copper. The gas should be as little diluted with air as possible. If the roasting-kiln or muffle-furnace be connected with the stirring-tank by an earthenware tube which enters either the cover or the side of the tank at a point opposite to that by which a wooden tube (best connected with a flue) gives exit to the unconsumed gas, a sufficiently rapid current of the gas will be kept up, and will be readily absorbed by the liquid in the tank.

It is seldom, however, that the process is thus complicated by the necessity of using sulphurous acid gas, for unless the objectionable matters mentioned above are present in considerable quantities in the ore, this, if a sulphuret of copper, will yield by careful calcination, as already explained, enough sulphate of copper to compensate for the loss of chloride of iron which these would occasion.

By the introduction of steam for heating and of water for washing the residue, the volume of the bath becomes slowly augmented. To reduce this it is therefore necessary to resort to evaporation, and for this purpose it has been found that in the case of the three-heated reverberatory furnaces already described, the upper hearth may with advantage be used for this purpose. A shallow basin 6 inches deep, of which the upper hearth is the bottom, is built of brick lined with Roman cement prepared as already described for brick-leaching tanks, with silicate of soda and chloride of calcium. Through the middle of it passes a funnel or hopper connecting with the second hearth and opening on the roof of the furnace for the purpose of charging the ore. The roof over the pan should be higher than if it were over a calcining-hearth, in order to give ample room to use a scraper with which to remove the crystals of salt which separate during evaporation, and two doors instead of three should open at each end so as to give free access to the whole surface of the pan. Care should be taken to keep the floor of the pan free from all accumulations of salt, else a crust will be formed which is difficult to remove. When this arrangement is used, the liquors from the store-tank are run into the pan where they are exposed to the escaping current of hot air and gases by which they are rapidly evaporated, while at the same time they absorb a considerable amount of sulphuric acid, (which, together with sulphurous acid, is formed in the slow roasting of pyritous ores,) and thus become strongly acid. An evaporator of this kind, with a surface of 100 square feet, is easily and cheaply constructed, is tight and durable, and will evaporate a layer of 4 inches of liquid in 24 hours, by the waste-heat. If the three hearths are required for calcination, large shallow tanks of the kind described may be constructed between the furnaces and the stack, so that the whole current of the hot gases shall pass over the surface of the liquid, thus dispensing with the use of steam for heating the liquors and evaporating the bath at the same time.

Precipitating the copper.—The copper liquors, whether taken from the stirring or settling tanks or flowing from the leaching-vats, are received in tanks of any convenient size, where, in contact with metallic iron, the chlorides of copper are decomposed, and the copper is precipitated in crystalline grains, plates, or crusts, the texture of which will vary according to the strength of liquors. Wrought-iron precipitates the copper more rapidly than cast-iron, but where this latter is the cheaper, it should be used. If small scrap is employed, it must be spread on trays arranged in the vats. If the residue, after the extraction of the copper, is a nearly pure oxide of iron, this may be reduced to a spongy metallic iron by heating it for some hours at a red heat with pulverized coal in a closed vessel. This spongy iron, which may also be easily made from ordinary iron-ores, precipitates copper very rapidly from its solutions, and is used for that purpose in England, where it is prepared in a reverberatory furnace.

From the precipitating-vats the liquor, which has been deprived of its copper, and in this process has been recharged with protochloride of iron, is drawn off after twenty-four hours or more and pumped up into the store-tank, which should be at a higher level than the leach-vats. It is then ready for the treatment of fresh portions of ore. A working drawing of a cheap pump, made entirely of wood, is included in the plan annexed.

Melting and refining the copper.—The precipitating-tanks are emptied from time to time, the cement-copper is washed with water and, if small iron scrap has been used, is passed through a screen or sieve to separate any fragments of the latter. It is then dried at a gentle heat, when it is ready for refining. In the treatment of copper obtained in wet process it is customary to melt the cement with a portion of matte or sulphureted ore, and thus obtain a crude copper, which is refined by a second fusion. Experience on a large scale has, however, shown that the purity of the cement obtained by the present process is such that but a single fusion is required to convert it into fine copper. The dried or even the moist cement is melted down in a furnace such as is used for refining blister-copper, poled in the usual manner, and then cast into ingots. It is found advantageous to mix the cement with one or two hundredths of coal-dust, and if compressed into blocks, it can be handled with greater advantage than if in a loose powder.

Arrangement of plant.—It is well, when it can be done, to choose a hill-side as the site for works for carrying out this process, so as to place the leaching-vats below the level of the calcining-furnaces. Above these vats should be a water-tank and also a store-tank for bath, from which it can be made to flow into the vats placed in rows on the lower level. Below these should be placed the precipitating tanks, and still lower a large tank into which the bath when deprived of copper can be allowed to flow, and from which, by means of the wooden pump, it is to be pumped up into the store-tank for redistribution, thus establishing a continuous circulation. Wooden tubes securely coupled together are the best conductors for the bath. A horizontal line of such tubing should run above the leaching-vats and be connected with the store-tank by a piece of India-rubber tube or hose, which can be closed at will by a wooden squeezer. From this line of wooden tubing the bath is to be conducted to each leach-tank by an India-rubber tube, the flow through which is to be regulated by squeezers. From the leach-tanks the copper liquors should be conducted through similar India-rubber tubes into a covered trough or launder, running the whole length of the row of precipitating-vats. Such a trough is better for this purpose than a closed tube, for the reason that when the bath is too cool or does not hold a sufficient amount of salt to retain the whole of the dichloride of copper in solution, a portion of this may be deposited and fill up the tube, while the launder can be watched and this state of things guarded against.

In localities where a hill-side cannot be chosen for the site, it will be better to place both the leaching and precipitating vats on the same level with the calciners, for it is easier and cheaper to pump the copper liquors into the precipitating-tanks than to elevate tne ore. In the plan, however, for clearness of illustration, the tanks are shown on successive levels in a building of three stories.

CHEMISTRY OF THE PROCESS.

The peculiarity of this method is the use of a solution of *protochloride of iron* and chloride of sodium to render soluble the oxidized compounds of copper. In the wet process now generally adopted in Great Britain and mentioned on page 25, where the ores are calcined with common salt, this is in great part decomposed with the formation of sulphate of soda and chlorides of copper, which are, in their turn, decomposed when in solution, by contact with iron, with separation of metallic copper and production of protochloride of iron.*

The liquid thus obtained, holding an abundance of protochloride of iron with a little chloride of sodium, is found to have but a feeble solvent action upon the oxide of copper and is accordingly thrown away, polluting the rivers, and thus giving rise to serious difficulties in England. Various attempts have been made to utilize the chloride of iron in these waste liquors for chloridizing copper. Gossage patented a plan which consisted in evaporating them to dryness and heating the residue in contact with air to low redness, by which means there is obtained a mixture of insoluble peroxide and soluble *perchloride of iron*, (see page 24.) Henderson effects the same result by the action of air on the liquors at ordinary temperatures. He also, by decomposing the evaporated waste liquors at a strong red heat in contact with siliceous matters, gets perchloride of iron in vapor with some hydrochloric acid and free chlorine, and dissolves these in a solution of protochloride of iron,

* The concentrated liquid obtained by leaching the ores in this process, at Widnes, in England, gave, according to Claudet, for a liter of specific gravity 1.24, sulphate of soda, 14.41 grams; chloride of sodium, 6.39; chlorides of copper and other metals 12.75, containing chlorine 6.61, copper 5.28, zinc 0.68, lead 0.057, iron 0.045, silver 0.004, besides a little gold, and small but undetermined quantities of arsenic, antimony, and bismuth. Of the copper, 0.580 was in the state of dichloride. The silver extracted from this solution by Claudet's method, with iodine, contains about 1.3 per cent. of gold. (*Chemical News*, vol. xxii, p. 184.)

thus getting a solution of *perchloride of iron*, the solvent action of which on oxide of copper is well known. (British patent of May, 1865, No. 1255, and United States patent, December, 1866, No. 60514.)

To dispense with these tedious and costly processes and enable liquor containing *protochloride of iron* to be directly used for the solution of copper, was much to be desired. It was found that when a solution of protochloride of iron is brought in contact with either protoxide or dinoxide of copper, dichloride of copper is formed, which, being insoluble in water, soon coats over the oxide and arrests the chloridizing process. To overcome this difficulty, however, it was only necessary to add a hot and strong solution of common salt, in which (as in all other solutions of chlorides) the dichloride of copper has a considerable degree of solubility. The reactions of the two oxides of copper with protochloride of iron are unlike. Three equivalents of the protoxide, containing 95.25 of copper, when brought in contact with an excess of solution of the protochloride under the conditions just explained, react with two equivalents of it, containing 56.00 of iron, and yield one equivalent of the protochloride of copper, which is readily soluble in water, and contains 31.75 of copper and 35.50 of chlorine, and one equivalent of the insoluble dichloride, in which the same amount of chlorine is united with twice as much, or 63.50, of copper. When the copper is in the state of dinoxide, only one-half as much protochloride of iron is consumed, and there is formed for the same amount of dichloride as before one equivalent, or 31.75 of metallic copper. This would remain undissolved if the dinoxide alone were treated, but metallic copper in presence of an excess of protochloride of copper is at once converted into the dichloride, so that if one-half of the oxidized copper in a mixture treated with an excess of protochloride of iron is protoxide and one-half dinoxide, the whole of the copper passes into the state of dichloride.* For this reason it is necessary, in submitting dinoxide ores to this process, either to mix them with a sufficient amount of ores containing protoxide, or to calcine them slightly in the air, so as to convert one-half or more of the dinoxide into protoxide of copper.

In the reaction between the oxide of copper and protochloride of iron, the iron of the latter separates from the solution as a reddish-brown insoluble precipitate of hydrous peroxide, which carries with it a small portion of chlorine in the form of an oxychloride of iron, due to secondary reactions and in part to the action of the air upon the solution of protochloride of iron. The amount of chlorine thus removed, and consequently lost to the bath, was found, in carefully-conducted experiments, to vary from 5 to 10 per cent. of that originally united with the iron, that is to say, for 100 parts of protochloride of iron consumed in chloridizing copper, the regenerated bath will contain from 90 to 95 parts. This loss of chlorine must in all cases be supplied if the strength of the bath is to be kept up, an end which is readily obtained in one or two ways. When sulphureted ores are oxidized there is always formed a portion of sulphate of copper, which, with careful roasting, (page 10,) may equal one-fourth or even one-half of the copper present. This sulphate when decomposed by metallic iron gives protosulphate of

* The reactions between protochloride of iron and the oxides of copper are thus expressed in chemical symbols, using the older notation, in which Cu = 31.75, Fe = 28, Cl = 35.5, and O = 8:

For the protoxide of copper,

$$3Cu_2O_2 + 4FeCl = 2Fe_2O_3 + 2Cu_2Cl + 2CuCl.$$

For the dinoxide of copper,

$$3Cu_2O + 2FeCl = Fe_2O_3 + 2Cu_2Cl + 2Cu.$$

In the reaction between the protochloride of copper and the metallic copper,

$$2CuCl + 2Cu = 2Cu_2Cl.$$

iron, which, by its reaction with salt, yields, as we have seen in the preparation of the bath, sulphate of soda and protochloride of iron, which in ordinary cases more than suffices to supply any loss of chlorine. If, as sometimes happens, there is found too large a portion of these compounds, this may be corrected by adding to the bath, *previously freed from copper*, a small quantity of slaked lime, by which means the excess of sulphate and of iron are precipitated in the form of sulphate of lime and protoxide of iron, from which the clear liquid may be drawn or filtered off.

The bath made, as already described, with 280 pounds of copperas (equal to 56 pounds of iron) and 320 pounds of salt in 2,000 pounds of water, has a specific gravity of about 22° Beaumé or 1.150 at ordinary temperatures, water being 1.000. A cubic foot of it weighs 1,150 ounces avoirdupois, and contains 3.52 pounds of protochloride of iron (besides an equal quantity of sulphate of soda) and about 5½ pounds of salt. This amount of protochloride contains 1.54 pounds, or 10,780 grains of metallic iron, and as a cubic foot is equal to almost exactly 1,000 fluid-ounces, each fluid-ounce holds in solution 10.78 grains of iron as protochloride. By the method of assay described above, the amount of iron held in solution by a fluid-ounce of the liquid is very easily determined, and in this way the efficiency of a bath is most conveniently designated. Solutions containing 5.0 grains, and even 3.0 grains, of dissolved iron to the fluid-ounce may be used, but the strongest are most efficient.

The protochloride of iron serves to chloridize the oxide of copper in the ore. A cubic foot of bath containing 10,780 grains of dissolved iron will chloridize 18,287 grains (or 2.61 pounds) of copper in the state of protoxide, converting one-third of it into protochloride, and two-thirds of it into dichloride of copper, of which latter compound (consisting of copper 63.5, chlorine 35.5) there will be formed 29,057 grains, or about 4.15 pounds. The dichloride is insoluble in water, though readily soluble in strong brine, especially if this be heated; hence the necessity of a large excess of salt in the bath. A cubic foot of saturated brine at a temperature of 194° F. will dissolve about 10.0 pounds, and at 104° F. about 5.0 pounds of the dichloride, while a cubic foot of brine holding 15 per cent. of salt will dissolve at 194° F. 6.25 pounds, at 184° F. 3.75 pounds, and at 57° F. 2.18 pounds of dichloride of copper, and the same amount of brine holding only 5 per cent. of salt will dissolve at 198° 1.65 pounds, and at 104° 0.70 pounds of dichloride. The bath above described, with 5½ pounds of salt to the cubic foot, contains not quite 8 per cent. of salt. It will thus be understood why in some cases it may become necessary to increase the amount of salt in the bath in order to augment its solvent power for the dichloride. Both by cooling and by dilution with water the dichloride separates in the form of a white heavy crystalline powder, which is readily converted by simple contact with metallic iron into pure crystalline copper.

In treating copper ores which contain no sulphur and consequently form no soluble sulphate in roasting, the loss of the bath in chlorine may be supplied by adding, from time to time, small portions of protosulphate of iron, or still better by passing over or through the liquid in the stirring or leaching vats, as already described, (page 16,) a current of sulphurous acid gas. This, being absorbed, converts the separated hydrous peroxide of iron into a mixture of protosulphate and protosulphite of iron, at the same time liberating the combined chlorine of the oxychloride in the form of soluble protochloride.

As the protoxide of copper is a comparatively feeble base, the solutions of the protochloride are readily decomposed by the oxides of zinc and lead, which are often present in roasted ores. These cause the separation from the solutions of a green insoluble oxychloride composed of oxide and protochloride of copper, chloride of zinc or of lead being formed at the same time. In the presence of an excess of protochloride of iron this oxychloride of copper is immediately dissolved, as oxide of copper would be, but in the reaction a certain amount of chlorine is consumed in forming the chlorides of zinc and lead. An excess of oxide of copper also unites with protochloride of copper to form this oxychloride, so that in leaching ores charged with oxide, the protochloride of copper formed is at first retained in a form insoluble in water and in brine, but as it is completely dissolved in an excess of protochloride of iron, this reaction gives rise to no difficulty in working.

In like manner carbonate of lime, though without action on solutions of protochloride of iron below 212° F., readily decomposes protochloride of copper at 140° F., with separation of a similar oxychloride, which requires protochloride of iron to redissolve it. In this way the presence of carbonate of lime in copper-ore *indirectly* causes a loss of protochloride of iron, which must be supplied in one of the ways already set forth. The action of carbonate of magnesia is similar to that of the carbonate of lime. Neither these substances nor the oxides of lead or zinc separate the copper from the dichloride.

In the precipitation of the copper by metallic iron 28 parts of this metal unite with 35.5 parts of chlorine, and in so doing separate from a solution of the protochloride 31.75 of copper, and from the dichloride twice that amount. Hence to obtain 100 parts of copper from the first requires 88.2 parts, and from the second 44.1 parts of iron, while from solutions in which one-half the copper exists as protochloride and one-half as dichloride the amount of iron required will be the mean of these two, or about 66 parts for 100 of copper.

In the roasting of sulphureted copper-ores the greater part of the copper (apart from the sulphate) is obtained as protoxide, besides a variable amount of dinoxide, sometimes, according to Plattner, as much as 20 or 30 per cent. of the copper.* Such a mixture when treated in the bath gives rise, of course, to a correspondingly large amount of dichloride, which is, however, generally nearly counterbalanced by the protochloride resulting from the reaction between the sulphate of copper and the salt of the bath, so that the proportion of iron required to separate 100 parts of copper from the solution of such roasted ores varies from 60 to 70 parts. Hence the present process presents, in this respect, a great economy over the ordinary wet methods in which the precipitation of 100 parts of copper requires 100 and often 120 or more parts of metallic iron.

A solution of protochloride of copper when mixed with salt not only has the power of chloridizing and dissolving metallic copper, as already described, but readily takes up the copper from sulphureted ores, such as the vitreous and variegated species, and from copper matte or regulus, with separation of sulphur and formation of dichloride. This reaction may, in some cases, be taken advantage of by causing a hot solution, nearly saturated with salt and holding protochloride of copper, to filter through a layer of such ore or regulus in coarse powder. The metal is

*In some cases we have found in such roasted ores a portion of sulphate of dinoxide of copper. This remains when the ordinary sulphate (of protoxide) has been removed by water, and may be dissolved from the residue by a hot solution of common salt, by which this insoluble sulphate is converted into dichloride. Some copper-ores of 15 or 20 per cent. have yielded as much as 1 per cent. of copper in this form, which is of course readily soluble in the protochloride of iron bath.

rapidly taken up, and solutions obtained in which the whole of the copper is present as dichloride. In this way an additional amount of copper is dissolved and may be separated in the metallic state with very little cost. The 66 parts of iron required to precipitate 100 of copper from the ordinary solutions of mixed protochloride and dichloride will separate from solutions of pure dichloride 150 parts of copper.

WHAT ORES OF COPPER MAY BE TREATED BY THIS PROCESS.

The forms in which copper occurs in nature may be conveniently grouped in three classes, to each of which, under certain conditions, the Hunt and Douglas process may be advantageously applied.

In the first class may be included the various sulphureted ores, such as copper pyrites (often mixed with iron pyrites) and the variegated and vitreous sulphurets, all of which are readily oxidized by calcination. In addition to these are the fahl-ores, which contain, besides sulphur, arsenic and antimony. These objectionable elements by calcination are either expelled or rendered insoluble. All the above-named ores yield their copper after oxidation to the Hunt and Douglas bath. The question of the comparative fitness of this method for rich and poor ores has already been discussed on page 396.

In the second class are included the oxidized compounds of copper, such as the red and black oxides, the green and blue carbonates, salts like the oxychloride, and also silicates of copper like chrysocolla. All of these are readily attacked by the bath without previous calcination; but in the case of the red or dinoxide, as already explained above, it should either be mixed with protoxide ores or in part converted into protoxide by a slight calcination, in order to render the copper wholly soluble. The carbonates of copper, which are readily dissolved in the bath, give off their carbonic acid so as to cause frothing, to prevent which it may be well to give them a slight calcination or roasting. Heating them to low redness in a kiln or furnace for a few minutes will be sufficient to convert the carbonates into protoxide.

The common silicate of copper called chrysocolla readily gives up its copper to the bath of protochloride of iron and salt, so that its treatment, whether alone or mixed with other ores, presents no difficulty. A peculiar ore which is now treated successfully by this process at Phœnixville, Pa., is a hydrated silicate of oxide of copper with magnesia, alumina, and peroxide of iron, containing when pure about 13 per cent. of copper. This mineral, which may be described as a copper-chlorite, is readily and completely decomposed by acids, but is not attacked by the bath of protochloride of iron. To extract the copper it is treated as follows: The crude ore, which is mixed with clay and sand and carries from 3 to 6 per cent. of copper, is heated to low redness for some hours in large vertical muffles, each holding 15,000 pounds, having been previously mixed with one-tenth its weight of coal in coarse powder, by which the combined oxide of copper is reduced to the metallic state. This, on withdrawing the heated charge, is at once oxidized by the air, yielding a mixture of protoxide and dinoxide of copper, which are readily and completely removed by the subsequent operation of leaching with the Hunt and Douglas bath. The copper is chiefly dissolved in the form of dichloride, as is shown by the fact that not more than 50 parts of metallic iron are required to precipitate 100 parts of copper from the solution.

The third class includes the deposits of native or metallic copper, which in almost all instances are most advantageously treated by mechanical means. In those rare cases in which the copper is too finely divided to be thus profitably extracted, it will be found that by careful calcination at a low red heat it may be oxidized so as to become soluble in the protochloride-of-iron bath. In this, as in all other cases of non-sulphureted ores, it is, as already explained, (page 401,) indispensable to supply the loss of chlorine by the use of sulphurous-acid fumes, or by the addition from time to time of a protosalt of iron.

The presence of carbonate of lime or carbonate of magnesia in any ore is objectionable, since, as already explained, (page 406,) it decomposes the protochloride of copper, and thus indirectly precipitates the iron from the bath. The action of oxides of lead and zinc, which come from the roasting of blende and galena when these are present in the ore, produces a similar effect. When not present in too large quantities the effect of all these substances may be corrected by careful roasting, which forms a large proportion of sulphates, or by the use of sulphurous fumes, but ores containing much carbonate of lime or carbonate of magnesia are not adapted to treatment by this or any other wet process.

PRACTICAL WORKING OF THE PROCESS.

The Hunt and Douglas process, after some experimental trials, was first worked continuously for a year, in 1872–'73, at the Davidson Mine in North Carolina, under the direction of the Messrs. Clayton. The ore, a pyritous copper in a slaty gangue, was dressed up to 5 or 6 per cent., crushed to pass through a sieve of forty meshes to the linear inch, roasted in three-hearth reverberatory furnaces so as to contain about one-fourth its copper as sulphate, and treated in stirring-vats in charges of 3,000 pounds. The loss of copper in the residue was found to be from 0.3 to 0.5 per cent., and the bath maintained its strength in chloride of iron without the use of copperas or sulphurous acid. The amount of iron consumed was equal to 70 per cent., and the salt, to supply unavoidable losses, to 25 per cent. of the copper produced. These details are from a letter from the manager of the works, Mr. James E. Clayton, published in the Engineering and Mining Journal for July, 1873, from which it appears that the entire cost of producing cement-copper from the dressed ore of 5½ per cent. was estimated to be 3⅜ cents a pound.

This mine was subsequently abandoned, and the same proprietors, in 1874, erected works with six calcining-furnaces for the treatment of 12 tons of pyritous ore daily by this process at the Ore Knob Mine in Ashe County, North Carolina. Up to the 1st of January, 1875, over 200 tons of copper had there been made by this process. In the report bearing that date of the directors of the Ore Knob Company, James E. Tyson, of Baltimore, president, it is said: "From the data furnished by the superintendent in his report from the mine, and a careful estimate made here, we find the cost of making copper, mining, and all expenses included, to be less than 8 cents a pound."

These works were soon after enlarged to nearly three times their former capacity; but in sinking below the water-line in the mine the ore, hitherto free from lime, was found to contain 30 per cent. or more of carbonate of lime, with some magnesia. The direct treatment of such an ore by any moist process was impracticable, and the reduction-works were accordingly suspended pending the erection of dressing-works, in which it is proposed to concentrate the ore by crushing and washing, removing thereby the carbonate of lime of the gangue. The concentrating machinery, as we are informed by the managing director of the Ore Knob Copper Company, Mr. James E. Clayton, will be in operation in June, 1876, when it is proposed to recommence at once the treatment of the purified ores by the Hunt and Douglas process.

Reduction-works are now in successful operation at Phœnixville, Pa., where copper-ores of two kinds are treated by the Hunt and Douglas process, the first of which is a magnetic-iron ore from Berks County, Pennsylvania, containing about 3 per cent. of copper, chiefly as copper pyrites, mixed, however, with a little carbonate and silicate of copper This ore, of which 20,000 pounds are treated daily, is crushed so as to pass through a sieve of seven meshes to the linear inch, roasted as already explained on page 398, and subsequently treated by leaching. The residue, which contains about 0.5 per cent. of copper, is a rich iron-ore, which is used for lining puddling-furnaces. The second ore is the peculiar hydrated silicate described on page 407, of which 15,000 pounds are treated daily. The leached residues of this do not retain over 0.3 per cent. of copper.

The works of the Stewart Reduction Company, at Georgetown, Colo., in which this process is applied to mixtures of silver and copper ores, will be again referred to.

TREATMENT OF SILVER AND GOLD ORES.

The use of soluble compounds of copper as an agent in treating silver-ores and rendering them fit for amalgamation, has long been known, and is the basis of the Mexican patio process and its modifications, as well as of the Washoe process, now largely employed in the West. The theory of the action of the copper salts in the first of these methods, where the materials are exposed for a long time to the action of the air, is still somewhat obscure. In the Washoe method sulphate of copper and common salt are added together to the ground ore mixed with water, and from these, by the reactions which take place in the pans, dichloride of copper is soon formed. This substance dissolved in brine is used directly with advantage in the treatment of silver-ores by Janin and by Kröncke. From the results of various experiments, it is clear that solutions, both of protochloride and dichloride of copper, mixed with common salt, when at an elevated temperature, effect a complete chlorination of sulphureted and arsenical silver-ores, or at least render them susceptible of ready and complete amalgamation.

The use of the chlorides of copper as hitherto applied presents, however, several difficulties: first, the sulphate of copper from which they are generally prepared is costly, and in some places difficult to procure; second, protochloride of copper is readily decomposed and separated from hot solutions as an insoluble oxychloride by the carbonate of lime often found with the ores; third, solutions of dichloride of copper in brine very readily absorb oxygen from the air, forming, besides, protochloride of copper, also an insoluble oxychloride. These oxychlorides are without action on silver-ores, though they attack the mercury when amalgamation is attempted simultaneously with the treatment by copper salts, forming an insoluble chloride of this metal, and thereby causing a considerable loss.

To meet these objections there is needed a cheap and ready method of preparing the chlorides of copper, and a simple means of preventing their precipitation in inert or noxious forms by the action of the air or carbonate of lime. It will be apparent from the preceding account of the chemistry of the Hunt and Douglas copper process, that the use of a heated solution of protochloride of iron and salt, aided by sulphurous acid, for the solution of the oxidized compounds of copper, meets the conditions of the problem in the following manner:

1. The Hunt and Douglas bath gives readily and cheaply strong solutions of the mixed protochloride and dichloride of copper wherever carbonates, oxides, or calcined sulphureted ore of this metal can be had.

2. It dissolves the oxychlorides of copper, by whatever means produced, changing them into a mixture of protochloride and dichloride of copper, and thus prevents any deterioration of the copper solution by the action of the air or of carbonate of lime.

The Hunt and Douglas bath may be advantageously applied:*

I. To effect more cheaply and more completely the chlorination and the amalgamation of such silver-ores as are now treated in the raw state with chemicals, as they are called—that is to say, sulphate or chloride of copper with common salt.

II. To chlorinate such silver-ores as have been calcined without the addition of salt.

III. To complete the chlorination of silver-ores which have been partially chlorinated by calcining with salt, thus securing a much more complete extraction of the silver than has hitherto been attained.

In all of these cases it will be understood that some oxidized form of copper, such as carbonate, native oxide or calcined sulphureted ore, is to be added, unless it is already present in the silver-ore to be treated. It may be added even in large quantities with advantage, and from the solutions charged with copper a portion, or the whole of this metal, may be precipitated from time to time by metallic iron as cement copper.

In localities where salts of iron are not readily obtained, and where sulphur-ores are abundant, it will be found that by passing sulphurous-acid gas into or over a solution of salt holding pulverized oxide or carbonate of copper in suspension, a solution of dichloride of copper will be readily formed, and this reaction may be rendered available for this treatment of silver-ores. By precipitating the copper solution thus obtained with metallic iron, protochloride of iron is at once readily and cheaply obtained.

Silver-ores chlorinated by the Hunt and Douglas bath may be subsequently treated, either by dissolving the silver from the washed residues by a solution of hyposulphite or of chloride of sodium, or by amalgamation. The use of mercury is to be preferred for ores holding, besides silver, a portion of gold. Such ores should be treated with the bath in the raw state, or after simple calcination, roasting with salt being for them objectionable.

United States letters-patent (No. 151,763) for the use of the Hunt and Douglas bath of protochloride of iron and common salt, conjointly with sulphurous acid, for the treatment of silver-ores, or silver and gold ores, mixed with oxidized ores of copper, were granted June 9, 1874, to James Douglas, jr., Thomas Sterry Hunt, and James Oscar Stewart. This process has now been most successfully applied for more than a year on a large scale in the working of silver-ores by Mr. Stewart, who will publish in the course of the summer of 1876 a detailed description of the method as adapted by him to various kinds of silver-ores. Copies of this (and also of the present pamphlet) may be had by addressing J. Oscar Stewart, Georgetown, Colo.

* Later observations show that this process may be advantageously applied to the treatment of the tellurides of silver and gold.

CHAPTER XIV.

EXPERIENCE WITH THE STETEFELDT FURNACE.

BY A. D. HODGES, JR.

These notes refer to the years 1871 and 1872, and to the Auburn Mill, situated at Reno, Nev. During that time the mill treated ores of the most varied nature and from very different localities. If an ore was considered very "rebellious" it was sent to the Auburn Mill for treatment, while more easily-worked material was kept at home. Large supplies were drawn from Utah, but the rise in the railroad freight tariff in the winter of 1871–'72 interfered materially with the shipments of the lower grades of ores, the increase in the freight charge being sufficient to counterbalance the small profit previously derived from such ores. From Humboldt County, Nevada, and from various places along the line of the Central Pacific Railroad, considerable amounts were derived. Very rich ore, running from $400 to $900 per ton, was received from Mono County, California. This was the partzite or stetefeldtite ore of which so much has been said. The most distant locality from which shipments were made was British Columbia, whence one lot of 20 tons was received.

The Utah ore held often considerable chloride of silver with oxidized silver, lead, minerals, and generally lime. This class of ore was the most difficult to treat. Ores (as much from Humboldt County) with quartz gangue and considerable sulphurets (of lead and zinc) worked well. The stetefeldtite ore, although causing some trouble with the men on account of the dust, which was claimed to be worse than from the usual run of rock, always roasted very well.

The general plan of working was this: The ore was broken in a Blake crusher, and carefully sampled for assay. It was then dried on the dry kiln on which was spread first the required amount of salt—from 6 to 10 per cent.; crushed under the stamps; carried in mechanical conveyers to the furnace and roasted; and, finally, amalgamated in Wheeler pans.

The plant of the mill was as follows: 1 Blake crusher; 20 stamps of 750 pounds each; 1 Stetefeldt furnace, with dry kiln, &c.; 12 small Wheeler pans; 6 settlers; 2 agitators; boiler; retort; overshot water-wheel of 28 feet diameter and 16 feet face, calculated to furnish 108 horse-power.

The ditch from the Truckee River is some two miles long, built to be 4 feet deep, 8 feet wide at the top and 6 feet wide at the bottom, with a fall of $\frac{3}{16}$ inch to the rod, and calculated to carry 4,000 inches of water per minute.

Sampling.—For sampling, the ore was crushed to a uniform size in the Blake crusher, and spread out evenly on the floor to a depth of 8 to 10 inches. Cuts of the width of a shovel were run through the pile in two directions and about 4 feet apart; from the ore obtained from these cuts another similar pile being made, and this being continued until a pile of about 100 pounds is obtained. The ore is now again crushed, spread out and reduced as before, until the amount is brought down to 20 or 30 pounds.

This is then taken to the assay-office, crushed fine, and resampled down to about one pound. Some of the customers preferred sampling from the battery, which was done when requested. But a battery sample never gave higher results than the other, and often somewhat lower ones. In case there are malleable minerals of the precious metals present, it is easy to see why the battery sample should be the poorer.

Crushing—The battery stamps weighed 750 pounds when new, had a fall of 8 inches, and dropped about 80 times per minute. The screens were No. 55 wire. The batteries were single discharge.

General experience teaches, I take it, that the most rapid crushing by stamps is effected when only sufficient ore is kept in the mortar to prevent the shoe and die from coming in contact. But one battery-feeder at this mill persisted in keeping the mortars so full that the foreman was in constant expectation of the choking of the batteries. Yet from this cause the stamps were hung up only once, and this feeder crushed 1½ tons to the stamp where no other feeder had been able to put through more than a ton.

The furnace.—The Stetefeldt furnace is 28 feet high and 4½ feet square at the base. It is of the old pattern, with two fire-places for wood at the base and one at the flue, using the old form of feeder—two simple wire screens. It was built in 1869, and although cracked a little by earthquake action, has stood the wear and tear extremely well, having needed no repairs of any consequence.

The amount of ore roasted daily was in practice 16 tons. Unquestionably the furnace will treat more, but during the time alluded to this was all which the batteries would crush, one battery of four stamps being hung up for repairs nearly all the time.

On each shift of twelve hours three workmen were employed, one tending the feeding apparatus, one firing, and one drawing out the roasted pulp, and wheeling it to the pans. Whites were employed for a long time, at $3 per day, but afterward Chinamen.

The amount of salt used averaged in practice 8 per cent., but this was undoubtedly in excess of what was needed in many cases, and may possibly have been injurious in the subsequent amalgamation. When the furnace was kept running night and day an average of 1½ cords per twenty-four hours was consumed, slab-wood answering all purposes. A charge was drawn every hour. The roasting expenses, when running on full time, may be given as follows, taking as data the actual work done at the Auburn Mill. Chinese labor is referred to:

2 firemen, at $2	$4 00
4 feeders and dischargers, at $1.75	7 00
8 per cent. salt=2,560 pounds, at 1½ cents	38 40
1½ cords of wood, at $5	7 50
Total expenses for 24 hours	56 50

or $3.56 per ton.

Roasting results.—With careful management this furnace gave excellent results. The chief requisites were: regular firing, sufficient heat, and controlling assays. In practice, it was found that the Chinese firemen maintained a more regular temperature than did the whites. So far as my experience went, the best results were obtained when the heat was as great as possible without causing the ore to cake. But the temperature must remain constant. Under these conditions the largest proportions of the base metals are volatilized. Any intelligent foreman, who is willing to be guided by assays and not from immature guesses can easily learn to manage the furnace.

With our workmen it is not possible to employ as high a heat in reverberatory furnaces—principally on account of the caking of the ore—as can be safely used in the Stetefeldt furnace. The advantages of high heat are that the base metals are more speedily and completely volatilized and oxidized, thus securing a finer bullion, the silver is more fully chloridized, and I have reason to believe an economy in salt can be secured. From the working at the Auburn Mill I was convinced that an unnecessary amount of this material was used. In reverberatories, for mechanical reasons, an excess of salt is requisite. But in the Stetefeldt furnace, not only is a good mixture of the salt and the ore easily obtained at the outset and maintained thereafter, but the whole of the chloridizing reagents as vapor come in most intimate contact with the fine ore-dust descending the shaft. My opinion as to the possible economy in salt has been confirmed by the results since obtained at the Surprise Mill at Panamint. Here, with base ores assaying $75 to $90 per ton, 2½ per cent. of salt was found sufficient to give a chlorination of 92 per cent., and in practice only 2¾ to 3 per cent. was used.

With a high heat in treating lead-ores, the bullion at the Auburn Mill was seldom under 600 fine. In reworking the tailings, (without roasting,) the bullion was often only 75 to 80 fine, but afterward Mr. Riotte, I am given to understand, by first roasting these tailings, raised the fineness to over 500. At Panamint the bullion produced from "rather base" ores was from 960 to 980 fine. In experimenting with these ores and roasting them at a low temperature, bullion only 300 to 500 fine was obtained.

The lots of ore worked at the Auburn Mill being of very varied character, the furnace was thoroughly tested as to its chloridizing capabilities. It in practice chloridized the silver to from 85 to 96½ per cent. The most difficult ores to treat were the oxidized ores containing lime. These needed an addition of sulphur in some form, but without this 85 per cent. was always obtained when proper care was exercised, the percentage rising from this to 88 or 89.

The best form in which to supply sulphur when required is that of pyrites. Mr. Stetefeldt has assured me that in common practice 1 to 1½ per cent. is sufficient. When pyrites cannot be obtained, Kustel's method of burning sulphur outside of the furnace and conducting the fumes into the shaft would appear to be a good one.

Ores containing oxide and peroxide of manganese seem to give good chloridizing results even without sulphur. Cupriferous ores have generally given very good results. A considerable portion of the copper is volatilized. Mr. O. Hoffman found that with an ore assaying 12 per cent. in copper 22 per cent. of this metal volatilized into the condensing chambers, 10 per cent. remained as chloride and subchloride, and the balance turned into oxide. I have found at times much larger percentages volatilized.

Ores containing lead are generally considered the most difficult to roast, yet we obtained very good results. The main trouble was the caking of the mass at the bottom of the furnace. With a constant and strong heat from 10 to 50 per cent. is volatilized. Ore containing 8 to 10 per cent. of lead (as sulphide) gave me the highest results of any treated. A lot of 40 tons of this kind chloridized to an average of 94½ per cent., commencing at 90½, then rising to 95, and reaching 96½. This average is the one obtained from all the numerous tests made of the samples taken for the guidance of the foreman. It may be relied on, and is, I think, as good an average as can be shown anywhere. Mr. Hoffman found that the addition of a little charcoal prevented any caking of ores rich in lead, the charcoal exercising only a mechanical action.

Ores containing 10 per cent. of zincblende, and even more, have been worked without trouble. Of the 40 tons just spoken of, about three-quarters, if I remember aright, contained 9 to 10 per cent. of zincblende, and had been sent to us because the shipper had failed to get any satisfactory results previously. (These figures are from memory. My notes and assays here are lost.) Another lot holding a large percentage of zincblende chloridized to over 90 per cent.

The fine dust in the flues was always well chloridized. The ores shipped to the mill generally held no gold, but a few tests with rock holding a little of this metal showed as much gold in the flue-dust as in the shaft-pulp. The percentage extracted I do not now remember. I have been told by Mr. Stetefeldt that in comparative tests made at Twin River from ore roasted in his furnace about 85 per cent. of the gold was obtained, while from the same ore roasted in a common reverberatory furnace only about one-quarter of this amount was extracted.

Amalgamation.—The amalgamation of the ores did not correspond with the results obtained in the furnace. In some instances very good returns were obtained, and I think that a lot of 100 tons, worked for the Mineral Hill Company, yielded considerably more than 85 per cent. of the assay-value. But the general yield was not over 80 per cent.

This result was due evidently to the imperfect working of the pans. The pulp was hardly ever of the proper consistency, being too thick in the commencement and too thin at the end. The charges were worked for six hours generally, in small Wheeler pans holding about 800 pounds. There was often a deficiency of quicksilver, and the pans were usually in poor condition. One reason for this state of affairs was the existence of a board of trustees in London, which tried to manage the mill from that distance, and considered it economy to spend nothing in the way of repairs or quicksilver.

The tailings often showed 10 to 15 per cent., and more, of the silver in them as a chloride. Whenever there was a lack of ore and a sufficiency of quicksilver, they were worked over, but as no account of the amounts was kept, I can give no percentages. Mr. Riotte has since worked these tailings, roasting them before amalgamating, and can probably give interesting results. I understand that he extracted about 80 per cent. of the assay-value, and obtained a bullion 500 to 700 fine.

The amalgamation results have been better in other mills, as at Austin and Panamint, so far as I can learn. At Panamint, the extraction by amalgamation was generally 2 per cent. below the chlorination. At Austin, the results have been less regular, for some reasons unknown to me, sometimes even exceeding the chlorination, sometimes falling 5 per cent., and in one case, July, 1874, nearly 9 per cent. lower.

It would seem very probable that humid extraction might profitably replace amalgamation in connection with this furnace. With this view I made a few tests of several tons at the Auburn Mill, and obtained favorable results as regards yield and fineness of bullion produced. Similar results have attended like experiments at Austin. But I believe that amalgamation is still retained universally north of the Mexican boundary.

One point more I mention with considerable hesitation. Out of three tests, two showed the presence of silver in the water coming from the pans. I have no knowledge of silver having been found thus in solution at other mills. I mention the fact here merely to call attention to the matter. At the time *a large amount of salt*—10 per cent. I think—was being used with the ore. I commenced a series of experiments subsequently in order to test the subject, but the mill was closed down, and in the excitement attendant on the occasion the sheriff managed to get hold of the vessels holding the test-liquor, and, by upsetting them, upset the experiment very effectually.

Expenses.—What the cost of working ore at the Auburn Mill actually was I am unable to state. The receipt of custom ore was very irregular, the mill was out of repair, so that only a part of the machinery could be run steadily, and the tailings were worked and reworked without any account of the amounts being kept. Still I will venture on an estimate of what could be done at this mill, based on the following general data, and applicable to conditions then actually existing:

The mill works rich custom ore at an average of 16 tons per day. It is situated about two miles from the railroad. The ore is received in small lots, keeping the assayer busy. The superintendent is obliged to travel considerable of the time in quest of ore, thus requiring a book-keeper.

General expenses include salary and traveling expenses of the superintendent, salaries and expenses of a book-keeper, a foreman, a hostler, a horse and wagon, and the office.

Assaying: An assayer, assistant, and assay-office.

Hauling: 2 teamsters, 2 wagons, and 6 horses.

Sampling and crushing: 4 samplers and dryers, 2 battery-feeders, castings, oil, &c.

Roasting: As before given.

Amalgamating: 2 amalgamators, 2 retorters and boiler-men, 1 blacksmith, fuel, castings, quicksilver, oil and lights, general repairs.

The cost of working per ton may be estimated as follows:

General	$2 40	Roasting	$3 56
Assaying	1 23	Amalgamating	4 37
Hauling	92		
Sampling and crushing	1 52	Total	14 00

Modifications of the furnace.—The furnace at Reno has always been very successful, although the first built. In furnaces constructed after this, some modifications have been made which it may be of interest to name in this connection.

The next furnaces after the one at Reno were those at Austin, Mineral Hill, White Pine, Belmont, Pioche, Pinto, and Troy. These were furnished with gas-generators, (in place of the simple wood fire-places,) and it was at first intended that charcoal alone should be used in these as fuel. But at Austin it was found more economical to use wood, cut in small pieces, together with the charcoal, in the proportion of one or two of wood to one of charcoal. It was found also that the use of wood in this manner gave with some ores better chloridizing results, an effect attributed to the generation of steam in the fire-gases, and thus a better formation of HCl. But although the generators always produced a steady heat and a good clear flame when properly managed, yet the difficulty of handling them with unskilled labor and the inability of the management in many cases led to a general return to the simpler wood-grate. At Austin, no trouble was experienced, and the gas-generators were retained, so far as I can learn.

Then, the grate for wood fires was placed lower than before, and an air slit introduced above the arch of the fire-place, so as to effect a complete burning of the flame, and introduce an excess of oxygen for desulphurizing purposes. Thus, I am told, with proper care, as regular a fire is obtained as from the gas-generators.

Still later, the height of the shaft was increased 10 feet where the ores worked were very base. The latest plan I know of shows a distance of 26½ feet from the fire-bridge to the top of the shaft. An automatic feeder, now generally used, dispenses with the labor of one man per shift.

In order to cheapen the construction, one fire-place only is built for small furnaces—those with a capacity of about 16 tons. The furnace at Belmont was constructed in this manner, and, I am told, gives good results as to the chloridizing action, but with the effect of driving the descending ore rather too much to the opposite side of the shaft, so that it descends somewhat unevenly. A similar furnace near Homansville, Tintic District, Utah, is said to do very good work. Still I am inclined to believe that the economy in construction and fuel will, in the long run, be counterbalanced by a more imperfect furnace-action.

The size of the auxiliary fire-place has been increased so as to obtain a higher heat here and a more perfect chlorination of the finest dust. A sample of this very fine dust, taken from the bottom of the draught-chimney at the Surprise Mill, Panamint, was chloridized to 96 per cent.

The last modification of which I have heard is an automatic discharge, by means of which the ore is kept hot a longer time at the bottom of the shaft, and none is withdrawn which has but recently dropped down the furnace.

In conclusion, I add a few examples of the working of the furnace, which I hope may be of some interest.

Mill.	Location.	Date.	Tons treated daily.	Total tons worked.	Chlorination percentages.			Authorities.
					Highest.	Lowest.	Average.	
Manhattan	Austin..	January to August, 1874	27¼	4, 351¼	*91. 7	*89. 0	90. 4	A. Trippel.
		January to Sept'r, 1875..	......	....	92. 8	89. 8	91. 3	
Surprise...	Panamint.	1875 to 1876	23	5, 000	96. 2	89. 0	92. 0	C. Weberling.
Auburn...	Reno	October, 1872............	16	40	96. 5	90. 5	94. 5	A. D. Hodges, jr.

* Monthly averages.

PART III.

MECHANICAL.

CHAPTER XV.

KROM'S CRUSHING AND CONCENTRATING APPARATUS.

Repeated allusions have been made in this series of reports to the concentrator invented by Mr. Stephen R. Krom, of New York, in which the medium employed is air. Impressed by the ingenuity, perseverance, and earnestness with which Mr. Krom has for many years pursued this branch of ore-dressing, and deeming his machine the best of its kind now before the public, while I did not fully admit the theoretical argument by which he sought to prove the inherent superiority of air to water as a medium of ore-dressing, I invited him to furnish an account of his whole system for this report. It was my purpose to accompany it with a critical analysis from the theoretical standpoint; but this I have had no opportunity to prepare; and I therefore publish Mr. Krom's statements and claims without comment, though some of them call in question propositions laid down in my former reports, chiefly on the authority of Rittenger. The subject will be discussed by Mr. Althaus in the reports on the Centennial Exposition, where Krom's machinery was exhibited and received an award.

With regard to the system of crushing introduced by Mr. Krom, I know but little in the way of practical experience. Of course his concentrator demands dry crushing, if the cost of drying the wet-crushed ore is to be avoided—to say nothing of the difficulty of so drying the pulp that it will behave properly in the air-concentrator. The superiority in dry-crushing of rolls over stamps has often been claimed; but the results of practice have seemed to leave the matter in doubt—principally on account of the unequal wear of the rolls. If Mr. Krom's graving and facing of his rolls obviate the difficulties heretofore experienced with that form of crusher, no doubt he can use them to advantage. But the merits of his concentrator, which are great, do not depend upon the other machinery which he sells in connection with it.

CRUSHING.

An ore to be concentrated must be granular instead of pulverized, and any system of crushing which diminishes the percentage of dust or "slimes" to the minimum amount, is the proper one to adopt.

The subject will be understood by a study of the following figures:

Ores from rollers, crushed to pass 100-mesh screen to the square inch, give:

Granular grains	88 to 90 per cent.
Flour and dust (which will pass screen of 10,000 meshes to square inch)	12 to 10 per cent.

And ores from rollers crushed to pass a screen with $\frac{5}{32}$-inch holes give:

Granular grains	92 per cent.
Dust passing screen of 10,000 meshes to square inch	8 per cent.

And according to Kustel (following Rittenger) wet crushing under stamps, through $\frac{5}{32}$-inch holes, gives:

Sand		32 per cent.
Flour	32 per cent.	68 per cent.
Dust	36 per cent.	

Again,

"The average loss at large of poor argentiferous ores in concentration by water is with

Coarse sands .... 40 per cent.
Middle fine .... 35 per cent.
Slimes .... 60 to 70 per cent."

From the above it will be seen that rollers produce in crushing through $\frac{5}{32}$-inch holes 8 per cent. of flour and dust, and that stamps produce in similar coarse crushing 68 per cent. of flour and dust, and that the loss in dust and flour is very much greater than in the coarse grades, amounting in *wet concentration* from 60 to 70 per cent.; or, to substitute data furnished by the dry concentration works at Star Cañon, Nevada, the tailings, from low grade De Soto ore, gave the following:

Coarse tailings, per ton	$3 23
Middle fine tailings, per ton	3 67
Fine tailings, per ton	8 00

It will therefore be observed that the finest grades of crushed ore are the most difficult to concentrate and in which the greatest loss occurs, and that, moreover, the very finest portion of the crushed product cannot be concentrated by any mechanical means whatever, as it is well known that some portions will float in the air, and a *much greater portion* will remain suspended in water. For example:

"Battery sands, crushed through a No. 6 slot screen, contain on an average of slimes which remain suspended after three minutes' rest in still water, 19 per cent."—(*Commissioner Raymond's Report of* 1873, page 332.)

It will not be necessary to further elaborate the subject, as it is well known that concentration depends on the difference of specific gravity, and that when ore is crushed so fine as practically to have lost its specific gravity, concentration is impracticable.

From the above statement it will be manifest that a granular condition of the ore is absolutely essential to concentrate with any degree of success, and our aim must be to employ the kind of machinery which will produce the least amount of floating dust.

It seems hardly necessary to explain the fact why rolls produce so small a percentage of dust in comparison with that from the stamp-mill, since the reason is obvious; the jaw-crusher, and also the rolls, when properly applied, simply break up the ore, and all particles which are fine enough fall immediately away, receiving no further crushing; whereas, in the use of the stamp-mill, the blows continue to fall on some portions after they are already too fine, simply because the manner in which the crushed particles escape from further blows is mostly accidental rather than positive. The stamps may fall repeatedly on the same particles after they are already fine enough, because the splashing which the fall of the stamp produces may not carry such at once through the screen.

Aside from the fact *that stamps are totally unfit for the purpose of preparing ore for concentration*, it is doubtful whether their use is advisable under *any* circumstances; but my purpose would be accomplished in showing in what manner ores should be crushed for concentration, and the proper machinery for the purppse. I shall, however, go a step further and institute a comparison in the matter of cost between the two systems of crushing, viz, wear and tear and power consumed, in order that the question of economy shall also be demonstrated and understood.

In regard to the wear, breakages, and power consumed in crushing with stamps, and other features incident to their use, I take some data from United States Commissioner Raymond's report of 1873, page 330, and report of 1874, page 179.

"A shoe lasts from 21 to 43 days—on an average 33 days—crushing 79 tons of rock. Wear, $1\frac{1}{3}$ pounds of iron per ton of rock. The die lasts on an average 7 weeks, crushing 100 tons; wear, $\frac{6}{10}$ pound of iron per ton of rock. The stem breaks generally square across the fiber near the upper face of the head, and wears, without breaking, about 60 weeks, crushing 864 tons. When the irons are new and of fine quality, the breakages are rarer, occurring, perhaps, but once in 120 weeks. The rewelding, including the necessary new iron, costs on an average $10. The stems, as well as the cams, last at least ten years. The battery-linings last six months. The tappets from two to three years.

It is seen, therefore, that shoe and die crush on an average $89\frac{1}{2}$ tons of ore, and the wear of the iron from shoe and die average $1\frac{3}{4}$ *pounds per ton of ore crushed;* but only about $\frac{2}{3}$ of the actual weight of shoe and die is worn in use. So, taking into account the portion cast aside with the portion worn, the consumption of iron amounts to 3 pounds per ton of ore crushed.

Again, the data furnished by Professor Trippel, found in Commissioner Raymond's Report of 1874, page 197, supply reliable statistics of the wear of stamps when crushing hard quartz:

Krom's Laboratory Crusher.

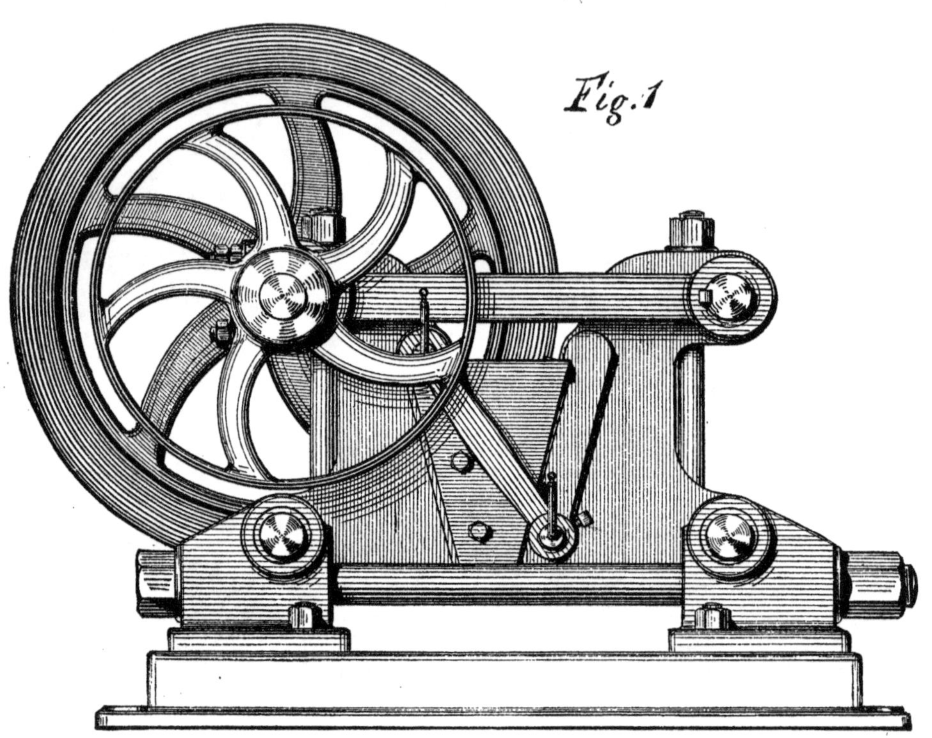

Fig. 1

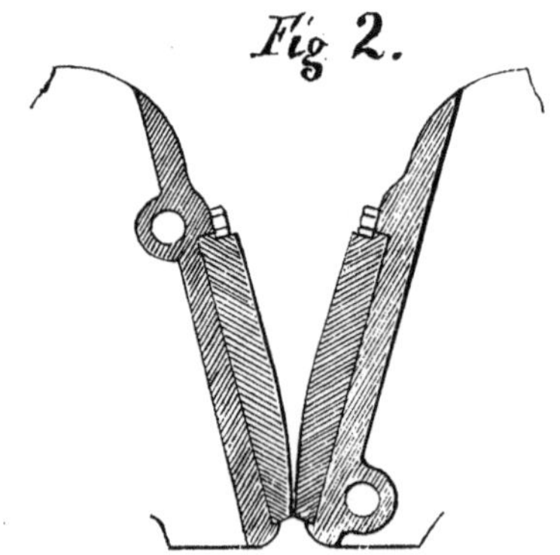

Fig 2.

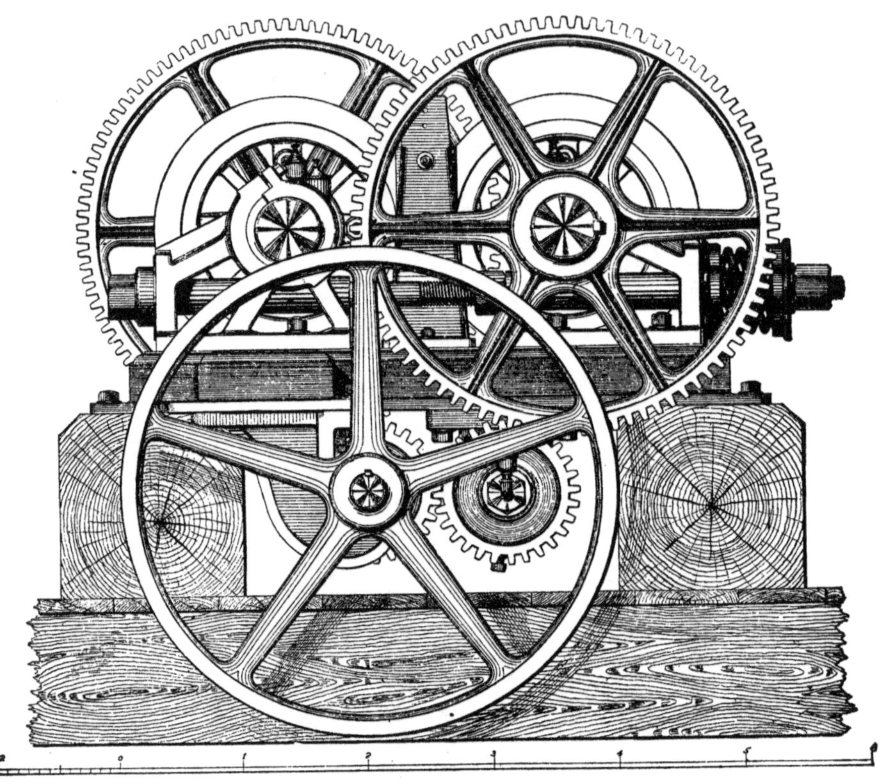

KROM'S STEEL CRUSHING-ROLLS

Manhattan Mill milling expenses per ton of raw ore.

1873.	Labor.	Fuel.	Supplies.	Quicksilver.	Salt.	Official labor.	Castings.	Hauling.	Average total.
January	$10 04	$10 32	$1 71	$3 33	$3 28	$1 02	$1 94	$1 36	$33 00
February	11 34	10 94	2 20	3 35	3 28	2 00	2 36	1 74	37 21
March	11 88	9 50	2 27	3 05	2 69	1 65	2 60	2 12	35 76
April	8 45	10 84	2 28	2 44	2 56	1 16	2 46	1 88	32 07
May	8 16	9 14	1 96	2 25	3 37	97	2 05	1 17	28 09
June	8 17	8 75	1 89	2 32	2 21	1 00	1 99	98	27 31
July	8 40	9 13	2 05	2 65	2 64	1 22	1 67	1 33	29 09
August	8 84	10 03	2 08	2 75	2 52	92	1 56	1 10	29 80
September	8 92	11 11	2 23	2 74	2 98	88	1 64	94	31 44
October	9 52	11 47	1 90	2 67	2 73	93	1 65	98	31 85
						average cost.	1 99		

Professor Trippel estimates the proportion of the cost due to crushing alone to be 85 *cents* per ton. And others estimate the *cost* with stamps, in wear, at 50 cents per *ton*, the wear and cost, of course, varying with the hardness of the ore.

Krom's laboratory crusher.—The accompanying view represents a crusher for laboratory use.

In this machine (unlike any other) both jaws oscillate on centers, fixed some distance from the crushing faces.

The principal feature is the employment of segments of circles, between which the ore is crushed on the same principle as rollers act.

It will be seen (Fig. 2) that the lower ends of the crushing-plates are true segments of circles, and throughout all the movement of the jaws they remain at fixed distances from each other, but the top part of the plates recede from each other with straight lines. The crusher can be adjusted, by means of the bolts, so as to produce either fine or coarse crushing.

It is the only machine in the market adapted for laboratory use.

Rolls.—Before describing the crushing-rolls, shown in the accompanying drawing, I will add, as before intimated, some more facts regarding the efficiency of rolls for crushing ores, and the qualities desirable in them. I speak of the rolls as more applicable for completing the crushing of the ore as it comes in small pieces from the jaw-breaker. For such purpose no other style or kind of machine can be equal to them, when properly constructed; since, first of all, my rolls not only bring into contact, within a given space of time, the largest amount of crushing surface, but also present this in the best manner to the material.

The efficiency of any machine for the crushing of ore depends, in general—first, on the condition in which it leaves the crushed product; secondly, on the durability of the crushing surfaces; and thirdly, on the rapidity with which it will perform the work. Rolls, by acting not to pulverize, but simply to break up finely, the previously divided material, leave the latter in the best possible condition for concentration, while they present surfaces as little liable to wear rapidly or unevenly, as any other form of crushing faces; and, the movement being continuous and rapid in one direction—so that there is no *loss motion*—the result is to secure crushing of the largest amount of ore, in a given time, and with the greatest economy.

In a similar manner to that in which the jaw-crusher operates so effectually on large pieces of ore, do the rolls act on small fragments; namely, as fast as the material becomes reduced fine enough to pass between the jaws, or in the small space left between the faces of the rolls, it immediately falls away, and receives no further comminution. Not so, however, with the stamp-mill, which continues to crush long after a large portion of the particles are already too fine; because, in it, the fine material escapes from the action of the stamps rather by accident than by any positive and certain means.

I will also call attention to the superior qualities in rolls not found in the jaw-crushers. It will be understood that in the latter all the ore must pass through the narrow opening at the bottom of the jaw; and the principal wear is at this point. It will be near enough correct to say that the last inch performs the final crushing before leaving the machine, and that the principal wear of the jaw is as indicated by the irregular lines. Assuming, then, that the last inch of the jaw controls the quantity delivered, we have, in a crusher 7 x 10 at the delivery point, 10 square inches, and this multiplied by the number of bites per minute, viz, 250, makes 2,500 square inches per minute of surface at the limit of delivery. Calculating the same for rolls we have in the circumference of 26-inch rolls $81\frac{9}{10}$ inches; this by 15 inches, the width of the face, equals 1,228 square inches in the surface of the roll, and this by the number of revolutions per minute (50) amounts to 61,425 square inches of crushing surface per minute in 26-inch rolls, as against only 2,500 in a jaw crusher of 7 x 10, running 250 revolutions per minute. Then, again, but a small proportion of the jaw or jaw-plates can be utilized, as shown by the irregular line of wear, viz, less than $\frac{1}{4}$ of the weight of the metal, whereas such rolls as herein described, over 80 per cent. of the steel tires is utilized. It will therefore be quite apparent that in all cases where the ore is not larger than say $1\frac{1}{2}$ inch in size, rolls should be used in preference to any other machine; and, for very extensive operations, the employment of rolls capable of taking pieces larger than $1\frac{1}{2}$ inch would be more economical than jaws.

Great economy, not to speak of other advantages, will be found in employing rolls of considerable size; since not only do such present the best form of surfaces for acting on the ore, but with them, also, the renewal of the surfaces will be less frequently required, on account of the large amount of material in them to wear upon, and thus trueing will be less frequently required.

The improved patented rolls, the employment of which I recommend, and which are herewith illustrated, may be described briefly, as follows:

1. First in importance is the improvement in the crushing-faces themselves. These consist of steel tires or rings, manufactured expressly for the purpose. It is confidently believed that these steel crushing-faces will continue to give the greatest satisfaction, because the material made use of is more tough and even in its texture than any heretofore employed for the purpose, and the wear of the faces, consequently, more even; and when, in the course of time, these do become worn uneven, the steel is not, as is the case with chilled surfaces, so hard as to prevent its being turned true again. The steel tires described are fitted to inner rings, or hubs, as clearly shown in the drawing, and with the aid of the tool (see Fig. 3 and 4) for keeping the rolls true they may be worn to $\frac{1}{2}$ inch in thickness before being cast off.

Chilled or hard rolls, when (as they will become in a short time) uneven by use, must be thrown aside, and that although but a small part of the thickness has been worn in actual service; and since the rings must in any case be about 3 inches thick, to have to cast them aside because already too uneven for further profitable use, when only about $\frac{1}{4}$ inch of the surface has been worn away, is evidently to subject the operator to frequent and very considerable expense and delay. And so it will clearly be seen that, by the employment of any material that will last equal to chilled or Franklinite iron, at the same time that it allows of turning true when uneven, and admits also of being worn quite thin before being cast aside, a really considerable margin is at once secured for the introduction, at the beginning, of crushing-faces that are in themselves more expensive. Therefore, although the first cost of steel faces is greater, there is great economy from their use. Still another point here, which should not be overlooked, is the fact of the great disadvantage of employing any material (such as chilled iron) that in wear must go from bad to worse in unevenness, until wholly unfit for use; that is, being obliged to use an imperfect roll for a long time before it can be put aside as entirely worthless.

2. The second improvement consists in the employment of steel shafts of large diameter, to prevent any spring or bending of the journal, and also to give a large bearing-surface, for enduring the great pressure on the journals. The shafts themselves, in the 26-inch roll, are $7\frac{3}{4}$ inches, and the journals $6\frac{1}{4}$ inches in diameter by 14 inches in length.

3. The improvement next to be considered is in the manner of gearing. Each of the rolls is driven, independently, by two 40-inch gear-wheels; which, again, receive their motion from two 13-inch pinions, secured upon the main shaft; one of the latter, that is to say, driving the 40-inch wheel on one side of the machine, and the other, on the opposite side, through an intermediate wheel, driving the second 40-inch wheel. The intermediate wheel, seen in Fig. 1 below and at the right, turns on a heavy pin, which is so arranged as to allow it to be lowered at pleasure. Accordingly, when the rolls wear, upon dropping the intermediate wheel, the movable roll (that to the right in the figure) can be drawn toward the fixed one (that to the left) by screwing upon the tie-bolts; and, the rolls having been thus again adjusted, the intermediate wheel is then also adjusted, to mesh properly with the large wheel. The left-hand roll, remaining stationary, is consequently at all times in proper gear; so that, by being able to adjust the right-hand roll, we secure perfect-fitting gear in all stages of the wear to which the rolls are subjected.

4. Another advantage is secured in the use of the cast-iron cups, which I have provided, placed under the nuts or heads of the tie-bolts; so that in case any undue strain should occur, as from the falling of iron, &c., between the rolls, these cups will first break, and thus prevent accidents otherwise possible, in the way of straining or

fracturing of some important part of the machine. Duplicate cups also are provided for such an emergency. I deem this an important improvement over the employment of rubber springs and weighted levers; since, while accidents are not very liable to occur, we by this means secure evenness of crushing, and save in time by crushing the ore at once, instead of being obliged to pass and repass through the rolls the same material; but when considered advisable springs may be employed, as shown in the figures. The importance of having rolls immovable when doing their regular and legitimate work, and also having them as true as possible, will be understood when we remember that all the ore which passes the rolls not crushed fine enough must pass over the screen and return to the rolls again—perhaps over and over again. Of course any unevenness or moving back of the rolls allows the material to pass untouched, and the screens, which are the most expensive to keep in repair, are worn out for no purpose, as well as the mill generally. The fact is, the very best machinery for crushing, and also for screening and concentrating, with the very best mechanical skill to operate the same, will be sure to pay the largest dividends.

5. The wrought-iron tie-bolts take all the strain due to crushing the ore, thereby securing the greatest strength with the least weight.

6. The sixth improvement consists in mounting the whole machine on a substantial cast frame, serving in a manner to render the machine complete within itself.

In addition to such improvements in the machine, I have provided, to be attached to the latter, a slide-rest, which, whenever the steel rings become worn uneven, is brought into use for turning them true again.

Durability of steel crushing-rolls.—Regarding the durability of steel crushing-rolls, although limited data can be furnished, as their introduction is of recent date, yet the data furnished indicate clearly the value and economy in using steel rolls. It was found, after crushing 2,000 tons of hard quartz at the dry concentrating-works at Star Cañon, Nevada, employing two sets of steel rolls, that their faces had worn one-quarter of an inch, reducing the diameter of the rolls one-half inch.

The steel tires are 26 inches in diameter, by 15 face, and 2½ inches thick, consequently—

	Pounds.
¼ inch wear on each tire equals	85½
¼ inch wear on four tires equals	342

Therefore, in crushing 2,000 tons of hard quartz, 342 pounds of steel were consumed, equal to $\frac{17}{100}$ pounds per ton of quartz crushed. At the same rate of wear the tires of two sets of rolls will crush 13,000 tons of quartz to pass through a 10-mesh screen to the linear inch.

As the tires (like shoes and dies of stamps) cannot be entirely worn out, in the above calculation I have allowed 648 pounds as the weight of metal not worn. This added to the actual wear will amount to $\frac{23}{100}$ of a pound per ton of ore crushed.

Therefore, in wear of crushing faces, the comparison will stand as follows:

In the first example, stamps require 3 pounds of metal per ton of ore crushed, which, at 6 cents per pound, equals	18 cents.
And in the second example, as furnished by Professor Trippel, the cost per ton for crushing Austin ore is	85 cents
Rolls required $\frac{23}{100}$ pound of steel per ton of ore crushed, which, at 16 cents per pound, equals, but not quite	4 cents.

Of the steel rolls used at the Star Cañon Mill, before referred to, Superintendent T. G. Negus says: "The rolls have worn better than I had any reason to expect. In working about 2,000 tons of ore we have turned them but once, and there is not to exceed ¼ inch worn away. I would judge a set of rings would be capable of working at least 10,000 tons of ore."

It will be within bounds, I think, to estimate that the tires of two sets of steel rollers, of the size mentioned, will be capable of crushing 12,000 tons of quartz fine enough to pass a screen of 100 holes to the square inch, and of ore of less hardness the same tires will crush at least 20,000 tons.

It will also be admitted that the breakages and the power consumed in doing the same amount of work, are very much greater with stamps than with crushing-rollers.

In the case of stamps, probably not more than half the power is consumed in useful effect; for example, the full amount of power is exerted in running the stamps, whether crushing any ore or not, and this, together with the fact that the stamps must fall part of the time on no ore at all, and often on ore already fine enough, shows clearly that the principle on which the stamps operate is defective; whereas in the case of rollers the power consumed is in proportion to the work done. If no ore is fed to them, the only power wasted is in overcoming the friction of the machine, and all ore reduced fine enough is never operated upon the second time. So if we should only realize for a moment the difference in the principle and the operation of the two machines, we would need no figures to demonstrate the economy in favor of rollers, either for crushing fine or coarse.

CONCENTRATION.

The mechanical concentration of ores is entirely based on differences of specific gravity, and the subject to be considered is the best means, practically and theoretically, to render available, for the separation of minerals from their accompanying gangue, whatever difference of specific gravity may exist.

Opinions differ, even among the learned, in regard to the process and the kind of machines best adapted for the separation of ores, and whether air or water is the best medium, since ores cannot be concentrated except through the agency of some fluid medium which offers resistance to the force of gravity. No principle has yet been discovered which is better adapted to the separation of minerals than the intermittent and impulsive action of some fluid medium on the crushed ore. The best results thus far obtained are from machines known as "jigs," which employ the above principle.

The reason why intermittent impulses, (of a fluid medium,) caused to act on the bed of crushed ore, prove more effectual in separating the minerals contained in it than do other methods, is found in the following facts: The ore is in this way subjected to repeated liftings and fallings before passing from the machine; the particles meanwhile constantly change position, so as to present the most favorable surfaces to the action of the medium. Again, in well-regulated "jigs," the impulses are given suddenly, having the effect to impart to the ore a succession of quick and sharp blows, lifting the lighter particles of gangue more freely than the heavy mineral; and finally, the action loosens and stirs up the mass of ore, and so favors, to a small degree, the gravitation of all heavy particles to the bottom, and the forcing to the surface, at the same time, the lighter material.

Similar results might be obtained (in separation of minerals) providing the ore particles were of some regular shape, by throwing them with great velocity, so as to send them quite a distance. It will be understood that the heavier the particles the greater distance they will be thrown; and the greater the projecting force, the greater will be the distance of the gangue from the mineral. If thrown with less violence, the nearer together will the ore and gangue fall. On the above principle, the machine spoken of acts, viz: At each impulse of the ore by the fluid medium, the gangue, or lighter portion, is lifted further or higher than the mineral, or heavier portion; and, by the successive liftings, the gangue is entirely separated, and the more sudden the impulses the more decided, complete, and rapid will be the separation. The intermittent and sudden lifting of the ore better facilitates the separation of *irregular-shaped* grains than any other kind of action.

The next branch of the subject which I will consider is, whether air or water is the best medium.

Those who believe water to be the best medium, advance the theory, and on which they found their conclusions, that "the most favorable possible condition under which ore could be dressed would be to have the valuable portion of the ore possessed of a specific gravity greater than the liquid in which the dressing is to be performed; and the worthless portion of a specific gravity less than that of the liquid. For example, let us suppose that an ore consisting of galena, the specific gravity of which is $7\frac{5}{10}$, and quartz of the specific gravity $2\frac{6}{10}$—so finely crushed that each particle consisted of one of the minerals alone—to be located first in a liquid of a specific gravity 5. It is evident that the quartz would remain floating on the surface, while the galena would be found at the bottom of the vessel containing the liquid. Practically, however, it would be found that pieces consisting partly of galena and partly of quartz, and whose specific gravity was less than that of the liquid, would remain floating, because it would be practically impossible to separate the minerals entirely by crushing, and fulfill one condition of our problem. It is evident, therefore, that if, even in the most favorable condition we can possibly imagine, the mechanical mixture of the ore is such that we can never divide it into pieces consisting entirely of one mineral, we cannot hope, by the ordinary appliances of dressing ore, to be able to achieve perfect results. Worthless and valuable minerals can never be entirely separated when they occur mixed together in an ore." * * * "Water and air are the most convenient and the cheapest media in which separation of ores can be made, and both of them have been employed for the purpose. The specific gravity of water, however, approaches more nearly to a mean between the specific gravities of ore and the accompanying gangue, and offers much more resistance to the action of gravity, and for these reasons it has generally been preferred to air, except for the dressing of certain ores." * * *—*U. S. Commissioner Raymond's Report*, 1873, pp. 427, 428.

It is assumed that the only difficulty in the way of making a successful separation of ores, by means of a liquid of intermediate specific gravity, arises from the fact that "it would be practically impossible to separate the mineral entirely by crushing," &c., whereas in the first place the whole theory is fallacious; and in the second place, if the theory were correct, the irregular shape of the grains would make the separation of ores by such a medium impossible. To demonstrate the fallacy of the theory, I will note a few examples, viz: Cubes of lignum-vitæ (specific gravity 1.333) will readily sink in water, while flat pieces will as readily float. Again, small cubes of pure gold and also of platinum will float on mercury. Mercury possesses a specific gravity of 13.580, gold 19.361, and platinum 22.069. Another example where a denser body will float on a less dense body is the case of cast iron floating on molten iron; and also, the well known tendency of substances when finely divided to lie on the surface of a liquid of less specific gravity.

So I think by these facts it can be demonstrated that dense liquids are the least suited as a medium for the concentration of ores. In the case of platinum and mercury we have a difference of 9 in specific gravity, which is a greater difference than what is named in the paragraph quoted as sufficient to cause separation.

In order to make another demonstration clear, which will prove the superiority of a less dense medium for the separation of ores, I again quote a paragraph from same report of United States Commissioner Raymond, of 1873, page 432:

"From a comparison of the ratio between the volumes and absolute weights of equal falling spheres of galena and quartz, in water and in air, it will be seen that in order to do good work with any machine for either wet or dry concentration, a previous accurate sizing of the stuff to be treated is necessary. More particularly is this the case in the dry process, for the difference in the size of equal falling bodies of different densities in air is so much less than in water. A quartz sphere must be four times as large in diameter, contain 68 times the volume, and weigh 23 times as much as a galena sphere that behaves in similar manner, in falling through a column of water. But in air the sphere would only have to be 2.8 times as large in diameter, contain 24 times the volume, and weigh 8.37 times as much. In either case, however, the importance of a careful sizing is at once apparent."

In the foregoing paragraph it is again asserted that water has a greater margin for separating ores than air, but practical results of dry concentration prove the reverse to be the case; and besides, some experiments lately instituted demonstrate, theoretically, that in air we have the greatest margin for separation.

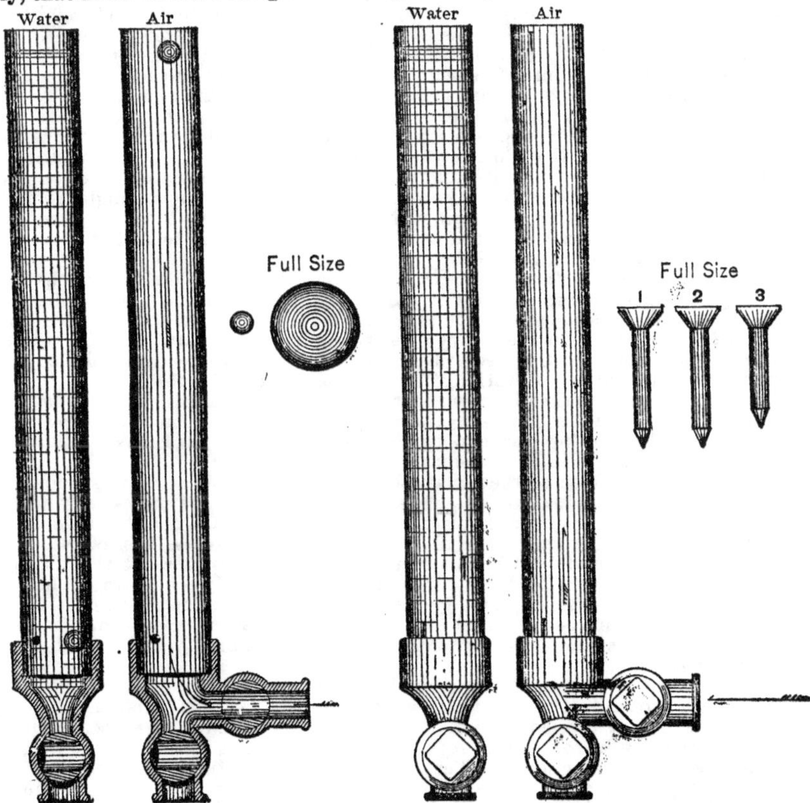

Experiment on the fall of bodies in water and in air.

To illustrate this theoretically I erected two glass tubes, each 2 inches in diameter and 8 feet high. One of those tubes I filled with water; through the other I forced a regulated blast of air. I found that, practically, as above stated, $\frac{1}{8}$ inch globule of galena, and $\frac{4}{8}$ inch globule of quartz, fall in equal time in the column of water. But when the blast of air was regulated to retard the galena in falling to the same extent as water, then the $\frac{4}{8}$ of quartz was sustained by the blast of air, and did not fall, while the galena fell as rapidly as in the tube of water. I also employed bodies of other forms, such as shown in the cut marked 1, 2, and 3.

In experimenting with these I regulated the current of air in the air-tube, to give the same resistance as water would to the falling bodies of equal weight and size, so that when I let fall two of equal weight and size, (1 and 2,) one in the water, the other in the current of air, both reached the bottom in equal time. I then let fall No. 1 and 3 in water, and when No. 1 reached the bottom No. 3 was about 10 inches behind; and next I let fall the same No. 1 and 3 in air; No. 1 fell in the same time in the air as it did in the water, but No. 2 did not fall at all. Thus demonstrating that instead of less margin, we have in air a much greater margin for separating ores than in water. Before making these experiments I expected to find a margin for separating ores in favor of air, but did not anticipate it would prove so great. But the experiment proved that $\frac{1}{8}$ globule of galena, and $\frac{4}{8}$ of quartz, which are equal-falling in still or moving water, can be separated by air. The results correspond exactly with the results obtained in practice—viz, that with less sizing, better results can be obtained with air than can possibly be reached with water. It should not, however, need the experiments just related to prove that air is the superior medium, for it should be understood by simple reference to what is already admitted in regard to the theory of concentration, viz, the requirements to effect separation are, first, differences of specific gravity; second, a proper agitation of the crushed ore by a fluid medium, so as to force the lighter gangue to the surface and allow the heavier to sink or remain at the bottom.

I need only discuss the latter condition. If air would not properly agitate or lift the ore intermittently, then air would be out of the question. But air is made to act upon the crushed ore so as to suspend it intermittently, in rapid succession, or a continuous blast will carry all before it just as a stream of water would. Therefore we have in air a medium which will act with sufficient force and power to properly agitate, suspend, and lift the ore, and, on account of its small density, the ore can be lifted and allowed to subside from 420 to 500 times per minute, and the medium does not, like water, afford a current or stream sufficient to carry away the mineral.

Another fact may also be properly mentioned, which is of some importance, viz, that dry ore particles in the operation of separation slide by each other more freely, that is, with less friction in air than they do in water. This may be proved by noting the angle at which a pile of dry ore will rest in air, and the same ore in water. Dry ore, sized between 10 and 20 mesh screens (to the linear inch) rests in air at an angle from base of $35\frac{1}{2}$ degrees, but in water at 2 degrees steeper angle. If wet ore in water flowed as freely as dry ore, the buoyancy of water would cause the same ore to rest at a less angle in water, instead of a greater angle.

By reference again to the quotation made, it will be seen that the idea is given that separation is due to the difference in time of falling of the mineral and gangue after each impulse or lift, whereas the separation takes place at each lift, on account of the lighter being lifted farther than the heavy; for when the impulses are properly adjusted, the lighter is the only portion decidedly raised, while the heavier is but slightly acted upon, and the amount of separation that takes place at each subsidence of the ore is too slight, if any, to be taken into consideration. It will be readily understood, then, that the buoyancy of water can be no aid in separating ores, but, on the contrary, it retards separation by limiting the lifts to 120 per minute, and, as I have already shown, in other respects is the inferior medium.

But a still farther illustration of the remarkable difference in favor of air as a concentrating medium is found in the fact that the air-jig concentrates successfully all the crushed ore except floating dust; that is, all that is not of a grade finer than about $\frac{1}{240}$ part of an inch in diameter is successfully treated by the air-process. In practice, at first, I employed a screen of 10,000 holes to the square inch, to take out the dust. All the granular particles up to 10,000 to the square inch are readily concentrated, but lately it is found practicable to employ a gentle current of air to remove the dust, so that all grains up to at least $\frac{1}{240}$ part of an inch go to the separators for concentration. But with water it becomes difficult to concentrate, with the jig, finer grains than $\frac{1}{25}$ of an inch, (or a 12-mesh screen.)

In several tests made in concentrating unsized ore—ranging from such as delivered through an 8-mesh screen to the finest slimes or dust—I have (with Gilpin County, Col., gold-ores) found that ten per cent. of the concentrations would pass a screen of 100 mesh, or 10,000 holes to the square inch, and much of which amount, of course, would pass a considerably finer screen. Yet all these mineral particles, so greatly differing in size, can by air be concentrated at one operation, in one pile, and the gangue in another—facts which establish conclusively, and beyond contradiction, that the rule applying with water does not meet the case in dry concentration. Nevertheless, for the best results sizing is indispensable, and I recommend the adoption of three or four grades.

So that, looking at the subject in every point of view, everything considered, both as to the results obtained practically and in a theoretical point of view, air is shown to possess superior advantages as a concentrating medium over that of water.

Superintendent T. G. Negus has furnished me the following reliable results of working three different lots of ore at the Dry Concentrating Mill at Star Cañon, Nevada:

66,800 lbs. of ore from De Soto mine, assay $72.24		$2,412 81
Mineral No. 1.—1,013 lbs., assay $722.71	$366 04	
Mineral No. 2.—1,092 lbs., assay $1,187.57	648 40	
Mineral No. 3.— 515 lbs., assay $1,204.54	305 35	
Dust from bin, 11,998 lbs., assay $138.17	828 88	
		2,148 67

Or 89.05 per cent. saved.

38,150 lbs. Sheba ore, assay value per T., 56.72		1,081 93
Mineral No. 1.—1,072 lbs., assay $441.09	$236 41	
Mineral No. 2.—1,077 lbs., assay $559.86	301 48	
Mineral No. 3.— 664 lbs., assay $780.40	251 28	
Dust from cham. 2,881 lbs., assay $96.56	139 09	
		928 26

Or 86 per cent. saved.

3,260 lbs. Seminole ore, assay value per T., $4.84		7 88
Mineral No. 1.—55 lbs., assay $32.32	$0 88	
Mineral No. 2.—49 lbs., assay $86.87	2 12	
Mineral No. 3.—48 lbs., assay $135.10	3 24	
		6 24

Or 80.47 per cent. saved.

Mr. Negus says: "I inclose the results of working three different lots of ore—one from De Soto, one from Sheba, and one small lot of very low grade ore from the Seminole. This I send, not that it is really of any practical value, but to show how very sensitive the machinery is in taking out the mineral where there is only the very smallest amount."

The De Soto and Sheba are the only mines in Star Cañon which furnish any ore. The ores are antimonial silver mixed with black sulphurets of silver, a class of ores exceedingly difficult to concentrate with water.

In Cornwall the concentrated tin-ores contain all the copper, iron, and arsenical pyrites. This concentrated product is charged into a reverberatory furnace and roasted, for the purpose of oxidizing the arsenical and sulphur combinations, in order to change the specific gravity. The roasted ore is again concentrated, and sometimes if the ore is very impure the roasting and concentrating is again repeated.

With air the concentration of Cornwall tin-ore is effected more completely without roasting.

Also, zinc blende is separated from galena with ease and rapidity.

Kryolite from spathic iron:

Specific gravity of kryolite	2.9
Specific gravity of spathic iron	3.9

Also the various sulphuret ores of silver, zinc, copper, and Colorado gold-ores are concentrated with a very small loss as compared with the loss following wet concentration.

Emery from quartz or iron-ore.

Coffee from stones.

Iron pyrites or nickel ores from hornblende.

Diamonds and other precious stones from sand, quartz, gravel, &c., and many other substances which have too slight a difference in specific gravity to be separated by means of water.

In addition to the advantages of saving a larger percentage of the value contained in such ores as have heretofore been concentrated by means of water, the successful separation or concentration of those which water cannot treat, and the greater rapidity of concentration, may be mentioned the greater convenience and simplicity secured in the use of air as the concentrating medium.

In some cases, no doubt, the percentage of loss in dry concentration will be greater than the results furnished by Mr. Negus. Then, again, in many cases, the loss will be less. The following example will illustrate the benefits following from dry concentration:

TABLE I.

Cost of concentrating 5 tons of ore into one ton, at $2 per ton	$10 00
Cost of smelting one ton of concentrated ore	35 00
Total cost of reducing 5 tons of ore	45 00
Cost of smelting 5 tons of ore, at $35	175 00
A difference in favor of concentration on 5 tons of ore of	130 00
Hence, on 50 tons of ore per day, (the work of one mill)	1,300 00
And on the total work of one year of 300 days, a saving of	390,000 00

Continuing the comparison between the two methods to the practical results to be secured by adopting the plan of dry concentration, I will assume that we have an ore of which the assay value is $100 per ton, and that a concentration of 5 tons into 1 is effected. I will allow a loss of 10 per cent. in concentration, while it will be fair to assume, again, that when the deleterious gangue rock is removed, the oneton of concentrated ore can be smelted or otherwise treated with no greater loss than 5 per cent. Accordingly, bringing in the aid of concentration, we shall have the following:

TABLE II.

Original value of 5 tons of ore at $100 per ton		$500 00
Cost of concentrating 5 tons into 1, at $2 per ton	$10 00	
Loss of 10 per cent. in 4 tons of tailings	50 00	
Cost of smelting, &c., 1 ton of concentrated ore	35 00	
Loss in smelting of 5 per cent. of concentrated ore	22 50	
Total cost of treating 5 tons of ore		117 50
Amount left over costs of reduction		382 50

WITHOUT CONCENTRATION.

Cost of smelting, &c., 5 tons of ore, at $35	$175 00	
Loss of 10 per cent. on 5 tons	50 00	
Total cost of treating 5 tons	225 00	
Amount left over costs of reduction		275 00
A difference in favor of first concentrating on 5 tons of ore		107 50

The above table will enable the reader to judge of the comparative cost of the two methods of treating ores.

In addition to such improvements in the machine, I have provided, to be attached to the latter, a slide-rest; this, whenever the steel rings become worn uneven, is brought into use for turning them true again.

Screens.—The plan of revolving screens is that which I have adopted, as best suited for the work to be performed; and perhaps the only features particularly requiring notice, in the department of screens, are those in respect to their systematic manufacture, and the adaptation of all their parts to the sizing they are intended to effect.

The screens are made larger at one end, in order to give the proper incline for discharging the ore, while allowing the shaft to be placed horizontal. By having the screens themselves cone-shaped, and the shafts accordingly horizontal and parallel with each other, the important advantages are secured of rendering it convenient to drive in the ordinary way by belts, and also of the facility of driving one shaft by the other, an arrangement shown in the Plan of Mill, where the lowermost one is driven directly from the main power, this in turn made to drive the next, and so on.

The bearings of these shafts, as with those throughout the mill, are self-adjusting; so that, in case the shafts spring or become out of line, the boxes will still bear truly on the journals.

To prevent clogging of the screen, I have arranged hammers or weights to slide on bolts hanging inside of the screen, the action of which is to jar out particles that may have stuck in the meshes. A light blow on the top of the screen serves best to loosen and throw out any particles sticking in the meshes, at the same time that (owing to some elasticity of the frame as a whole) it affects less the lower portion, as is desirable it should do, since whatever jar the screens receive when at the lowest point is likely to fasten the particles only the more firmly.

Rubber cushions or springs placed on the end of the bolt next to the screen soften the blow of the hammer at the lower side of the screen, as shown in the cut.

The dry concentrator.—The plate accompanying this description is a transverse sectional view.

The machine is composed essentially of the following parts: A receiver H, to hold the crushed ore; an ore-bed O, on which the ore is submitted to the action of air; the two gates G G, one to regulate the flow of ore from the receiver H, the other to determine the depth of ore on the ore-bed; a passage C, in which the concentrated ore descends, and roller R, to effect and regulate the discharge of the same; a fan B, to give the puffs of air; a trip-wheel, lever, and spring to operate the fan; and a ratchet-wheel and pawl to impart revolution to the roller R.

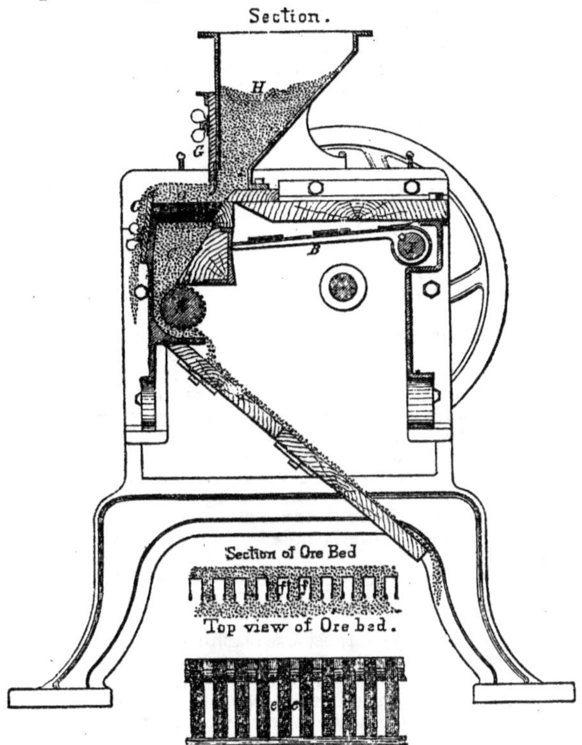

Cross-section of Krom's Concentrator.

The mode of operating the machine is as follows: Ore is placed in the receiver H, and the driving-pulley set in motion. The trip-wheel, fixed on the opposite end of the pulley-shaft, works by its cam-shaped teeth against the lever; and by the alternate action of this wheel, forcing the lever in one direction, and of the spring, which at once and suddenly carries it back again, the fan B is made to swing on the shaft I, sending at each upward movement a quick and sharp puff of air through the ore-bed, and lifting slightly the ore lying on it. As there are six projections upon the trip-wheel, it follows that the moderate speed of 70 to 80 revolutions of this per minute will give 420 to 480 upward movements of the fan in the same time, and consequently a corresponding number of puffs of air to agitate the ore; this rate is sufficient to secure steady motion of the heavy balance pulley, and yet not so fast as to produce any unpleasant jar or noise—the machine working smoothly and easily.

The ore-bed is composed of wire-gauze tubes, placed at distances from each other of $\frac{3}{16}$, $\frac{1}{4}$, $\frac{3}{8}$, and $\frac{1}{2}$ of an inch, according to the grade of ore to be concentrated—the finer requiring that the tubes be set nearer together, while the coarser allow of their being farther apart. The ore-bed, situated in front of the fan, as plainly shown in the sectional view, is formed by these tubes—their ends next to the fan being open, and the air from the bellows, entering these, escapes through the top and sides of the tubes, agitating the ore that lies on them, and also that between them near the surface.

The ore between the tubes rests on that immediately underneath, in the passage C, and sinks as fast as the roller R, at the bottom, effects its discharge. The tubes being open on the lower side, any fine ore passing through the meshes of wire gauze simply descends with the main body C, thus preventing any liability of the tubes to filling up.

In discharging the concentrated ore C, the roller R is operated (as mentioned above) by means of the ratchet-wheel and pawl, and, the latter being carried by a crank on the trip-wheel, it follows that its speed is governed by the speed of this wheel, which also gives motion to the fan B; by this connection the fan, which effects the concentration, and the roller, which discharges the concentrated ore, are made to act in concert with each other. The importance of this feature will be apparent, when it is remembered that the amount of ore concentrated in a given time depends on the number of puffs of air supplied per minute; so that, as the arrangement here secures, the motion of the discharge-roller should be controlled and regulated to correspond with the speed of the fan.

To accomplish more satisfactorily the result sought, the crank which carries the pawl can also be adjusted, by varying its length; so that the speed of the roller may be further regulated, according to the richness of the ore.

As already stated, the upper gate G governs the flow of ore from the receiver H to the ore-bed, whilst the lower gate G is so set as to determine the thickness of the stratum of ore lying upon the latter. The reason for this last arrangement is found in the necessity of increasing or diminishing the depth of the bed of ore operated on, according to the coarseness or fineness of grade—the finer the crushed ore the thinner should the stratum be.

The strap, with its screw fastenings, serves, first, to prevent the roller-attachment of the lever from striking the body of the trip-wheel as it falls from each of the cam-shaped projections; and secondly, to regulate the extent of movement of the fan. That is to say, the strap must in all cases be so adjusted that the small roller working against the trip-wheel shall not strike at the foot of the cam—the strap serving in this manner to cushion the blow and prevent noise. Further, by tightening up or slacking off by means of the screw-fastening, the fan is carried in its vibration through a greater or less space, producing accordingly a stronger or lighter puff of air.

It will of course be understood that the volume of the puff of air required varies with each grade of ore operated upon. Now, with the strap arrangement alone, the volume of the puff can be regulated to the exact requirements of different grades of material. But, as the finest grades of ore demand much less movement of the fan than do the coarser, it is preferable to have an additional means of control; and to supply such, trip-wheels of different sizes are provided along with each machine. It is, in working, better to select a trip-wheel which gives a movement corresponding most nearly to that required, and then to make the nicer adjustments by means of the screw and strap; but the roller must in no instance strike at the foot of the cam.

The novel features, then, to be particularly noted in this separator, are as follows:

1. The ore-bed, formed of wire-gauze tubes, which are set in a frame a short distance apart, thus allowing the ore to descend between them, is a novel and original device for securing the removal of the concentrated ore, as fast as the separation on the bed is completed.

The entire width of the ore-bed in the largest size machine is 4 feet, and along this the tubes, only $\frac{1}{2}$ inch wide, are set, with intervening spaces of from $\frac{3}{16}$ to $\frac{1}{2}$ of an inch; consequently, the total extent of openings through which the ore falls, amounts in the one case to $\frac{1}{3}$ and in the other to $\frac{1}{2}$ of the entire ore-bed. This construction gives a great amount of space through which to deliver the concentrated material, and of course distributes the discharge over such space; so that at no single point does the ore sink rapidly, and yet the action of the air is perfect and equal over the entire extent of the ore-bed.

2. The second feature in importance is the automatic discharge-roller R. This being driven by the motion that works the fan, and its rate of revolution being at the same time, and in the manner already explained, regulated according to the richness of the ore, it follows that the concentration of the material, and its discharge, are effected in concert; the result is, that when the general speed of the machine slackens, the concentration being of course less, the rate of delivery is (as it should be) correspondingly reduced.

3. The third feature is the general simplicity of the device for producing the puffs of air; namely, a fan or plate, furnished with rubber valves, swinging on its proper shaft, and directly actuated by means of a single lever L.

4. The next feature requiring notice is the combined operation of the trip-wheel and spring, in actuating the fan or bellows-plate. The wheel, by the gradual action of its cams, throws the lever L back, and consequently the fan or bellows-plate downward, with a movement as gentle as is possible for one so rapid, when, immediately after, the spring carries the fan quickly upward—the two motions, in this way, securing all the time practicable for the air to fill the space above the fan, and then the expulsion of this with a sudden impulse through the ore-bed, imparting a lift to the ore, as already explained.

The superiority of this particular device over cams, cranks, &c., arises from the fact that, with it, a considerable variation of the speed of the machine does not affect the quality of the concentration, but only the rate, and so, the quantity. If the trip-wheel revolves slowly, the number of vibrations of the fan is of course less; but as the spring causes the upward movement, the puff of air is of practically uniform strength, and we thereby obtain at all speeds what we may term a concentrating stroke of the bellows.

The more sharply or distinctly the jets of air are given, the more perfect and well-defined will be the separation, and the greater may be the varying sizes of the grains. And the more rapidly in succession are the jets of air repeated, the greater will be the amount of work done in a given time.

5. In reference to the action of the strap and adjusting-screw, although in itself important, the explanations already presented are deemed sufficient.

6. The gate on the hopper H compels the ore to flow on the ore-bed as an under-current, and as the puffs are regulated to agitate just perceptibly the heavy portion of the material, it follows that only the lighter portion will rise to the surface and be thrown (as tailings) over the lower gate G, while the heavy continues to sink through the ore-bed, and to be discharged below.

This feature of the under-flow of ore, just mentioned, enables us to concentrate perfectly with a very short travel of the material, or, in other words, to employ a short ore-bed, a condition of things which proves for several reasons of great advantage, viz:

By thus having a short ore-bed, we are allowed to extend what we can properly term the width of the bed, thereby greatly increasing the capacity of a machine of given size. All other experimenters have caused the delivery and discharge of the ore to take place over the shorter dimension of the machine, and the travel of the ore over the longer dimension; the exact reverse of this is secured in the machine here described, viz, the distance of travel of the ore over the bed is only 5 inches, while the line of overflow is extended to 4 feet, or can be at pleasure made still greater.

Again, a short ore-bed enables us to use a small fan or bellows; thereby reducing the size of the machine, as also the power required to run it, and the vibration attending rapid movement.

Finally, a more even and uniform agitation is secured, when the ore is confined within narrow limits; and consequently, more satisfactory results are for this reason also obtained.

7. The feature last considered leads us naturally to the shape of the machine, Since I have discovered that a short ore-bed, of only 5 or 6 inches length, is *not only sufficient, but in fact much superior*, for the purposes required, and that the width of the bed and extent of overflow can accordingly be greatly increased, thus largely increasing also the amount of concentration for a given size of machine, I am able so to place the fan and to group in compact form all the working parts, as very considerably to reduce the entire bulk of the machinery and frame, the whole being kept to a small and convenient size, in comparison with the amount of work performed.

8. The frame is made deep, and provided with a door to inclose the principal working parts, a feature, however, which is not considered essential.

Before leaving the subject of the concentrating-machine, attention should further be called to the fact, that with it the puffs of air, in agitating or lifting the ore, effect at the same time the delivery of fresh supplies from the receiver, and help to force the tailings over the lower gate, G.

The puffs of air are, at the start, regulated to agitate sufficiently the ore on the bed; but should the richness of the latter increase during working, or too large a supply collect at one time on the bed, the air ceases to lift or agitate the material so much as before; and thus a check is at once furnished to prevent loss by the overflowing of heavy ore in the tailings. No such check is possible in water concentration; because water moves practically as a solid, and carries all before it.

All the parts in this machine liable to wear in the course of time are manufactured to duplicate, and accordingly can be cheaply replaced.

The machine measures 6 feet in length over all, 3 feet in width, and 3 feet 10 inches height. It weighs, complete, 1,200 pounds, and is capable of concentrating ½ ton per hour with ⅓ horse-power. Besides the large machines, I manufacture smaller ones, of the weight of 150 pounds, for the requirements of laboratories and of mining prospectors.

DESCRIPTION OF MILL FOR DRY-CRUSHING AND CONCENTRATION OF ORES.

The accompanying plan of mill showing the best arrangement of the machinery for crushing, screening, and concentration of ores is designed with a view to economize in the labor and expense required to operate it.

In this plan some of the economical features introduced in practice are not shown for the purpose of better illustrating clearly the operation simply of crushing, sizing, and concentrating, including the means of drying the ore.

One important feature omitted is that for weighing after drying and crushing just previous to sizing. The plan adopted is simple and saves a great deal of trouble and expense, and secures greater accuracy in the weight of ore treated.

The mill is represented as built on the slope of a hill or mountain side, a course securing some conveniences. By this plan the ore is delivered in the third story, and at this point fed to the jaw-crusher, which breaks the ore into small fragments.

The ore thus broken falls into the drying-oven to release it from outside moisture.

The drying-oven is made of cast iron. The bottom, as plainly represented, is arranged in step fashion, so as to allow the hot air or fire to pass up through the spaces between the ore. It will be readily understood that such a system of drying will secure the most rapid and economical results. The heat, after it passes through the ore with the moisture it carries, is conducted away through a flue or pipe in the ordinary way.

At the bottom of the dryer is arranged a shute, capable of being adjusted at such an angle as just to deliver the ore to the endless belt in a comparatively thin stratum. This belt is adjusted in speed to carry the ore away from the dryer and deliver it to the first pair of rolls at the same rate it is fed to the crusher. If feeding at the crusher is stopped, the carrier belt should also be stopped, as it is essential to have the dryer always quite or nearly full. A shifting belt, which is under the immediate and easy control of the man at the crusher, supplies the means of starting and stopping the carrier-belt at pleasure.

The dryer will hold about 1½ tons, so, at a rate of crushing equal to 3 tons per hour, the ore will be half an hour traveling through the furnace, a space of time believed to be quite (and more than) sufficient to dry it.

After passing between the first pair of rolls the crushed ore (now about the size of corn) flows to the screen, and all that is fine enough taken out and allowed to flow at once to the elevator.

The coarse portion flows, by means of properly arranged and adjusted shutes, to the second pair of rolls, which complete the crushing.

The object in taking out the ore which has been crushed sufficiently by the first rolls is twofold, namely: The portion already so reduced should be saved from further crushing, to prevent making too much fine stuff; and, secondly, as each machine is adjusted to crush finer than the one preceding, it is not capable of operating on the same weight or bulk of ore. The elevator delivers all the crushed ore to the uppermost screen, which takes out any particles that may still be too coarse, such small percentage of coarse product being sent back through a shute (shown in the plate) to the first pair of rolls for recrushing. The portion passing through the meshes of the first screen flows to the second, and so much as goes through the second screen again to the third, and so on.

From the larger end of the second screen we get the first or coarsest grade of ore for concentration, and which flows to the bin. From the end of the third we obtain the second grade, and that from the end of the fourth screen is the third grade, and what passes through the meshes of the fourth screen is the fourth grade of ore, making in all 4 sizes, each size flowing to one of the four bins.

From the bins the ore flows directly downward to the separator, situated on the floor below.

The tailings from the first eight separators are removed by any convenient means from the building, but the concentrated ore, with some gangue with it, flows to the concentrators on the basement-floor, where it is reconcentrated to remove all the gangue.

In practice it is found to be more convenient and economical not to concentrate too highly in the first operation, but to allow some gangue to go with the concentrated mineral. If the mineral contains some gangue it is an evidence there is no loss of valuable ore going off with the tailings, so the rich concentrations are allowed to flow to a single set of machines below, and there reconcentrated.

In this operation is obtained a pure concentrated mineral and a small amount of rich tailings, but this latter (rich tailings) is sent back by the elevator to be concentrated over again on the machine above.

A few hours of the 24 is sufficient time to do all the reconcentrating, as the bulk, compared to the original ore, is greatly reduced.

This system of reconcentrating renders good concentration easy, serves as a check to loss in the tailing, and proves economical in practice.

The dust made by crushing is withdrawn through properly arranged dust-pipes. The exhaust-fan for removing the dust is connected with a main dust-pipe (not shown) placed against the elevator trunk, and all dust-pipes from crushers, separators, and screen-chambers lead into the main pipe.

The screens are provided with latticed hoppers, which allows a current of air to flow freely up through the screen-chambers, which removes the floating dust, but all which does not float in a gentle current flows to the bins, so that all grains not finer than $\frac{1}{240}$ part of an inch are concentrated. Each chamber is connected by separate dust-pipes directly with the main tube.

The dust withdrawn from the various parts of the mill is conveyed through a tube and carried outside of the building some distance away to a dust-chamber, as shown in the cut, where nearly all of it is settled and saved for subsequent treatment.

The importance of saving the dust, as well as the importance of making as little as possible in crushing, will be appreciated when it is understood that all the dust of ores assay always about double the value of the original in base and precious metals.

In order to produce as little dust as possible, in crushing at the rate of 2 to 2½ tons per hour, 2 sets of rolls are indispensable and even 3 sets preferable and more economical. In this way the ore is brought gradually from coarse lumps to fine sand.

The machinery throughout the mill is of the best possible workmanship; and each machine employed is constructed on the best known mechanical principles. No pains or money have been spared to bring each machine or other parts to a condition of working perfectly with all the rest, and also with the highest efficiency.

The mill, constructed and fitted up as shown in the plan, is capable of crushing and concentrating at the rate of from 2 to 3 tons per hour.

Machinery and plans for mills of less or greater capacity will be furnished as may be required.

The number of men required to keep in operation a mill crushing and concentrating at the rate of 3 tons per hour, and when steam is the motive power, is 6 men for day-work and 3 for night-work; and when water is the motive power, 5 men for day-work and 2 for night-work.

In Galena, Battle Mountain district, Nevada, as I learn from a report received since the preparation of the chapter on Nevada, (see page 172,) the White and Shilo Consolidated Company * had a Krom concentrating-mill built last summer by the Krom Concentrator Company, to dress the low-grade ore that had accumulated on the dumps of the mines. The ore consists of graywacke slate as a gangue, and contains sulphurets of silver, lead, iron, zinc, &c., with hardly any quartz. The machinery is propelled by a steam-engine, and works 40 tons in twelve hours, concentrating about 5 tons of rock into one. These concentrates contain about 30 per cent. of lead and about $130 silver per ton. There being no drying-kiln connected with the mill, the wet weather, coming in October last, forced the mill to stop. While operating the mill ran only twelve hours during the twenty-four, and about 500 tons of concentrations were shipped from Battle Mountain to San Francisco. The White Mine was worked about three months during the year, with only a few hands.

* I believe this is the company called on page 172 the Battle Mountain Company.—R. W. R.

CHAPTER XVI.

THE ACTION OF SMALL SPHERES OF SOLIDS IN ASCENDING CURRENTS OF FLUIDS AND IN FLUIDS AT REST.

By J. C. BARTLETT, A. M., *Cambridge, Mass.*

The following discussion* was suggested by an experiment of Mr. Krom, the manufacturer of air-jigs, to illustrate the superiority of air over water as a medium of concentration. The paper is written in the interest of no system of concentration, but simply to test the experiment, and, perchance, to add something to the general fund of information on the subject.

To speak of testing an experiment by a theoretical discussion may seem a misuse of terms, but the theories concerning falling bodies and the resistance of fluids are pretty well crystallized into laws, which may properly be used to show where experiments which seem to refute them were improperly performed, and that instead of refuting they only corroborate.

It is well known that a sphere of galena $\frac{1}{8}$ inch in diameter and a sphere of quartz $\frac{1}{2}$ inch in diameter are equal-falling in water; that is, these two spheres, being placed together in a column of water at rest or in motion, will practically remain together, falling or rising together or remaining in suspension. Mr. Krom, to show that these spheres could be separated in a current of air, and hence, as he supposes, to show that air is a better medium for separation than water, performed the following experiment. He says: "I erected two glass tubes, each 2 inches in diameter and 8 feet high. One of these tubes I filled with water, through the other I forced a regulated blast of air. I found that, practically, as above stated, $\frac{1}{8}$ inch globule of galena and $\frac{4}{8}$ inch globule of quartz fall in equal times in the column of water. But when the blast of air was regulated to retard the galena in falling to the same extent as water, then the $\frac{4}{8}$ of quartz was sustained by the blast of air and did not fall, while the galena fell as rapidly as in the tube of water."

It is a very remarkable coincidence that the quartz ball should be exactly held in suspension and the galena ball should be caused to fall in exactly the same time as in water by the same blast of air. It might be supposed that the quartz ball, the two balls being transferred from water to air, losing so much more sustaining force due to the buoyancy of the water than the galena, would tend to fall faster than the galena ball, and hence that a blast of air which held the former in suspension

*This mathematical discussion of the phenomena described by Mr. Krom in the preceding chapter was promised for the present report by Mr. Bartlett, but not received until the pages were in press. Like many other valuable contributions to this and former reports, it was also intended as a paper for the American Institute of Mining Engineers. The delay in the publication of the present volume has brought it to pass that several of its chapters have already appeared in the proceedings of that society. But they are not on that account any less valuable to the public for which these pages are intended.—R. W. R.

would cause the latter to rise. On the other hand, the sustaining force due to the velocity of the air would be much greater in the case of the quartz than the galena, so that a blast of air which would hold the former in suspension might allow the latter to fall. What the actual result would be can only be determined by a consideration of all the conditions together, and will appear from the following investigation.

In Rittinger's treatise on ore-dressing the following formulas are deduced for spherical solids in a rising stream of water. They are equally true for any other fluid, if we make the proper change in A and B for difference of density:

$$(1)\; v = \frac{A^2C^2 - 1}{A\left(\frac{\varepsilon^{2Bt}+1}{\varepsilon^{2Bt}-1} + AC\right)}$$

$$(2)\; s = \frac{AC+1}{A}t - \frac{1}{AB}\log\frac{(AC+1)\,\varepsilon^{2Bt} - (AC-1)}{2}$$

In (2) the logarithm is the Napierian, C is the velocity of the ascending current of fluid, v the velocity of the sphere at the end of t seconds, s the distance upward passed over by the sphere in t seconds,

$$A = \sqrt{\frac{3a\Delta}{2d\gamma(\delta - \Delta)}} \qquad B = \frac{g(\delta-\Delta)}{\delta}A.$$

In these values of A and B, $a = 25.5$, a constant determined by theory, and verified by experiment, being the force in kilograms exerted on a surface one meter square by water flowing directly against it with the velocity of one meter per second; Δ is the density of the fluid, δ the density of the sphere, γ is 1,000, the weight in kilograms of one cubic meter of water; g is the acceleration due to gravity, or 9,809 meters; d is the diameter of the sphere in meters, and ε is the Napierian base, or 2.71828. The reproduction of these formulas is somewhat lengthy, though not difficult, and will therefore not be given here. The reader who wishes to satisfy himself as to their correctness is referred to the above-mentioned work. From them simpler formulas for special cases will be deduced. The contraction log. indicates the Napierian logarithm.

If in (1) $C = 0$, or the fluid is at rest, we obtain

$$(3)\; u = -\frac{1}{A}\;\frac{\varepsilon^{2Bt}-1}{\varepsilon^{2Bt}-1},$$

and if 1 is very small compared with ε^{2Bt}, we obtain from this

$$(4)\; v = -\frac{1}{A}.$$

If in (1) 1 may be neglected in comparison with ε^{2Bt}, we obtain

$$(5)\; v = -C\frac{1}{A}.$$

If in (1) $v=0$, or the sphere is held in suspension in the fluid, we have

$$(6)\; C = \frac{1}{A}.$$

If C is greater than $\frac{1}{A}$, v is positive, and the sphere rises. If C is less than $\frac{1}{A}$, v is negative, and the sphere falls. If in (2) $C = 0$, we obtain

$$(7)\; s = -\frac{1}{AB}\log\frac{\varepsilon^{Bt}+\varepsilon^{-Bt}}{2}.$$

If we solve this for t, we get

$$(8)\ t = \frac{\log\left(\varepsilon^{-sAB} + \sqrt{\varepsilon^{-2sAB} - 1}\right)}{B}$$

If in (8) 1 may be negatived in comparison with ε^{-2sAB}, which is generally the case in practice, s being negative when $C = 0$, we obtain

$$(9)\ t = \frac{\log.\ 2}{B} - sA.$$

If in (2) we neglect $AC - 1$, which is generally small compared with $(AC + 1)\ \varepsilon^{2Bt}$, and solve for t, we get

$$(10)\ t = \frac{\log.\left(\frac{AC+1}{2}\right) + sAB}{B\,(AC - 1)}$$

and if in (10) $C = 0$, it reduces to (9). By approximations (2) may be reduced to

$$(11)\ s = \left(C - \frac{1}{A}\right)t,$$

or, for those cases where the velocity of the sphere may be regarded as constant, we may write $s = vt$, and take the value of v from (5), thus obtaining (11).

For small spheres falling or rising in water, all the approximate formulas are accurate enough, but not always so when the fluid is air, and they must be used with caution. In the consideration of particular cases we shall see to what extent the approximate formulas are trustworthy. For the sake of clearness and brevity, the discussion is put in the form of problem and answer, all the work of computation being omitted. In the following cases the densities of water, air, quartz, and galena are taken as 1, 0.00125, 2.6, and 7.5, respectively.

I. What must be the velocity of an ascending current of air to keep in suspension a quartz ball ½ inch in diameter? From (6) we find $C =$ 86.2 feet per second.

II. What will be the action of a galena ball ⅛ inch in diameter in an ascending current of air having a velocity of 86.2 feet per second? For the galena ball the value of $\frac{1}{A}$ is 73.21; hence C is greater than $\frac{1}{A}$ and the galena will rise with an increasing velocity, the limit of which is $C - \frac{1}{A}$ or 13 feet per second.

III. In what time will a ball of galena ⅛ inch in diameter fall 8 feet in water at rest? From (11) we get $t = 3.32$, and from the more exact formula (9) $t = 3.38$. As in this case $- 2\,s\,A\,B = 76.8$, we see that 1 may be omitted under the radical sign in (8), and (9) may be used without appreciable error. By applying (9) to the case of a quartz ball ½ inch in diameter falling with the galena, we find $t = 3.43$, a difference of 0.05 second. A part of this difference is due to the fact that the two balls are not exactly equal-falling theoretically, the ratio of the diameters of equal-falling spheres of quartz and galena being 4.0625 : 1, and not 4 : 1, as assumed. If we substitute the ratio 4.0625 : 1, we get $t = 3.40$ instead of 3.43. The rest of the slight difference is easily accounted for by explaining the meaning of equal-falling bodies. Two equal-falling bodies are not necessarily two bodies which fall from rest through the same distance in the same time; but they are two bodies such that the limit of the velocity which they acquire by falling from rest in any fluid is the same for both. This limit of velocity is found by making t infinite in (1), and is $C - \frac{1}{A}$ or $-\frac{1}{A}$ if $C = 0$. To illustrate this point with another example, it may be asked:

IV. What will be the velocity of an ascending current of water to keep in suspension a $\frac{1}{8}$-inch galena ball, and what will be the action of a $\frac{1}{2}$-inch quartz ball in this stream of water? From (6) we find that the velocity is 2.41 feet per second, and from (5) we find that the quartz ball would rise, its maximum velocity being 0.0187 foot per second. Practically, of course, they would remain together. If we reverse the problem, asking the velocity necessary to keep the quartz ball in suspension, we find 2.39 feet per second, and that the galena will fall with a maximum velocity of 0.0187 foot per second.

V. What will be the velocity of an ascending current of air to keep a $\frac{1}{8}$-inch galena ball in suspension, and what will be the action of a $\frac{1}{2}$-inch quartz ball in this current? By (6) we get, as before, 73.21 feet, and if we substitute this value in the exact formula, (1), with the proper value of A, we find:

When $t = \frac{1}{2}$ $v = -\ 3.83$.
When $t = 1$ $v = -\ 6.57$.
When $t = 2$ $v = -\ 9.82$.
When $t = 4$ $v = -12.28$.

The limit which v continually approaches, and practically reaches after a few seconds, is -12.98. This illustrates how soon, even in air, the velocity of small spheres becomes practically constant.

VI. What will be the diameter of a galena ball which will be held in suspension by an ascending current of air which will sustain a quartz ball $\frac{1}{2}$ inch in diameter; that is, having a velocity of 86.2 feet per second? Solving (6) for d, which is contained in A, we get $d = 1.386$ eighths of an inch.

VII. What is the diameter of a galena ball which, in an ascending current of air which keeps a quartz ball $\frac{1}{2}$ inch in diameter in suspension, will fall with the same velocity as in water at rest? If we assume that the velocity has become practically constant, we may employ (5) to solve the problem. For the galena falling in water at rest we have, $v = -\frac{1}{A}$, which may be written $-\frac{1}{A_w}$, the subscript w denoting that A is taken with reference to water. In the same way we shall have A_a for A taken with reference to air. Hence, (5) will become $-\frac{1}{A_w} = C - \frac{1}{A_a}$ or $\frac{1}{A_a} - \frac{1}{A_w} = C$. Solving this for d, which is contained in A_a and A_w, we get $d = 1.48$ eighths of an inch.

VIII. What is the diameter of a galena ball which, in an ascending current of air which keeps a $\frac{1}{2}$-inch quartz ball in suspension, will fall from rest through 8 feet in the same time it would fall 8 feet in water at rest? Formula (2) is the one to apply to this question, A and B being functions of the required diameter, and s, C, and t being given: $s = 8$ feet, $C = 86.2$ feet, $t = 3.38$ seconds. In this case $AC - 1$ may be neglected, and we may employ (10). Though we cannot solve this last question directly for d, we may find the value of d by approximations, starting with the value obtained in the preceding question.

Solving for s we have

$$(12)\ s = \left(C - \frac{1}{A}\right) t - \frac{1}{AB} \log. \left(\frac{AC+1}{2}\right)$$

In this the value d, 1.52 eighths of an inch, gives $s = 7.996$, instead of 8 feet as given in the data. This answer, 1.52 eighths inch, is practically the same as that found in the preceding question, 1.48 eighths inch. The difference between the two questions should be noticed, and the reason why d should have a little larger value in the latter will be understood upon a moment's reflection.

IX. What will be the velocity of an ascending current of air in order that in it a $\frac{1}{8}$-inch galena ball shall fall 8 feet in the same timeas in water at rest? Taking formula (12) and substituting the known values of A, B, t, and s, we find $C = 69.62$ feet.

X. In what time will a $\frac{1}{2}$ inch quartz ball fall 8 feet in an ascending current of air, having the velocity of 69.62 feet per second? From (10) we obtain $t = 0.9209$, or nearly one second.

XI. Compare the velocities of spheres of galena and quartz falling in an ascending current of air having a velocity of 20 meters per second, the spheres being equal-falling in water, the galena having a diameter of 4^{mm}., and the quartz $16\frac{1}{4}^{mm}$. From (1) we find:

For $t = 1$, $v = -2.606^{m}$. for galena; $v = -4.263^{m}$. for quartz.
For $t = 2$, $v = -3.901^{m}$. for galena; $v = -6.761^{m}$. for quartz.
For $t = 4$, $v = -4.801^{m}$. for galena; $v = -8.899^{m}$. for quartz.

The limit of the velocity of the galena is -5.045, and for the quartz -9.714.

To sum up the results thus far, we see that the velocity of an ascending current of air to keep a $\frac{1}{2}$-inch quartz ball in suspension is 86.2 feet per second, and that in this current a $\frac{1}{8}$-inch galena ball will rise with an increasing velocity, which never exceeds 13 feet per second. We also find that the galena would fall 8 feet in still water in 3.38 seconds, and that, practically, the quartz ball would fall in the same time, being only 0.05 of a second behind. We see that, practically, the quartz and galena are equal-falling, that they remain together in a column of water, whether at rest or in motion. From XI, we see that the two balls of quartz and galena, which are theoretically equal-falling in water, may be separated by a stream of air, the falling velocity of the quartz being nearly twice as great as that of the galena. We also see that the velocity of an ascending current of air which will keep a $\frac{1}{8}$-inch galena ball in suspension is about 13 feet less per second than is required to keep a $\frac{1}{2}$-inch quartz ball in suspension; that in this current the quartz ball would fall with a rapidly-increasing velocity, and that, practically, this velocity becomes constant after a few seconds, and is then about 13 feet per second, being the same velocity that the rising galena ball would attain in a stream of air which would sustain the quartz. We also see how very little the diameter of the galena would have to vary in order to have entirely different action in the current which sustains the quartz. If the diameter is $\frac{1}{8}$ inch, it rises; if the diameter is 1.39 eighths, it remains in suspension; and if the diameter is 1.52 eighths, it will fall as in still water. This illustrates how delicate a medium for separation air is compared with water. If the three galena balls were placed with the $\frac{1}{2}$-inch quartz ball in an ascending stream of water which would hold the quartz in suspension, they would separate very slowly, the heaviest galena ball having a maximum falling velocity of about 8 inches per second. But this sensitiveness of a stream of air is not necessarily an advantage, for it requires a correspondingly exact uniformity in the blast of air and the material to be worked, which is not attainable in practice. From IX and X we see that the blast of air necessary to cause the $\frac{1}{8}$ galena ball to be retarded to the same extent that it would be in water at rest, or, more exactly, to fall 8 feet in the same time as in water at rest, is 69.62 feet per second, and that in this stream the $\frac{1}{2}$-inch quartz would fall 8 feet in about 1 second. It did not fall in the experiment as performed, because the condition under which the experiment was tacitly supposed to have been performed, the condition upon which every discussion on the laws of bodies falling in fluids is based, was violated. This condition was that the air should be perfectly free to move, that the tension of the air below the ball should be the same as above it. In the case of the galena ball this condition was practically complied with, the section of the ball being only $\frac{1}{256}$ that of the tube, but in the case of the quartz ball its section was $\frac{1}{16}$ of the section of the tube. The quartz, when held in suspension, had the same effect in offering resistance to the passage of the air that it would have had if firmly fixed in the middle of the tube. It was held up against the force of gravity not only by the buoyancy of the air and by the force due to the velocity of the air, but also by the excess of tension below it. It was sustained in part by the same kind of force that impels a package through a pneumatic tube, or forces the cork out of a pop-gun. If the diameter of the tube had been 1 inch instead of 2, the velocity of the air necessary to sustain the quartz would have been much less than 69.62 feet, the section of the tube being only four times that of the sphere. That all the difference between the theoretical results and the result of the experiment as performed was due to this one cause cannot be asserted. There may have been some inaccuracy in measuring the small galena ball, and we have seen what a change in action a difference in diameter of $\frac{1}{16}$ inch makes. The balls may have been rough or not of spherical shape; indeed, from the brittle, crumbling nature of galena it must be quite impossible to make a small smooth sphere out of it.

But supposing that the theoretical results may all be verified by properly conducted experiments, the point which Mr. Krom made, namely, that, though the two balls could not be separated by water, they could be separated by air, remains the same, and it makes very little difference whether the galena goes up or down, if it only leaves the suspended quartz ball. After describing the experiment, he says: "Thus demonstrating that, instead of less margin, we have in air much greater margin for separating ores than in water. Before making these experiments I expected to find a margin for separating ores in favor of air, but did not anticipate it would prove so great. But the experiment proved that $\frac{1}{8}$ globule of galena and $\frac{4}{8}$ of quartz, which are equal-falling in still or moving water, can be separated by air. The results correspond exactly with the results obtained in practice, viz, that with less sizing better results can be obtained with air than can possibly be reached with water." The expression "greater margin" might be misleading. It is often applied, in speaking of difference in cost and selling price, to profits, where a large margin is desirable; it is a pleasing term, but the only meaning it can have in the case under consideration is, that the ratio between the sizes of quartz and galena which air will separate and water will not is greater than the ratio between the two sizes that water will separate and air will not. This is true, and if all the pieces of ore in a crushed heap were of two sizes only, and the quartz pieces were four times as large as the galena, air would be a better medium than water. But this is not the case in practice, and if it were, a screen would be the simplest separator. If the pieces of quartz were 2.88 eighths and the galena $\frac{1}{8}$ inch in diameter, air would not separate them, but water would; hence water, though offering less "margin," is in this case a better separator than air. That medium is the best for the separation of two substances for which the ratio of the diameters of equal-falling spheres is greatest, or, in other words, that medium is best which will separate most readily spheres of the two substances nearest in size. Hence, a fluid whose specific gravity lies between those of the substances is the best, and of two fluids, both lighter than the substances, that is better which is denser. As regards sizing, the lighter fluid requires a more careful sizing, the number of sizes required for the different fluids being inversely proportional to the ratios of equal-falling diameters. With any fluid the excellence of separation increases with the number of sizes, and the Germans have found by experience that it is advantageous to make ten sizes between 18^{mm} and 1^{mm}. The excellence of their work in concentration is remarkable, nearly all the loss being in the loss of the minute particles of ore which are carried away with the slimes of the gangue. Their system seems perfect in other respects, and now the problem is, to devise some way of saving those fine particles, which remain for a long time in suspension even in water at rest. In dry concentration the loss in this form is avoided; the ore-dust is removed with the gangue-dust, and both are saved—"saved for subsequent treatment" is the last operation it goes through generally. Now, it is proposed, however, by the manager of one system of *dry* concentration, to treat this dust in the *wet* way, thus employing water only in that part of the operation where it is most wasteful. If there is any place in which air can be economically used, it is in the treatment of the finest sizes, from 4^{mm} to $\frac{1}{2}^{mm}$, or as fine as can be well sized. From the great velocity of air necessary to raise or hold in suspension a quartz ball of from 12^{mm} to 16^{mm} diameter, it would seem quite impossible to treat such sizes economically by means of air.

To give an opportunity of testing the theoretical results as described by means of the preceding formulas, the following table has been calculated. Since perfect spheres of quartz and galena are difficult to make, four other substances have been taken—ivory, glass, zinc, and lead, from which, by turning or molding, very perfect and smooth spheres may be made. The first vertical column contains the name of the substances, the second their specific gravities, the third their diameters in millimeters, the fourth their weight in grams, introduced as a check. If the balls do not weigh as here given, either they have not been made of the right size or the specific gravity is different from that assumed here. As the specific gravity of these substances is quite uniform and well established, any great variation in weight would probably be due to error in size or shape. The fifth and sixth columns contain the suspension velocities for water and air respectively, in meters; by suspension velocity being understood the velocity of a vertically-ascending stream of the fluid necessary to keep the given sphere in suspension. The seventh, eighth, and ninth columns contain the times, in seconds, of falling from rest in water at rest through 3, 5, and 10 meters, respectively. These values were calculated from (9). Since s is negative for all cases, we may as well regard downward direction positive and write the formula

$$(13)\ t = s\,A + \frac{0.69315}{B}.$$

Substance.	Density.	Diameter in millimeters.	Weight, in grams.	Suspension velocity in meters.		Value of t for water when $C = 0$ and $s =$		
				Water.	Air.	3^m.	5^m.	10^m.
Ivory	1.87	2	0.0078	0.213	8.84	14.10	23.48	46.92
Glass	2.65	2	0.0111	0.294	10.53	10.25	17.06	34.08
Zinc	6.90	2	0.0289	0.5[illegible]5	16.99	5.45	9.05	18.05
Lead	11.35	2	0.0475	0.736	21.79	4.14	6.85	13.65
Ivory	1.87	4	0.0627	0.302	12.50	9.99	16.62	33.20
Glass	2.65	4	0.0888	0.415	14.89	7.27	12.08	24.12
Zinc	6.90	4	0.2312	0.786	24.02	3.88	6.43	12.83
Lead	11.35	4	0.3803	1.040	30.81	2.97	4.89	9.69
Ivory	1.87	8	0.5013	0.427	17.68	7.10	11.79	23.51
Glass	2.65	8	0.7104	0.587	21.05	5.17	8.58	17.09
Zinc	6.90	8	1.850	1.111	33.97	2.80	4.60	9.10
Lead	11.35	8	3.043	1.471	43.58	2.15	3.51	6.91
Ivory	1.87	12	1.692	0.522	21.46	5.82	9.65	19.22
Glass	2.65	12	2.398	0.720	25.78	4.25	7.03	13.98
Zinc	6.90	12	6.243	1.361	41.61	2.32	3.79	7.46
Lead	11.35	12	10.27	1.802	53.37	1.81	2.92	5.69
Ivory	1.87	16	4.011	0.603	25.00	5.07	8.38	16.67
Glass	2.65	16	5.683	0.831	29.77	3.71	6.11	12.13
Zinc	6.90	16	14.80	1.571	48.05	2.04	3.31	6.50
Lead	11.35	16	24.34	2.081	61.56	1.60	2.56	4.97

For all the cases assumed in the preceding table formula (13) is more than sufficiently accurate, but it would lead to wrong results if applied to bodies falling in air. In the exact formula (9) the value of $-2sAB$ varies, in the case of air, from 2.5 for ivory 2^{mm} in diameter falling 10 meters to 0.0155 for lead 16^{mm} falling 3 meters; hence, -1 cannot be neglected in comparison with ε^{-2sAB}. But for water $-2sAB$ varies in the same limits from 2006.5 to 12.4; hence, -1 may be neglected, and (9), deduced on this supposition, may be employed. As far as experimental verification is concerned, the formula $t = sA$ is sufficiently accurate for water, the value of the remaining term of (13) varying in the assumed cases between 0.032 for ivory 2^{mm} and 0.161 for lead 16^{mm}. When C is not equal to 0, we may employ (10) to find the falling time, provided $AC - 1$ may be neglected in comparison with $(AC + 1)\,\varepsilon^{2Bt}$; that is, when $AC - 1$ is nearly equal to 0, or $C = \frac{1}{A}$ nearly; that is, when the velocity of the current is somewhere near the suspension velocity. $AC - 1$ may also be neglected, though not very small, if $(AC + 1)\,\varepsilon^{2Bt}$ is large, or if B is large; or, as B is inversely proportioned to the square root of d, when the sphere is very small. Relatively to the density of the sphere, B is a maximum, in the case of water, when the density is 2. If the density of the sphere is less than that of the fluid, A and B are imaginary. The fundamental formulas (1) and (2) were deduced on the supposition that the density of the sphere was greater than that of the fluid, and they would assume an entirely different form, and the discussion would be quite different under the supposition that the density of the sphere is less than that of the fluid.

From the table we see that a blast of air which will keep in suspension a 2^{mm} lead ball will sustain a glass ball 8^{mm} in diameter, or an ivory ball 12^{mm} in diameter. The suspension velocity for the lead being 21.79^{m}, and for the other two 21.05^{m} and 21.46^{m}, the ivory and glass would rise, theoretically, with a slight velocity; but as perfect accuracy cannot be attained in the conditions, the results of well-conducted experiments might vary somewhat from the theoretical. From the table we also find that an ascending current of water which will support a 2^{mm} ball of lead will sustain a 12^{mm} glass ball, the glass rising slowly, perhaps. Similar experiments may be made in water with ivory 16^{mm} and glass 8^{mm}, with ivory 12^{mm} and zinc 2^{mm}, with lead 4^{mm} and zinc 8^{mm}. In water at rest, ivory 16^{mm} and glass 8^{mm} will fall 3 meters in about 5.1 seconds; glass 16^{mm} and zinc 4^{mm} will fall 10 meters in nearly the same time, between 12 and 13 seconds, the glass reaching the bottom about $\frac{3}{4}$ second sooner. Similarly a large number of experiments may be made up from the table to test the theoretical results. Experiments with very small and light balls, such as 2^{mm} ivory or glass, would probably not coincide very closely with theory, on account of unavoidable inaccuracy of measurement or the adhesion of air-bubbles.

The following may also serve for experimental tests:

XII. In an ascending current of air which will keep an 8^{mm} ivory ball in suspension, how long will it take a 4^{mm} zinc ball to fall 3^{m}? From (10) we find $t = 1.787$.

XIII. In a stream of air which will keep a 12^{mm} glass ball in suspension, how long will it take a 4^{mm} lead ball to fall from rest 3^{m} and 5^{m}? From (10) we find for 3^{m} $t = 2.235$, and for 5^{m} $t = 2.633$. From these two answers we see how nearly the lead ball has attained the limit of its velocity. The limit is $30.813 - 25.783$, or 5.03. It passes over the last two meters in $2.633 - 2.235$ seconds, or in 0.398 of a second, which is at the rate of 5.003 meters per second. Therefore, we may assume the velocity constant, and say, for instance, that it would fall through 10 meters in $2.63 + 1 = 3.63$ seconds.

XIV. In a stream of air which will support a 12^{mm} ivory ball, how long will it take a 12^{mm} glass ball to fall from rest through 3^{m}, 5^{m}, and 10^{m}? From the same formula (10) we find $t = 2.064$, 2.524, and 3.674.

XV. How long will it take a 16^{mm} ivory ball to fall from rest in air at rest through 30^{m}, 40^{m}, and 50^{m}? From (8), $t = 2.671$, 3.162, 3.623. In a vacuum these values would be 2.473, 2.856, and 3.193.

XVI. How long will it take a 4^{mm} ivory ball to fall from rest in air at rest through 30^{m}, 40^{m}, and 50^{m}? From (8), $t = 3.280$, 4.4081, 4.882. In a vacuum these values would be 2.473, 2.856, and 3.193.

CHAPTER XVII.

NOTES ON THE BRÜCKNER CYLINDER.

By N. H. Cone, *Nederland, Colorado.*

In addition to the report of the workings of the Nederland Mill, furnished by Mr. Cone, (see page 308 of this volume,) I take pleasure in publishing the following very practical hints on the proper handling of this apparatus from the same source. Mr. Cone's success in the technical management of the mill referred to renders his suggestions and opinions important to other metallurgists. Since its preparation this article has been communicated as a paper to the American Institute of Mining Engineers.

It is somewhat surprising that among the many mechanical devices that were brought into the State of Colorado the Brückner cylinders alone have stood the test for roasting ores. The brick walls of the Arey and Stetefeldt furnaces have been remodeled into reverberatories and compound reverberatories, their binding and anchor irons have been forged into hoes and shovels, while the Crosby and Thompson cylinders have been rent by the ruthless hand of the founderyman searching for a tough piece of boiler-plate. Two only of these furnaces remain in operation of the large stock that came into Colorado by car-loads several years ago, and they occupy only a subordinate position to some reverberatories on the North Boulder Creek.

But to-day there are in Colorado, in active operation, ten Brückner cylinders, and two or three more running part of the time. During the past year they have handled nearly one-half of the number of tons of silver-ore that has been mined.

Four of the cylinders I have been using in the Nederland Mill, in which I have roasted nearly four thousand tons of silver-ore during the past year, with results more favorable than have hitherto been attained.

The Nederland Mill is similar to many others in Colorado and Nevada. The plant consists of a Blake crusher, three batteries of five stamps each, four Brückner cylinders, and fourteen amalgamating-pans, with settlers, agitators, &c. The ore, after being dried on the drying-kiln, which is heated by the waste gases of the furnaces and an auxiliary fire, is weighed and feed into the batteries, which are dry-crushing, (size of screens 40 meshes to linear inch,) and thence carried by conveyors and an elevator to sheet-iron hoppers over the cylinders. The size of the cylinders is twelve feet long by five feet six inches in diameter. Mr. J. M. Locke has given an excellent description of them in a paper read before the institute, (vol. ii, Transactions,) and as during the coming year some very material changes will be made in their construction by reducing the weight, thereby reducing the cost of freight, and in the driving-gear, I will not go over the same ground.

After several trials I found that 3,700 pounds was the limit that could be handled for a charge in the cylinders of ores from Caribou Hill, and with several small lots of custom-ore I reduced it to 3,500 pounds. From these trials I very soon saw that to handle the cylinders not only to their utmost capacity, but to do thorough work, it was necessary to charge an amount of ore that, when it reached its largest volume in smelting, it would barely run out of the back nozzle of the cylinder. I have sometimes been delayed by small charges that it seemed almost impossible to finish.

The addition of salt I varied according to the value and quality of the ore; usually it was 175 pounds to the charge, occasionally 200 pounds. The time of roasting ranged all the way from 8 hours to 12 hours. I gave my men strict orders never to draw a charge till it was thoroughly *done*, if it took a week; fortunately this circumstance never happened.

When I first took charge of the mill, the diaphragms to the cylinders were entirely eaten away. For some reason "*basic scale*" would not form on those pipes and plates, nor on the new diaphragms that I put in last September. The stumps of the pipes that remained gave me a great deal of trouble by working loose in their sockets, and allowing the half-roasted ore to leak out, so that I finally removed every vestige of the diaphragms, and run the cylinders for over six months with nothing but a lining of common red brick. Having never enjoyed the benefits of a new set of diaphragms, I was very anxious to try them; so in last September I put in a complete set all around, and relined the cylinders, and during the next 60 days saw them rapidly disappear, and I was obliged to clean out the dust-chambers twice as often, and take out three times as much as ever before, and since November, 1875, I have been running on the good old plan.

The class of ore that I have been treating contains about 11 per cent. of mineral matter on the average for the year.

Galena........ 5 per cent.
Blende........ 4 per cent. } = 11 per cent.
Copper-pyrites 2 per cent.

I have occasionally had custom-ore that would reach up to 30 or 40 per cent. of mineral matter, and have been very successful in roasting it, the only difference being that it required a little longer time.

Part of the year I have had 8-hour shifts on, and the rest of the time 12-hour shifts. The advantage of 8-hour shifts is that the men watch the charges closer, and in case one is sick, or it becomes necessary to discharge one, the two can be put on 12 hours, and the work will go along surer than if a new man from some other part of the mill was put on.

I have adopted the following plan for taking samples, after trying different methods. The roaster opens the first door that approaches him, and, as it passes around and commences to dump the ore into the car the second time, a sample is taken with a long-handled shovel, allowed to cool, and then wrapped up in paper and the number of the charge marked on it. A regular list is kept of all charges, giving date, quantity, time charged, time discharged, quantity of salt used, workman's name that charged and discharged the ore, with remarks whether Caribou or custom ore had been used. Assays for chlorinations are made of each man's work, and the average recorded on the office book.

I changed the diameter of the nozzles several times. The flue to the dry-kiln leads off from the dust-chambers near No. 4 cylinder, so that the gases from No. 1 cylinder have the greatest distance to travel.

No. 1 cylinder, fire-box nozzle, 16 inches; back nozzle, 17 inches.
No. 2 cylinder, fire-box nozzle, 16 inches; back nozzle, 12 inches.
No. 3 cylinder, fire-box nozzle, 16 inches; back nozzle, 18 inches.
No. 4 cylinder, fire-box nozzle, 15 inches; back nozzle, 17 inches.

I have arranged the year's work under the following table, so that the work of different months can be easily compared. I also give the maximum and minimum of chlorinations and fineness of bullion, as well as the monthly averages.

Month.	Maximum, minimum and average.	Per cent.	Weight in tons.	Assay.	Fineness of bullion.	Time of roasting.	Barrels of salt used.
January..	Maximum of chlorination....	92.5	9.031	147	828	8½	137
	Minimum of chlorination....	87.8	5.093	30	713		
	Averages	90.	396.8	52	744		
February.	Maximum of chlorination....	95.4	11.231	152	831	8¾	108
	Minimum of chlorination	89.7	10.344	50	788		
	Averages..................	91.0	318.2	70	812		
March....	Maximum of chlorination....	91.2	12.595	74	821	9	137
	Minimum of chlorination	87.1	11.102	37	740		
	Averages..................	88.	371.2	46	790		
April.....	Maximum of chlorination....	93.2	8.505	92	847	9	136
	Minimum of chlorination	89.8	12.027	34	766		
	Averages..................	91.0	353.4	58	807		
May	Maximum of chlorination....	94.5	10.214	168	842	9½	140
	Minimum of chlorination	86.8	7.361	26	763		
	Averages..................	89.4	329.8	54	825		
June	Maximum of chlorination....	90.8	5.980	42	815	10¼	138
	Minimum of chlorination....	85.9	10.580	32	773		
	Averages..................	88.3	393.9	37	794		
July	Averages..................	88.8	362.7	42	820	9½	136
August...	Maximum of chlorination....	92.	10.	41	866	10½	100
	Minimum of chlorination....	87.6	12.148	27	836		
	Averages..................	89.1	319.9	36	854		

Month.	Maximum, minimum and average.	Per cent.	Weight in tons.	Assay.	Fineness of bullion.	Time of roasting.	Barrels of salt used.
September	Maximum of chlorination....	91.4	12.540	56	928	11	98
	Minimum of chlorination....	85.5	14.605	26	858		
	Averages....................	89.1	246.2	51	893		
October ..	Maximum of chlorination....	92.	11.880	65	946	10½	96
	Minimum of chlorination....	87.5	8.580	56	868		
	Averages....................	89.1	300.8	43	902		
November	Maximum of chlorination....	95.9	12.600	31	873	11	106
	Minimum of chlorination....	89.	6.930	21	814		
	Averages....................	92.8	305.3	41	853		
December	Maximum of chlorination....	92.4	14.300	48	822	10	42
	Minimum of chlorination....	89.3	14.520	56	777		
	Averages....................	91.5	120.9	53	804		

The consumption of wood is about a cord and one-half to five tons of ore; this, of course, depends on how constantly the cylinders are kept running.

The expenses for treating ore has been, per ton—

Labor	$6 18	Oil, candles, &c	$0 37
Quicksilver.....................	0 76	Repairs	1 68
Salt	2 09		
Wood	3 43	Per ton..........................	14 51

By wetting the ash-pit I have been enabled sometimes to get a current of steam to pass into the cylinders, and have found it a very good way to regulate the fires.

I have had no difficulty in teaching men how to roast; they very soon take hold of it, and there seems to be a general desire among the workmen to learn.

CHAPTER XVIII.

DRY ORE-CONCENTRATION AT THE MANHATTAN SILVER-MILL, NEVADA.

By A. TRIPPEL, *Mining Engineer, New York.*

The following figures, showing the working results of the Manhattan Mill at Austin, Nev., in 1875, were taken from the books of the Manhattan Silver-Mining Company, by kind permission of its agent, Allen A. Curtis, esq. The peculiar character and great richness of the Reese River district ores worked in this mill are well known and need no new description. It may be well to call attention to the fact that the fuel used for the Stetefeldt furnace in this mill is wood and charcoal combined. Of the whole wood and charcoal consumed, about nine cords of wood are used daily for the motive-power, and a small quantity of charcoal for the melting-furnace and assay-room; the remainder is used for the roasting of ores. It should also be mentioned that the cord of wood costs $12, and charcoal 30 cents the bushel, while labor is generally paid $4 per shift.

1875.	Pounds ore reduced.	Assay-value.	Bullion obtained.	Value tailings.	Bullion and tailings.	Amount lost.	Average mill-test.
January	1, 126, 000	$100, 364 29	$87, 036 37	$10, 359 20	$97, 395 57	$2, 968 72	$178 23
February	893, 500	78, 296 62	70, 120 38	7, 795 78	77, 916 16	380 46	177 93
March	1, 236, 250	127, 602 00	111, 087 37	12, 387 23	123, 474 60	4, 127 40	203 20
April	117, 500	116, 669 94	106, 654 69	9, 067 93	115, 722 62	947 32	209 94
May	966, 000	105, 277 64	94, 613 13	10, 413 48	105, 026 61	251 03	209 81
June	1, 167, 000	137, 087 70	114, 997 89	12, 965 37	127, 903 26	9, 124 44	230 04
July	1, 136, 500	130, 935 71	111, 874 53	11, 688 90	123, 563 43	7, 372 28	227 04
August	959, 500	94, 384 64	81, 935 72	9, 105 75	91, 041 47	3, 343 17	196 12
September	1, 120, 750	110, 256 54	96, 907 49	10, 495 82	107, 403 31	2, 853 23	198 07
October	1, 255, 750	139, 871 26	120, 435 49	10, 868 49	131, 303 98	8, 567 28	221 35
November	1, 094, 500	110, 401 10	96, 178 62	9, 303 25	105, 481 87	4, 919 23	202 01
December	1, 176, 500	122, 818 20	112, 812 50	8, 970 81	121, 783 31	1, 034 89	205 78
Totals and averages	12, 249, 750	....	1, 204, 654 18	....	....	....	....

1875.	Per cent. of bullion.	Per cent. of tailings.	Per cent. of loss.	Per cent. of chlorination.	Wood consumed. Cords.	Charcoal consumed. Bushels.	Pan-charges. Pounds.	Pounds crushed per hour.	Cost of milling.	
January	86. 72	10. 6	2. 67	89. 8	628	4, 800	2, 000	1, 592	Labor	$8 68
February	89. 55	10. 2	0. 27	90.	363	3, 500	1, 787	1, 731	Fuel	12 78
March	87. 05	10. 3	2. 64	90. 6	528	4, 727	1, 719	1, 816	Supplies	2 02
April	91. 41	7. 7	0. 884	90. 8	483	4, 025	1, 650	1, 839	Quicksilver	3 03
May	89. 87	10. 2	......	91. 6	436	3, 840	1, 785	1, 898	Salt	2 56
June	83. 88	9. 4	6. 71	92. 8	453	4, 700	1, 690	1, 885	Office labor	92
July	85. 44	8. 9	5. 65	92. 3	587	4, 964	1, 716	1, 800	Castings	83
August	86. 81	9. 7	3. 48	91. 8	461	4, 931	1, 586	1, 719	Hauling	90
September	87. 89	9. 7	2. 40	91. 5	463	5, 400	1, 729	1, 916		
October	87. 03	8. 4	4. 56	93. 8	458	6, 300	1, 794	2, 137		31 72
November	87. 11	8. 8	4. 08	92. 6	413	5, 230	1, 852	2, 130		
December	91. 85	7. 7	0. 44	94	451	5, 100	1, 761	1, 890		
Totals and averages	87. 67	......	......	91. 8	......	....	....	....		

At the present time the expenses of milling the ore must be less, as the company now has its own iron-foundery on the spot, and an extensive, well-appointed repair-shop. With regard to the percentage of silver produced, there is no doubt that the Manhattan is far ahead of any other mill in Nevada, and its working results may, therefore, be the more interesting.

The most important feature in Reese River district was the introduction of "Krom's" dry separation or concentration of ore at the Manhattan Mills. It has already been stated in last year's report that previous tests with Lander Hill ores in Krom's establishment at the Sheba Mine, near Unionville, had given satisfactory results, and it was expected that equal results would be obtained at Austin with the same ore. These results (of which I give the details in the appended table) were a total product of concentrations, including dust, equaling about 83 per cent. of the assay-value of the worked ore. The ore which was used on that occasion was a mixture from the three principal mines then worked by the Manhattan Company, having a mean assay-value of $120 per ton. Of this mixture a little over five tons were treated. The mineral in the ore consisted of sulphurets of iron, copper, lead, fahlore, antimonial silver and ruby silver, finely distributed through the quartz, yet most of the particles were easily visible, and could be well distinguished from each other. The results being as favorable as could be expected, it was decided to construct works with a capacity to treat 50 tons of ore per day, and during the winter the machinery, or most of it, was constructed in New York, and erected the following summer in the building formerly known as the "Boston Mill," and expressly purchased for that purpose by the Manhattan Company. The main part of this building is a massive structure 116 by 44 feet, with a large extension on the east side, and spacious rooms for steam engine and boilers. The motive-power was furnished by two engines, one of 80 horse-power for the crushing, and another of 15 horse-power for the concentrators proper. The first was partly rebuilt by Booth & Co., of San Francisco, from the engine on hand in the mill-building, and was provided with the best modern improvements; the smaller one was an ordinary engine. The arrangements for feeding the boilers were exceedingly well made, and everything done to economize fuel, which at Austin is very expensive. The machinery for crushing and concentrating was distributed mainly on two floors of the main building, with a loft and screen-tower, with bins for ore and tailings, and the main portion of the screening and sizing arrangements. The building being on a hillside, it was arranged that the ore be dumped high up on a platform in the rear of the same, and delivered through chutes on the second floor next to the ore-breaker—one of Blake's largest size.

From the ore-breaker the ore went through a chute to the first set of steel rolls below, and subsequently through another chute into an elevator, raising it again to the second floor to a rotary screen, which separated all above a certain size from all that was finer, delivering the latter to a second and general elevator, while the coarser part went to the second pair of steel rolls on the second floor. This rotary screen had at one of its ends a very coarse, three-quarter inch sieve, for the purpose of throwing out any larger bodies, among which were generally bits of steel from mining-tools. The ore which passed the second rolls descended to another rotary screen, and finally to the third rolls, from which all was elevated some seventy feet to the top of the screen-tower. The screens in the tower were four; one having 16 meshes, the next 25, the third 50, and the fourth 100 meshes to the linear inch. All too coarse to pass the first went back down to the third crusher; the balance was screened into three sizes on its way down, and each size was received in a separate ore-bin on the third floor or loft. Connected with the crushing, screening, or sizing apparatus were branches of large pipes, leading to an exhauster, which carried the dust into a large dust-chamber, situated immediately under the roof. The concentrators proper received their charge continuously from the different bins through wooden tubes. The concentrations from eight machines of three sizes fell into hoppers, and from these into three concentrators on the lower floor, where they were reconcentrated, while the tailings fell on endless-belt carriers, and from there to elevators and bins arranged to receive each sort of tailings, from day or night work, separate. From these bins they were carried off outside. The sampling of the tailings and the different sizes of ore and the dust (which comprised all ore finer than passed a hundred-mesh screen) were done in the most careful manner, so that the assays represent the actual results of every day's and night's work. I should mention that the *dust* had to be taken as it was, as any further concentration of such fine stuff was entirely impracticable.

The whole machinery was unquestionably of fine make, and on the whole well arranged. In my opinion, the high tower for screening it was objectionable, being, if not inaccessible, as least laborious to reach in its upper parts, and especially because the whole screening-machinery was out of sight, and not fully under control in case of accidents.

Neither were the arrangements to prevent the dust as complete as could be. In the successive crushing by a breaker and three steel rollesr, care should be taken that right from the beginning no stuff should pass the *next* crusher which is fine enough for the *second* ahead. This idea, well carried out, not only prevents much dust, when the chutes and screens are well boxed, but the forming of impalpable powder, or at least very fine ore, which cannot be concentrated any further. The regulation of the large Sturtevant exhauster is not an easy task at all; either its force is not sufficient to suck up all the dust when the place becomes intolerably dusty, or it is too much and the dust is carried far off through the opening at the farthest end of the chamber. The steel rollers of Mr. Krom are exceedingly well constructed, and many parts are of cast steel; the diameter of the rolls was 26 inches, with a tire 2½ inches, made of cast steel. They are undoubtedly the finest crushers ever made, well proportioned, and very powerful. I think, however, that their diameter should diminish as the stuff becomes finer, so that, for instance, the present diameter be maintained for the first pair, about 22 inches for the second, and but 18 inches for the third pair. I am fully convinced that such a diminution in size would be most beneficial where the ore has to be crushed fine. The face of the rolls was 15 inches, and the tire composed of two pieces, joined in the center, it having been found difficult to make cast-steel tires of the right temper as much as 15 inches wide. There was a marked difference in the behavior of the different steel tires; some, thought to be too soft at the beginning, stood the best, and worked off the most uniformly; others, which seemed to withstand the hard quartz well at the start, showed themselves to be brittle, and the edges broke off on some of them. It is not a too hard metal which is wanted; a medium temper and great toughness seem to be most desirable. The wear and tear of the three pairs of rollers, after the crushing of over 1,200 tons of quartz, averaged about $\frac{3}{16}$ of an inch on the surface; they were turned down, but it was found necessary to use titanium steel tools to do this successfully. The gear being so arranged as to suit a continuous decrease of diameter, it is not doubted that these rolls would crush over 8,000 tons before the tire should be renewed, and, where the gangue is not too hard, much more.

The arrangements to prevent fractures consisted essentially in the use of powerful steel springs, behind which were breaking-cups, which not unfrequently proved their usefulness, and likewise the danger of being in too near proximity to them. The third pair of rolls, for fine crushing, should, in my opinion, have no elasticity, but be screwed tight, or nearly so, provided the feeding is well regulated, and care be taken that no larger bodies than those intended come between the rolls. Most frequently stoppages occur by over-feeding, not so much by the coarse stuff as by the fine. The velocity which Mr. Krom gives to his rolls is rather excessive, and would puzzle such authorities as Rittinger. While I believe in a high velocity for small rolls and fine crushing, I hold a more moderate speed for coarse work preferable. A speed uniformly at 50 revolutions seems rather too high.

The speed for the rotary screens was variously tried and deserves all attention; while a too sluggish movement permits too great accumulation of ore, and in consequence an imperfect screening, too high speed throws the stuff violently from one face to another without giving it time to pass the meshes. It was found that about sixteen to eighteen revolutions was the most satisfactory rate.

The material subjected to Krom's dry concentration was not the same as that used on the preliminary trial. It was merely waste ore from a few mines—ore in which the mineral was so exceedingly finely disseminated that it appeared rather as a light-grayish streak, developing under the microscope an aggregate of minute particles of sulphurets. There was a steady value in that part of the ore, an assay-value which might have averaged perhaps $9 per ton, and it was nearly the same whether the *whole* assay-value of the ore was $15 or $40, the increase in the value of the ore being caused by more coarse (though still fine) particles of mineral. This fine part of mineral was as much as lost; although our coarsest size was already finer crushed than most ore for concentration is intended to be crushed, the particles showed plainly under the magnifier these grayish colors undetached from the more white quartz, and not sufficiently different in specific gravity to permit any successful separation. This fact will, I think, sufficiently explain why the tailings of the *lowest* grade were not much different from those of the higher grade ore, understanding that the two figures given above represent the two extremes in this case.

Other obstacles in the way of success were the absence of any drying apparatus, without which, as is well known, neither a stamp-mill nor a crusher, much less various sets of fine screens, can work satisfactorily. Some of the waste ore was delivered not many hours after it was hoisted from the mines, and in some instances thoroughly wet. In addition to that, no care was taken to separate the country-rock—in this case more or less decomposed granite—from the quartzose ore, which not only increased the dust considerably, but caused more difficulties in the screening.

From these facts it will be seen that this test of dry concentration was, to say the least, an uncommonly severe one, and would have been the same for any method of concentration.

Mr. Krom's concentrators proper are decidedly well constructed, and admit of the finest variations of movement in point of speed and strength, according to the different character of the ore; still there are some details which, in my opinion, could be materially improved. The greatest difficulty, however, seems to me to be the screening and the separation of all dust or dust-like ore before it passes into the concentrators and there causes an imperfect working. Even if that dust *is* separated, its disposition, in the absence of reduction-works on the spot, will be embarrassing and cause more or less loss. In this case, the dust, including all that passed a screen with 100 meshes to the linear inch, amounted to about 17 per cent. of the worked ore, and its average assay-value was about 48 to 50 per cent. above that of the value of the ore. It should be said that samples of dust, taken at a distance from the surroundings of the buildings, assayed the same as those taken from the nearest spot in the dust-chamber, proving how eminently *fine* the mineral particles were. All that class of product was sacked and milled without any other preparation than roasting in the Stetefeldt furnace.

A most interesting comparative test with wet concentration was made side by side with the dry process. A well-constructed automatic-working triple jig was used; the water, being scarce, was continually pumped back in the reservoir, and, as the ore was comparatively free from dust, no difficulty was experienced in doing so. The general result was that the product was equal to that made in three of Krom's separators; the average tailings were a trifle poorer, but the concentrations were by far lower in value than in Krom's machines, and my impression is that the work done by the latter is preferable for that class of ore.

The average assay-values for wet and dry tailings, under precisely the same circumstances and the same ore, were as follows during six days' regular work:

Average dry tailings.	Average wet tailings.		Average dry tailings.	Average wet tailings.
$12 55	$11 76		$10 20	$8 61
11 76	11 76		15 71	9 16
11 78	10 59			
10 98	9 43	Mean,	12 16	Mean, 10 22

A synopsis of the general results of three months' working will show as follows:

In 61 working days were crushed and concentrated......	1,210 tons.
Average crushed in 10 hours..............................	20 tons.
Consumption of pine wood per day...................	2¼ cords.
The average assay-value of the ore	$29.16
Average assay-value of dust-like ore....................	$46.00
Of this dust was produced about	17 per cent.
Of real concentrations................................	4.9 per cent.
Assay-value of concentrations varied between $108 and $560, and averaged approximately..................	$250.00.

A comparison between concentrations made by dry and by wet process will show the following values:

Dry concentrations.		Wet concentrations.	
Coarse	$141 35	Coarse ore, 1st box..............	$53 41
Medium	442 96	2d box..............	157 08
Fine	251 33	3d box..............	34 56
		Coarse ore, 1st box..............	72 26
		2d box..............	196 34
		3d box..............	62 83

The value of the combined product, consisting of the concentrations proper and the dust-like ore, which was delivered as product, amounted to about 56 per cent. of the assay-value of the ore received; the loss, therefore, was considerably larger than that sustained at a previous trial made with a better class of ore. I have already called attention to the fact that there was no proportionate difference in the value of tailings, whether the ore was worth $17 or $40, as the following figures will show, these figures being computed from the daily working during 61 days:

Ore averaging from—	Tailings were—	Ore averaging from—	Tailings were—
$15 to $18 85	$10 98	$28 to $30	$13 49
20 to 22 00	12 95	30 to 33	12 93
23 to 24 00	12 38	33 to 36	14 44
25 to 26 00	11 79	36 to 39	14 26
26 to 28 00	12 86	39 to 50	14 49

The entire cost of crushing and concentration per ton of ore, including hauling from the mines, varied between $4.50 and $5. It should be said that this estimate includes the first month of working, during which many delays occurred and numberless difficulties had to be overcome. The financial result for the Manhattan Company, although not entirely satisfactory to them, was, nevertheless, very fair, inasmuch as even that class of ore which could not have been worked without considerable loss in the usual way paid its own way, was made productive, and left a small profit. I am satisfied that the concentration of better ore, or what is called second class in Austin, would prove of great advantage, while admitting that the so-called dump-ore, which was exclusively worked, will never give the results expected by the parties erecting the works, nor will any other method give better results. An important fact which was developed on this trial is the apparent practicability and advantage in substituting a systematic crushing by steel rolls for stamp-batteries. If only the crushing had been the object in this case, it would not have cost over $2 per ton to make pulp fine enough to pass a 100-mesh screen. With every possible effort to avoid making such fine ore, we nevertheless produced 17 per cent. of it, much to our dislike, and crushed, say, 20 tons of ore in 10 hours, with but two cords of wood at the highest calculation, the rest being consumed by the concentrators and screens. When it is considered that the ore was delivered partly in large lumps, being mostly very hard quartz, together with the small wear and tear compared with stamp-mills, these results speak favorably for the adoption of crushing by rolls.

Another interesting feature for mill-men has been well proven by this trial; it is the substitution of the exhaust-fan in the place of the finer sort of screen. Not that this idea is new, but I think it has never commanded the attention it deserves from mill-men. Screening through fine screens is, at best, a very imperfect and troublesome operation, and expensive at that, while I have fully satisfied myself that a proper application of the exhaust-fan would produce a uniformly-sized pulp with far less dust and at a much less cost.

APPENDIX.

MISCELLANEOUS STATISTICS.

THE BULLION PRODUCT.

The following is the estimate of the bullion product of 1875, published by Mr. Valentine, general superintendent of Wells, Fargo & Co.'s express.

OFFICE WELLS, FARGO & CO.,
San Francisco, December 30, 1875.

DEAR SIR: We inclose you herewith a copy of our annual statement of precious metals produced in the States and Territories west of the Missouri River, including British Columbia and the west coast of Mexico, during 1875, which shows an aggregate yield of $80,889,037, being an excess of $6,487,982 over 1874, the greatest previous annual yield in the history of the coast. Nevada, Colorado, Mexico, Oregon, British Columbia, Montana, and Arizona increased, while California, Idaho, Utah, and Washington decreased. The increase is actual except for Mexico, Oregon, and Arizona, where it is apparent rather than real as compared with other years, a regular product being accounted for and reported herein, hitherto omitted. The decrease in California was in the main occasioned by a stinted supply of water for placer and hydraulic mining. The increase in Colorado and Nevada is notable, also the fact that Nevada yields more than half of the whole product of the country.

Professor R. W. Raymond credits New Mexico (omitted in our statement) and Arizona combined with $987,000, which is a liberal allowance. We have been unable to obtain any data that justifies a showing so favorable.

Present prospects indicate an aggregate yield of $90,000,000 for 1876, of which Nevada will doubtless produce $50,000,000.

Respectfully yours,

JOHN J. VALENTINE,
General Superintendent.

Statement of the amount of precious metals produced in the States and Territories west of the Missouri River during 1875.

States and Territories.	Gold dust and bullion by express.	Gold dust and bullion by other conveyances.	Silver bullion by express.	Ores and base bullion by freight.	Total.
California	$14, 842, 010	$1, 484, 201	$387, 768	$1, 039, 172	$17, 753, 151
Nevada	196, 858	19, 685	35, 283, 193	4, 978, 633	40, 478, 369
Oregon	759, 133	405, 913	....	....	1, 165, 046
Washington	74, 517	7, 415	....	....	81, 932
Idaho	1, 163, 698	116, 369	230, 835	44, 000	1, 554, 902
Montana	2, 235, 609	500, 000	88, 000	750, 000	3, 573, 609
Utah	43, 686	4, 368	764, 041	4, 875, 399	5, 687, 494
Arizona	23, 500	....	....	85, 593	109, 093
Colorado	2, 627, 444	....	2, 610, 266	1, 062, 107	6, 299, 817
Mexico	68, 117	....	1, 716, 184	624, 370	2, 408, 671
British Columbia	1, 615, 412	161, 541	....	....	1, 776, 953
	23, 649, 984	2, 699, 492	41, 080, 287	13, 459, 274	80, 889, 037

The criticisms of Mr. Valentine concerning the product of New Mexico and Arizona are elsewhere considered. (See chapter X.)

My own estimate for the year 1875 is given in the introductory letter to this report. It is repeated in the following table, combined with the reports of the previous years since 1868. For the grounds on which the estimate of product for each State and Territory is based the reader is referred to the respective chapters of this report.

States and Territories.	1869.	1870.	1871.	1872.	1873.	1874.	1875.
Arizona	$1,000,000	$800,000	$800,000	$625,000	$500,000	$487,000	$750,000
California	22,500,000	25,000,000	20,000,000	19,049,098	18,025,722	20,300,531	17,753,151
Colorado	*4,000,000	3,675,000	4,663,000	4,661,465	4,020,263	5,188,510	5,302,810
Idaho	7,000,000	6,000,000	5,000,000	2,695,870	2,500,000	1,880,004	1,750,000
Montana	9,000,000	9,100,000	8,050,000	6,068,339	5,178,047	3,844,722	3,573,600
Nevada	14,000,000	16,000,000	22,500,000	25,548,801	35,254,507	35,452,233	40,478,369
New Mexico	500,000	500,000	500,000	500,000	500,000	500,000	325,000
Oregon and Washington.	3,000,000	3,000,000	2,500,000	2,000,000	1,585,784	763,605	1,246,978
Wyoming	....	100,000	100,000	100,000	50,000	....	....
Utah	....	1,300,000	2,300,000	2,445,284	3,778,200	3,911,601	3,137,688
Other sources	500,000	525,000	250,000	250,000	250,000	100,000	500,000
Total	61,500,000	66,000,000	66,663,000	63,943,857	71,642,523	72,428,206	74,817,596

* Including Wyoming.

[From the San Francisco Commercial Herald.]

Receipts of treasure.

The following table comprises the receipts of treasure in this city, through Wells, Fargo & Co.'s express, during 1875:

FROM THE NORTHERN AND SOUTHERN MINES.

1875.	Silver bullion.	Gold bars, &c.	Coin.	Totals.
January	$973,166	$445,904	$971,741	$2,390,811
February	1,518,589	519,086	911,631	2,949,306
March	2,467,843	501,004	835,564	3,804,411
April	1,801,893	573,311	1,210,686	3,585,890
May	1,798,868	774,949	1,560,291	4,134,108
June	1,305,982	713,334	1,134,066	3,153,382
July	1,323,529	653,635	1,228,664	3,205,828
August	2,033,299	597,593	1,078,644	3,709,536
September	1,767,539	292,449	2,158,658	4,518,646
October	2,325,807	558,544	1,303,024	4,187,375
November	1,655,296	384,425	1,163,911	3,204,632
December	1,270,204	547,854	1,029,725	2,847,783
Totals	20,242,015	6,863,088	14,586,605	41,691,708
Totals, 1874	18,269,054	7,092,924	9,259,352	34,621,330
Totals, 1873	11,749,320	8,290,258	6,636,143	26,675,721
Totals, 1872	6,386,704	14,843,835	6,769,641	28,000,270
Totals, 1871	14,609,809	13,872,648	7,125,928	35,608,385
Totals, 1870	14,152,984	17,762,131	6,487,037	38,402,152

FROM THE NORTHERN COAST.

1875.	Silver bullion.	Gold bars, &c.	Coin.	Totals.
January	....	$184,998	$37,023	$222,021
February	....	45,027	243,394	288,421
March	....	108,681	159,371	268,052
April	....	136,782	65,004	201,786
May	....	96,176	87,156	183,322
June	....	44,428	37,065	81,493
July	....	119,353	34,321	153,674
August	....	85,764	57,698	143,462
September	....	98,873	79,828	178,701
October	....	204,855	74,777	279,632
November	....	230,516	72,653	303,169
December	$750	99,614	45,049	145,413
Totals	750	1,455,067	993,339	2,449,156
Totals, 1874	300	1,548,430	657,482	2,206,212
Totals, 1873	4,200	1,441,438	878,377	2,324,015
Totals, 1872	....	2,305,414	661,889	2,967,303
Totals, 1871	9,785	2,552,668	708,096	3,270,549
Totals, 1870	....	3,380,566	532,901	3,913,467

FROM THE SOUTHERN COAST.

1875.	Silver bullion.	Gold bars, &c.	Coin.	Totals.
January	1,200	16,410	39,854	57,464
February	....	3,515	20,251	23,766
March	....	10,895	24,952	35,847
April	1,685	9,930	21,839	33,454
May	2,300	8,705	43,458	54,463
June	5,000	11,324	48,655	64,979
July	3,550	10,296	30,394	44,240
August	477	17,434	38,416	56,327
September	1,200	17,747	50,766	69,713
October	13,211	17,764	32,811	63,786
November	13,000	10,278	53,047	76,325
December	19,237	15,109	142,675	177,021
Totals	60,860	149,407	547,118	757,385
Totals, 1874	9,547	208,445	383,465	601,457
Totals, 1873	3,688	180,537	570,013	754,238
Totals, 1872	3,884	274,249	564,477	842,610
Totals, 1871	5,750	347,627	551,413	904,790
Totals, 1870	....	399,888	844,548	1,244,436

Currency movement.

The annexed table exhibits the interior and coastwise receipts, (Wells, Fargo & Co.,) imports, (foreign,) and exports for the years 1873, 1874, and 1875:

	1873.	1874.	1875.
Interior receipts	$28,755,679	$36,097,261	$43,466,378
Imports, (foreign)	5,539,147	5,473,482	5,223,875
Totals	34,294,826	41,570,743	48,690,253
Exports	24,715,126	30,180,032	42,911,048
Currency movement, (increase)	9,579,700	11,390,111	5,779,205

Movement of coin in the interior.

The following has been the circulation of coin, through Wells, Fargo & Co.'s express, during 1875, as compared with the same period in 1874:

	1874.		1875.	
	To interior.	From interior and coastwise.	To interior.	From interior and coastwise.
January	$1,394,487	$714,862	$1,802,652	$1,048,618
February	1,108,611	714,944	1,249,485	1,175,276
March	963,314	575,643	3,180,038	1,019,887
April	1,312,070	661,032	1,611,934	1,297,529
May	1,573,629	837,327	2,297,097	1,690,905
June	1,552,281	922,986	1,697,166	1,219,786
July	1,917,597	857,834	2,393,840	1,293,379
August	2,001,436	934,119	2,552,520	1,174,758
September	2,055,615	980,914	3,671,205	2,289,252
October	2,294,193	1,010,046	2,300,546	1,410,612
November	1,950,220	1,005,496	2,284,189	1,289,611
December	1,813,910	1,085,096	2,269,130	1,217,449
Totals	19,937,363	10,300,299	26,709,802	16,127,062

Mint statistics.

The coinage at the branch mint in this city for 1875 compares with that in 1872, 1873, and 1874 as follows:

	1872.	1873.	1874.	1875.
January	$840,750	$900,000	$279,000	$2,355,000
February	1,210,000	1,219,400	1,994,000	1,681,000
March	1,127,750	1,140,000	3,958,000	2,482,000
April	1,420,000	1,282,000	1,752,000	3,458,000
May	2,020,000	2,772,000	367,000	2,794,000
June	666,000	652,000	2,393,000	1,172,000
July	2,245,000	3,082,000	2,309,000	2,508,000
August	730,000	2,131,000	4,320,000	4,510,000
September	1,264,500	2,264,500	2,570,000	2,648,000
October	1,895,000	2,658,000	3,204,000	3,118,000
November	1,525,000	254,500	96,000	2,623,000
December	1,436,600	3,720,000	4,087,000	2,720,000
Totals	16,380,600	22,075,400	27,329,000	32,069,000

The description of coinage for 1872, 1873, 1874, and 1875 was as follows:

	1872.	1873.	1874.	1875.
Double-eagles	$15,600,000	$20,812,000	$24,375,000	$24,600,000
Eagles	173,000	120,000	50,000	....
Half-eagles	202,000	155,000	35,000	45,000
Quarter-eagles	95,000	67,500	....	29,000
Half-dollars	290,000	116,500	197,000	1,600,000
Quarter-dollars	26,250	39,000	98,000	170,000
Dimes	19,000	45,500	24,000	907,000
Half-dimes	36,350	16,200	....	....
Silver dollars	9,000	700	....	....
Trade-dollars	....	703,000	2,550,000	4,487,000
Twenty-cent pieces	....	....	....	231,000
Totals	16,380,600	22,075,400	27,329,000	32,069,000

Exports of treasure.

Statement of the amount of treasure exported from San Francisco, through public channels, to eastern domestic and foreign ports during the year 1875, exclusive of shipments through United States mail:

TO NEW YORK.		
In January	$940,432 95	
In February	5,023,547 14	
In March	5,697,596 15	
In April	2,435,050 22	
In May	2,569,698 54	
In June	5,703,670 99	
In July	2,461,868 70	
In August	794,727 83	
In September	1,320,834 25	
In October	5,861,703 96	
In November	859,825 09	
In December	899,638 55	
		$34,568,594 37
TO ENGLAND.		
In January	$15,537 38	
In February	16,404 46	
In March	15,503 68	
In April	11,532 85	
In May	12,973 95	
In June	18,101 42	
In July	20,417 37	
In August	16,798 73	
In September	20,490 88	
In October	25,385 92	
		173,146 64
TO PANAMA.		
In February	$1,031 18	
In August	1,750 00	
In September	1,000 00	
In December	3,182 04	
		6,963 22
TO CENTRAL AMERICA.		
In January	$40,000 00	
In March	38,190 03	
In April	15,670 00	
In June	15,311 85	
In August	14,000 00	
In October	10,000 00	
		133,171 88
TO HONOLULU.		
In January	$10,000 00	
In September	10,000 00	
In October	10,000 00	
In November	10,000 00	
		40,000 00
TO MEXICO.		
In January	$6,000 00	
In March	27,000 00	
		33,000 00
TO GERMANY.		
In December		10,591 04
TO JAPAN.		
In August		2,070 00
TO CHINA.		
In February	$749,704 50	
In March	169,831 00	
In April	695,746 00	

In May	$584,583 70	
In June	679,265 82	
In July	423,512 08	
In August	566,532 05	
In September	625,056 40	
In October	737,036 25	
In November	872,002 48	
In December	729,859 00	
		$7,652,953 38
TO VICTORIA.		
In September	$50,000 00	
In October	35,000 00	
In November	40,000 00	
		125,000 00
TO PERU.		
In October	$165,000 00	
In November	200 00	
		165,200 00
TO MARQUESAS ISLANDS.		
In February		357 36
Total, 1875		42,911,047 89
Total, 1874		30,180,632 23
Increase this year		12,730,415 66

OTHER MINERAL STATISTICS OF THE PACIFIC COAST.

[From the San Francisco Commercial Herald.]

BORAX.

The entire product of merchantable borax produced on this coast, being wholly from the States of California and Nevada, amounted last year to about 5,000,000 pounds. Of this quantity, 1,300,000 pounds was the product of the Slate Range district, San Bernadino County, California, the balance coming nearly all from the Teel and the Fish Lake marshes, in the State of Nevada. Of the Slate Range production, 1,200,000 pounds were manufactured by the Riddle Company, while of the quantity made in Nevada, 2,140,000 pounds came from Teel's and 1,079,000 pounds from the Fish Lake marsh, some 500,000 pounds having been turned out at various other localities. William T. Coleman & Co., as agents of the principal Nevada companies, report shipments during the year 1875 as follows: To Liverpool and London, 2,659,375 pounds; to Hamburg, 215,799 pounds; to Bremen, 10,000 pounds; to China and Japan, 7,000 pounds; to Australia, 1,500 pounds; to Mexico, 1,300 pounds; to New York, 814,760 pounds; to Philadelphia, 124,158 pounds; besides 1,598,866 pounds sent east by rail, making a total of 5,433,658 pounds. Adding to this 627,685 pounds shipped by other parties, mostly by the Riddell Company, we have 6,051,343 pounds to represent the entire exports for the year. The Riddell Company, which made 600 tons last year, will increase their product to 1,000 tons the present year, the Nevada companies promising some, but not as large a percentage of increase, both the extent and the richness of the deposits there, as well as in California, appearing to have been considerably overrated by those who first examined and reported upon them. While these borate fields cover a broad area, the crude material is much less abundant and of lower grade than was at first supposed, admonishing the owners of these valuable salines to economy in disposing of their contents. The mistaken notions in regard to the available quantities of these borates that early prevailed, filling foreign dealers with apprehensions of an immediate over-production, caused the rapid decline in price that has been going on for the past three years, during which this commodity fell from 28 cents to 6¼ cents per pound. The correction of this erroneous idea has already caused a stiffening of prices, which, it is believed in well-informed quarters, must soon experience a material advance. Under vigorous working, the surface-deposits of our borate fields begin to show signs of early exhaustion, while those of South America, the only quarter in which we have reason to fear competition, cannot, by reason of their poverty in the borate of soda and their inaccessible position, be made available as sources of large supply at present prices. The Riddell Company having filled a considerable contract at 6⅜ cents per pound, decline to renew the same or take orders at 6½ cents, thinking better terms may soon be obtained. This company is in a prosperous condition; and having lately enlarged their works, as well as introduced some improvements in the methods of manufacturing, anticipate an increased production at somewhat lessened pro rata of cost. They have, furthermore, the benefit of skill and intelligence in the field and able financial management at headquarters. In disposing of their product the past year this company has sold some to British buyers here and sent the balance to eastern markets. At present they are separated from the railroad terminus by a space of 120 miles. As the track is advanced, this distance is being diminished, and will next year be reduced to 80 miles. This borax as it enters the market contains 95 per cent. boracic acid. Some small portions intended for special uses or certain branches of the trade being further purified and refined at the establishments here and in Oakland, an extra price is obtained for this commodity, though for most uses it is no better, and for some not so good as the ordinary article of commerce. As the dealer here has to find his principal market abroad, he is forced to place himself in accord with the foreign agent, subordinating his views and line of policy to those of the latter. Just now certain European scientists are exercising themselves to discover some new uses to which this substance can be economically applied, and it is not unlikely that their endeavors will be rewarded with success. Until it shall appear, however, that there is likely to occur a much greater production than now seems probable, these efforts can hereby be considered well directed. At the close we quote concentrated, in sacks, by the car-load, 6¾@7 cents. The regular agency price for concentrated by the car-load is 7½@8½ cents; refined 9¼@9¾ cents.

Exports by sea during 1874 and 1875.

To—	1874.			1875.		
	Cases.	Packages.	Value.	Cases.	Packages.	Value.
New York	3, 517	2, 012	$101, 546	262	5, 489	$61, 450
England	8, 632	2, 031	146, 126	3, 571	17, 114	212, 665
China	225	45	3, 892	62	....	559
Japan	160	72	3, 231	17	....	168
Mexico	27	....	898	17	....	220
Germany	1, 944	1, 034	40, 229	1, 406	348	16, 436
Belgium	60	....	720	....	....	....
Australia	42	....	504	15	....	283
British Columbia	6	....	76	2	1	39
Peru	10	5	235	....	....	....
Society Islands	1	....	15	....	....	....
Totals	14, 624	5, 199	297, 472	4, 992	22, 952	294, 770

CEMENT, PLASTER, AND LIME.

	Barrels.
Imports in 1871	32,602
Imports in 1872	54,740
Imports in 1873	61,911
Imports in 1874	79,435
Imports in 1875	96,984

The receipts of both Rosendale and Portland cement during 1875 show a large increase over those of the previous year, Prices in consequence have ruled low and unremunerative all the year; stocks large. The manufacture of cement upon this coast now is a perfect success, the Golden Gate Mill making a first-class article, fit for every purpose, out of gypsum, and is selling at $3@$3.25 per barrel, and can be supplied in any quantity. The ship Oriflamme has arrived from London with 2,250 barrels Portland cement. This article is largely used for making Frear (patent) stone, and is preferred to all other for fine work. It may be quoted ex ship at $4@$4.50 per barrel, while Hoffman's Rosendale is held at $3@$3.25, and Lawrenceville do. at $2.50@$2.75. Lime is produced here in endless quantity from Santa Cruz marble, and is of very superior quality, commanding $2@$2.25 per barrel. The Doune Castle from London has 2,000 barrels Portland cement.

Our monthly receipts of California lime compare as follows:

Months.	1874.	1875.	Months.	1874.	1875.
	Bbls.	*Bbls.*		*Bbls.*	*Bbls.*
January	5,440	8,797	July	14,098	21,245
February	5,500	9,529	August	11,624	24,061
March	6,250	11,532	September	16,102	18,966
April	8,128	15,153	October	17,005	13,440
May	12,682	21,341	November	12,613	7,906
June	19,182	22,541	December	14,899	8,120
Totals				143,513	182,631
Increase in 1875				......	39,118

COAL.

Annual receipts of coal at San Francisco.

Years.	Mount Diablo.	Coos Bay.	Bellingham Bay.	Vancouver Island.	Chili.	Australia.	English.	Cumberland.	Anthracite.	Seattle.	Rocky Mountain.	Other countries.	Total.
	Tons.	*Tons.*	*Tons.*	*Tons.*	*Tons.*	*Tons.*	*Tons.*	*Tons.*	*Tons.*	*Tons.*	*Tons.*	*Tons.*	*Tons.*
1860	....	3,145	5,490	6,655	1,900	7,850	6,640	5,970	39,985	......	......	......	77,635
1861	6,620	4,630	10,055	6,475	12,495	23,370	23,565	2,975	26,060	......	......	......	116,245
1862	23,400	2,815	10,050	8,870	5,110	12,590	16,055	4,970	36,685	......	......	......	120,545
1863	43,200	1,185	7,750	5,74	1,790	16,890	14,660	5,670	38,660	......	......	......	135,550
1864	50,700	1,200	11,845	12,785	2,323	21,160	18,330	7,275	41,680	......	......	......	167,298
1865	60,530	1,500	14,446	18,181	1,410	17,610	9,655	4,230	22,585	......	......	......	150,147
1866	84,020	2,120	11,380	10,852	1,480	53,709	7,400	9,524	12,124	......	......	......	192,601
1867	109,490	5,415	8,899	14,829	14,949	26,619	7,302	12,177	48,518	......	.....	727	248,925
1868	132,537	10,524	13,866	23,348	8,511	31,590	29,561	2,292	29,592	......	.....	204	286,025
1869	148,722	14,821	20,552	14,880	1,114	75,115	17,386	11,536	24,844	......	......	......	328,973
1870	129,761	20,567	14,355	12,640	7,350	83,982	31,196	9,322	21,320	......	......	......	320,493
1871	133,485	28,690	20,284	15,621	4,161	38,942	54,191	6,060	7,231	4,918	1,025	583	315,194
1872	177,232	32,562	4,100	26,008	3,682	115,332	29,190	10,051	19,618	14,830	1,862	......	434,467
1873	171,741	38,066	21,211	31,435	400	96,435	52,616	8,857	18,295	13,572	1,904	50	454,582
1874	206,255	44,857	13,685	51,017	......	139,109	37,826	15,475	14,263	9,027	433	......	531,947
1875	142,808	32,869	10,445	61,072	......	136,869	57,849	10,328	18,810	67,106	53	......	538,209

In making this exhibit, it should be stated that the Central Pacific Railroad handled much of their own coal, bringing it from the Lincoln Mine, California, and Rocky Mountain, from Wyoming Territory. They also use more or less Mount Diablo; and of all this consumed by the railroad we take no account in our statistics. The Pacific Mail Company have a contract with the Wellington (V. I.) coal-mine for a large monthly supply, and only what is landed here enters into our statistics. The same company are now seeking to make a like contract with the Seattle Mine, Washington Territory. The Coos Bay Company have been much interrupted the past six months in getting their coal to market, by reason of loss of one of their best steam-colliers, adverse winds, stormy weather, and bad luck generally. The great falling off in the Mount Diablo product is remarkable, and at this writing we have no cause to assign for it. The Seattle mines, Washington Territory, show a large increase in their product, as do also the Wellington and Nanaimo mines of Vancouver Island. These three last-named bituminous enter very largely into local use for household purposes. There have been times during the year when Lehigh ran short of supply by reason of the non-arrival of ships, causing very high prices to rule, and necessitating the bringing of a few car-loads across the continent by rail; but all that is now remedied and overcome by reason of fresh arrivals by sea—the Centennial having some 500 tons, and the ship Golden Fleece 1,750 tons Lehigh. These, with other lesser invoices recently at hand, have caused prices to drop from $25 to $15 per ton; in fact, we doubt whether these cargo parcels could be placed better than $12. So, also, in regard to Cumberland, by reason of the non-arrival of the ship Itasca, 253 days out from Baltimore, supplies threatened to give out; but dealers in the trade purchased from outsiders 1,000 tons or more, and now that the ship has safely arrived in port, and no more to arrive in some four months, prices of Cumberland in casks have been fixed to dealers at $22, and in bulk at $18. The supply of Sydney has been very constant all the year, and during the last quarter thereof cargo sales of steam were made as low as $8.50@$8.75. At this writing, Wallsend may be quoted at $9.25@$9.50, ex ship. The importation of Australian steam-coals during the year has not been profitable, and the same remarks are, no doubt, applicable to both Scotch and English steam. We quote: Bellingham Bay at $8.50; Coos Bay, $10; California Mount Diablo steam, $6.25@$8.25 for fine and coarse, respectively; English and Scotch steam, $9@$10; Nanaimo, $9.50@$10; Seattle, $9.50@$10; Anthracite, $12@$15; Lehigh, $15@$16. Imports during the week embrace the following: Prince Robert, 600 tons Wellington; Gem of the Ocean, 1,011 tons Seattle; Hannibal, from Newcastle, N. S. W., 1,662 tons; Marmion, 1,200 tons from Seattle.

QUICKSILVER PRODUCTION AND TRADE OF CALIFORNIA.

The exports to the different countries for 1875 and the three previous years were as follows:

To—	1872.	1873.	1874.	1875.
New York	1,202	....	315	287
China	4,810	1,900	1,200	18,190
Mexico	5,038	3,761	4,104	5,757
South America	1,300	508	738	2,149
Australia	643	105	100	832
British Columbia	2	11	2	17
Other countries	103	74	311	1,728
Total flasks	13,098	6,359	6,770	28,960

And our exports previously have been:

	Flasks.		Flasks.
In 1871	15,205	In 1861	35,995
In 1870	13,788	In 1860	9,448
In 1869	24,415	In 1859	3,399
In 1868	44,506	In 1858	24,142
In 1867	28,853	In 1857	27,262
In 1866	30,287	In 1856	23,740
In 1865	42,469	In 1855	27,165
In 1864	36,927	In 1854	20,963
In 1863	26,014	In 1853	12,737
In 1862	33,747	In 1852	900

Exports by sea during 1874 *and* 1875.

To—	1874.		1875.	
	Flasks.	Value.	Flasks.	Value.
New York	315	$35,696	287	$17,253
Mexico	4,104	426,249	5,757	375,120
Chili	404	39,888	355	24,803
New Zealand	51	5,345	258	14,074
Bolivia	134	13,805	....	....
China	1,200	135,878	18,190	1,003,842
Japan	248	27,751	968	56,116
Central America	12	1,195	34	1,794
British Columbia	2	207	17	931
England	....	....	100	7,650
South America	200	22,185	2,149	154,184
Australia	100	11,475	832	47,905
Calcutta	....	....	10	550
Russian Asia	....	....	3	195
Totals	6,770	719,674	28,960	1,704,417

The total receipts at the tide-water from all the cinnabar-mines of the State exceed 50,000 flasks, while the exports by sea are 35,000. The shipments east overland during the year have been larger than usual, while the consumption of the "bonanza" and other mines has been considerably more than ever before, and promises to be even greater in the near future. Colorado gets her supply via New York cheaper than it can be procured from this coast, owing to lessened transportation-charges. Our accumulated stock is very small, the export trade and home consumption thus far taking it off as fast as brought to market. This shows conclusively that a low price greatly favors increased consumption in China, Mexico, and in fact the world over. The overland exports of 1875 were 10,434 flasks; of 1874, 5,859 flasks; increase in 1875, 4,575 flasks. Our monthly receipts of this article compare with 1874 as follows:

Months.	1874.		1875.	
	Bay.	Coast.	Bay.	Coast.
	Flasks.	*Flasks.*	*Flasks.*	*Flasks.*
January	972	25	1,605	2
February	1,709	....	3,284	309
March	1,830	....	3,779	465
April	1,862	....	3,718	100
May	1,964	20	3,298	303
June	1,845	....	3,776	320
July	1,923	....	4,229	428
August	2,132	15	4,016	269
September	2,849	24	4,746	292
October	2,821	9	4,899	151
November	2,095	....	5,278	205
December	2,089	....	4,537	241
Totals	23,591	93	47,165	3,085
Increase in 1875	....	....	23,574	2,995

SALT.

Imports.

	1874.	1875.
Tons	2,811	3,092
Sacks	15,390	24,814
Cases	200	60

Exports.

	1874.	1875.
Tons	220	147
Bags	911	1,597

Prices December 31, 1875: California, $12.50 per ton; Liverpool coarse, $12 to $15; factory filled, $17 to $18.50 per ton.

Tabular statement of assessments and dividends, from the Daily Stock Report assessment-list, San Francisco, January 17, 1876.

Companies.	Number assessment.	Number feet in mine.	Number shares in mine.	Last assessment levied.	Amount per share.	Number dividends.	Last dividend.	Amount per share.	Total amount assessments levied.	Total amount dividends disbursed.	Amount assessment per share.	Amount dividend per share.
CALIFORNIA MINES.												
Booth	1		40, 000	Mar. 31, 1875	$0 15				$6, 000		$0 15	
Consolidated Amador		1, 850	30, 000			9	Apr. 8, 1874	$0 50		$210, 000		$27 00
Bellevue	11	8, 000	20, 000	Feb. 17, 1875	50				111, 000		5 55	
Calistoga		3, 600	60, 000									
Cederberg	5		24, 000	Nov. 9, 1875	50	4	Feb. 6, 1873	50	48, 000	24, 000	2 00	1 00
Chariot Mill	5		30, 000	Dec. 11, 1875	10	4	Nov. 16, 1874	40	48, 000	51, 000	1 60	1 70
Defiance		1, 500	100, 000									
Eureka		1, 680	20, 000			76	Dec. 8, 1873	1 00		2, 054, 000		102 70
Genesee Valley			25, 000			1	May 3, 1875	20				
Independent	9	1, 800	25, 000	Sept. 11, 1875	50				108, 000		4 32	
Keystone Quartz			10, 000			10	Feb. 10, 1874	50		5, 000		50
Mansfield	4	3, 300	66, 000	Oct. 9, 1875	50				72, 600		1 10	
New Coso	1		100, 000	Oct. 28, 1875	50				50, 000		50	
St. Patrick	11	1, 800	20, 000	Aug. 12, 1875					160, 000		8 00	
Wonder Consolidated		5, 250	100, 000									
Wyoming Consolidated		10, 500	100, 000									
Yule Gravel	5	400	10, 000	Nov. 9, 1874	10	9	Apr. 10, 1872	50	9, 000	40, 000	90	4 06
WASHOE MINES.												
Alamo	1	3, 000	30, 000	Nov. 2, 1872	25				7, 500		25	
Amazon Consolidated	1	1, 500	60, 000	Sept. 20, 1875	10				6, 000		10	
American Flat South		1, 200	48, 000									
Alpha Consolidated	7	306	30, 000	Aug. 12, 1875	1 00				180, 000		6 00	
Alta	2	1, 800	108, 000	Aug. 23, 1875	50				21 600		20	
American Flat	6	500	30, 000	Apr. 10, 1875	1 00				165, 000		5 50	
Andes	6	2, 000	100, 000	Dec. 30, 1875	50				225, 000		2 25	
Bacon Mill and Mining Company	3	65	25, 000	Mar. 9, 1875	50				12, 500		50	
Baltic Consolidated	2	2, 100	37, 000	Oct. 9, 1875	10							
Baltimore Consolidated	10	1, 050	84, 000	Oct. 7, 1875	1 00				573, 000		6 82½	
Beach & Paxton		233	60, 000									
Best & Belcher	9	540	100, 800	July 13, 1874	50				136, 192		6 08	
Belcher	8	1, 040	104, 000	Apr. 14, 1871	4 00	34	Jan. 10, 1876	1 00	660, 400	15, 085, 200	6 35	136 01
Bonanza		1, 140	100, 000									
Bowers		20	5, 000									

Bullion	45	943½	100,000	Aug. 6, 1872	1 50				1,802,000		18 02	
Buckeye	16	3,000	48,600	Dec. 28, 1875	50				260,000		13 25	
Caledonia	15	2,188	20,000	Nov. 1, 1875	3 00				950,000		47 50	
California		600	540,000									
Central Comstock		2,000	50,000									
Challenge Consolidated		90	50,000									
Chollar-Potosi	8	1,400	28,000	Oct. 14, 1875	5 00	44	Feb. 10, 1872	1 00	1,022,000	3,080,000	36 50	110 00
Columbia		1,200	100,000									
Comstock		750	100,000									
Confidence	10	130	24,960	Mar. 18, 1873	1 00	6	May 1, 1865	08⅔	243,840	78,000	9 75	3 12
Consolidated Virginia	15	710	108,000	June 11, 1873	3 00	21	Jan. 11, 1876	10 00	411,200	14,040,000	3 81	130 00
Consolidated Gold Hill Quartz	1	34⅓	20,000	Aug. 4, 1873	75							
Consolidated Washoe		1,200	40,000									
Cosmopolitan	2	1,800	100,000	Aug. 11, 1875	25				50,000		50	
Cromer			100,000									
Crown Point Extension		500	40,000									
Crown Point	24	541	100,000	Jan. 10, 1876	1 00	50	Jan. 12, 1875	2 00	773,370	11,588,000	7 73	115 88
Crown Point Ravine	3	1,200	30,000	Dec. 7, 1875	25				37,500		1 25	
Daney	15	2,000	24,000	Dec. 20, 1875	50	2	July 1, 1863	1 16⅔	252,000	56,000	10 50	2 33
Dayton	4	1,600	100,000	Sept. 15, 1875	1 00				400,000		4 00	
Dexter	1	1,200	60,000	Dec. 20, 1875	20				12,000		20	
Dardanelles	2	1,200	60,000	Feb. 5, 1875	1 00				120,000		2 00	
Eclipse Winters Plato	1	70	25,000	Oct. 17, 1873	50				12,500		50	
Empire Mill	20	75	50,000	Sept. 4, 1875	50	21	May 15, 1867	6 00	491,400	713,500	9 82	14 27
Europa	4	1,000	100,000	July 23, 1875	25				60,000		60	
Exchequer	10	400	100,000	Feb. 9, 1874	3 00				180,000		1 80	
Fairmount		250	15,000									
Florida	3	1,300	50,000	Nov. 5, 1875	50				112,500		2 25	
Franklin		1,200	30,000									
Genesee		800	30,000									
Glasgow	1	1,500	60,000	Sept. 20, 1875	10				6,000		10	
Globe Consolidated	7	4,300	38,000	Dec. 3, 1875	50				190,000		5 00	
Georgia	1	1,200	100,000	July 29, 1875	10				10,000		10	
Golden Fleece	9			June 16, 1875	10							
Gould & Curry	24	612	108,000	Oct. 25, 1875	1 00	36	Oct. 10, 1870	10 00	1,640,000	3,826,800	15 18	35 43
Green	1	1,634	20,000	Oct. 7, 1874	50				10,000		50	
Grenada		2,500	50,000									
Hale & Norcross	48	400	16,000	Nov. 9, 1875	5 00	36	Apr. 10, 1871	5 00	1,770,000	1,598,000	110 62	99 88
Hartford	3	1,400	35,000	June 26, 1875	30				10,500		30	
Imperial	25	184	100,000	Nov. 9, 1875	1 00	30	June 10, 1868	6 00	1,670,000	1,067,500	16 70	10 67
Independent and Omega		2,400	60,000									
Insurance	2	2,000	30,000	Sept. 13, 1873	10				10,500		35	
Jacob Little Consolidated	1	3,280	100,000	May 31, 1875	10				10,000		10	
Julia Consolidated	22	3,000	110,000	May 12, 1875	2 00				548,700		18 29	
Justice	17	2,100	105,000	Nov. 26, 1875	1 00				872,500		8 67½	
Kentuck	12	95	30,000	Dec. 3, 1874	1 00	32	Mar. 10, 1870	5 00	270,000	1,252,000	9 00	41 73
Knickerbocker	14	1,200	24,000	Dec. 28, 1875	1 00				372,000		15 50	
Kossuth	5	2,700	108,000	Oct. 4, 1875	75				297,000		2 75	
Lady Bryan	10	5,000	100,000	Nov. 30, 1875	1 00				450,000		4 50	
Lady Washington	6	1,223	60,000	Nov. 4, 1875	50				138,000		3 50	
Leo	4	1,600	32,000	Sept. 6, 1875	50				43,200		1 35	
Leviathan	2	2,000	100,000	Jan. 13, 1876	50				100,000		1 00	

Tabular statement of assessments and dividends, &c.—Continued.

Companies.	Number assessment.	Number feet in mine.	Number shares in mine.	Last assessment levied.	Amount per share.	Number dividends.	Last dividend.	Amount per share.	Total amount assessments levied.	Total amount dividends disbursed.	Amount assessment per share.	Amount dividend per share.
WASHOE MINES—Continued.												
Lower Comstock	...	1,300	86,000			...						
Maryland	...	900	54,000			...						
Mexican	1	600	108,000	Mar. 22, 1875	$0 50	...			$54,000		$0 50	
Mides	...	200	30,000			...						
Mint	12	1,200	50,000	Jan. 6, 1876	20	...			80,000		1 50	
Monumental	1	1,500	90,000	Apr. 17, 1875	25	...			22,500		25	
Morning Star	...	1,600	80,000			...						
Nevada	1	3,000	40,000	June 3, 1875	25	...			10,000		25	
New York	7	1,000	100,000	Oct. 27, 1875	75	...			420,000		4 20	
Niagara	1	1,500	60,000	Apr. 16, 1875	50	...			30,000		50	
North Carson	3	1,500	100,000	Dec. 16, 1875	10	...			45,000		45	
North Consolidated Virginia	1	1,500	100,000	Oct. 6, 1875	50	...			50,000		50	
North Utah	...	1,500	60,000			...						
Occidental	3	1,706	40,000	Feb. 2, 1875	50	...			62,500		1 00	
Og Gold Hill	4	3,000	30,000	Aug. 26, 1875	50	...			60,000		2 00	
Ophir	29	675	100,800	May 14, 1875	2 00	22	Mar. 9, 1864	$4 00	2,034,400	$1,394,400	20 18	$13 83
Original Flowery	...	1,000	50,000			...						
Overman	33	1,200	38,400	Oct. 12, 1875	3 00	...			1,876,680		48 86	
Pacific	...	1,200	100,000			...						
Patten	1	1,200	50,000	Feb. 3, 1875	20	...			10,000		20	
Phil. Sheridan	3	1,200	24,000	Aug. 6, 1875	50	...			42,000		1 75	
Pictou	9	2,000	30,000	Nov. 26, 1875	25	...			65,700		2 02½	
Pioneer Consolidated	...	1,500	100,000			...						
Prospect	...	1,000	100,000			...						
Rock Island	10	1,200	100,000	Jan. 8, 1876	50	...			280,000		2 80	
Savage	21	771	112,000	Dec. 17, 1875	1 00	52	June 11, 1869	3 00	2,186,000	4,460,000	19 51⅓	39 82
Scorpion	2	4,000	40,000	May 26, 1875	25	...			14,000		35	
Segregated Belcher	14	160	6,400	July 20, 1871	5 00	...			212,800		33 25	
Senator	12	1,200	24,000	Aug. 27, 1875	50	...			99,600		4 15	
Segregated Caledonia	2	100	10,000	June 22, 1874	10	...			1,000		10	
Segregated Gold Hill	...	1,000	60,000			...						
Segregated Rock Island	...	600	60,000			...						
South California	...	1,500	50,000			...						
South Comstock	3	1,636	40,000	Nov. 12, 1875	25	...			40,000		1 00	
South Justice	...	400	50,000			...						

South Overman	3	1,500	30,000	Aug. 6, 1875	1 00				60,000		2 00
South Star		1,200	48,000								
Sutro	2	2,400	24,000	Feb. 17, 1875	50				24,000		1 00
Silver Central Consolidated	2	3,000	110,000	Aug. 3, 1875	10				16,500		15
Silver Cloud		3,000	32,000	Mar. 19, 1874	25				8,000		25
Silver Hill	7	5,400	54,000	Oct. 1, 1875	1 00				702,000		13 00
Sierra Nevada	42	3,300	100,000	Oct. 1, 1875	1 00	11	Jan. 16, 1871	1 00	1,000,000	102,500	10 00	1 02
Succor Mill and Mining	13	3,800	68,400	Dec. 20, 1875	50	2	Oct. 16, 1871	50	370,500	22,800	5 42	1 00
Trench	1	20	5,000	Oct. 17, 1873	1 00				5,000		1 00	
Tyler	8	2,200	33,000	Dec. 21, 1875	30				72,600		2 20	
Union Consolidated	8	600	100,000	Oct. 11, 1875	50				160,000		1 60	
Utah	11	1,000	20,000	Oct. 19, 1875	2 00				300,000		15 00	
Ward		1,200	40,000									
Wells Fargo	3	1,500	108,000	Sept. 14, 1875	20				32,400		30	
Whitman		1,800	100,000									
Woodville	12	1,700	120,000	Nov. 4, 1875	1 00				681,000		5 67	
Yellow Jacket	21	957	24,000	Sept. 20, 1875	5 00	25	Aug. 10, 1871	2 50	2,358,000	2,184,000	98 25	91 00
WHITE PINE MINES.											
General Lee	6	1,000	20,000	Jan. 9, 1873	25				15,000		75	
Geneva Consolidated	6	3,000	50,000	Oct. 11, 1875	20				72,500		1 45	
Hayes	7	1,000	40,000	Aug. 18, 1875	20				66,000		1 65	
Mammoth	19	1,800	36,000	Aug. 18, 1875	15				104,400		2 90	
Or Hidden Treasure	11		21,333	Oct. 12, 1874	1 00	1	June 10, 1870	1 50	330,061	31,999	15 50	1 50
Silver Wave	12	1,600	20,000	July 31, 1875	25				165,000		8 25	
Ward Ellis	3	2,000	40,000	Feb. 10, 1875	5				10,000		25	
IDAHO MINES.											
Empire	12		25,000	Jan. 5, 1876	25				307,500		12 75	
Golden Chariot	15	1,820	90,000	Dec. 13, 1875	75	13	Oct. 24, 1873	2 50	577,500	500,000	6 41⅔	5 55½
Ida Ellmore	19		30,000	Oct. 16, 1875	50	6	Feb. 8, 1870	1 00	730,000	60,000	17 66	6 00
Illinois Central	4	1,000	30,000	Oct. 12, 1875	50				37,500		1 25	
Mahogany	16	720	50,000	July 15, 1875	2 00	1	Aug. 5, 1872	1 50	240,000	15,000	9 00	1 50
Pauper	6	1,600	50,000	Nov. 9, 1875	20				25,000		50	
Poor Man	4		50,000	Nov. 24, 1875	50				125,000		2 50	
Silver Cord	10		24,000	July 20, 1875	1 00				174,000		8 50	
South Chariot	15	660	50,000	Sept. 13, 1875	25				350,000		11 50	
South Mountain Consolidated	1		100,000	Aug. 9, 1875	2 00				200,000		2 00	
War Eagle	10	1,000	20,000	June 30, 1875	1 00				120,000		12 00	
Red Jacket	8	1,600	20,000	Dec. 16, 1875	25				115,000		5 75	
CORNUCOPIA DISTRICT.											
Constitution	2	1,500	50,000	Oct. 29, 1875	10				12,500		25	
Cornucopia Consolidated		3,000	100,000									
Hussey						2	July 15, 1875	50		50,000		1 00
Leopard		1,500	50,000									
Panther	2	1,500	50,000	Oct. 29, 1875	25				22,500		45	
Tiger	2	1,500	50,000	Oct. 29, 1875	10				12,500		25	
Beaver		1,500	50,000									

Tabular statement of assessments and dividends, &c.—Continued.

Companies.	Number assessment.	Number feet in mine.	Number shares in mine.	Last assessment levied.	Amount per share.	Number dividends.	Last dividend.	Amount per share.	Total amount assessments levied.	Total amount dividends disbursed.	Amount assessment per share.	Amount dividend per share.
ELY DISTRICT.												
American Flag	7		40,000	Mar. 26, 1875	$0 50				$260,000		$6 50	
Alps	8	800	30,000	Feb. 10, 1875	25				105,000		3 50	
Bowery	6		30,000	Dec. 15, 1874	20				94,500		3 15	
Chapman	4		30,000	July 28, 1873	25				37,500		1 25	
Chief of the Hill	6		30,000	Mar. 26, 1875	25				75,000		2 50	
Condor	4		25,000	July 9, 1875	50				50,000		2 00	
Huhn & Hunt	11	3,000	30,000	May 7, 1875	50				294,000		7 55	
Ingomar	7	1,000	40,000	May 4, 1874	25				70,000	$50,000	1 75	
Louise	3	2,400	30,000	Sept. 15, 1872	50				21,000		70	
Meadow Valley	10		60,000	Dec. 28, 1875	50	17	June 16, 1873	$1 00	1,290,000	1,200,000	6 00	$20 00
Newark	12	800	32,000	Sept. 14, 1875	50				304,600		9 55	
Page & Panaca	8	24,000	40,000	Oct. 6, 1874	75				190,000		4 75	
Phœnix	14		50,000	Apr. 21, 1874	50				337,500		6 75	
Pioche	11	1,000	20,000	Dec. 1, 1875	50	3	Aug. 5, 1872	1 00	230,000		11 50	3 00
Pioche West Extension	8		35,000	July 12, 1875	2 00				171,500		4 90	
Portland	5		30,000	Aug. 21, 1874	25				71,000		2 36	
Raymond & Ely	5	5,000	30,000	Nov. 5, 1875	3 00	23	Sept. 10, 1873	3 00	510,000	3,075,000	17 00	102 50
Silver Peak	6		30,000	Mar. 29, 1875	50				105,000		3 50	
Silver West Consolidated	5		50,000	Dec. 7, 1875	10				42,500		85	
Spring Mountain Tunnel	9		20,000	May 22, 1874	10				32,000		7 35	
Washington and Creole	15	1,520	30,000	Sept. 27, 1875	75				315,000		10 50	
Watson	1		30,000	Nov. 16, 1874	1 00				30,000		1 00	
MISCELLANEOUS.												
Wellington	4		50,000	Feb. 17, 1874	25				55,000		1 10	
Adams Hill	6		50,000	Feb. 16, 1875	15				57,000		1 15	
Eureka Consolidated			50,000			22	Aug. 5, 1875	1 00		1,000,000		20 00
Jackson	7		50,000	June 25, 1875	50				102,500		1 55	
K. K. Consolidated	1		50,000	Apr. 3, 1875	1 00	4	Sept. 15, 1873	25	50,000	50,000	1 00	1 00
Rye Patch	4	1,000	30,000	July 30, 1875	50	4	Mar. 5, 1875	25	82,500	37,500	2 75	1 25
Belmont	7		50,000	Dec. 9, 1875	50				325,000		6 50	
El Dorado, north	1		25,000	Aug. 4, 1874	50				12,500		50	
El Dorado, south, consolidated	8	2,600	40,000	Dec. 31, 1875	1 00				357,500		8 75	
Josephine	1		25,000	July 20, 1874	15				3,750		15	

North Belmont	2		50,000	Sept. 30, 1874	10				10,000		20	
Prussian	6		30,000	Jan. 5, 1876	50				112,500		3 75	
Quintero	3	2,000	50,000	Sept. 30, 1874	10				15,000		30	
Monitor Belmont	4	6,400	50,000	Mar. 16, 1875	50	3	Dec. 1, 1873	50	100,000	75,000	2 00	1 50
Juniata Consolidated	3	5,000	50,000	Sept. 20, 1875					95,000		1 90	
Tybo Consolidated			50,000									
Advance		12,000	100,000									
Western Almaden		10,000	200,000									
Webfoot	2		50,000	Nov. 11, 1875	20				22,500		45	
Northern Belle		1,600	50,000			8	Jan. 15, 1876	1 00		400,000		8 00
Virtue	4	2,600	20,000	Jan. 20, 1874	1 00				120,000		6 00	
Cherry Creek	5	1,000	30,000	Oct. 21, 1875	25				82,500		2 75	
Gila			100,000			2	Aug. 16, 1875	25		50,000		50
Jefferson		8,182	50,000			2	May 15, 1875	50		50,000		1 00

The ratios of gold to silver from 1760 *to* 1833.

[From the Report of the Director of the Mint.]

Years.	Pure gold to pure silver.	Years.	Pure gold to pure silver.
1760	1 to 14. 29	1797	1 to 15. 45
1761	1 to 13. 94	1798	1 to 15. 45
1762	1 to 14. 63	1799	1 to 14. 29
1763	1 to 14. 71	1800	1 to 14. 81
1764	1 to 14. 91	1801	1 to 14. 47
1765	1 to 14. 69	1802	1 to 15. 23
1766	1 to 14. 41	1803	1 to 14. 47
1767	1 to 14. 45	1804	1 to 14. 67
1768	1 to 14. 58	1805	1 to 15. 14
1769	1 to 14. 45	1806	1 to 14. 25
1770	1 to 14. 35	1807	1 to 14. 46
1771	1 to 14. 36	1808	1 to 14. 79
1772	1 to 14. 19	1809	1 to 16. 25
1773	1 to 14. 73	1810	1 to 16. 15
1774	1 to 15. 05	1811	1 to 15. 72
1775	1 to 14. 62	1812	1 to 15. 04
1776	1 to 14. 34	1813	1 to 14. 53
1777	1 to 14. 04	1814	1 to 15. 85
1778	1 to 14. 34	1815	1 to 16. 30
1779	1 to 14. 89	1816	1 to 13. 64
1780	1 to 14. 43	1817	1 to 15. 58
1781	1 to 13. 33	1818	1 to 15. 42
1782	1 to 13. 54	1819	1 to 15. 82
1783	1 to 13. 78	1820	1 to 15. 71
1784	1 to 14. 90	1821	1 to 15. 98
1785	1 to 15. 21	1822	1 to 15. 91
1786	1 to 14. 89	1823	1 to 15. 91
1787	1 to 14. 83	1824	1 to 15. 64
1788	1 to 14. 71	1825	1 to 15. 69
1789	1 to 14. 89	1826	1 to 15. 69
1790	1 to 15. 01	1827	1 to 15. 77
1791	1 to 14. 95	1828	1 to 15. 77
1792	1 to 14. 43	1829	1 to 15. 95
1793	1 to 15. 01	1830	1 to 15. 73
1794	1 to 15. 32	1831	1 to 15. 73
1795	1 to 14. 77	1832	1 to 15. 73
1796	1 to 14. 77	1833	1 to 15. 93

NOTE.—The highest value of silver compared with gold, from 1760 to 1833, was in 1781, when 13.33 ounces of the former were equal to one of the latter. In 1809 it required 16¼ ounces of silver to purchase an ounce of gold; the difference represents a change of 14½ per cent. Taking 1771 as the year of the highest relative valuation of silver and the average of the first seven months of 1876 as the lowest, shows a change within a period of 95 years of 34 per cent.

Table showing the yearly averages of the price of silver from 1834 *to* 1876, *and the corresponding relative values of gold to silver, (prepared from quotations furnished by Pixley & Abell, London.)*

[From the Report of the Director of the Mint.]

Years.	Price per ounce, British standard.	Price per ounce, United States standard, in United States gold coin.	Value of a silver dollar of 412½ grains.	Relative value of gold to silver.
	Pence.	*Cents.*	*Cents.*	
1834	59 15-16	118.25	101.62	1 to 15.73
1835	59 11-16	117.76	101.20	1 to 15.79
1836	60	118.37	101.72	1 to 15.71
1837	59 9-16	117.51	100.98	1 to 15.83
1838	59 1-2	117.39	100.88	1 to 15.85
1839	60 3-8	119.11	102.36	1 to 15.61
1840	60 3-8	119.11	102.36	1 to 15.61
1841	60 1-16	118.50	101.83	1 to 15.70
1842	59 7-16	117.26	100.77	1 to 15.86
1843	59 3-16	116.77	100.34	1 to 15.93
1844	59 1-2	117.39	100.88	1 to 15.85
1845	59 1-4	116.90	100.46	1 to 15.91
1846	59 5-16	117.02	100.56	1 to 15.89
1847	59 11-16	117.76	101.20	1 to 15.79
1848	59 1-2	117.39	100.88	1 to 15.85
1849	59 3-4	117.88	101.30	1 to 15.78
1850	60 1-16	118.50	101.83	1 to 15.70
1851	61	120.35	103.42	1 to 15.46
1852	60 1-2	119.36	102.57	1 to 15.58
1853	61 1-2	121.33	104.26	1 to 15.33
1854	61 1-2	121.33	104.26	1 to 15.33
1855	61 5-16	120.96	103.95	1 to 15.38
1856	61 5-16	120.96	103.95	1 to 15.38
1857	61 3-4	121.83	104.69	1 to 15.27
1858	61 5-16	120.96	103.95	1 to 15.38
1859	62 1-16	122.44	105.22	1 to 15.19
1860	61 11-16	121.70	104.58	1 to 15.28
1861	60 13-16	119.98	103.10	1 to 15.50
1862	61 7-16	121.21	104.16	1 to 15.35
1863	61 3-8	121.09	104.06	1 to 15.36
1864	61 3-8	121.09	104.06	1 to 15.36
1865	61 1-16	120.47	103.52	1 to 15.44
1866	61 1-8	120.59	103.63	1 to 15.42
1867	60 9-16	119.48	102.67	1 to 15.57
1868	60 1-2	119.36	102.57	1 to 15.58
1869	60 7-16	119.24	102.47	1 to 15.60
1870	60 9-16	119.48	102.67	1 to 15.57
1871	60 1-2	119.36	102.57	1 to 15.58
1872	60 5-16	118.99	102.25	1 to 15.63
1873	59 1-4	116.90	100.46	1 to 15.91
1874	58 5-16	115.04	98.86	1 to 16.17
1875	56 7-8	112.21	96.43	1 to 16.58
1876, (7 months)	52 13-16	104.19	89.53	1 to 17.85

During the above period the ratio for the highest monthly average, July, 1859, was 1 to 15.11, at which rate a silver dollar of 412½ grains was equivalent to $1.05¾ gold. The ratio for the lowest monthly average, July, 1876, was 1 to 19.19, at which the dollar was worth 83¼ cents.

During this latter month there were sales of silver in London at 46¾ pence per ounce, British standard, at which price the relative value was 1 to 20.17, and the gold value of the old silver dollar 79¼ cents.

Table for ascertaining the gold value of an ounce of silver, United States standard, from London quotations of an ounce, British standard.

[From the Report of the Director of the Mint.]

One ounce British standard, 925 M.	One ounce United States standard, 900 M.	One ounce British standard, 925 M.	One ounce United States standard, 900 M.	One ounce British standard, 925 M.	One ounce United States standard, 900 M.	One ounce British standard, 925 M.	One ounce United States standard, 900 M.
Pence.	*Cents.*	*Pence.*	*Cents.*	*Pence.*	*Cents.*	*Pence.*	*Cents.*
45	88.78	49¼	97.16	53½	105.55	57¾	113.94
45⅛	89.02	49⅜	97.41	53⅝	105.80	57⅞	114.18
45¼	89.27	49½	97.66	53¾	106.04	58	114.43
45⅜	89.52	49⅝	97.90	53⅞	106.29	58⅛	114.68
45½	89.77	49¾	98.15	54	106.54	58¼	114.92
45⅝	90.01	49⅞	98.30	54⅛	106.78	58⅜	115.17
45¾	90.26	50	98.64	54¼	107.03	58½	115.42
45⅞	90.51	50⅛	98.89	54⅜	107.28	58⅝	115.66
46	90.75	50¼	99.14	54½	107.52	58¾	115.91
46⅛	91.00	50⅜	99.38	54⅝	107.77	58⅞	116.16
46¼	91.25	50½	99.63	54¾	108.02	59	116.40
46⅜	91.49	50⅝	99.88	54⅞	108.26	59⅛	116.65
46½	91.74	50¾	100.12	55	108.51	59¼	116.90
46⅝	91.99	50⅞	100.37	55⅛	108.76	59⅜	117.14
46¾	92.23	51	100.62	55¼	109.00	59½	117.39
46⅞	92.48	51⅛	100.86	55⅜	109.25	59⅝	117.63
47	92.73	51¼	101.11	55½	109.50	59¾	117.88
47⅛	92.97	51⅜	101.36	55⅝	109.74	59⅞	118.13
47¼	93.22	51½	101.60	55¾	109.99	60	118.37
47⅜	93.46	51⅝	101.85	55⅞	110.24	60⅛	118.62
47½	93.71	51¾	102.10	56	110.48	60¼	118.87
47⅝	93.96	51⅞	102.34	56⅛	110.73	60⅜	119.14
47¾	94.21	52	102.59	56¼	110.98	60½	119.36
47⅞	94.45	52⅛	102.84	56⅜	111.22	60⅝	119.61
48	94.70	52¼	103.08	56½	111.47	60¾	119.85
48⅛	94.94	52⅜	103.33	56⅝	111.72	60⅞	120.10
48¼	95.19	52½	103.58	56¾	111.96	61	120.35
48⅜	95.44	52⅝	103.82	56⅞	112.21	61⅛	120.59
48½	95.68	52¾	104.07	57	112.46	61¼	120.84
48⅝	95.93	52⅞	104.32	57⅛	112.70	61⅜	121.09
48¾	96.18	53	104.56	57¼	112.95	61½	121.33
48⅞	96.42	53⅛	104.81	57⅜	113.20	61⅝	121.58
49	96.67	53¼	105.06	57½	113.44	61¾	121.83
49⅛	96.91	53⅜	105.30	57⅝	113.69	61⅞	122.07

General summary of the returns of the mineral produce of the United Kingdom for 1875.

[From the report of Robert Hunt, F. R. S., keeper of mining-records.]

Minerals.	Quantities.	Values.
	Tons. Cwt.	
Coal	131, 867, 105 0	£46, 163, 486
Iron-ore	15, 821, 060 3	5, 975, 410
Copper-ore	71, 528 0	333, 414
Tin-ore, (black tin)	13, 995 10	735, 606
Lead-ore	77, 746 4	1, 202, 148
Zinc-ore	23, 978 8	75, 110
Iron pyrites	48, 035 16	35, 136
Arsenic	5, 061 5	31, 174
Manganese	3, 205 11	15, 906
Ocher and umber	5, 315 12	7, 185
Wolfram and tungstate	46 2	382
Plumbago	20 0	None sold.
Fluor-spar	358 18	188
Clays, (porcelain and fire clays)	3, 008, 444 0	753, 957
Oil shales	442, 336 0	200, 000
Salt	2, 316, 644 0	1, 158, 322
Barytes	15, 549 5	14, 089
Coprolites, &c	250, 122 0	628, 000
Sundry minerals, estimated	....	3, 500
Total value of the minerals produced in 1875	....	57, 333, 013

Metals obtained from the ores produced in the United Kingdom in 1875.

Minerals.	Quantities.	Values.
Gold ....ounces..	579	£2, 105
Pig-iron ....tons..	6, 365, 462	15, 645, 774
Copper ....do..	4, 322	388, 984
Copper and silver precipitate ....do...	54	3, 207
Tin ....do...	9, 614	866, 266
Lead ....do...	57, 435	1, 290, 373
Zinc ....do...	6, 713	162, 790
Silver........do...	487, 358	115, 247
Other metals, (estimated)	....	1, 500
Total value	....	18, 476, 746

Total value of minerals and metals obtained from the mines, &c., of the United Kingdom in 1875.

Metals, value as above	£18, 476, 746
Coal........	46, 163, 486
Minerals not reduced, earthy, &c	2, 847, 456
Total value........	67, 487, 688

INDEX OF MINES, MILLS, WORKS, ETC.

[NOTE.—This index contains the names of such individual enterprises as are alluded to in the foregoing report. In most cases, the counties in which the mines or works are situated are also given. Reduction-works belonging to mines may be sought under the names of the mines.]

A.

D.

E.

F.

G.

H.

I.

J.

K.

L.

M.

N.

O.

Q.

R.

T.

U.

V.

Y.

Z.

INDEX OF COUNTIES, DISTRICTS, ETC.

A.

B.

C.

D.

E.

F.

G.

H.

I.

J.

K.

L.

M.

Q.

R.

T.

INDEX OF SUBJECTS.

A.

B.

C.

O.

P.

Q.

S.

T.

U.

W.

Z.

www.ingramcontent.com/pod-product-compliance
Lightning Source LLC
LaVergne TN
LVHW021302110826
845150LV00003B/459

* 9 7 8 1 4 2 5 5 6 0 0 2 7 *